HOME OF THE INFANTRY

Peggy A. Stelpflug

Richard Hyatt

MERCER
UNIVERSITY PRESS

Endowed by
TOM WATSON BROWN
and
THE WATSON-BROWN FOUNDATION, INC.

HOME OF THE
INFANTRY

THE HISTORY
OF FORT BENNING

PEGGY A. STELPFLUG AND RICHARD HYATT

MERCER UNIVERSITY PRESS
MACON, GEORGIA

WITH

THE HISTORIC CHATTAHOOCHEE COMMISSION

AND

THE NATIONAL INFANTRY ASSOCIATION

MERCER

© 2007 MERCER UNIVERSITY PRESS
1400 Coleman Avenue
Macon, Georgia 31207
with
The Historic Chattahoochee Commission
and
the National Infantry Association

First Edition.

Books published by Mercer University Press are printed
on acid free paper that meets the requirements of
American National Standard for Information Sciences—
Permanence of Paper for Printed Library Materials.

MUP/H741
ISBN 978-088146-087-2

CIP data are available from the Library of Congress

Peggy A. Stelpflug:

To my husband, Lieutenant Colonel William J. Stelpflug, USAF, and our son, Lance Corporal Bill J. Stelpflug, USMC

Richard Hyatt:

To Frank G. Lumpkin, Jr.

Contents

Prologue

Columbus, Georgia, was minding its own business. Another day on the calendar. War and terrorism were overseas, not in the States. But while these days started off like any other, these twenty-four-hour segments became unforgettable landmarks, dates by which the world would forever set its clock: December 7, 1941; September 11, 2001. These dates made history. These dates, never to be forgotten, turned peace to war for the United States of America.

On a quiet Sunday morning in 1941, Pearl Harbor was blindsided by Japanese planes, wounding the pride of a nation that thought itself invincible. Sixty years later, another attack shook the mainland. Passenger planes piloted by terrorists took down the twin towers of New York City's World Trade Center. On that same Tuesday in 200l, a similar attack occurred at the Pentagon just outside Washington, and a third was thwarted in the skies over Pennsylvania by a group of valiant passengers willing to give their own lives.

Americans of two generations felt violated and angry. Knowing that life would never be as it was before, Americans looked to its leaders for guidance, and the leaders turned to the men and women in uniform. Ultimately, they looked to Fort Benning. Tucked away on Georgia's western border, Fort Benning appeared isolated from the events of either date. Instead, this sprawling army installation found itself at the heart of the actions that followed. War was inevitable with its necessary training and preparation, whether the battlefield was in Europe, Asia, or the Mid-East. Fort Benning's mission was training.

December 1941

On Saturday, December 6, Columbus merchants prepared for the rush of Christmas shoppers. With eighteen shopping days left, traffic was heavy on the sidewalks and the streets. It was soldier payday, so uniformed post personnel joined the shoppers and the diners. The soldiers seemed so very young. It was unspoken, but citizen and soldier alike realized that somewhere, sometime, those young men would put their lives on the line.

These young men lived in garage apartments in Wynnton and Lakebottom. They danced with local girls during parties at the Country Club of Columbus. They sat on the next stool at the soda fountain at Dinglewood pharmacy. They cheered at Memorial Stadium when the Georgia and Auburn football teams clashed. They worshipped in the pew next to you on Sundays. The city and the rambling post had always been neighbors. Soon they would become family, but for now rumbles of war were in distant Europe and Asia.

People were more concerned about what to buy loved ones for Christmas. For the undecided GI, Kirven's Department Store advertised that Kitty Kay and her corps of personal shoppers could select the right gift. Restaurants were swamped—S&S Cafeteria featured veal cutlet, macaroni and cheese, string beans, bread and butter, apple cobbler, and a drink for a quarter. George Monoxelos locked the door at the Empire Café on 12th Street, unlocking it for one customer to enter as another paid his bill. The ingenious went to McCoy's Grocery for a Royal Crown Cola, pouring Tom's peanuts into the bottle for nourishment. As the day went on, Scott Rivers and his ten-piece band played "Harlem Rhythms" at Idle Hour Park in Phenix City. Johnny Mack's orchestra was held over at the Club Maytag. At Memorial Stadium, Morris Brown defeated North Carolina College 7-6 in the Peach Blossom Classic, winning the National Negro Football Championship. For those in need of rest, the Rankin Hotel advertised deluxe rooms for two dollars.

At Fort Benning, members of the 2nd Armored Division were too tired to go to town because they had been on maneuvers for sixteen demanding weeks. Colonel George Patton, who arrived on post July 27, 1940, rode them hard, warning them what war would be like, "You'll be up to your necks in blood and guts."[1]

Sunday came. It was a day of rest, of family, of worship and, as it began, a day of peace. Members of Saint Paul Methodist Church worshipped in the main sanctuary though the new carpet was not completely in place. The title of the Reverend Kenneth McGregor's sermon was "Enjoying the Peace We Have." After church, the first hints of Pearl Harbor reached the area. With no instant communications, no somber television anchors, no live reports

---

[1] Richard Hyatt, "Three Days that Changed Columbus," *Columbus Ledger-Enquirer*, December 8 1991, E-4.

from CNN, news in 1941 came in choppy, broken paragraphs delivered on clattering wire service machines that sounded like machine guns. Henry "Happy Hank" East had the afternoon shift at WRBL, the city's oldest radio station. While East monitored the network signal, his sleepy afternoon was interrupted around 1:30 by the clanging of the wire machine bells.

"The Columbia Symphony was on CBS," East recalled. "I began to hear the bells ringing on the news machines. I went over and looked and all it said was 'Pearl Harbor bombed.' I didn't lose any time. I broke into the symphony broadcast and read the bulletin on the air. Right after that, the network broke in for the first time with the details."[2]

Brigadier General Omar Bradley, Fort Benning's commander, was also informed of the bombing. Sent to Fort Benning by his mentor, US Army chief of staff General George C. Marshall, Bradley's assignment was to update and streamline the ways troops were trained, putting in place OCS, Officer Candidate School. Bradley was pruning flowers with his wife, Mary, on the grounds of "Riverside," the mansion that was—and is—home to post commanders. A colleague stopped and told him the news. Bradley went right to work securing and readying the fort.

Private First Class Samuel Tackitt of the 2nd Armored Division was walking a battery street on post when he heard. Two months before he turned down a fifteen-day leave because he preferred the army to harvest time at home in Arkansas. He huddled around a radio, knowing plans for a Christmas leave were vanishing.

West Point honor student Captain James Gavin, recent graduate of Fort Benning's Paratrooper School, was with his wife and daughter at a theater in downtown Columbus when the owner abruptly cut off the projector. "He stepped on stage to announce the attack," Gavin recalled. "I was shocked. We left to return to Fort Benning, expecting orders of some kind. To the contrary. All the aircraft we had been using for training were taken away and all of Washington's attentions seemed to be concentrated on the Pacific and the West Coast."[3]

W. C. Tucker, editor of the morning *Enquirer*, was on post for the funeral of Clinton Taylor, a twenty-one-year-old mess sergeant who was

---

[2] Hyatt, "Three Days that Changed Columbus," E-1.

[3] T. Michael Booth and Duncan Spencer, *Paratrooper* (New York: Simon & Schuster, 1994) 78.

killed in a collision with a rural school bus. Back in town, Tucker called the newsroom and was told the news. The hard-boiled newsman slammed down the phone, rushed to the office and called in the staff. It would be morning before the *Enquirer* rolled off the press, but Tucker and co-workers rushed two four-page "Extras" to the streets. The first, selling for a dime, contained essentials. The second, sold for a nickel, reported more details.

In eight-inch block letters was one word: WAR.

After shock came fear. The leader of the Civil Defense Council said the city needed to be watchful as if Japanese planes hovered in the clouds. Lawmen stood guard at public utilities. The State Defense Corps—100 men strong—surveyed the area and reported to Georgia Governor Ellis Arnall that no Japanese were living in Muscogee County. Sunday evening, Fort Benning suffered its first casualty—Staff Sergeant Thomas O'Leary, a World War I vet who died in his living room while listening to radio accounts of the attack.

People awoke Monday to a different world.

Age would keep many out of active duty, but old soldiers at the Charles S. Harrison Post of the American Legion were ready to help. At Jordan High, senior Joe Posey led a campaign for students to buy government saving stamps. Within an hour, the school was 100 percent, the first in the country to do so.

On Monday, Herbert Solon Sturkie, a twenty-five-year-old electrician at a local cotton mill, knew what he had to do. He became the first enlistee in Columbus—a moment captured in Tuesday's *Enquirer*. "I think this is an appropriate time for every able bodied man to come to the aid of his country," he said.[4] Less than a week later, Sturkie was on his way to basic training. Sturkie would stay in the army thirty-two years, retiring as a major and decorated veteran of three wars, and receiving full military honors at his death.

Over the next four years, Fort Benning graduated 200 lieutenants a day from OCS, turning them out like an assembly line. Around town, soldiers couldn't buy a meal or a tank of gas without someone offering to pay. Construction workers, trying vainly to keep up with the influx of trainees, threw up barracks and other facilities. An installation that had been a source

---

[4] Hyatt, "Three Days that Changed Columbus," E-4.

of interesting dinner guests or a place to hunt became the community's connection with the world and with history.

In the weeks that followed, anxious young men from every stop on the map got off trains in Columbus. They didn't know where they would be in the future, but right then they were bound for Splinter Villages that popped up all over Fort Benning. With them, a relationship was forged, one that would never end in the hearts of those who passed through. It began that weekend in December.

September 2001

News came instantly. Destruction was as near as a big-screen TV. So was the dying. On local television, the Columbus Council was directing city business. Mayor Bobby Peters was away, so Mayor pro tem Jack Rodgers held the gavel. J. Edward Wilson, a former radio newsman who now worked for the mayor, appeared on the screen and whispered into Rodgers's ear. Looking into the camera, Rodgers told viewers the news at the same time he did his fellow councilors. A plane had flown into one of the towers at the World Trade Center in New York.

Rodgers "asked the city to be in prayer."[5]

It was 9:33 A.M., Tuesday, the 11th day of September, sixty years after bombs and death were dumped on Pearl Harbor. The intervening years had hardly been peaceful. Americans died in Korea, Vietnam, Lebanon, Iraq, and Somalia. But the deaths that Tuesday were not on a cold mountainside in Korea or in a sweaty jungle in Southeast Asia. This was in Manhattan, a few blocks from Wall Street, and everyone watched it unfold on television.

Lieutenant General John LeMoyne, commandant of Fort Benning, was in an airplane between Fort Leavenworth and Fort Benning when the pilot advised passengers of the shocking news. While still in the air, LeMoyne issued a directive that placed Fort Benning on Delta, the army's highest order of security. Although threats to the post were minimal, Lieutenant Colonel Randy Macoz recognized the potential for continued terrorist

---

[5] "Columbus Council Meeting," *Columbus Ledger-Enquirer*, September 12 2001, 6.

attacks. "We are a historic location, and we've got some capabilities many posts don't have," he said. "We can't let down our guard."[6]

Being on guard was the first thought of city officials, too. After Rodgers offered a prayer for New York, Councilor Bob Poydashaff, a former lawyer at Fort Benning, asked about security at Columbus: "We're close and symbiotic with Fort Benning, one of the world's major military installations. We ought to be sure we have plans in place."[7]

Six minutes after officials were told of the first plane hitting the World Trade Center, a Muscogee County sheriff's deputy came into the council chambers with news about the second tower and the Pentagon. Chief Deputy Jimmy Griffin advised that local security measures already were being taken. Before the meeting was over, City Manager Carmen Cavezza, a former commanding general at Benning, issued orders to secure the Government Center. Within the hour, patrol cars blocked entrances and sawhorses and barricades circled the building.

Four floors above the council chambers, Sheriff Ralph Johnson and Griffin watched events unfold as they huddled around a television. Five years earlier, the city had been a venue for the 1996 Atlanta Olympic Games. Preparing a security plan for the Women's Fast Pitch Softball event, the city identified vital locations. Though Columbus was not a major metropolitan center, it had several potential targets. Fort Benning would take care of itself, but in addition to the army post, there were public utilities, the US Corps of Engineer dams on the Chattahoochee River, communication centers such as TSYS and AFLAC, a Fortune 500 corporation with international ties. Johnson's personnel and officers from the Columbus Police Department were dispatched to those key spots. Also Columbus Municipal Airport, moving to its highest level of security, Level 4, stopped air traffic on orders of the Federal Aviation Administration.

At 10:15 A.M., representatives from the various public agencies gathered for a press conference at the Public Safety Building, four blocks from the Government Center. Officials assured the community that the necessary steps were being taken to keep local people safe and secure. "I

---

[6] Eddie Daniels, "Officials Discuss Post Security," *Columbus Ledger-Enquirer*, September 15 2001, B-1.

[7] "Columbus Council Meeting," 6.

wasn't alive for Pearl Harbor, but those people must have been having the same feelings," noted Riley Land, Emergency Management Director.[8]

Ralph Puckett did remember Pearl Harbor. A day shy of his sixteenth birthday, he was on the ninth green of a golf course in Tifton, Georgia, when his father told him of the attack. The retired army colonel assumed that people's memory of September 11 would be just as keen as his generation's recall was of December 7.

"Pearl Harbor was the kick-off of a world war," Puckett said. "While we may consider ourselves at war with terrorists. I can't imagine this turning into a world war. For God's sake, I hope not."[9] War, however, was on the mind of Lieutenant General LeMoyne. On Thursday, LeMoyne held a question-and-answer session in his sixth-floor office at Infantry Hall. The commanding general bluntly stated the United States was at war. "There was a planned, a coordinated and a synchronized attack against the American people and America's heartland," the thirty-seven-year army veteran said.[10] LeMoyne was awaiting congressional approval before moving to his next assignment. What he did not reveal was that he had lost a close friend in the action at the Pentagon. In the coming weeks, LeMoyne would move into his late colleague's job. In September 2001, Le Moyne's responsibility was Fort Benning, just as it was Omar Bradley's generations before. War had changed, but leadership had not. Talking with the reporter, LeMoyne's words were clear: "As we have always done in the past, our petty differences have been put aside. We will be better for this."[11]

The terrorism in New York affected both young and old. Leaving a PTA meeting on the night of September 11, a middle school student looked to the sky. All day students had watched the horror. She took her father's hand and asked a question he dreaded. "Daddy," Kaitlin Hyatt asked, "should we be scared of every plane that comes over?"[12]

---

[8] Richard Hyatt, "Memories of Pearl Harbor Resurrected," *Columbus Ledger-Enquirer*, September 12 2001, A-13.

[9] Hyatt, "Memories of Pearl Harbor Resurrected," A-13.

[10] Richard Hyatt, "Life Will Never Be the Way it Was," *Columbus Ledger-Enquirer*, September 13 2001, A-13.

[11] Ibid., A-1.

[12] Richard Hyatt, conversation with his daughter Kaitlyn Hyatt, September 11 2001.

Former artillery sergeant Robert Sellers had come through such moments before. He was at Pearl Harbor that Sunday morning in 1941, trying to guard men and planes. "I was there. I saw it all," he said. He knew what he wanted to do. He knew there would be war, just as there was when he was young. "I wish I could go," he said. "I'm just too old."[13]

---

[13] Hyatt, "Memories of Pearl Harbor Resurrected," A-13.

1.

The Camp Comes to Columbus

John Betjeman was easy to overlook.

Though he rubbed shoulders with the leaders of business and politics, Betjeman was a hired hand, a civil engineer brought to Columbus to manage the Jordan Company, a prosperous development firm owned by one of the community's oldest families. He limped and he smiled, both with ease, overcoming his physical handicap with liberal doses of personality and persistence.

"He was a born ambassador," wrote journalist W. C. Woodall. "He limped with an elegance and air of distinction that I have never seen fully equaled."[1] So when it came time for the city of Columbus to undertake a high-stakes venture to alter its future, the city leaders turned to John A. Betjeman. In the halls of the US Congress, Betjeman would earn the honorary title of the "Ambassador from Columbus" and would secure a military institution vital to its neighbors and to the world.

When John A. Betjeman arrived from Albany, Georgia, in 1917, Columbus was a cotton town and cotton was a royal crop. Its riverfront was lined with textile mills that paid bills on both sides of the Chattahoochee River. Locals also considered themselves patriots. In frontier days, Fort Mitchell was located on an Alabama hilltop overlooking the river. In 1888, during the Spanish-American War, Camp Conrad was located in North Highlands, a mill village that flanked the massive Bibb Mill.

Columbus remembered Camp Conrad as good for the country and good for local bank accounts. "With the influx of several thousand troops, business became brisk and Columbus became quite military minded.... Dress parades and reviews became a part of the city's social life, and ball

---

[1] William Clyde Woodall, *Hometown and Other Sketches* (Columbus GA: Columbus Office Supply Company, 1935) 236.

games and barbecues were planned for the soldiers' entertainment."[2] World
War I was on the horizon in early 1917. As the country prepared, army
bases sprang up all over the South, including Macon and Montgomery.
Columbus leaders wondered why their community was not on the list. In
late March, S. A. Spivey, secretary of the Columbus Chamber of Commerce,
wrote a letter to the editor of the *Columbus Ledger*, pointing out advantages
the city offered to an army post. Days later at a chamber meeting, Josiah
Flournoy introduced a resolution proposing Columbus as a military site
because of its number of railroads, "radiating in seven directions to all points
of the compass from Columbus."[3] He also touted the area's good weather
and good location. His resolution called for authorities to consider
quartering at least a brigade of troops in Columbus.[4]

In May, after the resolution was adopted, Columbus newspapers
announced that the chief center of army training camps would be in the
southeast. Of sixteen proposed camps in the southeast, fourteen had been
chosen, including Fort McPherson in Atlanta. Congressman W. C.
Adamson received a telegram requesting him to arrange inspections by the
War Department of potential campsites near Columbus. Another telegram
was sent to Major General Leonard Wood, commander of the Southeastern
Department in Charleston, South Carolina, requesting Wood to send
someone to help elect a suitable campsite near Columbus. Wood
recommended Major C. E. Kilbourne.

Believing a personal visit would fortify their written request, a
committee headed by Mayor Lucius H. Chappell left for Charleston on May
24 to meet with Kilbourne. On that day, a lengthy questionnaire sent by
Kilbourne arrived in Columbus. Little time was spent on it due to the arrival
of Major Guthrie, who was stationed at Mobile with the Corps of Engineers.
Encouraged by Wood and Kilbourne, the War Department ordered
Guthrie to conduct an inspection of the Columbus area. Guthrie was the
first official to respond to the chamber's effort, and his one-day visit made

---

[2] Margaret Laney Whitehead and Barbara Bogart, *City of Progress, a History of
Columbus, Georgia, 1828–1978* (Columbus GA: Columbus Office Supply Company,
1979) 247–48.

[3] Loretto Lamar Chappell, "Notes from Scrap-book, Chamber of Commerce,"
Fort Benning Folders, Chappell File, Genealogy Department, Columbus Public
Library, Columbus GA, 3–4.

[4] Ibid.

the chamber's Military Committee realize it needed more specific information about available land. Members carefully completed Kilbourne's questionnaire, giving details of electrical and water supplies and listing land suitable for rifle ranges. An impressive tract of land east of the city was recommended by Marshall Morton, a county tax equalizer and real estate agent who later was city manager.

In June, local businessmen met to discuss funding the effort to attract the base and hoped to raise $50,000. This group evolved into the Chamber of Commerce's Military Committee. Members included Chairman Leighton W. MacPherson, R. C. Jordan, Walter A. Richards, Robert E. Dismukes, Homer R. McClatchey, J. Homer Dimon, R. M. Page, T. G. Reeves, W. J. Fielder, Reynolds Flournoy, H. C. Smith, and Rhodes Browne. Later that month, Wood's aide-de-camp inspected the Columbus area. He approved the tract of land recommended by Morton as suitable for a wartime cantonment. Columbus was not chosen as one of the sixteen sites, however. Still determined, George C. Palmer and J. B. Key returned to Charleston. Wood informed them that he had recommended Columbus and that the decision now rested with the War Department. Palmer and Key then went to Washington, coming home with secretary of the army Newton Baker's assurance that if the chosen sites failed to meet requirements, or if another was needed, Columbus would be selected.

If selected, Columbus desired the infantry and machine-gun firing school. General John J. Pershing, commander of the Expeditionary Force, emphasized the need for these additional firing schools in cables he sent to the War Department. He wanted troops trained to fire a rifle and a machine gun, the most destructive weapon of World War I's new technology, accounting for 90 of every 100 casualties during the conflict. In his September 25 cable, Pershing wrote, "Infantry soldiers should be excellent shots.... Therefore strongly review my previous recommendations that all troops be given complete course rifle practice...before leaving the United States."[5] On October 21, he defined a need not only for firing schools but also for an infantry school to train officers who would in turn train their men.[6] Pershing's cable foretold the mission of the Infantry School, but

---

[5] Senate Committee on Military Affairs, *Land for Artillery Training Fields*, 65th Congress, 3rd sess., 1919, 160.

[6] Senate Committee on Military Affairs, *Land for Artillery Training Fields*, 160–61.

chamber members could not have imagined this outcome as they struggled to "sell" the city as a site for the small-arms firing school. In December, an Encampment Committee of the Columbus Chamber of Commerce traveled to Washington. Making the trip were A. F. Kunze, H. R. McClatchey, Marshall Morton, Henry B. Crawford, Albert Kirven, Frank U. Garrard, T. T. Miller, J. Ralston Cargill, and John A. Betjeman.

Going "hat in hand," to meet impressive dignitaries, they were relieved to find a familiar face working in the nation's capital. Spotting Major J. Norman Pease behind a desk at one of the offices, the Columbus men observed, "That's no dignitary—that's Norman Pease."[7] Interestingly, this home boy was the grandnephew of General Henry L. Benning and kept close ties with Columbus since his mother, Anna Pease, lived there.

Although Pease eased the way for the men in Washington, their attempt seemed futile. Morton, Betjeman, and Kirven were the last to leave. Kirven, who caught a severe cold due to the Washington weather, developed pneumonia and died. However, on May 21, 1918, the War Department issued Special Orders 119, appointing Colonel Henry E. Eames to head a board of officers meeting at Fort Sill "for the purpose of selecting a site for the Infantry School of Arms."[8]

In the summer of 1918, when news reached Columbus that the Infantry School of Arms was leaving Oklahoma, the chamber sent Betjeman back to Washington as its resident agent. At the nation's capital for nearly three months, Betjeman provided valuable information to the chamber. When relocation of the Infantry School of Arms became a necessity due to overcrowding at Fort Sill, Oklahoma, the War Department considered Columbus. General Richard M. Blatchford, former commandant of the School of Musketry, a predecessor of the School of Arms, visited Columbus and approved the location. J. Norman Pease received a telegram from the War Department that same month ordering him to Columbus "for the purpose of carrying out the instructions of chief of staff in connection with

---

[7] J. Norman Pease, Columbus attorney and nephew of J. Norman Pease, telephone interview by Peggy Stelpflug, December 2 1999.

[8] Copy of orders found in LeRoy W. Yarborough, in collaboration with Truman Smith, *A History of the Infantry School, Fort Benning, Georgia* (Ft. Benning: The Infantry School, 1931) 307.

examination of site offered for a School of Musketry and preparation of estimates for construction necessary if site found suitable."[9]

Although other inspections of Columbus as a wartime cantonment were carried out, Blatchford and Pease were the first to inspect Columbus as a potential site of the Infantry School of Arms. Columbus now competed with Fayetteville, North Carolina, and West Point, Kentucky. In July 1918, Eames announced Fayetteville as his first choice and Columbus as his second. Aware of Eames' praise of Fayetteville, Colonel E. P. King, Jr., an artilleryman, requested Fayetteville as a training ground for the field artillery. General Peyton March, War Department chief of staff, also an artilleryman, is credited with saying, "If Fayetteville is all that damned good and the infantry wants it, maybe the artillery should have it."[10] Secretary of War Baker approved King's request, ending the battle between the artillery and the infantry. With Fayetteville no longer a contender, Columbus was first choice for the Infantry School of Arms.

As Betjeman continued negotiating and lobbying in Washington, Columbus businessman Frank G. Lumpkin was influential behind the scenes. As head of Willcox-Lumpkin Company, an insurance business started by his stepfather Dewitt Fisk Willcox in 1848, Lumpkin enlisted the aid of William J. Harris. A Cedartown native and University of Georgia graduate, Harris worked in banking and insurance, later serving as private secretary to US Senator A. D. Clay. Lumpkin helped Harris campaign for the US Senate in 1918, believing a senator from this part of Georgia would determine the fate of the Columbus post since Columbus received little support from Georgia senators busy with camps near their homes. Lumpkin, therefore, campaigned for his "own" senator.

---

[9] "Early History of Fort Benning," *Army, Navy, Air Force Register* 76/3920 (January 22 1955): 6. The telegram to Maj. Pease, Quartermaster Reserve Corps, and a copy of travel orders issued to Maj. Gen. Richard N. Blatchford, chief of industry, were found in Pease's personal papers in 1955. These documents are believed to be the first authorizing travel to Columbus GA, for the purpose of locating the Infantry School of Arms. Maj. Guthrie's visit, ordered by the War Department, May 29 1917, is considered the first inspection of Columbus GA as a potential army training site.

[10] Charles White, "The Origins of Fort Benning" White delivered his paper at Columbus College (Columbus State University) March 1998. *Muscogiana* 6/324 (Fall 1995): 57–81.

Together Lumpkin and Harris "arranged a party in Washington for selected military and civilian leaders. Georgia hospitality, which included some of Mr. Lumpkin's finest corn whiskey, proved decisive."[11] Betjeman's diligence and Lumpkin's hospitality were successful. On August 17, 1918, Betjeman advised the Chamber of Commerce of the General Staff's approval to locate the Infantry School of Arms near Columbus. Next morning's headline in the *Enquirer-Sun* was "Columbus Gets Big Camp." Columbus was expected to provide quarters for about 25,000 men and to secure $50,000. On August 27, the War Department's orders designating Columbus as the location for the army's School of Arms were approved.

Betjeman wrote his wife on September 1 from the Cochran Hotel in Washington: "Glad cold better. Please take care for all the effort and all the sacrifice is for you...this finer than I ever dare hope and worth more than any project yet started."[12]

On September 18, the War Department directed the Infantry School of Arms at Fort Sill, Oklahoma, to move "all its personnel, property, and equipment to Columbus, Georgia, by October first."[13] Eames, arriving September 21, informed Major J. Paul Jones of the move. Appointed construction quartermaster, Jones was in charge of the $11,000,000 project. His task was to build a temporary post to accommodate 1200 men.

In his "Final Report on the Construction of Camp Benning, Georgia," Jones wrote that he was in Washington working on plans and estimates for the Infantry School of Arms when he was informed that troops were en route and that "although there had been no money allotment made, nor had the project been formally approved by the Secretary of War, yet the troops would have to be taken care of."[14] Jones learned that the W. Z. Williams Company of Macon "would undertake the construction of the temporary camp and wait for their money until proper authorization had been obtained to repay them."[15] The offer was accepted.

---

[11] White, "The Origins of Fort Benning," 11.

[12] Chappell, "Notes from Scrap-book, Chamber of Commerce," 2.

[13] Yarborough, *History of the Infantry School*, 75.

[14] John Paul Jones, "Final Report of Major J. Paul Jones of the Construction of Camp Benning, GA," December 8 1919, Microfilm, Udgg FU (Item 4), Donovan Technical Library, Fort Benning GA, 1.

[15] Ibid.

On September 23, Jones purchased a carload of pipe and materials in Columbus. Appealing to "town pride and their patriotism," Jones purchased lumber from local companies at thirty dollars per thousand board feet rather than the thirty-five-dollar asking price. The Williams Company arranged for teams and trucks to haul needed lumber the next morning. The following day, local newspapers ran free ads for common and skilled labor while M. Reynolds Flournoy, representing the chamber, accompanied Eames and Jones to select a site: "The site finally determined on contained about eighty-four acres and was owned by Mr. Alex Reid. This site was situated on the Macon Road about three miles from the heart of Columbus and within less than a mile from the city water supply, street car service, etc."[16]

Flournoy arranged a six-month lease by the chamber, paying Reid a thousand dollars. Eames, Jones, and Reid agreed upon a settlement of two thousand dollars for damages paid by the W. Z. Williams Company. With the immediate purchase of the land, Jones mused that for the Reid family it was "quite a surprise...to wake up in the morning expecting to live in this old home the balance of their lives and by ten o'clock to be moved out."[17] With no time to harvest his sweet potato or cotton crop, Reid moved from his home and fields. By noon 200 men were on the job building the first mess hall.

On September 25, War Construction Division, Project Number 209–1, authorized the expenditure of $100,000 "to provide temporary accommodations for troops at Columbus, Georgia."[18] The *Ledger* reported on September 30, "Temporary quarters will be finished tonight and ready for troops. What was a cotton patch last Thursday is today covered in buildings."[19] The camp was completed in an impressive fourteen days. It included four warehouses, five mess halls, eight latrines, eight baths, a garage, a two-story infirmary, two standard stables, a fenced corral, sixty-five officers' pyramidal tent floors, 300 enlisted men's tent floors and approximately two miles of gravel roads.

---

[16] Ibid., 3.

[17] Ibid., 4.

[18] Jones, "Final Report of Major John Paul Jones of the Construction of Camp Benning, GA," 4.

[19] "Small Camp Is Near Complete," *Columbus Ledger*, September 30 1918, 3.

Jones, crediting Eames, wrote,

> This could not have been accomplished by the constructing
> Quartermaster without the cooperation and help of Colonel Eames
> himself, as he assisted the Constructing Quartermaster in many ways
> and dropped all rank and formality on the work and talked as builder
> to builder, and not as is often the case, as Commanding Officer to a
> Reserve Corps Major. Eames' counsel and his knowledge of what the
> school was to be saved at least 50 percent of lost motion which
> generally occurs in starting construction at other camps.[20]

On October 4, 1918, instructors from Fort Sill arrived in Columbus,
and the following day Eames was appointed commandant of the Infantry
School of Arms, succeeding Colonel S. W. Miller, who had not come to
Columbus. On October 6, the first troops arrived from Fort Sill, "a splendid
body of men, all being hearty, strong and in excellent shape."[21] The first
installment of 400 men led by Captain Albert Kindervater arrived by train
just after 6:00 A.M. The Red Cross canteen corps served breakfast in the Old
Southern Depot Building. After eating, the men marched to the camp. On
October 19, the *Enquirer-Sun* reported that J. W. Riley, adjutant general of
the War Department, wrote Chamber of Commerce Secretary S. A. Spivey
to inform him that the camp would be named Camp Benning.

The naming of the post for Civil War General Henry Lewis Benning
was suggested by the Confederate Veterans and the United Daughters of the
Confederacy. Winnifred Moore Minter, a UDC member, presented the
written proposal to the Secretary of War and members of Congress. The
Rotary Club, led by J. Homer Dimon, also requested that the camp honor
Benning, a local lawyer, judge, and soldier.

As the school moved into its new home, most Columbus citizens
accepted the post. In the newspaper column "Personals," Eames' new
residence was described: "Col. E. H. Eames has rented the lovely bungalow
of Mr. John Hinds on Wildwood Circle which he and his wife will occupy.
The Hinds home is one of the prettiest in Columbus and most
advantageously situated near the camp."[22]

---

[20] Ibid., 5.
[21] "Troops Reach City on Time," *Columbus Ledger*, October 7 1918, 5.
[22] "Personals," *Columbus Ledger*, October 6 1918, 14.

Eames was wise to rent since in mid-October he knew the camp soon would move from Macon Road to a site eight miles south of Columbus and five miles east of Bradley Landing. Jones was to head construction at the new site. News from the top didn't excite the soldiers. They had settled into their routines at the temporary quarters. They played baseball with teams from nearby posts, and some soldiers turned to poetry. In "Nuts and Bugs," a local news column, a poem titled "We Don't Know" appeared:

Some people were made to be soldiers
And the Irish were made to be cops
Saur kraut was made for the Germans
And Spaghetti was made for the Wops.

Fish were made to drink water
And men were made to drink booze.
Banks were made to hold money
And beds were made for a snooze.

Everything was made for something
There's even use for a misery
God made Wilson for President
But who in hell made the Kaiser.[23]

---

[23] "Nuts and Bugs: Camp Benning News," *Columbus Enquirer-Sun*, October 28 1918, 2.

2.

The Camp Gets a Name

Henry Lewis Benning was controversial in life and death. In his sixty-one years, he debated the politics of slavery, believed a republic based on slavery could be established, and went to war as a loyal officer in the Confederate army to stand up for those beliefs. When he returned home, he dedicated his life as a lawyer to his family and to the people of Columbus, Georgia. Then, in death, the name of this radical secessionist who feared giving power to slaves was attached to a military installation belonging to the nation Benning swore to oppose.

Writing in her thesis *Henry Lewis Benning: State Rights Advocate and Soldier*, Marie W. Kerrison captures the irony of that 1918 decision. She states, "It is interesting to note that one of the largest infantry schools in this country—federal property—is named for one of the staunchest state right advocates of the South and a brigadier general of infantry of the Confederate States Army."[1]

After government confirmation of the name Camp Benning, suggested by Winnifred Moore Minter and endorsed by the Chamber of Commerce, the *Columbus Ledger* published a historical commentary of Benning by Lucius Henry Chappell, president of the Columbus Historical Society. A two-term mayor, Chappell was called the "Father of modern Columbus."[2] To explain the mystique of this Southern general, Chappell presented information from the *Confederate Military History* published in 1899. Chappell wrote, "General Benning was one of nature's noblemen formed in her finest mould and most lavish prodigality. As an attorney, he was open,

---

[1] Marie W. Kerrison, preface to "Henry Lewis Benning: States Rights Advocate and Soldier" (thesis, Emory University, 1937).

[2] Etta Blanchard Worsley, *Columbus on the Chattahoochee* (Columbus GA: Columbus Office Supply Company, 1951) 397.

candid, and fair; as a jurist, spotless and impartial; as a warrior and patriot, brave, disinterested, and sincere; as a man and citizen, his whole life produced in those who knew him, the constant vibration of those chords which answer to all that is true and noble, generous and manly."[3]

Henry Lewis Benning was born April 2, 1814, in Columbia County near Sparta, Georgia. He was the third child and third son of eleven children born to Pleasant Moon and Malinda Lewis Meriweather White Benning. Attending Mount Zion Academy in Hancock County, Benning received the best education available. At age seventeen, he entered Franklin College, now the University of Georgia, as a sophomore.

In 1834, Benning, at the age of twenty, graduated with "first honors" from the university. After graduation, he studied law with George W. Towns in Talbotton. Towns, who served as a member of Congress and governor of Georgia, believed in the "reserved rights of the States," a belief his student shared.[4] In 1835, Benning was admitted to the bar in Columbus. His association with the popular Towns "made him welcome in the best circles in Columbus, and he made no secret of his fondness for mingling with the elite."[5] He was appointed solicitor general of the Chattahoochee Circuit in 1837 and a year later elected by the General Assembly to serve a full four-year term.

In 1839, Benning married Mary Howard Jones, who at age eight threw flowers along the path of Marquis de Lafayette on his visit to Milledgeville. She was the only daughter of the rich and respected Columbus lawyer and planter Seaborn Jones. After their marriage, the young couple moved in with Mary Howard's parents, who lived in Eldorado—a colonial house completed in 1833 by Seaborn Jones' slaves, who made bricks from the land and cut oak and cedar trees for window frames and the interior. The couple had one son,

---

[3] Lucius Henry Chappell, "Brief Sketch of General Benning for Whom Camp at Columbus Has Been Named," *Columbus Ledger*, October 20 1918, 5. Chappell cites Joseph T. Derry, author of "Georgia" in *Confederate Military History*, a Library of Confederate States History, 12 vols., ed. Gen. Clement A. Evans (Atlanta GA: Atlanta Confederate Publishing Co., 1899) 6:397.

[4] A. B. Caldwell, "George Washington Towns" *Men of Mark in Georgia: A Complete and Elaborate History of the State From Its Settlement to the Present Time*, 7 vols., ed. William J. Northen (Atlanta: A. B. Caldwell, 1910) 2:400.

[5] James C. Cobb, "The Making of a Secessionist: Henry L. Benning and the Coming of the Civil War," *Georgia Historical Quarterly* 60/4 (Winter 1976): 314.

Seaborn Jones Benning, and nine daughters (though only five of the girls survived: Mary Howard, Louisa Vivian, Augusta Jane, Anna Caroline, and Sarah).

Like his father-in-law, a member of the US Congress, Benning was interested in politics and government, especially in states' rights concerning slavery. To preserve his way of life, Benning wrote Congressman Howell Cobb, a classmate at Franklin College, proposing a separate consolidated republic that would put "slavery under the control of those most interested in it."[6] In 1849 he told Cobb, "The only safety of the South from abolition universal is to be found in an early dissolution of the Union...."[7] Cobb wanted the Union unchanged. He believed his influence in Congress would preserve slavery and that staying in the Union was the best way to fight abolition and defend slavery. Benning, convinced that bankruptcy and racial wars would follow if slavery were abolished, left the established Democratic Party and organized the Muscogee Southern Rights Association. In 1851, his "fire-eating" party, eager to fight, nominated him for Congress. In July 1851, the *Columbus Times* reported that Benning "will be true to his states. He will not sell out."[8] Benning, however, lost the election.

As a conservative regarding slavery and a radical concerning secession, Benning was not ready to share power with former slaves. Georgia had slaves when it entered the Union, so he believed slavery was neither illegal nor immoral. Benning had eighty-nine slaves valued at nearly $100,000. His old friend, Cobb—determined to keep Georgia in the Union—won a landslide victory as governor in 1851. Two years after his unsuccessful campaign for Congress, Benning, thirty-nine, was elected associate justice of the Georgia Supreme Court, the youngest man up to that time to hold the office. After serving six years, he was defeated in 1859.

After Abraham Lincoln was elected president in 1860, Benning, convinced of the moral and legal right as well as the economic need to retain slavery, spoke on behalf of secession before the Georgia State Legislature.

---

[6] Ulrich Bonnell Phillips, ed., *The Correspondence of Robert Toombs, Alexander Stephens, and Howell Cobb* (New York: DaCapo Press, 1970) 171.

[7] Phillips, ed. *The Correspondence of Robert Toombs, Alexander H. Stephens, and Howell Cobb*, 169.

[8] *Columbus Times*, July 22 1851. Title of article and page unknown. Newspaper name and date cited in Marie W. Kerrison, *Henry Louis Benning: State Rights Advocate and Soldier*, 37.

He argued the South had more arms, better military knowledge, better military schools, and financial power and resources. Without cotton provided for the industrial east, Benning reasoned, it would go bankrupt. England would provide aid to the South as it also needed cotton.

Benning helped draft Georgia's ordinance of secession, adopted in 1861. He was sent to Virginia to urge secession, stating that Georgia seceded because "a separation from the north was the only thing that could prevent the abolition of her slavery." In addition to the familiar arguments of a black takeover leading to social chaos, Benning argued that formation of a Southern Confederacy would help Virginia "materially, socially, politically, and religiously" since slavery would not be viewed as evil or morally wrong.[9]

When the Civil War started, Benning recruited men to form the 7th Regiment of Georgia volunteers. Appointed a colonel, he helped raise a loan for $5,000,000 from the Columbus district, personally donating more than 1500 bales of cotton for his cause. The unit was assigned to Toombs' Brigade of the army in Virginia. He fought in eleven major battles and later attained the rank of major general. He was at the Appomattox Court House and in command of his Georgia brigade when Lee's army surrendered.

Returning to Columbus, he "found his property burned, his family in poverty." His wife, Mary Howard, buried her father in 1864, nursed her son (who was wounded at Gettysburg), and cared for her mother as well as her brother's wife and their eight children. His daughter Anna Caroline Benning, then fourteen, later wrote that her mother "passed away June 28, 1867, as truly a victim of the war as was her gallant brother [Colonel James A. Jones] who had fallen in Gettysburg."[10]

Unable to maintain Eldorado without slaves and his horses and carriages gone, Benning moved his family into town on Broad Street. His dream of a separate republic—a South free to decide its own destiny—was

---

[9] H. L. Benning, speech to the Virginia State Convention, February 13, 1861, in Fulton Anderson, *Addresses Delivered before the Virginia State Convention* (Richmond: Wyatt M. Elliott, Printer, 1861); microfilm: New Haven CT: Research Publication 1974, reel 62, no. 2257, documents, Ralph Brown Draughon Library, Auburn University, Auburn AL.

[10] Anna C. Benning, "Henry L. Benning," *Men of Mark in Georgia: A Complete and Elaborate History of the State From Its Settlement to the Present Time*, 7 vols., ed. William J. Northen (Atlanta: A. B. Caldwell, 1911) 3:262–63.

over. Benning returned to his law practice and in 1865 was an unsuccessful candidate for judge of the Supreme Court of Georgia. He died July 10, 1875, at the age of sixty-one, having suffered a stroke while walking to the Muscogee County courthouse to try a case. He was buried at Linwood Cemetery. Later, Anna Benning in *Men of Mark in Georgia*, recalled her father's funeral. She remembered that "on a beautiful Sabbath morning, all classes in the city of Columbus—high and low, rich and poor, black and white, all denominations, religious, social, and military—took part in it...."[11]

Forty-three years after Benning's death and fifty-three years after the end of the Civil War, admirers proposed that the new army camp on the fringe of Columbus be named for him. At the time of the dedication at Camp Benning, Miss Benning—a true daughter of the Confederacy—was sixty-five years old. She had witnessed and written of her father's career as a lawyer, judge, soldier, and patriot.

On December 12, 1918, a formal "Flag Day" ceremony was celebrated at Camp Benning. Mrs. Rhodes Brown, president of the Woman's Federated Clubs, presented Eames with a flag for the camp's 102-foot flag pole made of Georgia pine. Columbus native Anna Caroline Benning, daughter of the Confederate general, raised the Stars and Stripes over the United States Army's Infantry School of Arms at Camp Benning, Georgia. The flag unfurled "in a lovely wave—a good omen forever for Fort Benning."[12]

Years later, Columbus native Louise Gunby Jones Dubose wrote of the 1918 ceremony. As author of the *A History of Columbus, Georgia, 1828–1928*,

---

[11] Ibid.

[12] "With Impressive Ceremony Flag Formally Presented to Fort Benning Thursday," *Columbus Enquirer-Sun*, December 13 1918, 1. The only detailed reference to a formal flag raising at Camp Benning is found in this article. Various dates are given elsewhere for the formal flag raising. Robert Holcombe's "An Outline History of Fort Benning, Georgia, and the Infantry School Concept" (a typed and duplicated booklet compiled for the National Infantry Museum, Fort Benning GA, 1990) lists October 18; The *Benning Leader* (October 1 1993, 16) says October 7; the *Bayonet* (October 8 1993, A-3) states October 19 as do Margaret Laney Whitehead and Barbara Bogart in *City of Progress* (249) and L. Albert Scipio in *The 24th Infantry at Ft. Benning, Georgia* (86); John Paul Jones in his "Final Report of the Construction of Camp Benning, Georgia," puts the date "a few days after the completion of the temporary camp" (5); and Etta Blanchard Worsley's *Columbus on the Chattahoochee* says "not long after the arrival of the soldiers," referring to October 6 1918 (412).

she used the pen name Nancy Telfair. In *Women in Columbus, 1828–1928*, Dubose revealed that not all Columbus citizens cheered the founding of the US School of Infantry near their city. Dubose described it this way:

> A great parade was held on Broad Street and among the spectators were my grandmother and aunt, the former a completely unreconstructed rebel. Opposite the old Transfer Station they stood and spotted Miss Tina (or Caroline) Benning in the lead car behind a big United States flag. My grandmother, a timid, old-fashioned lady who wore widow's weeds and a long black veil could not control her emotion. She stepped off the curb, shook her fist at her long-time friend and cried out, "Tina Benning, I'm ashamed of you—riding down Broad Street behind that old rag," and she pointed at the Stars and Stripes.[13]

Dubose illustrates how Columbus's past and Camp Benning's future melded in 1918. Amid the concerns of citizens like Dubose's grandmother, who looked to the past, and the courage of Anna Benning, who looked to the future, Camp Benning took root and grew.

---

[13] Louise Gunby Jones DuBose (Nancy Telfair), "Women in Columbus 1828–1928," 24–25, unpublished manuscript, n.d., MCI Folder l, archives of Simon Schwob Memorial Library, Columbus State University, Columbus GA. The *Columbus Enquirer*, November 10 1975, reports Telfair gave a seminar at Columbus college with "data concerning women from 1829–1928" on "Women in the History of Columbus, Georgia." Although DuBose refers to Anna Caroline Benning as "Tina," others, including Ms. Benning, use the name "Tiny."

3.

A Peacetime Valley Forge

With soldiers training in their backyards, some Columbus folks began to have second thoughts about Camp Benning. Cotton mill owners worried about their skilled white workers, "the only kind used in the cotton and woolen mills of Georgia," leaving low-paying jobs for higher-paying government jobs.[1] Although Columbus was the state's fifth largest city in the early 1900s, it was second in the South in the manufacture of cotton goods, exceeded only by Augusta, Georgia. Mill owners, fearing changes in local economic conditions would threaten productivity, wanted business as usual.

Since the 1850s, Columbus was a textile center with mills such as the Eagle & Phenix Manufacturing Company, Muscogee Mills, Swift Mills, and Columbus Manufacturing Company. Aside from farming, these mills provided most of the jobs in the area. People were sympathetic to the concerns of the mill owners, but most members of the Chamber of Commerce—the organization that worked the hardest to secure the camp—were bankers, realtors or insurance men who would benefit from the growth.

Plantation and farm-owners in Muscogee and Chattahoochee counties also feared government encroachment. Thousands of acres of land owned by families for generations were subject to condemnation and eventual government ownership. Less than fifty-five years had passed since the Civil War and the Union Army's partial destruction of Columbus. Citizens of the southern town did not want to be "destroyed" again by unnecessary action of the federal government. Nor was the military a favorite of single men. More men meant more competition for local Romeos who disliked the

---

[1] O. B. Stevens, commissioner, R. F. Wright, Department of Agriculture, *Georgia: Historical and Industrial* (Atlanta: George W. Harrison, State Printer, The Franklin Printing and Publishing Co., 1901) 774.

military taking their land and their women. Numerous local women married Benning soldiers, so many in fact that Columbus would become known as the "Mother-in-law of the Army."

Lieutenant LeRoy W. Yarborough, who wrote *A History of the Infantry School, Fort Benning, Georgia* in collaboration with Major Truman Smith in 1931, reported that "local opponents denounced the post" as a menace to religion, home and womanhood.[2] When Columbus businessman Frank G. Lumpkin read Yarborough's manuscript in 1931, he wanted this comment eliminated since it was "not seriously made by any representative group."[3] Lumpkin believed most citizens went out of their way to excuse or protect soldiers rather than accuse them of wrongdoing.

Lumpkin told of the city's response to the post's request to keep sexual diseases—brought into town by soldiers—from affecting other soldiers. Lumpkin wrote, "many women were actually locked in a high-wire fence at the old City Jail because it was said they were contaminated by army men." He added, "Much more could be said on this subject, but the post has the cooperation of the Columbus people at all times and sometimes to a point where it even appeared unreasonable. It would therefore be more accurate, also more dignified, to eliminate this from the history."[4]

The action Lumpkin referred to was considered appropriate at the time. After the Commission of Training Camp Activities (CTCA) was created April 1917, a law enforcement division enabled the forced treatment of infected prostitutes by putting them in jails or "lock hospitals." The CTCA would have approved of Columbus's attempt to create "moral zones" free of prostitution around its military cantonment.[5]

The Chamber of Commerce kept support alive. Secretary S. A. Spivey wrote for advice to J. T. Slatter of the chamber in Columbia, South Carolina, home of Camp Jackson and also a cotton-mill town. On October

---

[2] LeRoy Yarborough, in collaboration with Truman Smith, *A History of the Infantry School, Fort Benning, Georgia* (Ft. Benning: The Infantry School, 1931) 78.

[3] Frank G. Lumpkin Sr., written communication to Col. H. E. Knight, December 4 1931, in Lumpkin's personal files, Willcox-Lumpkin Company, Columbus GA, 1, regarding the manuscript *A History of the Infantry School, Fort Benning, Georgia* by LeRoy W. Yarborough, in collaboration with Truman Smith (Ft. Benning: The Infantry School, 1931).

[4] Ibid.

[5] Allan M. Brandt, *No Magic Bullet* (Oxford: Oxford University Press, 1985) 44.

6, as troops were arriving, the *Columbus Ledger* published a story called "Camp to Bring Big Prosperity," along with Slatter's response. Slatter explained that people are drawn to an army camp to build homes, find employment, or start a business. He argued the camp would serve as a stimulus for business and not harm cotton mill interests, writing, "Tell your people they are standing in the way of their own interests if they do not give you their full and unstinted support in securing the location of an army camp."[6]

Though some citizens doubted the camp's value, Colonel Henry E. Eames did not. Determined to make Benning a permanent post, Eames believed its demise would mean the extinction of the School of Infantry concept. Enlarging the camp was a deliberate move to preserve it. Congress could easily eliminate Camp Benning as it existed in 1918 but might reconsider a larger camp that prepared men for war or peace. Eames began searching for a permanent site. The camp on Macon Road was sufficient for war training but not for the technical training required for students of the Infantry School of Arms. Eames found an area on the south side of Columbus, the site of the Bussey Plantation, a location suggested by B. S. Miller, a lawyer who specialized in farm loans. Miller, whose clientele included Arthur Bussey, personally guided Eames, "a frequent visitor to Miller's house," around the plantation.[7]

In October 1918, Eames told Jones to stop construction of the railroad near the temporary camp until he met with the Construction Division and the War College officers in Washington. There they agreed to relocate the camp to the Bussey Plantation, nine miles south of Columbus in Muscogee and Chattahoochee counties, "generally to the south and east of the confluence of Upatoi Creek and the Chattahoochee River."[8]

In 1907, Arthur Bussey bought a 1,782-acre plot that once belonged to John Woolfolk and two years later built "Riverside." He began with a two-story meeting-house built on Lumpkin Road in the 1800s. It was rolled on

---

[6] "Camp to Bring Big Prosperity," *Columbus Ledger*, October 6 1918, 10.

[7] "Site for Fort Benning Was Suggested to Col. Eames by B. S. Miller," *Industrial Index*, July 28 1954, 59.

[8] LeRoy W. Yarborough, in collaboration with Truman Smith, *A History of the Infantry School, Fort Benning, Georgia* (Ft. Benning: The Infantry School, 1931) 131.

logs pulled by mules "without damaging a single tree" to its present location on Vibbert Avenue where it became an essential part of "Riverside."[9]

Bussey raised cotton, corn, and sugar cane and supported a dairy herd that provided milk and butter. The plantation, with a grove of large trees, had its own cotton gin, the Riverside Trading Post, housing for its black workers, a good spring for water, a storage tank, and other buildings. Bussey asked $878,000 for his land, home, tenant quarters, and barn. Jones, again proving his talents, offered to pay half. Bussey accepted.

On October 19, 1918, a year and a half after America entered World War I, the assistant secretary of war approved $3,600,000 for the purchase of 115,000 acres, including Bussey Plantation, for Camp Benning. With nearly 98,000 acres accounted for but not entirely paid for, the reservation could obtain 17,000 more acres—60 percent in Chattahoochee County with the remainder in Muscogee. On October 30, an additional $9,19,875 was authorized for a proposed 25,000 men at the Infantry School of Arms.

Condemnation proceedings to acquire 115,000 acres of local land began November 2. Aided by Reynolds Flournoy of the chamber, Eames began the acquisition. Teams of appraisers helped arrive at a fair price for landowners who responded favorably in most cases because of the "duty" to the war effort. Actual construction of the new post on the Bussey Plantation started November 2—nine days before the war ended.

One stipulation brought quick resentment. It required that one percent of the money received by a landowner in the sale of his property be paid to a title insurance company engaged by the government. This was contrary to the legal custom in Georgia that required a fee, if any, to be paid by the buyer instead of the seller. Landowners thought the requirement unjust. Families who owned their property for generations thought payment of a title examination was extortion. Refusing to enter in negotiations, these landowners contested their cases in court, slowing the camp's land acquisition.[10]

With the arrival of 40 officers and 700 men of the Small Arms Firing School from Camp Perry, Ohio, on October 26, the *Columbus Ledger*

---

[9] George McBurney, "Riverside," news release, November 26 1962, documents, information section, Donovan Library, U. S. Army Infantry Center, Fort Benning GA, 3–5.

[10] Yarborough, *A History of the Infantry School, Fort Benning, Georgia*, 132.

announced the reality of a permanent post: "With the coming of the Ohio troops in Columbus, which included many rifle experts, the Camp Perry Infantry School of Arms is no more. Instead Camp Benning looms upon the military horizon as the location of that necessary prerequisite of the military establishment."[11]

The Selden-Breck Construction Company of St. Louis, Missouri, started to work November 2 at the camp's new location where 5,000 workmen strived to build a camp planned for 10,000 men, 2,000 officers, and 2,000 non-commissioned officers. A two-story office, constructed from materials brought by wagon from Columbus, was the first construction at the new camp. Not surprisingly, it served as an office for Jones and later became the camp's headquarters.

World War I ended on the eleventh hour of the eleventh day of the eleventh month: "At the designated moment, the entire western front opened up with gunfire as war-worn troops sought to fire the last shot."[12] Though the war ended, military training continued. In December 1918, the camp's first class arrived: 125 officers and 1,200 men welcomed 100 recent West Point graduates, the first students enrolled in the Infantry School of Arms at Camp Benning, Georgia.

Many area citizens who viewed Camp Benning as a mere WWI training camp wished it would simply go away. Constituents wrote to their congressmen, praising or condemning the camp. Historian LeRoy Yarborough wrote that the fate of the camp "several times lay on the lap of the gods, and the gods were not inclined to be friendly."[13] He described a divided community: "Columbus, no longer presenting a united front, had entered a new contest, marked by acrimony and rancor...friends of the camp had to make many concessions and sacrifices, not the least of which was the assumption of liability for damages resulting from the government's tentative occupation of some 17,000 acres of valuable land near the city."[14]

In December, mill owner G. Gunby Jordan was toastmaster at a banquet for Betjeman held at the Cricket, a popular new dining spot. Betjeman was honored for his part in obtaining Camp Benning for

---

[11] "Camp Perry Troops Here," *Columbus Ledger*, October 27 1918, 1.
[12] Gorton Carruth, *What Happened When* (New York: Signet, 1991) 657.
[13] Yarborough, *A History of the Infantry School*, 79.
[14] Ibid., 113.

Columbus. At the dinner, 200 business and political leaders honored the city's foremost ambassador and lobbyist, presenting him with a silver loving cup and a check for $2,500. A lineup of speakers—some in uniforms, some in suits from Chancellor's clothing store—eulogized their guest. Dr. C. N. Howard of Chattahoochee County, an early supporter, sounded less mirthful than others, saying he hoped the camp would not "ruin the county I love by destroying it."[15]

Soon after the festivities, Betjeman received a letter from J. N. Pease of the War Department's Construction Division saying estimates for new camp construction had not gone to the General Staff. Pease thought Congress would block the action and said it was rumored that the Senate Committee on Military Affairs wanted to abandon Camp Benning. Pease asked for Betjeman's help: "I suggest that you use your good offices to rush this procedure, if possible from where you are; if not, think it wise for you to come to Washington immediately after the holidays to get this whole business settled finally so that Congress cannot 'spill the beans.'"[16]

Shortly after the holidays, Betjeman returned to Washington with Eames and Major John Paul Jones to attend meetings held by the Senate Committee on Military Affairs. They provided high drama played out by leading men from politics and the military. The cast included Senators Hoke Smith of Georgia and Kenneth D. McKellar of Tennessee; Colonels Henry E. Eames and Morton C. Mumma; and civilians B. S. Miller, Joe S. Bergin, and C. C. Minter.

Secretary of War Newton Baker appeared before the committee on January 7, 1919, asking approval to continue plans for permanent developments in Kentucky and North Carolina as well as machine gun training and establishment of a tank corps at Columbus, Georgia. Baker noted, "The military men all feel that the three projects are necessary," since after peacetime reductions, 500,000 would use these facilities.[17]

---

[15] "Appreciative Citizens Give Loving Cup and Check to Betjeman," *Columbus Enquirer-Sun*, December 7 1918, 1.

[16] J. N. Pease to John A. Betjeman, letter written December 17 1918, "Notes from Clippings, Telegrams, and Letters Preserved in a Scrapbook Belonging to Mrs. John A. Betjeman," Fort Benning Folders, Chappell File, Genealogy Department, Columbus Public Library, Columbus GA, 5.

[17] Senate Committee on Military Affairs, *Land for Artillery Training Fields*, 65th Congress, 3rd sess., 1919, 7.

Senator Charles S. Thomas of Colorado supported Baker. He said the camps were necessary to back up the League of Nations, Wilson's plan to prevent future wars. Committee members, however, favored abandoning Benning since only $1 million of its estimated cost of more than $14 million had been spent. McKellar asked if a camp "already built and paid for" could serve as the school site "rather than spend twenty-odd millions of dollars or whatever the amount it, in building a new one at Columbus?"[18]

Assistant Secretary of War Benedict Crowell reminded McKellar "none of them have the acreage that is involved here for this school of fire," referring to the 115,000 acres available at Columbus.[19] Committee chairman George E. Chamberlain of Oregon asked Crowell if he thought Camp Benning might be abandoned.

"Yes, sir," Crowell replied.

McKellar interrupted. "We think your work at Benning ought to be stopped," he said. "If you want a resolution, I think we can pass it instantly."

"If you will pass the resolution, I will stop the work tonight," the army officer answered.

McKellar proceeded. "Then Mr. Chairman," he said, "I move that the Secretary of War be requested not to proceed further with the work at Camp Benning, Georgia."[20]

The motion was seconded, put to a vote, and unanimously prevailed. On January 9, Congressional action ordered Major J. Paul Jones, the constructing quartermaster, to salvage and abandon the camp. Jones "upon receiving the order to salvage Camp Benning consulted the dictionary and found the word 'salvage' meant to 'save.' Armed with this definition, Jones ordered that all buildings be painted to 'save' them."[21] Senator-elect William Harris "assured Jones that while he could not order the Major to disobey his instructions, he could get him out of any trouble he might find himself in."[22]

---

[18] Ibid., 60.

[19] Ibid., 60–61.

[20] Ibid.

[21] L. Albert Scipio, *The 24th Infantry at Ft. Benning* (Silver Spring MD: Roman Publications, 1986) 9.

[22] Charles White, "The Origins of Fort Benning" White delivered his paper at Columbus College (Columbus State University) March 1998. *Muscogiana* 6/324 (Fall 1995): 57–81.

On January 10, hearings reconvened at the request of Senator Hoke Smith of Georgia. In a change of heart, he now spoke in defense of the camp. At this point, the school had been reduced from 30,000 officers and men to 25,000, then 10,000. The US Government, according to Yarborough, actually owned only 2,217 acres of the planned 115,000 acres and had paid the two owners $29,818.75 for their land, acknowledging, "Now because of peacetime even more reductions would come."[23] Senator Smith said Columbus citizens wanted to sell their land to the government and some already had made other provisions since condemnation proceedings began. Warning of "the ruin of these people unless the government goes on in good faith with its purchase," Smith, a former Georgia governor, urged government support for completion of the camp.[24]

Colonel Eames patiently and professionally answered committee members and reaffirmed his support for Benning. "There is no other place that I know of where we could put this school," he said, explaining the search process used in selecting Columbus, a search that stretched from the Pacific to the Atlantic.[25] Senator William F. Kirby of Arkansas questioned Eames about the necessity of an infantry school, asking the army colonel about the purpose of West Point.

"West Point is the foundation school which has nothing to do with the teaching of the technical use of arms," Eames explained. "Every officer who comes into the service must go through these schools."

"And it is the only school in the country where you train men?" Kirby asked.

"It is the only school," Eames replied, explaining that considerable land was needed to train a substantial number of men in the most effective way to use machine guns, automatic rifles, grenades, 37 mm guns, and 3 inch trench mortars.[26]

Opponents also testified. C. C. Minter, a Cusseta attorney and farmer representing his county of 8,000 people, said Chattahoochee people "do not want their land taken over," adding that three-fourths of the population of Columbus oppose the camp, and "every mill in that town is opposed to it,"

---

[23] Yarborough, *A History of the Infantry School*, 133.
[24] Senate Committee on Military Affairs, *Land for Artillery Training Fields*, 63.
[25] Ibid., 74–75.
[26] Ibid., 76–78.

cotton mills and the Southern Plow Works, since "it might make labor higher."[27] Minter, a Georgia state senator, concluded that $200,000 to $300,000 would cover damages if the camp closed: "There are only a few people who have been actually damaged, whose property has been torn up. Mr. Arthur Bussey is perhaps the largest one, and a few others where they have gone through with the railroad."

"You want to be left alone?" asked McKellar.

"Yes, sir," Minter said.[28]

Also appearing before the committee were Frank U. Garrard, E. J. Wynn and G. H. Howard. They, like Columbus lawyer B. S. Miller, favored the camp. Representing fifteen landowners, including Bussey and W. C. Bradley, Miller said the condemned land was sparsely populated and that his clients wanted to sell to the government since they saw Camp Benning "as an economical asset to the civilian community and as a necessary part of the military establishment."[29] Miller defended supporters of the post, "I think, very naturally, that the people of Columbus think that they have a great site and think it would be a great acquisition for the government to own it, and to have this great Gibraltar built on the Chattahoochee, just as we have that great Gibraltar on the Hudson."[30]

With hearings over, the contest between friends and foes of the camp carried on intermittently in Congress for more than a year.[31] On January 18, the omnipresent Betjeman sent his wife a telegram: "I am very much encouraged and am beginning to win again. Betting is 2 to 1 in our favor."[32] Betjeman was right about the odds. On January 27, the construction division of the General Staff, assisted by Eames and Jones, revised the plan, calling for a peacetime post of about 5,000 men and 98,000 acres.

The West Point cadets who arrived in December graduated from the Infantry School of Arms on February 22, 1919, the first class to graduate

---

[27] Ibid., 116.

[28] Ibid., 115.

[29] Yarborough, *A History of the Infantry School*, 124.

[30] Senate Committee on Military Affairs, *Land for Artillery Training Fields*, 145.

[31] Yarborough, *A History of the Infantry School*, 127.

[32] John A. Betjeman, telegram to his wife, "Notes from Clippings, Telegrams, and Letters Preserved in a Scrapbook Belonging to Mrs. John A. Betjeman," Fort Benning Folders, Chappell File, Genealogy Department, Columbus Public Library, Columbus GA.

from Camp Benning. Lumpkin recalled that when West Point cadets first came to Columbus they were strictly supervised. "Later," he said, "they were allowed to come to Columbus and a group came frequently to our house where they could immediately hustle out of their uniforms and put on old golf clothes and be comfortable."[33]

On the first of March, Betjeman again wired his wife: "Have had dandy day and am winning in hard fight. Do not expect to finish until Wednesday. Both houses work all day Sunday and so do I." Betjeman was right. On March 8, the Senate Committee on Military Affairs authorized resumption of the purchase of lands and continuation of construction for the Infantry School of Arms. This plan, which Eames and Jones helped design, allowed the camp to continue to grow. It was taking shape, at least on paper.

As things were progressing at the new camp, trouble occurred in Alabama. On March 4, the *Enquirer-Sun* reported that soldiers had been called to restore order in Girard on the outskirts of Phenix City. Girard had an infamous history. In 1833, F. L. Cherry described it in unpleasant terms: "Girard was originally what might be compared to a cess-pool, which received the scum and filth from Columbus…a convenient and measurably secure place of refuge from the majesty of the law. Here a conglomerated mixture of gambler, black-leg, murderer, thief and drunkard…produced a moral odor offensive to the very idea of good morals, and secured for the place, for several years, the appellation of 'Sodom' which in all probability is well deserved."[34]

In 1916, Alabama's Attorney General, Logan Martin, who led a cleanup of Girard, called upon the National Guard to destroy 265,000 gallons of moonshine liquor and to crack "the biggest illegal liquor ring ever to operate in the South." But by the time troops began moving into Camp Benning, "bootleg liquor was again flowing free."[35]

In March, Jones was made Land Acquisition Officer. He created six boards of appraisal, one for each 16,000-acre division. Each board consisted

---

[33] Frank G. Lumpkin, Sr., to Jimmy Alfonte, June 18 1944, Lumpkin's personal files, Willcox-Lumpkin Company, Columbus GA.

[34] Rev. F. L. Cherry, "The History of Opelika and her Agricultural Tributary Territory," *Alabama Historical Quarterly* 15/1 (Spring 1953): 183.

[35] Edwin Strickland and Gene Wortsman, *Phenix City, the Wickedest City in America* (Birmingham AL: Vulcan Press, 1955) 196.

of two civilians, a farmer, real estate agent, and an army officer as chairman. A Board of Review was also organized. Many agreements were made as the appraisal boards walked with the owner and agreed on an amount of purchase. Appraisal board members, paid ten dollars a day, were farmers who lived at least ten miles away since local farmers found it difficult to judge their neighbors' property.

The need for land was made clear in March 1919 when the 1st Battalion, 29th Infantry Regiment arrived from Camp Shelby, Mississippi. As a demonstration regiment, it provided school cadre, demonstration troops, and faculty members. A month later, 200 men of the Machine Gun School from Camp Hancock, Georgia, arrived. Accompanied by officers, instructors, and students, it provided two demonstration machine-gun companies for the school—one animal-drawn, one motorized.

Eames' mission was accomplished. Appointed executive officer and assistant commandant, Eames relinquished his command of commandant to Major General Charles S. Farnsworth on April 22. A graduate of the US Military Academy in 1887, Farnsworth's résumé included numerous commands. By appointing a general, Pershing established the importance of the infantry school—and the infantry—to the rest of the army. Farnsworth was given specific instructions to make Benning the largest and most influential post in the country. To assist, Colonel Paul Bernard Malone, a handsome bona fide warrior of World War I, was recalled from duty with the Army of Occupation in Germany to become assistant commandant of the Infantry School of Arms. At Pershing's request, Malone acted as liaison officer between the War Department and Congress from July 1919 to February 1920 before assuming duties at the camp. To help promote Camp Benning, Malone prepared the army's case before Congress. During this time, Eames acted as assistant commandant.

With the new commanders came new technology. In May 1919, telephone lines were installed, and electric power lines were under construction. The railroad was completed to the camp and tracks for the narrow gauge or "light train" were installed to distribute supplies within the camp. Communication now included airmail.

Actual training was minimal. To present a good face, a class of officers that entered March 15 was retained for an additional three-month course to keep the camp looking busy. According to Yarborough, the class that should have graduated June 15 gave the appearance, as intended, "of intensive training activity" to visiting observers.[36] Due to the demands of the survival of the school, students did not receive major attention. Frank Lumpkin observed, "at times, the officers of the school were so busy engaged with citizens of Columbus in making trips between Columbus and Washington trying to hold the post that the students were badly neglected."[37]

On June 5, the land acquirement officer was told to spend as much as needed to procure 98,000 acres for the new camp. The Bussey transaction was concluded June 17 with the transfer of the 1800-acre plantation and house to the federal government—a transaction that began in late 1918. Bussey deposited a check for $439,000 with the First National Bank, "the largest single deposit in the history of the bank to that time."[38]

The big event came later. Beginning June 17, 1919, the camp was transferred to its present location. During the move, students enjoyed a two-week holiday. But on June 30, during hot summer days, they returned to their classes of bayonet combat, drills and firing of weapons. Finding shelter for camp personnel was a serious problem. First priority went to Farnsworth, the first of the school's commandants to live at Riverside, Bussey's former summer home. Other troops lived in barracks, but when barracks were not available, tent camps were erected—a tradition that lasted ten years after the move to the new camp. Tents for single officers and for officers whose families did not accompany them to Benning were pitched in the grove near the commandant's quarters.

About 100 officers lived in town, renting rooms or apartments at very high rates. Student officers on post, even those with families living in town, could not leave camp except on weekends. Lack of transportation was a continuous problem. Roads were bad even in good weather and unusable in wet weather. Although automobiles were popular, few officers owned them, and the railroad extended only to Benning Junction, about four miles from Columbus.

---

[36] Yarborough, *A History of the Infantry School*, 91.

[37] Frank G. Lumpkin, Sr., written communication to Col. H. E. Knight, December 4 1931, Lumpkin's personal files, Willcox-Lumpkin Company, Columbus GA, 2, regarding Yarborough's manuscript *A History of the Infantry School, Fort Benning, Georgia*.

[38] Etta Blanchard Worsley, *Columbus on the Chattahoochee* (Columbus GA: Columbus Office Supply Company, 1951) 422.

Married officers of the 29th, required to stand reveille and retreat with their companies, shared the problems of the married students who were separated from their families. Housing problems were constant. Shacks once used by black workers were assigned to non-commissioned officers. About ten other officers were permitted to live in old farm buildings on untitled government land. They had to take out fire insurance at their own expense to protect the owners.

Yarborough's history described the move from the temporary camp to the new, yet primitive, site on the Bussey plantation as "a frank and deliberate scheme" to save the camp. "The actual occupation and use of the camp by the school troops, the faculty, students, and families were expected to make its discontinuance a far more difficult matter than the mere abandonment of a camp that was neither used nor occupied," he wrote. "This move was one of the details of a bold plan which had been evolved by the school authorities in their efforts to save the new Camp Benning."[39]

However, rumors of closing continued. In July an order to cease construction was issued. Contracts were cancelled and workmen were discharged. An official ban was placed on the purchase of land. Yarborough described the shutdown: "The abrupt cessation of general construction gave to the camp an appearance of chaotic waste. Frames of partially finished building stood like raggedly clothed skeletons. Heaps of unused materials lay haphazardly about. Miles of ditches yawned for the unlaid pipes and sewers. Everywhere was a profusion of litter. The departure of the workmen left inhabited buildings, without water, sewer, or lights."[40] Malone, in his role as liaison, continued to inform Congress of the need for the training offered by the Infantry School of Arms: "The Infantry School is one of the twelve absolutely necessary education institutions to be preserved in time of peace, no matter what the size of the army may be."[41]

People on post again prevailed in an attempt to overcome harsh restrictions. With materials found around camp, personnel improved their living conditions. Despite the construction ban, they accomplished much before another winter. By July 5, the government had acquired nearly 80

---

[39] Yarborough, *A History of the Infantry School*, 153.

[40] Ibid., 154.

[41] Malone, "What Camp Benning Means to the Infantry," *Infantry Journal* 16/6 (December 1919): 440.

percent of the reservation. It owned 76,417 acres purchased from 200 farmers, paying $2,558,974.20. The government paid an average of $33.94 per acre for land it owned. Land under contract cost about $40.00 per acre. The remainder would cost about $20.00.[42] In the early 1900s, farmland in Muscogee County could be bought from $5 to $40 an acre, so the government paid near top price.

Maintaining the temporary camp and trying to build the new one while fielding criticism was challenging. Farnsworth, therefore, was happy to report completion of the sewer system on July 10. Using only available equipment and material, he had organized a team effort with troops from the 29th assisted by 150 county convicts. Other available equipment was used to install plumbing, grade grounds and construct new roads. Wages and prices of material were rising as delays continued, resulting in more reductions. As designed, nearly all of the buildings of the camp were to have concrete foundations and stucco exteriors. Stucco had to be omitted. Total cost of the uncompleted camp in 1919 was $6,566,000.[43]

Camp Benning was a "peace-time Valley Forge." Word spread to men entering service or about to be transferred to avoid this Georgia post. In September 1919, a congressional committee visited and saw for themselves "the gaunt skeleton of the Infantry School of Arms" and "the hovels which sheltered the devoted and self-sacrificing personnel.[44] The committee recommended continuance.

Malone knew his mission was successful when the War Department issued General Orders, No. 112 on September 25, 1919, permitting the infantry to continue its own school in order "to develop and standardize the instruction and training of officers in the technique and tactics of their respective arm or service."[45] To cement Benning's acceptance and permanence, General John J. Pershing visited the camp on December 10 to honor the efforts of Farnsworth and Malone. City leaders met at Union Station in Columbus to greet the general's party, consisting of his staff, Senator Hoke Smith, and others. Later, Pershing spoke at the Ralston Hotel. With Pershing came rain and floods: "Seas of mud, overflowing

---

[42] Yarborough, *A History of the Infantry School*, 136.

[43] Ibid., 160.

[44] Ibid., 128.

[45] Ibid., 95.

streams, liquid roads, and a sodden camp awaited him. The heavy rain before his visit took its toll, and his arrival, then and later, was referred to as the 'Pershing Flood.'"[46] With him too was a man who would one day return: George C. Marshall.

---

[46] Ibid., 95–96.

4.

West Point's Finishing School: Progress to Permanence

For the first time Camp Benning seemed to have a future. The Infantry School of Arms, renamed by the War Department on January 30, 1920, was now called the Infantry School, reflecting a broader concept in infantry training than the original "school of fire" or "school of arms." Nearly a month later, Congress approved the continuation of construction work, maintenance of the camp, and the purchase of land to complete Camp Benning.

"Congress ended this dark period of doubt and uncertainty, and invested it with stability by authorizing the retention of Camp Benning as a permanent military post.... Thus with one handsome gesture did Congress sweep aside the foes of Camp Benning and assure the future of the Infantry School," wrote LeRoy Yarborough.[1] The treasury secretary's request of funds for Camp Benning as a permanent post gave way to a wish list including $3,362,940 for 204 five-room apartments for student commissioned officers to $26,050 for a veterinary hospital, a list totaling $7,502,320.[2]

In addition to the name change, on April 22, 1920, the War Department reorganized the entire Infantry School. The result was the Departments of Military Arts, Research, General Subjects, the School

---

[1] LeRoy Yarborough in collaboration with Truman Smith, *A History of the Infantry School, Fort Benning, Georgia* (Ft. Benning: The Infantry School, 1931) 129.

[2] David F. Houston, secretary of the treasury, to the speaker of the House of Representatives and added letters of Newton D. Baker, secretary of war, and Maj. Gen.George W. Burr, assistant chief of staff, "Buildings for Infantry Schools, Camp Benning, GA," document no. 725, 66th Congress, 2nd sess. (Washington: Government Printing Press, April 15 1921) 1–3.

Troops and School Detachment, and the Military Reservation, Camp Benning, Georgia.[3] The Department of Experiment functioned independently of the school and camp to furnish the Infantry Board (established in 1919) and the chief of infantry with recommendations to adopt, reject, adapt, or develop any article suggested for use by infantry troops. With its new name, updated organization, and financial security, the school now offered more services.

One concept tested at the "new" Infantry School in 1920 was aerial techniques and tactics. Machine-gun technology before and during World War I dominated the training agenda, but the war introduced a military novelty—the airplane. No longer was the soldier confined to the earth's surface. He could fly. With this new dimension available to observe and attack, new training was incorporated. Preparing for the aerial concept, the 32 Balloon Company, with 3 officers, 100 men, and complete flying equipment arrived March 24, 1920, to determine if data obtained by a balloon observation benefited infantry troops engaged in battle.

Observation balloons, used as early as the Civil War, and airplanes, used in the Spanish-American War and World War I, were now part of postwar training. On May 12, the post's first air detachment arrived at the unpaved airstrip with ten DeHaviland DH-4 airplanes—observation planes dubbed the "flying coffin."[4] Ten days later, the 22nd Observation Squadron arrived. The army's interest in airplanes reflected recent events. On September 7, 1920, the first New York-to-California mail plane, piloted by men who learned to fly in the war, left New York City. Airmail service and air transportation now were staples rather than exotics.

Not everything was left "up in the air" at the Infantry School, however. In April, the 344th Tank Battalion, later designated the 15th Tank Battalion, arrived from Camp Meade, Maryland, and later in the month, Company D, 7th Engineers reported. Since preparing for war meant simulating battle and simulated battle meant wounded soldiers, the urgent

---

[3] War Department, Special Regulations no. 14, section 9, regulations governing the Infantry School, Camp Benning GA, April 22 1920; copy in Yarborough, *A History of the Infantry School, Fort Benning, Georgia*, 315.

[4] Russell F. Weigley, *History of the United States Army* (Bloomington: Indiana University Press, 1984) 363.

need of medical facilities was met by the arrival of the Medical Demonstration Detachment on November 1.

The following day, the 1st Battalion, 83rd Field Artillery arrived, proving their stamina by a 630-mile march from Camp Knox, Kentucky, "the longest yet attempted by a motorized battalion of field artillery." The 1st Battalion would provide for the "first time in the history of the United States Army" barrages of high explosive shell fired over the heads of friendly troops.[5]

On June 5, 1920, Colonel Henry E. Eames left the post he helped build, and on July 1, Major General Charles Farnsworth was appointed chief of infantry, a position created by the National Defense Act of 1920. Brigadier General Walter H. Gordon took command of the Infantry School in September. Paul Malone stayed on as assistant commander. To alleviate housing and classroom problems, Farnsworth wrote Gordon this suggestion: "I believe that the tent camp should be constructed by use of labor from the Labor Battalion, or, if necessary, by adding a little to that labor from the 29th Infantry. I can see in my mind's eye Malone tearing his hair when the suggestion is made, but...."[6]

Malone did not want to see members of the 29th involved in post labor since they were needed for demonstrations. Post laborers were mainly from the Infantry School Detachment, black soldiers commanded by white officers. Black soldiers worked for the departments, labored for the camp in general, and built their own housing with tents and shacks in "Cashtown," an area near the stables. Several men of the School Detachment were detailed to the Infantry School Stables, "a plum assignment" since "it was a lot better than cutting logs, digging, or hauling materials."[7] Sergeant Willie

---

[5] "The First Battalion, 83rd Field Artillery," *The Doughboy 1920–21* (Fort Benning GA: The Infantry School, 1921).

[6] Major R. L. Hillman, "A Haphazard Review of Some Tribulations Which Beset the Infantry School in the Early Years and Have Been, In Part, Retained," correspondents: Maj. Gen. Charles S. Farnsworth, Brig. Gen. Walter H. Gordon, and Col. Paul B. Malone, 1920–1921, unpublished manuscript, November 1 1961, at Donovan Technical Library, Fort Benning GA, 5.

[7] L. Albert Scipio, *The 24th Infantry at Ft. Benning* (Silver Spring MD: Roman Publications, 1986) 71.

B. "Fez" Wood organized the first orchestra and quartet in July 1920 for the detachment's entertainment.[8]

Officers often hired black soldiers to help them build homes now allowed on post. "This resulted in sporadic growths which sprinkled the landscape with architectural creations limited only in size and design by the resources and imaginations of their builders," Yarborough wrote.[9] Troops of the 29th were moved into the tent camp south of the barracks to free the buildings for use as classrooms and unmarried student housing. Fifty tent-houses were erected for married officers. According to Yarborough, when one hopeful officer applied for a tent house, he was told, "there were only three tent houses available and there are 178 applications."[10] When married officers repaired farm buildings to live in, they were ask to take in others. However, a sense of permanency prevailed when Service Club No. 1, designed for enlisted men, was completed in May 1923. Biglerville Mess Hall, another early permanent structure, was completed April 11, 1921.

In November, Gordon wrote to Farnsworth about the school's readiness and its enrollment. There were 92 field officers, 81 company officers, 42 National Guard officers, and 487 newly commissioned officers. The 702 men composed "the largest body of student officers ever assembled in America in time of peace for training in the art of war."[11] Another sign of progress was the publication of the *Doughboy, 1920–1921*, a student yearbook. Names and pictures of instructors, students, support units, and civilian staff members were documented under the direction of Lieutenant Henry Wyatt Isbell, editor-in-chief, and Major Robert J. Halpin, general supervisor. Doughboy, a term for infantryman, originated from a corruption of the words "doughball," a type of button worn on infantry overcoats in the early 1800s or from the use of pipe-clay, known as dough, to whiten trouser stripes on dress uniforms. The yearbook cover featured a shield with the words "Follow Me" above a bayonet pointing down. Later, the bayonet, now raised, and the words "Follow Me" became school symbols.

"We 'doughboys,'" the book states, "are not dependent upon any thing but the equipment we were born with.... If we are a little slower than some,

---

[8] Ibid., 153.

[9] Yarborough, *A History of the Infantry School*, 163.

[10] Ibid., 171–72.

[11] Hillman, "A Haphazard Review," 3.

why we'll just stick around a little longer, that's all."[12] Pointing out 31 out of 100 infantrymen were killed or wounded in World War I, the *Doughboy* author notes the need of the Infantry School of Arms: "While first hand experience gained in actual warfare is perhaps the best teacher, the course is a terribly expensive one and the diploma as often as not must be forwarded to the next of kin."[13]

The camp's "permanency," did not do away with the threat of peacetime cuts. In January 1921, over the objections of Pershing and Secretary of War Newton D. Baker, the US Senate voted to limit the army to 150,000—only 50,000 more than Germany had after the Treaty of Versailles.[14] Farnsworth wrote, "recruiting has been entirely stopped and all recruiting officers are being relieved and ordered to other duty."[15] The War Department freely granted discharges to any soldier who desired to leave service.

But because of an economic recession in 1921–1922, young men sought jobs and adventure in the military. Although word was out to enlistees and regulars to avoid Camp Benning because of its primitive conditions, some were attracted to the post by its 1921 enlistment poster that promised, "A motorized regiment. No guard. No fatigue. Over $7,000,000 worth new barracks nearly completed."[16] In reality there were tents instead of wood buildings and "open ditches, five or six feet in depth criss-crossed the barracks area to provide for surface drainage."[17]

Though newcomers found good hunting and swimming—as advertised—and thirty-four basketball teams, driving into Columbus was difficult and visiting Atlanta, nearly impossible. "Many a promising—or promised—young man made an informal departure, never more to

---

[12] "Why 'Doughboy'?" *The Doughboy 1920–1921* (Ft. Benning: The Infantry School, 1921) n.p.

[13] "The Department of Research," *The Doughboy 1920–1921* (Fort Benning GA: The Infantry School, 1921) n.p.

[14] "Army of 150,000 Voted by Senate after Long Fight," *Columbus Enquirer-Sun*, January 15 1921, 1.

[15] Hillman, "A Haphazard Review," 3.

[16] A copy of the 1921 enlistment poster can be found in Yarborough, *A History of the Infantry School*, 414.

[17] Ibid., 172.

return—voluntarily."[18] Restricted funds also meant reduction of the 29th to a two-battalion regiment, the disbandment of the Medical Demonstration Detachment, and the withdrawal of the Air Service Detachment, reducing troop demonstrations.

Problems also existed between Gordon and Farnsworth, now stationed in Washington, DC. Farnsworth reprimanded Gordon in a letter, writing, "The personal appearance of the officers at Benning is the worst we have seen in the army."[19]

In addition to his concern of the physical appearance of Benning troops, Farnsworth warned Gordon about the health and reputation of Benning soldiers concerning venereal illness. The high incidence of the disease at Benning, Farnsworth said, was creating a bad impression in Washington: "The future of the school very largely depends upon stamping out that disease, both at camp and in Columbus."[20]

"You have my sincere sympathy; that and prostitution gave me more trouble and occupied more of my time than any other subject while at Camp Benning," Farnsworth added.[21] Farnsworth and Gordon also differed on post priorities. Farnsworth was interested in improving the camp laundry facilities, but Gordon wanted to improve the tent camp. The laundry won out. Again the perseverance and creativity of tent city inhabitants would "make do" with materials found in the camp.

Mrs. Lloyd R. Fredenall, wife of a major who was an instructor in Military Art, was asked how she liked living at Camp Benning. "Like it?" she said. "I helped build it!" She described how she and her husband placed newspapers on the tent floor, then covered them with scraps of tarpaper picked up from construction sites. After painting, shellacking, and waxing the 'floor,' they had a proper place to put their Oriental rugs.[22]

Yarborough praised the military wives in his history of the early post: "Tribute must be paid to the women of the infantry who endured unforgettable inconveniences and even hardships for the sake of the Infantry School, for its story is theirs, too. In less spectacular environment than that

---

[18] Ibid., 172–73.

[19] Ibid., 105.

[20] Ibid.

[21] Hillman, "A Haphazard Review," 7.

[22] "The School Came to Benning," *Benning Herald*, October 1949, 14.

of their men in war, they endure none the less heroically, the hardships of army life in peace."[23]

Another peacetime hardship was Prohibition. On January 16, 1921, Congress passed the Volstead Act, prohibiting the sale of alcohol. Prohibition aggravated criminal behavior rather than curtailed it, and bootleggers made money from inferior and at times dangerous liquor. People made bathtub gin or homebrew. Between 1920 and 1930, half a million people were arrested for violating the Volstead Act. In January 1921, authorities destroyed 10,000 gallons of mash beer and 11 stills in Columbus.

Louise Gunby Jones DuBose, a Columbus reporter and writer who used the pen name "Nancy Telfair," discovered bootleggers hung their stock in the Chattahoochee. She writes, "Liquor was brought up from the Gulf, sometimes put in crocus sacks and tied below waterline to the deck of the houseboat anchored in the middle of the river. Also, at other points, these sacks would be tied to limbs of willow trees that naturally hung into the current."[24]

Transportation problems, like Prohibition, had creative solutions. When individual drivers were allowed to provide service, "soon scores of nondescript vehicles, operated by persons of no particular responsibility, were haphazardly engaged in carrying passengers between Camp Benning and Columbus on roads that defied description."[25] Soldiers and officers were in the taxi business, running jitneys between post and Columbus. Farnsworth wrote Gordon to stop it: "I regard it below the dignity and entirely out of place of an officer and sure to lead to trouble."[26] In August, Gordon gave independent operators ninety days to withdraw. Gordon accepted the recommendation of the city's Camp Activities Committee chaired by J. B. Key, president of the Merchants and Mechanics Bank. The committee supported Atlanta businessman Troup Howard's proposal to establish regular passenger bus service between Camp Benning and Columbus. His friend Thurston C. Crawford took over as manager of the

---

[23] Yarborough, *A History of the Infantry School*, 174–75.

[24] Louise Gunby Jones DuBose (Nancy Telfair) "Women in Columbus 1828–1928," 27, unpublished manuscript, MCI Folder 1, archives of Simon Schwob Memorial Library, Columbus State University, Columbus GA.

[25] Yarborough, *A History of the Infantry School*, 102.

[26] Hillman, "A Haphazard Review," 7.

Howard Taxi and Bus Corporation. Four years later, Crawford would own the company, operating under the name of Howard Bus Line.[27]

A narrow gauge train, built in World War I by the Davenport Locomotive Works of Davenport, Iowa, eased post transportation when it moved to Benning in 1921. Designed to help the camp's internal transportation problem, it "hauled loads of logs, bricks, cement, and glass over the twenty-six miles of sixty-centimeter track to assist in the creation of the world's most complete military installation."[28]

Purchase of post lands was completed July 19, 1921, when $357,523.55 in vouchers arrived from Washington to pay forty-five property owners. These payments were made possible by a letter from Secretary of War John W. Weeks to the speaker of the House of Representatives. Weeks described the status of the condemnation proceedings in connection with the acquisition of land for Camp Benning.[29] With additional rulings, the Infantry School legally possessed the camp it had occupied for two and a half years.

To celebrate Camp Benning's third anniversary, President Warren G. Harding inspected the post on October 27, 1921. He was the first United States president to visit the camp. Senator William J. Harris invited Harding on behalf of the Columbus Chamber of Commerce. In reply, Harding expressed interest in the camp: "I think a number of such camps ought to be made permanent institutions and be thoroughly kept up."[30]

Arriving on a special train, Harding kept his visit "low-key" due to limited army funds. Still, many people turned out to meet him and his wife,

---

[27] Frank G. Lumpkin, Sr. written communication to Col. H. E. Knight, Fort Benning GA, December 4 1931, Lumpkin's personal files, Willcox-Lumpkin Company, Columbus GA, 2, regarding the manuscript *A History of the Infantry School*, by L. W. Yarborough in collaboration with Truman Smith.

[28] "Little Railroad War Veteran Helped to Build Fort Benning," (Name of paper not included.) December 31 1943, copy in Lumpkin file.

[29] John W. Weeks, "Acquisition of Land for Camp Benning, GA," letter from the secretary of war to the speaker of the House of Representatives, May 31 1921, 67th Cong., 1st sess. (Washington DC, April 11–November 23 1921), document 90, House Documents, vol. 14, 7946, referred to the Committees on Appropriations and Military Affairs (Washington: Government Printing Office, June 2 1921) 1.

[30] "Harding Would Make Benning Permanent," *Columbus Enquirer-Sun*, January 6 1921, 1.

Florence, who fascinated Columbus women "by wearing her much-talked of veil which she was said not to raise even at meals!"[31] The following month, Harding proclaimed November 11, Armistice Day, a legal holiday. In Columbus, services were held to honor the heroes. Malone gave a memorial address at Temple B'nai Israel in which he described his fighting in the Meuse-Argonne Campaign on the last two days of the war.

Of Malone's remarks, a reporter wrote: "He saw a group of American soldiers who had died because of a commander's mistake and says that he took a vow to himself at that time that he would devote all of his energies to the training of men for group leadership. This is the reason he is now at Camp Benning."[32]

Racial Issues Revealed

On December 1, 1921, the 3rd Battalion, 24th Infantry Regiment was organized from the Infantry School Detachment (Colored). Seven officers and 354 enlisted men were transferred into the 3rd Battalion. Their duties remained the same. Black troops continued to live separately from the white troops, eat in separate messes, and form their own athletic teams. No serious problems existed because black soldiers were in Columbus or at the camp. However, Georgia led the United States in lynching in 1918 when eighteen blacks and whites were hanged.[33] Though the number declined by half in 1920, Georgia ranked second in the country.[34]

These grim statistics were not ignored. Voices like newspaper reporter Julian Harris spoke out against members of the Klan who condoned lynching. His articles and editorials in the *Enquirer-Sun* prevented Columbus from coming under the influence of the Klan. The *Enquirer-Sun* was "the first and only Georgian newspaper to openly attack the Ku Klux

---

[31] Etta Blanchard Worsley, *Columbus on the Chattahoochee* (Columbus GA: Columbus Office Supply Company, 1951) 431.

[32] "Memorial Services in Columbus for World War Heroes," *Columbus Enquirer-Sun*, November 12 1921, 1.

[33] S. Zadak, "Lynchings for 1918," letter to the editor, *Montgomery Advertiser*, January 10 1919, 4.

[34] Julian Harris, "Lynchings in 1920," editorial, *Columbus Enquirer-Sun*, January 4 1921, 4.

Klan,"[35] and Harris later won the Pulitzer Prize in Journalism for his efforts. Some Southern editors said Harris gave comfort to those who disliked the South, but Harris would not accept the Klan as a social, do-gooder club. He created a climate that fostered reason and good sense, helping Columbus and Camp Benning to grow.

A Permanent Post

Celebration was in order in January when War Department General Order No. 1 made Camp Benning a permanent military installation. Final credibility came on February 8, 1922, when Secretary of War John W. Weeks announced Camp Benning was now *Fort* Benning. Assured of its location, its funding, and its identification, the post still faced troop reduction and funding adjustments, factors common to peacetime armies.

New plans for permanent buildings in what is known as Fort Benning's Second Construction Period (1922–1925) included ten double sets of brick quarters for regular and noncommissioned officers. Railroad shops, a steel-trussed bridge across Upatoi Creek, a gymnasium and a theatre were also built in 1922. The new 29th Infantry Theatre, a Main Post movie palace with 2,300 seats—the largest seating capacity in the south—advertised "room for everybody."[36] For fifteen cents, viewers sat in comfortable chairs in the "coolest place at Fort Benning" to see moving pictures or vaudeville.[37] A reserved section for officers and ladies with escorts was available.

General John J. Pershing returned on March 6, 1922, for his first inspection of *Fort* Benning. With him came downpours, just as in 1919. Although this visit was called the "Second Pershing Flood" rain could not spoil Pershing's parade.[38]

Unrest in Town and Post

General Gordon, meanwhile, continued his effort to eliminate vice in Columbus. "Social purity" became a local political issue, associated with the change of Columbus's government from a ward and mayor type to a

---

[35] Clement Charlton Moseley, "The Political Influence of the Ku Klux Klan in Georgia, 1915–1925," *Georgia Historical Quarterly* 57/2 (Summer 1973): 237.

[36] "Post Theatre," *Fort Benning News*, October 6 1921, 1.

[37] Ibid.

[38] Yarborough, *A History of the Infantry School*, 178.

commission-manager form. Five commissioners, elected at large, would appoint a city manager. That first commission consisted of Anna H. Griffin, a leader in woman's suffrage; J. Homer Dimon, R. E. Dismukes, Marshall Morton and Reuben Kyle. Dimon was named mayor. Gordon Hinkle, a specialist in municipal management, was selected the first city manager. Resentment grew because of his salary, "larger than that of anyone else," and because he was an outsider, a "Yankee" from Pennsylvania, hired to tell people in Columbus how to run their town.[39]

Unrest persisted. In April 1922, Hinkle was attacked with an attempt to kidnap him. A bomb blew away Dimon's front porch. Other commissioners were threatened. Failed efforts to blow up the Dimon Court Apartments, owned by the mayor, and the residence of Julian Harris, the crusading editor, left city leaders shaken. The Ku Klux Klan was blamed for the violence since its hooded members were suspicious of this new government that they claimed was under control of the "elite." Another suspect was a group that benefited financially from bootlegging and prostitution and objected to the clean-up program supported by members of the city government, the mayor, and Fort Benning's commanding general.

Gordon, in fact, was taken to the police station by a Columbus police officer a few days after the bombing at Dimon's home. The general's car, well marked, was returning from Atlanta. Officers said the driver was speeding, but Gordon said they were following other cars doing twelve miles an hour and those cars were not stopped. Although Gordon protested, he and his party were escorted to headquarters. From there the general phoned the mayor and obtained their prompt release.

In response to his arrest, Gordon wrote:

> I realize that I have been very active in instigating in the city and county the fight against vice, and no doubt, at least indirectly, the change in the form of city government may be traced to this agitation.... However, I feel that I am in good company with Mr. Hinkle and Mayor Dimon, and with other good people of Columbus. I am prepared to continue my part of the fight until we make Columbus what it should be, and the good people would like it to be.[40]

---

[39] Worsley, *Columbus on the Chattahoochee*, 456.
[40] Yarborough, *A History of the Infantry School*, 180–81.

To show no hard feelings, Gordon attended the city's Confederate Memorial Day exercises and parade. He also sent a band and a detachment of troops: "I was very proud of the appearance of our soldiers. They were all well dressed, well set up, marched well, and looked to be clean up-standing young men, worthy of our infantrymen."[41]

Malone Leaves Post

Meanwhile, Paul Malone was trying—literally—to keep the home fires burning on post. On October 14, 1922, Malone wrote Farnsworth in Washington to request a furnace in his quarters: "For the last two years, I have had to spend about one hour a day, personally, in stoking the six stoves which are necessary to keep my very open and airy home fit to live in. This is too much of an expenditure of energy."[42] Perhaps Gordon had complaints such as Malone's in mind when he wrote in the *Doughboy, 1922*: "Living conditions at Camp Benning are not easy. We are pioneers."[43] Malone, now a brigadier general, did not need to worry about heating problems much longer. On November 22, Colonel William H. Fassett assumed Malone's duties. In the *Doughboy, 1923*, Malone was honored: "His work has been indelibly impressed on the Infantry School, and the 'Days of Malone' will never be forgotten."[44]

Malone's replacement, Colonel William M. Fassett did not stay long. In September 1923, Colonel Alfred W. Bjornstad relieved him. The new commandant's wife, Pearl Ladd Sabin Bjornstad, is credited with originating the Benning Woman's Club, which sponsored riding classes, bridge club, and a dramatic club. Although pleasant diversions were available, serious housing problems continued. The intrusion of skunks, raccoon, possum, and other Georgia wildlife made life interesting in the tent housing and in the wooden homes. With several families sharing common bathhouses heated by Sibley stoves, long-lived memories were created.

Laura M. Bailey described housing in the 1920s:

---

[41] Ibid., 181.

[42] Hillman, "A Haphazard Review," 2.

[43] "Message from Walter H. Gordon," *Doughboy, 1922* (Atlanta: Press of Foote and Davies Co., 1922) n.p.

[44] "An Appreciation," *Doughboy, 1923* (Ft. Benning: The Infantry School, 1923) n.p.

As crude as the quarters were, the wives of those days considered themselves lucky to occupy them, for they were living on the Post. Eligibility for such quarters was based on the size of the family. If one had two children they were entitled to a tent house (covered with tar paper). If the family was larger, they were assigned to the wooden shacks hastily erected by the labor battalions.... Many an Army family slept under raincoats and umbrellas during the heavy rains.[45]

Great parties, however, took place in the tent homes. Couples who lived in wooden houses would bring their babies to the parties for fear of fires starting in their homes while they were gone. In addition to "house parties," Saturday night dances were held at the Officers' Club and the Service Club. Although some entertainment was available on the young post, work still needed to be done—and much was done in 1923. In addition to the barracks building, engineers and the post quartermaster, supplementing their own small forces by troop labor, completed a steel-trussed, double-draw bridge across Upatoi Creek, replacing the original wooden bridge leading to Columbus. Officials from both ends of the bridge, town and post, dedicated it on January 20, 1922.

In November 1923, Brigadier General Briant H. Wells replaced Gordon as commandant. Wells, like Gordon, wanted to clean up the post. His solution was a beautification project and making Girard and Phenix City off-limits to Fort Benning personnel. For his first project, Wells enlisted the aid of William H. Atkinson, a Columbus nurseryman. The civilian was put in charge of planting shrubs and trees in the main post area. Trees were planted twice as close as normal to achieve a wooded effect. Native trees were transplanted to the sides of the roads, and, under Wells's direction, pink crepe myrtles and mimosa trees were added.

The post's natural beauty was challenged by a military installation growing with little direction. Wells, with Farnsworth's approval, presented a plan for the post, including an immense apartment house for married student officers. Modeled on the newly adopted cuartel design "it could be built in separate sections, with appropriate interior divisions, while presenting from the outside, when completed, the appearance of one continuous C-shaped building partially enclosing an interior parade

---

[45] Worsley, *Columbus on the Chattahoochee*, 428.

ground."[46] Wells, with "an eye for the beautiful," wisely predicted, "There remains a staggering amount of work to be done but time will eventually make this one of the finest posts in the Army."[47]

Wells's second project included the cleanup of Girard and Phenix City, where crime and vice, despite Gordon's efforts, flourished. Naïve and drunken soldiers were often beaten and swindled of their paychecks in hovels across the state line. The Alabama villages offered illegal liquor and law-breaking women. Such temptations would plague young soldiers for generations to come. An unmarried Benning soldier wrote a humorous article for the school yearbook titled "Letter of a Lonely Bachelor." It told of soldiers going "to the village—home of Chero Cola and Cheri-Corn—to squander weekly earnings."[48] The routine, as reported, was dinner at the Cricket, then to the Poor Man's Club (Ralston Hotel) to talk about "the hysterical research department." The bachelor then looked for a bootlegger or attended a dance: "The dissipation over, we take the Rolls Royce Omnibus back to camp—in the box cars which serve as our temporary domiciles."[49]

Another soldier told of ending a night in Girard: "Scouts have been alert, they report no MPs on Girard bridge and everything O.K."[50] Wells's solution was to order his troops not to cross the Chattahoochee River. With soldiers ordered not to cross into the border towns, the communities soon felt the loss of revenue brought in by soldiers. People of Columbus, seeing the misfortune of the Alabama towns, were determined to keep the troops—and their money—coming to their city.

Upon taking command, Wells personally inspected the uniform of each student, a policy he continued in order to improve the appearance of the officers as previously criticized by Farnsworth. That year marked the first in which no student officer was tried by court-martial, a testimony to Wells's direction, his scrutiny, and his support of increased athletic activities for post personnel. To promote athletics at Fort Benning in order to keep soldiers

---

[46] Yarborough, *A History of the Infantry School, Fort Benning, Georgia*, 199.

[47] Ibid., 184.

[48] "Letter of a Lonely Bachelor," *Doughboy, 1922* (Atlanta: Foote and Davies Co., 1922) n.p.

[49] Ibid.

[50] "A Week End in Columbus" *Doughboy, 1922* (Atlanta: Foote and Davies Co., 1922) n.p.

on post, a post gymnasium was completed in April 1923 and the Officers' Club nine-hole golf course opened that December. In March 1924, ground was broken for Doughboy Stadium and Gowdy Field. When finished, the two fields were valued at $200,000.

When John A. Betjeman died in 1924, William C. Woodall, newspaper columnist, wrote about the successful lobbyist who—appropriately—died in Washington on business connected to the installation he helped secure for "the city he served so well." Betjeman was buried in Linwood Cemetery. Woodall went on to describe Fort Benning as "the finishing school for West Point" and told how Columbus had grown accustomed to army high-brows: "We have captains for breakfast, colonels for dinner and generals for supper."[51]

Getting back and forth from town to post remained a problem. The pig trail from Columbus to the post was filled with potholes and was impassable in rainy weather. After the city helped pay for a paved road to Cusseta, an editorial in the post newspaper questioned why Columbus had ignored the road to the post, pointing out that from a monthly Fort Benning payroll of $439,413.99, Columbus got 70 or 75 percent of it. Local newspapers picked up the cause and so did Columbus leaders such as Frank G. Lumpkin. At last, a bid was awarded and grading began July 22, 1924.

As this neighborly relationship grew, there were reminders of change. In the early morning of September 12, 1924, the wooden building that since 1919 had served as post headquarters was destroyed by fire. It was the first building built and used by Major John Paul Jones. An alarm was turned in, but high winds caused a total loss.

The world of the 1920s, stalled by the Great Depression, was again unsettled by unrest emanating from Europe with the rise of fascism and communism led by Mussolini and Stalin. Americans did not want to get involved so soon after the war that was supposed to end all wars. The idea of a strong military was not appealing. To those who claimed "the Army wants a war," Lieutenant John W. Elkins, editor of the *Infantry School News* offered a response. "The Army," he wrote, "does not want a war because very few

---

[51] William C. Woodall, "The Truth About Columbus, Georgia," *Home Town* (Columbus: Columbus Office Supply Co., 1935) 5.

people outside of the Army can even realize just what horrors the next war will bring forth and which no doubt will exceed our expectation."[52]

---

[52] Lt. John W. Elkins, Jr., "War?" *Fort Benning News*, January 12 1923, 4.

5.

A Dog's Life

He put down three and carried one, and only Calculator knew which one he was going to carry.

In Fort Benning's early years, this legendary dog was as much a part of the post as its mud. He rode the trains. He showed up at mess halls. He went to class. He marched in parades. It was during those years, according to Colonel B. A. Byrne, that he developed that distinctive style of walking.

"His habit of traveling on three legs was purely a physical idiosyncrasy. The leg he chose to carry was entirely a matter of momentary whim and could be observed on a long trip changing from leg to leg to rest one at a time. I knew this character extremely well and was in fact one of his guardians," Byrne said.[1]

Although other dogs tried to enlist, Calculator captured completely the soldiers' hearts. Calling him a "real pal," a *Bayonet* article recalled Calculator's steadfast character: "Legend has it that Calculator attended, at one time or another, every demonstration and problem given by the school. To attend all these classes, he made countless spectacular leaps aboard the moving 'Chattahoochee Choo-Choo.'"[2]

In 1922, Captain John Singletary noted the legendary canine's train rides: "I can see him now, riding to Biglerville mess with us on the Contour special.... He would hang around and beg for a handout...then ride back to class with us...it was said that when a bus driver shouted, 'One more and we'll go,' Calculator jumped on to make the busload complete."[3]

---

[1] Richard Brill, "Calculator—'He made a better dog of us all,'" *Bayonet*, October 8 1993, B-2.

[2] "Calculator—the School's 'Dog of All Dogs'—A Real Pal," *Bayonet*, September 29 1961, 34.

[3] Leonard L. Norwood, "Why Fort Benning Built a Monument to a Dog," *Atlanta Constitution*, November 2 1958, 50.

In summer 1923, Calculator jumped on buses or trains no more. The post mascot died from strychnine poisoning on August 29. No one knew what happened.

An article in the *Benning News* asked for donations of a quarter, and they came from all over the world. Coming from Regular Army and National Guard soldiers, more than 1,000 quarters were donated. Donations included sixteen pesos from the 45th Infantry in the Philippine Islands and another eight in gold—all for a dog that during its reign panhandled and hitchhiked his way into the hearts of Fort Benning and its people.

In July 1924, four officers were appointed to a panel charged with selecting a suitable memorial. One suggested a drinking fountain or a trough for dogs and horses with the inscription "Calculator was a friend of the masses as well as the classes."[4]

Although funding and impetus lagged at times, the memorial finally was completed. Referred to as the "first monument on the grounds of Fort Benning," a granite shaft was selected with the inscription: "Calculator—Born? Died Aug. 29, 1923/ He Made Better Dogs of Us All."

The monument was placed on the parade ground reminding viewers of the harshness of the early camp and of the soldiers and their mascot who led a "dog's life."[5] Later, the monument to Calculator was moved to the family entrance of the Infantry School Building after its completion in 1935. In December 1984, it was moved from the rear of Building 35, the site of the School of Americas, to the front of the National Infantry Museum, Building 396. Old-timers opposed the move in 1984, but officials believed the monument would be better displayed at the museum. Calculator had found his way to the heart of Fort Benning's history.

Calculator was not the only dog to gain legend status. Another first was witnessed at the post when Max, the "parachutist pooch," became the first dog to qualify for Airborne. Max, "coaxed" out of the aircraft door the required five times, wore a special harness designed for the "courageous

---

[4] "Officers Are Appointed on 'Calc' Board," *Infantry School News*, July 18 1924, 1.

[5] Norwood, "Why Fort Benning Built a Monument to a Dog," 50. Various dates have been given for the dedication of the monument, ranging from 1923 to 1930. In reference to the article "He Made Better Dogs of Us All," *Infantry School News*, June 6 1930, the year 1929 or 1930 seems most probable.

canine." After making three additional jumps, Max survived a hit-and-run driver, overcoming a broken leg and shattered jawbone.

Max received letters of condolence and monetary gifts from troops across the country. After leaving the hospital in February 1943, he adopted the 505th Parachute Infantry Regiment on TDY (temporary duty) at Fort Benning. Max, a real trooper, jumped again with the 505th back at Fort Bragg.

6.

Sealed with a Kiss

When Benning Boulevard was finished, both sides, post and town, sensed this long-awaited roadway would connect the civilian and military communities of Columbus and Fort Benning in ways beyond a mere paved road.

So why not celebrate with a wedding and seal the union with a kiss?

The gala ceremony was celebrated June 2, 1925, at the Springer Opera House in Columbus, a theater graced by luminaries such as William Jennings Bryan and Edwin Booth, brother of John Wilkes Booth. There was a bride, a groom, a best man and a father of the bride. There was a United States Congressman to officiate, and the 29th Infantry Band provided appropriate melodies, including, of course, the "Wedding March" from Wagner's *Lohengrin*.

Official papers for the new road were already in place. General Orders No. 10 had named it on April 18. The only thing pending was the celebratory nuptials in June at the Springer. General Briant Wells, on the Pacific Coast for his son's wedding, appointed Colonel A. B. Warfield to stand in for him as the groom. Colonel George Helms was best man. Judge C. Frank McLaughlin portrayed the blushing bride. G. Gunby Jordan was father of the bride, and Congressman W. C. Wright officiated.

As reported in the newspaper, "A real honest-to-goodness kiss of the bride and bridegroom sealed the vows and brought to a close a fitting union between the two communities (of) Fort Benning and Columbus." Once the couple was officially proclaimed man and wife, Wright intoned, "What the paved road has joined together, let no man put asunder."[1]

---

[1] "Benning-Columbus Step to Wedding March," *Infantry School News*, June 5 1925, 4.

The road was needed badly. Model Ts and Chevrolets were everywhere. Signs of "transportation past" and "transportation future" were seen in the Infantry School newspaper's admonishment to post personnel not to run a car over the grass or tie a horse to one of the newly planted trees. Troops were reminded that a horse's "chomping at the bit will disturb the young tree and retard its growth or even endanger it life."[2]

With the new road replacing the bumpy old pathway, life was easier for drivers going in both directions. Most thankful were the 250 civilian employees who worked on post and made the daily trip back and forth. The military population on post could now drive to town and visit popular places of entertainment like the Muscogee Club with its oyster pan roasts and the Ralston Hotel with its "fresh Chicago meat" and nightly music. More importantly, this road opened wide the gates of Fort Benning so that people in town could share in parades, demonstrations, and plain old cordial visits. The comfortable boulevard meant that close friendships, forged by the years both sides shared securing Fort Benning's future, would continue.

Quality Courses for Future Leaders

On post, the training and education Fort Benning soldiers received increased in quality. Standing departments were eliminated and new ones were created. As the level of training increased so did the rank of the men doing the teaching. Instructors now held the rank of captain or above, and tactic instructors were field officers—majors, colonels, and Fort Leavenworth graduates.

It was also a time in the army when key leaders of the future were being groomed, officers who would cut their teeth on the grounds of Fort Benning. Among the 1925 graduates of the Infantry School was Major Omar Nelson Bradley, a mathematics instructor at West Point before he attended the advanced course at Benning. Graduating second in his class at Benning, Bradley left for the 27th Infantry of the Hawaiian Division, serving with George C. Patton in the "Pineapple Army." Bradley also knew Dwight David Eisenhower, a West Point classmate. Their class of 1915 was known as "the class the stars fell on" with fifty-nine of its graduates earning the rank of general. Both men were made five-star generals during their careers.

---

[2] "The Reservation," *Infantry School News*, March 13 1925, 4.

Captain Matthew Bunker Ridgway also was a 1925 Benning graduate. After completing the company officers course, he was given command of a company in the 15th Infantry in Tientsin, China, serving with Lieutenant Colonel George C. Marshall.

The year 1925 began with little fanfare. The Infantry School's assistant commandant, Colonel Alfred W. Bjornstad, was promoted to brigadier general on January 17, following in the footsteps of Paul Malone who also was promoted while serving in that role. On February 20, Bjornstad left for his new assignment as commander of the 14th Brigade in Fort Omaha, Nebraska.

In his two years at Benning, Bjornstad was involved in several important ventures. He reorganized the old Athletic Council into the Athletic Association and served as its head. Under his oversight, work proceeded on Doughboy Stadium and Gowdy Field, structures envisioned by Wells and Malone. Acting as general-manager, Bjornstad was determined to help complete the projects: "As its new pilot the general began work on the big Doughboy Stadium and also Gowdy Field. He evolved and set forth a large Infantry School Athletic program."[3] In addition to Bjornstad's contribution to the athletic program, he introduced training management courses into the curriculum and perfected the general instructional methods of the school.

Construction on post continued. A new officers' club was started in January 1925 and a month later work began on the 29th Infantry Regiment barracks. Although money was available, the word "salvage" still instilled action in Benning troops. In February, fifty-five men of the 24th Infantry, led by Captain S. S. Eberle, went to Muscle Shoals, Alabama, to salvage equipment from two nitrate plants. Loading several trucks, they brought home tools, bricks, plumbing fixtures, roofing material, and office supplies—all for future use.

As spring came, a 100-foot steel flagpole was erected March 3, under direction of Lieutenant Colonel A. B. Warfield, the same officer who served as the groom in the Columbus mock wedding ceremony. He stepped in after an earlier attempt to erect the flagpole failed. During one attempt, students were excused from class when the pole tilted perilously close to classrooms.

---

[3] "General Bjornstad Leaves for New Station," *Infantry School News*, February 20 1925, 2.

The pole, which had been stored for nearly two years, became a symbol of another of the school's accomplishments: "No longer will it be necessary to write odes and verse—the job is done—the pole is up, its shining golden ball tops the reservation."[4]

A more lasting accomplishment was completion of the main hospital in May, a major medical improvement for the post. Located on Rickett Hill, it offered the best view of the Benning Reservation, including the Chattahoochee and Upatoi valleys. Congress added $275,000 to the Army Appropriation Bill for the hospital in 1923.

The fireproof building was equipped with concrete foundations, hollow tile and stucco walls, a terra cotta tile roof, and steel frames for its doors and windows. A large solarium, operating rooms, big kitchen, and mess halls made the hospital "one of the finest in service."[5] It held 102 beds and had its own boiler house, steam heating plant, and hot water system. Lieutenant Colonel Paul S. Halloran was commanding officer of the Medical Detachment. Unfortunately the facility lacked the space and equipment necessary to meet the needs of post personnel. The *Infantry School News* reported "existing space is only half of what the garrison requires."[6]

Gowdy Field Opener

With spring came baseball. With the new baseball field and construction of a football field, the Infantry School in 1925 was said to have the "Army's Greatest Athletic Plant." Paul Malone, former assistant commander and athletic director, accepted a stadium box and an honorary life membership in the Officers' Club. "One of the most beloved leaders ever doing duty at the Infantry School," Malone was one of the first to develop the fort's athletic activities "with a vision which (was) typically his."[7]

The baseball field was named for Hank Gowdy, the first major leaguer to enlist in the first world war. He served with the Rainbow Division,

---

[4] "New Steel Flag Pole Now Graces the Fort," *Infantry School News*, March 6 1925, 6.

[5] "Big Plantation Transformed Within Six Years," *Infantry School News*, September 17 1926, 13.

[6] Ibid.

[7] "General Malone Takes Stadium Box and Club Membership," *Infantry School News*, April 17 1925, 1.

fighting at the front during his unit's major offensives and rising to the rank of color sergeant. Gowdy Field was dedicated on March 27, 1925, with games with Georgia teams. General Wells threw out the first ball, and the 24th Infantry band played. The infantrymen, coached by Rabbit Fountain, won their games, 15-0 and 17-4, with Piedmont College of Demorest, Georgia. The second series of games was with the University of Georgia "because of the long friendship existing between the two institutions."[8] Georgia won both games by close scores, 7-6 and 2-1.

Perhaps "the greatest sports event in Benning history," was held March 31, reported as "Gowdy Day at Benning Gala Event." The game was between the New York Giants and the Washington Senators. An audience of 6,500 fans, "combining grace, beauty, and feminine pulchritude of the South, with the masculine sporting spirit witnessed the great event and packed Gowdy Field."[9] The Giants won 9-6. The Senators went on to the 1925 World Series, losing to the Pittsburgh Pirates. Gowdy caught for the Giants that day. Before the game's first pitch, he raised the flag in center field. To commemorate the day, a silver service was presented to the catcher and his wife, a personal gift from the officers and men of Fort Benning.

Technology and Pyrotechnics

For the soldiers, there was always training. In May, using modern devices such as field radio telegraph and telephone stations, troops held exercises at Sulphur Springs and Harmony Church. Such communication equipment led to the development of commercial transatlantic telephone service between New York City and London in 1927.

In July, the 83rd Field Artillery commanded by Major E. P. King, Jr., walked 500 miles from the fort to Port St. Joe, Florida. However, the previous record set in April 1920 by the unit with its 630-mile hike from Camp Knox, Kentucky, to Camp Benning remained unbroken. After a week's stay at the Gulf town, the marchers returned.

Fourth of July fireworks revisited the fort on August 19, with an explosion at the ammunition dump in a small concrete chemical ware shed used by Co. F, 1st Gas Regiment. The shed stored four-inch Stokes mortal

---

[8] "Gowdy Field to Be Dedicated in Game with Georgia Today," *Infantry School News*, March 27 1925, 1.

[9] "Gowdy Day at Benning Gala Event," *Infantry School News*, April 3 1925, 1.

smoke shells, HN and FC phosphorus shells, Livens projector shells, tear gas shells, propellant charges, and pyrotechnics.

Captain D. Lee Hooper, commanding officer of the Chemical Warfare Service detachment, "was sure the explosions were started by a leaky phosphorus shell occasioned by the extreme heat."[10] The result was spectacular. "The larger bombs and shells blew up with a dull roar while the propelling charges went off with a rat-tat-tat resembling machine guns." The fire occurred nearly a year after one that destroyed the headquarters building in 1924.[11]

Doughboy Stadium Dedicated

Doughboy Stadium was christened on September 16 with the Benning team defeating Stetson University (Florida) 51-7. On October 10, the Doughboy eleven beat Transylvania (Kentucky) 33-0. Dutch Smythe, "the Blue Streak," was the Doughboy's backfield star. On October 17, with military and civilian personnel present, the stadium was formally dedicated. In the dedicatory game, the Blue Tide defeated Oglethorpe University (Georgia) 27-6.

Congressman W. C. Wright attended the dedication along with Columbus Mayor Homer Dimon, viewing the finished stadium that held 40 bays and 320 boxes with a seating capacity of 8,500. Bjornstad, the former assistant commandant who worked with Wells to make it possible, also attended. Many who were unable to be present sent congratulatory letters, recognizing the "living" memorial for those soldiers who died in World War I.

Doughboy Stadium put Fort Benning on the list of preferred posts, and the *Infantry Journal* honored it in its October 1925 issue. Captain F. J. Pearson told of the fort's good post school, vicinity to large towns, transportation to the post proper by an "excellent new concrete highway, good bus service, and the Central of Georgia," round trip daily.[12] After mentioning the inexpensive servants, laundry facilities, fraternal

---

[10] "Extreme Heat Causes Combustion and Fire in Ammunition Dump," *Infantry School News*, August 21 1925, 1–2.

[11] Ibid.

[12] Capt. F. J. Pearson, "Intimate Glimpses of Garrison Life," *Infantry Journal* 27/4 (October 1925): 412.

organizations, the hospital, golf, polo games and fishing, Pearson singled out hawk hunting, noting, "using a stuffed owl mounted on a pole or in a tree, affords great sport."[13] After seven years of growing pains, Fort Benning was now a favorite of enlistees, with army personnel, and the City of Columbus.

---

[13] Ibid.

7.

The Arrival of Coach Ike

World War I passed him by and the disappointed major with the winning smile worried his army career would be spent coaching football and growing fat in a desk job.

With his belongings packed into a new Buick, Dwight David Eisenhower and his wife, Mamie, made a cross-country trek to his new assignment as battalion commander of the 24th Infantry Regiment at Fort Benning. His destination was 206 Austin Loop, not far from Riverside, the old plantation house that since 1919 was home to post commanders. This was Eisenhower's second trip to Fort Benning. On his first, he brought three Renault tanks from Fort Dix, New Jersey. That train trip to Georgia in the winter of 1919 was something he never forgot, one replayed in his book *At Ease*. "The train trip lasted for almost four days, each a year long," he wrote. "There were no lights, no heat, no hot water."[1]

During World War I, Eisenhower trained tankers at Camp Meade, Maryland, and Camp Colt, Pennsylvania, men who went overseas, leaving him behind. As the war ended, he and remnants of his tank corps were transferred to Camp Dix, New Jersey, and later to Georgia. Eisenhower described the transfer to Fort Benning as "only an interim until the War Department found a permanent post for the remains of the infant Tank Corps."[2]

At the struggling Georgia post, the arrival of the tanks was a significant event even if the officer who came with them was at the time obscure. The *Infantry School News* reported "In January 1919, Major Eisenhower brought

---

[1] Dwight D. Eisenhower, *At Ease* (Garden City NY: Doubleday Company, Inc., 1967) 153–54.

[2] Ibid., 147.

to Camp Benning a Detachment of Tanks which were [sic] the first to be stationed at this Post."[3]

Eisenhower spent his first stint at Benning considering his future. The ambitious captain was considering a change of careers, figuring his future in the army was anything but promising. "I was older than my classmates, was still bothered on occasion by a bad knee, and saw myself in the years ahead putting on weight in a meaningless chair-bound assignment, shuffling papers, and filling out forms," he wrote. "If not depressed, I was mad, disappointed and resented the fact that the war had passed me by."[4]

Before Eisenhower left Benning, Colonel Henry Eames, his commanding officer, offered this evaluation of the captain from Kansas: "Although a young officer and ranking above his classmates, he was well-liked, had his command well in hand, disciplined and of high morale and efficiency."[5]

The Eisenhower who returned seven years later was more seasoned. He had suffered the loss of his son Doud Dwight—"Icky"—in 1920. He had worked through the disappointment of missing frontline service. He had made up his mind that the army would be his life. Now accompanied by their four-year-old son John, Dwight and Mamie Eisenhower were overjoyed with their quarters on Austin Loop. But soon came a call he dreaded; they wanted him to coach football.

At West Point, Eisenhower was a promising halfback. Sportswriters touted him as a potential All-American. Those dreams ended when he injured his knee, first twisting it in a game against the legendary Olympian Jim Thorpe playing with the Carlisle Indians, then breaking it in the following game. His football experience followed him to every army assignment where, in addition to his other duties, he coached the base team. Eisenhower did not see himself as a "first-rate coach." He followed one basic practice: "Whenever I could find a good passer, I always tried to open up the game.... That lesson I had learned once and for all when Knute Rockne and Gus Dorais of Notre Dame had stunned the country's football

---

[3] "Who's Who," *Infantry School News*, October 15 1926, 67.

[4] Eisenhower, *At Ease*, 155.

[5] Merle Miller, *Ike the Soldier* (New York: G.P. Putnam's Sons, 1987) 175.

fans—and me, sitting on the bench—by their two-man defeat of West Point in 1913."[6]

Eisenhower came to Benning in 1926 from the Army's Command and General Staff School at Fort Leavenworth where he graduated first in a class of 275. His next assignment was not defined, wrote historian Stephen Ambrose, who noted Eisenhower had more than one offer: "He could go a northwestern university as a ROTC instructor and coach its football team, the duty to include coaching the university's football team at an additional salary of $3,500 per year, or he could take command of a battalion at Fort Benning. He chose Benning."[7]

After turning down the college job, Eisenhower hoped he could put football behind him, fearing he would be labeled a coach instead of an officer. Then, within a week of his return to Fort Benning, he received the familiar request. "I was told that I would have to coach the soldier football team. With an enormous effort of will, I said quietly that I just turned down $3,500 a year additional to do the same thing."[8] But he reminded himself of a basic lesson of the military: "that the proper place for a soldier is where he is ordered by his superiors."[9] Relenting, he accepted the coaching job. He did, however, decline the responsibilities of being head coach. Instead, he took charge of the backfield and offensive tactics.

At Benning, with "Fat" Franz, flank guard, receiving "Kelly" Kjelstrom's "rifle shot passes," Eisenhower hoped the team, "willing, but raw," would do well.[10] Kjelstrom and Franz had played together in infantry and battalion teams for years, but their efforts failed to impress Carson Newman in the opening game. The soldiers lost 7-0.

The school paper reported, "Last Saturday's Tennessee visitors were rough, rude, and rowdy and so little appreciative of doughboy hospitality that they took a victory away with them."[11] The next game produced a win, however, with a score of 20-0 over King College (Tennessee) with the help

---

[6] Eisenhower, *At Ease*, 197.

[7] Stephen E. Ambrose, *Eisenhower*, vol. 1 (New York: Simon and Schuster, 1983) 82.

[8] Eisenhower, *At Ease*, 204.

[9] Ibid., 155.

[10] Ibid., 204.

[11] "Mountain Tornado Blows into Fort for Gridiron Clash," *Infantry School News*, October 8 1926, 1.

of star linesman "Big Bertha Bertelman, a rushing, driving, fighting machine."[12]

Benning lost to Loyola of New Orleans but came back to defeat Mercer University (Georgia) and the University of Tennessee Doctors. When the marines from Parris Island won 16-7, Fort Benning ended its season at 3-3. For the marines, victory was almost a dream come true. It was their first in five years. For Benning, it meant more practice. As a sportswriter saw it, "It wasn't that they didn't fight hard, for they did. In fact they were fighting so hard that in the fourth quarter scarcely a play was run on which a marine wasn't knocked out and carried off the field. This without any dirty football too."[13]

The All-army team went on to play for the President's Cup at Washington, DC. The year before, the Benning squad had lost to the marines. In 1926, they hoped for better results. But when the game ended, the President's Cup remained with the "Sea Soldiers." Eisenhower summed up the season by saying it "was not one to divert attention from Notre Dame, Wisconsin, West Point, and the others. Fortunately, I didn't have to face another."[14]

Though that would be his final year as a coach, Dwight David Eisenhower's military career did not end. He commanded the largest force ever assembled in World War II—the invasion of Normandy. His uniform was decorated with five stars, one of only a handful of officers to earn that distinction. He was a college president. He was president of the United States.

His legacies are legend, but as battalion commander of Fort Benning's 24th Infantry Regiment, Eisenhower left behind one not often mentioned by historians trying to capture the essence of this smiling leader.

Private First Class Tom Fields, a black soldier, served in the 24th Infantry. Running "afoul of the army's strict regulations," he had to report to Major Dwight D. Eisenhower, his battalion commander. Fields was given

---

[12] "Berry Musketeers Beat Kin by Strong Last Half Attack," *Infantry School News*, October 15 1926, 1.

[13] "Marines Realize Their Five Year Dream and Defeat the Doughboys," *Infantry School News*, November 19 1926, 12.

[14] Eisenhower, *At Ease*, 204.

"a stern lecture, a stiff warning and was 'busted in rank.'"[15] Less than a month later, Fields was caught in an off-limits place "across the river," either in Phenix City or Girard, "centers in the manufacturing and marketing of corn liquor."[16] Again, he stood in front of his commanding officer. Fields promised Eisenhower if he would let him go he would never come back before him again. The private was given another chance, and the major's confidence was rewarded. Fields remained in the military with no further disciplinary problems for the next twenty-three years. In 1949, Fields was honorably discharged from the army after thirty-two years of service. He remained at Fort Benning as the popular "major domo" at the main Officers' Open Mess. Fields said he owed his army career to Eisenhower. "I would never have wanted to soldier under a better officer. You just played your little number and he wouldn't bother you."[17]

---

[15] Kathy Aure, "Death of 'Generals' Friend Marks End of Era," *Columbus Enquirer*, December 9 1971, 8.

[16] Charles F. Pekor, Jr., "An Adventure in Georgia," *American Mercury*, ed. H. D. Mencken, 8/32 (August 1926): 409.

[17] Kathy Aure, "Death of 'Generals' Friend Marks End of Era," *Columbus Enquirer*, December 9 1971, 8.

8.

A Revolution in the Classroom

Arthur Bussey would never recognize the old place. Roads were paved. First-run films and live performances entertained the troops. Golf was popular, and there was a new telephone building, a new bakery, and new barracks. The first camp for college ROTC opened and preparatory classes for West Point were offered. There was a shortage of soldiers in the ranks, but there was no shortage of activity.

There was even time for history. In May 1927, the Daughters of the American Revolution and Lizzie Rutherford Chapter of United Daughters of the Confederacy presented a tablet to commemorate General Henry L. Benning, the post's namesake. Anna Caroline Benning unveiled the tablet given in honor of her father.

Later in the year, a bronze tablet dedicated to General Marquis Lafayette by the Georgia Daughters of the American Revolution was erected. It recorded his reaction to the Revolution: "At the First News My Heart was Enrolled."[1] On a visit to the United States in 1825, Lafayette walked on the Federal Road, "Down the First Division Road to its junction with the Lumpkin Road (near Riverside) and hence directly west across the 29th Infantry area and on toward the Bradley farm."[2]

The Federal Road, authorized by Congress in 1805, opened as a bridal path in 1807 and became a main traffic route in 1811. It provided a route for emigrants and settlers moving from the Atlantic coast to the Lower Mississippi Valley. To protect the frontier, Fort Mitchell—a predecessor to Fort Benning—was built on the Federal Road in 1813 at a site across the Chattahoochee River from what is now Lawson Army Air Field.

---

[1] "Memorial Tablets To Be Established at Cross Roads," *Infantry School News*, February 26 1926, 1.

[2] Ibid.

Though conditions on post had improved greatly in 1926, "muddy walks and rutted roads" were common.[3] The school newspaper, taking an optimistic view, saw progress: "Benning is not a settled place. It is still growing.... Mr. Bussey would never recognize his farm today. But Benning has only started its growth and the visitor ten years hence will find the finest post in the Army as the construction proceeds."[4]

With modernization came new challenges and innovative solutions. The Ford Model A posed a problem soon solved by Captain James F. Hyde, commander of the 7th Engineers. Rigging a giant two-ton magnet to a trailer attached to a truck, he designed a way to pick up nails and other metallic objects to prevent punctures in the tires of the popular car. The post exchange provided free gasoline for Hyde's road-magnet rig.

Old problems continued, however. In July, the post sawmill was destroyed by fire. The abundance of trees on post land provided not only generous building material but also continuous threats of fire. In an attempt to preserve the post forest, the Benning National Forest was created in 1924. The War Department and Department of Agriculture had dual control of about 90 percent of Infantry School land. The agreement was unsatisfactory from a military viewpoint, and on December 2, 1927, by order of President Calvin Coolidge in Executive order 4776, the forest reserve was restored to its former status as part of the Fort Benning Military Reservation.

In March 1926, Brigadier General Edgar F. Collins assumed command of Fort Benning. He replaced Brigadier General Briant H. Wells, who became chief of the Supply Division of the War Department General Staff. A West Point graduate, Collins studied at Benning in 1924. A decorated veteran of World War I, his previous assignment was as commander of the Field Artillery Brigade of the First Division. Assistant commandant Colonel Frank Cocheu stayed on, continuing his important contributions to the way classes were taught. Under his direction, regular classes were supplemented by refresher classes of varying length and a series of infantry correspondence courses were added. He also established a map reproduction plant, operated by personnel from Company A, 7th Engineers, and replaced obsolete

---

[3] "Big Plantation Is Transformed within Six Years," *Infantry School News*, September 17 1926, 13.

[4] Ibid.

training films. A reserve officer who in civilian life worked with a motion picture news agency directed the production of the new films.

Military historian Geoffrey Perret claims Cocheu's biggest innovation was an improved method of instruction destined to reshape military education:

> It was known as demonstration, explanation, performance. Textbooks and long-winded professorial lectures were out. Henceforth, wherever possible, instructors would demonstrate what students were expected to learn, such as use of machine guns in an attack or how to make an opposed river crossing. Then the students took over. They explained the lessons back to the instructors. After which the students proved how well they'd learned the lesson by performing the operation in question using school troops.[5]

An extreme shortage of enlisted men existed in those demonstration units. This led to the garrison drawing extra duty in 1927. The 29th Infantry Regiment alone lacked 987 men in mid-summer. Leaves and some holidays were curtailed. Extra hours meant long days. Complaints were few, however. The positive reaction from troops brought praise from Collins, the new commanding general: "These officers and soldiers have worked with a cheerfulness, loyalty, and high-minded sense of duty as to earn for them the highest official commendation and my lasting personal gratitude and thanks."[6]

Even with the shortage of manpower, troops managed to help when a hurricane hit South Florida in July. The death toll hit 370 with 6,000 people injured and 18,000 families left homeless. Cost estimates were $165 million in damages. In September, soldiers at Benning loaded tents, cots, blankets, and kitchen supplies on to a boxcar provided by the Central of Georgia. The boxcar was connected to the Seminole Limited and sent on to Miami to help storm victims.

On post, there was also time for soldiers to help each other. Private Joseph Wiggins of the Quartermaster Corps gained recognition when he saved the life of Sergeant Frank Lavender's eighteen-month-old baby. The

---

[5] Geoffrey Perret, *There's a War to Be Won* (New York: Random House, 1991) 11–12.

[6] LeRoy W. Yarborough, in collaboration with Truman Smith, *A History of the Infantry School, Fort Benning, Georgia* (Ft. Benning: The Infantry School, 1931) 188.

toddler, looking for adventure, went through a hole in the screen door of his family's home.

"Wiggins, at the throttle of the post's narrow gauge train, noticed an infant crawling on the tracks ahead and immediately applied the brakes," a post reporter wrote. "Because of the angle of the grade, the train would not stop. Wiggins jumped out and ran ahead of the train to snatch the baby just in the nick of time."[7] Lavendar, a non-com with Co. H 29th Infantry, tried to talk to Wiggins, who got back on the train and kept on going. He had a job to do, and it had nothing to do with being a hero. Wiggins later explained: "I didn't have time to answer any dee fool questions. I had to get that load of sand and gravel out where I was going."[8]

Nor was time wasted when George C. Marshall replaced Cocheu as assistant commandant in November 1927. Marshall succeeded in the classroom revolution initiated by Cocheu at Fort Benning's Infantry School. His methods changed the way company-grade officers were taught and ultimately changed the way the army fought its battles. While serving overseas, Marshall observed over elaborate planning and too much writing of plans and operations. Forrest Pogue, Marshall's biographer, said his greatest lesson "was the need for simplicity in the techniques of troop leading."[9]

Marshall previously expressed his thoughts in a 1921 *Infantry Journal* article: "Our troops suffered much from the delays involved in preparing long and complicated orders, due to the failure of the Staff concerned to recognize that speed was more important than technique."[10] Fort Leavenworth instructor Major John F. Morrison inspired in Marshall "simplicity and dispersion." Marshall would say, "I was a Morrison man," and would add, "He taught me all I have ever known of tactics."[11]

In defining his mission at Benning, Marshall clashed with traditional teachings. He called for techniques so simple and brief "that the citizen

---

[7] "Pvt. Joseph H. Wiggins Quartermaster Corps Heroic Engineer," *Infantry School News*, September 17 1926, 11.

[8] Ibid.

[9] Forrest C. Pogue, *George C. Marshall: Education of a General* (New York: the Viking Press, 1963) 249.

[10] Maj. George C. Marshall, "Profiting By War Experiences," *Infantry Journal* 18/1 (June 1921): 36.

[11] Pogue, *George C. Marshall: Education of a General*, 99.

officer of good common sense can readily grasp the idea."[12] Keeping things simple went against the military pedagogy of the time, so Marshall was patient.

Marshall successfully fought for smaller classes and better classroom conditions. In early August 1929, reorgan-ization of the infantry regiment became one of the most important projects yet undertaken by the Infantry School. Under the plan, the square divisions used in World War I would be scrapped in favor of a triangular structure. Marshall believed the triangular division with the addition of weapons gave unity to a command: "A divided command on the battlefield is out of the question...only homogeneous units can fight with a maximum of efficiency."[13]

Marshall also approved of new drill regulations that "substituted a few simple movements for the earlier complicated formations that had been continued, almost without change, since the time of Prussia's Frederick the Great," in the 1700s. The new drill used squads and platoons to cover and conceal rather than formal mass formations, "which depended primarily upon shock action for results."[14]

In a lecture on tactics, Marshall summed up his philosophy of military preparedness based on his experiences and his idea of future warfare. They proved to be visionary. Tactics of the future, he said, need

> brief, concise oral orders, based on the ground you can see or on maps with very little detail.... They involve the necessity for very perfect teamwork between the infantry on the one side and the artillery, aviators and various commanders on the other.... They compel a constant tactical readiness in security arrangements as well as in battle tactics, in preparations for the sudden appearance of tanks or other mechanized units in front, flank, or rear. In all these matters, speed of thought, speed of action and direction and speed of operation is essential to success.[15]

---

[12] Forrest C. Pogue, *George C. Marshal: Education of a General* (New York: Viking Press, 1963) 251.

[13] Perret, *There's a War to Be Won*, 16.

[14] "Tests of Semi-Automatic Rifles," 16, History of the Infantry School papers located in vault, Donovan Library, Fort Benning GA.

[15] George C. Marshall, *The Papers of George Catlett Marshall*, vol. 1, ed. Larry I. Bland (Baltimore: John Hopkins University Press, 1981) 338.

Marshall deemed four things necessary for training for men to carry into battle: "discipline that triumphs over fatigue and danger, a thorough grasp of the technique involved, and a knowledge of two vitally important matters—real simplicity and correct methods for maintaining control."[16]

As the revolution in training continued, the post continued to grow. Sections F and G of the 29th Infantry cuartel barracks were completed in early 1929. That summer, the Infantry School Academic Library and a new gymnasium were opened. Troop labor rebuilt Russ Pool, enlarged several assembly halls for the Academic Building, and constructed a building for the servants of Block 23.

As a sad reminder of how far the once struggling post had come, word came of the death of Colonel Henry E. Eames, Camp Benning's first commanding officer. Eames, fifty-seven, died May 9, 1928, in Fort Sheridan, Illinois. After leaving Georgia, Eames led the 45th Infantry in the Philippines and directed recruiting in his home state of Missouri. He was forever remembered as a founder of the Infantry School—a fact his wife included on his tombstone.

One day after Eames's death, a demonstration was held that he would have applauded. Included in the annual Air Corps demonstration were seventy-three airplanes of all descriptions under command of Brigadier General Benjamin D. Foulois. As part of the show, there were attacks on targets and planes, aerial acrobatics including "a three-mile smoke screen laid along Lumpkin Road."[17]

But from the beginning, Fort Benning was a community of soldiers as well as a training installation. Families lived and worshipped on post. Children went to school there and explored its neighborhoods. Desiring an attractive community for everyone, the army hired city planner George B. Ford, who "completed his grand scheme for the post in 1929."[18] Although his plan for harmonious buildings did not see fruition until the 1930s, his ideas for the grouping of buildings, straight avenues, and open spaces prevail.[19]

---

[16] Ibid., 337.

[17] "Air Corps Maneuvers Held Thursday," *Infantry School News*, May 11 1928, 1.

[18] Sharyn Kane and Richard Keeton, *Fort Benning: The Land and the People* (Tallahassee FL: Southeast Archeological Center, 1998) 175.

[19] Ibid.

In 1929, Ward 1 and 2 of the main hospital were completed and work was started on Ward 3 and the nurses' quarters. Contractors paved and constructed storm sewers on Vibbert Avenue and a water filtration plant was built. With a ready supply of timber, by 1929, the post's average yearly production of building lumber was close to 1,500,000 board feet. Sand and gravel produced at the rate of about 5000 cubic yards a year also figured into the production of building materials. Members of the 24th Infantry Regiment ran the lumberyard as well as the sand and gravel pits.

With its reputation spreading, important guests came to visit. Franklin D. Roosevelt, the governor of New York, drove to Fort Benning in 1929 on his way to Warm Springs, Georgia. Former Columbus resident George Foster Peabody, a famous banker and philanthropist, had recommended the soothing springs there to the future president who suffered the lingering effects of polio. Also in 1929, Secretary of War Dwight L. Davis and Assistant Secretary Trubee Davidson inspected the post. During this time, March again proved petulant when severe rain brought flooding, causing Harp Pond to break with the loss of thousands of fish. On that same day, Herbert Clark Hoover was inaugurated as the thirty-first president of the United States. Consequently, the deluge was called the Hoover Flood with the Chattahoochee reaching a high water mark of 53 feet, breaking the record of 51.2 set during the Pershing Flood in 1919.

Marshall rose above the inclement weather conditions by flying out of the Fort Benning Airfield—the assistant secretary of war provided the plane—to begin a tour of military schools. Looking for ways to improve the Infantry School program, Marshall visited Fort Sill, Oklahoma; Fort Leavenworth, Kansas; Fort Humphrey, Virginia; and Langley Field, Virginia.

In May 1929, General Campbell King, a 1923 graduate of the General Officers' Class, took command, succeeding Collins, who was bound for the Philippines. The commanding general was leaving, but Assistant Commandant George C. Marshall was staying, and in the 1930s, Marshall's Men would lead the way.

9.

Workhorse and Show horse

The young army officer was totally befuddled. He was trying to relay a change in orders to his troops and he was as confused as the orders he was delivering. Adding to his nervousness was the presence of Lieutenant Colonel George C. Marshall, acting commander of the 15th Infantry. They were involved in a training exercise in China, and like every soldier there, he knew Marshall's reputation as a tactician. But Marshall was not as concerned about tactics as he was this confused young officer.

It was a moment Marshall vividly recalled: "I learned that he had stood first at Benning, and I, then and there, formed an intense desire to get my hands on Benning. The man was no fool, but he had been taught an absurd system, which proved futile the moment a normal situation of warfare of movement arose."[1]

Near the end of 1927, George Catlett Marshall did get his hands on Fort Benning. After visiting the post several times as an aide to General John J. Pershing, Marshall was now assistant commandant, and, though no one realized it, the "Benning Revolution" was about to begin. His name already was magical. In World War I, Marshall had carried out what was thought of an impossible assignment—referred to by some as the greatest single achievement of American staff work in France. In order to take the Germans by surprise, he planned and directed a shift from the Saint-Mihiel area to the Meuse-Argonne area, transferring men and guns in less than two weeks.

In September 1918, Colonels Fox Conner, Hugh A. Drum, Walter S. Grant, and Marshall, a temporary colonel, moved 600,000 troops, 3,000 guns, and 40,000 tons of ammunition—at night and without lights.

---

[1] Forrest C. Pogue, *George C. Marshall: Education of a General* (New York: Viking Press, 1963) 250–51.

Historian Russell Weigley notes, "Pershing as well as Foch doubted that the shift could be accomplished."[2] The operation was "the special responsibility" of Marshall, and "It was done."[3]

Marshall had his choice of assignments in 1927: The Army War College, chief of staff, a corps, or Benning. There was also an offer to be an aide to General Henry Stimson, governor general of the Philippines. Later Marshall wrote Stimson explaining that he had been an aide to three other generals: "Now if I become an aide for the fourth time I fear, in fact I feel sure, that to the army at large I would be convicted of being only an aide and never a commander."[4]

Remembering that experience in China, Marshall knew what he wanted to accomplish—changes at Fort Benning and in the way the army did business. There were also personal reasons he needed to be there. Elizabeth "Lily" Marshall, his wife of twenty-six years, died September 15, 1927, after undergoing goiter surgery at Walter Reed Hospital in Washington. Writing Mrs. Thomas B. Coles—his late wife's Aunt Lottie—Marshall said. "I thought it best professionally and in my present frame of mind to go to Benning."[5]

When Marshall arrived, he wore a black armband in Lily's honor. After moving into a house once part of the Bussey Plantation, he inherited an orderly, a cook, and a Cadillac with a driver. He immersed himself in country living, enjoying horseback riding, polo matches, and baseball games on the post. As he wrote a friend, "You can fish, shoot, find lovely walks or shoot wildcats."[6]

Marshall gave a "thumbnail sketch" of Fort Benning to Aunt Lottie: "Benning is near Columbus, Georgia, 125 miles southwest of Atlanta…there are 600 officers at Benning of whom 450 are students in the school which will be my direct charge. There is a war strength regiment (3,500 men) at Benning, also a peace strength regiment, a battalion of artillery, a company

---

[2] Russell F. Weigley, *History of the United States Army* (Bloomington: Indiana University Press, 1984) 388–89.

[3] Ibid.

[4] George C. Marshall, *The Papers of George Catlett Marshall*, vol. 1, ed. Larry I. Bland (Baltimore: John Hopkins University Press, 1981) 322.

[5] Ibid., 316.

[6] Ibid., 321.

of tanks, and a squadron of aeroplanes."[7]

Students were at mid-term when Marshall arrived in November 1927. Before leaving for a Christmas holiday, he wrote a memo to the commandant that would ultimately change the face of the post. For the short term, he expressed concerns about transportation. He requested the purchase of eleven buses, each seating twenty-five passengers. His memo presented arguments for improved mobility: "With existing means of transportation, about one-half of the available terrain is only occasionally employed in tactical training."[8] Land close to the post, available by horse or narrow gauge railroad, usually was closed to tactical training because of the firing on the experimental and school ranges. Students were therefore limited to a restricted area, which was "over-familiar and of which the students soon tire."[9] If his mission was to prepare men for the unexpected, new and unexplored training fields were needed.

Buses would also service students who lived in town. Before Marshall, nearly 200 student officers lived off base, paying high rent for apartments or houses in Columbus. He noted off-post soldiers "are personally obligated to provide their own means of transportation to and from post six days a week.... This particular situation has always adversely affected morale among the students, to the disadvantage of the school. It should be remedied."[10] His memo received twenty-one endorsements, but its only outcome was permission to train additional enlisted men to care for existing post vehicles.[11]

Fulfilling the post's primary function to train company-grade infantry officers in the art of leading small units, Marshall, over a period of nearly five years, gradually changed instructional style and tactical concepts. Marshall was both a workhorse and a show horse. While revolutionizing the training and education of the officers at Benning, he also was well-known for the colorful pageants he conducted for visitors. Guests in one flourish could see exhibitions of the garrison's social and athletic life.

---

[7] Ibid., 316.

[8] George C. Marshall, *The Papers of George Catlett Marshall*, vol. 1, ed. Larry I. Bland (Baltimore: John Hopkins University Press, 1981) 323.

[9] Ibid.

[10] Ibid., 323–24.

[11] Ibid.

"Staged for visiting dignitaries in place of formal military reviews…the pageant consisted of a series of acts," Pogue wrote. "In one of these, students marched by with their weapons, tennis players with the rackets, polo ponies and riders, basketball players, baseball players—and then as a climax, a pack of hounds following a scent laid down earlier in the day burst through the crowd, followed by huntsmen."[12]

Marshall was pleased with life at Fort Benning. In a letter to Brigadier General Frank R. McCoy, he praised Major Henry J. M. Smith, who taught Equitation, a required course for student officers, and described the 180 ladies in equitation class as making "the Italian Cavalry envious of their daring riding, particularly up and down slides."[13] Even the PTA president traveled on horseback. As Sara Spano, a former Fort Benning teacher recalled in a 1970 column in the *Ledger-Enquirer*, the woman arrived for meetings at full gallop. "Tying the horse to a convenient tree in the school yard," Spano wrote, "she would stride in and conduct the meeting with efficiency and dispatch. At the close of the meeting, she would leap back on her steed to finish her ride."[14] Marshall rode eight to ten miles daily and encouraged horse shows, trail hunts, and cross-country pursuit of foxes. Pogue told of Marshall "returning from a treasure hunt on horseback, wearing a Japanese kimono and Filipino hat, and carrying a bird cage."[15]

Not all Benning officers shared Marshall's enthusiasm for horses. Omar Bradley, who preferred playing golf to riding, was delighted to discover that Joe Stilwell believed, "If there is a woodener, less intelligent animal on earth than a god-damned hammer-headed horse, show him to me. All prance and fart and no sense."[16]

Bradley and Stilwell taught at Benning in 1929. Both graduated from previous Infantry School courses and both were extremely capable although exactly opposite in temperament. Marshall held the position of Tactical Section head open for a year until Stilwell, an "old China hand," was available. Bradley, in his first year, was assigned to Stilwell's section to teach

---

[12] Pogue, *George C. Marshall: Education of a General*, 261.

[13] Marshall, *Papers of George Catlett Marshall*, 341.

[14] Sara Spano, *I Could've Written "Gone with the Wind," but Cousin Margaret Beat Me to It* (Ann Arbor MI: McNaughton & Gunn, 1990) 74–75.

[15] Pogue, *George C. Marshall: Education of a General*, 261.

[16] Omar Bradley, with collaborator Clay Blair, *A General's Life* (New York: Simon and Schuster, 1983) 66.

senior officers "Battalion in the Attack." Marshall also requested Major Dwight D. Eisenhower as an instructor, but he was in Paris.

In 1929, Marshall attended a small dinner party at the home of Mr. And Mrs. T. (Tom) Charlton Hudson in Dinglewood, a wooded neighborhood near downtown Columbus. At the party he met Katherine Tupper Brown, an attractive guest who was visiting friends in Columbus. When Marshall declined to smoke or drink, Mrs. Brown observed, "You are a rather unusual Army officer, aren't you? I have never known one to refuse a cocktail before."

"How many have you known?" he asked.

"Not many," she confessed.

After dinner, Marshall asked to drive her to the home of Mrs. William R. Blanchard, a family friend with whom she was staying. After an hour of driving around town, Mrs. Brown asked Marshall how long he had been stationed at Benning.

"Two years," he replied.

"Well," she said, "after two years haven't you learned your way around Columbus?"

"Extremely well," he answered, "or I could not have stayed off the block where Mrs. Blanchard lives!"[17]

The dinner partners kept in touch after that evening. Both had been married and both had experienced personal tragedy in the loss of their spouses. Clifton S. Brown, a lawyer, was shot and killed June 4, 1928, by "a dissatisfied client."[18]

With her children Molly, Clifton Junior, and Alan Tupper Brown, Katherine Brown continued to live in Baltimore and to vacation at their cottage in Fire Island. Before her marriage, Tupper—a graduate of Hollins College in Virginia and the American Academy of Dramatic Arts in New York—performed in theatrical companies in England, Chicago, and New York. Friends in Georgia remembered her in summer productions of the Columbus Dramatic Club: "There was a notable local cast, and the Tupper sisters, those stylish Virginia-born girls who made their home in New York,

---

[17] Katherine Tupper Marshall, *Together: Annals of an Army Wife* (New York: Tupper and Love, Inc., 1947) 2–3.

[18] "Client Kills Lawyer Who Charged $2,500," *New York Times*, June 5 1928, 59:2.

came down to take occasional leads in the amateur plays."[19]

On June 12, 1929, Marshall left Fort Benning to deliver the graduation address at Virginia Military Institute, his alma mater. Later in the month, Marshall wrote Pershing, "I have had a very busy spring and feel much in need of a respite, so I am leaving in two days for the Eaton Ranch near Sheridan, Wyoming." In the same letter he encouraged Pershing to visit him at Fort Benning: "I can give you privacy, gaiety, delightful young people, fine horses, and pretty constant diversions, as you might elect."[20]

In June 1930, Marshall requested a captain to forward his mail, "Care Mrs. Clifton S. Brown, Ocean Beach, Fire Island, New York." Marshall was invited to spend five weeks with Mrs. Brown and her children. The stay provided an opportunity for Marshall to win over Allen, the youngest of the three children, who wanted things to remain as they were. Allen, however, soon changed his mind and invited Marshall to come: "I hope you will come to Fire Island. Don't be nervous, it is okay with me. A friend in need is a friend indeed, Allen Brown."[21] Only Allen freely called Marshall by his first name. Even FDR hesitated to call him George. Instructors and their wives also observed this etiquette at formal and informal setting although privately some called him "Uncle George" due to his formal behavior, disciplined nature, and often lonely demeanor.[22]

By September, a wedding date was confirmed. Marshall wrote Pershing, asking for a favor: "We are to be married in Baltimore the afternoon of October 15th. I would count it a great honor if you would stand up with me. The wedding is to be quiet with only family and very intimate friends of hers—no invitations.... My sister alone of my family knows anything about it."[23]

Marshall also wrote Lily's Aunt Lottie to reassure her that he was not "walking out" on her. He told her of his garden: "For my exercise I have been gardening violently this last week, getting in the annuals to insure early

---

[19] Etta Blanchard Worsley, *Columbus on the Chattahoochee* (Columbus GA: Columbus Office Supply Company, 1951) 363.

[20] Marshall, *Papers of George Catlett Marshall*, 343.

[21] Katherine Tupper Marshall, *Together: Annals of an Army Wife*, 3.

[22] Pogue, *George C. Marshall: Education of a General*, 262.

[23] George Marshall to Gen. Pershing, October 20 1930, in *Papers of George Catlett Marshall*, 358.

blooming next spring. My hands are blisters and raw spots. I swim late in the evening."[24]

As planned, Katherine Tupper Brown, forty-eight, and George Catlett Marshall, fifty, were married on October 15. General John J. Pershing was best man. Not planned was the crowd of reporters and admirers. After the wedding they rode overnight on a train from Baltimore to Atlanta, then drove from Atlanta to Fort Benning. Awaiting the couple were bouquets of flowers and cards in honor of their marriage. One bouquet contained a poem by Major Forrest Harding, who served in China with Marshall:

> If you rise with the dawn for a cross-country ride,
> If you stay up past midnight and dance;
> If you swim and play golf, and shoot quail on the wing,
> And read through a book at a glance;
> If you're keen about horse shows, like amateur plays
> And understand polo and art;
> If you sparkle at dinner (which I'm sure you do)
> Then I know you're the Queen of his Heart.[25]

After admiring their gifts, the Marshalls prepared for the al fresco reception where they shook hands with 1,000 people on the commandant's lawn. Attending the party were former staff members from China, young student officers with their wives, and other Infantry School instructors accompanied by their wives, especially one who was the mother of triplets.

To give his special friends proper recognition, Marshall would whisper in Katherine's ear to identify persons passing by in the reception line. She was to reply, "You served with Colonel Marshall in China, didn't you?" or "Thank you for your lovely flowers."[26] The reception was memorable for Mrs. Marshall. "I shall never forget that night. The reception was given on the lawn with a full moon shining through the huge oak and magnolia trees. Floodlights illumined the dance floor, which the army bandsmen in their

---

[24] George Marshall to Mrs. Thomas B. Coles, September 25 1930, in *Papers of George Catlett Marshall*, 358.

[25] Katherine Tupper Marshall, *Together: Annals of an Army Wife*, 5.

[26] Ibid., 6.

smart uniforms played soft music."[27]

Things went well with the first 500 guests. Then she felt her smile freeze and her husband's voice blur while whispering, "China...staff... flowers." When she heard the word "triplets," she replied, "Oh, thank you so much for your lovely triplets."[28] Both exhausted and exhilarated, Katherine Marshall survived her "first touch of the Army."[29]

The next morning, while eating breakfast outside, Marshall informed his wife that a class of colonels attending the Infantry School for a short course were invited, with their wives, to a reception at the Marshall home. Everything was arranged, but Mrs. Marshall was to call some instructors' wives to ask them to assist her in receiving the "Refresher Class." At her first call she said, "Colonel Marshall tells me you will be good enough to assist me at the tea in honor of the Refreshment Class this afternoon."

"Refresher Class," said Marshall in a loud whisper.

Covering the phone she insisted, "There is no word in the English language such as 'refresher.'"

"It is *refresher*, not *refreshment*," Marshall replied.

She corrected herself. "I am not quite responsible. I mean Refresher Class." By teatime, she discovered that her "Refreshment Class" gaffe was all over the post.[30]

Omar Bradley said marriage did nothing to mellow Marshall: "He remained his same formal, aloof self."[31] Stiffness was part of who Marshall was. So were vision and his ability to group around him leaders and thinkers. Fort Benning was a place he wanted to change, and he and his band of followers were affecting those changes. Even then, those who came in touch with George C. Marshall knew he had much to offer his army and his nation.

Pershing wrote Marshall in 1930, "Although I do not write often, you are in my thoughts frequently and I am hoping that some of these days you

[27] Ibid.

[28] Ibid.

[29] Marshall, *Papers of George Catlett Marshall*, 359.

[30] Ibid., 7.

[31] Bradley, *A General's Life*, 70.

will come into your own.... I think it is only a question of time when you will be repaid for your patience."[32]

[32] Gen. Pershing to George Marshall, February 28 1930, in *Papers of George Catlett Marshall*, 351.

10.

A Military Metropolis

Marshall's Men had gathered.

It was a group of officers he considered "the most brilliant, interesting, and thoroughly competent collection of men."[1] At that moment, they were together at Fort Benning. In the coming decade, these men and their influence would be scattered all over the world.

Lieutenant Colonel Joseph Stilwell headed the First Section, the Tactical Section; Lieutenant Colonel M. C. Stayer, Second Section, Logistics; Major Omar Bradley, Third Section, Weapons; and Major Forrest Harding, Fourth Section, Military History and Publications. Their styles were different and so were their backgrounds. What they shared was the confidence of their mentor—George C. Marshall.

No stranger to Benning, Stilwell was also an "Old China Hand," since serving with Marshall with the 15th Infantry in China. Stilwell, later called "Vinegar Joe," was a nonconformist. At times he could be near insubordination, but Marshall admired him for his brilliance and individuality.

Stayer was Marshall's personal physician. He treated Marshall's thyroid condition and irregular pulse and helped control the nervous facial tic that had plagued Marshall since France. Stayer's instructors included Captain Willard Paul and Major Harold R. Bull. Marshall gave Bull credit "for creating a simplified supply system for the Army," and for reducing a 120-page supply manual to 12 pages.[2] Bull also impressed Marshall when he "threw away the book" in a training battle in which umpires said Bull failed

---

[1] Forrest C. Pogue, *George C. Marshall: Education of a General* (New York: Viking Press, 1963) 259.

[2] Ibid., 256–58.

but Marshall approved of his innovations.[3]

Bradley taught under Stilwell and "received the highest possible personal honor" when Marshall selected him chief of the weapons section.[4] Bradley felt "the cold blue eyes of George Marshall" on the back of his neck, but on the whole appreciated Marshall's style—"when he gave a man a job, he let him alone...."[5] Marshall said Bradley was "conspicuous for his ability to handle people and his ability to do things simply and clearly."[6] In the next fifteen years, Marshall would rely often on Bradley's talent to get things done.

Harding was another "Old China Hand" and a talented writer. He wrote for numerous post publications and from 1934 to 1938 was editor of the *Infantry Journal*. It was Harding's section, under Marshall's direction, that prepared the influential publication *Infantry in Battle*. Earlier, as a second lieutenant, he had been an inspiration to Bradley when they both served at Fort Wright in Washington. Bradley would forever cite his influence.

Creativity was in the air, and new ideas were welcomed, even demanded. People sensed there was a "Spirit of Benning." Captain Joseph Lawton Collins, an instructor in Stilwell's section, who later distinguished himself as a corps commander in World War II and then as chief of staff, praised "the Spirit of Benning which was a marvelous thing, because if anybody had any new ideas he was willing to try them...."[7] Whereas Collins and others thrived on this creative atmosphere, some students and staff disapproved of Marshall's rewarding the individual who bucked tradition.

In many ways, the Infantry School was evolving into a hybrid of a traditional university campus. Freethinking was encouraged within the restraints of discipline. Instructors were expected to teach and demonstrate instead of lecture, and they and the students were encouraged to publish or perish. During this period Lieutenant LeRoy Yarborough in collaboration with Major Truman Smith was given time and resources to write *The History*

---

[3] Ibid.

[4] Bradley, *A General's Life*, 67.

[5] Omar Bradley, with collaborator Clay Blair, *A General's Life* (New York: Simon and Schuster, 1983) 68.

[6] Pogue, *George C. Marshall: Education of a General*, 258.

[7] Ibid., 256.

of Fort Benning.

Marshall continued going against past practices. Students were allowed to leave early if instructors finished a lecture and questions before the allowed time. Marshall no longer adhered to the policy of checking instructor's submitted lecture, encouraging them to work from cards, rather than reading the lecture. When cards got in the way, Marshall suppressed them too, believing "it was many times more effective when a man talked off the cuff, as it were, although it was a very well ironed cuff."[8]

The monograph, a traditional required paper in which students wrote on some aspect of military history, ranging from the Mesopotamian campaigns to World War I, also underwent changes. Marshall wanted the monograph delivered orally in a class lecture, limited to twenty minutes. When students complained they needed more time, Marshall stood in front of the class and outlined the Civil War in five minutes.

Marshall attended as many presentations as he could. His appearances were announced in the school paper. He especially enjoyed one given by Walter Bedell Smith, a student of Bradley, who stayed on as an instructor. Smith came through the ranks in the National Guard and fought in the world war. "Smith could express himself easily and well, both orally and in writing" Bradley said. He recommended Smith as an instructor before Marshall did so, noting, "I was elated. I had 'discovered' Smith before he had!"[9]

Harding, the writer, had the last word on the monograph. Dubbed "Poet Laureate" by Marshall for his talent of writing doggerels in China, Harding included an officers' prayer at the end of his short play about student life in the Infantry School: "Now into my bunk I creep/ To catch an hour or so to sleep/ And dream about my monograph./ Help me, O Lord, to stand the gaff."[10] Despite the pressure of writing and researching under Marshall, "there were no nervous breakdowns and no divorces among the monographers of the class of 1930."[11]

Teaching was designed to engage the student, not create note-takers. Marshall wanted students to have the confidence to think. On the field, they

---

[8] Pogue, *George C. Marshall: Education of a General*, 254.

[9] Bradley, *A General's Life*, 69.

[10] Pogue, *George C. Marshall: Education of a General*, 255.

[11] "The Advanced Class, In Retrospection," *Infantry School News*, June 6 1930, 6.

learned to improvise in order to deal with the real problems in the confusion of battle. For variety, troops from Fort McPherson in Atlanta were invited to "fight" with the 29th in 1930 exercises. Working with all types of maps and at times with no maps, the men were introduced to unfamiliar terrain to prevent complacency. When tanks suddenly appeared (probably the same Renaults Eisenhower brought to the post in 1919), it was up to the officers to rally their men and restore their position.

Matthew Ridgway, an advanced course graduate in 1930 at Fort Benning, commented on this "mental conditioning." He said it "cut down the time in which you have to think things out, so that your decisions come out almost instantaneously, and they are sound decisions, if you have worked your brain through this...before."[12]

Such a response was Marshall's goal. He believed the unexpected was normal in the field and wanted the men to think on their feet and to avoid the experience of the confused Benning soldier he had observed in China. *When* to make the decision was as important as *which* decision to make. Also, rather than fighting the last war, Marshall preached "study the first six months of the next war."[13] While Marshall was changing the atmosphere at Fort Benning, its graduates—5,064 through 1930—"had gone on to disseminate the teachings of the school in every corner of the United States and its possessions."[14]

Things were going well at the post. Seventy-two percent of the soldiers discharged in January 1930 re-enlisted. Under the leadership of General Campbell King and Marshall, Fort Benning experienced halcyon days in spite of the depression plaguing the nation. On post, officers wore Sam Browne belts and knee-high riding boots. Enlisted soldiers, wearing washbasin helmets and leggings, carried Springfield rifles; and officers on well-groomed horses reviewed the troops. Although "misery, mud, and mess kits" were prevalent, a construction boom in the coming decade brought great change. As Captain Ralph B. Lovett explained in his article "Up from the Primitive," the "Santa Claus who made possible the working of this miracle to the Infantry School and the post of Fort Benning was the Public

---

[12] Pogue, *George C. Marshall: Education of a General*, 252.
[13] Ibid., 253.
[14] "The School Came to Benning," *Benning Herald*, October 1949, 35.

Works Administration."[15]

On April 1, the construction of forty-one sets of quarters began at Miller Loop. Congress approved a barracks bill the following month. In June, the US House of Representatives approved $700,000 to cover additional construction of quarters. As Yarborough noted in the *Infantry School News*, Fort Benning with its nearly 7,000 inhabitants was becoming a "military metropolis."[16]

Entertainment modernized too. In January, more than 1,700 paid patrons squeezed into the 1,200-seat main theatre to see—and hear—talking pictures for the first time. Adults paid a quarter and children, a dime, to see *Oh Yeah*, starring Robert Armstrong and James Gleason and two other features. The post was the first of eighty-five army theatres to install the new sound equipment. The post's Drama Club presented productions such as *Captain Applejack* and *Shall We Join the Ladies*, both starring Forrest Harding. Charles Bolte, another talented actor, appeared in *The Best People*.

The Campbell King Horse Show Bowl, completed by the Service Company of the 24th Infantry, held its first show in May. Named for the commandant, a fine horseman, the bowl held two show rings set in an amphitheatre surrounded by shade trees, providing a permanent place for the post horse show, a tradition since 1923. In the May show, Mrs. B. W. Venable won the jumping sweepstakes, and Miss Sue Brandt excelled in riding and jumping. The Fort Benning Polo Club, part of the Southeastern Circuit of the United States Polo Association, provided entertainment twice a week for equestrians and their followers. Successful shows contributed to Fort Benning's "fast growing" status as "one of the most desirable posts in the service."[17] On Sunday mornings, officers and their ladies enjoyed recreational horseback riding. Enlisted men, who hardly ever saw an officer and rarely talked to one, were always on hand on the stables to saddle the horses, assist the young ladies on the saddles, and to show off their own horsemanship.

---

[15] Capt. Ralph B. Lovett, "Up from the Primitive," *Infantry Journal* 42/3 (May/June 1935): 217.

[16] LeRoy W. Yarborough, "Military Metropolis," *Infantry School News*, February 14 1930, 6.

[17] Capt. F. J. Pearson, "Intimate Glimpses of Garrison Life," *Infantry Journal* 27/4 (October 1925): 413.

As the year ended for the 220 children in the post school in May 1930, King presented twenty diplomas on the lawn of Riverside with the help of Miss Annie Lou Grimes, principal at Benning since 1920.

To close the year at the Infantry School, its faculty had a picnic at the academic department camp, "situated in a virgin pine grove on the banks of the Upatoi" twenty-two miles away from post proper.[18] It offered "a cool and pleasant retreat for overworked and harassed faculty members, their wives and families."[19] Jake Moon, wearing his bright green bathing suit, gave rides in his motorboat; Forrest Harding led a spelling bee; and Marshall himself pitched in a baseball game. While Marshall "held most of the batters helpless until someone forgot himself and socked a home run," Majors Bradley and St. John made "spectacular catches."[20]

For his part in making the school year a success, Marshall received an outstanding efficiency report from King: "The chiefs of sections are men of unusual qualifications and they are supported by a clearly superior group of instructors, supervised and directed by an assistant commandant, Lieutenant Colonel George C. Marshall, whose own qualifications for this work are certainly not surpassed and probably not equaled by any other officer in our service."[21]

---

[18] "Faculty Doffs Its Dignity At Picnic Beside the Upatoi," *Infantry School News*, May 23 1930, 1,3.

[19] Ibid.

[20] Ibid.

[21] Annual Report of the Infantry School, June 30 1930, Fort Benning Folder titled "Office of the Commandant," vault, Donovan Library, Ft. Benning GA, 28.

11.

A New Face for the Infantry

The face of the United States Infantry was changing and so was Fort Benning's. As fighting units updated with the emergence of air power and tanks, Fort Benning met these evolving needs. Both were evident on the post in the early 1930s. Most important, perhaps, was the official establishment of Lawson Army Airfield in 1931. Replacing the old Benning Airstrip, it was named for Captain Walter Rolls Lawson, a World War I aviator from Glen Alta, Georgia. Lawson attended flight school with the 41st French Escadrille and twice was awarded the Distinguished Service Cross for heroism displayed in the Meuse-Argonne and St. Michel sectors. At the age of twenty-eight, Lawson was killed in an air crash in 1921 in Dayton, Ohio.

Lawson Field consisted of two small hangars with the unit mess vegetable garden located behind them. With no runways, airstrips, or parking aprons, the field was "a small grass clearing, where two tiny hangars were a rendezvous for Saturday night dances."[1] The area, previous home to Kasihta (Cussetah) Indians, was known as Kasihta Fields. In 1813, across the Chattahoochee River, soldiers from Fort Mitchell observed these peaceful Lower Creek natives from a hill rising 225 feet above the river.

Twenty-five enlisted men and five officers of Flight B, 16th Observation Squadron moved to Benning. With the new air troops and the new official name, Benning prepared for its aerial future. Infantry officers and instructors soon were detailed for duty with the air corps as well as artillery units to acquaint them with updated technology.

On the ground, the emphasis on firepower dominated the 1920s, but between 1929 and 1935, the concept of greater mobility was again favored. Once considered as an infantry support weapon to overcome machine guns,

---

[1] "Flying Field's Growth Parallels AAF History," *Bayonet*, August 2 1945, 8.

armored vehicles were now used also in reconnaissance and for breaking through enemy lines just as George Patton and Dwight Eisenhower, experienced tank officers, predicted after World War I.

In June 1932, the tank school at Fort Meade moved to Fort Benning, a move many believed was overdue. Omar Bradley saw the need for tank training in 1924 when he attended the Advanced Class at the Infantry School: "There was a tank battalion at Benning, but its equipment was utterly obsolete and our contact with the unit was limited to watching rolling demonstrations—mere parades in the boondocks."[2]

Supplies were obtained from Fort McPherson, Muscle Shoals, and other government facilities. The December 19, 1931, *Army, Navy Register* reported, "The location of the two schools at Fort Benning is regarded as one of the most important steps made in recent years toward improving the facilities for training the infantry."[3]

With arrival of the tank school, infantry students were given preliminary tank and infantry instruction. Thirty-five students with the highest grades were chosen to attend the tank section for five months. Tank students often combined instruction with community chores, driving the tanks and collecting the garbage.

Marshall, meanwhile, continued "to get [his] hands on Benning."[4] For a week in October 1931, student officers, armed with notebooks and pencils, left formal classroom studies to attend a series of troop demonstrations held on diverse locations on the reservation. Daily exercises included tanks, anti-tank guns, field artillery support, defense against air attacks, and problems of supply. Each day brought new situations and solutions to experienced and inexperienced troops, just as Marshall wanted it.

For the infantryman in the 1930s, some things—like very long marches—did not change. The 29th Infantry Regiment left on a 235-mile round trip in May 1931. Nine days were allowed for the march to Atlanta. Not to be outdone, in August, the 2nd Battalion, 1st Tank Regiment left for

---

[2] Omar Bradley, with collaborator Clay Blair, *A General's Life* (New York: Simon and Schuster, 1983) 56.

[3] "News and Comments—The Tank School," *Army and Navy Register* 90/2682 (December 19 1931): 584.

[4] Forrest C. Pogue, *George C. Marshall: Education of a General* (New York: Viking Press, 1963) 250.

an 800-mile road march to Fort Barrancas in Pensacola, Florida. Forrest Shivers saw the troops march through his hometown, Sparta, Georgia, and never forgot it. He looked on with amazement and admiration of the military, its men, and open vehicles. After serving five years in the army, Shivers was a member of the Foreign Service, retiring after a distinguished career of thirty years. His memory of the Fort Benning troops never dimmed.[5]

Like the rest of the world, Fort Benning's 6,630 troops and its civilian workforce were affected by the country's troubled economy. Many soldiers took cuts in pay. Forrest Harding noted in the post newspaper, "We get little sympathy from our civilian friends, all of whom have taken their salary cuts of considerably greater proportion or losses in business which make our eight and one-third percent cut seem trivial."[6]

Marshall's tour of duty as assistant commandant now ended. His assignment had extended to five years with the permission of King, who assigned Marshall—in name only—to the 29th Infantry so Marshall could carry on as usual in the academic department. His five years as assistant commandant at Fort Benning remain the longest tour recorded for that position. Unlike his predecessors, Malone and Bjornstad, Marshall arrived and departed a lieutenant colonel. On September 1, 1933, he was promoted to colonel and later was promoted to brigadier general on October 1, 1936.

Marshall's replacement, Colonel Charles W. Weeks was a professor of military science and training at the University of Illinois. As a graduate of the University of Nebraska, Weeks enlisted in the army as a private and later rose to sergeant. Returning to civilian life, he won an appointment to the regular army in competitive exams and received his commission as 2nd lieutenant of infantry.

On June 12, 1932, Marshall was honored with a review of the 29th Infantry on Gordon Field. He addressed the troops and congratulated them on their appearance, development, and their training of thousands of National Guard and Reserve Officers. He told them, "A Corporal of the

---

[5] Personal communication of Forrest Shivers and Peggy Stelpflug, summer 1995.

[6] Forrest Harding, "The Flair: Reflections on the Pay Cut," *Benning Herald*, August 12 1932, 4.

29th Infantry is not merely a leader of seven men. He leads in the training of 100 squads scattered throughout the country."[7]

Writing of their life at Fort Benning, Katherine Marshall defined Marshall's tour of duty there: "My husband's years at Benning, where he had been in close association with hundreds of young officers, were of incalculable value later in choosing his higher commanders."[8] At the end of her two years at Fort Benning, Mrs. Marshall evaluated herself: "I was a fair Army wife. At least I had learned many things, among them to be on time, to listen rather than express opinions, that lieutenants do not dance with colonels' wives for pleasure, that acquiring a good seat in the saddle takes endurance beyond the power of man to express."[9]

Marshall's new assignment was Fort Screven, near Savannah, Georgia. He took command of a battalion of the 8th Infantry and CCC District "F" of the IV Corps Area. Though he moved on, Marshall's impact on Fort Benning and the army would be felt for years to come. "In addition to the 155 future generals of World War II who were students at the Infantry School and another 50 who were instructors during this five-year period, future field-grade officers also felt the impress of Marshall's Benning when they were learning the basis of their trade," military historian Forrest C. Pogue wrote.[10]

History records Marshall's storied future. During World War II, as army chief of staff, he was President Franklin D. Roosevelt's most trusted adviser, directing the strategies of a force scattered over the globe. Leaving his uniform behind, he turned to diplomacy, serving as secretary of defense and secretary of state under President Harry Truman. His enduring legacy was "The Marshall Plan," a blueprint for the restoration of post-war Europe. But he never forgot Fort Benning.

In 1978, at the 139th anniversary of the Virginia Military Institute—his alma mater and the site of the Marshall Library—people were reminded of Marshall's Benning years: "Perhaps his most important assignment between

---

[7] "Colonel Marshall Goes to New Command," *Benning Herald*, June 17 1932, 1.

[8] Katherine Tupper Marshall, *Together: Annals of an Army Wife* (New York: Tupper and Love, Inc., 1947) 9.

[9] Ibid.

[10] George C. Marshall, *Interviews and Reminiscences for Forrest C. Pogue*, ed. Larry I Bland (Lexington VA: George C. Marshall Research Foundation, 1991) 244.

wars came in the period 1927–1932 when he was Assistant Commandant of the Infantry School, Fort Benning, Georgia, where he had charge of instruction. With a faculty and staff of men who were to be leaders of World War II—a group including Generals Bradley, Ridgway, Collins, Stilwell and Bedell Smith—he instituted methods of instruction still in use today."[11] On June 12, 1932, as Marshall prepared to leave Benning, Commanding General Campbell King regaled Marshall's accomplishments to date: "He has been a vital force in developing and maintaining the conditions which make Benning one of the most sought after stations in the Army."[12]

---

[11] "The 139th Anniversary of the Virginia Military Institute, 11 November, 1978," pamphlet written for this occasion found in Marshall File at National Infantry Museum, Fort Benning GA.

[12] "Colonel Marshall Goes to New Command," *Benning Herald*, June 17 1932, 1.

12.

Problems Inside the Gate

The Devastation of Benning

The edict arrived like a bolt from the blue,
And assigned us by scores to the woodpecker crew;
And it closed up the School and sent the boys forth,
By overland travel, South, East, West and North.

Like leaves of the forest when summer is green,
The students one morn with diplomas were seen;
Like leaves of the forest when autumn has flown,
The students at sunset were vanished and gone.

Then more orders came on the waves of the air,
Which called on the shock troops for all they could spare;
And the Faculty too and the chair-warming Staff
Were caught in the whirlwind and scattered like chaff.

And all who had orders, that took them away
Were told to clear out by the last day of May
And haste to their posts to become CCCs
And forget about tactics and learn to plant trees.

And widows of Benning are loud in their wail
On tennis courts, golf course and Upatoi trail,
For the Army is out to deliver the goods

And the flower of the service has gone to the woods.[1]
—Forrest Harding, 1933

As noted in Harding's amusing poem in the *Benning Herald*, the rambling fields of Fort Benning were filled with civilians in 1933—civilians who wanted a job, not a free bowl of soup. Roosevelt promised them that and that was what they received.

In the 1932 presidential election, Franklin D. Roosevelt carried all but seven states, receiving 472 votes in the Electoral College to 59 for the incumbent Herbert Hoover. Democrats also held comfortable margins in both wings of Congress. Voters spoke loudly: the country needed a change. Americans wanted a New Deal.

Around Georgia, FDR was that guy up the road. He had found solace in the waters of Warm Springs. Investing two-thirds of his fortune, he assembled a center that would treat other polio victims like him. Roosevelt found something else in that small hamlet. He became a neighbor, sneaking away from bodyguards and riding the back roads of Meriwether County where he was treated like one of the locals. There he learned lessons that helped him with the nation's burgeoning problems and found leisure to ease the pressures he felt as one of the leaders of a troubled world.

Knowing the country needed reassurance and hope, Roosevelt wanted to speak to them like friends over a cup of coffee. He began his Fireside Chats on March 12, 1933. He chatted on the radio, entering American living rooms and creating an intimacy that assured listeners things would get better. He explained this New Deal, as he called it, spelling out its programs in ways folks could understand. One of the first was the CCC—the Civilian Conservation Corps. This and other programs were made possible by passage of the 1933 Emergency Conservation Work Act. This gave the president the authority and means to provide work for the unemployed.

The Department of War was responsible for organizing the CCC, and over the next nine years it achieved great success with programs of flood control, forestry, and soil conservation. It would build more than 8,000 parks.

---

[1] Forrest Harding, "The Devastation of Benning," *Benning Herald*, May 26 1933, 4.

Labor organizations complained about the army's disciplining and training of enrollees since this would lead to a "regimentation of labor" under military control and keep wages as low as army wages. Other lawmakers disliked the entry of the government into public relief, comparing such action to socialism.

Americans without jobs disregarded these issues. Nearly 300,000 signed up for the CCC. Fort Benning became a regional center, and in the summer of 1933, 10,000 of its members passed through the post, about 800 a day. A tent city on the reservation housed 8,000 men, most on their way to forest camps. Some stayed and worked on projects such as the reconstruction of Harp's Pond, completed in 1934.

The country's problems were no longer outside of Fort Benning's gates. Now they were inside, and the commander-in-chief expected the military to respond. Leaves were cancelled, including those of Omar Bradley, who completed a tour at the Infantry School, and also Joe Stilwell's, whose son was graduating from West Point.

Honest about his feelings, Bradley said, "The Army was not happy at being saddled with the CCC." At the Infantry School, sixty-nine of the eighty officers on the faculty were ordered to CCC duty; so although the enrollment at the service schools was cut, the post with its new construction and land projects, was improved. Bradley explained,

> Fort Benning became a focal point of CCC activity; the base was flooded with CCC applicants, almost all black. I was placed in command of six all-black companies, men who had arrived from the poorest farm area of Georgia and Alabama. We organized them, issued clothing, established pay accounts (the CCC men were paid thirty dollars a month, in contrast to the twenty-one dollars a private in the army received), gave them physicals and a couple of weeks "training," then shipped them to camps in the field. Some of these men had not had a square meal for at least a year.[2]

In spite of difficulties, Bradley expressed the satisfaction of doing a job right: "The Army's magnificent performance with the CCC in the summer of 1933, undertaken so reluctantly, was one of the highlights of its peacetime

---

[2] Omar Bradley, with collaborator Clay Blair, *A General's Life* (New York: Simon and Schuster, 1983) 72.

years."[3] By mobilizing men in peacetime, the army was ready for the task six years later when preparing for war.

To further raise employment and purchasing power in 1933, the Public Works Administration (PWA) was set up for the construction of useful public works. At Benning, these public works included new quarters, an apartment building, hangars for the Air Corps, a heating plant for the tank section, a veterinary hospital, and a theatre for the 24th Infantry. Plans for a new bridge across Upatoi Creek and a post headquarters were in the works. Columbus historian Clason Kyle notes, "the construction work at Fort Benning was a godsend to the local labor pools as the textile economy in Columbus was badly damaged by the Depression."[4]

In addition, at Roosevelt's bidding, troops at Fort Benning and throughout the army, took a one-month furlough without pay. Spread over twelve months, officers such as Bradley received $290 a month. Bradley and his fellow officers did not complain: "With the various benefits provided by the army—housing, medical and dental care, discounted groceries, and other items at the commissary and PX—our standard of living was not substantially curtailed.... We prepared to leave Fort Benning with a mild feeling of disquiet and loss. These had been four wonderful and constructive years."[5]

Fort Benning soldiers, willing to share their good fortune during this difficult time, opened their hearts and wallets to prepare Christmas dinner for the needy. The *Benning Herald* reported their good deed: "By voluntarily giving up two full meals, one on Christmas Day, the soldiers made 1,000 poverty-stricken people of Columbus, hard hit by the depression, happier on Monday, when the latter were served a complete meal at two stations in the city. The meals were cooked at Benning and transported to Columbus in rolling kitchens and served by the soldiers under the directions of the Salvation Army."[6]

Like the rest of the country, soldiers sought escape. With a Golden Age of Sports in America, men like Babe Ruth, Jack Dempsey, and Georgian

---

[3] Bradley, *A General's Life*, 72.

[4] F. Clason Kyle, *Images, A Pictorial History of Columbus, Georgia* (Norfolk VA: The Donning Company/Publisher, 1986) 174.

[5] Bradley, *A General's Life*, 72.

[6] "The School Came to Benning," *Benning Herald*, October 1949, 36.

Bobby Jones were gods. On post, soldiers also turned to sports and entertainment, playing golf on the new eighteen-hole golf course and attending football and boxing events at Doughboy Stadium.

In an evening of thirty-six bouts, handsome Bob Godwin, a native of Cairo, Georgia, and the tenth-ranked heavyweight in the world, met Walker "Cyclone" Smith of Fort Benning in the main event. Godwin handled Smith "as though he were an infant," and stopped him in the seventh round.[7] He gave a "sharp, dynamic left hook to the chin that sent Smith's mouthpiece spiraling from the ring among spectators in the fourth row at the ringside."[8] Smith met the second loss of his career with "both eyes closed and a swollen face."[9] Captain Phillip T. Fry, post athletic officer, was praised for the caliber of those fights.

It was also a time of change at the command level. Bradley left for the War College in Washington, DC, not imagining that he would one day return at the request of his mentor, George C. Marshall. That spring, General Campbell King made known that he was ready to retire. In a farewell tribute, Forrest Harding wrote that King made the Benning garrison "a happy family" and commanded with tact, diplomacy, and understanding, taking with him into his retirement "the affection as well as the esteem of his last command."[10]

When Columbus business leader Frank Lumpkin discovered King was leaving, he wrote General Douglas MacArthur to request that Major General Briant H. Wells, former commandant, be reassigned to Fort Benning. Lumpkin's second choice was General George H. Estes, who, as Lumpkin said, came from "our neighboring county."[11] Estes was related to Mrs. Homer Dimon, wife of a Columbus city commissioner. MacArthur informed Lumpkin in July that Wells wanted to stay in Hawaii. Lumpkin then wrote Wells, "We thought we knew it was all fixed and that you would soon be among your Columbus friends again."[12]

---

[7] "Godwin Puts Bug on Smith in 7th Stanza," *Benning Herald*, August 12 1932, 8.

[8] Ibid.

[9] Ibid.

[10] Forrest Harding, "The Flair," *Benning Herald*, June 2 1933, 4.

[11] Gen. MacArthur and Gen. Wells to Frank G. Lumpkin, found in Lumpkin's personal files, Willcox-Lumpkin Company, Columbus GA.

[12] Ibid.

Wells answered Lumpkin saying Estes would be a good choice for Benning: "In this way he and I will be pleased and satisfied—the other way it would have been only I.... I am sure you will not indicate in any way that I love Benning the less or that I love Hawaii more."[13] The following year, Wells retired and took a position with the Hawaii Sugar Planters Association.

Estes, the new commandant, was born in nearby Eufaula, Alabama, but moved to Columbus at an early age. According to local historian Etta Blanchard Worsley, the West Point graduate's ancestors were among the city's original settlers.

According to Worsley, with Estes in command of the post and Homer Dimon as mayor of Columbus "an exceptional spirit of cooperation and friendliness" existed between the communities.[14] Tea dances, organized by Mrs. Leighton MacPherson, were held at the Country Club of Columbus. At these fetes, senior West Point cadets on post for field training danced and mingled with local girls. In return, dances were held at Fort Benning's brand new Officers' Club that opened to members on July 12, 1934. Unlike the construction of many buildings in this era, it was built with funds donated by private donors and dues rather that the WPA or government sources. The cost was $250,000.

For officers, the club's initiation fee was $10, or $100 for a life membership. Well-known names in Columbus became life members and many more were invited to join. Dimon with other civilian life members presented Estes a silver service that cost more than $1,000 as a gift for the new club. Consisting of a banquet hall, dance floor, billiard room, library, a card room, a beauty parlor, barbershop, and modern grill, the new attraction was a rarity for its time and place. Contributions also established the golf course, tennis courts, two swimming pools, polo fields, and kennels.

George A. Sheddan, a well-known New York designer, created its Spanish-type structure. Architect L. D. Raines drew the plans while Constructing Quartermaster Captain Carl H. Jabelonsky carried out the plans with the help of supervisors Captain H. J. Golightly, Lieutenant A. E. O'Flaherty, and Master Sergeant Otis R. Glenn. Soldiers were free to do the

---

[13] Ibid.

[14] Etta Blanchard Worsley, *Columbus on the Chattahoochee* (Columbus GA: Columbus Office Supply Co., 1951) 439.

labor since WPA (Work Projects Administration) and PWA (Public Works Administration) funds kept civilian workers busy on other needed post construction. Though an officers' club was present on post since 1925, Worsley noted the new facility was "a dream come true" and "one of the finest club buildings in the whole country."[15]

Equally beautiful was the new post chapel, formally dedicated in November 1934. Built at a cost of $81,169, it was home to Protestant, Catholic, and Jewish services. It was modeled after the Bull Street Presbyterian Church in Savannah, Georgia.

In spring of 1934, work began on "one of the most important buildings in the whole construction program."[16] Built of reinforced concrete, covered with stucco, decorated with Indiana limestone, and topped with a tile roof, the Infantry School Building was ready for occupancy in July 1935. This handsome building—three stories high with floor space equal to an average ten-story office building—contained the commandant's office along with the academic department, classrooms, large lecture and study rooms, and a library with a collection of 13,000 books.

In the June 1935 issue of *Infantry Journal*, writer Ralph Lovett recalled the post in the 1920s. Comparing the present with the past, he described the new academic building as "an imposing structure, eminently suited to house the activities of the greatest Infantry School on earth."[17] Lovett described "a modern looking community" noting, "the last tent as a permanent installation has passed into oblivion."[18] By that point, the major permanent buildings on main post were complete—a miracle he attributed to the Works Progress Administration. WPA funding for Fort Benning totaled nearly $7 million. These funds also made possible the planned modernization of "Buzzard's Row," a neighborhood of homes where it took an eagle on the shoulder to rate a house.[19]

By 1935, the enlisted men's cuartel-type barracks were finished, complete with cross-ventilation and continuous open balconies.

---

[15] Ibid., 438.

[16] "The School Came to Benning," *Benning Herald*, October 1949, 39.

[17] Capt. Ralph B. Lovett, "Up from the Primitive," *Infantry Journal* 42/3 (May/June 1935): 221.

[18] Ibid., 217.

[19] Ibid., 217.

Nevertheless 1,057 enlisted men still needed housing.[20] Seventy years later, this trio of architecturally beautiful structures—the Officers' Club, the Main Post Chapel, and the former headquarters building—remain the anchors of the historic main post. The old headquarters building is now home to the Western Hemisphere Institute for Security and Cooperation.

When those buildings were new, the nearby streets were sometimes filled with the 24th Infantry Regiment band. Soldiers and spectators who witnessed these full-dress parades in the mid-1930s were "fortunate individuals," according to historian Louis Scipio, Jr.[21] Given the command to march, they would strike up John Philip Sousa's "The Thunderer." "Old Slone Williams would be in front to the band as drum major, marking the cadence," recalls Scipio. "This was a sight to behold. The power of the band could be heard at great distances. It set pulses throbbing as almost everyone within sound distance shared in its command for attention."[22]

When they were not marching in parades, the band broke into jazz combos and dance bands. Its musicians played for dances and parties all over the post. At this time, the 24th Infantry band was the largest regiment band in the US Army.

Music helped block out the economic sadness that blanketed the country, but bleak news of the Depression was not the only event making headlines. Emerging leader Adolph Hitler and a new political force called the Nazi Party were making headlines in Germany and around the world. In Italy, Benito Mussolini delivered bombastic speeches extolling the doctrine of Fascism.

A dubious reminder of those faraway voices was a nearby lecture by Mussolini's biographer at the Chase Conservatory of Music in Columbus. George Raffolovich predicted that 1933 would be the "crucial year for Europe."[23] He believed Mussolini was the most likely leader to bring order

---

[20] "Post evolves from plantation to modern facility," *Bayonet*, October 8 1993, A-7.

[21] L. Albert Scipio, *The 24th Infantry at Ft. Benning* (Silver Spring MD: Roman Publications, 1986) 153.

[22] Ibid.

[23] "Biographies of Mussolini to Appear at Columbus with Russian Singer," *Benning Herald*, August 12 1932, 4.

to "that old, war-shocked continent." Without a leader like Mussolini, he warned, the only alternative would be "war and chaos."[24]

Part of his premise would prove correct.

---

[24] Ibid.

13.

The Coming of the Belly-Flopper

As the 1930s marched on, frequent reminders of Fort Benning's past and harbingers of its future generated interesting times.

Reminding observers of the post's early years were a pair of local milestones. First was the death of Anna Caroline Benning in 1935 at age eighty-two. In 1918, she helped dedicate the post in honor of her father, Confederate General Henry L. Benning. Second was the 1937 naming of a bridge connecting the military reservation with the civilian community for John Betjeman—the most faithful and effective lobbyist for the establishment of Fort Benning. Naming of the bridge over Upatoi Creek came fourteen years after his untimely death at age forty-four.

The appointment of Lieutenant Benjamin O. Davis, Jr., a West Point graduate, to the officer staff of the 24th Infantry Regiment in 1936 brought a promise of things to come. Davis, the fourth African-American graduate of West Point, served as a recruit instructor, a position usually held by white officers. His father, Colonel Benjamin O. Davis, Sr., was professor of military science and tactics at Tuskegee Institute, Alabama. Davis and his father were the only two black line officers in the US Army in 1936.

A pair of technical advances in weaponry and mobility that proved valuable to contemporary soldiers arose in 1937. Following years of testing—much of it at Fort Benning—the Garand M1 rifle was adopted as the army's standard weapon, replacing the Springfield Model 1903, the bolt-action rifle that was the friend of World War I Doughboys. The Garand MI rifle increased a soldier's firepower 100 percent with little effect on his mobility. The 29th Infantry tested the weapon in the field, and the Infantry School played a key role in its research and development. Designed by John C. Garand, the M1 enabled men in actual combat to accomplish "the same thing in a much shorter time and less physical exhaustion than a similar group armed with the M1903."[1]

That same year, using spare automobile parts retrieved from the scrap heap at Benning, Captain Robert G. Howie and Master Sergeant Melvin C. Wiley built a machine gun carrier they called the "Belly Flopper." Although the Infantry Board recommended more testing, Assistant Commandant Walter Short saw its possibilities. Short invited Delmar Roos, chief engineer of Willys-Overland Motors, to Georgia for a demonstration. Roos, recognizing the potential of a general-purpose vehicle, took the first step toward the development of the Jeep, the wheels of the military for years to come.[2] Willys-Overland Motors produced about 360,000 military jeeps by 1945.[3]

The 1930s were years when advancements in military technology were on the drawing board, and the Spanish Civil War turned into a testing ground for many of them. The conflict began in July 1936 and was the first notable war in Europe since the World War. Generalissimo Franco, leader of the revolt and head of a fascist faction, fought against the loyalists. The war in Spain lasted nearly three years and was considered by some as the opening battle of World War II. Sides were taken. Italy and Germany supported Franco as did wealthy Spaniards. The International Brigades, composed of Americans and others, fought with the loyalists, as did France, Russia, and the Basque Republic.

Weapons tested in the Spanish Civil War appeared on the battlefields of World War II. Advanced models of tanks, artillery, planes, and other weapons were put to work in Spain, killing more than a million people. American citizens were also drawn into the action, sending US dollars to support the various factions. In Columbus, Frank Lumpkin, Jr., one of the first locals to hold a private pilot's license, decided to sell his airplane to those fighting in the war. Later, he wasn't sure which side bought it: "When

---

[1] "Tests of Semi-Automatic Rifles," 5, History of the Infantry School papers located in vault, Donovan Library, Fort Benning GA.

[2] "Wiley Carrier 'Belly Flopper,'" National Infantry Museum Official Tour Guide Book, typescript spiral-bound book for museum staff and volunteer tour guides, Fort Benning GA, 1–12.

[3] Willys-Overland Motors, "Willys Overland History," http://www.willysoverland.com/index.php/wo/history/ (accessed May 20 2007).

they started the war in Spain, I sold it for about ten times what I paid for it."[4]

Colonel Walter Short, an early advocate of the infantry school concept, replaced Weeks as assistant commandant in July 1936. His stay was, as indicated by his name, short. Promoted to brigadier general, he left after just seven months. Colonel Charles F. Thompson, who replaced Short, also had a brief stay. In July 1938, Colonel Courtney H. Hodges was named assistant commandant. Born in Perry, Georgia, Hodges was an instructor at Benning in 1925–1926.

Commander General George Estes left in September 1936, retiring from active duty by the end of the year. After Estes retired, his successor, General Asa L. Singleton, was "the only native Georgian holding general officer rank in the regular army of the United States."[5] Born in nearby Taylor County, Singleton was a graduate of Emory University in Atlanta. He enlisted as a private in the Spanish-American War, and served two tours of duty at Fort Benning, one as commander of the 29th Infantry.

In 1938—the same year President Franklin D. Roosevelt paid the post a neighborly visit—Fort Benning was on the list of 181 posts to get building funds from a designated $120,000,000 to correct "worse housing conditions than exist in the worst slums of our cities."[6] Funding came from $450,000,000 Roosevelt requested for the Public Works Appropriation.

The new Main Post Theatre opened September 1938. Built with government funds and the US Army Motion Picture Service, the theatre was the largest structure of its kind in the army, seating over 1,500 people. Soon, buildings of steel, concrete, and brick replaced many of the original tents and temporary wooden structures on post.

Social Priorities

ROTC cadets from colleges and universities from throughout the United States arrived on the post every summer for exercises that supplemented

---

[4] Frank G. Lumpkin Jr. interview by Peggy Stelpflug, spring 1994, typed transcript, Columbus GA.

[5] "The Story of Fort Benning Home of the Infantry School of the U.S. Army," *Industrial Index* 34/24 (November 29 1939): 50.

[6] "Fort Benning to Get $1,200,000 for Buildings," *Columbus Enquirer*, June 2 1930, 1.

their classes on campus. Ed Williamson was among that group in the summer of 1938. Williamson, later a military historian and Auburn University history professor, came from the University of Florida. He lived in a tent, and during his stay at Benning he saw his first army general. He also argued with an instructor that horses were obsolete when he saw guns still being towed by horsepower. The good-natured instructor told Williamson of a recent incident when horses could get through muddy roads and vehicles could not.

While adventurous friends made their way to the honky-tonks in Phenix City, Williamson said most did not have enough money to go. The only trouble he got into was at a dance at the Officers' Club. The dance, arranged by ROTC leaders and officers, included local lovelies and young women whose fathers were stationed at the post.

The evening was well planned, and the 24th infantry Band played dance music. However, instead of being "social," Williamson fell in with "bad companions," led by a ROTC hotshot who organized a private crap game that lured away many of the college guys. Williamson did remember dancing to a single song: "Stick Out Your Can, Here Comes the Garbage Man." The next morning, his commanding officer, displeased with the crap game, gave the guilty cadets five demerits and assigned them—as the song might have suggested—to the garbage detail.[7]

Not every soldier was so innocent with his carousing. Phenix City was a wide open town, openly run by a criminal element that controlled the mayor, the police, and the courts while operating night clubs that offered anything a young GI might desire. Keeping their troops from being targets of unscrupulous figures in the neighboring Alabama town was a problem faced by Benning's commanding generals for two decades.

On April 21, 1938, tragedy occurred in Phenix City when the walls the Ritz Café collapsed. Twenty people were killed and eighty were hurt. The café was a spot where players, predominantly black, gathered to enjoy "The Bug," an illegal lottery. The scene at the Ritz was bedlam. The newspaper reported, complete with dialect, the comments of a woman "preaching to an eager group of listeners" at the scene: "I's been telling you sumthing was gonna happen. I knowed it was going to happen. I's through. De Bug ain't

---

[7] Ed Williamson, interview by Peggy Stelpflug, spring 1995, typed transcript, Auburn University Library Archives, Auburn AL.

worth tht to me. No sur."[8] In the aftermath of the building's collapse, Fort Benning units were called to assist local authorities in the cleanup.[9]

Across the Atlantic Ocean, another type of trouble was growing. Americans had not taken Chancellor Hitler and his goose-stepping followers seriously, and some even considered him a leader they could follow. In 1934, the August 17 front page of the *Benning Herald* featured a photograph of several young boys with a counselor at the German-American camp. A group known as "friends of Germany" sponsored the youth camp and the newspaper caption openly promoted Nazism in the United States.[10] The article caused no alarm, for many Americans were convinced that leaders like Mussolini and Hitler would restore order and economic recovery to their nations.

Even the army's War College seemed unconcerned with Hitler in 1933 when he became Reich Chancellor and leader of the National Socialist German Workers' Party, also called the Nazi Party. While at the War College, Omar Bradley said student reports on Hitler concluded, "Hitler could be discounted because he was mentally unstable."[11]

After watching Hitler's menace grow as his forces marched unopposed into neighboring countries, American military leaders privately acknowledged one day US forces would face the Germans on a European battlefield. With that in mind, training at Fort Benning was altered. Time spent on the tactics of small units such as the rifle platoon and company was increased, and instruction in pistol, grenades, and bayonets was eliminated. A fifty-two-hour motor maintenance course was introduced, and signal communication, map, and aerial photo reading were emphasized. In the military history course, the regiment and its component parts were researched and presented in conjunction with tactical instruction.

Many young men believed war was inevitable. In the fall of 1938, Frank G. Lumpkin, Jr.—rejected by the army in 1924 at the age of sixteen—wrote a letter to the British ambassador to the United States to volunteer as a pilot

---

[8] "Phenix City Crash Toll Mounts to 20 Dead and 4 Score Injured," *Columbus Enquirer*, April 22 1938, 1.

[9] Ibid.

[10] "Naziism in the United States," *Benning Herald*, August 17 1934, 1.

[11] Omar Bradley, with collaborator Clay Blair, *A General's Life* (New York: Simon and Schuster, 1983) 74–75.

in the Royal Air Corps: "I am in the prime of life, in good physical condition and have flying experience, with some 4,365 flying hours. I understand what dangers and hazards and hardships there would be flying in a war at this time.... Of course, I owe my first allegiance to the United States and always will, but...there is no doubt that you are on the right side."[12] His answer came in early October. The letter informed the Columbus native that "only British subjects are eligible for entry in the Royal Air Force, and that in their case, it is necessary for them to proceed to England at their own expense in order to take the necessary physical and educational examinations."[13] Lumpkin was rejected again. But like thousands of other young Americans, his time in the military was soon to come.

---

[12] Frank G. Lumpkin Jr. to Sir Ronald Lindsay, British Ambassador to the US, September 27 1938, personal files at Willcox-Lumpkin Company, Columbus GA.

[13] Correspondence found in Lumpkin's personal files, Willcox-Lumpkin Company, Columbus GA.

14.

Sweet Pea Becomes a Soldier

A soldier named Sweet Pea was in for a fight. So it was for Matthew St. Clair, a fifteen-year-old recruit who received his nickname from the baby Swee' Pea in the Popeye comic strip. His nickname was not his only burden. He was an immigrant from Germany, was reared in West Virginia coal country, and was educated in a Catholic boys' school.

"The fact that I was educated, originated from somewhere outside of Dixie, and owed my true allegiance to the Pope in Rome made me an 'outsider,' a 'Yankee,' and my personal life was difficult," St. Clair recalled in an interview many years later, remembering vividly the humid day he arrived at Fort Benning in 1937.[1]

Among plowboys from Georgia, Tennessee, and Alabama, St. Clair might as well have been an alien. His accent was different and so was he, something that did not sit well with the fellows of Battery B, 83rd Horse-Artillery to which he was assigned. His troubles worsened when his sergeant decided it was time for the nine recruits to meet their four-legged superior officers. For those introductions, they were marched to the paddock, an oval arena with sloped sides and a hard-packed sand floor. St. Clair and other newcomers were positioned atop the paddock walls. Once everybody was in place, a corporal brought in a horse, one they called a single mount. The horse wore only a leatherhead harness with a three-foot length of rope, called a halter shank, snapped to it. Then Sergeant Nahling took over. A crusty veteran of a World War I cavalry unit, Nahling was their professor at the Benning School for Boys, the man who gave them their formal education. In the paddock, he lectured about parts and functions of the

---

[1] Matthew St. Clair, interview by Peggy Stelpflug, December 11 1998, Donovan Library, Fort Benning GA, typed transcript and audio cassette, Auburn AL. The remainder of the quotations in this chapter are from this interview.

animal, explaining that their horse would be their primary means of transportation.

"His needs and wants will always come first and you will faithfully see to it. You recruits will never, ever, under any circumstances, strike or in any other way abuse this animal. He has cost the American taxpayer $120. You [expletive deleted], we can find on any street corner and buy you for $21 a month with three 'hots' and a cot thrown in. And don't forget it!"

Now it was time to get better acquainted. Each recruit, one by one, was called from the wall and told to mount the horse and take it a lap around the paddock. The others howled like wild Comanches leaping on to the horse and galloping around the ring. Who needed reins or a saddle? When it was Sweet Pea's turn, there was one problem: He was scared of horses. The only ones he had ever seen were the ones the mine police rode when they bowled over striking coal miners back in the hills.

"Falling off each time I attempted to mount the horse, I was gleefully and maliciously hoisted back on," St. Clair said. His buddies were snickering. They were farm boys, Southern Baptists. They knew horses before they knew Jesus. What was wrong with this guy? St. Clair lived by a code. Six months shy of his sixteenth birthday, he had to be a man. "It was considered very imprudent, or unmanly, to show any visible pain or emotion. Nothing personal," St. Clair explained. "That was just the way it was, for everybody."

Matthew "Sweet Pea" St. Clair rode that horse. Not the first time or the second, but he conquered it: "I did in time because it was absolutely essential to master the art. I became quite good at it." He spent hours every day on a horse loping around the woods and fields of Fort Benning. But horses were not his primary problem; his challenge was the troops of Battery B, and it was a challenge he would meet with his fists.

The unit's supply sergeant, Sergeant Lein, saw to that. Instead of a horse paddock, he took the young recruit to the post gym. Inside the boxing ring, he gave St. Clair a pair of gloves and taught him to fight. Not box—but fight. Sweet Pea was taught to butt with his head, dig elbows into opponents' ribs and jaws, push thumbs and laces up against the nose, or hit with the side of the thumb right in the eye. A roll of quarters palmed inside each glove also improved his punch. With his sergeant as trainer, coach, and friend, St. Clair entered the battalion and regimental tournaments as a 135-

pound lightweight. "I was never knocked down," he said, "and I never lost a fight."

He was Fort Benning's Lightweight Champion for 1938–1939 and won the Knox Trophy twice. His trophies and awards were proudly hung in Doughboy stadium. "And I never, ever again had any personal problems with my fellow soldiers," he said. "Nobody messed with me in that battery. They were terrified of me."

Sweet Pea was sweet no more.

Word of his success as a boxer spread, even reaching the brass. His battalion commander set him up for a grudge match with "Foots" Cantrell another ground-pounder from the 29th. For St. Clair that was the saddest day of his life. "This man hit me with everything but the water bucket. I stayed three rounds but spent three weeks recovering in the post hospital. I never again went into boxing. I still remember 'Foots' because of the scar tissue," he said.

But his mission was accomplished. "The harassing ended from then on, and I was promoted to private first class at thirty dollars a month—an almost unheard of event for someone with only eighteen months in the regular Army. I became one of the guys, and I became very capable as a soldier."

With improving skills on a horse and prowess in the ring, St. Clair became a popular member of his barracks. Along the way, he discovered a bonus of hanging out around horse barns. When the new Main Post Theatre opened in September 1938, it was a showplace. It was air-conditioned, held 1,500 people, and showed movies in Technicolor. Everybody wanted to go but seats were scarce—unless you were an aromatic member of the Horse-Drawn artillery. "When we trooped into the post theatre," St. Clair explained, "everyone else immediately got up from around us and moved as far away as possible."

Not everybody was interested in seeing what movie was showing at the post theatre. To some, Phenix City's twinkling neon was a lighthouse that guided them to Alabama every time there was money in their pockets. Prohibition was no more, and liquor flowed as freely as the Chattahoochee. Working girls hung out in the clubs, and they celebrated soldier paydays as if Christmas came twelve times a year. It could be fun, but it also could be dangerous. Stories of GIs found floating in the river were more than legend. Their sergeants lectured them, but St. Clair and his crowd remained faithful patrons of the Alabama nightspots.

"We were very good soldiers for twenty-nine days of the month, but when payday rolled around—look out! The barracks became a beehive of activity. Everyone shaved and showered and shampooed and prettied up. Not just to Phenix City alone. Prostitution was as close as you could reach out—anywhere," he said.

One of the most notorious spots in Phenix City was "Ma Beachie's." Its owner, Beachie Howard, ran her place from a stool near the door, pistol close at hand. She was a town character. Twenty years later, when Hollywood made a movie of the law and order cleanup of Phenix City, she did a cameo, playing, who else, Ma Beachie.

His buddies wanted Ma to meet Sweet Pea.

"When I went to Beachie Howard's in Phenix City, I was a very naïve, innocent young boy and my buddies couldn't wait to get me over there and let those little girls see me, telling them, 'Look what we've got for you.'"

Fort Benning authorities patrolled the bridges crossing from Columbus to Phenix City and made regular tours of the favorite haunts. But according to St. Clair, soldiers did policing of their own. "To see that troops behaved, two MPs were stationed outside the place. Also, every battery brought its own 'gook' or 'goon,' someone built like a gorilla who evened the odds in case of a fight."

When the night was over, fellows had to make it back to the post, some ten miles from the bridges that brought them back into Columbus. The Howard Bus Line ran regular routes from the 13th Street Bridge to Fort Benning. But what if a GI left his last money on a craps table in some joint across the river? St. Clair said smart ones stopped at the bus station before leaving post and bought a ten-cent return ticket that was tucked in his shoe for safekeeping.

Though Matthew St. Clair answered to Sweet Pea, he was worldlier than the typical teenaged soldier. During his three years in Battery B, he began to provide entertainment on nights fellows could not get to Phenix City.

"Everybody in those days had a wrinkle. Everybody," he explained. "I dealt blackjack. I paid $800 for a car, got a table and four chairs, furnished cards, sandwiches, and chewing gum for the players. We cut the Blackjack in the day room on post. It was open gambling with money exchanged, but no one cared. After payday, the power sergeants would take over the gambling for three days until all the money was gone."

St. Clair learned more than how to shuffle and deal or how to care for "Dan," the horse that for three years was his transportation. Before drills, he learned to "simonize" his boots instead of polishing them. There was one catch: the wax finish would crack if you wore them much. To combat that, they carried their boots to inspections.

"We looked beautiful," he bragged.

But this peacetime army of the late 1930s also taught him about human nature, including his own. He spoke with a German accent and knew more about mining coal than digging peanuts, but living in a barracks taught him about people different from himself and how to get along with them. "You could lay a wallet, money, your watch, your ring, your mama's picture, your girlfriend's picture in the middle of the bed and go down the hall and talk to somebody for hours and nothing would be disturbed. It just didn't happen. Those Florida, Georgia, and Alabama plowboys were completely honest," he said.

Finally, he was a veteran, watching new guys, many of them plowboys like the ones that had once harassed him. Only now he saw them differently: "They all had a great sense of personal honor. I used to watch the new ones arrive. They would eat and eat. Those kids had lived on corn bread and molasses where they came from, and they never seemed to get filled up, and I never said a word. I never had been hungry so I didn't know, but they didn't care. They ate."

Sweet Pea was no longer a fifteen-year-old kid. Matthew St. Clair was a soldier. Using box stirrups to ride, post, and gallop, he and "Dan" covered many miles on Fort Benning's rutted, unpaved roads. Looking back on those days, he confessed: "I have not ever been on the back of a horse again! But all in all, it was the best three years of my entire life."

Colonel Henry Eames did yeoman duty as the camp's first commandant in 1918.

HENRY L. BENNING

In 1918, the new camp was named
for Confederate Major General Henry Lewis Benning of Columbus.

MISS ANNA CAROLINE BENNING

Anna Caroline Benning, the daughter of the camp's namesake,
raised the flag during a Flag Day Ceremony in 1918.

Major General Charles S. Farnsworth, the second commandant
of the Infantry School 1919-1920, was appointed the Army's first
Chief of Infantry on July 1, 1920.

Housing conditions on post led one sarcastic soldier
to compare Camp Benning to Valley Forge.

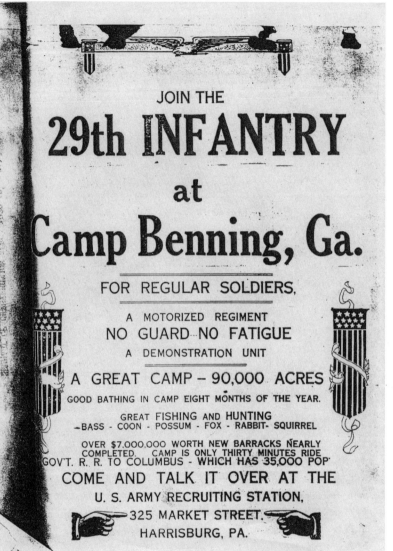

A 1920's recruiting poster in Pennsylvania is not exactly truthful in its glowing descriptions of Camp Benning.

On October 27, 1921, President Warren G. Harding, holding his cane, was the first
Chief Executive to visit the post. Next to him is Major General Walter H. Gordon,
Fort Benning commandant 1920-1923., and Columbus Mayor Rhodes Browne.
To the rear of Browne is Colonel Paul Malone.

Horse-drawn wagons were the mode of travel in the days before roads were paved.

The 29th Infantry Regiment has been part of post history since the 1920s when the unit lived in tents and crude wooden barracks.

This 1920 retirement ceremony said farewell to some of the earliest members
of the 29th Infantry who served on the post.

Flood waters frequently threatened the post in its early years—
especially when General John Pershing was visiting.

Ladies from Columbus and Phenix City join Army wives to greet President Warren G. Harding and his wife Florence who arrived on a special train in October 1921.

Built in 1920-1923, Service Club No. 1 Building 227 was one of the first permanent structures on post. Gowdy Field background. was completed in 1925.

Baseball champions of the post in 1925 were the Reds of the 24th Infantry, the earliest all-black unit at Benning.

Gowdy Field, dedicated in 1925, is named for Hank Gowdy, a catcher for the New York Giants and the first major league player to enlist in World War I.

In the Army that served between the world wars,
polo was a popular sport among the gentlemen officers.

Construction began in 1925 on the historic Cuartel Barracks, part of the beautification plan designed by Fort Benning Commandant Brigadier General Briant H. Wells 1923-1926. This unique facility, home to the 29th Infantry Regiment, replaced many traditional wooden barracks.

Major Dwight D. Eisenhower never dreamed of being President of the United States when he came to Benning in 1926.

When Dwight D. Eisenhower, wearing his West Point letter sweater, joined the Doughboy coaching staff, he feared he was being typecast as a football player instead of a soldier.

The group picture of the Infantry School faculty, 1928-1929, includes Assistant Commandant Lieutenant Colonel George C. Marshall, holding his riding crop. Many of "Marshall's men" became well-known leaders in World War II.

Brigadier General Campbell King popularized horse shows when
he commanded the post in 1929-1933.

Wearing their washbasin helmets and wrap-around leggings, soldiers of
the 29th Infantry ride to their classes in 1930.

This experimental vehicle used by the 29th Infantry in 1932 looks as if it is ready for a wagon train to the west.

Trucks replaced horse-driven vehicles on post in the 30's. Battery B, 83rd Horse Drawn Artillery was the first experimental motorized unit in the United States Army.

Fort Benning was once considered a lonely outpost—and so was its main gate.

Packs on their backs and canteens strapped to their belts, these grim-faced soldiers of the 29th Infantry Regiment rest between classes.

Riverside, longtime home to Benning's commanding generals, is draped with red, white and blue bunting during a ceremony honoring a visiting dignitary. Once the manor house of the former Bussey Plantation, Quarters 1 is on the National Register of Historic Places.

15.

It's Marshall's Army

Poland lived no more. Gallant Polish cavalrymen led charge after futile charge before being trampled by Germany's Guderian's panzers. It was over before the Poles realized it had begun—on the very day George C. Marshall took the oath as the US Army's chief of staff.

It wasn't irony. It was appropriate, for this brilliant general, whose cold demeanor could intimidate even his commander-in-chief, was about to put into place plans to gather an army that would inevitably have to deal with Hitler's relentless force.

"My day of induction into office was momentous, with the starting of what appears to be a World War," Marshall said, a statement based on knowledge rather than prophecy. Within forty-eight hours, "Great Britain and France honored Polish bravery by declaring war on Germany."[1]

It was September 1, 1939. Marshall had emerged from a field that included Hugh A. Drum and John L. DeWitt. Each was a key leader of the 1st Army in World War I and not a one of them was a graduate of the US Military Academy. That April, the choice was Marshall, architect of the "Benning Revolution" and a person who prepared for such a job since the day he entered the US Army. School was over. It was his army now.[2]

After his selection in April, Marshall carefully picked his team. That it included many of the officers he had surrounded himself with at Fort Benning surprised no one. Omar Bradley was assistant secretary of the General Staff, and Walter Bedell Smith was the liaison officer to the White

---

[1] "Germany's Invasion of Poland—September 1, 1939," National Infantry Museum Official Tour Guide Book, typescript spiral-bound book for museum staff and volunteer tour guides, Fort Benning GA, 6.

[2] Geoffrey Perret, *There's a War to Be Won* (New York: Random House, 1991) 25.

House and Treasury Department. Nor should it have been a surprise that the new chief of staff would turn to Fort Benning as an installation vital to the game plan he was about to unfold.

Benning's role was surmised even before his springtime selection. In February, Marshall wrote General Asa Singleton, Benning's commanding general, to inform him of Brigadier General Lesley McNair's upcoming visit. In line to be the next commandant at Fort Leavenworth, McNair was to be given "a good idea of the practical tactics and technique" taught at the Infantry School.[3] McNair was to see the briefly written orders, the concise summaries, supply details, and geological survey maps, all suggesting more of "contact with soldiers and the soil, than did the Leavenworth production."[4] Not a coincidence was the fact that these were innovations previously installed by Marshall.

Under directions from McNair, Leavenworth's instructors and students wrote more than 150 new field manuals that incorporated modern military doctrine in a "program of methodical training" for expanding units throughout the country.[5] Marshall's fingerprints were on every page. Taking a lesson from the Spanish Civil War and Hitler's September invasion of Poland, the army wanted tanks to sweep the battlefields. A month after Marshall took control, a medium tank outfit—Headquarters and Headquarters Company, 2nd Battalion and Company D of the 67th Infantry—was activated at Benning.

A week to the day after Germany roared into Poland, President Franklin D. Roosevelt delivered an emergency proclamation that authorized the Regular Army to increase from 210,000 officers and men to 227,000. It also allowed the National Guard to go from 190,000 to 235,000. Many of these new soldiers would pass through the gates of Fort Benning, Georgia.

In late October, the first contingent of the 1st Infantry Division arrived in Georgia for training. By the end of November, the entire division, consisting of 8,500 soldiers, occupied a new tent city built ten miles from main post at Kissick Pond. It was the first full infantry division ever to train

---

[3] Ibid.

[4] Ibid.

[5] George C. Marshall, *Interviews and Reminiscences for Forrest C. Pogue*, ed. Larry I Bland (Lexington VA: George C. Marshall Research Foundation, 1991) 306–307.

at Benning. In command was Major General Walter C. Short, a former assistant commandant of the Infantry School.

Benning was back where it started, only with many more people. The expanding military population outgrew existing barracks. With these new forces reporting for field training, post population doubled to 16,000. Behind the scenes, organization changes were being discussed. Experiments and studies at the Infantry School led to "development of new equipment, weapons, organizations and the application of tactical principles to these weapons produced a modern infantry capable of accomplishing its mission in a war of movement."[6] Quality, not numbers, determined a battle's outcome: "Superior hostile members may be overcome through greater mobility, better armament and equipment, more effective fire, higher morale and better leadership."[7] Responding to this theory, a major reorganization took effect. The triangular organization was implemented throughout the Regular Army. McNair was among those forging the "design to keep the army lean and simple...to achieve the best possible combination of fighting power with flexibility and maneuverability...."[8]

New weapons and equipment were combined with new organizational charts—many of them tested and improved at the Infantry School. The new infantry squad consisted of squad leader, assistant squad leader, a three-man automatic rifle team, and seven riflemen. The infantry regiment also was reorganized. The organization adopted in 1939 "became, with various modifications in names of units, armaments, and minor organizational changes, the basis for the organization of the infantry regiment during the period of the second World War."[9]

New drill regulations developed at the Infantry School by the 29th Infantry Regiment under the direction of J. Lawton Collins went into effect throughout the army. This simplified version replaced the traditional drill that stemmed from Friedrich Wilhelm Von Steuben's "Blue Book," published in 1779. Unlike the old drill that took time to learn and required

---

[6] "Tests of Semi-Automatic Rifles," 24, History of the Infantry School papers, vault, Donovan Library, Fort Benning GA.

[7] Ibid.

[8] Russell F. Weigley, *History of the United States Army* (New York: Macmillan Company, 1984) 461.

[9] "Tests of Semi-Automatic Rifles," 22.

constant practice, the new one made it easy to train large numbers of troops, including military novices, and "would assist the rapid deployment of platoons and companies in fast-moving triangular divisions."[10] Quickly, Fort Benning was becoming essential to the country's preparation for a war it was certain it would have to fight. Where and when was the question. But if these theories were to be tested, Marshall determined the army would have to undertake a field exercise more ambitious than any other it had ever put together.

The *Army and Navy Journal* published an article revealing plans for the largest peacetime field exercises ever conducted by the United States Army. It said five infantry divisions would be in training areas by November. According to the *Journal*, the exercises were proposed by Secretary of War Henry H. Woodring and Marshall "after consultation with and approval by General John J. Pershing, General of the Armies of the United States."[11] It would require mobilizing 164 units to form the five divisions.[12] The five divisions included the 1st Division of Fort Benning, commanded by Major General Walter C. Short; 2nd Division of Fort Sam Houston, commanded by Major General Walter Krueger; 3rd Division of Fort Lewis, Washington, commanded by Major General Walter C. Sweeney; 5th Division of Fort McClellan, Alabama, commanded by Major General Campbell B. Hodges; and 6th Division of Camp Jackson, South Carolina, commanded by Major General Clement A. Trott.

Fort Benning would be the site of this mass exercise. It was a post Marshall knew so very well. He had ridden his horse over most of its acreage. He knew the people there. He knew he could count on support from the civilian community. In December, he scheduled a visit to those familiar surroundings so last minute arrangements could be made. Meetings on post were set up with Singleton, Short, Brigadier General Bruce Magruder, executive officer of the Infantry School, and Brigadier General Karl Truesdell, infantry commander of the 1st Division.

Though Columbus newspapers reported "the distinguished visitor" and his wife were in town, Marshall asked Singleton to limit their social

---

[10] Perret, *There's a War to Be Won*, 16.

[11] "Divisions, Corps Units, Speed Movement South," *Army and Navy Journal* 77/7 (October 14 1939): 1.

[12] Ibid.

obligations: "We want to be polite and we must be considerate of our old friends in Columbus, but if there is any possible way in which Katherine and I can have a little peaceful time without entertaining, it will be greatly appreciated."[13] While on post, he did make time to ride the woodlands on horseback, to shoot his limit of doves, and to kill a pheasant. There was also a dinner for seventy-five friends at the home of Mr. and Mrs. Ernest Dismukes in the Peacock Woods neighborhood of Columbus.

Marshall, though generally pleased with what he saw on post, was concerned about housing conditions in winter for the 1st Infantry. Necessary shelter was not available on the overtaxed post. When Marshall returned to Benning for a second stop after Christmas, the troops had already endured a bitter early winter drop in temperatures. "Some of them almost froze up in the situation," he noted. Returning to Washington, he "had them make the corrections then, within the hour." His orders were followed, and the 1st Division received not only shelter but also a post officer and a first-aid setup.[14]

Weather issues were handled, but health concerns were another matter, and it was health that threatened the decision to locate the important maneuvers at Fort Benning. With the influx of soldiers on the post, incidences of venereal disease were steadily increasing. The surgeon general of the US Army asked Bascom Johnson of the American Social Hygiene Association to make a study in Columbus and Phenix City, explaining, "that wherever large bodies of troops assemble near a city there is bound to be a vice situation."[15] Colonel Myron P. Rudolph, division surgeon of the 1st Division, informed the group that he was in and out of Fort Benning for the past eighteen years and was quite familiar with the situation. "Unfortunately, it is not a desirable one, by any means," he said, noting venereal diseases contributed to 50 percent of the infectious ailments of soldiers.

---

[13] George C. Marshall, *The Papers of George Catlett Marshall*, vol. 2, ed. Larry I. Bland (Baltimore: John Hopkins University Press, 1981) 115.

[14] George C. Marshall, *Interviews and Reminiscences for Forrest C. Pogue*, ed. Larry I. Bland (Lexington VA: George C. Marshall Research Foundation, 1991) 511–12.

[15] "Drive against Vice Promised for Columbus," a newspaper clipping found in Frank G. Lumpkin's personal files, Willcox-Lumpkin Company, Columbus GA. Other than the year (1939), no other information was available.

Short, the division commander, worried about young men contracting the disease "because of the serious aftermath of their contracting syphilis."[16] He pointed out, "We're going to have some 40,000 men here for maneuvers," warning that if the venereal disease rate was too high, the government might choose another site for its exercises. Short defended the soldiers, saying they were on the "receiving" end rather than the "distributing" end since infected soldiers were confined and treated until non-infectious to civilians. Dr. L. E. Burney, loaned to the state board of health by the US Public Health Service, thought "it would be a good idea if this community"—Columbus and Phenix City—"made it known to prostitutes that their presence was unwanted here and would not be tolerated."[17]

Marshall saw the need for motorized transportation for the divisions and corps troops he organized "for the first time in the peace-time history of the Army," five Regular Army divisions and eighteen National Guard divisions.[18] Noting "that the German Army had opened its assault on Poland with animal-drawn divisions," he did not intend to eliminate animals and their caretakers completely.[19] To ease the movement of men and equipment, Battery B, 83rd Horse Drawn Artillery at Fort Benning became the first experimental motorized unit in the army.

Private Matthew St. Clair remembered the experiment well: "We were selected to become motorized as an experiment. Batteries A and C still had horses, but they took ours away and gave us these big old trucks. I had never ridden a horse or driven a car before coming into the service."[20] St. Clair recollected changes in weaponry as well as in transportation: "When we were motorized we still had the same old gun—the same kind used in World War I. But they turned around and gave us the split-trail 75 mm. We had four for the battery. During our training, the first sergeant and some others

---

[16] Ibid.

[17] Ibid.

[18] George C. Marshall, *The Papers of George Catlett Marshall*, vol. 1, ed. Larry I. Bland (Baltimore: Johns Hopkins University Press, 1981) 118.

[19] Ibid.

[20] Matthew St. Clair, interview by Peggy Stelpflug, December 11 1998, Donovan Library, Fort Benning GA, typed transcript and audio cassette, Auburn AL.

pitched horseshoes while the rest of us practiced firing the piece. The new gun was much better than the old one, much more stable."[21]

Marshall asked Congress for $16 million for motor vehicles, making a request to Kaufman T. Keller, the president and general manager of the Chrysler Corporation: "I hope that your people work one of those industrial miracles for which American industry has become famous, and give us deliveries at a much earlier date than we now anticipate."[22] Chrysler delivered, not only motor vehicles for the war but tanks as well.

---

[21] Ibid.
[22] Marshall, *The Papers of George Catlett Marshall*, vol. 2, 118.

16.

Airplanes and Indians

Before arriving in Georgia, these guys had never seen a parachute. Most of them had not even flown in an airplane. Now as US Army paratroopers, they would be jumping, en masse, out of a perfectly good airplane over Lawson Field.

On the night before the jump in August 1940, Private Aubrey Eberhardt and some buddies went to a movie at Fort Benning's main post theatre. It was a western, and in the film the cavalry and the cowboys were chasing Geronimo, a wily Apache chief. Leaving the theatre, guys teased as guys will do. Trying to seem brave, they picked at each other about the next day's jump. They were all nervous but trying not to let each other know it.

"To prove to you that I'm not scared out of my wits when I jump, I'm gonna yell 'Geronimo' as loud as hell when I go out the door tomorrow!" Private Aubrey Eberhardt told his buddies.[1]

The soldier who drew the winning straw froze at the open door of the C-33 when the test dummy's parachute failed to open. Master Sergeant William "Red" King, next in line, took his place, becoming the first enlisted man to jump as a paratrooper in the US Army. King followed Lieutenant William T. Ryder into the open air over Lawson and into the history books.

True to his word, as Eberhardt left the plane, he shouted "Geronimo," adding "an Indian war whoop." According to Gerald Devlin, author of *Paratrooper!*, "Without knowing it at the time, Eberhardt originated what was to become the jumping yell of the American paratroopers."[2]

At Fort Benning, a new era began—an era that would help the post reach new heights, literally and figuratively. It began on June 25, 1940, when the commandant of the Infantry School formed a volunteer Parachute Test

---

[1] Gerard M. Devlin, *Paratrooper!* (New York: St. Martin's Press, 1979) 70.
[2] Ibid.

Platoon from the 29th Regiment. The 29th again lived up to its reputation of "Let the 29th Infantry do it" by providing Ryder to lead the platoon and forty-eight enlisted men chosen from over 200 volunteers. Hobart B. Wade was platoon sergeant. Shortly afterward, 2nd Lieutenant James A. Bassett, who placed second to Ryder in the written exam, became assistant platoon leader. Requirements were stiff. Volunteers were required to have served a minimum of two years in the infantry, to weigh no more than 185 pounds, to be in excellent physical condition, and, due to the expected danger, to be unmarried.[3]

The hangar at Lawson field was cleaned and the platoon set up tents to prepare for training. Warrant Officer Harry "Tug" Wilson arrived from Kelly Field, Texas, to conduct the eight-week course designed by the Infantry Board. Wilson, the Army Air Corps's most experienced parachute jumper, faced a challenge since no platoon members "had ever seen a parachute before, or ridden in an airplane."[4]

Major Bill Lee was chosen to head the air infantry project in Washington. Lee fought in World War I and once taught at the Fort Benning Tank and Infantry School. Lee, whose "ambition then was to retire in a few years, at the rank of lieutenant colonel," would soon earn the rank of general and "would become known as the 'father' of American Airborne troops."[5]

The program was instantly popular. When it was known that a parachute battalion would be formed, branches and posts vied for it. So did the leaders. Major General Eugene Schley, chief of engineers; General Henry H. Arnold, air corps chief; and Major General George A. Lynch, chief of infantry, all wanted control of the program. Chief of Staff George C. Marshall, who brought brass from Washington to observe the final jump of the Parachute Test Platoon, finally announced the battalion was "under control of the Infantry Branch at Fort Benning."[6] The Airborne concept of vertical envelopment, mastered by Germany, was ready to take off in the American military.

---

[3] Ibid., 49.

[4] Ibid., 54.

[5] Ibid., 42.

[6] Ibid., 81.

A month after the first jump of the test platoon, the War Department approved formation of the 1st Parachute Battalion at Fort Benning. By September 26, it was redesignated the 501st Parachute Infantry Battalion, commanded by Colonel William Miley, Fort Benning's former athletic officer. With members of the test platoon as the cadre, Miley prepared the 501st. A major when he commanded the 501st, Miley, like Lee, was promoted rapidly. In thirty-six months, the 501st commander was a major general in command of the 17th Airborne Division. Of the 501st, Devlin noted, "No other battalion in any of the American armed services has ever produced more generals."[7]

The new unit quickly gave birth to its own traditions. One was the "prop blast." Devlin described its origin: "Just prior to the original prop blast, held in the horse-show cabin at Fort Benning, Lieutenant Carl Buechner of the 501st Parachute Battalion took a brass 75 mm shell casing into nearby Columbus. There he had two reserve parachute handles fastened to the sides of the casing and the names of fifteen battalion officers engraved on the front. This crude drinking became the hallowed 'Miley Mug.'"[8] At the first prop blast all fifteen officers, one at a time in order of rank, had to stand on a chair, jump off, tumble on the floor, get on his feet, and guzzle the contents of the mug. According to Devlin, Miley was the first to be "blasted." Over the years, prop blast ritualists jumped from tabletops, pianos, bars, and, according to Devlin, even the eighteen-foot high balcony in the main Fort Benning Officers' Club.[9]

Troops and equipment were arriving at Fort Benning on almost a daily basis in 1939 and 1940. To train more students, Lynch, the chief of infantry, ordered all nine-month courses cut to three or four months. The 1940–1941 courses for officers included rifle and heavy weapons, battalion commanders' and staff officers' class, communication, and motor maintenance. Classes for enlisted men included radio operators and motor mechanics.

More than infantrymen were arriving. Tank divisions along with armored and artillery divisions showed up, and the 4th Army's first Antitank Battalion was activated at Fort Benning in January 1940 under command of Lieutenant Colonel Leven C. Allen. In June 1940, the 20th

---

[7] Ibid., "Footnotes," Chapter 4, #3, 674.
[8] Ibid., 90.
[9] Ibid., 91.

Engineer Regiment Combat Unit was reactivated and assigned to the IV Corps.

Columbus historian Etta Blanchard Worsley noted the growth at Fort Benning: "By the time of the IV Corps maneuvers in the spring of 1940, nearly every type of unit was represented and there were 45,000 troops."[10] The IV Corps exercises, designed to familiarize troops with large operations, were "the first genuine Corps and Army maneuvers in the history of this country."[11]

To house the 22nd Infantry—still waiting in Alabama at Fort McClellan to join the 4th Division—sixty-two barracks, housing nearly 4,000 troops, were built under the direction of Post Quartermaster Colonel James R. Alfonte. "Rank," as Marshall noted to a friend "goes up the hill near the golf course."[12] On August 27, the National Guard was called into Federal Service with the first units inducted September 16, 1940, the same day President Roosevelt signed the Selective Service Act. With this first US peacetime draft, men between the age of twenty and thirty-six were required to register for a one-year tour. Within a year, tours were extended to eighteen months. With passage of the Selective Service Act, the army was authorized 1,400,000 men: 500,000 in the regular army, 270,000 in the National Guard, and 630,000 selectees. With new troops arriving daily, the post resembled a large construction site. In a fifteen-month period ending in October 1940, $5.6 million was spent on new construction. As the post became a pre-war boomtown, Columbus leaders wanted to solidify Fort Benning's future and its presence in their community.

Walter A Richards, a veteran of World War I and president of the Columbus Chamber of Commerce, wrote Frank Lumpkin, asking his view about the troops that might come to Fort Benning for permanent station: "We must interest ourselves in the social and personal lives of the army personnel so that we can keep them sold on the idea that Fort Benning is the

---

[10] Etta Blanchard Worsley, *Columbus on the Chattahoochee* (Columbus: Columbus Office Supply Company, 1951) 441.

[11] Katherine Tupper Marshall, *Together: Annals of an Army Wife* (New York: Tupper and Love, Inc., 1946) 62.

[12] George C. Marshall, *The Papers of George Catlett Marshall*, vol. 1, ed. Larry I. Bland (Baltimore: Johns Hopkins University Press, 1981).

best possible location for the headquarters for the infantry training of the United States Army."[13]

Richards wanted to better "community morals" by organizing civil organizations to help eliminate prostitution in Columbus. On May 10, General Walter Short, writing from IV Corps Headquarters, responded to Richards's proposal. Short approved of the chamber's offer of help in procuring additional land for the post and warned that the venereal disease rate at Fort Benning was "much higher than the average rate of the Army as a whole."[14] If the city did not try to control venereal disease, Short predicted, additional troops would not come to Benning, adding "from a purely business point of view, I am sure you will find it desirable to continue the movement."[15]

On the last day of August, Brigadier General Asa Singleton, who began his tour of duty at Benning in 1936, retired from the army; Brigadier General Courtney H. Hodges, former assistant commandant of the Infantry School, assumed command October 7. Slowly, city leaders were seeing old military friends leave the army, a feeling expressed in Lumpkin's lament, "Gone with the wind is a fitting description of many of our good friends leaving Fort Benning."[16]

The Infantry Board was separated from the post after Singleton's retirement and placed under direct supervision of the chief of infantry in Washington, DC. During this time, personnel at the Infantry School continued to write new manuals, study theory, and propose doctrine as well as carry on maneuvers and field training.

From comrades educated in Germany's buildup and tactics, George C. Marshall realized whatever direction he took, it would take firepower and manpower. In 1939, the United States had 2,500 airplanes, but by 1945 it would have 80,000. In 1939, the army had 174,000 men, but by 1945 would have 6,000,000. But the changes were more than numbers. After two

---

[13] Walter C. Short, copy of "confidential" letter to Walter A. Richards issued from Headquarters IV Corps, May 10 1940, stating concern that high venereal rate at Fort Benning would affect fort's growth. Located in Frank G. Lumpkin's personal files, Willcox-Lumpkin Company, Columbus GA.

[14] Ibid.

[15] Ibid.

[16] Frank Lumpkin to William E. Persons, retired Col. and director of Dept. of Corrections and Institutions in Atlanta, February 1 1940, Lumpkin file.

decades of peace, a youth movement was on the horizon, bringing with it a transfusion of new ideas. Since World War I, technology changed, tactics evolved, communications improved. Marshall realized the army must change, too. In 1940, with aging soldiers, the post had to open its doors to young men—many young men and, soon, many young women. As it trained them, Fort Benning would prove its worth—just as its early defenders had predicted.

17.

A Piano and the Post

Thomas and Henrietta shot baskets in their driveway next door, but Lulu Carson Smith stayed in her house, spending time with Mozart, Beethoven, Chopin, and Bach. Hours a day, she practiced. Whatever it took to get it right, whatever it took to be ready for her weekly piano lesson with the teacher she longed to please.

Lulu Carson Smith was a waif of a girl, frail and sickly. Her father owned a jewelry store in Columbus. The Smiths lived on Stark Avenue in a comfortable neighborhood a couple of blocks behind Columbus High School. She was thirteen years old when she became the only student of Mary Tucker, a concert pianist who left the stage to marry Albert S. J. Tucker. Her husband was a lieutenant colonel stationed at Fort Benning. Every Saturday, Carson went to the Tucker's home on Austin Loop, one of those stately two-story houses in that part of the post where the buzzards roost—colonels, who wear eagles on their shoulders. The Tuckers were known in town. Author Virginia Spencer Carr said Columbus, a town that "prided itself on its fine arts" welcomed Mary Tucker.[1] The talented Mrs. Tucker soon became active in the Three Arts League, a group of society women that through the years fostered a love of music and drama in a textile town reared on catfish and cornbread. Recognizing the withdrawn Carson's gift for music, she adopted the shy adolescent as her only pupil.

It was 1930, and the trek to Fort Benning was still a major excursion. For Carson, it was the highlight of her week. She loved the piano, but it was more than the music—she loved the time she spent there. Their relationship was formal and disciplined, like the music on the page. But after the lesson there was time to play with the Tucker children, Gin and Bud. Carson felt

---

[1] Virginia Spencer Carr, *The Lonely Hunter: A Biography of Carson McCullers* (Garden City NY: Doubleday & Co., Inc., 1975) 26.

like one of the family when she and Gin "would ride bicycles or walk to the pool, swim for a while, and then move on to the stables for an afternoon of riding."[2]

On one of those Saturdays in 1934, Mrs. Tucker shared news with her protégé that changed their relationship forever. Colonel Tucker was being transferred to Fort Howard, in Maryland. They would be moving soon, she said. The fragile adolescent was devastated. She was losing her other family and the teacher she worshipped. Carson retaliated. She announced to her music teacher that she would become a writer—not a pianist. Neither realized that Saturday what those words would someday mean. But in less than a decade, this tormented young woman would be acclaimed as one of America's most celebrated authors—Carson McCullers. She wrote about subjects she knew, Columbus and Fort Benning, but in her descriptions they are dark and moody places—a picture the town and post could not easily accept.

Friends back home were introduced to her work in 1940 when her first novel, *The Heart Is a Lonely Hunter*, brought her national fame. Published in 1941, her second book reflects a twisted Fort Benning that others had never seen. It was introduced in two parts, October and November 1940, in the monthly magazine *Harper's Bazaar*. It was called *Reflections in a Golden Eye*, but its original title was simply *Army Post*.[3]

McCullers' view of Fort Benning was more than the one she had enjoyed those carefree Saturdays on Austin Loop. Her views included ones shared with her by James Reeves McCullers, Jr., her future husband. Like the withdrawn young Columbus girl, McCullers marched with his own demons. He enlisted in the army in 1931 after graduating from high school in Wetumpka, Alabama. Assigned to Fort Benning, Reeves McCullers met Carson Smith through Edwin Peacock, a CCC worker who knew the high school student through the Tuckers. At the age of seventeen, Carson went to New York to study writing at Columbia University but returned home to work as a reporter at the *Columbus Ledger*, a job at which she was unsuccessful. Returning to New York, Carson was soon followed by Reeves, who purchased his discharge from the army. The couple married in 1937 at her parents' home.

---

[2] Ibid., 27.
[3] Ibid.

When Carson and Reeves divorced in the early 1940s, Reeves re-enlisted in the army and attended Officer Candidate School at Fort Benning in 1942. He fought in three campaigns in World War II and was decorated for bravery. In 1945, the couple remarried, but eight years later, Reeves committed suicide in a Paris hotel room.

The idea for *Reflections in a Golden Eye* came from a story Carson's husband told her about a Fort Benning soldier peeking into an officer's quarters. His story morphed into a complicated tale about army captain Wendell Pendleton, who has a homosexual attraction to a young private. The private is revealed as the peeping tom, who, though he fears women, is attracted to the captain's wife, Lenora. Meanwhile, Lenora is having an affair with Major Morris Langdon. Langdon's wife, Alison, plans to leave the post with her devoted Filipino servant Anacleto, a dwarfed eunuch; but Alison dies before they can escape together.

Scenes in the novel are scenes common to the post—the stables, the horse trails, the housing, and the classrooms. In one scene, the captain follows the private to his quarters: "As he thought of the 2,000 men living together in this great quadrangle, he felt suddenly alone. He sat in the dark car and as he stared at the lighted, crowded rooms inside, as he heard the sounds of shouts and ringing voices, the tears came to his glassy eyes. A bitter loneliness gnawed in him. He drove quickly home."[4]

At the end of the novel, the captain kills the private who has entered the officer's bedroom to stare at Lenora as she sleeps. The southern army post, set in a lush woodland setting, reveals to one of McCullers's critics "the contrast between rigid discipline and the monotony of the military establishment as opposed to the uncontrollable natural universe and to the permissive and egocentric behavior of the people who live on the base."[5] McCullers said her novel, which revealed the stratified social life of the army, was written as a "comic fairy tale."[6] Reviewers referred to it as Southern Gothic, but most readers accepted it as creative fiction and marveled at the talent of the twenty-three-year-old author.

---

[4] Carson McCullers, *Reflections in a Golden Eye* (Boston: Riverside Press, 1941) 66.

[5] Margaret P. McDowell, *Carson McCullers* (Boston: Twayne Publishers, 1980) 45.

[6] Carr, *The Lonely Hunter*, 91.

Readers back home were not so benevolent. Carr reported, "Carson's father Lamar Smith threw the magazine in which it first appeared across the room in disgust and wondered how a child of his could have spun such a tale."[7] Mrs. George Patton, a recent arrival at the fort (and a writer) cancelled her subscription to *Harper's Bazaar* and "encouraged other wives at the fort to do the same thing."[8] George C. Marshall, who had met young Carson through the Tuckers, teased them about the book, wondering if "the whole post had gone to pot" after they left.[9]

Carson and her former piano teacher were estranged for years after the officer's wife told her they were leaving Fort Benning. Though Carson and Gin Tucker wrote often, the piano teacher and her pupil kept a distance until 1950. That spring, *A Member of the Wedding*, a play about an adolescent's sense of rejection, was presented in New York. Only then did her friendship with Mary Tucker resume. The play won the New York Drama Critics Circle Award and the Donaldson Annual Award for Best Drama. The author received the Gold Medal of Theatre Club, Inc. for best playwright of the year.

Carson McCullers died September 29, 1967. She was fifty years old. McCullers's words created a gulf between herself and her hometown that was never bridged. However, years after her death a historic marker was placed outside her former home on Stark Avenue, the house where Thomas and Henrietta Worsley heard Lulu endlessly practicing piano. Thornton Jordan, a Columbus State University literature professor, bought the house and turned it into a haven for writers and artists. In 2003, a citywide literacy campaign urged Columbus people to read *The Heart Is a Lonely Hunter*. But even her inclusion in a listing of the 100 best novels of the century did little to move older residents to forgive her or her words, nor did a revitalization of her fame brought on by her being named to Oprah Winfrey's book club in 2004.

By the end of the 1930s, the country club army that Carson McCullers depicted in her story was slowly disappearing. The primitive camp that became a comfortable fort shielded from problems faced by civilians was now facing reality. Some viewed the post as a "good ol' boys' club."

---

[7] Ibid.

[8] Ibid.

[9] Ibid.

Successful wives were accomplished equestrians and party givers. Men played polo and sipped drinks at the Officers' Club. With job security and a sense of community, each did what he or she was trained to do. The maxim was "Everybody works a little so nobody has to work too hard." Only war would disrupt the gentleman's army

18.

The Ghost of Benning

The brass buttons of his fitted pea-green jacket stretched from his waist up over the right shoulder. His jodhpurs, also green, billowed over brightly shined boots. An ivory-handled pistol dangled from a peculiar sling under his left arm. His helmet had a gold band around it that looked very much like a halo.

General Raymond S. McLain knew at once it was George Patton, tall and stately, leaning against a tree. The year was 1940. Patton, fifty-five, arrived at Fort Benning deeply concerned about George C. Marshall's youth movement. The careers of 500 senior officers abruptly ended because of it. Now Patton feared he would not get to command a combat force in a war that he sensed was around the next Georgia pine, a command he believed was "the apparent return of his destiny."[1]

Patton was an original. He and Omar Bradley were stationed together in Hawaii in the "Pineapple Army," featuring polo and parties. Bradley found Patton a fascinating although frustrating friend and fellow soldier: "As a soldier, a professional officer, Patton was the most fiercely ambitious man and the strangest duck I have ever known."[2] An open believer in reincarnation, Patton said he had fought alongside Alexander the Great, Genghis Khan, Caesar, Napoleon, and with his own grandfather in the Civil War. Such beliefs added to Patton's intuitive, almost mystic, approach to battle, not to mention his image—an image he fiercely protected. In his quirky way, Patton believed he was predestined to be in combat. In World War I he requested tank service and was the first American officer to receive

---

[1] Martin Blumenson, *The Man behind the Legend, 1885–1945* (New York: William Morrow & Co., 1985) 144.

[2] Omar Bradley, with collaborator Clay Blair, *A General's Life* (New York: Simon and Schuster, 1983) 98.

it. Using French tanks and know-how, Patton established the AEF Tank School at Langres and commanded the 304th Tank Brigade in Saint-Mihiel. On the first day Americans employed tanks in World War I, Patton, in support of the infantry, rode a tank into battle under fire. He also was in the Meuse-Argonne offensive: Patton's "little known army was the forerunner of the armored forces of the United States."[3]

Patton and his wife, Beatrice Ayer Patton, were both children of wealthy California winegrowers. Bradley described Patton's lifestyle thusly: "The incomes from the Patton and Ayer families probably made George the richest officer in the US Army. The Pattons had horses for riding, racing and showing, and a string of thoroughbred polo ponies. Everywhere, they had the highest social connections."[4] In his twenty months at Benning, the Pattons connected with local society. They attended costume parties in town dressed as Rhett Butler and Scarlett O'Hara or King Arthur and Guinevere. They also enjoyed eating "nearly every Sunday night" at Spano's, a downtown Columbus landmark founded in 1893 by Angelo Spano.[5]

Located near the historic old Springer Theatre, Spano's was a narrow café with marble tabletops and courtly waiters who knew everybody by name. Customers filled out their own tickets, usually asking for the bread pudding soaked in wine. Those who wanted a cocktail arrived with a bottle of their favorite poison in a brown bag. Spano's daughter-in-law Sara was a character in her own right, sometimes serving as a hostess at the restaurant. A former third- and fourth-grade teacher at Fort Benning, Sara Spano went on to become a beloved food editor and columnist for the *Columbus Ledger-Enquirer.*

The gregarious Spano found Patton an extraordinary customer. Spano remembered, "When things weren't too rushed I used to sit down at their table for a while. I had to get used to the General's method of conversation. When he was just talking about ordinary things he clamped his teeth together and spoke in a very low tone.... If he became excited over some point, he would suddenly pound on the table and yell out in a voice you

---

[3] "Hit the Deck," *Bayonet,* January 7 1943, 8.

[4] Bradley, *A General's Life,* 98.

[5] Sara Spano, *I Could've Written "Gone with the Wind," but Cousin Margaret Beat Me to It* (Ann Arbor MI: McNaughton & Gunn, 1990) 81.

could hear three blocks away. The first time he did that I nearly went over backwards in my chair."[6]

Although dyslexic, Patton was an avid reader and writer. He had read and generously annotated *Infantry in Battle*, written at Fort Benning under direction of George C. Marshall. He also made numerous notes in *Battle Leadership* by Captain Adolph von Schell of the German Army. This book consists of lectures given at Fort Benning by von Schell in the early 1930s. Patton underscored the words "confidence," "pride," "attack," and "speed," and to the statement "if a leader waits for complete information before issuing an order, he will never issue one." Patton made this part of his personal philosophy.[7]

Realizing the limitations of cavalry—his first love—and the army's need to modernize, Patton made an appeal to Brigadier General Adna Chaffee and Henry L. Stimson, who became secretary of war, for an assignment in the mechanized forces. Chaffee, in command of the Armored Force established by Marshall on July 10, 1940, wanted Patton to command an armored brigade and predicted Patton's World War II success: "With two light armored regiments and regiment of tanks employed in a mobile way, I think you could go to town."[8]

The Armored Force was composed of two divisions: the 1st Armored Division, commanded by infantryman Brigadier General Bruce Magruder, was stationed at Fort Knox, Kentucky. Brigadier General Charles L. Scott, a cavalryman, commanded the 2nd Armored Division at Fort Benning. The 2nd Armored Brigade, when first formed at Fort Benning, consisted of 350 officers, 5,500 men, 383 tanks, 202 armored cars, and 24 105 mm howitzers. Again, men from the 29th Infantry Regiment were out front. In addition to testing new weapons, providing troops for paratrooper school, serving as demonstration troops, and upholding the status of the best-trained infantry regiment of the regular army, troops from the 29th joined Patton's unit. On September 18, the division conducted its first dismounted review, assembling 8,000 men together for the first time. Later in the year, Patton assumed command of the 2nd Armored Division, earning the rank of

---

[6] Ibid.

[7] Roger H. Nye, *The Patton Mind* (Garden City Parks NY: Avery Publishing Group Inc., 1993) 101.

[8] Ibid., 113.

brigadier general. In December, he led a march from Columbus to Panama City, a round-trip of 400 miles, accompanied with more than 1,000 vehicles, including tanks and half-tracks. Patton considered the attention he and his men received from people and newspapers along the way as good publicity for the army and the 2nd Armored Division. He confided to a friend, "I think this outfit now has the popular imagination, and will go far."[9]

Patton's persona was forever building. Everyone who served at Benning during his stint seemed to have a story. Some talked of the paradox between the legend that he threatened to take his tanks into Phenix city to clean up the town and the whispers that working girls from the so-called "Sin City" visited his private headquarters on post. His was an image that would culminate with a classic film starring George C. Scott simply titled *Patton.* In his Academy Award-winning performance, Scott turns the colorful general into a character larger than life. To his men, Patton *was* larger than life.

Donald E. Houston, author of *Hell on Wheels,* a name given to the 2nd Armored Division, explains how Patton received his enduring nickname, "Old Blood and Guts." Patton often told young officers they would be "up to their necks in blood and guts." One Monday evening, while drinking beer in the bachelor officers' quarters, Lieutenant Al Kirchner looked at his watch and said that it was about time to go hear "old Blood and Guts." His remark was greeted with a burst of laughter. Houston states, "To that time Patton was called the Green Hornet because of the tank suit he had designed and because of his propensity for roaring around the training area in his light tank with its siren blaring."[10]

Beatrice Patton, an accomplished musician and pianist, also contributed to the post's musical library. In January 1941, Patton staged a division parade with 1,300 vehicles passing flawlessly before the reviewing stand. The band played Mrs. Patton's "The March of the Armored Force," a piece that became the official 2nd Armored Division march. Scored to open with the wail of a tank siren and the firing of guns, her lyrics were

---

[9] Martin Blumenson, *The Patton Papers* (Boston: Houghton Mifflin Co., 1974) 18.
[10] Donald E. Houston, *Hell on Wheels* (San Rafael CA: Presidio Press, 1977) 40.

triumphant: "Glorious! Glorious/ In War we're ever victorious/ We move right in fight like sin/ In the great Armored Corps."[11]

In late spring 1941, Patton took his troops on maneuvers. They were trained from small unit to division, including night bivouacs and a predawn assault river crossing: "The problems were the nearest thing to actual combat.... The division suffered four dead, three in accidents, while one could not stand the strain and committed suicide. In addition there were some twenty-one broken bones caused by accidents."[12] The 4th Infantry Division also took part, and in his critique, Major General Lesley J. McNair, commanding general of Army Ground Forces, stated that "the 2nd Armored and the 4th Infantry Division were among the most ready for battle."[13]

In June 1941, Patton took the 2nd Armored Division and an infantry division to Camp Forest, near Tullahoma, Tennessee: "He was pitted against a large force that consisted almost entirely of infantry. With his tanks and a few light bombers he created a mini-blitzkrieg, routed the larger force, and brought the maneuvers to an abrupt end...."[14]

Patton's style attracted the attention of national newsmakers. He appeared on the cover of the July issue of *Life* magazine. He was riding a tank, wearing his "snappy helmet and costume."[15] His men were proud of his fame, and the article gave high praise of his unit: "Along with its counterparts, the First, Third and Fourth Armored Division ... the second Armored Division is the most encouraging news of the year."[16] Comparing it to a German Panzer Division, *Life* noted: "Along with its tanks and scout cars, it has its own infantry, its own artillery, its own engineer supply, and medical corps. It even has scouting and bombardment aviation."[17] Patton

---

[11] Maj. Verne D. Campbell, "Armor and Cavalry Music," part 2, *Armor* 8/3 (May-June 1971): 37.

[12] Donald E. Houston, *Hell on Wheels* (San Rafael CA: Presidio Press, 1977) 56–57.

[13] Ibid.

[14] Geoffrey Perret, *There's a War To Be Won* (New York: Random House, 1991) 42.

[15] "Armored Forces: U. S. Army Stages Its Own Brand of Blitz," *Life*, Defense Issue 11/1 (July 7 1941): 72.

[16] Ibid.

[17] Ibid.

defined his 385 tanks and 1,900 vehicles as "the strongest force ever devised by man."[18]

In August 1941, Patton and his troops participated in the Louisiana maneuvers. Geoffrey Perret points out the advantages of Patton's private income: "He burned up all the gas provided for his tanks long before they got back into Louisiana. Spending his own money, he refueled his division at roadside gas stations."[19] He also brought parts for tanks with his own money, often ordering from Sears, and used his private plane "to experiment with controlling armored columns from the sky by two-way radio."[20]

Patton clearly demonstrated his ability as a tank commander or leader of men in battle, reaffirming Marshall's confidence in this "old" warrior. Perret describes the importance of the Louisiana maneuvers: "Some men's reputations were made in Louisiana, others were ruined, just as surely as if it had been a real campaign. The commanding generals of five National Guard divisions were relieved. Dozens of colonels and scores of lieutenant colonels were sacked."[21] The army chief of staff also understood the importance of the exercises. In many ways, it was a dress rehearsal for an opening night yet to come. George C. Marshall knew that it was better to learn how to fight in Louisiana than on the unforgiving battlegrounds of Europe.

Patton, wearing the stars of a brigadier general, learned of his nomination for major general before leaving Fort Benning in March 1942 to establish the Desert Training Center near Indio, California.[22]

Patton was ready to go and ready for action. As he had written to a friend earlier, "All that is now needed is a nice juicy war."[23] The day Patton left Fort Benning, old-timers remember the men of the 2nd Armored Division lining the streets, waving and cheering their charismatic leader. To some observers, he was something more. Father Joseph P. Symes took a different tack. A Catholic priest and history professor, Symes was assigned to Saint Patrick's, a small parish in Phenix City. Over the years, he was

---

[18] Ibid.

[19] Perret, *There's a War to Be Won*, 25.

[20] Ibid.

[21] Ibid., 44.

[22] "General Patton Will Command Desert Corps," *Columbus Ledger*, March 27 1942, 1.

[23] Martin Blumenson, *Patton: The Man behind the Legend, 1885–1945* (New York: William Morrow and Company, Inc., 1985) 147.

closely affiliated with the nearby post. "Patton," offered Symes, "is the ghost that haunts Fort Benning."[24]

---

[24] Fr. Joseph P. Symes, conversation with Peggy Stelpflug, Auburn AL, summer 1994.

19.

Bradley Leads the Way

The first time Omar Nelson Bradley came to Fort Benning, he rediscovered confidence. This time, he began to find his page in history. A young captain when he arrived in 1924, Bradley was forty-eight when he returned in the spring of 1941, a brigadier general for a matter of days and for twenty-six years a soldier. The nation was close to war, and he was close to emerging as one of its legends.

Bradley became post commander, replacing Major General Courtney Hodges, who soon became chief of infantry. Bradley was serving as assistant secretary of the General Staff in the office of George C. Marshall when the army chief of staff promoted him from lieutenant colonel, believing he was the man to get an important job done back at the post they both knew so well. Challenges were ahead, but Bradley was ready. In so many ways his preparations had begun on this same installation seventeen years before he took the new command. Those preparations came at a time in his life when the young captain did not know where his career or his future was going.

Like Dwight Eisenhower, his West Point classmate, Bradley was left behind when his army went to war in 1917. The young officer assumed his military career was over since he never made it to the frontlines in France. All of these feelings he brought with him when he reported to Benning in 1924. What he found in the Infantry School classes was a different kind of warfare, one based on fire and movement instead of the confining trenches of World War I.

"We found that quite a lot of the people who had been overseas were sort of locked in. It was more difficult for them to forget and get into open warfare than it was for some of us that had not had that battle experience," Bradley said.[1] At Benning, Bradley found his tactical judgment as good as

---

[1] "Omar Bradley," *Bayonet*, April 17 1981, 17.

those who had fought in the war: "The confidence I needed had been restored. I never suffered a faint heart again."[2]

Starting in 1941, under his direction, thousands of young men would be instilled with the diligence and skill such as he found years ago at the post. For months after his return, Fort Benning began producing officers like a leadership assembly line. Every ninety days, a new group of 2nd lieutenants graduated—"90 Day Wonders," they were dubbed.[3] But the fact that Omar Nelson Bradley was at the helm was neither wonder nor coincidence. Fate, in this instance, went by the name of George C. Marshall.

The idea for an infantry Officer Candidate School was projected in 1938 when Brigadier General Asa L. Singleton submitted a plan to Chief of Infantry Major General George A. Lynch. The proposal lay dormant until 1940 when Hodges—then Benning's assistant commandant—revived it. Marshall knew the country would need new leaders in this war it was about to fight and he turned over the implementation of the OCS plan to Bradley. On July 1, the first 3-month course began with 200 students. Its job was to provide training for the enlisted privates, corporals, and sergeants who would be replacing aging soldiers with rank.[4]

In his biennial report, Marshall described the new course:

> To provide additional officer personnel, to offer a fair opportunity to the man in the ranks, and most important of all, to utilize a rare opportunity for securing outstanding leaders, The War Department has established a series of officers' candidate schools, the students for which are selected from enlisted men of the army who have given positive evidence of marked capacity as leaders. In a series of three-month courses these schools will produce a minimum of 10,000 officers a year and are capable of rapid expansion if the situation demands.[5]

---

[2] Charles E. Kirkpatrick, "Omar Nelson Bradley," (Washington DC: U. S. Army, 1992) 5. Written in remembrance of the hundredth anniversary of Bradley's birth. Article found in the vault, Donovan Library, Fort Benning GA.

[3] Bradley, *A General's Life*, 97.

[4] "Benning OCS Program 30 Years Old," *Bayonet*, September 24 1971, 32.

[5] Gen. George C. Marshall, *Report on the Army*, July 1 1939, to June 30 1943 (Washington: The Infantry Journal, 1943) 27.   .

Marshall had been following Bradley's career since their earlier service together at Fort Benning. More than once, Marshall had turned to Bradley to fill a particular assignment, and Bradley had never let him down. That Bradley would become a headmaster for such a school should not have been surprising. He was the son of a Missouri teacher, and much of his military career had been spent as an instructor—including a stint as a mathematics professor at West Point.

Bradley graduated from West Point in 1915, finishing 44th in a class of 164. He played a year of football for the cadets and lettered three years in baseball, hitting a resounding .383 one season. After being commissioned a 2nd lieutenant, he was sent to Fort George Wright in Spokane, Washington. At Fort Wright, he fell under the tutelage of Edwin Forrest Harding, who held the same rank but was six years older. Harding—well known for his gift for words and writing—was a natural teacher. Few people influenced Bradley more than Harding, who convinced him that an officer should study at the beginning of his career and continue to study to master the profession. That advice served him well when Bradley first met Marshall, his future mentor.

At Benning, Bradley was an instructor, a job for which Marshall held great expectations, especially for a section head such as Bradley. Bradley told how he prepared for his first lecture: "I was so edgy at my first lecture that I cheated. I made several cards with subject matter headings in large letters and placed them on the floor at my feet!"[6] Such was the intimidation of Marshall whose cold demeanor followed Bradley and his career. But just as he had faced the rigors of West Point, Bradley the teacher flourished under the demands of Marshall.

Though he could not have known it at the time, he was finding a military home. He and Mary, his childhood sweetheart, melted into the day-to-day routine. Sara Spano was teaching third grade in the Fort Benning school, and Mary Bradley was the PTA room mother for her class that year. Spano's class was determined to win the monthly PTA attendance prize so they could buy a two-dollar fishbowl. For the first five months of the school year other classes won the prize, so Mary Bradley went to work. She urged the third grade families to be at the monthly meeting—including her own

---

[6] Bradley, *A General's Life*, 66.

husband. Captain Bradley showed up and helped the class get the money for the fishbowl.

"He was the only man present," Spano said. "He spent the whole afternoon with his six-foot frame doubled up in a kindergarten chair. That afternoon, surrounded by all those women, he was the most scared looking individual I ever saw. One word from anybody and he would have jumped through the window—bars and all."[7] But when Spano thanked him for attending, he did not receive her gratitude very kindly: "He brusquely informed me that if the third grade needed any more equipment to please consult him."[8]

When he reported for class in 1941, it was not third graders waiting to be taught, and the prize these young men would be fighting for would be much more than a fishbowl. Bradley was back at Benning to put together final plans for the OCS. Bradley soon developed a school that would serve as a model for similar schools throughout the army—ones that would turn out the thousands of lieutenants needed to lead the platoons for a US Army that eventually would be composed of eighty-nine divisions.

Explaining the success of the OCS plan, Bradley said: "All you do is, for example, a class comes in on Monday and one group of instructors would take them through the schedule one week at a time. We had a group in charge of each week, and at the end of that week they would turn over their students to the next group and pick up that class that entered one week later. All I had to do was get an extra group of instructors—I believe it took 106 for all twelve weeks of instruction. You would take in another class on Tuesday and start them through, and another one on Wednesday, and finally we were taking in five classes a week, each one with 1,200 students."[9]

In his brief tour as Benning's commander, Bradley also supported the new Airborne forces and the training of tank forces—including the 2nd Armored Division headed by is former colleague from Hawaii, George Patton. Following Marshall's style of leadership, Bradley developed a hands-off style of command and did not interfere as long as the officer performed

---

[7] Sara Spano, *I Could've Written Gone with the Wind, But Cousin Margaret Beat Me to It* (Ann Arbor: McNaughton & Gunn, Inc., 1990) 75.

[8] Ibid.

[9] "Omar Bradley," *Bayonet*, April 17 1981, 17.

well. But it was his establishment of the school for officers that was most memorable.

Marshall was attending the Louisiana maneuvers and was unable to deliver his address to the graduates of the first Officer Candidate School on September 27. Bradley expressed his regrets to Marshall: "All three groups of candidates will be assembled and your address will be read to them. Each candidate will also receive a copy."[10]

Marshall's address evoked a desire reminiscent of another former Fort Benning leader, General Paul Malone. It was the desire for the proper leadership to avoid American soldiers dying because of a commander's inability to command:

> You are about to assume the most important duty that our officers are called upon to perform—the direct command of combat units of American soldiers.... Modern battles are fought by platoon leaders...if you know your business of weapons and tactics, if you have inspired the complete confidence and loyalty of your men, things will go well on that section of the front.... Good luck to you. We expect great things of you. Your class is the first of which I believe will be the finest group of troop leaders in the world.[11]

Students for the Officer Candidate program arrived daily and with the expanded training of men in the parachute and tank units, life moved at a fast pace. Though everyone—citizen and soldier alike—kept an eye on events in Europe, there were other things to do. For Bradley, there was time to visit friends in Columbus, an occasional round of golf at the Country Club of Columbus, or the annual Georgia-Auburn football game at Memorial Stadium that November.

Like the players prepared for that football game, soldiers at Fort Benning prepared for war. It started at the top. With Bradley pushing them, instructors pushed the officer-candidates, but Bradley still did not take himself seriously. An oft-repeated legend about that period explained Bradley's enduring nickname as the "GI's General."

---

[10] George C. Marshall, *The Papers of George Catlett Marshall*, vol. 1, ed. Larry I. Bland (Baltimore: Johns Hopkins University Press, 1981) 622.

[11] George C. Marshall, *Selected Speeches and Statements of General of the Army George C. Marshall* (Washington: The Infantry Journal, 1945) 175–77.

A twenty-five-mile march was ordered and, naturally, it rained. As troops trudged along, red Georgia mud splattered over their ponchos, covering up rank. A private, complaining as privates will do, could not see the other soldier's stars.

"They ought to shoot the son-of-a-bitch that ordered this march," he said.

"Yeah," answered Bradley, "they ought to hang him."[12]

Ten weeks after the first OCS graduation, on a lazy Sunday afternoon, the Bradleys were busy on the grounds of Riverside when Pink and Betty Bull drove past. Seeing his old friends in the flower garden, Bull stopped. Walking over to Bradley, the logistics officer asked the general if he had heard about Pearl Harbor. Though he recognized that war was inevitable, news of the attack was a shock. "Like all Americans that day, I was stunned," Bradley wrote, "I immediately put on my uniform and hurried to post headquarters. My staff was already there, speaking in hushed, somber tones."[13]

Bradley ordered "Emergency Plan White" into effect. Designed by post planner Lieutenant Colonel Truman C. "Tubby" Thorson, it not only secured Fort Benning but also dispatched troops to guard key statewide facilities such as electrical generating plants, bridges, and dams. Though Bradley was confident espionage was unlikely, he went by the book and executed the emergency order. One thought reassured him: "When I finally got to bed and closed my eyes, I thought how lucky we were to have George Catlett Marshall as chief of staff. In just two and a half years in command, he had laid the necessary groundwork for us to go to war."[14]

OCS classes were in place. More than 100,000 candidates enrolled in the program between 1941 and 1947. Of that number, 67 percent graduated as 2nd lieutenants. In the two years following Bradley's departure, officer candidate courses became the Infantry School's major function. More than 1,000 new officers graduated each week, representing every corps area and foreign station in the army. Its peak was from September 28, 1942, to December 27, 1942. There were sixty-nine classes with 14,309 candidates

---

[12] "'Soldier's General' in Command When Hawaii Attack Launched," *Bayonet*, October 4 1968, 31.

[13] Bradley, *A General's Life*, 102.

[14] Ibid., 102–103.

and 12,569 graduates. Looking back, Bradley was pleased with the results: "I considered the founding of the Fort Benning OCS my greatest contribution to the mobilization effort."[15]

Having accomplished the job Marshall assigned him, Bradley was promoted to temporary major general and was given command of the 82nd Division in February 1942. The 82nd was activated at Camp Claiborne, a new post near Alexandria, Louisiana. Marshall again wanted Bradley "to get the job done" as division commander—"the epitome for an infantry officer"—of the first full-scaled Airborne division in the United States Army.[16]

The OCS was left in the capable hands of OCS Director Richard R. Coursey, and, at the request of Marshall, Bradley handpicked his successor as commandant of the Infantry School: Major General Levan Allen, a familiar figure on the post.

During the war years, Bradley was a key leader on many fronts. So were Eisenhower, his academy classmate, and Patton, his colorful but unusual colleague. And always there was Marshall, pulling the strings. Bradley would become army chief of staff and chairman of the joint chiefs of staffs. He also served as head of the Veterans Administration.

Bradley returned to Fort Benning many times over the years. He often came back to hunt quail with J. Ralph Richards and Leighton McPherson in Alabama or to enjoy a round of golf with Frank Lumpkin, Jr. He would serve the longest of any American soldier in history. Observers believe he will prove to be the country's last five-star general.

---

[15] Ibid., 97.
[16] Ibid., 102.

20.

Fighting with Real Bullets

When Japanese planes swooped down on Pearl Harbor, it shocked the world. At Fort Benning, once the anger subsided, the surprise attack was a confirmation of all they had been doing for two years. America, a nation now at war, would need soldiers trained to fight and that was the mission at an outpost where so many of the country's primary military leaders were gathered that Sunday in December. These were men future historians would write about and men who would lead this nation in war. Legends were not yet earned. Assignments were not as important as vision. Ranks were not as important as character.

Omar Bradley was there, commanding a post he referred to as home. So was George Patton, fresh off his swaggering march from Louisiana. Matthew Bunker Ridgway, on temporary duty with the War Department General Staff, heard of the attack during dinner at the Fort Benning's Officers' Club. Ridgway, a "Marshall man," once helped his mentor win a 1936 military exercise "by talking General Motors executives in Detroit into lending Marshall 200 brand-new trucks."[1]

"Gentleman Jim" Gavin—his nickname at Benning because of his perfectly polished brown jump boots and his glider patch—was a newly graduated paratrooper in town at a movie when the theatre owner stopped the film and announced the attack.

George C. Marshall was not there that Sunday in 1941, but his presence shrouded the post like a morning fog.

Another figure from Fort Benning's past was also absent on that fateful December 7th. Lieutenant General Walter Short, assistant commandant in 1936–1937, was commanding the Hawaiian Department during the attack

---

[1] Clay Blair, *Ridgway's Paratroopers: The American Airborne in World War II* (Garden City NY: Doubleday, 1985) 9.

on Pearl Harbor, helpless to do anything to defend the American ships, planes, and men lost that morning.

The months leading up to Pearl Harbor had been hectic around Fort Benning. Men were being dispersed and new ones were taking their place. In January, the Infantry School Service Command was activated, replacing the Infantry School Detachment—a unit whose history reflected that of the Infantry School, dating back to 1826. In February, the $1 million expansion of Lawson Field began. The airfield was busy and would get busier.

In May 1941, the Battle of Crete took place. A German airborne invasion, including 30,000 men and 500 transport aircraft, seized the Island of Crete. British forces evacuated by sea. The Germans, in spite of their victory, endured great losses. The bittersweet German success "contributed to the fact they never again made a major airborne assault."[2] A month later, Congress set up the Army Air Forces in response to Germany's aerial success.

Benning also reacted to the Crete invasion. By the end of May two steel jump towers were operating for parachute training, and by June, the Parachute School was placed on permanent basis. On July 1, the 502nd Parachute Battalion was activated under the command of Major George P. Howell, Jr., former executive officer of the 501st. It joined the 501st as part of the Provisional Parachute Group. Nine days later, the Parachute Section of the Infantry School was activated. With aerial invasions gaining importance, the units looked for ways to establish an identity, an esprit de corps. In 1941, when a paratrooper completed training, he received a certificate signed by Major William Miley. To visually identify these troops, Miley authorized his troops to wear jumping boots with their dress uniform.

Former paratrooper and author Gerald Devlin described the proper care for the boots: "These boots became known as the symbol of the paratroops. All paratroopers took great pride in their special boots, and they spent many hours spit-shining them to a high gloss from toe to heel."[3] Not only were the boots highly shined but also precisely laced with the "trousers properly bloused over the tops of the boots," as a former jumper recalls.

---

[2] Richard Holmes, *The World Atlas of Warfare* (New York: Viking Studio Books, 1988) 200.

[3] Gerard M. Devlin, *Paratrooper!* (New York: St. Martin's Press, 1979) 95.

Paratroopers called non-jumpers "legs" or "straight legs."[4] The boots were so special that paratroopers were insulted if anyone wore them "who had not paid their dues."[5] Miley also asked William P. Yarborough to create a parachute badge. The badge held "a bold parachute with strong eagle-like wings extending from the base of the parachute and curving upward to touch the canopy."[6] This badge became the paratroopers "wings." Yarborough, who earlier designed the boots, also came up with a two-piece jump suit with extra-large pockets on the jacket and on the sides of the trouser legs that was issued until 1945.

When the troopers were not jumping out of airplanes, they were partying; when they were partying, they were probably singing. Devlin reported "Beautiful Streamer" and "Blood on the Risers" were favorite hits.[7] In "Beautiful Streamer," the lyrics were the last words of a paratrooper who was praying hard that his parachute would open. The song, typical of gallows humor and its grim bravado, does not have a happy ending. "Blood on the Risers" was sung with feeling to the tune of "The Battle Hymn of the Republic." Its lyrics, according to Devlin, "were rather grisly and were also about a paratrooper whose parachute failed to open." The chorus was blunt and to the point: "Gory, gory what/ a helluva way to die,/ he ain't gonna jump no more!"[8]

By August, the 503rd Parachute Infantry Battalion was activated and then commanded by Major Robert F. Sink, a former member of the 501st. Enhancing Benning's Airborne program, Brigadier General William Lee recruited 172 men as jumpers from the 9th Infantry Division at Fort Bragg, North Carolina: "The response to Lee's effort was startling. More than 1,000 men, including officers, answered his call for volunteers."[9]

Gentleman Jim Gavin—formally known as Captain James M. Gavin—volunteered as a paratrooper in April. At the age of thirty-four, he reported for Parachute School at Benning and graduated that August. He

---

[4] Frank Mastin, Jr., "Paratroopers no place for jumpy," *Montgomery Advertiser*, June 6 1994, 2C.

[5] Ibid.

[6] Devlin, *Paratrooper!*, 93.

[7] Ibid.

[8] Ibid., 123–24.

[9] "Paratroops A Colorful Transition," (Columbus GA) *Sunday Ledger-Enquirer*, October 6 1968, 21.

recalled that after "being banged around a bit, I completed my training unscathed and as a young parachute captain reported to the 503rd Parachute Infantry as a company commander."[10] Soon he moved to Airborne headquarters, the Provisional Parachute group headed by Brigadier General William Lee.[11]

Gavin, who enlisted in the army at seventeen, won a competitive examination to West Point. His first sergeant, "Chief Williams," an American Indian "over six feet tall and hefty" told Gavin about the exam and wanted him to "go up and take a look at it."[12] Another soldier, Lieutenant Percy Black, "a born pedagogue," helped Gavin prepare.[13] Three years after graduating from West Point in 1929, Gavin was assigned as a student to the Infantry School: "At Fort Benning, Gavin at last found the army he was looking for, an army that was actively seeking new directions and had started on a course of self-improvement."[14]

"Vinegar Joe" Stilwell was still head of the tactical section when Gavin arrived in 1929. Gavin adopted an enduring philosophy from Stilwell, "a belief that the leader must be as tough as, if not tougher than, the troops he is trying to inspire."[15] Before coming to Benning to volunteer as a paratrooper, Gavin was a faculty member in the Department of Tactics at West Point. He was promoted to major in October. Gavin continued to train soldiers by writing his first book, a manual called *Tactics and Technique of Air-Borne Troops*. Written at the request of Lee, it was one of the "first textbooks on Airborne training and tactics."[16] Lee credits Gavin for being one of the "architects" of the parachute group and later the Airborne command.[17]

"Paratroopers," according to Gavin's biographers, T. Michael Booth and Duncan Spencer, "with their mystique of danger and ruthlessness,

---

[10] James Gavin, *On to Berlin* (New York: Bantam Books, 1978) 2.

[11] Ibid.

[12] T. Michael Booth and Duncan Spencer, *Paratrooper* (New York: Simon & Schuster, 1994) 38.

[13] Ibid., 39.

[14] Ibid., 54.

[15] Ibid., 55.

[16] William C. Lee, "Introduction," in Maj. Gen. James M. Gavin, *Airborne Warfare* (Washington: Infantry Journal Press, 1947) ix.

[17] Ibid.

became part of American folklore."[18] However, other Fort Benning units also felt "special." Friendly rivalries quickly developed. The 2nd Armored Division and the 4th Infantry Division (Motorized) tried to outdo each other in field maneuvers. Gavin also told of "run-ins" between the parachute groups with troops of the 2nd Armored commanded by George Patton: "Inevitably small collisions occurred in the bars and fleshpots of Phenix City, but many friendships were made, and later we were glad to see one another in Sicily."[19]

On October 10, the first Airborne infantry battalion, designated a glider infantry unit, was activated at Fort Benning. It was officially designated the 88th Infantry Airborne Battalion under the command of Lieutenant General E. G. Chapman. Officers of the command toured the east coast by airplane to contact men desiring this duty. Unloading heavy infantry equipment, often in dangerous circumstances, members of the 88th had to be quick and reliable. In May 1942, the battalion moved to Fort Bragg, North Carolina. Enlarged to 1,000 men, it was renamed the 88th Glider Infantry Regiment.

Still another big maneuver was held in November 1941 at the North Carolina maneuver area. Using blanks for ammunition, wielding wooden guns and toting bags of flour to use as bombs and grenades, soldiers had a dress rehearsal for World War II. The maneuver also offered a chance to gauge the performance of equipment that would be valuable when the shooting began. The 200,000 men of the 1st Army, commanded by Hugh Drum, overcame the 1st Armored Division, but the 2nd Armored Division, which also took "heavy losses," redeemed itself by capturing Drum.[20]

Reporting for Duty

When Fort Benning reported for duty on December 8, 1941, a new energy was evident. With one swift kick, the Japanese stepped up the post to wartime tempo. Dr. Cyril Floyd remembered it as a sudden jolt. A former engineering student at Auburn University, Floyd went on to medical school at Tulane University in New Orleans. He first served in the Medical Corps reserve. Working the CCC in Mississippi, he took care of the men, fished,

---

[18] Booth and Spencer, *Paratrooper*, 67.

[19] Gavin, *On to Berlin*, 5–6.

[20] Donald E. Houston, *Hell on Wheels* (San Rafael CA: Presidio Press, 1977) 97–98.

and made friends with the locals who urged him to run for sheriff. Floyd was promised that a clinic would be built for him if he would stay.

Coming to Benning in 1940, Floyd's schedule was more hectic than in the CCC. His day began with a 6 A.M. sick call for Company Officers' School and continued past 5 P.M. when he made house calls. Talking to foreign officers at Benning, Floyd grew familiar with their way of thought and life. "For I knew well and good that our involvement was just inevitable. But when it came, it was still a sudden, terrific jolt."[21]

Though Fort Benning was inhabited with men confident in their leadership and the tactics they would follow—men such as Bradley, Gavin, Stilwell, and Lee—thousands more were untried but equally ready. They too realized the deeper meaning of that unholy Sunday.

When the final practice session was over and a weary George Patton returned from maneuvers that November, he left his men a sobering message. It was appropriate for the young men stationed there as war finally began at the end of 1941.

"This is the last time you will fight with blank ammunition," he warned. "The next time we meet like this the bullets will be real."[22]

---

[21] Cyril Floyd, *Dr. Floyd's Journal: Memoirs of Dr. Cyril Floyd 1925–1941*, copy of unpublished, handwritten manuscript, accession no. 93-31, Auburn University Library Special Collections, Auburn AL.

[22] Houston, *Hell on Wheels*, 40.

21.

Diagnosis for Combat

Paratroopers Ready for Action

Sleep was out of the question. Men of the 505th Parachute Regiment were on the march. James Gavin was in command. He said march; they marched. Through the dense woods of Fort Benning, his men skillfully maneuvered and seized an airfield. Then they defended it from a counterattack while carrying full combat loads on their backs and living off reserve rations. Their training as full-fledged paratroopers was nearly over.

Benning's Parachute School, after two years of testing and experimenting, was detached from the Infantry School and activated as a separate unit on May 15, 1942. Colonel George P. Howell, Jr., was commandant. Officers and enlisted men from all eligible branches were qualified as parachutists in a four-week course: "Parachute trainees go through an intensive course of learning how to tumble, how to jump from the free and controlled towers, how to pack a chute, and how to run five miles with a full field pack. By the time they get around to the actual jump, falling out of a plane at 1,200 feet is practically child's play."[1]

In early July 1942, the 505th Parachute Infantry Regiment was activated. Gavin, its first commanding officer, described the unit's *esprit de corps*: "Its training program was just about as thorough and demanding as we could make it. The troopers responded well. However, despite the rigor of their training, they always seemed to have enough energy left to get into fights in Phenix city, Alabama, and its environs during time off."[2]

---

[1] "America's Most Colorful Post," *Fort Benning, Georgia, Pictorial Revue* (Columbus: Columbus Office Supply, 1942) 17, found in Special Collections, Auburn University Library, Auburn AL.

[2] James Gavin, *On to Berlin* (New York: Bantam Books, 1978) 4.

When a paratrooper from the 505th was mistreated at Phenix City's Cotton Fish Camp, his buddies tried "to take over the place."[3] Authorities arrested the troopers and jailed them overnight in the post guardhouse. Obtaining their release the next day, Gavin "marched them back to camp and took the entire regiment on an all-night march down through the canebrakes in the bottoms of the Chattahoochee River."[4] When Gavin's troops returned to camp that Sunday evening, many were still ready for action: "Later in the evening I noted quite a few of them in dress uniforms, wearing polished boots on their way to the bus stop to go to Phenix City. Some time later one of them drew a sketch of a campaign ribbon for the battle of Cotton Fish Camp."[5]

Gavin knew his men were ready for action when the 505th joined the 82nd Airborne Division at Fort Bragg, North Carolina. By April 1943, they were off to North Africa.

Lowering the Draft

The army doors continued to revolve. In 1942, men between the ages of thirty-five and forty were being drafted. Chief of Staff George C. Marshall realized men that age "however willing had not the resistance or stamina for this lightning war."[6] Marshall appeared before the Military Affairs committees of the house and Senate to ask Congress to lower the draft age to eighteen—an unpopular proposal politically and emotionally. When the bill was finally passed, Marshall received a short note from President Roosevelt saying, "Dear George: You win again. F. D. R."[7]

Benning Alumni Lead the Way

While draftees and enlisted men were trained, experienced units were reassigned. As the men of the 505th were leaving Fort Benning, other units were arriving; and Benning alumni were in leadership positions on every front. Dwight D. Eisenhower was Allied commander for the invasion of

---

[3] Ibid.

[4] Ibid.

[5] Ibid.

[6] Katherine Tupper Marshall, *Together: Annals of an Army Wife* (New York: Tupper and Love, Inc., 1946) 126–27.

[7] Ibid.

North Africa. Alexander Patch was in the Pacific. Forrest Harding commanded the 32nd Infantry. Courtney Hodges was commander of X Corps. Matthew Ridgway was commander of the 82nd Airborne. Joseph Stilwell commanded US forces in the China-Burma-India Theater. Bedell Smith was chief of staff in the European Theater. George Patton was preparing for the invasion of Sicily.

A review of the post later said, "The battlefields of North Africa were the proving grounds of principles that had been advocated at the Infantry School. For that matter, the course in mobilization and training, taught long before the draft, was of inestimable help in the orderly processing of civilians into soldiers, soldiers who could fight under any type of conditions on all type of terrain."[8] Historian Geoffrey Perret confirmed this readiness: "By 1942 the infantrymen of a triangular division were well armed...they had more firepower in their own hands than infantry anywhere else in the world."[9]

On a lighter note, it was announced all post soldiers would be issued khaki underwear since white underwear "were a danger on the battlefield because they could be easily seen by enemy bombers when hung out to dry in combat Zones."[10]

War Department Reorganization

Important changes were made when troop buildup led to a reorganization of the War Department and the army in 1942. Two central training headquarters were established: Army Ground Force and the Army Air Force. Lieutenant General Lesley J. McNair, commander of Army Ground Forces, ordered the formation of the Airborne Command at Fort Benning, naming Colonel William C. Lee as commander. Lee, commander of the Provisional Parachute Group since its inception at Fort Benning, now led all parachute units, plus the 88th Infantry Airborne Battalion.

On April 9, 1942, the Airborne Command moved to Fort Bragg, North Carolina. The Parachute School remained at Benning to continue its mission of training "fillers" for parachute battalions. As Devlin explained,

---

[8] "The School Came to Benning: 1937," *Benning Herald*, October 1949, 43.

[9] Geoffrey Perret, *There's a War to Be Won* (New York: Random House, 1991) 85.

[10] Richard Brill, "Fort Benning in the 1940s," *Bayonet*, October 8 1993, B-5.

"Under this arrangement, separate parachute battalions would be formed and jump-trained at Benning. The battalions would then be shipped to Bragg for tactical training and testing by the Airborne Command."[11]

In July 1943, Allied Forces invaded Sicily. Patton's 7th Army and British Field Marshal Bernard Law Montgomery's 8th Army led the way. The 82nd Airborne Division also played an important role. Lee, father of the Airborne, described emotions "old timers" experienced upon hearing the news: "There was not a man of the pioneer group whose heart did not swell with the fiercest pride in the realization of a dream come true...unsung pioneers who blazed the early trails from the skies to the red clay hills of Georgia and the sand hills of North Carolina deserve at the very least a modest tribute."[12] Although Italian troops surrendered unconditionally on September 8, 1943, German troops fought on in the Battle of Salerno.

Longtime Regiments Leave Post

With the ongoing shift of manpower in 1942 and 1943, two dramatic changes occurred: the departure of the 24th Infantry Regiment in April 1942 and that of the 29th Infantry in May 1943. Each marked the end of an era at Fort Benning. In April 1942, the 24th was the first black infantry regiment sent overseas. After twenty years at Fort Benning, the regiment arrived in the South Pacific in May, serving on a number of Pacific islands.

In May 1943, the 29th Infantry was relieved from the post and moved to Fort Jackson, South Carolina, a port of embarkation for overseas duty. It was assigned to the 2nd Army and attached to the 12th Corps during World War II. The unit's motto, "We Lead the Way," found credence when the unit was fully trained and prepared, distinguished as the only war-ready regiment in the army. Its troops provided the first paratroopers in the US Army and helped fill the ranks of the 2nd Armored Division. On May 4, 1943, the 176th Infantry Regiment occupied the cuartel, barracks located in the heart of Fort Benning formerly occupied by units of the 29th as early as 1925. In October, the 131st Infantry arrived to serve as the school's demonstration unit.

---

[11] Gerard M. Devlin, *Paratrooper!* (New York: St. Martin's Press, 1979) 115.

[12] William C. Lee, "Introduction," in Major General James M. Gavin, *Airborne Warfare* (Washington: Infantry Journal Press, 1947) viii.

Visitors Relieve Post's Isolation

With the condemnation of adjoining acres of civilian property, Fort Benning grew to more than 200,000 acres to support 90,000 troops and 8,000 civilian workers. In 1942, Fort Benning was designated a prohibited zone by the Eastern Defense Command. All post civilians age twelve and over were required to have permits and identification cards to enter the post. This security fostered the post's isolation from the town. With gas rationing, few local people could afford the fuel to make a trip to the post even if invited.

The post became more isolated, but it was not entirely cut off from the outside world. Artist Norman Rockwell spent time there in early 1943, capturing military life with his talented pen for the readers of the *Saturday Evening Post*. Concert violinist Jascha Heifetz appeared at the Main Post Theater in March while the legendary Bob Hope and his troupe of radio regulars, including singer Frances Langford and comedian Jerry Colona, made frequent visits.[13]

Other visitors came too. President Roosevelt came calling and so did General Marshall. With Marshall were British Foreign Secretary (later Prime Minister) Anthony Eden and Field Marshall John Dill, who visited the post in 1942. While viewing the 10th Armored Division, commanded by Major General Paul W. Newgarden, Eden left the group and jumped up onto a training platform and began questioning private William McHugh, a student from Detroit, Michigan: "Afterwards, McHugh was so excited that he had difficulty in spelling his name for the visiting cameramen."[14]

While at Benning, Eden spoke to 200 officer candidates: "I want you to know that you should be proud because you are training to lead American soldiers. There is no higher or bigger job. Our folks at home in England are with you. We're proud to be with you and will see the war through to victory."[15]

During his visit, Marshall asked to see Master Sergeant Thomas Tweed, a veteran game warden, who lived on the post with his wife, Lillian Luise. Tweed joined the army in 1915 and was at Camp Benning with the

---

[13] "Post to See Bob Hope Show," *Bayonet*, April 8 1943, 1.

[14] "Anthony Eden, General Marshall, Sir John Dill Tour Fort Benning," *Bayonet*, March 25 1943, 1.

[15] Ibid.

29th Infantry in 1919. Friends since Marshall's arrival at Fort Benning in 1926, the two men again found time to hunt together. Two of Tweed's sons were in the army, one in training, and one at war. When Marshall was ready to leave on his plane, Tweed presented him with a wild turkey.

More than dignitaries came to the post. The enemy also came to Fort Benning in the person of captured Italian soldiers. In July 1943, the Italian Prisoner of War Camp was established with Colonel George M. Chescheir serving as commander. The prisoners helped farmers in the local area during the day, harvesting peanuts and cotton. Some of the farmers they helped had sons overseas. The Italian prisoners also organized an orchestra with the help of Chaplain Roderick McEachen, who appealed to Chescheir to allow the men this recreation.

Skilled Italian prisoners helped rebuild the chapel Private Stadnik constructed in the 1920s in gratitude for his recovery from a serious illness. The cathedral had three carved towers, four to six feet tall. The chapel was large enough for one man to enter and kneel at a hewn altar. The shrine was dedicated to Saint Hubert, patron saint of horsemen, and to former members of Fort Benning's military riding classes who died in battle.

Recognizing Leadership

As the need for officers spread around the world, key leaders were kept on the move. On September 30, 1943, Major General Charles H. Bonesteel, former commanding officer of the United Nations forces in Iceland, succeeded Infantry School Commandant Major General Leven Allen, who took a command in Europe.

Past post leaders were in the news as 1943 ended. After directing Allied invasions of Sicily and Italy, Dwight D. Eisenhower returned to England in November to resume planning for the invasion of France. On December 24, he received a unique Christmas present: he was named supreme commander of Allied Forces for the invasion of Europe. However, *Time* magazine picked General George C. Marshall—not Ike—as its "Man of the Year" for 1943: "The American people do not, as a general rule, like or trust the military. But they like and trust George Marshall."[16]

---

[16] "The General," *Time* 43/1 (January 3 1944): 16–18.

Marshall, with forty-two years of service from lieutenant to general, was credited with rebuilding the army, providing necessary training, and refusing "to send out green and half-equipped troops...."[17] Marshall was not chosen supreme commander because F. D. R. and the US needed Marshall at home: "He was the one and only citizen who could get a unanimous vote of confidence from Congress."[18] Marshall "had armed the Republic...kept faith with the people...and gained the world's undivided respect.... In the name of soldiers who had died, General Catlett Marshall was entitled to accept his own nation's gratitude."[19]

---

[17] Ibid.
[18] Ibid.
[19] Ibid.

22.

War and Duty

Ourselves—
The infantry.
We, who do all the dying.
Yes, it's the infantry always that does all the dying.
The poor bloody infantry.
—Conrad Aiken
"The Soldier," 1944[1]

To some, it was the last good war, fought by men who were part of what newsman Tom Brokaw would one day describe as the greatest generation. Duty was clear. So was purpose. There was right and there was wrong, but it was still war, and as Georgia poet Conrad Aiken noted, in war men do die.

Reminders of war were everywhere: in telegrams from the War Department that made knocks on the door fearful, in newspaper reports, in fallen friends and family members, and even in the daily training of young soldiers who soon would be frontline replacements. More than 500,000 soldiers passed through Fort Benning on their way to war. More than 50,000 men enrolled in Officer Candidate School, and nearly 200,000 students were trained at the Infantry School and Parachute School.[2]

Trainees who were unable to read or write English at a fourth-grade level or who got Grade V on the Army General Classification Test were assigned to Fort Benning's Special Training Unit. The unit graduated over 20,000 men in 1943–44. The trainees, however, were not sent to normal

---

[1] Conrad Aiken, "IV: The Wars," *The Soldier* (Norfolk CT: New Directions, 1944) 23.

[2] "Fort Benning," *Army and Navy Register*, October 28 1944, 1.

army assignments "until they developed the required proficiency to undertake a regular course in training."[3]

The challenges of running a training center and a community were great. General William H. Hobson, the post commander, had 500 staff officers. However, civilians helped make it work. Hobson explained the importance of civilians: "Civilians play the major role in the operation of our shops, our offices, our hospitals, our laundries, our stores and shops, our signal system, our fire system, our warehousing, our utilities, and our transportation. It would be hopeless for us to try operating without them."[4] Civilians equaled two regiments in size with a payroll of nearly $7,000,000. Nearly one-third of them were women, and half of those were military wives.[5]

With every major campaign came lists of casualties. By the end of the war, the US Army lost 234,874 men while 565,861 were wounded. Too often, Columbus folks saw familiar names on these lists. No home was immune, from the home of retail clerks to the homes of army generals. People of Columbus devoured military news since it was not only their sons and daughters who were serving but also the adopted sons and daughters they had come to know through Fort Benning. Almost daily, headlines traced the exploits of young men who passed through on their way to battle.

There were thousands like Jesse P. Sweat of Columbus. Sweat was the former manager of the drapery and curtain department at Kirven's, the popular department store in downtown Columbus. Sweat was killed in Belgium on September 10, 1944. Day after day, throughout the war, local newspapers printed names such as his. He was a soldier, but at home he was the boy who used to play ball in the front yard or cut the grass on hot Columbus afternoons.

The McCorkles of nearby Buena Vista were one of the thousands of grieving families. Within three months, Mr. and Mrs. William Andrew McCorkle lost two sons—Eugene in the Pacific, Pruitt on the beaches of Normandy. Eugene was a marine who fought at Iwo Jima and was killed April 1 while trying to rescue a wounded buddy. Pruitt, a member of the 2nd

---

[3] Ibid., 2.
[4] Ibid.
[5] Ibid.

Ranger Battalion, died on June 8. An escort from Fort Benning and a lone bugler were in the memorial for the two sons on Father's Day 1944.

That August, General Alexander "Sandy" Patch successfully led the US 7th Army in the invasion of southern France. Friends in Georgia celebrated his success as they did other Benning alumni. But on October 24, a headline in the *Columbus Ledger* delivered news of another kind involving that family: "Mac Patch Buried Near Dad's Army... Columbus knew him well."[6]

The article told how the young soldier died: "Captain Alexander M. Patch, Jr., only son of the Lieutenant General commanding the Seventh army was buried in the American Cemetery behind the southern sector of the western front where his father's forces are fighting. The twenty-four-year-old company commander was killed by a direct hit from a German 75 mm antitank gun while leading an attack in the Vonges hills. Patch had been treated for wounds previously."[7]

A graduate of West Point, Patch attended Columbus schools when his father (who died a year after Mac's death), then a major, was stationed at Fort Benning. Mac Patch and his wife, Virginia Spalding, attended classes together at Columbus High School. Returning to Columbus in spring of 1943, Patch lived in Benning Hills with his wife and son until he went overseas.

Tragic news also reached the home of Katherine and George Marshall in Washington. On May 29, 1944, Katherine Marshall's son 2nd Lieutenant Allen Tupper Brown died in a tank battle on the road to Rome. Allied forces entered the legendary city six days later. Brown was awarded the Bronze Star. Surviving was his wife and two-year-old son, Tupper. Allen, the youngest of Katherine's three children, had sent her an Easter letter days before his death: "God did make beautiful things when he made Mothers."[8]

With news of casualties came news of heroic deeds, including those of two graduates of Fort Benning who were awarded the Medal of Honor. Paul B. Huff of Cleveland, Tennessee, who earned his boots and wings in jump school, was the first American paratrooper awarded the Medal of Honor.[9]

---

[6] "Mac Patch Buried Near Dad's Army," *Columbus Ledger*, October 24 1944, 1.

[7] Ibid.

[8] Katherine Tupper Marshall, *Together: Annals of an Army Wife* (New York: Tupper and Love, 1946) 191.

[9] Gerard M. Devlin, *Paratrooper!* (New York: St. Martin's Press, 1979) 350.

On December 14, Robert P. Nett, a graduate of Officer Candidate School, led an attack with rifle and bayonet against protected Japanese troops while fighting in the Philippines. The Medal of Honor recipient, though severely wounded, "provided an inspiring example for his men" while capturing an enemy stronghold.[10]

Huff, a corporal with the 509th Parachute Infantry Battalion, led a six-man patrol near Carano, Italy, in full view of the enemy. Attacked by machine gun fire and small arms, Huff went alone through a minefield, killed the German crew with his submachine gun, and destroyed all the guns. He purposely took tank fire from another enemy company in order to spot its location. Huff then returned to this patrol and led them to safety. Later his patrol found the enemy company, killed twenty-seven Germans, and captured twenty-one with a loss of only three of Huff's patrol members.

Nett killed seven of the enemy, and though wounded, led the attack until the objective was reached. He then walked back to the rear, unaided, to seek medical treatment. After retiring in Columbus as a colonel, Nett recalled, "I was so relieved after all the combat, I was just grateful to lead a normal life and leave all this behind me."[11] Nearly sixty years later, Nett frequently speaks to graduates of the OCS program in which he earned his bars.

John Eisenhower Visits Dad in England

As supreme commander of the Allied Expeditionary Force, General Dwight D. Eisenhower oversaw the D-Day landing on June 6, "the largest amphibious operation in the history of warfare," and planned the attacks that led to eventual surrender of Germany about a year later.[12] The order to his troops on D-Day gave this reminder. "The eyes of the world are upon you. The hopes and prayers of liberty-loving people everywhere march with you."[13]

---

[10] "Georgia Valor," Georgia Public Broadcasting, http://www.gpb.org/programs/valor/rnett.htm (accessed May 20 2007).

[11] "Filipinos re-enact the return of MacArthur to Philippines," (Raleigh NC) *News & Observer*, October 21 1994.

[12] Stephen E. Ambrose, *Eisenhower*, vol. 1 (New York: Simon and Schuster, 1983) 361–62.

[13] Ibid.

Shortly after D-Day, John Eisenhower, the general's son, reported to Fort Benning just as his father had. After graduating from West Point on June 9, Marshall arranged for the second lieutenant to spend his two-week graduation leave in England with his father, whom he had last seen in 1942.

In early 1945, the 71st Infantry Division, John Eisenhower's unit, received orders to deploy to Europe. The young Eisenhower would serve as a rifle platoon leader. Aware that General Patch was devastated by the death of his son, General Omar Bradley was opposed to Ike's son serving in "so risky a slot." He believed "if John were killed, the psychological impact on Ike might seriously jeopardize our operations." Bradley also feared Nazi propaganda if John were captured. To avoid these issues, Bradley said that, "Ike and I had arranged that John would be assigned to me as a staff officer."[14]

Fort Benning Generals Advance

On September 8, Lieutenant General George S. Patton's 3rd Army unit, XX Corps, led by Walton Walker, crossed the Moselle River, followed by five battalions the following day.[15] On September 12, the US 1st Army, commanded by former Benning commandant Courtney Hodges, engaged in fighting hostile troops and citizens on German soil. Patton continued "pushing to support Hodges" on Hodges's drive to Cologne and Bonn to attack the Ruhr.[16]

Stilwell Ends China-Burma Command

In October, General Joseph W. Stilwell, a military favorite in Columbus, was taken from his China-Burma command for a new assignment. Stilwell served his second tour at Benning as chief of the Tactics Department, 1929 to 1932, and was active in the community. He and his wife had five children. His son, Joseph Jr., attended Fort Benning schools, graduated from West Point, and was stationed at the post as a second lieutenant.

---

[14] Omar Bradley, with collaborator Clay Blair, *A General's Life* (New York: Simon and Schuster, 1983) 396–97.

[15] George S. Patton, *The Patton Papers* (1940–1945), ed. Martin Blumenson (Boston: Houghton Mifflin Co., 1974) 546.

[16] Ibid., 550.

While attending social events at Fort Benning and Columbus during 1933 and 1934, Joseph Stilwell, Jr., met Mira MacPherson. Her parents, Postmaster and Mrs. Leighton MacPherson, were friends of General and Mrs. George Marshall and of President and Mrs. Franklin Roosevelt. After their marriage in Columbus in 1935, Joseph Stilwell, Jr., was assigned to the 15th Infantry Regiment in Tientsin, China, for a three-year tour. His father, "Vinegar Joe" Stilwell, who left Benning in 1932, was promoted to colonel and was made military attaché in China, living in Beijing when his son and his bride were "at home" in China.

In 1942, Stilwell led American forces in China and commanded the Chinese V and VI Army Corps. When Burma lost to Japan, Stilwell walked 140 miles with his soldiers to India. There, he began the Ledo Road from India to the Burma Road. Chiang Kai Shek later named the Ledo Road the Stilwell Road. Engineer General Lewis A. Pick, Sr., from Auburn, Alabama, completed the road, which was called "one of the great engineering feats in World War II."[17] Stilwell directed the gasoline pipeline laid next to the road, providing needed fuel for US planes. The road, costing $37,000,000, closed November 1, 1945.

World War II Officer Commands Post

Also important was the appointment of Major General Fred L. Walker. In July, he became the first combat officer of World War II to lead the Infantry School. General William H. Hobson remained post commander. Walker, who commanded the 36th Infantry Division in fierce battles from Salerno to Rome, "made one of the toughest amphibious landings of the war—under the fire of the enemy's guns at Salerno."

Interviewed in Columbus, Walker said, "Our soldiers are more cheerful, more confident, and better marksmen.... I feel confident they are capable of being made into the best soldiers in the world."[18] Walker was a student at the Infantry School in 1923 and graduated from the officers' advanced course. His son, Colonel Fred L. Walker, Jr., was an instructor at Benning in 1944. His other son, 1st Lieutenant Charles Walker, was in Italy.

---

[17] "Stilwell Road," *World Book Encyclopedia*, vol. 17 (Chicago: Field Enterprises Educational Corporation, 1963) 702.

[18] Ibid.

Holding down the Fort

While their peers were at the front, their counterparts at Fort Benning were also busy. Milestones were also being recorded at Fort Benning. On September 15, Angus J. McIntosh became the 50,000th graduate of the officer candidate course at Fort Benning. To celebrate, Lieutenant General Ben Lear, commanding general of the Army Ground Forces, attended the ceremony.

Also in September, award-winning movie actress Bette Davis visited her boyfriend, Corporal Louis A. Riley, creating a stir at the 1944 Georgia-Auburn football game. The Hollywood star, who stayed at a private home in Phenix City, denied being married to Riley. She had her sister buy a cake at Federal Bakery in Columbus to give to her boyfriend's company.

In November, Frank Lumpkin wrote Manfred Eddy, scion of the famous Eddy insurance family, to invite him to his Georgia-Auburn luncheon party. It was a playful letter as Lumpkin was very aware of the general's whereabouts. Eddy, married to a Columbus woman, received the Distinguished Service Medal for his leadership in the 9th Infantry Division's action in Chersbourg where his men captured several Nazi generals. Eddy's reply arrived in mid-December. He wrote Lumpkin that he would like to have attended but "we were playing quite a little game with Germans, and still are."[19]

It was a bloody game that thankfully was about to end.

---

[19] Manton Eddy to Frank G. Lumpkin, December 18 1944, in Lumpkin's personal files, Willcox-Lumpkin Company, Columbus GA.

23.

Benning and the Bomb

Paul Tibbets III was old enough to know but not old enough to understand. He was four years old but wanted to be older. He needed to be, for he was the man of the house on Francis Street in Columbus.

His daddy, Paul Tibbets, Jr., was away fighting the war as a lot of daddies were in 1945. Paul III didn't know the grown-up at their house who was talking with his mother. The man said he worked for the newspaper, that he wrote stories. He asked the little boy a question, and little Paul gave him an answer more profound than the pre-schooler could grasp. The reporter asked young Paul when his father would be home. "Daddy has dropped his bomb," the boy said. "Now I guess he'll be home tomorrow, won't he, Mother?"[1]

Colonel Paul Tibbets, Jr., would not be home the next day. There was still work to do. But because of his mission, thousands of other Americans would come home. He was, to so many people of that generation, the man who won the war. Flying the *Enola Gay*—a B-29 flying fortress named for the little fellow's grandmother—Paul Tibbets, Jr., delivered the world's first atomic bomb on August 6, 1945, less than a month after he had flown into Lawson Army Airfield to visit Lucy and their two boys. Eight days after Tibbets and his crew dropped the bomb on Hiroshima followed by another American crew doing the same to Nagasaki on August 9, President Harry Truman announced the surrender of Japan.

War was over. Peace was at hand.

When stationed at Lawson Airfield before the war, Tibbets met and married Columbus native Lucy Wingate. Attached to Flight B 16th Observation Squadron, it was his first assignment as an army aviator.

---

[1] "Family of 'Atomic Pilot' Thrilled by Jap Offer," *Columbus Ledger*, August 10 1945, 9.

Tibbets was there from 1938 until April 1941 when he was sent to Hunter Field in Savannah.

Born in Quincy, Illinois, in 1915, he first felt the lure of the sky at the age of twelve in Miami, Florida. A barnstorming pilot was hired to drop Baby Ruth candy bars over the racetrack at Hialeah. Tibbets tied tiny parachutes to the candy bars and went up with the pilot to drop the candy out of the plane. Right then, he knew what he wanted to do with his life. He had to fly.

After two years in pre-med studies in Florida and Ohio, Tibbets joined the Army Air Corps in 1937. He came to Fort Benning from Kelly Field in Texas. A shotgun enthusiast, Tibbets soon made friends with Colonel George Patton. The two spent hours together at the skeet range where Patton would get furious when he lost bets to the cocky young lieutenant. Tibbets soon became Patton's personal pilot, flying him to maneuvers all over the region.[2]

After Pearl Harbor, Tibbets took part in the North African and European campaigns. He received the Distinguished Flying Cross with cluster (a cluster represents an additional award of that particular medal), the Air Medal with three clusters, and the Purple Heart. In 1942, he flew the first daylight bombing run over Germany. He piloted Dwight D. Eisenhower and Mark Clark. With his reputation as a pilot spreading, it was no accident that a year later, General Jimmie Doolittle sent Tibbets back to the US to train on the new B29, an aircraft known as the Flying Fortress. It was a massive plane with four 2,200-horsepower engines.

When President Franklin D. Roosevelt died April 12, 1945, the decision of whether to use this deadly device was left to President Harry Truman. The war in Europe had ended in May and American military leaders were cautious about a full-scale invasion of Japan. The A-bomb was seen as a way to spare the blood of thousands of American troops as well the blood of enemy civilians.

Tibbets was at the controls on August 6 with a well-trained crew of eleven—only three of whom knew what they were carrying. The B-29 that carried the bomb he dubbed the *Enola Gay*, named for his mother, the former Enola Gay Haggard. Taking off from Tinian, an obscure island in the Pacific Ocean, he flew a 2,000-mile journey that took six tedious hours.

---

[2] "Paul Tibbets," http://www.acepilots.com/usaf_tibbets.html.

Also on board were twelve cyanide pills the crew would take rather than be captured by the Japanese.

The plan was to be over the city at 8:15 A.M. The load was dropped on Hiroshima at 8:15 A.M., plus seventeen seconds. "The city was hidden by that awful cloud...boiling up, mushrooming, terrible and incredibly tall," Tibbets recalled.[3]

That mission brought the reporter to the Wingate's house on Francis Street in August 1945. Paul Tibbets, Jr., was front-page news in Columbus and around the world. He was awarded the Distinguished Service Cross when he stepped out of his B-29 in Guam. Now Lucy Tibbets, holding sixteen-month-old Gene on her lap, was posing for newspaper photographs herself with her other son at her knee.

The *Columbus Enquirer* reporter who wrote the article, was Jesse Helms—years before he became a stalwart in the United States Senate. In 1945, the North Carolina native was a naval recruiting officer in Columbus by day and the sports editor of the *Enquirer* at night. He not only reported on the Tibbets, he also rendered a colorful account of V-E Day in Columbus.

Mrs. Tibbets was bewildered, Helms wrote.

"He's the one who deserves the publicity," she said repeatedly, referring to her secretive husband. When Helms asked Paul III about the event, the little guy said, "I'm gonna bust these picture bulbs."[4]

Many of his peers considered Paul Tibbets, Jr., to be the man who ended the war. Men weary from campaigns in Europe faced an uncertain battlefield in Japan. Had the allies invaded, it would have been a bloodbath. The A-bombs led to an early surrender of Japan. Yet Tibbets or the crew of the *Enola Gay* received no ticker-tape parades or testimonial dinners. He had done a job and he came home. Tibbets did receive one invitation to the White House right after the war. President Truman was his host.

"We met in an irregular-shaped room," Tibbets said. "I suppose it was the Oval Office. It was short and quick. He offered me some coffee."[5] As

---

[3] "Hiroshima/Nagasaki," *Dothan Eagle*, August 6 1995, 8-A.

[4] Jesse Helms, "Columbus Woman's Husband Flies First Plane to Drop Atomic Bomb," *Columbus Enquirer*, August 8 1945, 1.

[5] Bob Greene, *Duty: A Father, His Son, and the Man Who Won the War* (New York: Harper Collins, 2000) 21.

they chatted, Truman asked the pilot if anyone was giving him a hard time—saying unpleasant things to him because of the bomb and the hundreds of thousands of deaths it caused.

"I said, 'Oh, once in a while.'"

Truman said, "You tell them that if they have anything to say, they should call me. I'm the one who sent you."[6]

Over the years, Paul III distanced himself from his father. But Tibbets's grandson, Paul IV, is an air force pilot. Retiring as a brigadier general in 1966, Paul Tibbets, Jr., chose to live in Columbus, Ohio. In many ways, he is a symbol of the nuclear age.

In *Duty: A Father, His Son, and the Man Who Won the War*, a 2000 book by *Chicago Tribune* newspaper columnist Bob Greene, Tibbets talked about the emotions he carries and the answer he gives if someone asks why he did not say no when he was ordered to drop the bomb: "'That's when I really know that they don't understand. It's usually younger people who say that to me. Because in those days—during World War II—you didn't tell your superiors that you didn't want to do something. That's reason number one. Reason number two is more important. The reason I didn't tell them that I didn't want to do it is that I wanted to do it.'"[7]

---

[6] Ibid.
[7] Ibid., 19.

24.

Good and Over

In a red school building in a small French village, Lieutenant General Walter Bedell Smith signed his name for himself, his superiors, his army, and his country. With a swipe of his pen, peace came to Europe.

It was May 7, 1945. Germany had surrendered. May 8th was designated the official V-E Day, a day that happily coincided with President Harry Truman's sixty-first birthday. Smith—remembered as Omar Bradley's "discovery" at Fort Benning's Infantry School in 1930—was serving as Dwight D. Eisenhower's chief of staff. He represented the Allies in that schoolhouse in Reims.

The world had waited for that day. But there was still Japan. With that in mind, Mayor Sterling Albrecht said Columbus would observe rather than celebrate the peace in Europe: "This is not a time for great rejoicing, as the war is only half through."[1]

When President Truman announced the Japanese surrender on August 14, there was no holding back the celebration at Fort Benning and Columbus. Soldiers came to town to celebrate. With restrictions lifted, thousands got free transportation on the Howard Bus Line. Reporter Virginia Bailey described the scene downtown: "Soldiers on Broadway offered their dog tags for sale at exorbitant prices. Automobile and bus horns tooted loud and long—even cowbells were resurrected and clanged away. Trumpets blared—firecrackers exploded—blank pistols were discharged. Waves of confetti drifted through the air like rice at a wedding. This was the biggest news that ever came to Columbus, and the town let its hair down."[2]

---

[1] "Columbus Is Ready To Observe V-E Day," *Columbus Enquirer*, May 8 1945, 1.

[2] Virginia Bailey, "Columbus Lifts Lid in Big Celebration," *Columbus Enquirer*, August 15 1945, 1.

To celebrate victory, on the day after the surrender, the Muscogee County Commission renamed the boulevard extending from town to Fort Benning as Victory Drive. Commissioner L. R. Aldridge made the motion, and it passed unanimously. "No time could be more appropriate than the day following the night when we know victory is ours," he said.[3] On post General Hobson responded to the gesture: "We believe that so designating the highway as 'Victory Drive' will be long-lived testimonial to the men and women of Georgia, and the men and women who have trained at Fort Benning during World War II, for their contributions to Victory."[4]

It was a year of shifting emotions. On April 12, President Franklin D. Roosevelt died in his fourth term of office, less than a month before the war ended in Europe and only four months before the end of the war in the Pacific. He died at the Little White House in Warm Springs, hardly an hour from the post. Fort Benning soldiers formed an honor guard and marched in his funeral procession to the Warm Spring train station where his casket was draped with a flag brought by the soldiers, thus replacing the flag taken from the flagpole in front of the Little White House.[5] The train carrying his body left Warm Springs for the White House in Washington DC. Katherine Marshall, who was present there, reported, "The casket had no flowers; it was covered only by a United States flag."[6]

Hitler hoped Roosevelt's death would cause dissension, but Vice President Harry Truman, a former US Senator from Missouri, proved a worthy successor. With George Marshall's continued guidance, the allied commitment remained strong. On April 30, Hitler committed suicide with his mistress Eva Braun. Joseph Goebbels, propaganda leader of the Nazi party, poisoned himself and his family on May 2. Earlier, on April 28, Italian Dictator Benito Mussolini was tried by members of the Italian underground, who then shot Mussolini and his mistress, Clara Petacci, hanging their bodies by the heels in front of a garage in Milan.

---

[3] "Hobson Praises Naming Highway 'Victory Drive,'" *Columbus Ledger*, August 20 1945, 2.

[4] Ibid.

[5] Author's personal communication with Roosevelt State Park Ranger and Little White House guide, April 2007.

[6] Katherine Tupper Marshall, *Together: Annals of an Army Wife* (New York: Tupper and Love, Inc., 1946) 244.

On September 2, General Douglas MacArthur presided over the Japanese surrender. Benning was well represented on the *USS Missouri* with General Joseph Stilwell, former head of tactics at the Infantry School, and General Courtney Hodges, a former Fort Benning Commandant.[7]

In July 1945, Major General John W. O'Daniel succeeded General Fred Walker as Infantry School commandant. O'Daniel, who enlisted in the National Guard in 1916, attended the Infantry School in 1927 and in 1941 commanded a battalion of the 24th Infantry at Fort Benning. In World War II, O'Daniel led the 3rd Infantry Division in battle from southern France to Germany, capturing Nuremberg, Augsburg, and Munich. He earned the nickname "Iron Mike" for his unfaltering leadership. In Columbus, he recalled a war story about the French invasion, telling of one battalion of the infantry arriving during the night at one end of a French town while at the other end a company of Germans rode in on bicycles. "Next morning our men were riding bicycles," the general said.[8]

Fort Benning had much to celebrate. Men trained there helped gain a hard-fought victory. One of those was Captain Robert "Bobbie" Brown. Frank Hanner, curator of the National Infantry Museum, said, "Brown had the most enduring ties of any Medal of Honor winner to Fort Benning, having served here throughout the 1920s and '30s, where he won minor fame as a boxer with thirty-nine wins."[9] Brown lied about his age and enlisted in the army at age fifteen in 1922 when "the Army was hungry for recruits."[10]

At Benning, Brown made the All-Army football team with scholarship offers from several colleges before they discovered he had left after the seventh grade. In the early 1940s, he was first sergeant for the Headquarters Company of the 2nd Armored Division commanded by George Patton at Benning. During the war, he fought in North Africa and led his company across Omaha Beach on D-Day, earning a battlefield promotion to captain. On August 23, Brown received the Medal of Honor from President Truman

---

[7] "Courtney Hodges," http://en.wikipedia.org/wiki/Courtney_Hodges (accessed May 21 2007).

[8] "Maj. Gen. O'Daniel Tells About Invasion of France," *Columbus Enquirer*, July 28 1945, 3.

[9] Clint Claybrook, "Post has turned out its share of heroes," *Benning Leader*, October 1 1993, 80.

[10] Ibid.

at the White House. Brown was the hero of Crucifix Hill in Germany. He eliminated three pillboxes (concrete emplacements for machine guns) in full view of the enemy and received the Purple Heart eight times.

Seventeen Fort Benning OCS graduates also received the Medal of Honor in World War II. The list included Orville E. Bloch; Cecil H. Bolton; Frank Burke; Victor L. Kandle; Jimmy W. Monteith; Charles P. Murray, Jr.; Robert B. Nett; Carlos C. Ogden, Sr.; Bernard J. Ray; Paul F. Riordan; Robert S. Scott; John J. Tominac; Robert M. Viale; Keith L. Ware; Robert T. Waugh; Eli Whitely; and Thomas W. Wigle.[11]

In August, gas rationing ended, and two months later the first new cars arrived in local showrooms. Meat and shoe rationing continued, but tires and radios were soon available. Washing machines and bobby pins were on sale again. With a backlog of civilian orders, Columbus mills expected to keep busy after the war. At the post, the forty-eight-hour workweek for civilian employees was reduced to forty-four hours. By this reduction, Benning expected to save a million dollars a year. On Labor Day, the Infantry School scheduled a forty-hour week.

During World War II, nylon replaced silk for parachutes made for the US armed forces, and nylon stockings became scarce. This was evident in a rush on a Columbus department store. The day after an ad in the *Ledger-Enquirer* notified the public that Kirven's would have more than 1,000 pairs of nylon stockings for sale, store employees arrived at work at 8 A.M. to find crowds of women standing in the rain at every door.

By the time the war was over, the South had a healthy economy for the first time since the Civil War. During World War II, 320,000 or more Georgians served in the armed forces and were now eligible for "further education, home ownership and other benefits."[12] Civilians found jobs in war industries or at military bases: "The fortuitous arrival of World War II and other developments fueled the state's long-awaited transformation into an urban, industrial, and diverse society."[13]

---

[11] List courtesy of Rebecca O. Pennington, secretary, National Infantry Museum, Fort Benning GA.

[12] Numan V. Bartley, *The Creation of Modern Georgia*, 2nd ed. (Athens: University of Georgia Press, 1990) 180.

[13] Ibid.

After the declaration of a national emergency before America entered the war, Benning trained 600,000 troops, and the Infantry School graduated approximately 59,000 2nd lieutenants. The post's population varied from 45,000 in 1939 to 90,000 or 100,000 in 1945. During World War II, 36,000 soldiers were treated annually at the hospital.

Fort Benning was one of the large separation centers located throughout the nation as the army and Fort Benning decreased in size. In 1945, soldiers returning home were granted a ninety-day leave and thirty days to decide if they would remain in uniform. Those who stayed at Benning got on with their lives. Military wives had babies at the post hospital, children attended post schools, men and women did their jobs, and all witnessed changes at the fort. Although normalcy returned, veterans carried the memories of battle, the loss of friends, and the realization of the devastation of war.

Novelist James Jones, a US Army infantryman who served in the Pacific, said that more than any medal, the Combat Infantryman's Badge, a rifle on a field of blue with a silver wreath around it, was preferred over the Bronze Star or the Purple Heart. The author of *From Here to Eternity*, a novel of army life in Hawaii on the eve of the attack on Pearl Harbor, described the medal's importance. "It's the only one we wore when we shipped home.... It was a point of pride, you see—better than all the rest. It spoke for itself. It really meant something. It was just an unspoken rule."[14]

Many returning soldiers never recovered from their experiences. As Bill Schmitzer, who at twenty-one was a Coast Guard veteran of nearly three years of war, stated, "You were there to kill people...too many...the closest bar was the rehabilitation center."[15] Schmitzer was part of the crew of a LCI, landing craft infantry, delivering troops to the islands in the South Pacific. Medical authorities were slow to relate stress to war. In World War I soldiers suffering from stress were referred to as being "shell-shocked." In World War II, soldiers suffered from battle fatigue. Post-traumatic stress disorder (PTSD) was not recognized until 1980 when the term first appeared in the diagnostic manual of psychiatry. It was estimated that

---

[14] Willie Morris, "From James Jones: A Friendship," in *Modern War*, ed. Paul Fussell (New York: W. W. Norton Company, 1991) 646.

[15] William P. Schmitzer, a WWII veteran, in conversation with Peggy Stelpflug, his sister-in-law, Neenah WI, summer 1993.

210,000 World War II survivors "suffer full-blown symptoms of traumatic stress," but these men and women did not receive treatment.[16]

On November 26, President Truman awarded Marshall the oak leaf cluster and the Distinguished Service Medal for his outstanding performance as chief of staff. Marshall, by his own request, was relieved from that duty by General of the Army Dwight D. Eisenhower. In his citation, Truman spoke candidly of Marshall's accomplishments:

> He was the first to see the technological cunning and consequent greater danger of the Nazi enemy. He was the master proponent of a ground assault across the English Channel into the plains of Western Europe directed by a single Supreme Allied Commander.... He obtained from Congress the stupendous sums that made possible the atomic bomb, well knowing that failure would be his full responsibility.... To him, as much as any individual, the United States owes its future. He takes his place at the head of the great commanders of history.[17]

Truman appointed Marshall his special ambassadorial envoy to China. Marshall, however, was unsuccessful in his attempt to seek an end of the civil war and to encourage a coalition government. After failing to dissuade Chairman Mao Tse-tung from establishing Communism in China, he returned home in 1947.

When Marshall became chief of staff in 1939, the US Army consisted of 13,000 officers and 174,000 enlisted men. At war's end, over 8 million men were in the army. By convincing Congress and the American people, Marshall built America from what he considered a third-rate power to the most powerful nation in the world. Yet Marshall was the first to understand that fewer soldiers would be needed in peacetime. The new factor at the end of World War II was the emphasis on the air force and navy—the air force had over 69,000 planes in 1945—and the atomic bomb. Infantry no longer got top billing, and some military professionals made the unlikely premise that the infantry was no longer needed.

Many veterans, feeling unneeded after the war, experienced problems at home. Some men who were reported dead returned to find their wives

---

[16] David Gelman, "Reliving the Painful Past," *Newsweek* 123/24 (June 13 1994): 20.

[17] Marshall, *Together: Annals of an Army Wife*, 290–91.

married to other men. Many marriages did not stand the test of long separations. For most, it was a stark transition to civilian life. A Canadian who served in World War I wrote to his son who fought from Italy to Holland. He warned his son of what it was like to leave the battlefield and return home: "You will, for a time, be homesick for the army.... It gets to be like a distant green field because of the male companionship and camaraderie, which you lose when you become 'mister' and can never regain in any other walk of life...that feeling of oneness with the finest of mankind will live with you forever.... And this is a gift reserved in its fullness for the infantryman."[18]

---

[18] Farley Mowat, *My Father's Son* (Toronto: Seal Books, 1992) 102.

25.

A Peacetime Post

As Americans returned to life in a peaceful world, so did Fort Benning. And as the post looked to the future, it was reminded of the past. In early 1946, many soldiers due to be discharged were still in uniform impatiently waiting for their paperwork to be processed. Since V-E Day, the Infantry School had discharged more than 12,000 soldiers. Others were on hold. Just waiting. On February 19, a fire caused $5,000 in damages to a wing of Lawson Field Headquarters. But to many fellows on post, the fire threatened more than just a building. Enlisted men awaiting processing for discharge dashed in "to help salvage voluminous records to insure that their discharge will not be delayed by lost records."[1]

Discharged soldiers received ongoing help from General Omar Bradley, who, when the war in Europe ended, became administrator of the Veterans Administration. Helping veterans readjust to a normal life was a necessary part of war, Bradley believed. With the support of President Truman and Chief of Staff Dwight D. Eisenhower, Bradley accomplished much: "Nothing I have done in my life gave me more satisfaction than the knowledge that I had done my utmost to ease their way when they came home."[2] Under Bradley, medical facilities for servicemen also improved. Medical journalists praised Bradley in *Reader's Digest*: "In two years General Omar N. Bradley has transformed the medical service of the Veterans Administration from a national scandal to a model establishment."[3]

---

[1] Robert Holcombe, Jr., *An Outline History of Fort Benning, Georgia, and the Infantry School Concept*, unpublished manuscript compiled for the National Infantry Museum, 1990, 22–23.

[2] Omar Bradley, with collaborator Clay Blair, *A General's Life* (New York: Simon and Schuster, 1983) 462.

[3] Ibid.

Another assist for returning soldiers was the GI Bill of Rights, lobbied for by veterans groups. The program included economic assistance programs in education, jobs and job training, disability pensions, loans, and insurance. It eased the problem of placing millions of men trained to kill back into civilian life.

A reminder of the days when the fledgling post and city leaders were constantly concerned about Benning's existence was present in 1946. On November 22, the *Columbus Enquirer* reported the Officers Training School and the officers' basic course would transfer to Fort Riley, Kansas.[4] Fort Benning would lose more than 2,500 personnel through course transfers and closings.

Maynard R. Ashworth, publisher of the *Columbus Ledger-Enquirer*, T. G. Reeves, and Richard E. Tukey, executive director of the Chamber of Commerce—all members of the Chamber of Commerce Military Affairs Committee—met with General Jacob Devers. The committee of three reasoned, "For a long time it has been the feeling of the Columbus Chamber of Commerce that we should maintain closer liaison with the high ups in the army and the War Department and in this way be in position to do a better job here at home in our relations with Benning."[5]

The committee accepted that wartime training courses would end, "but heatedly challenged transfer of the AOC, Army Officer Candidate School at Fort Benning, to Fort Riley as an economy measure."[6] The committee argued, "We have the ranges, in fact more than we need; the buildings and the know-how are adequate and could be added to or altered to suit peace time needs at little or no expense."[7] The committee pointed out that facilities and equipment were already established at Fort Benning while Fort Riley did not have the school, the quarters, or the housing facilities for families and dependents. Fort Benning offered housing for military personnel at Baker Village—a $3 million housing project with 1,042 units.

---

[4] "Benning Will Lose OCS, Basic Officers' Course in Transfers," *Columbus Enquirer*, November 22 1946, 1.

[5] Maynard Ashworth, "Why the Army Plans 'OCS' Move," *Columbus Enquirer*, December 15 1946, 2-D.

[6] "Fight Launched to Save Officer Candidate Course for Benning," *Columbus Enquirer*, November 23 1946, 1.

[7] Maynard R. Ashworth, "Why the Army Plans 'OCS' Move," (Columbus GA) *Sunday Ledger-Enquirer*, December 15 1946, 2-D.

Other favorable considerations were abundant and diverse terrain and climate for year-round training as well as the proximity to a city like Columbus, in contrast to Junction City, Kansas—the closest civilian town to Fort Riley with a population of only 8,507. Devers, however, told them that the $1 million cutback of army appropriations was secondary to the real purpose for the move. In a newspaper article, Ashworth explained:

> The whole move is based, according to General Devers, on the thinking that Benning should be a Divisional School for Infantry, like Knox for the Armored, and Sill for the Artillery. Riley should have the OCS and the Basic Course (BI) as it is not a function of the Divisional Schools to teach other than what applies direct to Divisional training so far as their branch is concerned. Riley will teach what all Army Ground Force Officers should know and the Divisional Schools will pick up from there and give the officers and some enlisted men what they should know as Infantry Officers in an Infantry Division and the Armored and Artillery will do likewise at their two Divisional Schools.... It seems that General Devers thinks that this move is best for the efficiency of the training of the Army Ground Forces.[8]

Despite local efforts, OCS program—a hallmark of World War II mobilization—was transferred in September 1947. From the opening of OCS at Fort Benning in 1941 until its move, 102,751 candidates enrolled in 488 classes. Of these candidates, 67,056 were graduated and commissioned 2nd lieutenants in the US Army. Adjusting to the loss of the OCS and BOC, the Infantry School offered a curriculum geared for 10,000 officers and enlisted soldiers expected to attend the 1947–1948 academic year.

While OCS was on its way to Kansas, the parachute program prospered. Brigadier General Gerald "Jerry" J. Higgins—the youngest general officer in the Army Ground Forces when promoted in August 1944 at age thirty-four—was commandant of the Parachute School in 1945. Higgins, a pioneer paratrooper, joined the 501st in March 1941 as a captain and was chief of staff of 101st Airborne Division on D-Day on June 6.

In December 1945, Higgins announced the proposed designation of the Parachute School as the Airborne School. Plans included a revised training program and centralization of the enlisted personnel into one

---

[8] Ibid.

regiment. Officially renamed the Airborne School in January 1946, the school's mission was to train both paratroopers and air landing personnel. Airborne School graduates were entitled to wear the wings of either Airborne component.

In early March, Private First Class William Charles Blackwell of College Park, Georgia, became the first graduate of the new eight-week paratrooper and glider program initiated three months before.[9] Blackwell was presented with both paratrooper and glider wings by Major General E. Gerry Chapman. However, due to postwar cutbacks, the Airborne School was eliminated effective eleven months later, and the Airborne Department was established. All courses underway in the Airborne School were transferred to the Infantry School.

After Congress passed the Armed Forces Voluntary Recruitment Act, new enlistments gave the United States the biggest volunteer army in the world with over 600,000 members. The *Bayonet* advertised for the "Peacetime Army": "For adventure, travel, and a job with a future, the Regular Army has a good 'deal' for men seventeen to thirty-four years of age, inclusive."[10] After three years as a "Guardian of Victory," the volunteer enlistee could attend college, business, or professional school of his choice, free. A retiree's monthly income after twenty years was $89.70 and after thirty years, $155.25 a month for life.

The OCS was not the only institution leaving. Benning's narrow gauge railroad was retired in 1946. The little railroad began its twenty-five-year tour of duty when the 7th Engineers laid the tracks for the miniature in 1921. Deciding that Camp Benning would be a good place to use the train, the War Department ordered army personnel "to remove the tracks, cars, and locos to Benning for use in building a permanent fort out of a temporary camp."[11]

The train was the world's longest narrow-gauge railroad. In addition to its 32 coaches, 53 flat cars, 105 gondolas, 4 tank cars, 1 work car, and 10 locomotives, a special observation car was constructed in 1935 for visiting dignitaries. The master mechanic of the train was Fred Whitaker, who

---

[9] "TABS Graduates First 'Double Wing' Troopers," *Bayonet*, March 8 1946, 1.

[10] "Peacetime Army," *Bayonet*, March 8 1946, 2.

[11] "Benning Railroad, Combat Veteran, 8 Fogeys, Retires," *Bayonet*, November 28 1946, 1.

serviced the train during its lifetime at Benning. Saving gas and tires, the "Chattahoochee Choo-Choo" transported officer candidates to their classrooms in the field, reducing traffic on the post.

Other endearing names were the Dinky Line, Old Fuss and Feathers, Bull's-eye Limited, Toonerville Trolley, and the Contour Special. According to military historian L. Albert Scipio, "The railroad tracks and spur lines were removed during the latter part of 1946 and turned over to the district Engineer in Savannah, Georgia, for disposal. The railroad system was sold in late 1946 and later moved by a contractor to Cuba for use in the operation of a sugar plantation."[12] The legend of the post's narrow gauge train, however, lived on—No. 1902, one of the old engines that was a part of this system, was placed in front of the National Infantry Museum on upper Wold Avenue, site of the old base hospital.

On December 9, Post Headquarters at Fort Benning ceased to exist. Due to an order for consolidation throughout the army "for the sake of economy," three separate headquarters at the post—Post Headquarters, the Infantry School, and the Infantry Center—were combined under the Infantry Center with Major General John W. O'Daniel as commanding general. Although many offices remained in the same buildings, some, like the post coordinator and the records section, moved to the Infantry School Building. Moving involved "six-by-six trucks by the score lined up in front of the Post Headquarters buildings throwing off and taking on all sorts of office equipment and supplies ranging from huge metal files to tiny paper clips."[13]

For civilians, though ration books were no longer bestsellers, there were still shortages. As 1946 ended, Staff Sergeant Carl E. "Lucky" Senior was pictured in the *Bayonet* writing a letter home: "I'm worried about the poor civilians—they've just got over a meat shortage, sugar shortage, butter shortage. Now they're facing a coal shortage along with a housing shortage, and I've just got to write 'em a nice letter—just like they used to write me when I was overseas and suffering the same things."[14]

---

[12] L. Albert Scipio, *The 24th Infantry at Ft. Benning* (Silver Spring MD: Roman Publications, 1986) 79.

[13] "Post Hq. Closes; TIC Takes Over," *Bayonet*, December 12 1946, 1.

[14] "Home Sweet Home," *Bayonet*, December 12 1946, 7.

In early January 1947, Frank Lumpkin wrote George C. Marshall to congratulate him on his appointment as secretary of state. Marshall replied on January 30, "I wish I could go back to some of our pleasant days in Benning and Columbus."[15] On June 5, Marshall, in a speech at Harvard University, proposed a plan for the reconstruction of Europe with US economic aid. Known as the Marshall Plan, it was in effect until 1951.

Marshall was not the only Fort Benning legend in the news. To help celebrate army week in April, General Dwight D. Eisenhower, army chief of staff since 1945, toured the post.

Another person of note on post was Walter Benning, a grandnephew of General Henry L. Benning, the post's namesake. Young Benning entered the Army Air Forces in 1944 at age seventeen. After completing his enlistment in 1946, he joined the army. During his service career he worked as a physical training instructor, winning the light-heavyweight title in the San Antonio district of the Texas State Golden Gloves. Benning was the sixth member of his family to receive a commission at the Officer Candidate School at Benning. The *Bayonet* reported that Benning avoided special attention and was "determined to win his gold bars on his own merit, thereby adding another Benning to the list of graduates who have carved their careers in the best traditions of the Confederate general."[16]

On July 4th, the 1918 camp named for Walter Benning's ancestor was remembered in stone. To mark the original site, a six-foot granite slab weighing two tons was installed at the intersection of Macon Road and Dixon Drive in Columbus. Major Elvin A. Kreilick, stationed at Benning since 1919 when he came to the Infantry School as an enlisted machine gun student, unveiled the marker. Maynard R. Ashworth, Columbus newspaper publisher, led the dedication of the marker, and Judge J. Arthur Lynch, first commander of the Charles S. Harrison post of the American Legion, acted as master of ceremonies.

The inscription, decorated with the infantry insignia of crossed rifles, read, "Camp Benning. Established on this site in 1918 as the US Army Infantry School originally embracing eighty-five adjoining acres. In 1919, the garrison was permanently located nine miles southeast of Columbus and

---

[15] Frank G. Lumpkin's personal files, Willcox-Lumpkin Company, Columbus GA.

[16] "Post Pupil Grand-Nephew of Benning Namesake," *Bayonet*, April 10 1947, 11.

is now designated Fort Benning. The tablet was donated by the Columbus Chamber of Commerce, 1947."[17]

During the ceremony, O'Daniel said, "The same spirit of teamwork that existed in 1917 may be seen here today."[18] He then "paid tribute to the Columbus men who were responsible for making Fort Benning a permanent installation," introducing former Columbus mayor J. Homer Dimon, Postmaster L. W. McPherson, and Columbus businessman Frank G. Lumpkin to the nearly fifty people attending the ceremony.[19]

Post tradition continued when members of the original Parachute Test Platoon gathered in 1947 for a reunion, their first postwar get-together. Devlin, their historian, noted the importance of their meeting: "The good luck experienced by the platoon during its training and experimentation in 1940 had continued during the war. Although several platoon members had been wounded, none had been killed in action."[20]

As new traditions were established, others disappeared. Army horses in the Infantry Center Stable were sold at auction under the War Assets Administration on August 1. Horses for auction included ninety-five of the Infantry School and seventeen of the Quarter Master Corps. There were thirty mules on post, but fifteen were kept for general purposes. No private mounts were allowed at the stables after that date. Hunts—established since 1923 during October through March and recognized by the master of Fox Hounds Association of America—were no longer conducted. Polo games, horse shows, and riding classes all ended. Ribbons and trophies awarded to the mounts and riders from the Infantry Center stables were turned over to the Officers' Club. Enlisted personnel at the stables were absorbed into the 25th Infantry.

Change also occurred in the national military organization. On September 18, 1947, the United States Air Force was created as a separate branch under the National Security Act. Under that act, "the services agreed to recognize each other's obvious primary functions—land, sea, and air

---

[17] "Original Post Site Dedicated July 4," *Bayonet*, July 10 1947, 1.

[18] Ibid.

[19] Ibid.

[20] Gerard M. Devlin, *Paratrooper!* (New York: St. Martin's Press, 1979) 77.

warfare…but that none was to develop weapons and capabilities that could serve it only in a secondary mission."[21]

On December 7, 1947—the sixth anniversary of the attack on Pearl Harbor—Omar Bradley, Benning's commanding general at the time of the attack, arrived for a tour of Fort Benning. Bradley had ended his job at the Veterans Administration and awaited approval of his appointment as army chief of staff. Bradley received a warm welcome at the post and was awarded a key to the City of Columbus.

Beatrice Patton also visited in 1947. Columbus historian Etta Worsley recalled her return: "Her visit was two years after her distinguished husband had been accidentally and tragically killed in Germany and buried among his men…. Again there was a gathering at Patton House, and Columbus friends were there."[22]

General George S. Patton, sixty, died December 21, 1945, at the military hospital in Heidelberg, Germany, from injuries he suffered as a passenger with his new driver in a car accident that occurred on his way to hunt pheasant. His longtime chauffeur, Master Sergeant John L. Mims, his driver since Fort Benning, had left for home in May.

Patton's book *War As I Knew It* appeared in 1947. In it he defines bravery and courage, two qualities both Patton and his wife knew well: "If we take the generally accepted definition of bravery as a quality which knows not fear, I have never seen a brave man. All men are frightened. The more intelligent they are, the more they are frightened. The courageous man is the man who forces himself, in spite of his fear, to carry on. Discipline, pride, self-respect, self-confidence, and the love of glory are attributes which will make a man courageous even when he is afraid."[23]

On January 10, 1948, the 325th Infantry Regiment, commanded by Colonel Charles H. Royce and the 319th Field Artillery Battalion, commanded by Lieutenant Colonel John A. Gloriod were reactivated at Benning with personnel from the now-defunct 37th Infantry and the 83rd

---

[21] Russell F. Weigley, *History of the United States Army* (Bloomington: Indiana University Press, 1984) 494.

[22] Etta Blanchard Worsley, *Columbus on the Chattahoochee* (Columbus GA: Office Supply Co., 1951) 446.

[23] George S. Patton, Jr., *War As I Knew It* (Boston: Houghton Mifflin Company, 1947) 340.

Artillery Battalion. Each was made part of the 82nd Airborne Division with Commander James M. Gavin presenting the colors. The 82nd, headquartered at Fort Bragg, North Carolina, was back to wartime strength due to "the consolidation, reorganization, and the absorbing of units of School Troops" at Benning.[24] Also the 3rd Division transferred to Benning for reorganization as a regular army division.

When the Airborne Requirements Board was established and was consolidated with the Infantry Requirements Board, now called the Infantry Airborne Requirements Committee, its mission was to assist the commandant in the development of infantry and Airborne tactics and techniques. It consisted of three permanent members and twelve associate members representing infantry, artillery, armor, cavalry, engineers, signal, medical organizations, and quartermaster branches.

On June 26, 1948, the Berlin airlift began. There was a deep concern of war with Russia. With the Soviet blockade of Berlin, the US airlifted supplies to the city, breaking the blockade. After O'Daniel finished his tour as commandant of Fort Benning, he was sent to Russia in June as military attaché in Moscow.

In July 1948, Major General Withers A. Burress became commanding general of the Infantry Center and commandant of the Infantry School. Burress was assistant commandant from October 1941 to February 1942. After serving in World War I, Burress attended the Infantry School and later the Army War College. In 1922, he married Virginia Collier "Ginger" Chappell, a Columbus girl. In 1949, their only daughter, Cynthia Kent Burress, married Major Wellborn Griffin Dolvin, formerly of Greene County, Georgia, in a wedding on post.[25]

In November 1948, President Harry S. Truman was reelected, defeating his Republican opponent, Governor Thomas E. Dewey of New York. Although George C. Marshall would soon retire as secretary of state due to health problems, Truman remained committed to implementation of the Marshall Plan, the Foreign Assistance Act of 1948, which provided a European Recovery Program.

The year 1948 marked the death of General John J. Pershing, a longtime friend and inspirational supporter of Benning. Born at the

---

[24] "Units to Receive Colors Saturday," *Bayonet*, January 8 1948, 1.

[25] Worsley, *Columbus on the Chattahoochee*, 431.

beginning of the Civil War, Pershing at eighty-eight died at the beginning of the Cold War. Marshall gave an enduring tribute to Pershing when writing from Benning on the general's seventieth birthday—September 13, 1930. It was the same letter in which he asked Pershing to be best man at his wedding to Katherine Tupper Brown: "There have been pitfalls without number, but the dignity and modesty of your course has carried you steadily upward in the public mind.... Yours must be a great satisfaction."[26]

In 1947, the Department of War (established in 1798) became the Department of the Army. The Departments of the Army, Navy, and Air Force were unified under the National Military Establishment. In August 1949, Congress changed the National Military Establishment to the Department of Defense, making it an executive department of the government. In 1949, Departments of the Army, Navy, and Air Force—no longer executive departments although remaining separately administered—became departments within the Department of Defense. The secretary of defense, with the help of a deputy and three assistant secretaries, strived to unify the services and prevent duplication. At the same time, in an effort to improve the joint chiefs of staff, a chairman that did not represent any single service was authorized to head the joint chiefs. As army historian Russell Weigley pointed out, "Congress explicitly prohibited the creation of a single chief of staff over the armed forces or an armed forces general staff," such as had existed in Hitler's Germany.[27]

The man chosen as first chairman of the joint chiefs of staff, was the man who got "the job done" as commandant at Fort Benning and as a commander in World War II: Omar N. Bradley. James Forrestal, secretary of defense from 1947 to 1949, who recommended the change to the Department of Defense, resigned because of poor health. Two months later Forrestal committed suicide, an act perhaps brought about by stress of the job. Louis A. Johnson then took over as secretary of defense.

In the early part of 1949, Fort Benning experienced a tremendous expansion of personnel brought on by establishment of a peacetime draft. The Selective Service Act, passed in June 1948 after the wartime draft ended in 1947, provided for the registration of all men between eighteen and

---

[26] George C. Marshall, *The Papers of George Catlett Marshall*, vol. 1, ed. Larry I. Bland (Baltimore: Johns Hopkins University Press, 1981) 358.

[27] Weigley, *History of the United States Army*, 495.

twenty-five and the draft of enough men for an army of 837,000, a navy and
Marine Corps of 666,882, and an air force of 502,000. The number of
personnel at Fort Benning would reach its highest peak since the early days
of World War II.

The influx of troops in 1949 and 1950 resulted in an acute housing
shortage. The House Armed Services Committee soon approved a $28.7
million construction program on post. It included additional housing,
bridges, training utilities, hospital facilities, and the construction of new
schools. Draftees were sent to training units or tactical units. Benning was
designated as a tactical unit. Soldiers in tactical units were formed into
recruit squads or platoons for their training. Men who attended tactical units
rather than training units received more weapons instruction, tactics of the
squad, platoon, company, and battalion and eventually were welded into a
combat team or division. During twelve months of training, men in tactical
units participated in field maneuvers on divisional or combat team level.
Some men further trained in tactical units were eligible to enter army
school, "specializing in everything from cooking and baking to
electronics."[28] Some received OCS commissions.

The world was entering a new phase of saber-rattling diplomacy.
Events after the war pointed to a standoff between the Soviet Union and the
rest of Europe. A term included in a speech by Bernard M. Baruch on
October 24, 1948, when he appeared before the Senate War Investigating
Committee was coined to describe the alarming situation: "Although the
war is over, we are in the midst of a cold war which is getting warmer."[29]

And the heat would soon grow stronger.

---

[28] Hanson W. Baldwin, "What Draftees Will Do," *New York Times*, July 8 1948,
2.

[29] Gorton Carruth, *What Happened When* (New York: Harper & Row, Publishers,
1987) 818.

26.

Training for Korea

This was a peacetime army, still recovering from the rigors of war. The leaders of World War II were aging and so was the technology that soldiers were depending upon more and more. This war was cold—and the battlefields ahead would be cold.

At Fort Benning, training continued—war or no war.

Not even a devastating accident could keep Private Victor Root from his training. Eleven students from the Student Training Regiment's Airborne Battalion were killed on January 13, 1950, during a glider indoctrination flight at Lawson field. An Airborne instructor and the glider's pilot also died, bringing the toll to thirteen.

Four men survived the crash, but one survivor died shortly afterward. The remaining three men—Ernest Stuehlmeyer, Paul Romero, and Root—received care at the Infantry Center Hospital and were treated later at Walter Reed Hospital in Washington, DC.

In a special bedside ceremony soon after the accident, Root received his paratrooper wings from Airborne Department Director Lieutenant Colonel Patrick F. Cassidy. After mending, Root was back at Fort Benning in March to continue his duty as a paratrooper. "I am very enthusiastic about it," the private said. "I suppose I've been through the worst part, so I might as well go through the rest. I wanted to come back real bad...they said I could, so here I am."[1]

Following a memorial for the fallen Airborne students, a dedication was held in honor of Major General William C. Lee at Lee Field with its 250-foot jump towers. Lee, known as the "father of the American Airborne Armies," was the first commander of Benning's Parachute School. During World War II, Lee activated and directed the 101st Airborne Battalion,

---

[1] "Crash Survivor Returns to Resume Parachuting," *Bayonet*, March 23 1950, 1.

serving as the unit's commander until a heart attack in February 1944 caused his early retirement in March 1945. Due to his illness, he missed his unit's jumps at D-Day at Normandy and at Bastogne in the Battle of the Bulge. Lee, fifty-three, died in 1948.

During the ceremony, a seven-foot stone monument, covered with two combat-type camouflaged parachutes, was unveiled. Master Sergeants Albert H. Miller and William Odom, members of the 101st and veterans of the jump at the Battle of the Bulge, did the honors. Miller, one of Benning's first paratroopers, was Lee's jumpmaster when Lee made his first jump in 1941. After the unveiling, 100 combat veteran paratroopers performed a mass drop from three C-82 troop-carrying planes.

In April, an exciting event involved the entire post. Fort Benning, selected by the Defense Department to represent the army, hosted a high-level civilian and military conference. Harry Truman, the nation's thirty-third president, was the headliner. His cabinet members, congressional and military leaders, as well as business and professional leaders attended the Joint Orientation Conference on April 21, including the Armed Forces Staff College and the Civilian Component Group.

Infantry School Commandant Withers A. Burress and Assistant Commandant J. S. Bradley were the official hosts. Other distinguished visitors were Georgia Governor Herman Talmadge, Secretary of Defense Louis Johnson, Army Secretary Frank Pace, Secretary of the Treasury John W. Snyder, Secretary of Agriculture Charles I. Brannan, Secretary of Labor Maurice J. Tobin, Secretary of the Navy Francis Matthews, Secretary of the Air Force W. Stuart Symington, and US Attorney General J. Howard McGrath. Representatives of the military included three men familiar to the post: General Omar Bradley, chairman of the joint chiefs of staff; army chief of staff J. Lawton Collins; and General James Gavin, commander of the 82nd Airborne Division.[2]

A writer for the *Bayonet* was impressed: "An assemblage of such importance has never visited here during the post's thirty-one years of life."[3] President Truman was treated to an "Infantry-Artillery-Tank Team in Attack" and a 3rd Division review, reviews not seen by a United States commander-in-chief since President Roosevelt's visit in 1943.

---

[2] "Truman Concludes Benning Visit," *Bayonet*, April 27 1950, 1.
[3] Ibid.

On June 1, the *Bayonet* announced the merger of the Post Exchange Grocery and Quartermaster Commissary, scheduled for a grand opening on July 5. A luxury of the "old" post came to a halt when it was announced, "The Commissary will be unable to make deliveries, as did the Grocery, because allotted personnel is insufficient."[4] The centralized facility, in addition to the commissary, included the main PX, Howard Bus Station, barber shops, shoe repair, and dry cleaning shops. The first Post Exchange, which opened in 1920 on the corner of Vibbert Avenue and Ingersoll Street, later was moved to the brick building in the Student Training Regiment area.

A member of Benning's "family" who remembered well the first Post Exchange visited in June. General Paul Malone, former Infantry School assistant commandant, was a special guest of Burress, who recognized Malone's importance in the founding of Fort Benning. Malone addressed members of the faculty and staff in Pratt Hall. Recalling the thousands of men and women trained at the post during World War II, Malone generously praised the military installation he helped create and sustain: "There is no place in the world so important to America as Fort Benning."[5]

His observation soon was put to the test.

On June 25, 1950, North Koreans crossed the 38th Parallel and invaded South Korea, capturing Seoul, the capital of South Korea, three days later. The United Nations protested the action of the North Koreans. Consequently, the United States, one of the fifty-three nations joined together to help each other in peace and war, sent forces to defend South Korea against communist aggression. General Douglas MacArthur was appointed commander of the United Nations Forces in Korea. This was the first war fought by the US as a member of the United Nations.

US Forces had occupied the southern portion of the Korean peninsula since the end of World War II, but had withdrawn on June 29, 1949—almost a year ago to the day of the breakthrough. Only a military mission remained there until the arrival of ground forces on July 1, 1950. The 24th Infantry Regiment, long-time resident at Fort Benning, headed for Korea. Stationed in Okinawa during World War II and afterwards

---

[4] "PX Market, Commissary to Merge," *Bayonet*, June 1 1950, 10.

[5] Etta Blanchard Worsley, *Columbus on the Chattahoochee* (Columbus GA: Columbus Office Supply Company, 1951) 427.

assigned to the 25th Infantry Division for occupation duty in Japan, its service in Korea began July 13, 1950. The 24th liberated the first South Korean city—Yechon—from North Korean forces on July 20. The last of the six original Colored Regulars created after the Civil War, the 24th was inactivated in Chipori, Korea, on October 1, 1951, one month short of its eighty-second birthday. The move meant the elimination of separated black units in Korea.

Military bases like Fort Benning again prepared to train thousands of young men. In August, the army called up 62,000 enlisted reserves for twenty-one months of active duty as part of US Forces in Korea. At the Infantry School, classes increased from 104 in 1950 to 247 in 1951. Glider orientation flights, a requirement of Airborne training at Benning ended August 3. Gliders, usually made of wood and incapable of "go a-rounds," were extremely vulnerable, especially under battle conditions.[6] The loss of life in the glider crash in January brought this home.

A new mode of air transportation now performed the duties of a glider, transporting men and equipment, but with less vulnerability. The helicopter, introduced in World War II, provided vertical mobility so the pilot could take off and land in a limited space. The helicopter, "having come of age in Korea, appeared to be the army's best hope for future battlefield mobility."[7] A "new" machine, though existing in man's imagination for over 400 years, sketched by Leonardo da Vinci (1452–1519), the helicopter was used in Korea for transportation, observation, and rescue, including medical purposes. Major General James Gavin, who supported airmobile warfare, tested thirteen Bell YR-13s, later called H-13 by the army, in the 82nd Airborne at Fort Bragg from 1946 to 1948. In Korea, the H-13 "became the Army's rotary-wing workhorse and caused the world to understand the contribution of the helicopter to modern warfare."[8]

In September, US forces landed at Inchon and recaptured Seoul. Because of these battles, Fort Benning prepared to receive hundreds of wounded soldiers from Korea. To accommodate the wounded, the post

---

[6] Gerard M. Devlin, *Paratrooper!* (New York: St. Martin's Press, 1979) 119.

[7] James W. Bradin, *From Hot Air to Hellfire* (Novato CA: Presidio Press, 1994) 77.

[8] Ibid., 87.

hospital was ordered to increase its number of beds by an additional 2,000 by December.

Because of the Korean crisis, Truman asked George C. Marshall, the legendary Infantry School assistant commandant, to take over as secretary of defense when Louis A. Johnson resigned. Marshall served as president of the American Red Cross from 1949 to 1950, but for his new assignment "special legislation was passed waiving—in his case only—the prohibition against a military man serving as head of defense."[9] Summoned again from retirement, Marshall was sixty-nine years old. He agreed to stay one year, until September 12, 1951. With little rest since the war, Marshall once more chose to serve, now as secretary of defense.

Building up the Army

William B. Steele, a country boy from Georgia, had trained in 1949 in Harmony Church area in a ROTC unit at Benning. At times his troops used broomsticks instead of guns. When he entered the army in 1950, he returned to Benning and was assigned as a platoon leader in the same company area where he had been a ROTC student. "I knew the terrain, but that's about all I knew. It's a familiar experience for Fort Benning," Steele explained.[10] "The size of the army after World War II had been reduced tremendously, and the army got lulled into this peaceful living and all of a sudden Korea came along and Benning found itself with the job of building up the army."[11]

Steele was assigned to the 4th Infantry Division, a unit preparing to go to Europe as the first division of the NATO forces. One of his first assignments as a twenty-one-year-old 2nd lieutenant was to put on a pistol and go to Phenix City to "make sure the troops didn't get into trouble."[12] Steele also found it difficult to deal with property accountability. He found that the 3rd Infantry Division, the first Benning unit sent to Korea, left the

---

[9] "Marshall, George Catlett," *Dictionary of American Military Biography*, vol. 2, 736. Because of his 5-star status, Marshall was on permanent military status.

[10] Gen. (Ret.) William B. Steele, interview by Peggy Stelpflug, October 5 1998, Donovan Technical Library, Infantry Hall, Fort Benning, GA. Written transcript and audio cassette, Auburn AL.

[11] Ibid.

[12] Ibid.

post without turning in a lot of equipment. Some of the equipment was misplaced, some unaccounted for, and some, Steele believed, left post with the 3rd Division.[13]

People coming in from ROTC like Steele normally would go to the Infantry School's officers' basic course. Men ordered to Korea did take the course, but the Infantry School lacked time and capacity to service all the troops, especially those headed for Europe. "They were trying," Steele said, "to send people to Korea who had had basic training, who had the various schools, who were more qualified to go into war situation as opposed to a relatively peacetime, no-war situation."[14]

When Steele joined the 4th Infantry Division in 1950, it was composed of people pulled from the reserves, army World War II veterans, and new second lieutenants. "With very few regular army 1st lieutenants, captains, majors," Steele explained, "you had people suffering from back ailments, leg problems, and brand new lieutenants who didn't know how to write the date the army way."[15]

The Infantry School converted to a forty-four-hour academic week because of the demands of war. While unnecessary courses were eliminated, most courses were intensified but reduced in length. The Infantry School's program of instruction emphasized weapons, small unit tactics, physical fitness, night operations, defensive combat, and combined arms teamwork.

Still concerned that Korea was a distraction from the real threat of the Soviet Union, world leaders established the North Atlantic Treaty Organization (NATO) to give allies protection against possible attacks by Russia or other enemies. Dwight D. Eisenhower, who resigned from the army in 1948 to become president of Columbia University, was recalled in 1950 as NATO commander.

During the turmoil and uncertainty of 1950, relief was found in routine activities. The Infantry School Detachment mess hall conducted a test to see if black-eyed peas should be added to the regular menu. Of 471 soldiers served, 397 ate the peas, so the traditional Southern dish was included in the post's chow lines.[16]

---

[13] Ibid.

[14] Ibid.

[15] Ibid.

[16] Richard Brill, "Fort Benning in the 1950s," *Bayonet*, October 8 1993, B-6.

The world had more to worry about than Fort Benning's menu, however. The possibility of another world war loomed when Chinese Communist troops took over Inchon and Kimpo Airfield and recaptured Seoul. MacArthur wanted to attack China territory, but President Truman and other military leaders felt Russia, which had an alliance with China, would enter the war. Therefore, the idea of a war with limited objectives in a nuclear age seemed a reasonable resolution.

At the same time, Benning marked a change of command. In January 1951, Fort Benning's new commanding officer Major General John H. Church arrived at the Infantry School from the battlefields of Korea. Church, former commander of the 24th Division, returned stateside "under a program to give Army training camps and schools the advantage leadership by men who have had experience in the current conflict and at the same time give younger generals a chance at combat experience."[17] Major General Withers A. Burress, a Benning pioneer and former champion horseman, left on January 21, to assume command of the reactivated 6th Corps at Camp Atterbury, Indiana.

In February 1951, Officer Candidate School returned to Benning with the establishment of the 1st Officer Candidate Company by the Infantry School, General Orders No. 9. Plans called for twelve classes of infantry officer candidates yearly. By August 2, more than 200 men, the first OCS class to graduate at Benning since the end of World War II, received their second lieutenant bars. The schedule included twenty-two weeks of classes designed for combat leadership with emphasis on weapons, tactics, physical fitness, and character guidance. The unspoken school motto was "if a man cannot discipline himself under any and all conditions he is not fit to be a leader."[18] During the height of the Korean War, 1951–1953, more than 7,000 young officers graduated from OCS.

In February 1951, the 325th Airborne Infantry Regiment returned to Fort Benning for six months' temporary duty with the Infantry School as school troops. The group was formerly stationed at Fort Benning as the 325th Infantry Regiment before its transfer in 1948 to the 82nd Airborne Division at Fort Bragg. Under command of Colonel Thomas Mifflin, 400 trucks helped move the 325th from Fort Bragg. An overnight stop was made

---

[17] "Gen. Church Given Benning Command," *Bayonet*, January 25 1951, 1.
[18] "OCS Is Resumed," *Benning Herald*, March 1951, 19.

at Camp Gordon, Georgia. After their arrival, men were billeted in the cuartels on the Main Post, their "old barracks."[19]

Classes at the Infantry School increased from 104 in 1950 to 247 in 1951 since all newly commissioned officers coming on active duty were ordered to attend the associate infantry company officers' classes. Two new courses, the field grade officers' refresher course and the company grade officers' refresher course, lasting one month, acquainted recalled World War II officers with the latest infantry tactics and techniques. Troops, preparing for war, followed news carefully. Seoul was recaptured by U. N. Forces in March 1951, and the enemy was pushed back to North Korea, past the 38th parallel. MacArthur, believing a total victory was necessary, tried to convince Congress to support his views rather than those of the president.[20]

Truman relieved MacArthur of his Far Eastern commands. Defense Secretary George C. Marshall, Secretary of State Dean Acheson, army chief of staff J. Lawton Collins, and 8th Army commander General Matthew Ridgway supported the president's decision. Four of these men—Marshall, Bradley, Collins, and Ridgway—were at Fort Benning in 1930, all playing a part in "the Benning Revolution" which prepared them for World War II, Korea, and for decisions affecting civilian control of the military. To replace MacArthur, the president turned to General Matthew Ridgway. MacArthur, still popular with a majority of Americans, presented a televised farewell before Congress. He concluded his speech by saying, "Old soldiers never die, they just fade away. And like the old soldier of that ballad, I now close my military career and just fade away—an old soldier who tried to do his duty as God gave him the light to see that duty."[21]

As fighting continued in Korea, more casualties (those killed and wounded) occurred. By 1951, with more than 100,000 American casualties, Americans were ready to end the war. With the UN's decision not to attack Chinese bases and with Truman's support of the decision, the war was a limited war. Truce negotiations began in June 1951 under Ridgway's

---

[19] "325th Returns as School Unit," *Bayonet*, February 15 1951, 1.

[20] Russell F. Weigley, *History of the United States Army* (Bloomington: Indiana University Press, 1984) 517.

[21] Douglas MacArthur, "Old Soldiers Never Die; They Just Fade Away," farewell address to Congress, April 19 1951. Accessed May 21: 2007: http://www.americanrhetoric.com/speeches/douglasmacarthurfarewelladdress.htm.

command. On June 5, Secretary of Defense Marshall went with Ridgway to Korea for his "last view of an active battle front."[22]

Marshall was again in news but it was not celebratory. On June 15, 1951, the *Columbus Enquirer* headlined, "McCarthy Hurls Charge of 'Liars' at Marshall, Secretary Acheson." Joseph McCarthy, a Wisconsin senator who led a frenzied crusade against Communism in the United States, attacked George Marshall and other loyal Americans.

McCarthy began his attack in an after-dinner speech in February 1950 when he waved what he said was a list of Communists in the State Department known to the Secretary of State Dean G. Acheson. On the Senate floor on June 14, 1951, he attacked Secretary of Defense Marshall as "grim and solitary man," who led "a conspiracy of infamy."[23] He accused Marshall of supporting Russia and of destroying our relationship with China. McCarthy's speech was titled "America's Retreat from Victory: The Story of George Catlett Marshall," a manuscript of more than 60,000 words that was sent to daily newspapers and to the Wisconsin schools.[24]

Marshall, a powerful figure during World War II, was no longer immune from criticism. American people ready to place blame on government officials for the devastating attack on Pearl Harbor, the "sell-outs" to Russia, the spread of Communism in China (where Marshall tried to intervene), and in Europe (where Marshall fostered the Marshall Plan) allowed McCarthyism, "the exploitation of a nation's fears" to dominate American politics for the following three years.[25]

Wounded and ill soldiers from Korea continued to arrive at Benning's post hospital. In 1951, 25,000 casualties were cared for at the facility. The hospital, completed in 1925, added a nearby temporary building and an annex in the Harmony Church area to treat 36,000 soldiers annually during World War II. The Harmony Church annex was reactivated during the Korean conflict.

---

[22] Forrest C. Pogue, *George C. Marshall: Statesman* (New York: Viking, 1987) 488.

[23] "Modern History Sourcebook: Senator Joseph McCarthy: The History of George Catlett Marshall, 1951." Accessed May 21, 2007: http://www.fordham.edu/halsall/mod/1951mccarthy-marshall.htm.

[24] Joseph R. McCarthy, *America's Retreat from Victory* (Milwaukee WI: Educational Foundation, Inc., 1951) 3–4.

[25] Time-Life Books, *This Fabulous Century 1950–1960* (Alexandria VA: Time-Life Books, 1970) 117.

Bringing comedy relief to the war, movie stars Dean Martin and Jerry Lewis filmed *Jumping Jacks*, featuring the comedy duo as paratroopers. Martin and Lewis rode to the top of the Benning's 250-foot control tower and were awarded certificates as Qualified Buddy Seat Riders and Honorary Parachutists, earning their wings from Lieutenant Colonel Richard J. Seita, director of the Airborne Department. Colonel Robert J. Whitus, coordinator and project officer for the Paramount production, provided props such as airplanes, pontoon bridges, tanks, artillery, and kitchen utensils. "This," he said, "has been one of the most interesting jobs of my Army career."[26]

---

[26] "Operations Officers Amazed," *Bayonet*, December 20 1951, 6.

27.

"Don't Forget Nothing"

Squad leader, rifleman or grunt, Ralph Puckett didn't care. He was a young and eager lieutenant with the dust of West Point still on his boots, but he knew what he wanted to be. He wanted to be a paratrooper, an infantryman, and most of all, a Ranger.

Lieutenant Colonel John McGee, on the 8th Army Staff, was putting together a special unit to go into Korea's Pohang Pocket and he wanted a special breed of soldier. As for Puckett, he was a farm boy from Tift County, Georgia. He had captained the 1949 West Point boxing team, so McGee knew he would fight. After leaving the academy, Puckett went to the branch and material course at Fort Riley then graduated from the basic infantry course at Fort Benning, the same place where he had taken his physical and academic tests for West Point. After his basic course ended on a Friday, Puckett entered Jump School on Monday. During his training, North Korea invaded South Korea. He was not assigned to Korea, but Puckett requested a change of orders so he could go to war.[1]

That was the extent of his military background when he sat down with McGee.

"I knew I wasn't a captain and knew I had no experience, but I really wanted to be a Ranger," Puckett said, remembering the brashness of the twenty-three-year-old lieutenant.[2] McGee liked what he saw and selected Puckett as commander. Puckett requested Lieutenants Charles N. Bunn and Bernard Cummings—his West Point classmates—to serve as the company's platoon leaders. Puckett, Bunn, and Cummings were key components in

---

[1] Col. (Ret.) Ralph Puckett, interview by Peggy Stelpflug, May 28 1996, National Infantry Museum, Fort Benning GA, written transcript and audio cassette, Auburn AL.

[2] Ibid.

what proved to be the army's first Ranger company since World War II, the 8th Army Ranger Company.

With his experience in the 6th Army during World War II with the Alamo Scouts, McGee looked for the unit's table of organization, an official document that gives unit recognition and organization, including positions, rank structure, and equipment. McGee could not find a table for the Alamo Scouts, but he did find one for a Ranger company.

"That's why we were Rangers rather than Alamo Scouts," Puckett said.

Puckett's 8th Army Ranger Company was organized at Camp Drake, Japan, under the directive of the commanding general of the 8th Army, General Walton Walker. Although organized according to a Ranger unit, it was formed under a table of distribution, unauthorized by the Department of the Army. As Puckett explains, "We were something the 8th Army took out of its hide, so to speak. It says, 'I want this unit. I will do this, and I will take the troops from other units to go into this.' So the 8th Army Ranger Company is not part of the official lineage."[3]

When Puckett began organizing his Ranger Company at Camp Drake, Japan, qualified infantrymen were not available due to a shortage of trained riflemen. Selectees came from all service units in Japan—quartermaster, signal, engineer, and ordinance.

"The Army of occupation in Japan was not well-trained because World War II was over. The attitude was 'we're not going to fight any more wars. Let's live it up. Let's have a good time.' So the Army there was not well-trained or physically fit."[4] Puckett's company was among the first integrated units in Korea. According to its company's organization, his unit was allowed three officers and seventy-four enlisted men. "We only had seventy-three that we actually took into the company. Of those seventy-three, two of them were black soldiers, Wilbert Clanton and Allen Waters. Clanton was killed on Hill 205. They were good, good men. They pulled their weight. They did just as well as the rest of the Rangers in my company," Puckett recalls.

---

[3] Col. (Ret.) Ralph Puckett, interview by Peggy Stelpflug, May 28 1996, National Infantry Museum, Fort Benning GA, written transcript and audio cassette, Auburn AL.

[4] Ibid.

His unit was typical of America. "We had WASPS, Italian-Americans, Hispanics, German-Americans, Hawaiian-Americans, every kind of hyphenated Americans you can find plus those two black guys. We didn't look on them as hyphenated Americans, and we didn't look at ourselves as hyphenated Americans. We were all Americans. The blood was the same color—red. We had the same aspirations. Everybody wanted to get home to their families. Everybody wanted a better life for their kids," said Puckett, now retired in Columbus.[5]

The battle for Hill 205 was the company's biggest battle. It took place November 25–26, a time when General Douglas MacArthur was saying troops would be home by Christmas. Puckett's Rangers were attached to the 25th Division. US forces had invaded North Korea across the 38th parallel in early October and reached the Yalu River on the Manchurian border by November 20. But Puckett knew from listening to the Armed Forces Radio that four corps of Chinese, opposed to the US crossing, were between them and the Yalu River.

"I knew that in the 25th Division Sector we were outnumbered abut three to two and also knew—something I learned at Benning—that the doctrine said we should outnumber them two or three to one," he said.

Wounded in the battle, Puckett was rescued by two of his men, Privates Billy G. Walls and David L. Pollock, who dragged Puckett down the hill. After ordering the tank platoon sergeant to call in artillery fire on the Chinese, Puckett was taken to the Battalion Aid Station. Three or four days later, Puckett was in Japan. A week later he was on his way to Fort Benning Hospital, which he had requested in order to be close to his family in Tifton. As he journeyed home, US forces retreated to the south due to the massive Chinese Communist offensive. But his time as an Army Ranger was only beginning.

The action on Hill 205 is not part of the official Ranger heritage. Nor did the concept of the elite force rise out of Korea. Early in World War II, George C. Marshall chose General Lucian Truscott to organize an elite fighting unit. Truscott did just that, with help from Major William Darby, who selected and trained Darby's Rangers, leading his unit in North Africa,

---

[5] Ibid.

Sicily, and Anzio until his death in battle on April 30, 1945.[6]

At the request from General Dwight D. Eisenhower not to name the unit after the British Commandos, Truscott picked the name Rangers. He viewed it as a "compliment to those in American history who exemplified such high standards of individual courage, initiative, determination, ruggedness, fighting ability and achievement...few words have a more glamorous connotation in American military history."[7] Ranger heritage is traced back to colonial America when the British employed Ranger units from the colonies. Early Ranger leaders were Robert Rogers, Dan Morgan, Thomas Knowlton, Francis Marion, and Benjamin Whitcomb. Rogers's Rangers are often referred to as the inspiration for the US Rangers. However, Rogers's request to fight with American forces in the Revolutionary War was turned down by George Washington, who along with his officers, believed Rogers "is not to be sufficiently relied on."[8] Rogers, in turn, chose to fight for the British. As a result, he is not considered the sole inspiration for the US Rangers, but is, perhaps, the most well known.

Three writers, Francis Parkman, Kenneth Roberts, and Rogers himself, memorialized the Rangers. In his journal, Rogers told of fighting the Indians and the French in pre-Revolutionary times in North America. He listed his nineteen rules and guidelines, "Standing Orders" for Rogers. Rangers, including "Don't forget nothing," and "Let the enemy come till he's almost close enough to touch. Then let him have it, and jump out and finish him up with your hatchet."

Parkman, an American historian who wrote about the French and Indian Wars in his books in the late 1800s, "secured the place of the Rangers in American folklore." [9]Finally, when Kenneth Roberts published *Northwest Passage* in 1937, a novel about a young man who fought with Rogers' Rangers, he portrayed Rogers as a tragic hero rather than "untrustworthy"

---

[6] William O. Darby and William H. Baumer, *Darby's Rangers: We Led the Way* (San Rafael CA: Presidio Press, 1980) 179–80.

[7] Lt. Gen. Lucian K. Truscott, Jr., *Command Missions* (New York: E.P. Dutton and Company, Inc. 1954) 40.

[8] "Rogers' Rangers," http://en.wikipedia.org/wiki/Rogers%27_Rangers (accessed May 21 2007).

[9] David W. Hogan, Jr., *Raiders or Elite Infantry?* (Westport CT: Greenwood Press, 1992) 7.

as Washington viewed him. As America grew closer to World War II, Spencer Tracy, a popular actor, played Rogers in the screen version of Roberts' book.

The Rangers adopted their motto, "Rangers Lead the Way," from the command General Norman Cota, leader of the 29th Infantry Division, gave to Lieutenant Colonel Max F. Schneider, an original member of Darby's 1st Battalion. Cota ordered Schneider, commander of the 5th Ranger Battalion, "Lead the way, Rangers," after the landing on Omaha Beach, D-Day, June 6, 1944.

Like commandos, Rangers were not well received by many military leaders, who believed the special unit drained the best men from other units. However, Marshall and other key military leaders who supported innovative units, actively supported the Rangers. On September 21, 1950, the day Marshall became secretary of defense, Colonel John G. Van Houten was hand-picked by Chief of Staff General J. Lawton Collins to start the Ranger Training Program at Fort Benning. Its headquarters would be in the Harmony Church area—the area used by the 1st Infantry Division in 1939.

Army historian David W. Hogan, Jr., explained the setup: "Most of the fifty instructors and administrative personnel who were initially available came from the Infantry Center. Additional help soon arrived as army personnel officers screened records for those who had served with the Rangers, Merrill's Marauders, 1st Special Service Force and O. S. S. [Office of Strategic Services] in World War II."[10]

Van Houten's deputy, Colonel Edwin Walker, had commanded the 1st Special Service Force, and Hogan explains, "Like many who were involved in special operations, he possessed little regard for the fine points of garrison protocol, an attitude that occasionally brought him into conflict with Van Houten."[11]

Major William Bond, a former member of Darby's Rangers, helped as soon as permission was given to form the Ranger Training Command at Fort Benning. Instructors also included Major James Y. Adams, Captain "Bull" Simons of the 6th Ranger Battalion, colorful Captain Wilbur "Coal Bin Willie" Wilson, and intense young Major John K. Singlaub, who had parachuted into France for the OSS.

---

[10] Darby, *Darby's Rangers*, 109.

[11] Ibid.

Organization of the mobile units, available to division commanders for special missions, consisted of 4 rifle companies, each with 5 officers and 110 enlisted men. Each company contained 3 platoons of 3 ten-man squads each. Each Ranger carried a light automatic rifle and each squad had a 60 mm mortar or a bazooka.

The first recruits were enlisted men from Airborne units, particularly the 82nd at Fort Bragg, North Carolina, and the 11th Airborne Division at Fort Campbell, Kentucky, as well as jump-qualified officers from all over the country. Van Houten and Walker were looking for rugged nineteen-year-olds with initiative, high test scores, and a knack for hand-to-hand combat. Among the Airborne formations, recruiters found numerous cocky young paratroopers who were eager to escape the routine of garrison duty and see some action. Those rejected were returned to their units.

African-American soldiers volunteered for the Rangers although many officers were concerned that they could not compete. They believed the army should not be used as an instrument of social change. Many African-American volunteers for the Ranger program came from the segregated 3rd Battalion of the 505th Airborne Infantry. Of the 491 enlisted recruits who went through training at Benning in mid-October, 27 percent were African-American. In accordance with army policy, African Americans formed a separate unit, initially called the 4th Ranger Company but redesignated the 2nd Ranger Infantry Company (Airborne). It was the only authorized, all-African-American Ranger unit in army history.[12]

In addition to traditional subjects, the Ranger course also covered escape and evasion, cooperation with natives, and the language and characteristics of the target area. The center allotted forty-eight hours per week for six weeks, with an abundance of night training. Pressure was controllable; no man was forced to remain a Ranger candidate. During training, there was a jeep with a white flag in the background, and anyone who decided he could not continue got into the jeep. He would be driven away, and his personal gear removed from the barracks before the other men returned.

On November 13, 1951, the first four companies trained at the Ranger training center at Harmony Church graduated: "For the first time since

---

[12] *75th Ranger Regiment: Rangers Lead the Way*, 10, information booklet, vertical file, Donovan Library, Fort Benning GA.

World War II the Rangers were on the march Monday.... Men receiving their Ranger shoulder patches Monday were members of four rifle companies which started training six weeks ago under Department of the Army plans which call for one Ranger company to be assigned to each infantry division. The graduating Ranger class was composed of volunteers, chosen on the basis of high mental and physical standards."[13]

The four Ranger companies were soon involved with fighting or training troops for the Korean conflict. The 1st Company was attached to the US 8th Army; the 3rd Company stayed at Benning to train new Rangers, and the 2nd and 4th Companies were assigned to the 187th Regimental Combat Team.

In May 1951, John Paul Vann, a friend of Puckett's, arrived with his family for duty at the Ranger Training Command. Vann's superior was Wilbur "Coal Bin Willie" Wilson. His nickname derived from his demand that the coal stacked in bins in the barracks slant downward at an exact angle, a discipline he used to help train his troops. Vann and Wilson's friendship survived until Vann's fatal helicopter accident in Vietnam.

Vann entered the advanced course at the Infantry School in the fall of 1951. He and Puckett resumed their friendship and visited socially, often barbecuing in Vann's backyard with the help of Vann's wife, Mary Jane, and Puckett's fiancée, Jeannie. Vann took command of Puckett's 8th Army Ranger Company in Korea after Puckett was wounded. Although envious of Puckett for being chosen to lead "the first Rangers" in Korea, Vann led his men in the tradition of the young commander from Georgia.[14] Aware of Puckett's bravery with his Rangers, Vann recommended Puckett for the Distinguished Service Medal Puckett received in September 1951. Vann's biographer Neil Sheehan said Vann also got "decorations for the two enlisted men who rescued Puckett."[15]

In March 1951, the 8th Army Ranger Company was deactivated. On July 25, General Order Number 584 was issued to inactivate the 1st, 2nd, 3rd, 4th, 5th, and 8th Ranger companies.[16] Commanding generals reassigned those men designated as parachutists to the 187th Airborne

---

[13] "First Rangers End Training," *Bayonet*, November 16 1950, 1.

[14] Neil Sheehan, *A Bright Shining Lie*, (New York: Random House, 1988) 453.

[15] Ibid., 468–69.

[16] Robert W. Black, *Rangers in Korea* (New York: Ivy Books, 1989) 203.

Regimental Combat Team. By September, the Ranger companies in Korea had been dissolved.

Robert Black, author of *Rangers in Korea*, gave his reason for dismissal of Ranger companies in Korea. He wrote, "By tradition, philosophy, and training, Rangers are designed to fight for victory. A man experiences too much in the process of becoming a Ranger to accept half measures of limited effort. In a war the United States and its allies decided not to win, there was no place for the spirit of the American Ranger."[17] Black describes the assembly of Rangers in Pusan, Korea, as a near riot: "As night fell, the sky glowed red and there were sirens and shots, shouts and screams. What the Chinese and North Koreans could not do, the Department of the Army was bringing to pass."[18] Black wrote, "The Rangers were taken out of Pusan in long, open-bed trucks called cattle cars. The Rangers mooed as each truck pulled away."[19]

Although Ranger companies no longer fought battles in Korea, Ranger training continued at Fort Benning. Responding to the need of well-trained small infantry unit leaders—and wanting to keep the Ranger program—Benning leaders proposed a plan to revise the Ranger Training Combat program by giving the Infantry School responsibility for individual Ranger training in the Ranger Training Department. By September 1, all Ranger infantry companies were deactivated. On August 31, 1951, a board of officers defined the purpose, the desired personnel, and the training specifications for Ranger training at the Infantry School. The board believed "a special course can be conducted at the Infantry School which will provide small infantry unit leaders of such ability that the Army Training Program can become much more effective."[20]

Volunteers would come from officers and NCOs. Officers were not to be over twenty-seven years of age and NCOs not over thirty. A score of not less than 250 on the Army Physical Fitness Test was expected of both, and both had to be able to swim. Both were expected to have excellent character,

---

[17] Black, *Rangers in Korea*, 202.

[18] Ibid.

[19] Robert W. Black, *Rangers in Korea* (New York: Ivy Books, 1989) 203.

[20] "Report of Board of Officers: Ranger Training, The Infantry School," August 31 1951, Fort Benning Folders, vault, Donovan Library, The Infantry School, Fort Benning GA.

no disciplinary actions or investigations pending. They were to have successfully passed the final physical exam for hazardous duty training. Officers and NCOs who passed the course would be assigned to infantry units to instruct others. The Ranger Department at the Infantry School was to provide "one Ranger-qualified officer per rifle company and one non-commissioned officer per platoon."[21]

In October 1951, Chief of Staff General J. Lawton Collins, responding to a recommended report of Ranger Training at the Infantry School, directed Colonel John G. Van Houten "to head the prospective Ranger Training Section."[22] He later directed the commandant of the Infantry School to establish a Ranger Department instruction to raise the standard of training in all combat units. In World War II, the concept was Ranger battalions. During Korea, the concept was Airborne-Ranger companies. Now it was individual training.

After months in and out of the hospital, Puckett was assigned to the Ranger Department. While a patient, Puckett experienced a life-changing experience—he fell in love. Puckett's picture was in the paper after his arrival at Benning, and Nan Strickland, the typing teacher at Columbus High School, recognized Puckett as her former seventh-grade English student. She asked Jeannie Martin, a senior student, to visit the young soldier.

Jeannie went with her friend Peggy Ashford, daughter of newspaper publisher Maynard Ashford. The girls came on a Sunday afternoon when Puckett's family was visiting. When the girls poked their heads around the door, Puckett's father said, "He's going to marry one of you." His dad said this because Puckett had told him about a fellow patient who read his palm. The fortuneteller had announced to Puckett, "You've been on a long trip. Pretty soon you're going to meet two beautiful girls. One's blond, one's brunette. You're going to marry one of them."

"Which one?" Puckett asked.

"I don't know," he replied, "but one of them has a lot of money."[23]

---

[21] John Aragon, "Ranger Said Tough Breed of Fighting Infantryman," *Bayonet*, October 4 1968, 71.

[22] Darby, *Darby's Rangers*, 108.

[23] Puckett interview.

Jeannie began to visit two or three times a week for the next six months.

When Puckett returned to duty at Fort Benning for three weeks, his skin grafts didn't hold up, so he returned to the hospital for another five months. Jeannie then visited him daily.

Finally well, Puckett started out as the Rangers Headquarters' Company commander, instructing at the Jungle and Amphibious Training Center in Florida. From there he was sent to the mountain camp in Dahlonega, Georgia, as camp commander. Later, as a tactical officer he took a group of students entering the Ranger Department and followed them through the entire course, helping with their evaluation.

"I was very fortunate in that I'd been a headquarters company commander, a mountain camp commander, an instructor at Benning and Florida, and a tactical officer. So I've seen it all," said Puckett, who half a century later still mentors young Rangers. The Ranger Department, according to Puckett, had a different concept than the Ranger Training Command: "It was to train individuals—infantrymen, leaders, company commanders, platoon leaders, and squad leaders. Then those soldiers, because of their improved leadership and trained capability, would return to their units and would improve that squad, platoon, company, whatever because the leader was better."[24]

This was an admirable goal, one that would continue until a Fort Benning Ranger named Kenneth Leuer received a new set of orders.

---

[24] Puckett interview.

28.

Ike Delivers Campaign Promise

David Hackworth was seldom at a loss for words. As a self-proclaimed military critic, he offered his opinions on the military to readers of newspapers and magazines. He also wrote bestselling books. As a twenty-one-year-old soldier, Hackworth arrived for Infantry School at Fort Benning in the spring of 1952. Even then, his opinions flowed as easily as sweat on a Georgia afternoon.

Hackworth, like many of his classmates in the 121st Student Officers' Course, received a battlefield commission in Korea. Now he was in a classroom. "We were one of the first classes back from the present 'Police Action'—a formidable bunch with one Medal of Honor, six DSCs, and limps, scars, and Purple Hearts attendant to the 100 Silver Stars (at least) among us," Hackworth remembered.[1]

Critical of the school, Hackworth said the "Benning School for Boys for us newly returned Korean vets, was an insult and a joke."[2] He said "old pros who packed these weapons across Europe, the Pacific, and Korea became resentful, then openly hostile...."[3] To amuse themselves, battle-tested students ridiculed the class "Eager Beavers." Classmates who sprang from their seats to answer questions such as "What is the muzzle velocity of the M-1 rifle?" were dubbed "Spring Butts." Hackworth admitted being one himself until Korea.[4]

According to Hackworth, men dealt with boredom and disappointment in a variety of ways: by watching soap operas ("the latest rage"); by avoiding "the entrapment of freshly appointed young officers by the fair city's

---

[1] David Hackworth, *About Face* (New York: Simon and Schuster, 1989) 212.
[2] Ibid., 212.
[3] Ibid.
[4] Ibid., 215.

southern belles"; by living with army wives maintaining homes in Columbus while their husbands were overseas; and by driving across the Chattahoochee River to Phenix City, Alabama.[5]

"Anything went there—gambling dens, red-light districts, crooked cops, murder, and intrigue—you name it, Phenix City had it. A visit there was excellent pre-combat training for Korea," the controversial ex-soldier said.[6]

When the course ended, 180 students graduated from a roster of 243. Hackworth, who graduated 108th in the class, said thinking was not required. "None of us had learned to think. It was not part of the required curriculum."[7]

Hackworth was not alone in his criticism.

Edward L. King, disillusioned with the military after serving in Korea, told his reaction in his book, *The Death of the Army*. "After returning from Korea I was sent to Fort Benning, Georgia, to attend the company-officer course and learn what I should have known before going to Korea two years before," he wrote. "After combat experience I found the course repetitive and so far removed from the reality of war as to be almost ridiculous."[8]

However, for most, training and classes went on as usual. In June 1952, Major General Robert Nicholas Young, a veteran of the Korean conflict, assumed his duties as commandant of the Infantry School. A 1922 graduate of the University of Maryland, Young was commissioned a second lieutenant in 1923, and he graduated from the Infantry School in 1933. A veteran of campaigns in France and Germany, he was assistant division commander of the 82nd Airborne Division and in 1951 commanded the 2nd Infantry Division in Korea.

A hero of the fighting in Korea was honored on September 15, 1952, when Faith Middle School was officially dedicated. The school was named for Lieutenant Colonel Don C. Faith, who was posthumously awarded the Medal of Honor on August 2 for his heroism in Korea near Hagaru-ri in 1950. Faith was commanding officer of the first battalion in the 32nd

---

[5] Ibid., 213.

[6] Ibid., 213–14.

[7] Ibid., 222.

[8] Edward L. King, *Death of the Army* (New York: Saturday Review Press, 1972) 18.

Infantry Regiment of the 7th Infantry Division. In World War II, Matthew Ridgway handpicked Faith from OCS at Fort Benning to be his aide-de-camp. A paratrooper, Faith jumped with Ridgway into Normandy. Faith, said historian Clay Blair "was a clone of Ridgway, intense, fearless, relentlessly aggressive, and unforgiving of error or caution."[9]

Ike Elected President

That fall, a leader of World War II and former Doughboy football coach was elected president of the United States. After consenting to become a Republican presidential nominee, Dwight D. Eisenhower narrowly won nomination over Senator Robert Taft of Ohio in his own party, but he overwhelmingly defeated Democrat Adlai Stevenson in the general election.

Henry Cabot lodge, stationed at Fort Benning in 1942 with the 66th Armored Regiment, helped persuade Eisenhower to run. Lodge, a manager in Ike's campaign, enjoyed telling the story about General George Patton's offer of $50 to anyone who captured Eisenhower, then a lieutenant colonel, in the Louisiana maneuvers in September 1941. Eisenhower named Lodge, a former US Senator from Massachusetts, as ambassador to the United Nations.

Assistant Commandant Major General Guy Meloy was appointed commandant of the Infantry School in January 1953. A 1927 graduate of West Point, Meloy served in World War II and was wounded in Korea. Prior to Benning in 1951, he was chief of the Civil Relations Office in the office of the chief of information at army headquarters.

January also saw Eisenhower sworn in as the country's thirty-fourth president. His was the first Republican administration in twenty-four years. Recalling his military days, he stressed the value of freedom in his inaugural address: "In the final choice a soldier's pack is not so heavy a burden as a prisoner's chain."[10]

Fulfilling a campaign promise to end the fighting in Korea, Eisenhower arranged a truce on June 27, leaving the country divided. A two-and-a-half-mile-wide buffer zone was created across Korea, giving South Korea nearly 1,500 square miles more territory than before the war. With no official

---

[9] Clay Blair, *The Forgotten War* (New York: Times Books, 1987) 292.
[10] Dwight D. Eisenhower, "January 20, 1953 Inaugural Address," http://www.eisenhower.utexas.edu/1stinaug.htm.

peace treaty signed, American troops remained in South Korea to monitor
North Korea's military actions. Those who died in the conflict numbered
54,246; wounded, 103,284; and missing in action, 5,178.

Eddy Back in Town

One former officer with close connections to post and town decided to
return permanently to the area. After retiring commander of the US Army
Forces in Europe, Lieutenant General Manton S. Eddy accepted an
executive position with Williams Lumber Company, the Williams
Construction Company and their affiliates. Eddy, who married Mamie
Peabody Buttolph of Columbus, planned to make Columbus his home.
Williams made two trips to Europe to visit with Eddy and praised the
general's accomplishments: "I had the privilege of seeing him in action, as
he controlled some 250,000 men. He is a magnificent executive. I know the
caliber of the man who is coming to us."[11] Money for post construction was
available due to the Korean conflict, and the Williams Company, an early
builder of the camp and fort, continued to do business with the army, now
with the help of one of its retired generals.

Recognition for Post Personnel

At the US Army Hospital at Benning, Alpharetta E. Slaats, Army Nurse
Corps ward administrator, received her Oak Leaves for her promotion to
major. Colonel Mack Green, hospital commanding officer, and Lieutenant
Colonel Marie Smith, chief nurse, presided. Slaats, when stationed at Tokyo
General Hospital during Korea, was photographed with the first wounded
North Koreans, giving "warm-hearted treatment."[12] The picture was used
on leaflets dropped over enemy lines. Any North Korean possessing a leaflet
was assured safe passage through American lines.

As Ranger training continued in 1953, 2nd Lieutenant Donald J. Wild
of Chippewa Falls, Wisconsin, a student in Ranger Officers Class Number
8, received a perfect score of 500 points in the army's physical fitness test,
"the first ever reported by the Infantry School's Ranger Department."[13]

---

[11] "Eddy Accepts Position Here with Williams," *Columbus Enquirer*, March 18
1953, 7.

[12] "Famed for Pix, Nurse at USAH Upped to Major," *Bayonet*, May 28 1953, 1.

[13] "Ranger Gets Perfect Score," *Bayonet*, June 4 1953, 7.

Wild also received a perfect score in October 1952 as an officer candidate at Fort Belvoir, Virginia. A member of the track team at St. John's University in Collegeville, Minnesota, before entering the army, Wild performed twenty pull-ups, seventy-five squat jumps, fifty-four push-ups, seventy-nine sit-ups in two minutes and a half-mile run—carrying rifle, bayonet, water canteen, field pack, and helmet—in 2:17.[14]

When the first atomic artillery shell was tested at Frenchman's Flat in Nevada in the spring of 1953, 114 enlisted men and 10 officers of Fort Benning were there. Wearing gas masks, they crouched in a five-foot deep slit in the sand. After the explosion, they recovered their balance but felt as though they were "in a box suspended above the ground and were being shaken to and from violently."[15]

On post, a celebration took place when a 100-woman detachment from ages eighteen to fifty-two celebrated the eleventh birthday of the Women's Army Corps (WAC) in April 1953. Founded in 1942, the WAC helped win World War II by doing essential jobs in the states and overseas. In 1953, nearly every section and department of the Infantry Center and Infantry School employed the WAC. First Lieutenant Jewel H. Wales commanded the Benning detachment. After graduating from the University of Southern California, she received a direct commission, followed by advance training at Fort Lee, Virginia.

Comings and Goings in 1954

With the opening of Airborne schools at Fort Campbell and Fort Bragg, only 250 new trainees a week were expected at Fort Benning in 1954—fewer than the weekly 300 to 350 trainees in 1953. While the number of Airborne students decreased, other men came. By mid-1954, 7,000 new troops had reported for assignment at Benning while 3,000 left for other assignments. The large number of veterans returning from overseas duty and a reduction in training at other installations attributed to the net gain of 4,000 men.

Major units of the 47th Infantry Division, commanded by Major General R. W. Stephen, transferred to Benning from Camp Rucker, Alabama, in the spring of 1954. The remainder of the 47th arrived in June. Called the Viking Division, the 47th Infantry Division, was a former

---

[14] Ibid., 7.

[15] Vic Jowers, "We Beheld Atom Blast in Nevada," *Bayonet*, June 4 1953, 1.

National Guard unit with personnel from Minnesota and North Dakota. It was ordered to active duty at Camp Rucker in January 1954. In March, more of its units, Companies A and B of the 582nd Combat Engineer Battalion, commanded by Major George S. Weyer, arrived from Rucker. In addition, the 164th Infantry Regiment from the 47th Division Headquarters moved to Benning in April, making its new home in the South Sand Hill area.

Major General Joseph H. Harper, new Infantry Center commander, was welcomed on Chapel field in June 1954 by a battalion of troops and a thirteen-gun salute fired by Battery C, 41st Field Artillery Battalion. It was the fourth tour of duty at Benning for the fifty-three-year-old general. In 1931, Harper attended the officers' course; in March 1946 he served as director of the Advanced Training Division of the old Airborne School, and in 1947 he became deputy chief of the staff of the Center. Prior to arriving at Benning in 1954, he commanded the 4th Infantry Division.

In July 1954, General Maxwell D. Taylor "made it mandatory that all newly commissioned Regular Army officers of infantry, armor, artillery, corps of engineers, and signal corps select and attend Airborne or Ranger training."[16] Although not volunteers, these officers secured the continuation of Airborne training at Fort Benning.

The *Army, Navy, Air Force Journal* reported in October 1954 that Harper had appointed a five-man board to review and coordinate helicopter instructional material used at the Infantry School. The board's mission was to supervise preparation of special texts and other training literature and to make recommendations at Fort Monroe, Virginia, for helicopter training tests. Benning's 506th Army Helicopter Company supported the Infantry School in training demonstrations and exercises.

29th Infantry Regiment Returns Home

As the year ended, several ceremonies were held on post. As the *Columbus Ledger* put it, "the Army played the numbers game on Fort Benning's French Field late yesterday afternoon."[17] On December 1, the colors of the 29th Infantry Regiment returned to Benning, replacing the 30th Infantry

---

[16] Ranger Manual, U.S. Army Infantry School, vault, Donovan Research Library, Fort Benning GA.

[17] "30th Becomes 29th; 47th Due to Become 3rd," *Columbus Ledger*, December 2 1954, 6.

Regiment. The 30th joined the 3rd Division in number only in a changeover ceremony that did not involve personnel. As the 30th regimental colors became part of the 3rd Division, Colonel Earl Sutton, former commander of the 30th and new commander of the 29th, accepted the colors of the 29th and its motto, "We Lead the Way."

The 30th Infantry Regiment celebrated its 141st Anniversary in January 1954. It had come to Benning in December 1948 with the 3rd Division and stayed as a training unit when the 3rd went to Korea. Supplying the Infantry School with school troops, the 30th was the center of the Combat Training Command formed in December 1950. In November 1952, the 41st Field Artillery Battalion and 406th Engineer Company joined the 30th Infantry Regiment to form the 30th Regimental Combat Team.

The 29th Infantry Regiment, organized in 1901, served as a demonstration unit at Benning for twenty-four years after arriving in March 1919. The 29th was one of the few infantry regiments retained at full combat strength after World War I and took part in organizational and equipment tests, such as implementing the triangular formation and the new drill regulations later used throughout the army. In addition, the 29th was the army's first unit to use motor vehicles instead of animals. In 1943, the 29th left Benning for Fort Jackson and then to Europe to serve in England, France, and Belgium. After World War II, the unit had duty in Germany, the Korean conflict, and Okinawa. The unit was away eleven years before returning "home" to Benning in 1954.

Another number's game involved the 41st Field Artillery Battalion. It was renamed the 23rd Field Artillery Battalion. The ceremony included a parade and a review of 4,000 troops by Harper who "trooped the line in modern fashion in a jeep."[18] When darkness fell on the ongoing ceremonies that began at 5 P.M., "spectators gave the Army a hand by pulling their cars to the edge of the field and turning on their car lights."[19]

3rd Division Home from Korea

In honor of the 3rd Division, December 3 was called "Marne Division Day" by Columbus Mayor Ralph Sayers. Secretary of the Army Robert T. Stevens was on hand to welcome the 3rd Division home from Korea. Because of his

---

[18] Ibid.
[19] Ibid.

appearance on televised Senate hearings in which Senator Joseph McCarthy confronted him and attacked the army, Stevens was well known. On post, Stevens said little about the hearings but assured everyone that "Fort Benning will not get penalized" since it had the backing of two important leaders: Senator Richard Russell (D-Georgia), and Representative Carl Vinson (D-Milledgeville), both slated to head the Armed Forces Committees in the Senate and House.[20]

Another important visitor, a real crowd-pleaser, was Captain Audie Murphy. While fighting with the 3rd Division's 15th Infantry Regiment in Italy, Murphy became the most decorated soldier of World War II. He was awarded the Medal of Honor for his actions in France on January 26, 1945, and received a battlefield commission. After the war, his legend of bravery and his good looks led him to Hollywood and to fame as an actor. While at Benning, Murphy visited with his friend Major General Haydon L. Boatner. Murphy and Boater discussed an ending for *Hell and Back*, a movie about the 3rd Division produced by Universal-International Studio. Murphy welcomed the 3rd Division when its ship docked at New Orleans earlier in the week. At ceremonies scheduled for December 3 on post, the young hero was again on hand to complete the division's homecoming. Although never stationed at Benning, Murphy defended the post's intense training of soldiers to prevent throwing them "into combat raw and untrained against highly organized troops of an enemy nation."[21]

Asked by *Columbus Ledger* reporter Mary Daly why he got out of service, Murphy, answered, "Well, ah—you know." However, he reassured her by saying, "I will always be available when the Army needs a helping hand, however."[22]

The 3rd Division, organized in 1917, served in World War I, World War II, and Korea. Columbus "opened its heart to the division immediately" when it came to Benning from Kentucky in 1948.[23]

---

[20] "Stevens Sees OK of New Draft Plan," *Columbus Ledger*, December 4 1954, 3.

[21] Mary Daly, "Audie Murphy Arrives to Help Welcome Third," *Columbus Ledger*, December 3 1954, 26.

[22] Ibid.

[23] "'Columbus' Own' Returns Home After Four Years," *Columbus Ledger*, December 3 1954, 9.

When the 3rd Division replaced the 47th Division at Benning, the men of the 47th Division removed their shoulder patches. The blue and white striped 3rd Division patches were sewn on underneath. Special ceremonies were scheduled in Minneapolis when the name and colors of the 47th returned to National Guard control of Minnesota and North Dakota.

Major General Robert H. Soule replaced Major General P. W. Clarkson as commander in 1950. Soule, leading his men in battle, received the Distinguished Service Cross (D. S. C.) in Korea. He won his first DSC for his leadership on Leyte in World War II. Soule, who died in 1952, did not return home with his troops.

Associated Press writers like Jim Becker and John Randolph caught the spirit of the 3rd and its feisty commander when they wrote in November 1954, "In the winter of 1950, it was the Third that fought the rear guard action in below zero weather and threw back the Chinese Reds. A little gamecock, a scholar, and a scraper led the Third Division in those darkest days of the war. He was Major General Robert (Shorty) Soule, now dead of a heart attack."[24]

In 1954, Fort Benning accommodated 41,000 troops, about 2,500 civilian employees, 8,918 dependents (quartered in Columbus and at the post), with 6,640 houses or apartments occupied in the vicinity, and 2,000 occupied on the post. The Benning staff consisted of 650 officers and 2,000 enlisted men. Fort Benning's monthly payroll was $6–$7 million—money that benefited the entire area.[25]

Three days before Christmas, three men stationed at Fort Benning celebrated a memorable tenth anniversary. Harper, who served in the 327th Glider Infantry Regiment in 1944, personally delivered a message to the Germans who demanded the Americans to surrender at the Battle of the Bulge. Major Oswald Y. Butler, operations officer of the Airborne Department, and Lieutenant Colonel James F. Adams, 6th Battalion commander of the 3rd Division were with the 327th. They escorted the Germans to General Anthony C. McAuliffe, commanding officer of the 101st, who answered "Nuts"—a message which McAuliffe's G-3 Colonel H. W. O. Kinnard found "hard to beat." Harper explained to the German

---

[24] Ibid.
[25] "Harper Tells Lions of Post Program," *Columbus Ledger*, December 1 1954, 2.

messenger, "If you don't understand what 'Nuts' means, in plain English, it is the same as 'go to hell.'"[26]

---

[26] "Three Now at Benning Had Roles 10 Years Ago at Bastogne," *Columbus Enquirer*, December 22 1954, 1.

29.

Infantry in the Sky

The infantry always relied on its feet. But visionaries realized the future infantry soldier would need to move faster than his two feet could carry him.

This vision put the army into conflict with the air force. In 1953, the army believed the air force, still mainly responsible for aviation training, "had drifted somewhat afield from training pilots and mechanics to operate and maintain aircraft in the field, the hallmark of army aviation."[1] Determined to gain control of its own airmobility, the army established the Aviation School at Fort Sill, Oklahoma. The school moved to Camp Rucker in 1954.

The army staff in the Pentagon knew army aviation spent "a good share of the army's annual appropriation," so the Aviation Staff Division was established: "Its first head, Major General Hamilton H. Howze, saw to it that army aviation had a voice when major decisions were made."[2]

When the US Air Force left Fort Benning's Lawson Air Field in February 1955, the army resumed operational control of the airfield and authorized its own changes under the command of Colonel Gilmon A. Huff. The basic taxiway system, with taxiway lights, was completed, and hangers were added along with a shop, two unit operations, aircraft parts supply buildings, a synthetic trainer, and a classroom building.

The Airborne and Army Aviation Department composed of the former Airborne Department and a newly organized Air Mobility Group was established at the Infantry School on February 14. The new department reflected the army's policy of increasing its airmobility, which military

---

[1] James W. Bradin, *From Hot Air to Hellfire* (Novato CA: Presideio Press, 1994) 91.

[2] Ibid., 91.

leaders believed necessary in the solution of modern conflicts—especially those related to an atomic war.

The Airborne School, directed by Colonel Leland G. Cagwin, continued to operate as it formerly did and kept its basic organization. New to the curriculum in 1954 was the Pathfinder course. Lieutenant Colonel Sammie N. Homan, a paratrooper since 1943, headed the Air Mobility Group, which planned to work with helicopters and with fixed wing planes of both the army and air force.

In October 1948, the army started a helicopter advanced tactical training course at Fort Sill, Oklahoma—site of the Infantry School in 1918 before its move to Camp Benning. Here Lieutenant Colonel Hubert D. Gaddis, instructed in 1946 by Bell Helicopter Company in the army's first formal helicopter pilot training course, developed a standardized flight training course for the army's first rotary wing instructor pilots.

When the Army Aviation School moved to Camp Rucker in September 1954, the south Alabama post was named the Army Aviation Center. It became a permanent post, training pilots and maintenance men for the army's own air force of small fixed-wing airplanes and helicopters. The rotary wing course, part of the flight department at Fort Sill, became a department in its own right.[3]

The Infantry School's Airborne and Army Aviation Department aided the Army Aviation School at Camp Rucker. It also cooperated with other service schools, including the newly opened Air Force Academy in Colorado, to develop new doctrines, procedures, and organizations for the army's airmobility operation. Colonel John J. Tolson, with fourteen years of Airborne experience, was chosen to head Benning's Airborne and Army Aviation Department where he developed tactical doctrine for helicopters in combat. A West Point graduate, Tolson took Airborne training and was company commander in the 504th Parachute Infantry Battalion at Fort Benning in 1941–1942.[4]

Before assuming his duties at the Infantry School as director of the Airborne and Army Aviation Department, Tolson was chief of the doctrines and combat developments branch of the army's G-3 Section in Washington,

---

[3] Ibid.

[4] "Airborne-Army Aviation Department," *Army-Navy-Air Force Register* 76/3930 (April 2 1955): 5.

DC. He was a master parachutist with three World War II jumps to his credit.

The feud between the army and the air force worsened in 1956. The army claimed the air force was not doing its job. Once possessing the third largest air force in the world, following the US Air Force and the Russian Air Force, the army was restricted to serviced aircraft missions in 1951. Weight restrictions determined the army's fixed-wing aircraft along with the helicopter's "performance of functions" in the 1952 agreement between the army and the air force.

Brigadier General Carl I. Hutton, the Aviation School commandant at Fort Rucker, believed "mobility was important, but armed aerial weapon platforms were more important."[5] Concerned that the air force did not provide the close air support the army desired, Hutton "reasoned that the helicopter was one way of getting around the prohibition against the Army's arming its aircraft."[6]

Colonel Jay D. Vanderpool, at the invitation of Hutton, became the first director of combat developments for the Aviation School and Center and named his organization the Armed Helicopter Mobile Task Force. As an army ground fighter, Vanderpool realized the need and substance of effective ground support for soldiers. His success in arming the helicopter had a direct effect on training tactics at Fort Benning where, in the future, after air assault tests were completed, the first air cavalry squadron was committed to combat in Vietnam.

When Major General Herbert B. Powell became commandant of the Infantry School, a student enrollment of 18,047 was expected for fiscal year 1956. At a talk to the Columbus Chapter, Military Order of World Wars, in October at the Main Officers' Mess at Fort Benning, Powell listed four objectives of a balanced and flexible force: deterrent to general war; deterrent to local aggression; defeat of local aggression; winning general war.[7]

---

[5] Bradin, *From Hot Air to Hellfire*, 94.

[6] Ibid.

[7] "Gen. Powell Cites Need for Flexible Force," *Columbus Ledger*, October 19 1956, 2.

A balanced and flexible force, Powell said, needed dispersion, improved communication and enemy observation and detection.[8] To realize these needs, Powell recommended development of lighter support weapons of reduced range. Powell saw the need for an air transportable weapon to "slug it out" with enemy heavy armor.

In a 1957 article for the *Army, Navy, Air Force Journal,* Powell explained that the Infantry School was meeting the demands of an atomic-age infantry by its Airborne-Army Aviation Department, which tried to make the infantry air transportable. "We believe that Army aviation will provide the necessary mobility, speed, and flexibility that the infantry needs for the movement of units and supplies in future combat operations," Powell wrote.[9]

Considering "the helicopter an Airborne jeep which can get us to our destination quicker and more efficiently," Powell stated the infantry was beginning to rely more and more on helicopters and small fixed wing aircraft as a means of transportation.[10] He also said more than 100 hours of instruction, dealing primarily with characteristics and capabilities of atomic weapons and delivery means, was common in advanced classes at the Infantry School in order to help in the transition to an atomic age battlefield. "To make atomic training more realistic," Powell wrote, "The Infantry School has developed an atomic burst simulator for use in instruction."[11]

Phenix City Attractions

Fort Benning was one of seven stateside army posts designated as a permanent home station for the army's tactical divisions under "Operation Gyroscope." Benning served as home station for two divisions, one in the US, the other overseas.

For those who stayed stateside, Benning, again experiencing peacetime, was a busy but relaxed post. On September 15, 1955, the *Columbus Ledger-Enquirer* reported, "Post Covers 182,000 acres." Land purchases in Georgia

---

[8] Ibid.

[9] Herbert B. Powell, "The Army's Infantry Center Takes An Atomic Age Look Ahead," *Army, Navy, Air Force Journal* 94/26 (February 23 1957): 27.

[10] Ibid.

[11] Ibid., 27.

were valued at \$4,474,878.97 and in Alabama at \$453,064.50. In 1955, the military reservation held 285 square miles, including 12,311 acres in Alabama. It was approximately 15 miles across from east to west and 20 miles from north to south. Including the Main Post, Sand Hill, and Harmony Church areas, the population of the military garrison was 56,069. Benning was a supervised city with its own stores, schools, recreation centers, churches, and plans for a new hospital.

Keeping those 56,069 soldiers on the straight and narrow had always been a challenge to Fort Benning's commanders—especially with the lure of the honky tonks in Phenix City providing round-the-clock temptations. That challenge existed for decades. During World War II, Fort Benning joined local crime-fighters to clean up a town where even law and order was under the thumb of the longstanding gambling element. In *Phenix City, the Wickedest City in America*, the authors wrote "of all the illicit industries, lottery was the biggest money maker. Following came other forms of gambling, such as dice, slot machines, and poker. Prostitution and dope were close behind. Illegal whiskey and beer sales marked up huge profits.[12] Raids on these establishments, however, were just for show, and the clubs soon were open again.

Not that Columbus was always pure. On January 4, 1945, T. H. Lacey, who represented a group of "Christian-minded Chicago businessmen" attacked the entertainment provided for servicemen in Columbus: "I recently looked in on one of your USO's formal dances," he said, "and was shocked to see that the soldiers had as companions women naked half-way down to the waist. Being a man of God, I could not associate with them."[13] Lacey appealed to the Columbus Rotary Club to open a Christian service center for soldiers.

Meanwhile, Phenix City was a wide-open town that thrived on soldier payday. There was prostitution, gambling, illegal booze, and drugs. Soldiers looking for a good time often found themselves bloody and beaten or in a Phenix City jail cell, courtesy of police on the underworld payroll. It was a billion-dollar industry doing business in a town that went to Columbus to

---

[12] Edwin Strickland and Gene Wortsman, *Phenix City, the Wickedest City in America* (Birmingham AL: Vulcan Press, 1955) 3–4.

[13] "The Longest Year: Home Front," *Columbus Ledger-Enquirer*, January 4 1995, A6.

buy groceries or a new Chevy. The local syndicate made money for years, but profits soared during the buildup of troops at Fort Benning during World War II and Korea.[14]

The town was dotted with clubs, casinos, and joints. Some neighborhood grocery stores even had slot machines young children could play as they stood on soft-drink crates. The most infamous club was Ma Beachie's, run by pistol-packing Beachie Howard. In her novel *Heartbreak Hotel*, set in 1956, Georgia author Anne River Siddons, a graduate of Auburn University, describes the evening college students Maggie and Delia went clubbing at Ma Beachie's with a young Yankee professor, Charles Peyton Tucker:

> The room was jammed with lean, prowling-eyed young soldiers, cool and mean and languid, in droves whistling and stamping and calling out matter-of-fact obscenities to the uninterested strippers. They were drinking hard. No beer now, not at Ma's. Just the house hard stuff. Ma's kept a few token bottles of call brands, but they were dusty and unused. Ma's prices were prohibitive. No one was mean drunk, fight drunk, but the chemistry of an evening is a delicate and unpredictable thing.[15]

A musician who played in the Phenix City area said,

> Mama Beachie was probably loved by more musicians than any other club operator in the entire area.... She employed more fine musicians than any other club in town. She had a heart as big as all outdoors and served the best home-made chili I ever ate.... Beachie paid a decent salary, but the big money came on weekend nights from the 'kitty' we kept on the bandstand.... Our main source of income to the band kitty were the vocals and parodies we did on many tunes. Most of the songs we played were a bit off-color, to say the least.... Just a straight one or two-chorus instrumental tune was worth one

---

[14] Phillip Rawls, "'Sin City' just a memory 50 years after assassination," *Opelike-Auburn News*, June 13 2004, 2.

[15] Anne Rivers Siddons, *The Heartbreak Hotel* (New York: Simon & Schuster, 1976) 38.

dollar in the kitty, while some of the off-color tunes were five-dollar tunes...those really were the days![16]

In the 1950s, another city cleanup group emerged: the Russell Betterment Association (RBA). Led by Hugh Bentley, owner of a sporting goods store in Columbus, the RBA enlisted the services of Albert Patterson, a lawyer who had at times represented some of the men they wanted to put out of business. Patterson was a fighter. Although permanently disabled from a leg wound in World War I, he took a stand against crime in Phenix City.[17]

With support from the *Columbus Ledger*—which would win a Pulitzer Prize for its crusade—Bentley, Patterson, and friends began to campaign against the rackets and the men who ran them. The influence of the gambling syndicate extended all the way to the Alabama State Capitol in Montgomery so the RBA decided it needed a statewide voice. Patterson, billing himself a man against crime, ran for state attorney general.[18] Overcoming a crooked election, Patterson won that race and became the Democratic nominee for state attorney general. People figured "Sin City" was about to be shut down. Patterson was not so optimistic. He predicted his own death on Thursday, June 17, 1954, in a talk at the Men's Club of the Phenix City First Methodist church. "I have only a 100-to-1 chance of ever being sworn in as attorney general," he said.[19]

By the next night, he was dead.

Patterson, shot twice in the mouth at close range, was left bleeding in an alley between his upstairs law office and the Elite Café, only blocks from the Russell County Court House.[20] In death, he was able to do something he might not have accomplished in life. His murder had a profound effect upon a town in which nearly every law agency was involved in some illegal operation. In forty-eight hours, the Alabama National Guard, led by Major

---

[16] Gene Kocian, *Memories of Jazz: The History of Swing & Jazz in the Columbus, Georgia, Area* (New York: Sewell Printers, 1989) 99.

[17] "Assassin's Bullet Ends Life of War One Hero," *Columbus Enquirer*, June 19 1954, 1.

[18] "Patterson Shot to Death in Car Alongside Office," *Columbus Enquirer*, June 19 1954, 1.

[19] Ibid.

[20] Ibid.

General Walter J. "Crack" Hanna, marched into town. Martial law was declared, the beginning of the end for the vice and corruption that plagued the town.[21]

Little was mentioned in the *Bayonet* about the situation in Phenix City other than to note that Phenix City was off-limits indefinitely. This action was in response to Alabama Governor Gordon Persons's request to restrict the visitation of Fort Benning soldiers to the troubled hamlet. Only military personnel who were residents of Phenix City were allowed special passes to enter. To enforce the order, military police were placed on the 14th Street and Dillingham bridges. Authorities also were stationed at the pontoon bridge across the Chattahoochee River behind Lawson Field.

In December 1954, former Russell County deputy Albert Fuller and Russell County circuit solicitor Arch Ferrell were charged with murder in the slaying of Albert Patterson.[22] Only Fuller was convicted and sentenced to life imprisonment.

While Phenix City was undergoing a metamorphosis, life went on at Fort Benning. In 1956, the Army Nurse Corps, the oldest of all the women's military services, celebrated its fifty-fifth birthday on February 2—the date it was established by Congress in 1901. The all-commissioned corps consisted of registered professional nurses. Nurses were on duty at Fort Benning for thirty-three years. Before 1923, nurses were procured for duty by contract with the Columbus City hospital. In 1956, sixty-nine nurses were stationed at Benning. Lieutenant Colonel Clara M. Kiely, chief nurse, and Major Augusta K. Peake, assistant chief nurse, were in charge of the sixty-nine women officers.

In October 1955, Fort Benning hosted the first national meeting of the Association of the United States Army (AUSA), an organization formed in 1950 from a merger of the Infantry Association and the Field Artillery Association. In attendance were Secretary of the Army Wilbur M. Brucker and some 100 general officers, including former army chief of staff J. Lawton Collins, then the US representative to the Military Committee and Standing Group of the North Atlantic Treaty organization (NATO). In addition to his regular duties, Collins served as special envoy to Vietnam

---

[21] Strickland and Wortsman, *Phenix City*, 7.

[22] "Ferrell, Fuller Indicted for Patterson Murder," *Columbus Ledger*, December 2 1954, 2.

with the rank of ambassador. Also present were Research and Development Chief Lieutenant James M. Gavin and army chief of staff General Maxwell Taylor.

Delegates saw firing demonstrations and displays of new weapons such as the Honest John bombardment rocket and the Corporal guided missile, both capable of using atomic warheads. Also displayed were the Nike anti-aircraft guided missile and the 280 mm gun, which could fire atomic shells. Various types of army aircraft, including helicopters, were also exhibited. At the meeting, army Secretary Brucker spoke to what was considered, "the largest gathering of top brass in the history of Fort Benning," assuring them, "There will always be an Army."

President Eisenhower sent a message to the group from a Denver hospital where he was recuperating from a heart attack. He greeted his former World War II comrades-in-arms, reminding them that their courage and patriotism "are more valuable than ever in this day of rapid change and global responsibility for the armed forces of the United States."[23] Attesting to the tactical changes in warfare, Brucker said, "Nothing has appeared to substitute for the soldier and ability to hold ground."[24]

Soldiers, however, who served faithfully and often brilliantly during World War I now questioned Eisenhower's plan to reduce the army, navy, and air force while refusing to spend money on missile development. Eisenhower's philosophy was to use the nuclear bomb to deter the Russians. The resignations of army chief of staff General Matthew Ridgway in 1955, General James Gavin in 1958, and army chief of staff General Maxwell Taylor in 1959 reflected the concern of army officers "who feared that the nation was reverting to the Army weakness that had invited attack in Korea."[25] Taylor, recalled to active duty by President Kennedy, later visited Benning as chairman of the joint chiefs of staff in 1962.

President Eisenhower was reelected in 1956 in a landslide over Adlai E. Stevenson. He continued to avoid international military conflicts and to produce a balanced national budget. Richard M. Nixon remained as vice-president. Eisenhower soon would face his first domestic crisis: the violent

---

[23] "Brucker Assures Role of Soldiers," *Columbus Ledger*, October 22 1955, 12.
[24] Ibid.
[25] Russell F. Weigley, *History of the United States Army* (Bloomington: Indiana University Press, 1984) 526.

reaction to the court-ordered racial integration of schools in Little Rock, Arkansas. International problems also existed. The Cold War seemed to heat up when Soviet troops marched into Hungary. American military forces were put on alert, but no action was taken. At Fort Benning, soldiers could do nothing but wait.

30.

A Tale of Two Soldiers

They were two very different soldiers. One arrived in 1957, the other a year later. Each had a ROTC background. Each came out of a university setting in New York City. Each would go on to greatness in arenas very different from Fort Benning.

After receiving his degree from Fordham University in 1956, Alphonse J. D'Abruzzo went to ROTC summer camp at Fort Bragg. That October, he entered the army a 2nd lieutenant, ready to serve his six-month stint on active duty. From Bragg he was sent to Benning. His wife, Arlene Weiss, did not accompany him to Georgia. A classically trained musician, she was performing with the Houston Symphony Orchestra, so she stayed in Texas. In April 1957, Fort Benning's theatrical group, The Masques, presented the melodrama, *Pure as the Driven Snow*. D'Abruzzo played the lead.

The young soldier came by the stage naturally. His father was Robert Aldo, a popular actor and singer who appeared as composer George Gershwin in the movie *Rhapsody in Blue* and in the Broadway production *Guys and Dolls*.[1] D'Abruzzo, known professionally as Alan Alda, went on to a successful acting career of his own. In the 1970s, relying on his army experience, he portrayed "Hawkeye Pierce," an outspoken army medical doctor serving near the front in Korea. The television series *M*A*S*H* (mobile army surgical hospital) entertained thousands of television viewers.

A year later, in June 1958, a young soldier destined to a distinguished military and public service career, began the eight-week infantry officers' basic course. It was Colin Powell's first tour of duty at the Georgia post. He was a ROTC graduate of City College of New York. He lived in the BOQ (Bachelor Officers' Quarters) across from the Airborne training ground.

---

[1] Millicent Scudder, "Al D'Abruzzo Played Lead in 'Driven Snow,'" *Benning Herald*, May 1957, 7.

Later, he lived in an apartment in Phenix City. He graduated from the basic course in the top ten of his class.

His training left a lifelong effect that he summed up in these maxims:

— Take charge of this post and all government property in
        view—The army's first general order.
— The mission is primary, followed by taking care of your soldiers.
— Don't stand there. Do something!
— Lead by example.
— "No excuse, sir."
— Officers always eat last.
— Never forget, you are an American infantryman, the best.
— And never be without a watch, a pencil, and a notepad.[2]

Alan Alda and Colin Powell epitomized the young soldiers who continued to pass through Fort Benning. Like Alda, thousands did their duty and moved on to other careers. Others, such as Powell, built a foundation for a life and a career in the military. Each found something at Fort Benning to carry with him.

The Fort Benning they experienced in the late 1950s was not as vibrant as a wartime post but was quietly fulfilling its mission. A new hospital was opened as was a museum dedicated to the infantry and a hall of fame for outstanding OCS graduates. Airborne divisions reorganized, and new schools for dependents appeared. In spring 1958, the 2nd Infantry Division was reorganized as a training division at Benning with personnel and equipment of the 10th Infantry Division returning from Germany.

Pentomic Army

The 2nd Infantry Division was part of the army's proposed modernization of the triangular division structure. Referred to the Pentomic Army, the Pentomic Infantry Division used a pentagonal structure designed to fight under atomic conditions. The infantry division numbered five combat or battle groups. Each battle group held five infantry companies plus a headquarters, service company, and mortar battery. Logistical support was

---

[2] Colin L. Powell with Joseph E. Persico, *My American Journal* (New York: Random House, 1995) 41.

centralized under a single Support Group responsible for all supply, evacuation, maintenance, medical services, and transportation. A separate Signal Battalion, with improved signal communications, handled the increased communication resulting from the five elements and their wider dispersion.

The proposed Pentomic Army Division called for 13,748 personnel, a reduction from the triangular division of 17,460. Although the cut in manpower was a concern, the Pentomic Infantry Division structure represented only a 21 percent reduction in manpower as compared to the Airborne division's 32 percent manpower reduction. More support-type groups were needed in relation to combat groups to maintain sophisticated weaponry and to help the larger number of dispersed subordinate units on the atomic battlefield.[3]

The Pentomic concept meant the combat zone, especially in an atomic war, would extend in depth with units dispersing to avoid detection and destruction by atomic weapons. These units would form small independent groups capable of operating for unlimited periods on the modern battlefield.

OCS Hall of Fame

Plans for Fort Benning's Officer Candidate School Hall of Fame began in the summer of 1957 with Colonel Waldron J. Winter, commanding officer of the 5th Student Battalion (OCS). Membership included officers commissioned from infantry OCS who attained the grade of colonel while serving on active duty, or were elected or appointed to an office of national prominence or have been the recipient of the Medal of Honor.

Major Robert B. Nett, assigned to the Platoon Tactics Committee at the Infantry School, was honored as one of the first outstanding Fort Benning OCS graduates. His picture, along with a copy of his Medal of Honor citation and a résumé of his career, was placed in Wigle Hall, named in honor of 2nd Lieutenant Thomas Wigle, like Nett, a World War II Medal of Honor recipient. Wigle Hall was dedicated June 2, 1958, as the Officer Candidate School of Fame.

In 1958, a new Infantry Museum was conceived, planned, and promoted by the US Army Infantry Museum Society. It was to depict "each

---

[3] "Details Told on New Organization," *Bayonet*, May 2 1957, 2.

period of the US Army and the nation's history." The project would include a memorial park and museum "to preserve the proud heritage of the US infantryman and his exploits from the Indian wars to the Korean conflict."[4] With the backing of the US Army Infantry Museum Society, the park and museum would become "one of the truly scenic sites of the South."[5] Unfortunately, insufficient funds halted the building plans. Treasured memorabilia, however, continued to be stored in Building 81, formerly the Visitors Information Center.

By 1959, the scaled-down museum was open. The new Infantry Museum, located in Pusan Hall on Ingersoll Street, was not the building supporters hoped for but did feature the first manufactured M-14 rifle and M-60 machine gun. In addition to the display of medals, flags, regimental colors, weapons, and documents, its art gallery exhibited contemporary paintings of infantry leaders and highlighted a portrait of Major General Henry L. Benning.

More than 3,000 Fort Benning civilian employees observed the seventy-fifth anniversary of civil service in 1958. Initiated on January 16, 1883, the Civil Service Act provided equitable government employment. In operation at Benning since 1919, civil service employees, serving under the Department of Defense, ranged from "street repairmen, water plant operators, laundrymen, postal clerks, firemen, educators, scientists, executives, and administrators."[6]

Representatives of long-time civilian employees were Lawrence L. Woolbright, administrative officer in the Administrative and Management Division of Quartermaster Section, who came in October 1922, and Mrs. Mattie H. Bray, a clerk in the army field printing plant, who began in August 1922.

In true Hollywood fashion, Major General William C. Westmoreland, the youngest major general in the army in 1958, made a parachute jump at Fort Benning during a March visit. Touring the Airborne-Air Mobility Department, as well as viewing artillery demonstrations, the designated commander of the 101st Airborne Division at Fort Campbell, Kentucky,

---

[4] "Post Begins on Edifice," *Bayonet*, January 9 1958, 1.

[5] Ibid.

[6] "3000 at Post Observe Civil Service Birth Today," *Bayonet*, January 15 1958, 1.

received briefings on the Infantry School's newest tactics and techniques.[7] Westmoreland took paratroop training at Fort Benning in 1946 and commanded the 504th Paratroop Infantry Regiment before becoming chief of staff of the 82nd Airborne Division at Fort Bragg in August 1947.

Doughboy Comes and Powell Leaves

On April 1, 1958, the Infantry School celebrated its fifth-first birthday since its beginning in 1907 as the School of Musketry at the Presidio of Monterey, California. The ceremony included the unveiling of the *Doughboy Statue*, a 9-foot, World War II soldier dressed in full combat dress, holding a M-1 rifle in the parade-rest position, a replica, cast in bronze, of the *American Doughboy Statue* that stood in Berlin, Germany. German sculptor Ernst Kunst used Staff Sergeant Thomas E. Love, a veteran combat member of the 26th Infantry Division, as his model. Placed in front of the Infantry School, the statue carries this inscription: "The American infantryman—this monument stands as a tribute to our nation's bravest soldiers."[8]

In April 1958, Major General Herbert B. Powell, Infantry Center commanding general and Infantry School commandant, received his new assignment as deputy commanding general for reserve components at Continental Army Command at Fort Monroe, Virginia. Powell, called a "soldier's general," served as a platoon leader of the 3rd Infantry Division in World War II and as commander of the 17th Infantry, 7th Infantry Division, in the Korean conflict.

Earning his third star while at Benning, Powell learned how to fly the helicopter at Lawson Field and earned his army aviator rating. Before departing, he was honored with a fly-by of aircraft from Lawson Army Airfield Command. On his day of departure, Infantry Center bands played at his quarters, and troops lined his route as he left post. His successor, Major General Paul L. Freeman, assumed command in May 1958. Freeman previously served as senior army member of the Weapons Systems Evaluation Group, Office of the Assistant Secretary of Defense for Research and Engineering in Washington, DC.

---

[7] "Infantry School Visited by Gen. Westmoreland," *Bayonet*, March 20 1958, 28.

[8] "Doughboy Statue Unveiling Held; Stands as Infantryman Memorial," *Bayonet*, April 3 1958, 1.

Preparing Post for Future

Four Fort Benning agencies were helping prepare the infantry of the future. The Combat Development Program increased the army's effectiveness in the field through innovative studies, field experiments, and testing material requirements. The Airborne Air Mobility Department tested and evaluated Airborne infantry's use of air transport, preparing for the battlefield of the future. The Infantry Board continued to test and recommend weapons, ammunition, combat clothing, rations, protective devices, and other individual equipment. Finally, the Human Research Unit, composed of civilian scientists and military personnel, improved methods of training, motivation, and morale.

On July 1, Martin Army Hospital formally opened. The former post hospital, begun in 1923 and completed in 1925, continued to serve as an outpatient clinic. The widow of Major General Joseph Martin unveiled the plaque and her husband's portrait. Martin was an Infantry School graduate and Medical Corps officer who worked in field medicine and in medical military education and training. Three sons, present at the ceremony, followed their father's profession: Lieutenant Colonel G. W. Martin, army physician at Fitzsimmons Army Hospital, Denver, Colorado; Captain Joseph I. Martin, Jr., Medical Service Corps at Fort Meade, Maryland; and SP2 Robert E. Martin of Brooke Army Medical Center, Fort Sam Houston, Texas. Guest speaker was Major General James P. Cooney, army deputy surgeon general.

Early Post Supporter Dies

That fall, Fort Benning lost one of its earliest advocates. On the day of the Georgia-Auburn football game that he helped bring to the city, Frank G. Lumpkin died. In a twist of fate, the game moved to the campus stadiums after the 1958 contest. His life reflected the history of Columbus and Georgia. He was born October 4, 1876, in Athens, Georgia, to Frank G. and Katherine DeWitt Willcox Lumpkin. The night Frank was born, his father died from injuries incurred in the Civil War. His mother returned to Columbus to live with her parents, Mr. And Mrs. D. F. Willcox.[9]

---

[9] "Death Claims Frank Lumpkin," *Columbus Ledger-Enquirer*, November 16 1958, A-1.

Lumpkin's grandfather, Joseph Henry Lumpkin, was the first chief justice of the Georgia Supreme Court. Lumpkin and his two sisters were believed to have been the only surviving grandchildren of the first chief justice of an original colony. The family name was given to a county, a city, and the University of Georgia's law school. On post, Lumpkin Road kept its "civilian" name by General Order #43 issued December 1939 and in 1942 by Special order #296 that recognized established roadways though most post roads were named for battles, war heroes or well known units.[10]

In 1900 young Lumpkin, who worked in the family's insurance company, married Annie Leonard Garrand of Columbus. They had two children, Frank Jr., and Ann. Ann died of malaria in Panama, where her husband, Jefferson D. Box, a soldier, was stationed in World War I. For years the Lumpkin family entertained before the Georgia-Auburn game. The tradition began in 1918 when Lumpkin threw a big party at his downtown office. The party, known as the "Basement Party," was held every year until the death of the company's treasurer, W. H. Thurman in 1951.

"We started in primarily for the boys at Fort Benning," Lumpkin explained. "They had absolutely no recreation at that time, so we figured we owed them a good time at least once a year."[11] In addition to enlisted men, his guest list included famous generals such as George C. Marshall, Omar N. Bradley, and George S. Patton.

After the death of his first wife in 1928, Lumpkin married Helen Dargan Lowndes of Atlanta in 1930. He headed one of Georgia's oldest insurance agencies for over fifty years, retiring in 1955. His son Frank G. Lumpkin, Jr., succeeded him as president of the Willcox-Lumpkin Insurance Company.

Conference of Civilian Aides Held

When not at war, the army trained for war or talked about war. Important conferences were held on post in 1958 to study the state of the modern army, especially how to move the foot soldier in smaller, lighter units, using greater firepower. In September, more than 110 key US business and civic

---

[10] LeRoy W. Yarborough, in collaboration with Truman Smith, *A History of the Infantry School, Fort Benning, Georgia* (Ft. Benning: The Infantry School, 1931) 371.

[11] Ray Jenkins, "Grid Series Owes Debt to Before-game Parties," *Columbus Ledger-Enquirer*, November 13 1955, C-3.

leaders and generals attended the Conference of Civilian aides to the secretary of army and army commanders. The civilians who attended served as advisory aides for two-year periods.

Prior to the exodus of 7,500 post personnel for the holidays, the World-Wide Infantry Conference was held December 2–6. Army secretary Wilber M. Brucker met with 80 US—7 wore 4 stars—and allied generals, in addition to 200 conferees. Freeman told the group, "Victory is a product of unity and cooperation between all branches of the Army and other services."[12]

Army chief of staff General Maxwell Taylor assured them the infantry was needed, now and tomorrow. "This function of the future, as well as today, remains to close with the enemy and to destroy or capture him, driving him from his position, and securing the ground wrested from him.... Thus to those who would say, 'The Queen is dead,' I would reply, 'Long Live the Queen!'"[13]

And as long as the Queen lived at Fort Benning, the relationship with the City of Columbus flourished. At the annual Columbus Rotary Club's Fort Benning Day in 1959, as reported in the *Bayonet*, "Fort Benning and Columbus patted each other on the back...and renewed their good neighbor policies."[14] Twenty-five officers were honored at the event held at the Ralston Hotel. In his speech that evening, Freeman said 9,000 military families lived off post and "own local property, pay local and state taxes, attend community churches, teach Sunday School, play on athletic teams and participate in Scouting."[15] Counting civilian and military, nearly 70,000 people were associated with Fort Benning.[16] Nearly 1,500 births in military families were registered each year in Chattahoochee County.[17]

Continuing to cite Benning's influence on Columbus, Freeman referred to the 12,000 students from thirty-eight nations present each year

---

[12] "Leaders Draft Means to Power New Army," *Bayonet*, December 11 1958, 2.

[13] "Chief of Staff Taylor gives the Word on the Future challenges of Infantry," *Army Navy Air Force Journal* 96/14 (December 6 1958): 11.

[14] "Post Integral in Columbus Community, Says Freeman," *Bayonet*, March 5 1959, 1.

[15] Ibid.

[16] Ibid.

[17] Ibid.

who "buy almost everything they can in this vicinity."[18] He also mentioned retirees who made Columbus their permanent home, no doubt influenced by the new post hospital and its other facilities, in addition to the city's hospitality and acceptance of the military. Their presence helped raise the area's economy above Georgia's 1959 median family income of $4,208.[19]

In 1959, the 4th Transportation Company (Medium Helicopter H-37 Mojave) was recognized as the outstanding unit at Lawson Army Airfield Command. Activated June 11, 1952, the 4th Transportation Company participated in projects Honest John, Little John, SS10, numerous air shows, and almost every major maneuver since 1952. Major James R. Woods, a veteran army flier, commanded the 4th Helicopter Company, the first company to use H-34s and the H-37s—the largest helicopters in the army.

After the 3rd Army inspection in 1959, the 4th Helicopter Company was rated outstanding and superior in all operational phases: "An H-37 helicopter, selected at random from the flight line, was found to have only one minor defect. The H-37 has more than 3,000 moving parts."[20]

Loyd School, the fourth dependents' educational facility on post, was dedicated in honor of 2nd Lieutenant Frank R. Loyd, Jr., killed in action in Korea in 1950. His parents, Colonel (Ret.) and Mrs. Frank R. Loyd of San Antonio, Texas, unveiled a plaque and accepted flowers from Miss Annie Lou Grimes. Miss Grimes was their son's principal when he was a student in the fourth and fifth grades in the main post school from 1937 to 1939. Her tenure as post principal in 1920 began when wives established a school for the younger children. Before this, school children on post were driven into town in a World War I reconnaissance car. After President Eisenhower declared Alaska a state in January 1959, the post's first forty-nine-star flag flew over Loyd School.

In April, Sergeant Major George C. Ferguson of the Army Advanced Marksmanship Unit's first, made history as the first E-9 to reenlist at the post and as the first noncommissioned officer promoted to the army's top enlisted pay grade at Fort Benning. Entering the army as a member of the 45th Infantry Division in 1940, Ferguson became a member of the famed

---

[18] Ibid., 2.

[19] Ibid.

[20] "4th Transportation Co. Named Outstanding Helicopter Company," *Bayonet*, March 5 1959, 6.

"Bushmasters," 158th Regiment Combat Team, in the South Pacific. He also served during the invasion of Normandy in 1944, receiving the Distinguished Service Cross, the Silver Star, Bronze Star with cluster, and four awards of the Purple Heart.[21]

Ferguson, who received a personal citation from General George Patton, Jr., said, "I have never regretted making the Army my career."[22] And he wasn't alone.

---

[21] "Sgt. Maj. Ferguson First E-9 to Re-up," *Bayonet*, April 30 1959, 1.
[22] Ibid.

31.

Big Birds and Benning

As the new decade began, so did the army's concentrated study of the helicopter. In January 1960, the Army Aircraft Requirements Review Board, chaired by Lieutenant General Gordon B. Rogers, evaluated designs of armed troop-carrying helicopters. The gas turbine engine now provided high power at low weight. Using gas turbine engines rather than reciprocal engines, "choppers" flew higher and faster with heavier loads. To advance army aviation, the Rogers Board suggested the army procure the Bell Helicopters turbine-powered UH-1 Huey utility helicopter as well as the deHaviland AC-1 Caribou, a troop-carrying short takeoff and landing aircraft.[1]

Benning's 2nd Infantry Division tested the new concept of army airmobility in January at Fort Steward, Georgia, teaming riflemen and support companies to give ground troops close support. An aerial weapons system developed by Colonel Jay D. Vanderpool and his team at the Fort Rucker Armed Helicopter Task Force armed helicopters with rockets and machine guns.

Under supervision of the US Continental Army Command, Major General R. H. Wienecke, commander of the 2nd Infantry Division, tested two major phases. The first phase tested the Aerial Reconnaissance and Security (ARS) Troop Unit as an organic element of the division reconnaissance squadron. The second tested the ARS Troop unit as a separate unit under division control. The 2nd Infantry Division's ARS Company was made a provisional company of the 2nd Division and was ready to demonstrate the tactical advantage of the helicopter for the close air support the US Army long desired.

---

[1] James W. Bradin, *From Hot Air to Hellfire, The History of Army Attack Aviation* (Novato CA: Presidio Press, 1994) 104.

In February, Wienecke left for his new assignment as chief of the Military Assistance Advisory Group in Pakistan. Major General Frederick W. Gibb assumed command of the 2nd Division in February. Gibb, who planned D-Day assault on Omaha Beach for the 1st Division—the "Big Red One"—later commanded the famed 16th Infantry that fought in Europe, earning an oak leaf cluster to the Legion of Merit.

On March 19, the army chief of staff approved the recommendations of the Rogers' Army Aircraft Requirements Review Board. Colonel John J. Tolson, former head of the Airborne and Army Aviation Department at the Infantry School, believed the Rogers Board was "a remarkable milestone in army airmobility. It set forward a chain of actions which had a profound effect on latter concepts."[2]

In April, plans for testing the Caribou aircraft were announced. Tests, scheduled to end in June 1961, included 46 realistic exercises simulating combat conditions.[3] In addition to helicopters, the Caribou, designed by deHaviland Aircraft Corporation of Canada as a short takeoff and landing aircraft (STOL), formed an army "air force" to provide the army air support and airlift mobility for small units in ground combat operations.

The US Air Force objected to the army's use of the Caribou, a thirty-two-passenger aircraft, and the Mohawk, originally designed as a visual reconnaissance aircraft with the potential of carrying sophisticated sensor systems and radar. However, Secretary of Defense Thomas S. Gates, Jr., approved the Mohawk and the Caribou for army aviation though both planes exceeded the 5,000-pound weight limitation set in 1952 for the army's fixed-wing aircraft. As John Tolson pointed out, "in the early 1960s the Caribou and the Mohawk were the two major symbols of army-air force disagreement and more time was devoted to these systems than to the entire airmobility concept itself."[4]

Commandant Major General Paul Freeman left Benning in April for his new assignment as deputy commanding general for Reserve Forces, Continental Army Command (CONARC), and Fort Monroe, Virginia. On Freeman's last day, members of the staff and their wives gathered at

---

[2] Lt. Gen. John J. Tolson, *Vietnam Studies: Airmobility 1961–1971* (Washington DC: Department of the Army, 1973) 9.

[3] "Caribou Troop Tests Evaluation Under Way," *Bayonet*, June 30 1961, 8.

[4] Ibid., 13.

Riverside to say goodbye. From there to Outpost No. 1, members of the Infantry Center band and the colors of all units on post and the guidon bearers lined the way in a last tribute to the general and his wife.

His successor, Major General Hugh P. Harris, arrived April 19. His previous duty was with CONARC at Fort Monroe, serving as deputy chief of staff since June 1958. Harris, a 1931 graduate of West Point, became the twenty-third commandant of the Infantry School and served as commanding general of the Infantry Center.

Dwight D. Eisenhower's "surprise one-day visit" on May 3, marked his fourth visit as president to Fort Benning although he had "unofficially" visited his son, Major John Eisenhower of the 30th Infantry Regiment, and his family on post.[5] The president's visit drew international attention to the army's Project MAN (Modern Army Needs), a massive show of the army's military might and progress. In the demonstrations, witnessed by hundreds of top ranking military and civilian leaders, the infantryman was called "the ultimate weapon."[6] Secretary of the Army Wilber M. Brucker stressed the "One Army" concept, referring to the Ready Reserve Forces—the Army National Guard and Army Reserve as well as the Active Army units.[7]

Following Eisenhower's visit, the *Infantryman Statue* (later named *Follow Me*) was officially unveiled and dedicated by Brucker. Its dimensions are impressive. The 3,000-pound, 22-foot statue (12 feet for the infantryman and 10 feet for the base) is made of polyester and glass fiber with a bronze impregnated resin finish. The rifle is 7 feet, 3 inches, and the raised right arm extends 5 feet, 8 inches. Circumference of the chest is 7 feet, 5 inches, helmet 5 feet, 5 inches, and the waist is 5 feet, 5 inches.

Specialists Manfred Bass and Karl H. Von Krog were the sculptors, and Officer Candidate Eugene J. Wyles served as the model. Bass and Von Krog made clay models from which Freeman, who initiated the project, made the selection. The infantryman depicts the "Follow Me" pose and wears equipment proved and tested in World War II and Korea "to express the

---

[5] Arlee Grubbs, "Man Presented Modern Army to Thousands," *Bayonet*, May 5 1960, 1.

[6] "Project MAN," *Bayonet*, May 5 1960, 11.

[7] "MAN Presented Modern Army to Thousands," *Bayonet*, May 5 1960, 2.

seriousness and attitude of a squad leader in combat."[8] The statue was installed on Eubanks Field near the Officer Candidate School headquarters, inspiring service men *and* women at Fort Benning.

In March 1961, Captain Madeline Barbour assumed duties as commander of the Woman's Army Corps (WAC) Company of the Infantry Center Troop command succeeding Captain Dorcas A. Stearns. Barbour previously served at Benning from June 1949 to July 1951 as a technician in the Infantry Center Signal Section's photographic laboratory. Prior to her present post assignment Barbour was posted in Germany as executive officer of the Intelligence Division of the Northern Area Command.

The highest-ranking WAC officer on post was Lieutenant Colonel Kathleen Burns, G-I Action Officer, assigned to the G-I (personnel) section of the Infantry Center Headquarters. Her duties involved "the multitudinous problems of personnel—their housing, morale, welfare and all the knotty situations that flesh is heir to."[9]At Benning since 1959, Burns joined the WAAC in 1943, serving tours in France and Germany.

In mid-March 1961, the 1st Aviation Company moved to McKenna and Dekkar Airstrips on the reservation for the second training problem in preparation for a troop test of the Caribou. Capable of landing in 500 to 600 feet and able to "clear a fifty-foot obstacle in 1,000 feet or less with no wind," the Caribou could aid paratroopers "alone out in the boondocks cut off from friendly lines."[10] On June 30, Troop Test Headquarters' evaluation of the army's Caribou aircraft was at its final stage with Lieutenant Colonel E. W. Smith as chief evaluator.

Major General Hugh P. Harris, in command since April 1960, left Fort Benning to assume command of I Corps in Korea, July 15, 1961. Harris was one of five Regular Army officers who volunteered for assignment in 1941 with the experimental 88th Airborne Battalion at Benning, later serving as chief of staff of the 13th Airborne Division in Europe in World War II.

---

[8] Arlee Grubbs, "*Infantryman Statue* Work Done Locally," *Bayonet*, May 5 1960, 2.

[9] Pat Abbot Ryan, "Top Lady Soldier," (Columbus GA) *Sunday Ledger-Enquirer Magazine*, June 18 1961, 10.

[10] "The Infantryman's Aerial Friend—The Caribou," *Bayonet*, September 22 1961, 5.

The largest fly-by in army aviation history, according to Lawson Army Aviation Command operations officials, honored Harris at his farewell review: "Fifty aircraft from all units of the major command took part in the formation flight, as some 2,300 troops from post units, marched in review."[11] Included in the fly-by were fixed-wing and rotary wing craft ranging from L-19 observation planes to the army's latest and largest cargo carrying Caribou, as well as H-12s and H-34s to the largest operational cargo helicopter, the H-37 Mohave.

On August 1, Major General Ben Harrell became the new commandant of the Infantry School and commanding general of the Infantry Center. He previously served as commander of the 101st Airborne Division at Fort Campbell, Kentucky. In 1943, he commanded the 3rd Division's 15th Infantry Regiment, and, as G-3 of VI Corps in 1944, planned the tactical maneuvers for the Anzio campaign and the capture of Rome. From December 1945 to July 1949, he was at the Infantry School. His son, 2nd Lieutenant Charles Harrell, a student in the Infantry School's Ranger Class No. 1, carried on the tradition.

In Exercise Swift Strike, held in August 1961, near Fort Bragg, North Carolina, more than 25,000 army and 10,000 air force personnel waged a mock war—the largest since the 1941 Louisiana maneuvers. The exercise displayed the preparedness of the Strategic Army Corps (STRAC) and Tactical Air Command (TAC). Composite Air Strike Force (CASF), used in the 1957 Lebanon Crisis by TAC, was employed in Swift Strike, including aerial tankers, reconnaissance and troop carrier aircraft as well as fighters.

The army's AC-1 Caribou "flew tons of supplies and hundreds of troops into unimproved areas where no fixed-wing aircraft had ever landed."[12] Flown by pilots of the 1st Aviation Company, Lawson Army Aviation Command, the Caribou was graded throughout the exercise for its tactical use. The aggressors, the 101st Airborne Division of Fort Campbell, faced the friendly force, the 82nd Airborne Division of Fort Bragg. The 4th Infantry Division, Fort Lewis, Washington, and other support elements also participated. During the "Swift Strike" maneuvers, the 3rd Transportation Battalion of Lawson, commanded by Lieutenant Colonel Donato N. Vincent, "hauled over 10,000 troops, 600 tons of supplies and flew over

---

[11] "'Fly-by' of 50 Called Largest Ever in Army," *Bayonet*, July 28 1961, 1.
[12] "Here's What LAAC Units Did," *Bayonet*, September 1 1961, 31.

1,300 hours."[13] In addition to the Caribou, Benning helicopters—H-37s of the 19th Transportation Company and H-34s of the 31st—demonstrated their abilities. Aircraft was maintained by Lawson's 138th, 593rd, and 507th Maintenance detachments.

Colonel Michael Paulick succeeded Lieutenant Colonel Harold E. Greer as director of the Infantry School's Airborne-Air Mobility Department. Paulick, Audie Murphy's battalion commander in Europe, acted as a technical adviser for Murphy's film *To Hell and Back* in 1954. Paulick previously commanded the 10th Special Forces Group (Airborne), 1st Special Forces, in Germany.

In late September, 46,000 troops from the National Guard and Army Reserves were called to active duty for stabilizing the Berlin Crisis. In early October, the first of approximately 2,500 officers and men of 12 Army Reserve and National Guard units arrived at Fort Benning. Supported by President John Kennedy, Secretary of Defense Robert S. McNamara ordered an increase of the Active Army in 1961 from 875,000 to a force of nearly a million.[14]

The buildup fit the Strategy of Flexible Response by General Maxwell Taylor—and adopted by Kennedy—in contrast to former president Eisenhower's plan for massive retaliation. To support flexibility, the Pentomic division, designed for the nuclear battleground, was replaced in 1961 by Reorganization Objectives Army Division (ROAD). Historian Russell F. Weigley defines ROAD as the army's return "to the triangular pattern that had served it well in World War II and Korea."[15]

In developing his policy of "special war," the young commander-in-chief looked to specialized counter-insurgency forces. As Weigley reported, "Kennedy especially became fascinated by guerrilla war."[16] On October 12, Kennedy attended a STRAC combat readiness demonstration of conventional and unconventional units at Fort Bragg. General William P. Yarborough, commander of the Special Warfare School there—wearing a green beret—greeted Kennedy. Years earlier, senior officers objected to the

---

[13] Ibid.

[14] Russell Weigley, *History of the United States Army* (Bloomington: Indiana University Press, 1984) 538.

[15] Ibid., 540.

[16] Ibid., 543.

"special" treatment given to "elite" soldiers, so the Special Forces had not been wearing berets.[17] Returning to Washington, Kennedy supported the green beret as "a symbol of excellence, the mark of distinction, the badge of courage. Army Regulations prescribed the color, shape, angle of droop, authorization to wear, and the insignia."[18] The official issue of the beret was "the first such distinctive headgear ever authorized by the Army."[19]

The Green Berets were not the only troops that pleased Kennedy that day. Fort Benning units also received praise. In a wire to Harrell, the president expressed his admiration for Benning soldiers: "I would like to especially commend the performance of Captain (Raymond F.) Spinks of your Weapons Department for his excellent presentation, and the Rangers, to a man, were the highlight of the afternoon."[20]

The *Bayonet* announced on December 8, "The Army's Airborne training, which first began here more than twenty years ago has returned to the post." With Airborne training phased out at Fort Bragg and Fort Campbell, the only basic Airborne training center in the continental United States was at Benning. Harrell was credited with the return. Though the return of Airborne training was important, airmobility became even more important—at Fort Benning and in the faraway country known as Vietnam.

---

[17] Aaron Bank, *From OSS to Green Berets* (Novata CA: Presidio Press, 1986) 203.

[18] Charles M. Simpson III, USA (Ret.), *Inside the Green Berets* (New York: Berkley Books, 1988) 34.

[19] Col. Aaron Bank, USA (Ret.) *From OSS to Green Berets* (Novato CA: Presidio Press, 1986) 203.

[20] "Infantry School Gets Presidential Citation," *Bayonet*, October 20 1961, 5.

32.

Invade Cuba—Not Mississippi

Cuba's Fidel Castro aimed Russian missiles at South Florida. James Meredith wanted to attend classes at the University of Mississippi. American boys were frequent casualties in Vietnam, and each episode was on the minds of Fort Benning soldiers in 1962, and each brought its own list of controversies to the table.

When Fort Benning troops returned from Mississippi in October, the Cuban Missile Crisis was prominent. The sentiment in Columbus was to send those soldiers to Havana. Cars in the Columbus area bore bumper stickers that read, "Send Troops to CUBA Not MISSISSIPPI." It was that kind of year, and it would be that kind of decade. America's mood was changing. Civil rights marchers soon would be in the streets and so would protesters of the escalating war in southeast Asia. Like it or not, Fort Benning found itself in the middle of change, conflict, and controversy.

In Vietnam, Americans were called "advisers" in 1962, but soon it was evident advisers can also bleed and die. First Lieutenant William F. Train III was one of the first casualties in the Fort Benning family. A West Point graduate, Train attended the Infantry School after graduation and stayed on for Airborne and Ranger training. Train was previously in Korea and "believed that his success with Koreans together with his facility in French would be of especial value to his country" in Vietnam.[1] He was killed in Vietnam on June 1, 1962.

His father, Major General William F. Train, Jr., replied to President John F. Kennedy's letter of condolence: "We are anxious that our nation remember him not just as another casualty of the cold war, nor ever only as

---

[1] Maj. Gen. William F. Train, "Casualty Portrait of Soldier," *Bayonet*, January 25 1963, 4.

our son, but rather as a loss to the Army and to the Nation of one of its promising courageous young officers."[2]

John Paul Vann, former instructor at the Ranger Training Command at Fort Benning, volunteered to serve as a senior adviser to a South Vietnamese infantry division in the Mekong Delta south of Saigon. In 1962, South Vietnamese peasants were resettled in defended towns protected from the Vietcong by US advisers and South Vietnamese soldiers. Biographer Neil Sheehan describes Vann's attitude toward US support of South Vietnam: "He manifested the faith and optimism of post-World War II America that any challenge would be overcome by will and by the disciplined application of intellect, technology, money, and, when necessary, armed force."[3]

Captain Colin Powell, a Benning graduate, also served in Vietnam in 1962. Eager to stop the communist conspiracy, Powell was ready to serve his country in its commitment to help achieve an independent South Vietnam: "It all had a compelling neatness and simplicity in 1962," he said.[4]

On Secretary of Defense Robert S. McNamara's fourth trip to Hawaii, he met with Frederick E. Nolting, US Ambassador to South Vietnam, and recently promoted four-star general Paul D. Harkins, commander of the US Military Assistance Command (MACV), a new US military command in Saigon. McNamara found Harkins "tall, handsome, and articulate; he looked and spoke exactly as a general should...he was very straightforward and persuasive."[5]

In response to his briefing, McNamara said, "I am pleased to learn that the Armed Forces of Vietnam are taking the offensive throughout the country, carrying the war to the Viet Cong, inflicting higher casualty rates and capturing Viet Cong weapons and supplies in greater numbers.... We

---

[2] Ibid.

[3] Neil Sheehan, *A Bright Shining Lie: John Paul Vann and America in Vietnam* (New York: Random House, 1988) 5.

[4] Colin Powell with Joseph E. Persico, *My American Journey* (New York: Random House, 1995) 75.

[5] Robert S. McNamara with Brian VanDeMark, *In Retrospect* (New York: Times Books, 1995) 47.

must not of course expect miracles overnight—a war of this kind takes time."[6]

Following a trip to Vietnam, McNamara sent a memorandum on April 19, 1962, to Secretary of the Army Elvis J. Stahr, Jr., strongly urging the army to substitute airmobile systems for traditional ground systems if it would improve capabilities and effectiveness.[7] He suggested a group study of the problem, naming several men to help the army's effort, including Lieutenant General Hamilton H. Howze. Within a week of McNamara's note, Howze became president of the ad hoc US Army Tactical Mobility Requirements Board. It reexamined the role of army aviation and aircraft requirements. "The Board," according to Howze, "has only a single, general conclusion. Adoption by the Army of the airmobile concept—however imperfectly it may be described and justified in this report—is necessary and desirable. In some respects the transition is inevitable, just as was that from animal mobility to motor."[8]

Howze's support for airmobility greatly affected Fort Benning for the next three years. In addition to the airmobile concept, the Howze Board issued its findings on special warfare concluding that for the army, "neither its indoctrination nor training is not altogether satisfactory for this mission...much of this concept is foreign to fundamental Army teaching practice."[9]

President Kennedy's wishes for counter-insurgency training as part of special warfare prevailed. Spurred by hints "that future promotions to general officer would depend on the individual's demonstrated competence in the field of counterinsurgency," the Department of the Army proposed the Military Assistance Training Advisors (MATA) course, approved by the Defense Department in January 1962.[10]

One of the students in these first counterinsurgency classes at Fort Bragg was Captain Russell Ramsey, previously assigned in Panama. Ramsey,

---

[6] "Changing Vietnam Pattern Seen Following Meetings in Pacific," *Bayonet*, April 6 1962, 1.

[7] Lt. Gen. John J. Tolson, *Vietnam Studies: Airmobility 1961–1971* (Washington DC: Department of the Army, 1973) 24.

[8] Ibid.

[9] Andrew F. Krepinevich, Jr., *The Army and Vietnam* (Baltimore: John Hopkins University Press, 1986) 44.

[10] Ibid., 32–33.

a 1958 graduate of Airborne and Ranger training, remembers Fort Benning Ranger instructor Tony Herbert, author of *Soldier*, as "a real rough and tough character."[11] After completing the course at Fort Bragg, Ramsey, proficient in Spanish, was assigned as anti-insurgency instructor at the School of Americas in Panama. When Robert Kennedy, a visitor at the school, observed the training, he put his arm around Ramsey, saying, "You're doing the president's program exactly right."[12]

In September 1962, Benning troops responded to a crisis in their own backyard. James Meredith, an African-American air force veteran of the Korean conflict, wanted to enroll at Ole Miss, a campus better known for Southern writer William Faulkner and Miss America contestants. The Supreme Court validated Meredith's desire, but university officials were not supportive. When he showed up on the tree-lined quadrangle, there was trouble. Fort Benning troops were to restore order during this national crisis. President Kennedy placed the Mississippi National Guard under federal control and sent a battle group as well as a command group of the combat-ready 2nd Infantry Division of Fort Benning to Oxford. Brigadier General Charles Billingslea, commanding general of the 2nd Infantry Division, was field commander of the operation. His command group included division chief of staff Colonel Louis A. Kunzig, Jr. The 2nd Battle Group of the 23rd Infantry, commanded by Colonel Lucien F. Keller, moved by motor convoy to Oxford with an attached unit, Company B, 2nd Battle Group, 9th Infantry, commanded by Lieutenant Robert L. Clarke.

Two Regular Army outfits from the 101st Airborne Division and the 2nd Battle Group, 1st Infantry, 2nd Infantry Division, stayed in Columbus, Mississippi, to prevent convoys led by White Citizens' Councils and other segregationist groups from Alabama or other neighboring states from entering the Oxford area. Commanded by Colonel Edgar R. Poole from Fort Benning, the 2nd Battle Group was joined by Company A, 2nd Battle Group, 9th Infantry, led by Captain Donald B. Smith, Jr.

In all, 16,000 federal troops, including the Mississippi National Guard plus other regulars from Fort Campbell, Fort Bragg, and Fort Dix, and 140

---

[11] Quoted by Dr. Russell Ramsey, interview by Peggy Stelpflug, March 4 1997, School of Americas, Fort Benning GA, handwritten transcript and audiocassette, Auburn AL.

[12] Ibid.

US Marines (who furnished 28 helicopters) were involved at a cost of $3 million. Howze, commander of STRAC and the 18th Airborne Corps at Fort Bragg, took charge of the operation from Billingslea. To emphasize the importance of the situation, Major General Creighton W. Abrams came to Oxford briefly as the personal representative of the army chief of staff.

In 1962, Sergeant James K. Hudson was an NCO in command of the Sand Hill swimming pool, an unexpected assignment that followed his expressing his opinion of the first sergeant. During the crisis he was assigned to a unit of the 23rd Infantry. Recalling the event, Hudson remembered he was interested in seeing Oxford, the home of William Faulkner, winner of the 1955 Pulitzer Prize in Letters, who died July 6, 1962. "Once we arrived, we formed a triangular formation on a corner of Oxford's town square where teenage boys assaulted us with empty Coke bottles placed conveniently outside the stores by Oxford merchants. A tear-gas grenade caused them to flee in panic," Hudson recalled.[13]

Locals objected to racially integrated units and wanted black soldiers removed. Orders came to relocate the black troops and things calmed down, but the compromise, Hudson explained, "was obviously against the principle the soldiers were defending. Especially upset were the black soldiers who were concerned about the safety of the soldiers left behind in the company when they departed the downtown square."[14]

Although two people were killed in the rioting—a French reporter and a local resident—order was restored. Ironically, Major General Edwin Walker, who commanded federal troops during the Little Rock desegregation crisis in 1957, came to support the Oxford protesters. Hudson said Walker, wearing a western style hat and business suit, told Hudson's squad, "It looks like you fellow have everything under control."[15] The former general was arrested but later released along with other protesters.

After restoring order, soldiers erected a tent city in a field outside Oxford with helicopters ready to transport the men if their assistance was required. The troops stayed eighteen days, keeping fit and maintaining readiness. In their free time, they read, wrote letters, and played cards. To

---

[13] James K. Hudson, interview by Peggy Stelpflug, April 3 1997, Donovan Library, Fort Benning GA, handwritten transcript and audiocassette, Auburn AL.

[14] Ibid.

[15] Quoted by Hudson.

avoid possible unnecessary harm, soldiers carried their weapons, but did not carry any ammunition.

This crisis was seen as "the bitterest federal-state clash since the Civil War."[16] Kennedy federalized the National Guard, "mainly to keep the guard out of the hands of Governor (Ross) Barnett," who defied federal efforts to integrate the all-white university.[17] Alabama Governor John Patterson, sympathetic to his neighboring state, wrote US Attorney General Robert Kennedy reminding him of his promise "never to use federal troops against the southern states."[18]

Although deploring the need to use federal troops to advance human rights in America, Signal Corps sergeant Joe "J. Q." Quarterman, stationed at Fort Benning in 1962 after a tour in Korea, believed the US government had to end segregation. "That's the only way this country could have dealt with communism. We had to sweep our own doorstep," he said. "Dealing with communism called for Civil Rights to advance at a more rapid rate."[19]

Quarterman, now retired in Columbus, believed if federal troops had been deployed in Alabama or Mississippi in 1957, rather than in Arkansas where the federal government made its first effort to integrate school, "much more bloodshed would have occurred."[20] Arkansas, less volatile than Alabama or Mississippi concerning integration, was a prudent choice for the first test. Although there was violence in Oxford, the people of Mississippi were better prepared for social change in 1962 than they were in 1958 because of dramatic outcomes in civil rights reported throughout the country by television and radio since the event in Little Rock, Arkansas.

By the time Fort Benning troops returned to Georgia, all post units were on alert because of the Cuban Missile Crisis. Hudson and his unit found themselves sitting on an airplane on the runway of Lawson Army Airfield ready to go to Cuba. Fortunately the alert was called off when

---

[16] John E. Jessup and Louise B. Ketz, "The Military and Civil Authority," *Encyclopedia of the American Military* (New York: Charles Scribner's Sons, 1994) 1825.

[17] Ibid.

[18] "Has Bobby Forgotten His Pledge?" (Columbus GA) *Sunday Ledger-Enquirer*, September 30 1962, 1.

[19] Joseph "J. Q." Quarterman, interview by Peggy Stelpflug, February 3 1997, Donovan Library, Fort Benning GA, handwritten transcript and audiocassette, Auburn AL.

[20] Ibid.

Russian premier Nikita Khrushchev removed the missiles from Cuba after Kennedy formed a naval blockade of the island and discussed the removal of US missiles from Turkey.

The only other excitement on post was the removal of one of Fort Benning's historic landmarks. The pontoon bridge, spanning the Chattahoochee River since 1942, was replaced by a permanent structure. The old bridge connected 82nd Airborne Division Road on the Georgia side with the 101st Airborne Division Road on the Alabama side. A ferry was used at the site before the pontoon bridge was built. Known as Whiskey Bridge because Alabama bootleggers once paddled across the river to bring illegal liquor to Georgia, the pontoon mooring often broke free to travel on its own. A part of it once floated to Florida. The old bridge remained in place until the new bridge, located a half-mile downstream, was completed in 1963.

The 197th Infantry Brigade, organized in March 1962, was activated September 24, under the Reorganization Objective Army Division (ROAD) concept, increasing the commander's control and the brigade's mobility. Supporting the Infantry School, the 197th insured students the best possible demonstration of infantry in combat.

In October 1962, the Student Brigade celebrated its twentieth anniversary. At one time or another, all army infantry officers were assigned to the Student Brigade. In October 1959, the School Brigade was redesignated the Student Brigade, and in February 1960, the Infantry School Detachment became the Infantry School Battalion. In 1962, the Student Brigade was composed of the 2nd Student Battalion, the 4th Student Battalion, the 5th Student Battalion, and the Infantry School Battalion: "The Student Brigade has as its mission, keeping the hundreds of students of the Infantry School fed, billeted, counseled, guided and disciplined by means of the finest facilities, physical and human, the Army offers."[21]

---

[21] Pvt. William Smyser, "Student Brigade Marks 20th Year," *Bayonet*, October 26 1962, 9.

33.

Replacing the Army Mule

Ten thousand troops passed in review on French Field. Herbert Powell, four stars twinkling on his shoulders, came home to Fort Benning, a post he once commanded, to end his distinguished military career.

More than foot soldiers were on that grassy field. There were missiles, engineer equipment, armored personnel carriers, tanks, artillery, and flybys with an assortment of aircraft from Lawson Army Aviation, the 2nd Infantry Division, and Fort Rucker, all reminders of change and progress. Powell noted the change: "The Army mule had been replaced by the jeep, the old bolt action rifles have become M-14s, and high collars and campaign hats have given way to modern Army greens."[1]

Powell praised the product of the Infantry School, the professional soldiers, the fighters, "men who have the know-how, the physical strength, and the guts to do the job."[2] Ending a forty-four-year career that started in 1919 when he enlisted in the Oregon National Guard, he complimented troops on their appearance, describing them "as fine a looking group of fighting men as it has ever been my privilege to stand tall with. It is a real privilege and honor to take this final salute from you."[3]

Major General Charles W. G. Rich took command on February 25, 1963, with the departure of Major General Harrell who was honored with four brigades of dismounted troops, three elements of mounted equipment, a thirty-aircraft flyby, and a composite colors unit that passed in review. Rich held the same job Harrell held before his arrival at

---

[1] "Faith in Fighting Man Expressed by Retiring General," *Bayonet*, January 25 1963, 1.

[2] Ibid.

[3] Ibid.

Benning—commanding general of the 101st Airborne Division at Fort Campbell.

Betty Rich, now at Riverside, recalled their quarters at her husband's assignment at Fort Benning in 1938: "They were not luxurious—far from it. Actually, they were old Army barracks converted from World War I. They have all been demolished."[4]

More than ceremonies and command changes went on. The first step in redoing the 2nd Division under the Reorganization Objective, Army Division (ROAD) concept was completed February 1. Members of the 9th Infantry and 23rd Infantry paraded for the first time in brigade formation. The changeover required no retirement of colors.

Counterinsurgency training in the 2nd Division was realized in early February as companies started the weeklong course, training in the tactics of action and reaction when confronted with guerrilla type warfare. Training was designed for any type of terrain. This was reflected in the shield created for the new course, the 2nd Division patch with the Indianhead replaced with mountains, crossed machetes and a hissing cobra.

When Brigadier General Harry W. O Kinnard, commander of the 11th Air Assault Division, arrived on base, he was greeted with an eleven-gun salute. Kinnard, a 1939 West Point graduate, was stationed in Hawaii when Pearl Harbor was attacked. He then came to Fort Benning for the infantry officers' basic course and afterwards enrolled in Airborne School. Friends told him, "the physical exam for parachutists consisted of two doctors, each looking in one your ears at the same time; if they saw each other plainly, you were a fit candidate to jump."[5]

During the war, Kinnard, a colonel at age twenty-nine, made jumps and captured a bridge—later name for him—in Holland. He received the Distinguished Service Cross and was knighted by the Dutch queen. Before assuming command of the 11th Air Assault Division, Kinnard was assistant division commander of the 101st Airborne Division. His new unit was formed at Fort Benning by the Department of the Army to test the air assault concept defined by the Howze Board, a result of a study ordered by Defense Secretary McNamara with the urging of President Kennedy. Kinnard found post personnel "very understanding and helpful as this new

---

[4] "Post's 'First Lady' Reminisces," *Bayonet*, August 30 1963, 13.
[5] "Retired general takes top infantry honor," *Bayonet*, June 23 1995, 1.

upstart elbowed its way onto Fort Benning, overloading training areas, building innumerable heliports and filling the skies with noisy helicopters."[6]

Colonel Elvy B. Roberts, a twenty-year Airborne veteran, was named chief of staff of the 11th Air Assault Division (Test). His career reflected the level of quality found in the division. After graduating from West Point in 1943, he attended the Infantry School's basic and Airborne courses. In World War II, he made two combat jumps with the 501st, first into Normandy and then into Holland. He was former commander of the 506th Airborne Battle Group, 101st Airborne Division. After the war, he attended the infantry officers' advanced course and served with the Airborne Department and the Infantry School's Airborne Air Mobility Department.

The 11th Air Assault Division featured three brigade headquarters to which combat units were attached. It had a normal complement of military police, signal and engineer units, and a division headquarters. Division artillery had three 105 mm howitzer battalions plus a battalion of helicopter-mounted aerial rockets and a Little John missile battalion. Eight air assault infantry battalions in the division relied on division aircraft to provide transportation. The support command provided supplies and maintenance.

The Aviation Group contained the division's assault and surveillance aircraft. Assault helicopters were capable of moving nearly one-third of the combat elements in a single lift. The Aviation Group consisted of a headquarters company, one surveillance and attack battalion, one assault support helicopter battalion, and two assault helicopter battalions. The Air Cavalry Squadron consisted of three air cavalry troops and a ground cavalry troop with the traditional cavalry missions for reconnaissance, screening, security, and limited assaults.

The Air Transport Brigade was not an organic part of the Air Assault Division but operated from an area to the rear and provided backup for the division for troop-lifts and re-supply. The airmobile concept, explained in a February *Bayonet* article, called for movement and support of combat movements in the battle area by helicopters and aircraft capable of operating in the soldier's environment: "Conceptually, the air vehicles used to provide air mobile units with their high degree of mobility will become as much a

---

[6] Ibid.

part of the unit as the truck, armored vehicles, cannons or to other ground equipment they replace."[7]

In March 1963, command and staff assignments of the growing unit were announced: commander of support command, Colonel Robert C. Shaw; commander of the 1st Air Assault Brigade (Test), Colonel George S. Beatty; and commander of the Division Aviation Group (Test), Colonel George P. Seneff. Formerly in charge of the Army Aviation Research and Development Program, Seneff shared James Gavin's ideas that "there were shortcomings and limitations in the practice of airborne warfare; but airmobile warfare could address most, if not all, of those limitations."[8]

In addition to Beatty, five officers—veterans of World War II and Korea—were given key posts in the Air Assault Division; G-1, Lieutenant Colonel Robert A. McDade; adjutant general, Lieutenant Colonel Malcolm R. Baer; signal officer, Lieutenant Colonel Tom M. Nichelson; G-2, Major Frederic Ackerson; G-3, air officer, Major Norman L. Williamson.

In support of the air assault concept, the 2nd Infantry Division was the first old-line army division to undergo extensive structure changes under the Army's Reorganization Objectives Army Division (ROAD) concept. On April 16, the activation of the 1st Brigade's Headquarters and Headquarters Company on Sand Hill marked "the date on which history and tradition [was] born for this new combat force."[9] Complete reorganization was due June 1963.

In May, under the ROAD concept, the 2nd Infantry Division's 7th Cavalry began providing the "Indianhead" Division with air cavalry troops prepared to add an air wing to the combined arms of the 7th Cavalry. By using airmobility concepts in cavalry tactics, air cavalry troops planned to increase reconnaissance and security of the armored cavalry. The "Garry Owen" tradition remained with the unit. When General George Armstrong Custer commanded the 7th Cavalry, he adopted "Garry Owen" as the regimental song. "Garry Owen" became the regimental greeting, password,

---

[7] "11th Air Assault Division Will Be Located on Post," *Bayonet*, February 8 1963, 1.

[8] Lt. Gen. Harold G. Moore, USA (Ret.) and Joseph L. Galloway, *We Were Soldiers Once...and Young* (New York: HarperPerennial, 1993) 11.

[9] Bob de Camara, "Officials Are Lining Up 1st Brigade," *Bayonet*, April 3 1963, 11.

and battle cry. Because of the song's popularity, the 7th Cavalry Regiment was known as the "Garry Owen."[10]

Organization Day ceremonies were held at Lawson Army Airfield on May 2—the designated official birthday of the 11th Air Assault Division (Test). It was a day when the men of the 11th showed the skills they were perfecting—skills that soon would be used on a battlefield because by March, 12,000 US military personnel were in the Republic of Vietnam, working in aviation or as advisers to Vietnamese forces. Tradition was changed when Kinnard and retired lieutenant general Joseph M. Swing trooped the line in a UH-1 IROQUOIS helicopter. In the past, generals such as King, Singleton, and Marshall trooped the line on horseback. Patton preferred a tank, and Bradley looked at home in a jeep. However, this was the first use of a helicopter to troop the line—a fitting twist for the newly activated Air Assault Division.

A mechanized light weapons carrier, "the modern Army mule," brought up the rear of the ground units.[11] A flyby led by Seneff, the Aviation Group commander, included division aircraft: seven OH-13 Sioux helicopters, twelve UH-1 Iroquois helicopters, six CH-34 Choctaw helicopters, three CH-37 Mojave helicopters, three CV-2 Caribou aircraft, and three OV-1 Mohawk aircraft. The Mohawks came in full throttle over the crowd, trailing colored smoke in front of the reviewing stand.

Swing, WW II commander of the 11th Airborne Division, commended the unit: "Today will be remembered throughout the years...as the entry into the greatest episode of your lives." In response, Kinnard said, "Ours is a proud heritage. We have the history and traditions of an illustrious fighting unit on which to model ourselves."[12]

The Trooper's Tub, a silver urn of the 11th Airborne Division until its deactivation in 1958, passed on to the new unit. Kinnard noted, "by accepting the 'Troopers Tub' we complete the 'passing of the baton' and we shall hold that baton high."[13]

---

[10] Moore, *We Were Soldiers Once...and Young*, 27–28.

[11] Ben Nichols, "Marching Units, Helicopters, Equipment Pass in Review on 11th's Organization Day," *Bayonet*, May 10 1963, 1.

[12] Ibid.

[13] "Gen. Harris Returns Famous Urn 'Home,'" *Bayonet*, June 7 1963, 3.

Even the new assistant commandant of the Infantry School had his airmobility credentials. On May 8, an eleven-gun salute welcomed Brigadier General John Norton. In 1962, Norton, a member of the Howze Board, defended the airmobility concept from "attacks by members of congress, the air force, and conservative elements within the Army."[14] A paratrooper who made combat jumps in Sicily, Italy, Normandy, and Holland, Norton was an army aviator and long-standing pioneer of airmobile warfare. He wore a Master Parachutist Badge and the Combat Infantryman Badge.[15]

Another newcomer, the CH-54 A, dubbed the "Flying Crane," arrived at Lawson Army Airfield for testing. A product of the Sikorsky Aircraft Division of United Aircraft corporation, the CH-F4A was the latest and largest helicopter in the United States. Capable of carrying sixty-eight combat-equipped troops and ten tons of cargo loads, the new helicopter, with its detachable pods ready for use as self-contained units for medical facilities, communication centers, or command posts, seemed ideally suited for the mission of the 11th Air Assault Division.[16]

On September 2, Sky Soldier I, the first test of the army's new air assault concept, began near Camp Oliver and Fort Stewart, Georgia. Tested were Kinnard's 11th Air Assault Division (Test) and the 10th Air Transport Brigade (Test), commanded by Colonel Kelbert L. Bristol. The 1st Air Assault Brigade was given the task of seizing a base area in "Stewartland," establishing it as a battalion base, then building it into a brigade base where future operations were run. The test was not large or complex. But it was considered "one of the biggest changes in tactical doctrine since the changeover from horse-flesh to horsepower."[17]

Continuing improvements for the sky soldiers included a new runway begun by the deactivated 806th Engineer Battalion and completed by the 577th Engineers. Covered with nylon, vinyl, and polyethylene fabric, the 2,400-foot runway had a life expectancy of six months to two years, capable of withstanding 22,000 landings of planes such as the Caribou and

---

[14] John J. Tolson, *Airmobility* (Washington DC: Department of the Army, 1973) 24.

[15] "Review Planned for Gen. Reynolds; Gen. Norton Named His Successor," *Bayonet*, May 3 1963, 1.

[16] "'Flying Crane' Helicopter Arrives Here for Testing," *Bayonet*, July 5 1963, 1.

[17] Maj. Ben Nichols, "The Sky's No Limit," *Infantry* 53/6 (November/December 1963): 3.

Mohawk.[18] To keep the sky soldiers mobile, more than 5,000 gallons of gas were dispensed daily from 11 rubber tanks holding 10,000 gallons each. A large mobile pump, operated by a generator, pumped 350 gallons of gas per minute. Smaller 500-gallon rubber tanks were available to load on the Caribou or Mohawk aircraft. This need of gas, its quantity and expense, was listed as a disadvantage.[19] Another disadvantage was vulnerability. Howze optimistically answered the question: "It is time indeed that we realize that nothing is more vulnerable to actual bullet strike than the individual infantryman; everything kills him. But he gets along by the skillful combination of fire and maneuver. So can the helicopter."[20]

In an effort to keep experienced men in service and to attract the young, the US House of Representatives passed the largest military pay increase in history. Military men and women with more than two years service received an average increase of 14.4 percent. The increase included a $55 monthly combat bonus for servicemen exposed to Viet Cong fire. Army strength grew from eleven to sixteen combat-ready divisions, balancing the power between the US and the USSR and adding new mobility to the army.

The 11th Air Assault Division continued to expand, and General Hamilton Howze predicted more divisions would follow. He also predicted something already present in the rich background of troops volunteering for the airmobility unit—that an assignment to these new tactical units "should be a most exciting and enjoyable experience to any young man who prefers life with spice and challenge in it."[21]

President John F. Kennedy, a strong supporter of the airmobility concept, was assassinated by Lee Harvey Oswald on November 22. Lyndon B. Johnson was sworn in aboard Air Force One at Dallas's Love Field. On Benning's Marne Field, an honor guard lowered its rifles while a message was read from the secretary of defense. Then, as reported in the *Bayonet*,

---

[18] "577th Engineers Finish Unique Airstrip Runway," *Bayonet*, October 18 1963, 1.

[19] "5,000 Gals. a Day Move Sky Soldiers," *Bayonet*, October 11 1963, 36.

[20] Gen. Hamilton Howze, "Tactical Employment of the Air Assault Division," *Army* 14/2 (September 1963): 53.

[21] Ibid., 36.

"the trumpet sounded 'Taps.' The rain came down harder on the saluting men, and a simple prayer was read."[22]

---

[22] Bob de Camara, "Loss of President; a Terrible Blow," *Bayonet*, November 29 1963, 15.

Private Matthew St. Clair, 83rd Field Artillery, rides his horse Dan in the 1930's. He declared his assignment at Fort Benning was "the best three years of my entire life."

Members of Fort Benning's 24th Infantry Band played for post military functions and for post parties. It was the largest regiment band in the U.S. Army.

Building 35, built by Depression-era public works programs in 1934-1935, served as the U.S. Army Infantry School from July 1935 to June 1964. The U.S. Army School of the Americas located there in 1984. In 1994 it was dedicated as Ridgway Hall in honor of General Matthew B. Ridgway for his outstanding work in Latin America.

Proud participants await their turn in Fort Benning's popular horse shows.

President Franklin D. Roosevelt motored from the Little White House at Warm Springs to Fort Benning in the summer of 1938. Georgia Governor Ed Rivers sits next to him. School Commandant Brigadier General Asa L. Singleton salutes in the foreground.

General George C. Marshall (left), former Fort Benning assistant commandant 1927-1932, walks next to post commander Brigadier General Asa Singleton 1936-1940. while visiting the post in 1940.

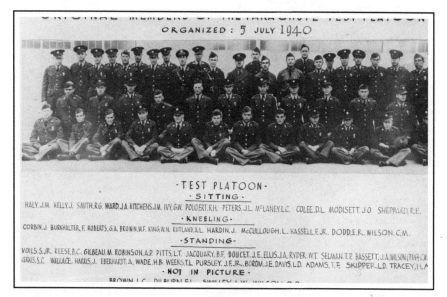

ORGANIZED: 5 JULY 1940

·TEST PLATOON·
·SITTING·
HALY,J.M. KELLY,J. SMITH,R.G. WARD,J.A. KITCHENS,J.M. IVY,G.W. POUDERT,R.H. PETERS,J.L. McLANEY,L.C. COLEE,D.L. MODISETT,J.O. SHEPPARD,R.E.
·KNEELING·
CORBIN,J. BURKHALTER,F. ROBERTS,G.A. BROWN,W.F. KING,W.N. RUTLAND,A.L. HARDIN,J. McCULLOUGH,L. KASSELL,E.JR. DODD,E.R. WILSON,C.M.
·STANDING·
VOILS,S.JR. REESE,R.C. GILBEAU,M. ROBINSON,A.P. PITTS,L.T. JACQUARY,B.F. DOUCET,J.E. ELLIS,J.A. RYDER,W.T. SELMAN,T.P. BASSETT,J.A.WILSON (TUG),C.W.
CERXIS,S.C. WALLACE, HARRIS,J. EBERHARDT,A. WADE,H.B. WEEKS,T.L. PURSLEY, J.F.JR.,BOROM,J.E.DAVIS,L.D. ADAMS,T.E. SKIPPER,L.D. TRACEY,H.A
·NOT IN PICTURE·
BROWN, L.C. DILRURN EL SWILLEY A W WILSON O B

All original members of the Parachute Test Platoon, formed at Fort Benning in July 1940, returned safely from action in World War II.

Members of the 501st Gold Parachute Battalion, 1941, stand poised in full regalia.

A series of boxing bouts between selectees from Fort Benning's Second Armored Division Replacement Center were held in the "piney woods" on the post's 100,000-acre reservation. Boxing was one of the most popular sports at the fort in the 30's and 40's.

Major General George S. Patton, Jr., commander of the 2nd Armored Division at Fort Benning, wears his self-styled "Green Hornet" tank suit.

Two-Star General James M. Gavin, World War II paratroop leader at Fort Benning, was stationed on post December 7, 1941. Three and a half years later he was one of the first American generals on French soil on D-Day, June 6, 1944, dropping in four hours before the main invasion began.

Brigadier General Courtney H. Hodges, Commander Infantry School (second from left), Brigadier Charles L. Scott, Commanding General 2nd Armored Division (third from left), and Colonel George S. Patton, Jr., Commander 2nd Armored Brigade, watch a review in 1940. Beatrice Patton, wearing a black hat, sits behind her husband.

Brigadier General Omar Bradley (left) stands at attention with paratroopers Major William Miley, Captain Strother, Captain Chase, Captain Michaelis, and Lieutenant Taylor in front of Fort Benning's wooden barracks in 1941.

Fort Benning Commander Brigadier General Omar Bradley views the 29th Infantry's demonstration of its 37mm gun in May 1941.

Major General George S. Patton, Jr. and his wife Beatrice, a popular couple in the social life at Fort Benning and Columbus during 1940-1942, sit together at a party.

An enthusiastic Columbus crowd cheers troops of the 29th Infantry Regiment during the Army Day parade held in downtown Columbus on Monday, April 7, 1941.

Soldiers and their dependents enjoy Russ Pool with its high dive tower in July 1941.

Soldiers in Officer Candidate School practice bayonet training with their M-1 rifles. Established in 1941 by Fort Benning Commander Omar Bradley 1941-1942, OCS was the Infantry School's major function, peaking in September-December 1942.

Non-commissioned officers of the 24th Infantry Regiment pose for a group picture. The 3rd Battalion, 24th Infantry Regiment was formed on post in December 1921. In April 1942, the 24th was the first black infantry regiment sent overseas.

UNITED STATES OF AMERICA
OFFICE OF PRICE ADMINISTRATION

(4 Nᵒ 705 485 BL

WAR RATION BOOK No. 3

Void if
altered

NOT
VALID
VALID
WITHOUT
STAMP

Identification of person to whom issued: PRINT IN FULL

Thomas E.   _Taylor_
(First name)   (Middle name)   (Last name)

Street number or rural route _1563 - Hilton Ave_

City or post office _Columbus_ State _Ga_

AGE	SEX	WEIGHT Lbs.	HEIGHT Ft. In.	OCCUPATION

SIGNATURE
(Person to whom book is issued. If such person is unable to sign because of age or incapacity, another may sign in his behalf.)

WARNING

This book is the property of the United States Government. It is unlawful to sell it to any other person, or to use it or permit anyone else to use it, except to obtain rationed goods in accordance with regulations of the Office of Price Administration. Any person who finds a lost War Ration Book must return it to the War Price and Rationing Board which issued it. Persons who violate rationing regulations are subject to $10,000 fine or imprisonment, or both.

LOCAL BOARD ACTION

Issued by
(Local board number)   (Date)

Street address

City   State

(Signature of issuing officer)

Ration Books were issued to individuals
for items difficult to obtain during World War II.

Fort Benning once again became a tent city during World War II.

Wartime expansion of the post in 1942 extended to the Sand Hill area of the reservation to accommodate troops sent to Fort Benning for training.

Four-Star General Mark Clark, who attended the Infantry School's Advanced Officers Course in 1924, checks out the troops of the First Student Brigade, OCS, during WWII training. Fort Benning was the first Army post and first home for Clark and his wife Maurine.

Dwight D. Eisenhower, Army Chief of Staff, and Katherine Tupper Marshall greet General George C. Marshall, March 15, 1946, on a return trip from China where Marshall served as President Truman's special representative in 1945-1947.

Fort Benning's Commanding General John "Iron Mike" O'Daniel (1945-1948)
and Mrs. O'Daniel greet Secretary of State George Marshall and his wife Katherine
Tupper Marshall at Lawson Field in 1948.

34.

Iron Mike's Home

Since 1960, he was a lonely sentry on Eubanks Field, an imposing fellow that offered a decisive "Follow Me," to anyone who passed. Four years later, the big guy was reassigned to Building 4, the new academic building. There was no enemy fire, but Iron Mike was injured nonetheless. On his way to his new position, the famous infantry statue was unceremoniously dropped while being hauled by a crane to a truck for his trip to Building 4. He received a chipped left elbow in the fall, and it took his creator to mend him. Manfred Bass, who built the landmark statue along with Karl H. Von Krog while both were stationed at Fort Benning, flew in from New Jersey and did the repair work. In addition to fixing the chip, Bass re-bronzed the *Follow Me* statue.

While the repairs were being made to Iron Mike, the Infantry School flagstaff was removed from Building 35, the headquarters for the Infantry School since 1935, and installed in front of the new $10 million headquarters building. With dedication of the new building on June 5, the Infantry School had an impressive new home with 1,900 parking spaces. The six-story "H"-shaped building took two years to build. It housed instructional and administrative departments of the school as well as elements of the Infantry Center Command. With access to closed-circuit television, it was the first service school to use telecasts as a teaching aide.

At the opening, "I Am the Infantry" was presented in tableau after an invocation by post chaplain Colonel Silas E. Decker. Major General Charles Rich introduced former Infantry School commandant General Hugh P. Harris, acting vice-chief of staff of the US Army, who delivered the principal address and took part in the ribbon cutting.

The building was conceived in 1951 during the tour of Major General John H. Church. During the tours of Major Generals Freeman and Harris, Cecil M. Sanders, Infantry School Operations Department's project officer, "appeared before twenty-two major hearings and various smaller ones in an effort to justify construction of the structure."[1]

As 1964 began, two guest speakers at the Infantry School addressed a topic of major importance. Each provided a supplement to the students' classroom and tactical training. Major General Robert H. York lectured on military operations in Vietnam, and Dr. Bernard B. Fall, professor of International Relations at Harvard University, discussed world-wide political trends.

York, commander of the 82nd Airborne Division at Fort Bragg, directed the Research Development Field Unit and Joint Operation Evaluation Group in Vietnam. Author Neil Sheehan said since York spent three-and-a-half years in country, he was "the only American general in Vietnam with any firsthand knowledge of a communist-led guerrilla insurgency in Asia."[2] York served as the US Army observer of the British campaign to suppress the guerrilla revolt by the Chinese minority in Malaya, a classic counterinsurgency success story.

Fall, a military historian and journalist, also spent time in Vietnam and published his acclaimed *Street Without Joy* in 1961.[3] He recounted key developments of the French War in Vietnam, including the Battle of Dien Bien Phu, a French defeat in 1954, marking the end of France's rule in Indochina. Addressing American involvement since 1957, he ended his book by writing, "And this is perhaps as good an epitaph as any for the men who had to walk down the joyless and hopeless road that was the Indochina War."[4] Fall died in Vietnam in 1967 when he stepped on a land mine.

In 1964, 23,310 US troops served in Vietnam. Casualty lists included 147 men killed and 22 helicopters lost. General William Westmoreland, fifty, a frequent visitor and lecturer at Fort Benning, succeeded General Paul D. Harkins as commander of American Advisory Forces in the Republic of Vietnam after serving as Harkins's deputy since 1963.

---

[1] John Holland, "Infantry School Building Finally Becomes a Reality After Spending 13 years in Planning and Construction, *Bayonet*, June 5 1964, 8.

[2] Neil Sheehan, *A Bright Shining Lie: John Paul Vann and America in Vietnam* (New York: Random House, 1995) 273.

[3] Bernard B. Fall, *Street without Joy* (Harrisburg PA: Stackpole Co., 1961) 310.

[4] Ibid.

The continued development of the 11th Air Assault dominated post activities in 1964. Colonel Richard T. Knowles, former 2nd Division Artillery commander was named acting assistant division commander of the 11th Air Assault Division effective February 10. Nominated for promotion to the rank of brigadier general, Knowles was a veteran of more than twenty-one years of army service.

The army's first Air Cavalry Squadron, the 3rd Squadron (AIR), 17th Cavalry, was officially activated in March as a part of the army's experimental 11th Air Assault Division. The strength of the 11th Air Assault Division (Test) in April 1964 was approximately 10,000 men. Additional troops would bring it to 14,500 by summer. These figures did not include 3,200 men assigned or to be assigned to the 10th Transport Brigade. Other elements brought the total number of personnel involved in Project Team to more than 18,500. Overall post population was a little less than 48,000 when all units were activated. Based on official statements, post military strength would reach 50,000, a figure referred to as "the 'Saturation Point' or maximum number of troops that may be maintained and supported adequately by Fort Benning's existing facilities."[5]

Brigadier General John T. Corley, assistant 2nd Division commander, received orders for his new assignment as chief of staff at 1st Army headquarters. One of the army's most decorated men, Corley was awarded two Distinguished Service Crosses, eight Silver Stars, and other medals in World War II and Korea. In Korea, September 1950, Corley took command of the 24th Infantry Regiment, a long-time Benning unit that "Finally got the commander it so desperately needed."[6]

While serving at Fort Benning, Corley helped move the 2nd Division to the ROAD structure. Because of his previous assignment as head of the Ranger Department, he remained a strong advocate of Ranger training for his troops. Corley, his wife, Mary, and their seven children helped with post and community activities. Mary Corley wrote, produced, and appeared in several plays and musicals during their stay.

In spring 1964, Colonel Hal Moore wrote Major General Harry Kinnard, his former boss at Fort Bragg, requesting an infantry battalion in

---

[5] "Status of Air Assault Unit Clarified," *Bayonet*, April 3 1964, 2.

[6] Joseph L. Galloway, "The Last of the Buffalo Soldiers," *U.S. News & World Report* 120/18 (May 6 1996): 46.

Kinnard's new division. Kinnard assigned Moore to command the 2nd Battalion, 23rd Infantry. Until quarters on post were available, Moore joined the unit on Kelley Hill while his wife, Julia, and their five children stayed with her parents in nearby Auburn, Alabama.

Moore believed he was in "on the birth of the concept of airmobility."[7] In 1957, after graduating from Command and General Staff College at Fort Leavenworth, Moore was assigned to the Pentagon office of the chief of research and development When he assumed command of his unit at Fort Benning in June, Moore was forty-two years old, a West Pointer with nineteen years of service and fourteen months of combat in Korea. He told his troops, "I will do my best. I expect the same from each of you."[8]

After a farewell ceremony on July 30 with more than 2,800 troops on Sightseeing Field, Major General Charles Rich assumed command of the 3rd Army at Fort McPherson, Georgia, with the rank of lieutenant general. At the elaborate ceremony, "Over 170 fixed-wing planes and helicopters took part in what is believed to be one of the largest concentrations of army aircraft ever to take part in an aerial parade."[9] In spirit with his role as test director for airmobility concepts since his arrival on post in 1963, Rich trooped the line in an UH-IB helicopter accompanied by Kinnard.

In August, Major General John A. Heintges, former commanding general of the 5th Infantry Division (Mechanized) and Fort Carson, Colorado, succeeded Rich. Heintges, the son of a US Army officer, now served his fourth tour at the Georgia post. A foreign language teacher at West Point after serving in World War II, Heintges greeted guests in Spanish when the Infantry School hosted the 1964 Conference of the American Armies with military personnel from seventeen Central and South American countries.

In mid-August, 1,000 troops from special units formed at Benning left for Vietnam, including several aviation companies equipped with Caribou aircraft and HU-1B (Iroquois) helicopters from the 11th Air Assault Division (Test) and the 10th Air Transport Brigade. Personnel from

---

[7] Lt. Gen. Harold G. Moore, USA (Ret.) and Joseph L. Galloway, *We Were Soldiers Once…and Young* (New York: HarperPerennial, 1993) 18.

[8] Moore and Galloway, *We Were Soldiers Once…and Young*, 20.

[9] Sgt. Maj. A. W. Spratky, "Post Bids Farewell to General Rich," *Bayonet*, July 31 1964, 1.

elsewhere in the United States were transferred to these units to refill them to their authorized strength to continue testing by the army for its airmobility concept. Testing was scheduled for completion at the end of 1964.

A new policy was adopted by the Department of the Army in 1964. All 500 graduates of the US Military Academy's Class of 1964 would come to Fort Benning for mandatory Ranger training during their first six months in the army. The new policy would cancel attendance for these West Point officers at the infantry officers' basic course and basic courses of other army branches.

A dire reminder of the growing Vietnam conflict came home to Benning when the widow of Captain Morris R. McBride accepted her husband's medals, the Distinguished Service Cross and the Vietnamese Medal of Honor First Class. His two young daughters and his parents, Colonel and Mrs. Otto L. McBride, were also present. McBride, thirty-four, was an adviser to a company in the army of the Republic of Vietnam. On March 3, 1964, when the company commander and others were wounded, he assumed command, removing the remainder of the company to safety. He was mortally wounded when he stopped to assist the wounded company commander. Commissioned a 2nd lieutenant after graduating from West Point in 1957, McBride graduated from the Infantry School's officers' basic, Airborne, Ranger, and career courses. He attended the Special Warfare School at Fort Bragg before leaving for Vietnam. The Morris R. McBride School, a $500,000 elementary school on Custer Road, was dedicated to the young soldier on January 7, 1966.

In another ceremony, the parade ground in front of Building 4 was named in honor of Alvin C. York, a hero of World War I awarded the Distinguished Service Cross and the Congressional Medal of Honor. His story, based on his diary, was told in the 1941 film *Sergeant York*, starring Gary Cooper who won a best actor Oscar for his portrayal of the mountain sharpshooter. York died at age seventy-six on September 2, 1964.

Another legend from the past, "Blackjack" Pershing, was recalled when his grandson, 2nd Lieutenant John W. Pershing III, attended the officers' basic course in 1964. He was following the path of both his father and grandfather. His grandfather was instrumental in creating the Infantry School and in locating it at Fort Benning. Neither fact impressed the 2nd lieutenant. A ROTC graduate of Boston University, he planned to attend

Airborne and Ranger Training. The elder Pershing, who was general of the armies of the United States, was not "famous" to his grandson, who commented, "To me he was just my grandfather."[10]

Lieutenant John W. Pershing was not the only member of that illustrious family to pass through Benning's gates during this era. In 1967, his brother 2nd Lieutenant Richard W. Pershing also trained there. Richard, a graduate of Yale University, went to Vietnam later that year with the 101st Airborne Division. On February 17, 1968, while searching for the body of a missing soldier from his unit, Richard Pershing was killed. He was twenty-six. Today, Lieutenant Richard Pershing lies on a grassy knoll with the same kind of government issued headstone as the man beside him—General of the Armies John J. Pershing, his grandfather. Next to them, in Section 34 of Arlington National Cemetery, rests John Warren Pershing III, an army colonel. He died in June 1999.

---

[10] Pvt. Frank L. Lombardi, "'Blackjack' Pershing's Grandson Maintains Tradition," *Bayonet*, November 6 1964, 14.

35.

Cavalry in the Sky

Soldiers called her the "Mother of the 1st Cavalry," and it was Mrs. Ben Dorcy who designed and sewed the yellow and black patch that men serving in the unit first wore in 1921. Soldiers proudly wore it for forty-four years, but the eighty-year-old wife of a former 7th Cavalry commander decided it was time for a change. "I couldn't see in 1921 that the division would be flying. They were riding horses then. Some changes are in order now," she said, accepting the colors of the old division on a Fort Benning parade field.[1]

Mrs. Dorcy was not the only person who couldn't see the division in the air. The concept of airmobility remained controversial, even in the army family. But since June 16—when the secretary of defense announced the 11th Air Assault Division would be redesignated the 1st Cavalry Division Air Mobile—change was pervasive at Benning.

The new division was organized and made combat ready "as expeditiously as possible" from the men and equipment of a regular infantry division. In addition to the 2nd Brigade only two other units of the 2nd Infantry Division—the 1st Battalion, 23rd Infantry and the 2nd Battalion, 9th Infantry—were tapped for roles. As of June 25, the only direct transfer of 2nd Division soldiers was limited to fill specific vacancies.

In the "Second Infantry Division News" published in the June 25 edition of the *Bayonet*, Major General John H. Chiles, 2nd Division commander since October 1964, argued against merging the 2nd Division and the Experimental 11th Air Assault Division to form the 1st Cavalry Division (Airmobile). Though he appealed to his longtime friend General Harold K. Johnson, army chief of staff, to halt the merger, his appeal was unsuccessful. Chiles, who fought with the 2nd Division in World War II and Korea, left in July to serve with the 3rd Army as chief of staff.

---

[1] "1st Cavalry's 'Mother' Hopes to Restyle Patch," *Bayonet*, July 9 1965, 24.

Controversies or not, airmobility was a reality. On July 3, the colors of the 11th Air Assault Division were retired, and its personnel along with members of the 2nd Infantry Division transferred to the 1st Cavalry Division (Airmobile). More than 10,000 civilian and military guests witnessed the colors of the 1st Cavalry Division pass to Major General Harry W. O. Kinnard, commander of the 1st Cavalry Division (Airmobile).

One of the guests was General Hamilton Howze, recently retired, who recommended the incorporation of airmobile units in the army combat force. His father, Major General Robert L. Howze, was commander of the 1st Cavalry Division at its birth September 13, 1921, in El Paso, Texas. The colors of the 2nd Infantry Division, which flew throughout the Korean War, were sent to Korea where the old 1st Cavalry Division, holding the front line in Korea, was renamed the 2nd Infantry Division.

The "First Team" was one of the earliest Cavalry units in the army. Robert E. Lee who resigned his commission at the beginning of the Civil War commanded its oldest regiment, the 5th, organized in 1855 as the 2nd Cavalry Regiment. The 7th Regiment, organized in 1866, was commanded by George Custer and fought at the Little Big Horn. The 8th Regiment, also organized in 1866, fought against Sitting Bull and took part in the Mexican Punitive Expedition.

Kinnard announced the command for the new 1st Cav: Colonel E. B. Roberts, 1st Brigade; Colonel George S. Beatty, Jr., chief of staff; Lieutenant Colonel John Hennessey, the Division Support Command; and Colonel Allen M. Burdett, Jr., the Aviation Group.

Excitement of the 1st Cavalry's formation attracted top generals. NBC Radio conducted an interview with Kinnard for the documentary *The New War in Vietnam*. Twelve US Congressmen, including Representatives William L. Dickinson of Alabama and Howard (Bo) Callaway of Georgia, took part in the training of the 1st Cavalry Division, rappelling the twenty-five-foot training tower and shooting the new M-16 assault rifle.

Everything done was planned with Vietnam in mind. But what the Vietnam 1st Cav would face was different from what soldiers found earlier. After Congress passed the Gulf of Tonkin resolution in August 1964, approving US action in Southeast Asia, 3,500 US Marines joined 23,500 American advisers in Vietnam in March 1965. Further involvement came in June 1965 with the first mass bombing raid on North Vietnam.

The *Bayonet*'s July 30 headline read, "Cav Viet Nam Bound." Upon hearing the news, Kinnard spoke for his troops. Though he was prepared to introduce the unit to combat, he held mixed feelings about the assignment: "Separation from your family is always a matter of heartache and hardship."

Hundreds of 1st Cavalry families remained in the Columbus-Fort Benning area, including Mrs. Harry W. O. Kinnard, the commander's wife, and their six children. Acting as "mama" to the wives of her husband's men, she remembered her own experiences: "I get cold shudders when I think back to the 1950s when so many young women were left to fend for themselves while their husbands struggled in Korea."[2] Mrs. Kinnard urged the women that if legal or financial concerns came up or if they had problems with housing or transportation, to consult Benning's Community Services Agency (CSA). Major Shirley Sneed was chief coordinator for the Agency.

The 1965 buildup was in response to President Johnson's desire to save Vietnam from Communism, to help commanders in the field, and to "get things happening." He did not want the United States to lose its first war on his watch. Ambassador Maxwell Taylor, reluctant to introduce US forces into a ground war in Southeast Asia, agreed to Westmoreland's request for more troops, going along with chiefs of staff Earle G. Wheeler (1962–1964) and Harold Johnson (1964–1968).[3]

As early as July 21, 1964, shortly after returning from Saigon, McNamara offered the president three alternatives: 1. To withdraw; 2. To continue at present levels; 3.To expand US forces. McNamara recommended the latter. Writing years later, he admitted "Subsequent events proved my judgment wrong."[4]

Although McNamara recommended a call-up of the reserves, he explained why it was not implemented: "President Johnson believed high defense appropriations would kill his proposals for the greatest social advance since the New Deal," legislation considered essential in preserving

---

[2] "Mrs. Kinnard Plans to Remain as Division's 'Mama,'" *Bayonet*, August 6 1965, 24.

[3] Andrew F. Krepinevich, Jr., *The Army and Vietnam* (Baltimore: John Hopkins University Press, 1986) 150.

[4] Robert S. NcNamara with Brian VanDeMark, *In Retrospect* (New York: Times Books, 1995) 204.

the country.[5] US strength in Vietnam rose to 125,000 troops in the summer of 1965. The draft doubled from 17,000 to 35,000 men a month.

Colonel Hal Moore, commander of the 1st Battalion, 7th Cavalry,

> began to suffer the consequences of President Johnson's refusal to declare a state of emergency and extend the active-duty tours of draftees and reserve officers. The order came down: Any soldier who had sixty days or less left to serve on his enlistment as of the date of deployment, August 16, must be left behind. We were sick at heart.... The very men who would be the most useful in combat—those who had trained longest in the new techniques of helicopter warfare—were by this order taken away from us.[6]

Politics or not, training heated up. On August 3, "a beautiful day...with bright sunshine and virtually no clouds," less than a month after their orders to Vietnam, more than 2,700 paratroopers led by the division's all-Airborne 1st Brigade made their first major mass parachute drop on Fryar Drop Zone as a major tactical organization: "At exactly 11:00 A.M. Colonel E. B. Roberts, brigade commander, exited the lead aircraft in a serial of ten C-130 air transports and the mass parachute operation was underway."[7]

Individuals in the 1st Cav were kept busy. They dyed underwear, handkerchiefs, socks, and fatigues a deep forest green. Edward Dennis Monsewicz, then seven years old, remembered his dad, Sergeant Lloyd Joel Monsewicz, "training for his mission, coming home and dyeing his tee-shirts green and sorting out his field gear."[8]

Colonel Kenneth D. Mertel, commander of the "Jumping Mustangs," the 1st Battalion, Airborne, 8th Cavalry, said this was a way to survive. "In addition, all insignia were colored a dark green or black to decrease the possibility of being spotted by the enemy. Thus we would make less of a

---

[5] Ibid., 198.

[6] Lt. Gen. Harold G. Moore, USA (Ret.) and Joseph L. Galloway, *We Were Soldiers Once...and Young* (New York: HarperPerennial, 1993) 28.

[7] Charles Jameson, "Initial Mass Jump Made by Division Paratroopers," *Bayonet*, August 6 1965, 1.

[8] Moore and Galloway, *We Were Soldiers Once...and Young*, 390.

target for snipers. I doubt if wives and girl friends of 1st Cavalry Sky Troopers ever forgot the color of green dye," he said.[9]

On August 18, the 1st Air Cavalry Division held its farewell review before its deployment to the Republic of Vietnam. Kinnard, who received the Distinguished Service Medal, the nation's highest decoration for meritorious service, on August 11, was presented with a "Follow Me" statuette by General York. In his remarks, Kinnard remembered friends and family members: "We leave behind us fond memories and our gratitude and thanks, but more important, many of our dependents, who have found as we did that Columbus is a hospitable place."[10] Vietnam was not.

On August 18, the day of the division's final review at Fort Benning, Major Donald G. Radcliff, a member of the division's advance party to Vietnam, was killed by ground fire that struck the UH-IB he was piloting. Radcliffe, executive officer of the 1st Squadron, 9th Cavalry, was the first casualty of the 1st Cavalry Division. Two days later, on August 20, final elements of the 1st Cavalry Division (Airmobile) departed Fort Benning for their 10,000-mile trip to Vietnam. Reacting to the change on post, the 197th Infantry Brigade, including some 3,500 soldiers, began moving to Kelley Hill to occupy the barracks formerly used by the 1st Cavalry Division. Brigade Commander Colonel Jacob I. Riley, Jr., said the move would be accomplished "without disrupting our support of the Infantry School's problems."

The 1st Cavalry Division arrived in Vietnam in mid-September, taking up positions "on Viet Cong infested Route 19 between Qui Nhon and Pleiku." Deploying more than 15,000 men, the unit was the first US division-sized element to arrive in Vietnam. After deciding bulldozers would turn the site into a mud pit, Assistant Division Commander Brigadier General John M. Wright led a force in clearing the jungle by hand. In 5 days they cleared 50 percent of the area. Some 600 native workers finished the helicopter pad in "Operation golf course."

An extensive barrier system of outposts and guards to keep the enemy beyond mortar range was planned for the fifty-square-kilometer campsite. Alas, there was one casualty, mistakenly shot by a nervous sentry from

---

[9] Col. Kenneth D. Mertel, *Year of the Horse—Vietnam* (New York: Exposition Press, 1968) 19.

[10] "Gen. Kinnard Gets Official Farewell," *Bayonet*, August 20 1965, 1.

Charlie Company. Dead was Colonel John Stockton's (commanded 1st Squadron, 9th Cavalry) beloved cavalry mascot, smuggled from Fort Benning to Vietnam. Maggie, the mule, was shot and killed as she wandered the perimeter on a dark night. Sergeant Major Boris Plumley personally reported Maggie's untimely demise to Moore: "She was challenged and didn't know the password."[11] And in those jungles she would not be the last to die.

The North Vietnamese army attacked the Pleime Special forces Camp twenty-five miles southwest of Pleiku on October 19. On October 27, the 1st Cavalry Division's mission was to seek and destroy the enemy force. This was the beginning of a month-long campaign known as the Battle of the Ia Drang Valley. This confrontation was described in the book *We were Soldiers...Once and Young* written by Hal Moore and Joe Galloway.[12] A movie starring actor Mel Gibson as Moore presented the conflict—one even Hollywood found difficult to portray—under Moore's supervision.

In a pivotal battle in mid-November, Moore's 1st Battalion, 7th Cavalry, killed 634 Viet Cong and captured 6. Of his men, 79 were killed, 121 wounded, and none missing.[13] Aa reporter and author Neil Sheehan noted, "Most of them were men whom Moore had schooled and led for a year and a half."[14] Sheehan also reported the losses suffered by the 2nd Batallion, 7th Cavalry: 151 killed and 121 wounded. "The battle of Ia Drang," he wrote, "had taken 230 American lives in four days."[15]

---

[11] Moore and Galloway, *We Were Soldiers Once...and Young*, 30.
[12] Ibid.
[13] Ibid., 233.
[14] Sheehan, *A Bright Shining Lie*, 578.
[15] Ibid., 579.

Moore affirmed that "for the first time since Dien Bien Phu in 1954, the North Vietnamese Army had taken the field in division strength."[16] Moore's words now echo: "Vietnam was now a whole new ball game militarily, politically, and diplomatically. Decisions…would have to be made soon."[17]

---

[16] Moore and Galloway, *We Were Soldiers Once…and Young*, 234.
[17] Ibid.

36.

Death Comes Calling in a City Cab

Death arrived at the wheel of a Yellow Cab. Soldiers were being killed in a faraway Asian jungle, and their wives and children back home were getting the news from a cab driver with a Western Union telegram in his hand.

Their husbands, members of the 1st Cav, engaged in bloody battles at LZ X-Ray and LZ Albany. These freshly cleared locations were landing zones for choppers in a Vietnamese valley known as Ia Drang where hundreds of Americans died. The routine procedure of Department of Defense called for a telegram to be sent to their loved ones.

Some family members who stayed behind at Fort Benning or Columbus met in a group they called the "Waiting Wives Club." Led by the wives of Major General Harry Kinnard and Colonel Hal Moore, they started gathering a month after their husbands left. In that first meeting at the Officers Club, they had—as a group—reacted to the first reported death since their husbands arrived in Vietnam. On November 4, days before the luncheon, Major Richard E. Steel, assigned to the 229th Helicopter Battalion, 1st Cav, was killed. The wives planned to attend his funeral service November 19 at the Fort Benning cemetery. They also made plans to send gift packages to orphans in Vietnam and found comfort in exchanging ordinary information. More than anything, the wives were trying to make a normal life for themselves and their children, trying not to think of the news following a knock at their door or a ringing of their doorbell.

Mrs. Kinnard felt responsible. She remembered the loneliness she felt while her husband was in Korea. It was not just that her husband was their husbands' commanding officer. These young wives became her daughters. She was joined by Julia Moore, wife of 1st Battalion, 7th Cavalry's commander; Emma Lee Henry, wife of the 2nd Battalion, 7th Cavalry's executive officer; and Kornelia Scott, wife of the 2nd Battalion's sergeant major. Together, they consoled families and attended funerals.

Hearing the scattered stories of uncaring or confused cabbies, they wanted to do something. Like good army wives, they made known their criticism through the chain of command. The army listened. Procedures changed. Instead of cab drivers, casualty notification teams were organized, consisting of a chaplain and a military representative.[1] Nothing could take away the shock and grief in such messages, but through the efforts of "the Waiting Wives," an element of care and concern came with the delivery.

The first funeral at Benning for a 1st Batallion casualty was that of Sergeant Jack Gell, a radio operator in Tony Nadal's Alpha Company. Gell died in the Battle of Ia Drang Valley. When Julie Moore saw Gell's funeral at the post cemetery shown on television, she called Survivors Assistance and told them to inform her of every 1st Batallion death notification.[2] After that, this only child of an army colonel never missed a local funeral or burial. She was always there—for the solder and his family.

Julia Moore was an army brat, born at Fort Sill, Oklahoma, in 1929. From the time she was twelve years old, she was sending the men she loved to war; first her father, then her husband, then her son, who fought in Panama and the Gulf War. Two of her three sons were army officers. She learned about separation, and she learned the risks of war. She met Hal Moore, a West Point graduate, when she attended college in North Carolina. Under crossed sabers, they were married in 1949. Her husband fought first in Korea then in Southeast Asia. So in 1965, when she found herself in Georgia alone with her five children, she was well versed in the role of an army wife, a role well documented in a move based on the book *We Were Soldiers Once...and Young* written by her husband General Hal Moore and reporter Joe Galloway.[3]

When Julia Moore died on 18 April 2004, at age seventy-five, her funeral was attended by her husband of fifty-five years, her five children, and by many dignitaries, military and civilian. Betty Jivens Mapson-Beers,

---

[1] Joseph L. Galloway, "Rest in peace, Julie Moore," *Columbus Ledger-Enquirer*, April 25 2004, F4.

[2] Lt. Gen. Harold G. Moore, USA (Ret.) and Joseph L. Galloway, *We Were Soldiers Once...and Young* (New York: HarperPerennial, 1993) 381.

[3] Galloway, "Rest in peace, Julie Moore," F4.

daughter of Jeremiah Jivens who died in Ia Drang, the so-called Valley of Death, also attended, explaining, "I remember seeing Mrs. Moore at my daddy's funeral at the post chapel. I wasn't about to miss hers."[4] Julia Moore was buried at Fort Benning, near the graves of her mother and father, Colonel and Mrs. Louis Compton, and among the graves of the soldiers who fought so long in Vietnam. Next to her was Sergeant Jack Earl Gell.[5]

The loss of life continued for the 1st Cavalry in 1966. In April, Mrs. Bernard J. Creed, Mrs. Lloyd J. Monsewicz, and Mrs. Herman L. Jefferson received their husbands' medals at posthumous award ceremonies. In another ceremony at Martin Army Hospital, Major General York presented Purple Hearts to 25 men wounded in Vietnam. Later, arriving at Atlanta Stadium with a police escort, 125 patients, many of them wounded veterans of Vietnam duty and Purple Heart recipients, were guests of the Braves baseball team. Team members autographed programs and visited with the men. For many of the men it was the first trip out of the hospital in several months.

On post, the mission remained training. Because of the Vietnam expansion, the Army Training Center located at Fort Benning in 1965 provided basic combat training to new recruits. Initially two training brigades moved into the Sand Hill and Harmony Church, areas vacated by the 1st Cavalry Division. A third was added in April 1966. Newly printed signs in the area read, "Welcome to the US Army." To train an estimated 1,300 basic trainees arriving weekly, 200 non-commissioned officers took an intensive five-week course as drill instructors at Fort Jackson, South Carolina. Airmobility pioneer John Tolson saw such training as essential: "Airmobility put a new dimension into ground warfare, but it did not change the nature of warfare itself.... The airmobile trooper, like the paratrooper before him, must be basically a professional infantryman."[6]

With increased funding, Lawson Field received a 2,000-foot expansion, a new control tower, new operations building, new field and approach lighting, and an Instrument Landing System. One of the buildings was

---

[4] "Moore, Buried among those she honored," *Columbus Ledger-Enquirer*, April 23 2004, A3.

[5] Galloway, "Rest in peace, Julie Moore," F4.

[6] Lt. Gen. John J. Tolson, *Vietnam Studies: Airmobility 1961–1971* (Washington DC: Department of the Army, 1973) 83.

named McCarthy Hall for Captain Thomas W. McCarthy, a senior adviser to a Vietnamese Airborne battalion killed in March 1964. Temporary buildings on post were replaced, and the destruction of 100 World War II buildings began in January. Removal of these wartime structures—meant to last five years—gave way to a park for dependent housing and new schools. Later in 1965, Building 86, the old main entrance guard post, was removed.

The post remained "home" to most infantrymen. On February 27, 1965, General Hugh P. Harris returned for his "last salute," honored in his farewell review with a seventeen-gun salute. More than 10,000 Fort Benning troops paraded before him. The 11th Air Assault Division and 10th Air Transport Battalion ended the review with a flyover of helicopters and fixed wing aircraft. The retiring commander of the US Continental Army Command served his country thirty-three years. Harris followed retired General Mark Clark as the president of The Citadel, a military college in Charleston, South Carolina.

Brigadier General George L. Forsythe arrived in early March to replace Brigadier General John Norton as assistant commandant of the Infantry School. Norton was assigned to the Army Support Command, Military Assistance Advisory Group (MAAG) in Vietnam. A World War II veteran, Forsythe taught at the Command and General Staff College and commanded the 502nd Airborne Infantry of the 101st Airborne Division. He also was the first senior adviser to the Field Command of the Vietnamese army. Prior to coming to Benning, he was assistant commander of the 25th Infantry Division in Hawaii.

A reminder of the price of military training occurred June 15. Fourteen soldiers from B and C Companies, 1st Battalion, 38th Infantry, 11th Air Assault Division, together with two pilots and two co-pilots from the 227th Assault Helicopter Battalion, died instantly when their two HUI-D copters collided in mid-air and crashed into a swampy area near King's Pond. It was the worst single air accident in Fort Benning history.

In July 1965, Major General Heintges, nominated for his third star, left for his assignment as commander of I Corps (Group) in Korea. His successor, Major General Robert H. York, took over duties as Fort Benning commander and commandant of the Infantry School. York, formerly commanded the 82nd Airborne Division at Fort Bragg. Born in Hartselle, Alabama, he was assigned to Fort Benning in 1956 and served successively as director of the Tactics Department of the Infantry School, assistant chief of staff, Infantry Center director of instruction, deputy assistant commandant TIS, and Infantry Center chief of staff.

Another person of note, Captain Roger Donlon, the first Medal of Honor recipient since the Korean War, was now a student in the career course for infantry officers. A former Special Forces member, Donlon earned his medal for heroic action when his Special Forces camp at Nam Dong, Vietnam, came under attack by the Viet Cong. Donlon was a graduate of Fort Benning's OCS.

Graduation for 396 students of the 35-week career course, including Donlon, was held in spring 1966. General Harold K. Johnson, army chief of staff, reminded the graduates, all with more than three years of service, that they were "the senior citizens of the Army.... With the buildup of the Army from 960,008 men to 1,200,000, 71 percent of all enlisted men and 40 percent of all officers have less than two years service."[7]

Because of the 235,000-man buildup in 1965, the post received 180 openings for officer candidates. The 180 were drawn from 2,300 eligible soldiers on post. A second OCS battalion was created under command of Lieutenant Colonel G. Abarr. Airborne training graduated 750 weekly compared to former classes of 500 graduates per week.[8] Another buildup occurred when the 37th Aviation Battalion became part of Fort Benning's 10th Aviation Group with the mission of supplying qualified aviators and aircraft technicians either individually or in units. Major Roy Miller commanded the 1,681-man battalion. The 10th Aviation Group was activated in 1965 to support the 1st Cavalry Division (Air Mobile).

With casualty reports from the 1st Cavalry Division came puzzling news. After all the high hopes, testing, and politics on the part of the army and its airmobility concept, the CV-2 Caribou, designed to get in and out of small, unimproved landing fields, was transferred to the air force, along with the CV-7 Buffalo. The transition training course, originally conducted at the Army Aviation Center at Fort Rucker was moved to Benning, under the

---

[7] David Ybarra, "Army Chief of Staff Addresses Graduates," *Bayonet*, March 27 1966, 27.

[8] "180 Spaces Open for Post Troops to Attend OCS," *Bayonet*, November 12 1965, 1; "Sky Trooper Battalions Commence Paratrooper Qualification Training," *Bayonet*, July 2 1965, 1; "Jump School Training Completed," *Bayonet*, July 16 1965, 21.

control of the 10th Aviation Group. The first of thirty-six select air force pilots graduated from the course in June, qualifying as instructors in the Caribou.

Also in June, the 199th Light Infantry Brigade was activated in the Kelley Hill area. The 3rd Battalion, 7th Infantry Regiment, the "Cottonbalers," was a member unit. Colonel George D. Rehkopf commanded the brigade. Although not a new concept like airmobility, the small organization trained with the idea of immediate replacement where needed, by airlifting or moving the unit as required. Rehkopf said by mid-October, "The 199th Light Infantry Brigade was expected to be fully trained and ready for whatever mission they might be assigned."[9] The unit was sent to Vietnam in November.

Preparing the post for Vietnam training was costly and spending was carefully supervised. The army's second highest award for meritorious civilian service was presented to Vernon G. Abrams, accounting officer for the Infantry Center finance and accounting section. Abrams played a large role in effectively utilizing $59 million to support the Infantry School, the 2nd Division, the reorganization and testing of the 11th Air Assault Division and other contingency missions.[10]

In August, the Army Training Center welcomed Brigadier General Charles M. Mount, a Vietnam veteran, in ceremony on York Field. Mount, a veteran of three wars, made known his pleasure of being at Benning. His views were typical of many: "Twenty-seven years ago this month, I reported to Fort Benning. I was married here, and my first son was born here. That will give you some idea of my fondness for this post."[11]

The post, however, was involved in a controversial plan suggested by Secretary of Defense Robert McNamara. He announced "Project 100,000" in a speech to the Veterans of Foreign Wars in New York City. The military services would accept 40,000 enlistees who were rejected in the current fiscal year (1966) and 100,000 each following year.[12]

---

[9] "Post to Get New Unit," *Bayonet*, May 27 1966, 1.

[10] "Finance Week Brings Accountant Army's Second Highest Civil Award," *Bayonet*, July 8 1966, 1.

[11] "General Mount Is Named ATC's New Commander," *Bayonet*, July 15 1966, 1–2.

[12] Janice H. Laurence and Peter F. Ramsberger, *Low-Aptitude Men in the Military* (New York: Praeger, 1991) 21.

McNamara argued that men entering service under reduced aptitude testing would have a "more fulfilling and productive civilian life after separation."[13] Other viewed it "as an exclusively cynical idea carried out only to provide 'cannon fodder' for Vietnam" since the project protected upper- and middle-class whites from the draft during Vietnam.[14] The army took about 66 percent of the lower aptitude men, assigning the slower soldiers to the infantry, many coming to Fort Benning. McNamara's plan ended in 1971.

In October, Airborne students took their first parachute jump from a C-141 flown from Lawson Field. When Lawson Field's 8,200-foot jet runway opened in September, General Paul D. Adams, commanding general of the US Strike Command, landed in a KC-135 jet, the military equivalent of a Boeing 707. After officially opening the runway, Adams visited his son, Captain Robert T. Adams, a student at the post.

With the continuing Vietnam buildup in 1967, new units were needed to assist the 197th Infantry Brigade and the Infantry School. To house these soldiers, the cuartel, built for the 29th Infantry Regiment in the 1920s, was converted into bachelor quarters with 628 air-conditioned rooms, private baths, and walk-in closets. The building, a mile around the outside, was termed the largest US Army POQ under one roof.

Better housing, better health care, and better technology impressed Chief Warrant Officer Phillip W. Foley of the 43rd Engineer Battalion, a subordinate unit of the Center Troop Command. The changes he witnessed during his career, from caring for horses in 1931 to maintaining helicopters with the 1st Air Cavalry in 1965, reflected growth he once thought impossible. "Thirty-six years ago," he said, "if anyone said I would think of rockets, helicopters, and three hot meals a day as normal military operations, I surely would have viewed him as a candidate for a lunacy discharge."[15]

Military operations in Vietnam now were openly questioned. In March, Senator Herman E. Talmadge of Georgia spoke at the semi-annual dinner meeting of the Columbus-Phenix City-Fort Benning Chapter, Association of the US Army (AUSA). He received enthusiastic applause when he

---

[13] Ibid.

[14] Ibid.

[15] "CWO Entered Army Life As Infantryman in 1931," *Bayonet*, February 24 1967, 11.

advocated that generals and admirals should get the country out of the 'mess" that politicians produced in Vietnam.[16] A navy combat veteran of World War II, Talmadge criticized the US policy of fighter bombers destroying small bridges that could be replaced overnight but bypassing the enemy's surface to air missiles that could destroy planes.[17]

The war, however, continued. Retired army general Maxwell D. Taylor, a special consultant to the president, addressed career course graduates, including his son Captain Thomas H. Taylor: "You are going forward, not from school, but to a sterner school—Vietnam—where only you can pass the test.... Today's young officer...must also consider the pig crop—the rice harvest—the village school."[18]

On Memorial Day 1967, Major General Robert York paid tribute to the nation's war dead at the post cemetery, saying it was "not for us to know" why some died and some were spared.[19] He asked for personal involvement to honor those who died and to "insure the flag and honor for our country."[20] A *Bayonet* reporter noted the ceremony included "active and retired military personnel and a number of parents and widow 'personally involved' in Memorial Day Service for the first time."[21]

Major General John McNair Wright, Jr., former assistant division commander of the 1st Cavalry Division (Airmobile) in Vietnam, succeeded York as Fort Benning commander and commandant of the Infantry School in July 1967. Due for promotion to lieutenant general, York would soon command the XVIII Airborne Corps at Fort Bragg.

Wright enlisted in the army in 1935 and graduated from West Point in 1940. He attended Airborne School in 1947, qualifying as a parachutist and gliderman. Following the Infantry School advanced course, he was battalion commander of the post's 508th Airborne Regimental Combat Team, a forerunner of the 11th Air Assault Division. He commanded the battery that fired the last shot on Corregidor before the Japanese took control and was a

---

[16] Ibid.

[17] Al Spratley, "Local AUSA Chapter Hails Speech by Senator Talmadge," *Bayonet*, March 31 1967, 1.

[18] "Maxwell Taylor Addresses Career Course Graduates," *Bayonet*, May 26 1967, 39.

[19] Al Spratley, "CG Speaks At Services," *Bayonet*, June 2 1967, 2.

[20] Ibid.

[21] Ibid.

prisoner of war for three and a half years. Wright was with the Department of Army Office of Force Development at the Pentagon prior to Benning.

Around the time Wright reported to Fort Benning, so did John Wayne. The Hollywood legend came to film *The Green Berets*—billed as "the first feature length movie on war as it is in Vietnam."[22] Shooting began on August 9 with a Special Forces team from Fort Bragg putting on a "Gabriel Show," a demonstration of unconventional warfare. Fort Benning's ranges, barracks, and woodlands substituted for Fort Bragg. For the Vietnam scenes, a Special Forces "A" Camp and a Montagnard village were built. Filming an OCS class performing routine helicopter assault pickups saved two days of special staging. The movie was inspired by the 1965 novel *The Green Berets* by Robin Moore, who went to Vietnam after completing Airborne training at Benning and attending the Special Forces Center at Fort Bragg. In the movie, Wayne plays Colonel Michael Kirby, a two-time Vietnam veteran, who handpicks specialists for a Special Forces team to take to Vietnam. The cast includes David Janssen, Aldo Ray, Jim Hutton, and Pat Wayne, the star's son. A month long premier of the movie was held on post in June 1968, a month before the 4th of July national premiere in Atlanta.

A true-life hero and former Benning soldier posthumously received the Medal of Honor at a White House ceremony in August. Staff sergeant Jimmy G. Stewart, Company B, 2nd Battalion, 12th Cavalry of the 1st Cavalry Division, was killed in combat in Vietnam on May 18, 1966. His wife and two sons lived in Columbus. Sightseeing Field, south of York Field, was renamed Stewart Field in his honor.

With troop buildup continuing in Vietnam, Benning's Officer Candidate School expanded, peaking in fiscal year 1967 when 8,000 candidates (65 classes) were commissioned. In addition, the Training Center graduated an average of 12,300 men weekly since December 1965. In an August ceremony, Brigadier General Charles M. Mount, Jr., commanding general of the Training Center, delivered the graduation address and presented an engraved plaque to the 100,000th graduate. On November 10, President Lyndon B. Johnson began a Veteran's Day weekend tour of stateside military posts. Fort Benning was first because "here is where it

---

[22] Larry Mahoney, "'Colonel Kirby' Directs Cameras on Eubanks Field," *Bayonet*, August 18 1967, 10.

starts...." Johnson referred to Fort Benning's alumni, the paratroopers, the Rangers, the basic trainees, the officer candidate graduates, combat infantrymen from buck private to career officer. "It is here," he said, "that so much of our hope for peace begins. It is here that so many dreams of freedom are refreshed. Here, in this vast arsenal of war, soldier and family devote life and honor to ending war." [23] Johnson was the fifth sitting president to visit the post, following Warren G. Harding, Franklin D. Roosevelt, Harry S. Truman, and Dwight D. Eisenhower.

After decorating fourteen Vietnam veterans, Johnson referred to Columbus as a "community of courage and family of patriots" and called the Infantry Center "a cradle, a college, and a crossroads...more than that, Benning is a family."[24]

And at that time, it was a family that often grieved.

---

[23] "Post Straightens Up Following LBJ Visit," *Bayonet*, November 17 1967, 1.
[24] Ibid.

37.

Tumult in the Air

Residents of the White House changed and so did political policies. There was talk of peace but sounds of battle. Still the trauma of war continued—for the nation and for Fort Benning.

On Veteran's Day, 1968, the *Bayonet* reprinted a Veteran's Day essay written by veteran reporter Al Spratley, a retired sergeant major. On October 11, a month before the holiday, Spratley died. The post newspaper decided to share with readers his essay that remembered the young soldiers who have to deal with the ageless trauma. Spratley wrote, "Young unshaven cheeks learn the feel of a smooth rifle stock.... Remember the veterans...pay tribute to the dead...but pray...pray...that their sleep will never again be disturbed...and give thanks...for freedom."[1]

Men and units still were leaving the post for the Vietnam War—now considered the longest war in the history of the United States. For the US, war in Vietnam officially began when James Thomas Davis from Tennessee was killed on December 22, 1961—the first of 25,000 American deaths as of June 23, 1968. The Revolutionary War, from the Battle of Lexington to the surrender of Cornwallis, lasted six and a half years. The Vietnam War, from December 22, 1961, to June 23, 1968, had lasted six and one-half years plus twenty-four hours, with no treaty in sight.

There was tumult in the air. The assassination of a reasoned voice of civil rights, Martin Luther King, Jr., led to rioting. Robert Kennedy, the brother of an assassinated president, was killed as he campaigned for the same office. The process of choosing a presidential candidate went from the floor of a convention to the streets of Chicago. Soldiers were being wounded and killed in Vietnamese jungles, and though no one knew it then,

---

[1] Sgt. Maj. (Ret.) Al Spratley, "Veterans Day Eulogy," *Bayonet*, November 8 1968, 16.

women and children were killed in a village called My Lai. By the end of January, attention shifted to South Vietnam. During Tet, the Vietnamese New Year, enemy forces attacked South Vietnam, including Saigon, Khe Sanh (US Marine Base), and Hue, the provincial capital. Although many Americans interpreted the attack as a show of enemy strength, communist forces of North Vietnam suffered devastating losses. Some 45,000 of the enemy were dead, and thousands were captured or wounded.[2]

General William Westmoreland praised the men and women of the Military Assistance Command, Vietnam (MACV) for their performance during the Tet Truce aggression that began January 29. "You have destroyed more of the enemy in seven days," he said, "than the United States has lost in the seven years of the war since January 1961."[3]

Nevertheless, to be on the safe side, Westmoreland requested 206,000 additional American soldiers, raising the total to 715,000 uniformed soldiers in Vietnam. The American people, however, after watching the Tet attacks on television, developed a strong antiwar sentiment and questioned the leaders who were asking for more troops. The administration shared some of those concerns. Following the Tet invasion, President Johnson booted Robert S. McNamara "upstairs" to head the World Bank. Clark Clifford became secretary of defense.

During this time, one of the largest major units on post and the largest brigade in the army—the 197th—was stationed at Kelley Hill, Harmony Church, and the Main Post. Its mission of primary troop support for the Infantry School began in September 1962 under the Reorganization Objective Army Division (ROAD) concept. Used for ceremony as well as training, the 197th traveled to Marietta, Georgia, in March for the unveiling of the Lockheed C-5A Galaxy super transport aircraft—the largest airplane in the world. To the army's satisfaction, the six-story tall subsonic jet, part of the air force's Military Airlift Command, was capable of moving men and equipment anywhere in the world within hours. This would not be the unit's last trip out of town in 1968.

On March 31, President Johnson announced he would not run for a second term. Devoted to his Great Society agenda and military action,

---

[2] Gen. William Westmoreland, "Gen. Westmoreland Lauds Troops for Tet Victory," *Bayonet*, March 6 1968, 12.

[3] Ibid.

including Operation Rolling Thunder, the bombing of North Vietnam, Johnson continued to support the war and to enact civil rights legislation.[4] On April 11, the Civil Rights Act ended racial discrimination in housing. Some saw its passage as a response to the murder of Dr. Martin Luther King, Jr., winner of the Nobel Peace Prize, who was thirty-nine when he was killed in Memphis on April 4.

Violence resulting from King's death hit the nation's capital on April 6. Five people died, and 350 were injured. Army troops were called to Washington to bring order and to end the looting and burning. On April 7, Fort Benning soldiers of the 197th Infantry Brigade deployed to Baltimore, Maryland, to reinforce overwhelmed law enforcement agencies. Commanded by Colonel Jack L. Treadwill, the 197th was joined by troops from Fort Bragg and the Maryland National Guard. Order was restored without a shot being fired. There were no civilian or military casualties and a minimal use of physical force. The entire operation took a week. All units returned to post by April 15.[5]

As peace talks to end the Vietnam conflict began in Paris, another enemy offensive, not as severe as Tet, occurred in May. Even with talk of peace, more men headed for Vietnam. The number of American military personnel in Vietnam was the highest since the war began. President Johnson was ready to negotiate an end to war. He was reacting to the American public and to the "wise men," an advisory group that included retired generals Matthew Ridgway and Maxwell Taylor. Creighton Abrams would succeed Westmoreland, who became army chief of staff. Abrams, respected World War II warrior and Korean negotiator, was to begin the Vietnamization[6] of the war and the withdrawal of forces from South Vietnam.[7]

Since men would still be needed for the successful withdrawal of troops, two of eight National Guard and Reserve units arrived at Fort

---

[4] Robert McNamara, *In Retrospect* (New York: Times Books, 1995) 173–74.

[5] "Post Soldiers Called to Baltimore to Quell Rioting, Civil Disobedience," *Bayonet*, April 19 1969, 20.

[6] Neil Sheehan, *A Bright Shining Lie* (New York: Random House, 1988) 731; "Changing of the Guard," *Time*, April 19 1968, 25. Newscaster Bob Schieffer says Melvin Laid, defense secretary, coined the term "Vietnamization" (Bob Schiefer, *This Just In* [New York: G. P. Putnam's Sons, 2003] 166).

[7] Sheehan, A Bright Shining Lie, 730–31.

Benning because of Johnson's mobilization order. They were part of 20,000 Reservists and National Guardsmen who reported to active duty at military installations in the United States.[8] The largest unit scheduled to come to Benning was the Massachusetts National Guard unit, the 1st Battalion of the 211th Artillery, consisting of 564 men. It was attached to the 197th Infantry Brigade with quarters at Harmony Church.

To remember those who died, a memorial fountain was built adjacent to the Georgia Welcome Center on Victory Drive. It honored the army's first airmobile unit as well as other members of the Armed Forces. Lieutenant General Harry O. Kinnard, commander of the 1st Cavalry at its creation and its first commander in Vietnam, attended the dedication on July 26. Jack Bell, chairman of the Memorial Committee and former president of the Columbus Chamber of Commerce, drew the original sketches that Ed Neal and Lewis Scarborough used to design the fountain.[9]

On October 6, light rain fell on a memorial service at Linwood Cemetery ceremony when honoring the fiftieth anniversary of Fort Benning and its namesake, Confederate general Henry Benning. Seventy people were under a tent, and thirty huddled under umbrellas, including Mrs. Henry Benning Crawford, the general's granddaughter. Referring to "our brave men in Vietnam," Columbus mayor B. Ed Johnson assured all present that "the people of Columbus have always shared the triumphs and the heartaches of the fort."[10]

During the three-day celebration, "Massed troops, military and civilian bands and floats carrying Southern belles marched along Broadway from Phenix City to the Columbus Municipal Auditorium" where the US Army band and chorus performed.[11] Leighton W. McPherson, a founder of the Columbus Chamber of Commerce Military Affairs Committee in 1918, was grand marshal of the parade. The public was invited to displays and demonstrations at Stewart, Watson, and York Fields. Eugene Becker, assistant secretary of the army, spoke on post in lieu of Westmoreland, who

---

[8] "Guard Reserve Units Answer Call," *Bayonet*, May 17 1968, 1.

[9] "Gen. Kinnard to Attend Dedication of 1st Air Cav Monument Today," *Bayonet*, July 26 1968, 1–2.

[10] "Benning Namesake Honored on Anniversary," *Columbus Ledger-Enquirer*, October 7 1968, 13.

[11] "Thousands Enjoy 50th Celebration," *Bayonet*, October 11 1968, 1–2; "Celebrating Benning's 50th: Fun for Everyone," *Bayonet*, October 11 1968, 21.

entered Walter Reed Army Hospital, October 4, for treatment of a recurring intestinal disorder.

On November 5, former vice-president Richard Nixon was elected president of the United States, narrowly defeating Hubert Humphrey. Nixon, proposing domestic unity and world peace, appealed to the silent majority for a return of order in the nation. A protester explained Nixon's victory: "Generally speaking, blue-collar kids weren't the ones out there chanting; they still wanted their piece of the American dream. (And they—and the poor—were, by and large, the kids doing the dying in Vietnam.) Nixon was right; there was a silent majority out there. And it agreed with him, not with us."[12]

The man Nixon served with earlier was again in the news. Fort Benning's flags were lowered to half-staff for thirty days following the announcement on March 28 that General Dwight D. Eisenhower died at age seventy-eight. From sunrise to sunset on Saturday, March 29, the cannon in front of Infantry Hall was fired on the half-hour. At noon Monday, the cannon was fired every minute for fifty minutes in respect of his place in history as president of the United States and supreme commander of Allied Expeditionary Forces in World War II.[13]

Post leader Major General John M. Wright, Jr., left Fort Benning in mid-May for Vietnam. Under Wright's command, the post expanded its officer training program, established the non-commissioned officer candidate course, hosted national and international conferences as well as the post's fiftieth anniversary, welcomed President Johnson to the post, and turned out what he called, "the finest combat infantryman in the world."[14]

Major General George Forsythe, a former assistant commandant of the Infantry School, succeeded Wright. Before coming back to Benning, he served as commander of the 1st Cavalry Division (Airmobile) in Vietnam. His tour on post was brief. In July 1969, he was nominated to lieutenant general and reassigned as commanding general of the US Combat Developments Command at Fort Belvoir, Virginia. In August he succeeded

---

[12] Scott Turow, "Where Have All the Radicals Gone?" *Newsweek* 128/10 (September 2 1996): 1.

[13] "Fort Benning Mourns Eisenhower," *Bayonet*, April 4 1969, 1–2.

[14] "Gen. Wright Will Depart in May," *Bayonet*, February 28 1969, 1.

Kinnard, who planned to retire September 11. For a second time, Brigadier General Oscar E. Davis served as Benning's acting commanding general.

Major General Orwin C. Talbott, who "served in combat with the 1st Infantry Division in the Republic of Vietnam longer than any other commandeer" arrived in September to take command of the US Army Infantry Center and Fort Benning.[15] In 1943, he attended the wartime infantry officers' advanced course at Fort Benning. He later was a rifle company commander during the Normandy Campaign and a battalion commander in the Battle of the Bulge and the battle of Central Europe. In 1947, Talbott attended the regular advanced course of the Infantry School. In April 1968, he was assistant commander and later commander of the 1st Infantry Division in Vietnam.

As 1969 ended, Dexter School, the newest of Fort Benning's eight elementary schools, was formally dedicated November 10 in honor of Major Herbert Dexter, a member of the 101st Airborne Division, killed in Vietnam. Dexter attended OCS at Fort Benning and received his commission at the post in 1952. Mrs. Dexter, with her five children, unveiled a plaque commemorating her husband.[16] Dexter was posthumously awarded the Distinguished Service Cross, the nation's second highest award for valor.

Reflecting signs of the times, the Army Training Center received notice of closure for March 31, 1970. The final closing date for the Reception Station was January 31. Lower draft calls due to the "Vietnamization of the war" was responsible for the reduction of troops. Since its organization in 1965, the Center produced nearly 190,000 trained combat soldiers.[17] Over 2,100 military and civilian personnel were responsible for turning civilians into soldiers.[18]

Post military and civilian personnel found their pay call was changing. Instead of cash disbursement—the army way—17,000 people on post received US Treasury checks delivered to their units. The US Army was the "largest paying agent in the world still involved in cash disbursement" until

---

[15] "General Talbott to Arrive Soon," *Bayonet*, September 5 1969, 1.

[16] Marian Jones, "Gen. Orwin Talbott Dedicates Dexter School in Honor of Infantryman Killed in Vietnam," *Bayonet*, November 14 1969, 1.

[17] "Traiing Center Closes March 31," *Bayonet*, December 12 1969, 2.

[18] Ibid., 1.

Fort Benning became the first army post to initiate the pay-by-check method.[19]

The Infantry Board observed its fiftieth anniversary in 1969. Although established in March 1903 at the US Army General Service and Staff College, Fort Leavenworth, Kansas, the War Department relocated the board to Camp Benning in 1919. During 1969, its testing "The Best for the Finest" included the antitank missile weapon TOW, a lightweight entrenching tool, a new jungle boot, a foxhole cover, a rifle grenade launcher, various reduced visibility and night vision sights. It continued the ongoing reduction of the soldier's pack, now known by an acronym—Project LINCLOE (lightweight individual combat clothing and equipment).[20]

The board liked to say it tested "The Best for the Finest."[21] Most of a soldier's gear passed through the board's tedious testing: "Whether he shoots it, rides it, sleeps in it, eats it, wears it, or uses it in some manner in combat conditions, the infantryman is using some item of equipment that has been tested for him by the Infantry Board."[22]

---

[19] "Benning Makes Switch to Check Pay System," *Bayonet*, January 12 1968, 1.

[20] Rex Ellis, "Infantry Board to Observe 50th Anniversary," *Bayonet*, October 17 1969, 21.

[21] Ibid.

[22] Ibid.

38.

The Soldier's Hero

Charlie Black's leathery face was as lined as a roadmap that would take you there and back. His voice and his unmistakable laugh were as rough as sixty-grit sandpaper, honed by years of strong coffee, cheap whiskey, and unfiltered cigarettes. At times in his life he was a marine recon man, in uniform for two wars. He walked narrow rafters as a high-flying steelworker. He reported the news on radio. He was a welder and public information officer.[1] But most of his life he was a newspaperman who could hunt and peck faster than your modern word processor. He wasn't "old school," for that would wrongly imply there were others like him. He was not some stuffy journalist with diplomas on the wall, but a gut-level reporter who went where the story was. Charlie Black's story was the Vietnam War and the men who fought it.[2]

The Vietnam War defined the career of this gypsy newsman, a story he told from the foxhole. As a correspondent for the *Columbus Ledger-Enquirer*, he was a small-town reporter covering a big-time story. His reports were full of names and full of hometowns, as much letters home as they were journalism.

As Marv Wolf, a former army PAQ, said, "Black was not what you would call a writer. He was more a reporter, a man who just put down what he saw and heard and felt, put it down in simple words. Who, what, when and where. Rarely why. Why didn't so much concern him. His readers, moms, dads, wives, kids back in Columbus—they knew why."[3]

---

[1] Ned Baxter Ennis, *Charlie Black: The Ernie Pyle of the Vietnam War* (Thesis, University of Georgia, 1987) 33–34.

[2] Glenn Vaughn, "Amazing Legend of Charlie Black Remember," *Columbus Ledger-Enquirer*, August 30 1987, B10.

[3] Marv Wolf, "A Man Called Charlie Black," *Military Media Review* 10/4 (October 1983): 22.

Black's own history sounds like one of the tales he was known to spin. He was, it is said, raised in the Ozarks by his grandmother, a Miami Indian named Mrs. Blue Crane. She would burn down her house when she tired of it then move on to the next one. It was a habit Black adopted, for through fifty-nine years he was known to leave everything behind him as he moved from place to place and job to job.

On a Saturday in 1963, Black drove to Columbus for an interview with the *Columbus Enquirer*. He talked with Ben Walburn, who in later years worked in Fort Benning's Public Affairs Office. Walburn was impressed, maybe because of clippings from Black's previous jobs, maybe because of Black's interesting and varied life. Or maybe because Black's application indicated he attended Drury College and the University of Missouri, a couple of "minor mistakes."[4] He got the job, and on June 15 of that year Black had his first byline in the *Enquirer*. Ten days later, his first story about the military appeared—an article about the spring meeting of the AUSA.[5]

That August, Fort Benning's 2nd Infantry Division was in South Carolina for Swift Strike III, an operation involving more than 80,000 troops. The *Enquirer* assigned John Coombs, its military reporter. Within a few days Black joined Coombs. On this assignment Black began to forge a relationship with the army, the soldiers, and the people who wanted to read about them. For the next twenty years, this would be his niche.

His stories from Swift Strike III were not gathered in the press tent. Black, a former marine who fought in World War II and Korea, went out in the field. He ate with the men. He talked with the men. He scratched chiggers with the men. He listened to them, not the officers with the bars and the birds. One article had fun at the expense of a first lieutenant named Julian Simerly, an aide to Brigadier General Robert Coffin. It was the story of a reconnaissance team that knew how to operate behind the lines, even if those lines were in rural South Carolina. An administrative truce was in place, and Simerly decided to get a haircut and pick up the general's laundry in a nearby town. He went by helicopter, and when the chopper landed in the square, the town came out to meet them. The reconnaissance team went straight to the barbershop, not to get their hair cut but to take a prisoner, Lieutenant Simerly. Firing blanks into the air, the troopers claimed the

---

[4] Ennis, *Charlie Black: The Ernie Pyle of the Vietnam War*, 42.
[5] Ibid., 44–45.

general's aide, the pilot, the helicopter, and the general's laundry as prisoners of war.[6]

A personal adventure for Black took place one afternoon in April 1964 when a man climbed WRBL-TV's 185-foot tower and said he was going to jump. Charles Hiott, twenty-two years old and a Fort Benning soldier, clutched the tower for two hours before Black arrived at the scene on 13th Avenue. Two city employees climbed up to talk with Hiott, but he was not budging. Black found Grover Knox, a Columbus police captain, and asked if he could go up to the young soldier.

"I work with that division," he said, "I am familiar with those boys. I know a lot of them by their first names. Maybe I can be of help?"

To everyone's surprise—Black included—Knox said yes.

Black intended to talk the young man out of launching himself and to avoid a handshake, fearing the GI would turn both of them into an express elevator going down. Clinging 185 feet above the ground, they dickered. A deal struck, they started down. Black came first, fast enough to keep out of range of Hiott's feet. Black was almost down when a flash bulb exploded. The red-haired soldier fell, aiming his body in the direction of the cameraman. On the ground, a quilt of blue uniforms covered him.

With that deed, Black was on his way to legend, which he noted years later in his unfinished memoirs: "There I was, suddenly and unalterably a hero, the first step, or climb, to all the rest of this. No one of which made much more sense than the beginning. The entire fourteen years that followed seemed to be planned by maniacs, executed by a fool, and supervised by the sister Fate who was the most incompetent asshole of the entire family. Once you get to be a hero, they don't let you quit. They are too curious about finding a way to cut you down."[7] For his bravery, Black got a bonus—and money was something newspaper publisher Maynard Ashworth clutched as tightly as Black did the rungs on that tower. He was honored by the city government and was the subject of laudatory letters to the editor.

---

[6] Charles L. Black, Jr., "Truce Announcement Sometimes Is Slow," *Columbus Enquirer*, August 15 1963, 1.

[7] Charles L. Black, Jr., introduction to unpublished manuscript, personal papers of Charles L. Black, Jr., Columbus GA.

Later that year, Black became acquainted with the newly formed Air Assault unit. He earned respect by his willingness to hike, rappel, and parachute alongside them. By the time they went to South Carolina for Hawk Star I, he was one of them. Black gave his reason for such personal engagement: "The only way I can get a true picture of what a particular sky soldier is like and what type of spectacular job he is doing, is to go out and do it myself."[8]

When they deployed to Vietnam, Black intended to be with them. He petitioned the Department of Defense. He called on old friends such as Major General Harry Kinnard, the commander of the 1st Cavalry Division. Black not only got permission, he was invited to fly with the 92nd Aviation Company—an unusual invitation for a reporter.[9]

Over the course of the next four years, Black spent about as much time in Vietnam as he did at home. He went to the jungles of Southeast Asia five times and spent sixteen months in country. If Fort Benning soldiers were there, so was Black. Banging on a portable typewriter, using whatever paper was available, he kept the families back home informed. He wasted no space, typing single-space instead of double. He penciled in sentences that trailed down the margins like a coffee stain. He used front and back, figuring a copy editor back in Columbus would decipher his scribbling.[10]

On November 20, 1965, Black was the subject of a story himself. Robin Mannock, an Associated Press reporter, wrote that Black took part in thirty-two patrols, sweeps, and attacks against the Viet Cong and that a chopper was shot out from under him. He wrote about the local reporter being caught in crossfire between the VC and another American unit. "I gave myself up for dead," Black told the AP reporter. "I've been shot at by Japanese, Chinese, Koreans, and Viet Cong, but American fire is by far the most terrifying and the most demoralizing."[11]

Black did all this on $130 a week—though Ashworth gave him a raise when *Newsweek* printed his salary in 1965. Charlie Black didn't care about

---

[8] Sgt. Chuck Lowenhagen, "Local Paper's Modern 'War' Correspondent Follows Sky Soldier Division Field Exercise," *Bayonet*, October 16 1964, 29.

[9] Ennis, *Charlie Black: The Ernie Pyle of the Vietnam War*, 56.

[10] Wolf, "A Man Called Charlie Black," 22.

[11] Robin Mannock, "'Charlie Black Club' in VN Is Least Exclusive in Highlands; Generals, Privates Are Members," *Columbus Enquirer*, October 9 1965, 1.

money; he had to smell the fuel of the choppers, see the blood, and hear the deafening sound of mortars. Joe Galloway, then of UPI, was one of the premier correspondents of the war. Now a consultant with Knight-Ridder Newspapers, he also spent time with the 1st Cav. From that experience, he and General Hal Moore co-authored *We Were Soldiers Once ...and Young*.

He remembered Black and his exploits:

> The Cav also brought along with them their home town reporter, a grizzled, and to we [sic] twenty-somethings, ancient World War II veteran Charlie Black of the *Columbus Ledger-Enquirer*.... Charlie would go out with a battalion on operations and stay for a week or ten days or two weeks. When he came back to An Khe he would sit down at a battered old typewriter and write endless dispatches, single-spaced on onionskin paper. His stories were full of names and hometowns. He would find a friendly GI who would frank the letter so it went home airmail for free. His editor would run every line, because his readers included the wives and kids of many of the troops.... Charlie was supposed to stay two or three weeks. He ended up staying more than a year that tour. The Cav troops would have happily passed the hat for donations if Charlie had gone totally broke. They loved him, and the love affair was mutual.[12]

J. D. Coleman was a public affairs officer with the Cav. He remembered how other reporters perceived Black—in the beginning contemptuous, finally respectful:

> His clothing, his actions, his words allow him, like the chameleon, to become part, as well as an observer, of the picture. He can talk the language of the soldier, and because he can, the soldier feels that Charlie is his friend. He'll ask a friend to help him split his last ration or to share a part of his poncho in a drenching tropical storm. He won't divulge confidences to a visiting journalist, or even some of his fellow squad members. But he will to a friend, and Charlie Black is such a friend.[13]

---

[12] Joe Galloway, *A Reporter's Journal from Hell*, http://www.digitaljournalist.org/issues0204/galloway2.htm.

[13] J. D. Coleman, "Charlie Black—The Soldier's Friend in Vietnam," *The Journalist* 11/4 (November 1967): 6–7.

Coleman, like others, compared Black to Ernie Pyle, the quintessential reporter of World War II. But while Pyle was nationally syndicated, Black wrote only for his readers in Columbus and Fort Benning. "And nobody wrote about the war like he did," wrote Wolf. "Nobody."[14]

"Like Ernie Pyle, getting PFC's story is Black's specialty," *Newsweek* wrote. "And with a straightforward, unadorned style, he puts his readers in the thick of the fight."[15]

Privates and generals alike revered Black. When Colonel William B. Steele commanded the 197th Infantry Brigade at Fort Benning, he often invited Black to join them for their maneuvers. "I enjoyed Charlie," Steele said. "He would come out on night problems with us and spend two or three days with us.... He would tell one story after another, very loquacious. A good fellow and a good friend of mine...a good friend of the army. He was a pretty straight-shooting guy. If you told him the facts, he'd print them just that way. When news people came out from CBS or NBC, you never knew how it was going to come out till you saw it on TV."[16]

That is why, decades after the war, this sinewy, weather-beaten reporter is a character soldiers remember. He was the subject of a master's thesis submitted in 1987 by army major Ned Ennis.[17] He was remembered by the survivors of the 1st Cav who gathered at Fort Benning in 2002 for a premiere showing of *We Were Soldiers Once...And Young*. When one of his daughters was introduced in the theater, she received an ovation.[18]

Those memories are why so many of them toasted his memory in October 1982 when Black died at the age of fifty-nine—not on a battlefield, but of a heart attack in his backyard in Phenix City. Like so many warriors, he was never able to find peace at home. When there were no more wars to cover, he lost that glint in his eye. He found a time of happiness with his third wife, Priscilla. Like him, she was a reporter and columnist in Columbus. His last stint as a newsman was with the *Valley Times* in Lanett, Alabama.

---

[14] Wolf, "A Man Called Charlie Black," 23.

[15] "Git or Git Got," *Newsweek* 66/23 (December 6 1965): 88.

[16] Gen. (Ret.) William B. Steele, interview by Peggy Stelpflug, October 5 1998, Donovan Technical Library, Fort Benning GA, handwritten transcript and audio cassette, Auburn AL.

[17] Ennis, *Charlie Black: The Ernie Pyle of the Vietnam War*.

[18] Richard Hyatt, *Columbus Ledger-Enquirer* reporter, Columbus GA.

A memorial service was held at Fort Benning's main post chapel, planned by Charlie himself. Newspaper friends were there, including some who were with him in Vietnam. So were the sky soldiers, Kinnard, Moore, Coleman, and others. Friends remembered his glory years. "Charlie Black told us the truth of the American soldier's bravery and success in Vietnam, both of which were considerable," said Millard Grimes, the editor who first sent him to the war.[19] "The wonder of it all was that Charlie Black lived long enough to die peaceably at home," wrote Bob Roos of the Associated Press, also a Vietnam correspondent.[20] "He told the truth," said Glenn Vaughn, retired publisher of the *Columbus Ledger-Enquirer*. He had a dimension of truth that no one else had because he stayed with the troops, ate with them slepth with them and fought with them.[21]

Charlie Black lived a life, of extremes. The mundane bored him and so did what others call peace. His writing of war made it difficult for Black to adjust to routine reporting. Judging from his own words, he understood "Once you get to be a hero, they don't let you quit." To the soldiers he wrote about and the families that pasted his articles in scrapbooks, he will always be that hero.

---

[19] Millard Grimes, "Charlie Black Knew a Secret," *Columbus Ledger*, November 28 1982.

[20] Glenn Vaughn, "Amazing Legend of Charlie Black Remembered," *Columbus Ledger-Enquirer*, August 30 1987, B-10.

[21] Ennis, *Charlie Black: The Ernie Pyle of the Vietnam War*, 151.

39.

A Country in Shambles

The United States Army was coming apart at the seams in 1970—but so was the country—because of a war that was never declared. As the new decade began, the Vietnam War, "America's least successful war," continued.[1] Approximately 39,642 American servicemen had been killed in action by the end of 1969.[2] The historic bond between the military and the government leaders who sent them to Vietnam was notably weakened.

Carrying "the major share of the military burdens of the entire non-Communist world,"[3] American soldiers frequently were away from family and friends, and frequent separations often led to divorces and splintered families. Rather than regarded as heroic defenders of American democracy as their counterparts in World War II, soldiers, as well as President Lyndon Johnson, were branded as "baby killers" by some anti-war protesters.[4] The soldiers were not greeted as they came home; they received no celebrations, parades, or marching bands. Those who were killed were termed "wasted" by their comrades.[5] Drugs and alcohol, readily available in Vietnam as well as it home in America, often became a destructive force in the lives of many of the demoralized warriors.[6]

---

[1] Russell F. Weigley, *History of the United States Army* (Bloomington: Indiana University Press, 1984) 558.

[2] "Statistical Information about Casualties of the Vietnam Conflict," www.archives.gove/research/vietnam-war/casualty-statistics.html.

[3] Ibid., 558–59.

[4] "American Experience—The Presidents—Lyndon B. Johnson, Foreign Affairs," www.pbs.org/wgbh/amex/presidents.

[5] William J. Stelpflug, Lt. Colonel USAF, F-4 Pilot Vietnam veteran (1968–1969).

[6] Col. David H. Hackworth, *About Face* (New York: Simon & Schuster, 1989) 573–74.

Despite the chaos around them, the majority of US servicemen continued to support the war.[7] Not wanting to identify with the draft dodgers who fled to Canada or with the peaceniks who railed against the war and the actions of the US government, the majority of soldiers answered the call to duty with only normal complaints. No ranking officer resigned his commission in protest of the policy or the operational rules related to US involvement in the Vietnam War.[8]

An example of the serviceman's commitment was that of a Fort Benning soldier with the allegorical name of Captain Buddy Allgood. He lost a foot in Vietnam when he stepped on an enemy land mine in 1965. Five years later, his injury did not stop him from completing Airborne training with the help of an artificial foot.[9]

Recognizing that so many troops coming home from Vietnam were troubled with addictions, the army acted. To combat some of the problems at Fort Benning concerning drugs and alcohol, the Benning House, a halfway house, was opened and supervised by Martin Army Hospital. Patients worked in their assigned units during the day but returned to the center after work for therapeutic programs such as Alcoholics Anonymous meetings and to stay the night. A special phone connecting on post, 545-DRUG, provided recorded information about drug misuse and addiction. Although the army assumed the number of alcoholics in the military matched those in civilian society, inexpensive alcoholic beverages available at stateside posts and overseas bases often complicated the problem.

After a peak of 550,000 troops in Vietnam in the summer of 1969, that number dropped to 475,000 by the end of the year and to 335,000 by the end of 1971.[10] This decrease of military strength in Vietnam also was reflected at Fort Benning. The Officer Candidate School program was reduced in 1970, and on February 6, the US Army Training Center (ATC) was officially closed. Since its organization on September 15, 1965, the ATC trained nearly 129,000 civilians to serve during the Vietnam War. Brigadier

---

[7] Ibid, 475–76.

[8] Erin Solaro, "Retired generals rising up against Iraq war," http://seattlepi.nwsource.com/opinion/266638–solarosub16.html.

[9] "Fort Benning in the 1970s," *Bayonet*, October 8 1993, B9.

[10] Google: Vietnam War Expedia; "Vietnamization and American Withdrawl," 1969–1973."

General Oscar E. Davis, commander of the ATC, was transferred to Fort Bragg to serve as chief of staff of the 18th Airborne Corps.

Other changes reflecting a change in mission included the reorganization of the 10th Aviation Group, once one of the largest army aviation units in the United States. It helped prepare the 11th Air Assault Division in 1962–1965, reaching a peak year in 1966 when it became a major aviation training command, providing aircraft transition, advanced flight formation flying, and gunnery training in the UH-1 (Huey) and CH-47 (Chinook) helicopters. On May 15, the headquarters and headquarters company of the 10th Aviation Group were inactivated. It was redesignated the US Army Infantry Center Aviation Command (USAICAC). USAICAC provided support for the Continental Army Command, the 3rd US Army, the Infantry Center, and Infantry School. It also operated Lawson Army Airfield, supervising the training of aviation units and individual aviators and providing aerial medical support for Benning.

Racial integration, introduced into the army in 1948, increased during the 1970s since many blacks, drafted into the army because of the Vietnam War, remained in service. An awareness of black history, publicized in the *Bayonet* and other publications helped troops appreciate the contribution of blacks to the United States. In addition, the Race Relations Council and Race Relations Coordinating Group were formed to "assist in identifying and correcting possible sources of racial tensions on post."[11] In another effort to combat racial prejudice, the Infantry School Leadership Department developed a class in race relations that could be adopted army-wide. Tested in the infantry officers' basic courses, the class helped junior leaders prevent or solve race-related problems in their units.[12]

Off-post housing for black soldiers also improved. In 1970, two-thirds of all military families resided off post in privately owned dwellings. Equal treatment regarding race, color, creed, or national origin for all military personnel who lived off post was guaranteed by the government, so civilian landlords were alerted that no soldier was allowed to rent or lease housing from anyone practicing unfair housing practices.[13] All servicemen were to receive equal treatment.

---

[11] "Race relations helps in solving problems," *Bayonet*, July 24 1970, 32.

[12] Ibid.

[13] "Army program insures equal treatment in housing," *Bayonet*, 1970.

A leader who implemented many of the new programs arrived on post in June 1970. Colonel John T. Carley, nominated for promotion to brigadier general, replaced Brigadier General Sidney Berry to become the thirtieth assistant commandant of the US Army Infantry School. Berry left for Vietnam to serve as assistant division commander of the 101st Infantry Division (Airmobile). Formerly with the 2nd Infantry Division in Korea and later commander of the 2nd Brigade, 1st Infantry Division in Vietnam, Carley had special duty with the Howze Board in 1962. He also served with the Washington War Plans Division under the secretary of the army, acted as director of the Infantry School's Weapons Department, and later was director of instruction until becoming assistant commandant. He attended Marion Military Institute in Alabama before entering the US Military Academy in 1942.

By October 1970, the 199th Infantry Brigade returned from Vietnam and was inactivated at Fort Benning, its colors retired in a ceremony held at York Field. Formed at Fort Benning in June 1966 under the command of Colonel George D. Rehkopf of Columbus, the "Redcatchers" went to Vietnam in December 1966. A member of that unit, Captain Angelo J. (Charlie) Liteky, with the 199th's 4th Battalion, 12th Infantry, became the first military chaplain awarded the Medal of Honor for service in Vietnam.[14] Years later, after relinquishing his medals, Liteky would return, standing outside the Main Gate as a pacifist and protester of4 the former School of the Americas.

With fewer troops on post, two major Benning commands became one unit in October 1970. The Candidate Brigade (TCB) and the School Brigade (TSB), the organizations to which all students of the Infantry School were assigned, combined into a single unit. Colonel Frank L. Garrison was named commander of the new organization that retained the name of the School Brigade. In another change, the 931st Engineer Group (Combat) assumed control of units from the former Center Troop Command and was elevated to major unit command status.

Fort Benning, one of three installations to develop a pilot program for a draft-free modern Volunteer Army (VOLAR), balanced mission and resources while attracting and retaining high-quality people. A welcomed

---

[14] Warren Steinhacker, "Welcome home 199th Inf. Bde," *Bayonet*, October 9 1970, 1.

8.1 percent pay raise for military personnel helped, plus other improvements on post. A $10 million construction and maintenance program improved barracks, added new housing units, repaired existing family housing units, fixed sidewalks, and sandblasted and painted Building 35, the former Infantry School. The Department of Defense was determined to keep men and women in service by providing pleasant homes, neat workplaces, and attractive surroundings.

The volunteer army also meant more opportunity for individual fashion. In 1970, the army set new hairstyles after outlawing compulsory white sidewall haircuts. With a mandate for a "neat and soldierly appearance at all times," a soldier had a choice of hairstyle.[15] Shaved heads or excessively short haircuts, unless desired by the individual, were a thing of the past. Neatly trimmed sideburns and mustaches were permitted but goatees and beards were not authorized. Rules for sideburns, stated in "army-speak" were daunting: "The base of the sideburns will not extend downwards beyond a line parallel to the ground and drawn horizontally through the center of the ear canal."[16]

In January 1971, Benning became the first army post to go completely to civilian KP (kitchen police) as part of VOLAR project. Leaders were to provide a different style when applying traditional leadership principles. As Colonel William B. Steele, then Leadership Department director, explained, "The pushup style of leadership just won't get it with today's young soldier."[17] Other changes included a welcome booth at the Columbus airport for incoming soldiers, a five-day workweek for soldiers and civilians, improved shuttle bus service, permission for students to drive to their classes, and the posting of all duty rosters three days in advance.

Carley, assistant commandant of the Infantry School, left Fort Benning in July 1971 for his second tour in Vietnam. His successor was Brigadier General Paul F. Gorman. Gorman served two years as a member of the US delegation to the Paris peace talks in Vietnam as battalion commander in the 25th Infantry Division and later as brigade commander in the 101st Airborne Division.

---

[15] "Army Sets New Hair Styles," *Bayonet*, June 5 1970, 34.

[16] "Army Sets New Hair Styles," *Bayonet*, June 5 1970, 34.

[17] "Can VOLAR end the draft?" *Columbus Ledger*, March 28 1971, 18.

Although Congress did not end the draft until late 1972, Fort Benning's C Company, 1st Battalion (mechanized), 58th Infantry (Patriots) of the 197th Infantry Brigade officially became the army's first all-volunteer unit on January 10, 1972, helping to fulfill the army's goal of attaining all-volunteer status by 1973. Company commander Captain Frederick W. Heath had been in charge of the 217-man unit since September 1971 when unit-of-choice volunteers arrived to replace draftees leaving the service. Soldiers in C Company, nicknamed the "Cougars," all enlisted under the 197th's unit-of-choice enlistment option, guaranteeing a fifteen-month tour of duty with the unit.

Brigadier General William R. Richardson, new assistant commandant of the Infantry School, arrived in July 1972, after leaving Fort Leonard Wood, Missouri, where he was deputy commanding general of the US Army Training Center, Engineer. A Vietnam veteran, he was chief of staff of the 23rd Infantry Division in Vietnam and commanding officer of the 198th Infantry Brigade, 23rd Division, before his tour at Fort Leonard Wood.[18]

Gorman was assigned to the US Department of Justice to assist the prosecution in the trial of Daniel Ellsberg for alledgedly releasing the Pentagon Papers to the news media. Robert McNamara, secretary of defense, ordered the study, officially called the "History of US Decision-Making Progress on Vietnam Policy," which later came to be known as the Pentagon Papers. He believed an unedited study of this controversial war would "help prevent similar errors in the future." However, he "never thought to mention the project to the president [Lyndon Johnson] or the secretary of state [Dean Rusk]."[19]

Ellsberg, a Vietnam veteran and research associate, worked on the study. He leaked its existence to *New York Times* correspondent Neil Sheehan, who covered the Vietnam War. The 7,000-page manuscript, filling 47 volumes, was printed serially in the *Times*, beginning June 13, 1971.[20] Although the Department of Justice tried to block publication, arguing the papers were damaging to National Security, the Supreme Court allowed the newspaper to print the study.[21]

---

[18] "Gen. Richardson named to replace Gen. Gorman," *Bayonet*, July 14, 1972, 1.
[19] Robert McNamara, *In Retrospect* (New York: Times Books, 1995) 280.
[20] Ibid., 281.
[21] Ibid., 281.

Ellsberg, a former US Marine company commander in Vietnam, was a close friend of John Paul Vann, who died June 9, 1972, in a helicopter crash in South Vietnam. Vann, a former instructor with Benning's Ranger Training Command and a graduate of the Infantry School, retired from the army but returned to Vietnam with the Agency for International Development (AID). In *A Bright Shining Lie*, Sheehan call Vann "the most important American in the country after the ambassador and the commanding general in Saigon."[22] Although critical of US policy in Vietnam, Vann believed America could win the war. Ellsberg sat with Vann's family the day of Vann's funeral at Arlington Cemetery. Many US dignitaries, military and civilian, attended. Sheehan said many "sensed that they were burying with John Vann the war and the decade of Vietnam."[23]

In 1972, determined to end America's involvement in Vietnam, President Richard Nixon offered a total cease-fire in Indochina with the withdrawal of all US and allied forces within six months of acceptance.[24] Anticipating the war's end, Infantry School planners replaced the noncommissioned officer course (NCOC), which provided junior NCOs during the Vietnam conflict, with the noncommissioned officer education system. The new system established a professional development program for career NCOs. The OCS program also was revised. Called the Branch Immaterial Officer Candidate, it trained individuals of all branches of the army. Graduates were commissioned second lieutenants and sent to appropriate branch schools for basic branch training.

In November 1972, President Nixon carried forty-nine of the fifty states and was re-elected in a landslide over Democratic challenger George McGovern. In an effort to end the war, a campaign promise of 1968 and 1972, Nixon resumed massive bombing in North Vietnam in April 1972 to make the North Vietnamese agree to a peace settlement.

Although Nixon carried Georgia by a huge margin, unknown Georgia Democrat Sam Nunn won the 1972 US Senate race. Nunn, a farmer, lawyer, businessman, and state legislator from Perry, entered the US Senate at age thirty-four. He was a graduate of Georgia Tech and Emory University's Lamar School of Law. In 1962–63, Nunn was legal counsel to

---

[22] Neil Sheehan, *A Bright Shining Lie* (New York: Random House, 1988) 7.
[23] Ibid., 4.
[24] Ibid., 784–85.

the US House Armed Services Committee, chaired by his great-uncle, Carl Vinson. As a member of the US Senate's Armed Services Committee and chairman of its subcommittee, Nunn would follow in the tradition of Vinson and Georgia's late Senator Richard B. Russell, "the most powerful voices in Congress for the armed services of the US."[25]

On January 27, 1973, a cease-fire in Vietnam was signed, ending the undeclared war. Afterward, envoys from the US and North Vietnam drank a champagne toast to peace and friendship. The exchange of prisoners and a withdrawal of all US forces soon followed, but America's military presence would not end until May 7, 1975. Just days before, the South Vietnamese surrendered to North Vietnam. There were 46,616 deaths from actions by hostile forces, and 10,000 deaths associated with the war. More than 600 US military personnel still were listed as missing.[26]

A celebration was held at York Field in 1973 marking the homecoming of Colonel Benjamin H. Purcell—the highest ranking army officer held prisoner during the Vietnam conflict. His wife, Eleanor Anne Purcell, Fort Benning's military wife of the year in 1970, and their five children were present at the ceremony.[27]

A new post commander was welcomed on February 16. Major General Thomas M. Tarpley succeeded Major General Orwin C. Talbott, who became deputy commander of the Training and Development Command (TRADOC). Talbott served since September 1969. Tarpley's previous assignment was commander of the Delta Regional Assistance Command.

In March 1973, the 197th Infantry Brigade became a Division Forces Strategic Army Forces (STRAF) brigade. Colonel William B. Steele, a Georgia native, assumed command from Colonel Edwin L. Kennedy who had served since November 1971. Steele, who first arrived at Fort Benning as a University of Georgia ROTC student, was a former senior aide to Chief of Staff William Westmoreland in Washington, DC. When Westmoreland asked Steele what he wanted for his next assignment, Steele replied, "I want

---

[25] Beau Cutts, "The Most Powerful Voices in Congress for the Armed Services of the U.S.," *Atlanta Journal and Atlanta Constitution*, June 8 1975, 3-A.

[26] "Statistical information about casualties of the Vietnam conflict," www.archives.gov/research/vietnam-war/casualty-statistics.html.

[27] "Professionalism and change, Soldiers saw a lot of both in 1973," *Bayonet*, December 1973, 14.

to go to Fort Benning."[28] Returning in 1970, Steele was director of the Infantry School's Leadership Department and secretary of the Infantry School before taking command of the 197th.

With Tarpley's support and Steele's leadership, the 197th grew as the army's first all-volunteer brigade-size unit. Steele rounded up his own people, sending troops to recruit all over Georgia, Alabama, and Louisiana. Some recruits wanted to join for the college tuition; others wanted to train for a job. Steele recalled, "Everybody we recruited, we earmarked. After they went through basic training, they came to us eventually as replacements."[29]

Trying to make the environment more conducive for the retention of the volunteer soldiers, Steele said, "I think in many ways we went overboard, really overboard. It got to the point we would say, 'What would you like the situation to be?' We didn't realize the thing that was most important to all was good training, good leadership, fairness—the very things the soldiers wanted. After six months we started to develop better training."[30]

Steele credited General William DePuy for his idea of having the Infantry School design specific segments and teaching points to help soldiers master basic military elements, believing that a soldier needed training to perform specific goals. Soldiers, using very practical skills, were graded on their progress in obtaining these goals. "The 197th was getting better by the day," Steele explained. He added, "Three or four years later with better training and better leadership, there was a world of difference. We probably had the best army that we've ever had."[31] Steele described the 197th as a heavy brigade: "I had a battalion of armor, a battalion of armored personnel infantry, a battalion of straight infantry. We had helicopters, engineers; it was a completely integrated unit with 5,000 troops. We were on alert to go different times to different places, participating in several good-sized maneuvers."[32]

With the coming of peace, the army began to change its structure. Major commands such as the 3rd US Army and Continental Army

---

[28] Brig. Gen. (Ret.) William B. Steele, interview by Peggy Stelpflug, October 5 1998, Donovan Technical Library, Fort Benning GA, handwritten transcript and audiocassette, Auburn AL.

[29] Ibid.

[30] Ibid.

[31] Ibid.

[32] Ibid.

Command (CONARC) were eliminated. Newly created commands included the US Army Health Services Command (MEDDAC). Since CONARC's size made it difficult to manage, Lieutenant General William DePuy, in operations, and General Walter "Dutch" Kerwin, in personnel, helped develop the new structure. A headquarters was set up to take care of schools, training, and the development of doctrine and equipment. It was called TRADOC.[33] The other headquarters, FORSCOM, commanded the fighting forces and units that supported them. To make this structure work, General William Westmoreland, army chief of staff, US Training and Doctrine Command, put DePuy in charge of TRADOC and Kerwin in charge of FORSCOM, US Army Forces Command. Since Benning included units with both missions, the Infantry School commandant worked with two bosses, DePuy and Kerwin.

Although still in shambles, scarred by the debacle in Vietnam and the antiwar controversies that plagued the nation, the army fought back. Facing these challenges, Colonel Kenneth C. Leuer was about to create an elite, proficient fighting unit that was an "infantry" in the traditional sense. As their slogan would come to say, these soldiers would lead the way.

---

[33] "Professionalism and changes, Soldiers saw a lot of both in 1973," 14.

40.

His Legacy and His Curse

His face is forever fleshy and young. His rank always will be that of an army 1st Lieutenant. He is an embarrassing symbol of an officer who went tragically astray in a war forever draped in controversy. William Laws Calley, Jr., is as connected to Fort Benning as he is to My Lai, the obscure village that his platoon rampaged on a hot spring day in 1968.[1] It was Fort Benning where he graduated from OCS and where he was brought after being plucked out of the jungle. It was Fort Benning where he was tried and convicted of killing innocent Vietnamese civilians and where he served under house arrest. It was in a federal courthouse ten miles from Fort Benning where he was set free. He has lived in neighboring Columbus where he sold expensive wedding gifts and took children to school in a car pool in which some parents didn't know who he was.[2]

The world knew Lieutenant Calley in 1971. He was the unlikely cover boy of the Vietnam War, a soldier charged by the army he served with killing children and babies, just like the war protesters were chanting. To sympathetic supporters, this undersized lieutenant was a scapegoat, sold out by US Army superiors who did not want this incident to march up the chain of command. His was a trial that is part of Fort Benning legend. Every day, reporters from around the world staked out Building 5, a military courtroom that came to known as "Calley hall."[3] In what was the longest court martial in American military history, he was charged with killing 109 civilians at My

---

[1] "Calmness Is Needed," *Columbus Ledger*, March 31 1971, 4.

[2] Richard Hyatt, *Columbus Ledger-Enquirer* reporter, recalling Calley's personal information.

[3] Richard Hyatt, *Columbus Ledger-Enquirer* reporter and resident.

Lai 4.[4] But in people's eyes, more than Calley was on trial—so too was the army and the war in Vietnam.

Calley was born June 8, 1943, in Miami, Florida. He graduated from Miami Edison High School in 1962 and briefly attended a local junior college. He held various jobs in Florida, California, and Texas before entering the army on July 26, 1966. He asked to become a clerk trainee and took basic training at Fort Bliss, Texas, before he was assigned to clerical school at Fort Lewis, Washington.[5] On March 16, 1967, Calley reported to Fort Benning's Officer Candidate School—one year before his unit was committed to a mission in My Lai. He was commissioned a second lieutenant on September 7, graduating 120th in his OCS class of 156. "He shouldn't have been there in the first place," said a Pentagon colonel, "But...holes in the screen got bigger and bigger and Calley slipped through."[6]

Calley seemed pleased with his Fort Benning training: "Call it harassment, but I learned here at OCS that if I *try* I can do almost anything."[7]

The newly-commissioned officer joined Charlie Company, 1st Battalion, 20th Infantry, 11th Brigade, for training in Hawaii where he said he was taught how to kill the enemy but not how to deal with civilians. Captain Ernest Medina, a Mexican-American career officer, led the unit. A former member of the National Guard, Medina volunteered for the draft in 1956 and enlisted as a private. After two tours in Germany, Medina entered Officer Candidate School at Fort Benning and graduated as a second lieutenant in March 1964. Arriving in Vietnam in December 1967, Calley was twenty-four years old, one of three platoon leaders assigned to Charlie Company. Although the unit had encounters with the enemy, My Lai was its first search-and-destroy mission. This mission followed the Tet offensive of January and February 1968. Such attacks involved looting, death, and torture of prisoners by the Viet Cong. After that, all Vietnamese men,

---

[4] Tom Dunking and Bob Payne, "Lt. Calley gets Life," *Columbus Ledger*, March 31 1971, 1.

[5] Allan Davidson, "National Defense: The Calley Case," *The 1972 World Book Year Book* (Chicago: Field Enterprises Educational Corporation, 1972) 447.

[6] Ibid.

[7] Arthur Everett, Kathryn Johnson, and Harry F. Rosenthal, *Calley* (New York: Dell Publishing Company, Inc., 1971) 49.

women, and children under Viet Cong influence were considered as enemy suspects to most American servicemen.

My Lai, a hamlet in the village of Son My in the Quang Ngai Province of South Vietnam, was thought to be a stronghold of the Viet Cong, specifically the 48th Viet Cong Battalion, which received rice and supplies from villagers. Whether they did so out of support or fear was not an issue that day. When the company prepared for the mission to rid My Lai of the Viet Cong, Calley remembers, "I never sat down and analyzed whether they were men, women and children.... They were the enemy."[8] He believed his orders from Medina were "to go in there and destroy the enemy."[9] Calley did not question Medina's orders. Nor did he testify later at Medina's trial.

At My Lai, on March 16, 1968, Calley an inexperienced leader, who by his own admission lacked the respect of his men, contributed to the deaths of over 200 civilian Vietnamese. Others were wounded, and some women were raped. "Personally, I didn't kill any Vietnamese that day," Calley said. "I represented the United States of America. My country."[10] What happened at My Lai that day was well known in-country by American and Vietnamese alike. Photos taken by Sergeant Ronald L. Haeberle confirmed the killing of women, children, and old men.

Helicopter pilot Hugh Thompson was also a witness to the unlawful massacre. He and his crew rescued many villagers. Thompson received a certificate for the soldiers medal but not until November 1997.[11] Despite its being common knowledge, the incident was not investigated until Ron Ridenhour, a Vietnam veteran and aspiring writer, heard the story from a soldier in Charlie Company. Ridenhour wrote a letter requesting an inquiry, sending copies to members of Congress and the chiefs of staff.

A quiet investigation began. Meanwhile, Calley, who extended his tour in Vietnam, was ordered home in June 1969. He arrived in Seattle with the mud of the jungle still on his boots. After appearing before a tribunal in Washington, he was sent to Fort Benning. Officially, no one knew where he

---

[8] Tom Dunkin, *The Trial of Lt. William Calley*, Sketches by Angelo Franco (Columbus GA: The R. W. Page Corporation, 1971) n.p.

[9] Ibid.

[10] John Sack, *Lieutenant Calley* (New York: The Viking Press, 1971) 106.

[11] "Forgotten hero finally getting medal," *Columbus Ledger-Enquirer*, March 2, 1998, A4.

was. In September, he was formally charged. While awaiting trial, Calley was assigned to the office of the deputy commander. He said that during those months at Benning, he "never had an officer down on me." He said many would say, "I'm with you."[12]

Fort Benning's Public Information Officer gave the first news release of Calley's involvement to the Georgia press on September 5, 1969—one day before he was supposed to be mustered out of the army and out of military jurisdiction. "1st Lt. Calley," the news release read, "who was to have been separated from the army on 6 Sep. 69, is charged with violation of Article 118, murder, for offenses allegedly committed against civilians while serving in Vietnam in March 1968."[13] Colonel Robert M. Lathop, the post's chief legal officer, wrote the charges. Major General Orwin C. Talbott, Fort Benning's commanding general, ordered the court-martial.[14]

Columbus Enquirer reporter Charles Black visited Calley before the trial. Black was the first reporter in the US to talk to the young lieutenant since his arrest. Although Black uncovered details of My Lai from Vietnam veterans of the American Division stationed at the post, he chose not to publish until the army's official release.[15]

When the historic trial began on November 12, 1970, the court martial jury was composed of six officers stationed at Fort Benning: Colonel Ford, deputy director of Operations and Training at the Infantry Center; Major Charles McIntosh, an instructor in the Infantry School Company Operations Department; Major Carl Ray Bierbaum, an evaluation officer, Directorate of Instruction for the Infantry School; Major Walter D. Kinard, a Columbus native and an executive officer for the 4th Student Battalion of the School Brigade; Major Harvey Gene Brown, a training officer in the nonresident Instruction Department of the Infantry School; and Captain

---

[12] Ibid., 9.

[13] Seymour M. Hersh, *My Lai 4* (New York: Random House, 1970) 128; "Post Lieutenant Charged with Murdering Vietnamese," *Columbus Ledger*, September 6 1969, 1.

[14] Lt. Gen. Wiliam R. Peers, *The My Lai Inquiry* (New York: W. W. Norton & Company, 1979) 8.

[15] Seymour M. Hersh, *My Lai 4*, 129, 103; Richard Hyatt, *Columbus Ledger-Enquirer* reporter.

Ronald J. Salem, an instructor in Land Navigation in the Company Operations Department of the Infantry School.[16]

Each juror was a veteran of two combat tours in Vietnam except Ford, who fought in World War II and served in Korea. Ford later received orders to Vietnam. Captain Aubrey M. Daniel III served as Calley's prosecutor while Colonel Reid W. Kennedy conducted the trial.

Four months after the trial began and three years to the day after the My Lai massacre, the jury began to ponder Calley's fate. It took them thirteen days. In a secret ballot, three-fourths of the panel found William Laws Calley, Jr., guilty of killing "not less than one" person at a trail intersection in the hamlet; guilty of killing "not less that twenty" Vietnamese in a group at a drainage ditch in the village; guilty of premeditated murder in the death of a monk; and guilty of an assault charge involving a child, also killed at the drainage ditch.[17] Two days later, on March 31, the jury announced its decision of a life sentence. The headline in the next morning's *Columbus Ledger* said, "Lt. Calley Gets Life."[18]

As Calley left the court building, a crowd of about 150 soldiers and civilians shouted, "Free Calley."[19] Because of an attempted cover-up of the incident and the revelation of missing unit documents, many felt Calley was made a fall guy for higher-ranking officers. He spent the following three nights and part of two days at the Fort Benning stockade.

Protest was immediate. Flags were lowered to half-staff. Politicians were flooded with letters from people slamming the verdict. In Columbus, a "Rally for Calley" was held at the Municipal Auditorium with Governor George Wallace of Alabama as the featured speaker. Bowing to pressure, president Richard Nixon ordered Calley released from the stockade and placed under house arrest in an apartment near Fort Benning's main gate.[20]

Lieutenant General William R. Peers, head of "The Department of the Army Review of the Preliminary Investigations into the My Lai Incident," later referred to as "the Peers Inquiry," said Nixon's decision made things difficult: "When the president thereafter appeared to sympathize with those

---

[16] Dunkin and Payne, "Lt. Calley gets Life," 48.

[17] Ibid., 48.

[18] Ibid., 1.

[19] "Crowd laments guilty verdict," *Columbus Ledger*, March 31, 10.

[20] Neil Sheehan, *A Bright Shining Lie* (New York: Random House, 1988) 689.

protesting Lieutenant Calley's conviction, the difficulties of obtaining convictions against Captain Medina, Colonel Henderson, and others became almost insurmountable. Thus the failures of leadership that characterized nearly every aspect of the My Lai incident itself had their counterpart at the highest level during the attempt to prosecute those responsible."[21]

On September 22, a military jury at Fort McPherson, Georgia, acquitted Medina of murdering 102 civilian Vietnamese.[22] Colonel Oran K. Henderson, former 11th Brigade commander, was brought to trial but was acquitted for alleged falsification of records to conceal mass civilian deaths.[23] Brigadier General Samuel W. Koster, former Americal division commander, was demoted one grade because of the controversy.[24]

Calley continued to live under house arrest near Fort Benning's main gate. He could receive visitors but could not leave the apartment. His folk-hero status continued despite the decision of the army court. On August 20, 1971, Calley's life sentence was changed to twenty years, and on April 15, 1974, Secretary of the Army Howard "Bo" Callaway reduced the sentence to ten years.[25]

Neither decision changed his status. But quietly, the legal machine was churning. On November 19, 1974, Calley was taken to US District Court in Columbus. He went before Judge J. Robert Elliott, a veteran jurist appointed to the court by President John F. Kennedy, who kept a portrait of Robert E. Lee hanging in his office. Calley, wearing a khaki dress suit, testified on his own behalf. Elliott did what other courts had not done. He set Calley free. After three years of house arrest, Calley was paroled.[26] By the time he was freed, Calley had spent much of his adult life in and around Fort Benning. He was sentenced there and he served his time there. There he found a base of support. Columbus had become home.

---

[21] Lt. Gen. William R. Peers, USA (Ret.) *The My Lai Inquiry* (New York: W. W. Norton & Company, 1979) 254.

[22] Guenter Lewy, *America in Vietnam* (New York: Oxford University Press, 1978) 359.

[23] Peers, *The My Lai Inquiry*, 252–53.

[24] Ibid., 221.

[25] Jack E. Swift, "Callaway to cut Calley sentence, source reveals," *Columbus Ledger*, April 16 1974, 1.

[26] "William Calley," http://en.wikipedia.org/wiki/William_Calley, 2.

Calley married Penny Vick, whose family owned an upscale Columbus jewelry store. The ceremony was held in a stately Methodist Church in a tree-shrouded neighborhood. The former sheriff of Muscogee County provided the special music. In attendance were the judge who freed him; the mayor of Columbus; a former mayor of Macon, Georgia; the retired publisher of the *Columbus Ledger-Enquirer*; and the mother of the president of Knight-Ridder newspapers.[27] Outside, roped off under the trees, was a band of reporters.

Most of the time, Calley has lived in a self-imposed anonymity. Now a certified gemologist, Calley manages V. V. Vick Jewelry Store in a Columbus strip mall. His son helps out in the family business. Calley has the charm of a local merchant, smiling at customers and calling them by name. On anniversary dates of My Lai or his trial, reporters stake out the store hoping for an interview, but Calley has steadfastly declined, and "refuses to discuss that day."[28] When controversy arose in an Iraqi prison in 2004, the memory of Calley was invoked but still he was quiet, although outside his Columbus home yellow ribbons were tied to the trees to honor the deployment of American troops.

These days, nothing about him demands a second look. His hair has taken an extended vacation. His pudginess makes him look shorter than he is. His body is soft, unlike the twenty-four-year-old OCS graduate. He is past the age of sixty, relegated to being an answer on Trivial Pursuit card or a question on *Jeopardy*. But like it or not, he will *always* be Lieutenant Calley. It is his legacy and his curse. More than anything, it is his punishment.

---

[27] Richard Hyatt, *Colubmus Ledger* reporter, recalling events related to Calley's personal life.

[28] George Esper, "Anniversary revives memories of massacre at My Lai village," *Birmingham News*, April 25 2000, 3A.

41.

Writing the Creed

Colonel Kenneth C. Leuer's orders were simple and clear. Carrying them out would not be so simple.

General Creighton Abrams, commander of the 3rd Armored Division in World War II and the former commander of US forces in Vietnam, was army chief of staff. He wanted Leuer to create the army's first Ranger battalion since World War II. He did not want any "hoodlums or brigands" in the unit.[1] He wanted an elite unit, with its own creed and own music—one that could fight. "The Ranger battalion is to be an elite, light, and the most proficient infantry battalion in the world," he said.[2]

Leuer, later a major general and commandant of Fort Benning, recognized that Abrams was giving him a tough assignment. "That task was not an easy one," Leuer said. "The Army was in shambles."[3] This order was carried out with flair, however. Leuer became commander of the 1st Battalion, 75th Infantry (Ranger), scheduled to train at Fort Benning until June 1974. He and an assembled group of officers and non-coms did what some thought was impossible in the 1974 army.

For music, Colonel Keith Nightingale, obtained "Rangers Go March," and Command Sergeant Major Neal Gentry wrote the Ranger Creed, later engraved on a granite column of the post's Ranger Memorial. Leuer praised Gentry, the battalion sergeant major, for accomplishing the impossible: "He proved to be everything that we needed at that battalion at the time. He was primarily responsible for the recruitment of the non-commissioned

---

[1] "Rangers Lead the Way: 75th Ranger Regiment Information Booklet," vault, Donovan Research Library, Fort Benning GA, 15.

[2] Ibid.

[3] Ann M. McDonald, "Former Benning commander addresses Rangers," *Bayonet*, August 17 1990, A3.

officers."[4] Leurer said success came with hard work: "The NCOs and officers trained and trained and we instituted something that scared everyone. Every exercise we did was with live rounds."[5]

When the 1st Battalion (Ranger), 75th Infantry completed training at Fort Benning, they flew across the state to Fort Stewart for the unit's official activation. The 2nd Battalion (Ranger), 75th Infantry, soon followed and was activated on October 1. Later, the 1st Battalion established its headquarters at Hunter Army Airfield, Georgia. The 2nd Battalion made its home at Fort Lewis, Washington. Abrams barely lived to see the Ranger Battalion he requested become a well-drilled reality. The decorated general died of lung cancer on September 4 and was buried in Arlington National Cemetery. However, his legacy as "the No. 1 fighting general in the army" in World War II and the "plain-speaking" negotiator in Korea and Vietnam lives on.[6]

A World War II Ranger was honored when Benning's Florida Ranger Camp at Eglin Air Force Base was renamed in memory of Major General James E. Rudder. He commanded the 2nd Ranger Battalion that captured the cliffs at Pont du Hoc in France on D-Day. The camp was officially dedicated as Camp James E. Rudder on June 22, 1974, commemorating the thirtieth anniversary of the bravery displayed by Rudder and his men.[7]

While the Rangers were returning, new opportunities were becoming available to women serving in the army. A list of "firsts" for women at Fort Benning occurred in 1974. Specialist Sylvia Campos, 139th Military Police Company, was the first woman in the 36th Engineer Group to be named soldier of the month. Second Lieutenant Deborah R. Olson became the first female officer assigned to the 197th Infantry Brigade, and Private June A.

---

[4] Kimball Perry, "Peers remember post Rangers' founding," *Columbus Ledger-Enquirer*, August 8 1990, D4.

[5] Ann M. McDonald, "Former Benning commander addresses Rangers," *Bayonet*, August 17 1990, A-3.

[6] "Changing of the guard," *Time*, April 19 1968, 25.

[7] "Chronology of Fort Benning Highlights, 1973–74" *Bayonet*, May 17 1974, 17; "Ranger camp will be renamed after Major General Rudder," *Bayonet*, June 14 1974, 1.

Wileman, 444th Transportation Company, was the first female in the 36th Engineer Group to graduate from the wheel vehicle mechanic's course.[8]

Married couples also benefited from the "new army." Private Fred Higgins and his wife, Joyce, were the first husband and wife team to graduate from the Infantry School Airborne Program, and they were the first married couple to make an official military jump together from an army aircraft.[9] First Sergeant Henry Caro made news when named the first noncommissioned officer to assume permanent command of a company at Fort Benning. Also noteworthy, with only twenty-four GS-13s at Fort Benning in 1974, Theresa Gunter was named chief of the recruitment and placement branch at the civilian personnel division. Gunter was the second woman in the history of the US Army Infantry Center to be promoted to the GS-13 level. Barbara Ennis, chief of the Program Budget Division in the comptroller's office, was the first.

Growth and construction were other earmarks of change. In March, the 43rd Engineer Company, 36th Engineer Group, completed the helipad at Martin Army Hospital. It was later named in honor of Specialist 4th Class Joseph G. LaPointe, Jr., killed in action in Vietnam and awarded the Medal of Honor posthumously.[10]

The new $11 million Fort Benning mall and commissary also opened in March, containing 240,000 square feet of space and featured many shops, a bank, a service station, and a bowling alley. Parking spaces for 1,500 cars surrounded the complex. Located on a forty-eight-acre site at the intersection of Marne and Santa Fe Roads, the modern "one-stop" shopping facility was convenient to Sand Hill, Kelley Hill, Harmony Church, and Main Post.[11]

Training sites likewise benefited from this spirit of new growth. Buckner Range, formerly a heavily wooded hilly area 300 meters wide and 1,000 meters long, was transformed into a unique training facility for the tools and techniques of firepower. Modeled on the range at the Army Field

---

[8] Becki Kellam, "Fort Benning events of 1974," *Bayonet*, December 27 1974, 12–13.

[9] Ibid., 13.

[10] Ibid., 12.

[11] Tim Purdon, "New mall scheduled for spring opening," *Bayonet*, November 30 1973, 17.

Artillery School at Fort Sill, it was built to scale, appearing to be 10,000 meters in length.

A familiar landmark also received recognition in 1974. Riverside, the plantation home used by commanding generals as their personal quarters, was officially dedicated as a National Historic Site. The house was placed on the National Register of Historic Places in June 1971.[12] One of Riverside's visitors in 1974 was Secretary of the Army Howard H. "Bo" Callaway of Pine Mountain, Georgia. He served as an Infantry School instructor during his last two years in the army and earned his Combat Infantryman's Badge as a platoon leader in Korea. Officially visiting the Infantry Center in May, Callaway discussed plans to dismiss remaining draftees before Thanksgiving.

Former prisoners of war in North Vietnam now enrolled in the infantry officers' advanced course. Among these was Lieutenant Colonel Floyd Thompson, the longest-held army prisoner captured during the Vietnam conflict. Thompson and Staff Sergeant Stanley A. Newell, both assigned to Benning in 1974, received a total of seven medals for gallantry as POWs in Southeast Asia.

A change of command in 1974 resulted in Paul J. Mueller's promotion to brigadier general and his assignment as assistant commandant of the Infantry School. Mueller succeeded Brigadier General William R. Richardson, who was assigned to the Canal Zone. Colonel Wallace F. Veaudry became assistant commander of the Infantry Center, and Colonel William B. Steele, commander of the 197th Infantry Brigade, was promoted to brigadier general. Steele left to serve as deputy commander of the Recruiting Command at Fort Sheridan, Illinois.

As America's longest war ended, training for future wars continued. The 197th Infantry Brigade, now commanded by Colonel Joseph E. Wasiak, conducted its first full-scale field training exercise off post. Traveling by vehicle convoy and C-130 aircraft, the "Forever Forward" brigade moved some 3,500 troops to Fort Stewart for the field Training Exercise "Label Cleaver."[13] They battled for a week with the 1/325th Infantry of the 82nd Airborne Division. The 197th Infantry Brigade was officially declared a

---

[12] Becki Kellam, "Fort Benning events of 1974," 13.

[13] W. R. Cage, "197th Inf Bde...the year 1974," *Bayonet*, December 27 1974, 13.

combat-ready Strategic Army Forces (STRAF) in April 1974 after weeks of testing, culminating a year of intensive training.[14]

As other missions were changing, the mission of the Infantry School stayed the same though the focus of the weaponry it tested was modernized. New technology introduced and implemented at Fort Benning, such as the new Bradley fighting vehicle, was no longer aimed at the low level fighting recommended in Vietnam.[15]

Colonel Burnet Quick, an aide to Tarpley, said future army doctrine was written in 1975. "There was a lot of rewrites of doctrine and how-to-fight manuals...a kind of revolution in the army at that time...and Fort Benning led the way. General Tarpley, General Bill Richardson and lots of colonels, smart young majors, and captains really wrote the doctrine for the army of the future," Quick said.

The military was preparing for the Soviet Union. Quick recalled,

> It was a total rewrite of the doctrine in case the cold war didn't work. Armor forces, mobile defense, studying World War II, studying all wars, developing doctrine to be sure we fought a combined arms war—that the air force, army, and navy would fight together—it was a real revolution in the 70s. I can remember standing at the old quadrangle with M-16s shooting lasers that later became the equipment we trained with in our maneuvers. The army was downsizing, new technology was there, as well as money to educate people and to do some things.[16]

Training programs for the mechanized infantry combat vehicle (MICV) plus the TOW and the Dragon (anti-tank missile systems) as well as other weapons systems were being closely coordinated at the Infantry School. Other items developed and tested were a squad automatic weapon, a lightweight mortar, a lightweight laser range finder, and a hand-held thermal viewer.[17]

---

[14] Ibid.

[15] *Fort Benning "Home of the Infantry," 1918–1976*, Infantry School Folder, history of the post plus current activities, vault, Donovan Research Library, Fort Benning GA, 36.

[16] Col. (Ret.) Burnet R. Quick, interview by Peggy Stelpflug, July 16 1998, Uptown Columbus GA.

[17] *Fort Benning "Home of the Infantry,"* 36.

The Army Research Institute awarded Benning's Human Resources Research Organization (HumRRO) an eleven-month contract to test a new computer-based training device designed to provide a realistic experience of tactical operations to battalion command groups and advance-course officers. The Combined Arms Tactical Training Simulator (CATTS) required highly trained controllers, so under the contract HumRRO researchers helped develop a handbook for controllers.[18]

The airmobile concept also was emphasized in the post-Vietnam Era. Work continued on development of the Utility Tactical Transport Aircraft System and the Advanced Attack Helicopter. A major change in the Infantry School was the Airborne Department's reorganization as the Airborne/Airmobility Department. It assumed responsibility for teaching, coordinating and testing of both airborne and airmobile doctrine. One accomplishment was its introduction of a more maneuverable parachute that offered fewer chances of malfunctioning.

Women in the "new" army continued to make headlines. The 197th Infantry Brigade welcomed its first female military policeman, Private First Class Michele D. Bradley.[19] The 283rd Army band received its first female member, Private First Class Joan C. Arno, who entered the army on the "Stars for Skills" program. First Lieutenant Linda Horan, one of only two WAC helicopter pilots in the army, was assigned to Fort Benning as a member of the 498th Medical Company, 34th Medical Battalion.[20]

Lieutenant Colonel Patricia Maybin, assistant information officer, received attention when she became the first female officer to serve as field officer of the day. Private First Class Barbara Hile of the US Army Marksmanship Training Unit retired in 1975. She was, as the *Bayonet* reported, "one of the finest women marksmen the army and the United States has ever produced," winning over twenty national championships and holding more than forty national shooting records.[21]

Another woman, a military wife, also made headlines. The role of military wives was evolving. Wives were getting involved in social causes that extended far beyond an afternoon tea. At Fort Benning, in the late

---

[18] "CATTS," *Bayonet*, January 17 1975, 12.
[19] "1975—a busy year for Ft. Benning," *Bayonet*, January 2 1976, 10–11.
[20] Ibid., 10–11.
[21] Ibid., 11.

1960s, the Waiting Wives' Club of the Armed Forces YMCA helped more than 1,000 Vietnamese orphans.[22] Under direction of Mrs. Jack Thornton, the club was composed mostly of wives whose husbands were in Vietnam although wives whose husbands were stationed overseas also were members. But the unmitigated passion of a single army wife would draw the greatest attention to the plight of children orphaned by war.

While working in the office of Senator Jacob Javits of New York, Betty Moul met Dr. Tom Dooley, already a legend for his compassion and his work with orphans in Vietnam, Laos, and Cambodia. When they met, she did what most folks did. "I gave five dollars," she said.[23] Only she could not forget this former navy lieutenant. She continued to give money; then she gave time. She was visiting the An Loc orphanage in Saigon in 1967 when she met widower Patrick Tisdale, then a medical officer with the 1st Infantry Division.[24] Two years later they married at the post chapel on Fort Benning where Tisdale was chief of pediatrics at Martin Army Hospital. She became mother to Tisdale's five sons.

Neither could forget the faces of the orphans in Vietnam. Betty Tisdale spoke out for them, knowing their voices could not be heard.[25] She and her husband adopted five orphan girls and helped other children from An Loc find homes in America. With the war winding down in Vietnam, she feared what would happen to these children, many of them fathered by American soldiers, making them outcasts on the streets of Saigon. Her greatest fear for the children was that, under communism, they would "grow up in a godless society.[26] Working with other army wives, agencies at Fort Benning, Columbus, and all over the United States, she was determined to keep them safe.

On April 12, 1975, her dreams landed at Lawson Army Air Field. Aboard a huge military transport aircraft were 219 children—the children of

---

[22] "Wives send goods to Viet Nam," *Bayonet*, April 1 1966; "1st Cavalry wives meet," *Bayonet*, November 12 1965, 7.

[23] Richard Hyatt, "100 people to remember Betty Tisdale," *Columbus Ledger-Enquirer*, Nobember 16 1999.

[24] Marian Jones, "Colonel's Wife helps 400 orphans," *Bayonet*, September 26 1969, 12.

[25] Ibid.

[26] Tony Adams, "Orphan Angel," *Columbus Ledger-Enquirer*, Nobember 16 1999.

An Loc, "the largest single airlift from one orphanage in history."[27] Working swiftly and methodically, Tisdale gained their release, deftly overcoming the bureaucracies of two countries, including Fort Benning.[28] Her job was to bring them "home."

Back in Saigon, soldiers had built cribs aboard the airplane so the infants could peacefully sleep on their flight. As it landed that evening, Fort Benning troops in combat dress went on board the plane, coming off with toddlers tenderly nestled in their arms. Loaded on to army buses, the children were taken to Wilbur School, near the main gate to the post, a building that now houses the administrative offices of the Fort Benning Schools. That night, the school was transformed into a nursery where the anxious children would stay until they were medically cleared. Only then would they be ready for trips to their adopted homes, the final leg of their journey of mercy.[29]

It was as if her entire life prepared Betty Tisdale for that important task. "I didn't have time to think if I would fail," she said.[30] Not that her work ended that night at Fort Benning. She invigorated a military installation and a community—even an entire nation. That May, elements of Fort Benning's 34th Medical Battalion and other units were dispatched to an army post in Pennsylvania to help care for additional Vietnamese refugees. To aid former allied soldiers, their families, or war orphans escaping from South Vietnam, Congress approved $405 million for Vietnamese refugee aid in 1975.[31]

A CBS movie *The Children of An Lac* told Tisdale's experiences. Actress Shirley Jones played the role of the woman who never considered "no" a proper answer. But the story of this army wife was not fiction. The Vietnam Association in Seattle honored her remarkable life in 2000, the year the

---

[27] Jason Robertson, one of the An Loc orphans lives in Columbus, GA, www.ricetogrits.com.

[28] Jack Swift, "Orphans Arrive Safely on Post, Prepare for a New Life," *Columbus Ledger-Enquirer*, April 13 1975, 1.

[29] Ibid., A-5; "Orphans involved in another 'war,'" *Columbus Ledger-Enquirer*, April 14 1975, 1.

[30] Richard Hyatt, "100 people to remember," *Columbus Ledger-Enquirer*, November 16 1999.

[31] Spencer Rich, "Senate votes $405 million refugee aid," *Washington Post*, May 17 1975, 1.

"Angel of Saigon" started HALO (Helping and Loving Orphans), an organization that reaches out to orphans around the world.[32] Betty Tisdale enlisted her Vietnam orphans to rescue children orphaned by today's wars. One of Betty's adoptees had become a physician, another a schoolteacher, another a social worker. One chose to work at an orphanage in Romania. Some, like Jason Robertson, adopted in 1973, live and work in Columbus.[33] In 2003, Tisdale returned to Columbus and Fort Benning. Waiting to visit her were children and families she touched through her efforts twenty-eight years before.[34] Her energy was the same and so was her passion.

President Ford Visists Post

On June 14, 1975, more than 25,000 people, including President Gerald Ford, helped Fort Benning celebrate the army's 200th birthday. Ford became the 38th president when Richard Nixon resigned on August 9, 1974, after revelation of his involvement in the Watergate cover-up. One of Ford's first official acts as president was to grant Nixon a pardon for any criminal offenses committed while in office. Ford also granted limited amnesty to Vietnam War draft evaders and military deserters. President Ford, attending the June celebration, viewed a Glorious Heritage Pageant and crowd-pleasing demonstrations by the Ranger Department, the Airborne-Airmobility Department, the Military Dog Detachment, the Silver Eagles of Fort Rucker, and the Golden Knights of Fort Bragg.

That August, Tarpley retired from active duty in ceremonies on York Field. Major General Willard Latham succeeded Tarpley, who served as commander since 1973. Latham's previous assignment was as commander of the 72nd Infantry Brigade in Alaska although he was known at Benning for his earlier leadership of the 197th. Another retiree was Grady E. Tolle, a supply supervisor for the Fort Benning schools. Although he did not receive the pomp and flair of a change of command, Tolle retired with fifty years

---

[32] Caroline F. Daniel, "An Angel Gets Her Wings," Google: "Betty Tisdale An Angel Gets Her Wings."

[33] Jason Robertson, www.ricetogrits.com.

[34] Richard Hyatt, "Angel of Saigon makes return visit to Columbus GA," *Columbus Ledger-Enquirer*, October 23 2001, 1.

federal service. He became the first person at the post to be awarded the fifty-year service pin.[35]

At the end of 1975, the army was ready to put Vietnam behind it—although debate continued how the war could have been won or whether US military should ever have been sent there. The army was still uncertain of its ability to attract and hold responsible people. One program, "Action 75," encouraged participation in post programs that resulted in mental, physical, and spiritual self-improvement. Participants received points for each completed activity and were eligible for various certificates and awards. Another strategy was Fort Benning's modernization program. Twenty-one dining facilities were renovated to look like English pubs, ski lodges, or European restaurants at a cost of over $4 million. Such facilities would hopefully encourage experienced soldiers to reenlist.

Secretary of the Army Martin R. Hoffman, Callaway's successor, "praised the quality and caliber of soldiers he encountered during 'rap sessions' here."[36] Although "old-timers" complained newcomers were too soft or not representative of the nation, the army's mission and the training of its soldiers remained the same as it did 200 years ago.

"Tactical and technical proficiency, physical strength, mental toughness and spiritual awareness are the mandatory qualities of the infantry leader," Hoffman said. "It is toward the development of these qualities in all infantrymen that the Infantry Center of today is dedicated."[37]

---

[35] "1975—a busy year for Ft. Benning," 11.

[36] Ibid.

[37] *Fort Benning "Home of the Infantry," 1918–1976,* Infantry School Folder, history of the post plus current activities, vault, Donovan Research Library, Fort Benning GA, 36.

42.

Winning the Next Battle

Willard Latham was a small man with large principles. There was no nonsense in his approach and a loud ring of authority in his manner. He believed and you should believe; he was prepared and you should be also. He ran and you too should run. That was the persona Major General Willard Latham brought to Building 4 in 1975. It brought him through Korea and Vietnam. It brought him through his other commands. That it might not succeed when he was chosen Fort Benning's commandant was something he never considered since previously it had served him well as chief of staff and deputy commander of the Infantry Center.[1] Latham wanted any soldier in any given unit to be physically able to make a forced march in full combat gear—as if their life depended on it, which Latham said it did. "Indeed the ultimate goal would be to have a soldier make such a march in full combat gear wearing his gas mask. That's not an eccentric requirement. That's the kind of battle we are preparing to defend ourselves against," Latham said.[2]

Latham installed a strict physical training program. All over post, men and women ran on a daily regimen. Latham ran among them, encouraging them and pushing them. There were no exceptions. Physicians were supposed to be in shape. Lawyers from the JAG office were required to run and so were the clerics from the chaplain corps. Latham's program, however caused "dissension in the ranks.[3]

There was new concern by September 1976 after eleven suicides had occurred on post in eight months. The post was tense. Losing personnel to

---

[1] "An Interview with the CG," *Bayonet*, October 1 1976, 6.

[2] Ibid.

[3] Gen. (Ret.) William B. Steele, interview by Peggy Stelpflug, October 5 1998, Donovan Technical Library, Fort Benning GA, handwritten transcript and audio cassette, Auburn AL.

their own hands was hard for the army community to accept. People whispered among themselves, and some began to talk openly with Jack Swift, an outspoken columnist in the *Columbus Ledger*. Swift began to report Fort Benning's alarming suicide rate, and other soldiers began to talk with him. His local columns attracted the attention of *Newsweek*, one of the most influential weekly news magazines in the country.[4]

"Fort Benning's suicide rate is about five times that of comparable army bases in the US," *Newsweek* reported. "About the only common thread linking some of the cases, army investigators said, is a history of marital problems."[5]

Five of the eleven deaths occurred in the 197th Infantry Brigade, which was reported to have poor morale. The magazine interviewed Specialist 4th Class Lamar Evans of Texas, who was in the same squad with one of the suicide victims. "Morale is about as low as the tile on this floor," Evans said.[6] The *Newsweek* article observed, "Only the continuing investigations (which will include psychological autopsies) will tell whether the making of a soldier, Fort Benning style, has any connection with the unusually high suicide rate at the base."[7]

Latham, commanding officer of Fort Benning's 20,000 soldiers, argued that the post showed a decline in the crime rate and the number of AWOLs. Reenlistments were up, and 70 percent of Benning's first term reenlistments were reenlisting to stay at Fort Benning. "We view this as a positive indicator of high morale," the general said. However, the *Newsweek* article added, "Some soldiers on the base suspect other causes. A few complain about the emphasis Latham has placed on physical fitness training since he took command two years ago."[8] Latham, on the other hand, believed the suicides were the result of serious marital problems, the excessive use of alcohol, and critical financial problems. He had no plans to change any programs at Fort Benning. "I am absolutely convinced that the product we are developing at Fort Benning is the quality of soldier and military unit that our country must have in order to have a creditable military posture so far as

---

[4] Richard Hyatt, *Columbus Ledger-Enquirer* reporter.
[5] "The Army: Fort Suicide?" *Newsweek* 88/13 (September 27 1976): 36.
[6] Ibid.
[7] Ibid.
[8] Ibid.

the Army is concerned. I believe Fort Benning leads the Army in that regard. And it will be a great tragedy if we are not successful," he said.[9]

Meanwhile, US Senators Herman Talmadge and Sam Nunn of Georgia—longtime supporters of the post—called on the army to investigate the deaths fully.

Latham's goals to produce a warrior stemmed from a personal experience in the Korean conflict. William B. Steele, Latham's classmate at the officers' advanced infantry course in 1957, remembered the story: "He saw a lot of people die who couldn't do in combat what they were supposed to be able to do physically. It made a big impression. Wherever he went, his soldiers were physically conditioned. In some cases he overdid it."[10]

In 1970, Latham commanded Fort Benning's 197th Infantry Brigade, guiding the unit in its role as the army's first all-volunteer command under the volunteer army program. As soldiers returned from Vietnam, difficult problems existed. Soldiers were ready to leave the service, and many wanted "out" immediately.[11] They chose not be "good soldiers" and caused problems and dissension while awaiting their official dismissal from the army. With incidents of drug abuse, suicide, robbery, and assault, no one dared to walk the streets at night.[12]

Determined to keep order, Latham used barbed wire in the 197th area. He placed guards armed with shotguns on tops of buildings. Part of his remedy for the problem was working the soldiers hard. The problem, Steele pointed out, was greatly improved when "most of those folks got out of the Army."[13] As post commandant, Latham continued to stress physical exercise. He wanted everybody running—including himself. Master Sergeant Bob Summers, age thirty in 1976 and chief instructor at Jump Committee,

---

[9] "An interview with the CG," *Bayonet*, October 1 1976, 6.

[10] Gen. (Ret.) William B. Steele, interview by Peggy Stelpflug, October 5 1998, Donovan Technical Library, Infantry Hall, Fort Benning GA, handwritten transcript and audiocassette, Auburn AL.

[11] Ibid.

[12] Ibid.

[13] Ibid.

recalled jumping with Latham on Friday afternoons on Friar Drop Zone then running to Building 4, a distance of ten to fifteen miles.[14]

Negative local headlines were somewhat unusual at Fort Benning. It was a post that from its earliest years prided itself on its strong relationship with the civilian community and the Columbus media. The Pentagon began monitoring news articles on a daily basis, hoping reports of the suicide and low morale would cease. In an unusual move, Latham, joined by several of his key commanders, personally visited the offices of the *Columbus Ledger-Enquirer* in a last-ditch attempt to explain his position and to mend fences with the community.[15]

One of Latham's friends, James Woodruff, a long-time supporter of Fort Benning, died in a car accident in October 1976. Woodruff helped create a National Infantry Museum Association for the construction of a national museum honoring the infantry soldier. Upon his death, his family requested that donations be given to the project. Woodruff also served as a civilian aide to the secretary of the army and was serving his third term as president of the national AUSA. He was also a charter member and chairman of the Civilian Military Council, a group of influential local people who met regularly to address problems that concerned the military and civilian communities. Woodruff was a spokesman for the all-volunteer army and supported the one-station unit concept for training. In addition, Woodruff owned WRBL radio and television.[16]

Latham issued a statement for his friend: "Jim Woodruff was a Fourth of July-type patriot 365 days a year.... Friend and counselor of commandants over the years, he was even more importantly vitally concerned with the welfare of all the soldiers at Fort Benning and their families.... His achievements for the Army deserve an honored place in the records of our affairs. Jim Woodruff was a rare man. We will miss him."[17]

Though controversy still swirled under Latham's leadership, the post continued its mission. Earlier, in January 1976, a ceremony activating the 1st

---

[14] Sgt. Maj. (Ret.) Bob Summers, interview by Peggy Stelpflug, February 24 2000, Donovan Technical Library, Fort Benning GA, handwritten transcript and audiocassette, Auburn AL.

[15] Richard Hyatt, *Columbus Ledger-Enquirer* reporter.

[16] "Army loses friend, champion," *Bayonet*, October 22 1976, 8.

[17] "Jim Woodruff—citizen, patriot, friend," *Bayonet*, October 22–28 1976, 1.

Advanced Individual Training Brigade (infantry) was held on York Field. Building and ranges were restored for the brigade that would consist of 5 battalions with 24 companies and 1,650 permanent support personnel. The unit received its first group in March when nearly 650 infantry trainees from basic training centers around the country reported for the seven-week course. Responding to the type of training the troops would receive, brigade commander Colonel Jack B. Farris stated, "Human dignity will be preserved, but soft pedaling is out. When they leave here they will be infantrymen through and through."[18]

To train incoming soldiers, the drill sergeant—distinguished by his campaign hat—returned. The post was a choice assignment for drill sergeants whose schedules reflected consideration—as much as possible—of their home life. Some of them found the youth of the 1970s more physically fit than in the 1960s due to the popularity of physical fitness programs and awareness of the ill effects of drugs, alcohol, and tobacco.[19]

Staff Sergeant Joseph Johnson, drill sergeant of A Company, 5th Battalion, 1st AIT Brigade, was willing to be married to an AIT platoon and put in grueling hours in a thankless job. "Because after graduation," he explained, "when the band has left, the speeches are finished, and the dignitaries have gone home, the guys come back to the barracks to talk about things. It's a good feeling."[20] In 1977, Sergeant 1st Class Michael Wagers, selected as Benning drill sergeant of the year, was later chosen the army's outstanding drill sergeant of the year and received an assignment to headquarters, TRADOC.[21]

A change of command occurred in spring 1976. Brigadier General Fred K. Mahaffey assumed duties as assistant commandant of the Infantry School, replacing Brigadier General Paul Mueller, Jr., who was assigned to Iran. Mahaffey, commander of infantry units from platoon through brigade size, was commander of the 2nd Brigade, 101st Airborne Division (Air Assault) at Fort Campbell, Kentucky, before coming to Benning.[22]

---

[18] Jerry Van Slyke, "AIT Brigade receives first trainees," *Bayonet*, March 19 1976, 1.

[19] "Yes!!! The drill sergeant is back," *Bayonet*, June 11, 1976, 15.

[20] Ibid.

[21] Pam Pegram, "Benning Drill Sergeant Selected as Army's Best," *Bayonet*, July 29–August 4, 1977, 1.

[22] "Deputy CG reassigned," *Bayonet*, April 23 1976, 1.

Recognitions once available only for military men were now awarded to military women. Sergeant Rita Lewis, an Airborne instructor, became the first woman to receive the Senior Parachutist's Badge while training at Benning. Private First Class Grace Hammack of Company B, Headquarters Command, a twenty-year-old parachute rigger, was selected as Fort Benning soldier of the year. Previously named post soldier of the quarter and honor graduate of the basic training class and Airborne school, Hammack was the first enlisted woman to achieve this honor. "I'm no women's libber," she said, "But I'm proud when women accomplish great things. My winning Post Soldier of the Year is good for women in general."[23]

Other awards were also earned. Helping the post's transition to the new volunteer army, Fort Benning's Word Processing Center (WPC) was rated as the best WPC in the army. In 1974, Benning was the first military installation in the country to utilize the new technology and its success led to its adoption by other army posts and branches of the military. Ron Companion, an installation administrative officer, spent three years researching, planning, and implementing the system that saved the post over $100,000 a year in manpower, money, and additional resources.[24]

At long last, the National Infantry Museum found a permanent home during the summer of 1977 after being housed in temporary wooden quarters for more than eighteen years. The move from Building 1234 to Building 396, the former hospital annex, represented years of planning by the Infantry Museum Association, Inc.—formerly led by James W. Woodruff. After Woodruff's death, Thomas Tarpley, former Fort Benning commandant, became head of the non-profit National Infantry Museum Association.[25]

In celebration of the event, platoons of Rangers, Airborne, light, and mechanized infantry and trainees from the 1st Advanced Individual Training Brigade and the branch immaterial officer candidate course passed in review as the 283rd Army band played on July 1. Major Generals Latham and Tarpley unveiled two plaques on the front of the museum. In a separate

---

[23] Madonna Simple, "Woman named year's top soldier," *Bayonet*, August 5 1977, 6.

[24] Debra Hilegman, "Computer System Supports Benning," *Bayonet*, November 18, 1977, 16.

[25] Marshall Jones, "Infantry museum to open today," *Bayonet*, July 1–7, 1977, 1.

ceremony for invited guests, the museum's 100-seat James W. Woodruff, Jr., Memorial Auditorium was unveiled by his widow, Peggy Woodruff, and by Latham.

General of the Army Omar N. Bradley, former Fort Benning commandant and World War II leader, led the list of dignitaries that day. Bradley officially opened the museum by cutting the ribbon with a Revolutionary War sword. Confined to a wheelchair since a stroke in 1973, Bradley told the crowd of 2,500, "For an infantryman, coming to Fort Benning is coming home."[26]

As the 283rd Infantry band played "The Star Spangled Banner," Bradley, always the soldier, rose from his wheelchair and stood at attention, offering a crisp hand salute. Later, while touring the museum with his second wife, Miss Kitty, and Dick Grube, museum director since 1972, Bradley donated his five-star insignia to be placed on his overcoat that was part of the museum's permanent exhibit. The aging five-star general—last of the legendary leaders of World War II—displayed his sense of humor when he overheard an unsuspecting officer complain about fewer promotions because of the cutback after Vietnam. "You're right," Bradley commented. "I haven't had a promotion in the last twenty-seven years."[27]

In late July 1977, Latham left the post for a position in Turkey. His replacement was Latham's antithesis. Major General William J. Livsey, Jr., assumed command on July 25. While Latham was intense, Livsey was mountain folksy. While Latham was all business, Livsey was fond of spinning a tale. While Latham was a Texan, Livsey was a native Georgian, a graduate of North Georgia College who received a master's degree in general psychology from Vanderbilt University. Before coming to Fort Benning, Livsey served as chief of staff, I Corps, in Korea. In Vietnam, he served as assistant chief of staff for plans and operations and later as commander with the 4th Division.[28]

In 1977, concerns continued. The lack of high quality recruits may have contributed to the growing number of drug users on post. During the first six months of 1977, $1,100 worth of marijuana plants and $8,000 in processed weed were confiscated by the Criminal Investigation Division on

---

[26] David Einhorn, "Bradley Dedicates Museum," *Columbus Ledger*, July 1 1977, 1.
[27] Ibid.
[28] "Livsey to assume command Monday," *Bayonet*, July 22–28 1977, 1.

or in the immediate area of Fort Benning.[29] As the year ended, close to $57,000 worth of illegal drugs and marijuana was found.[30] Some civilian offenders brought marijuana from town or tried to grow it on post.[31]

Major Robert Pegg, Military Police Operations officer, said 93 percent of his cases in 1977 involved marijuana. However, he added, "Alcohol is by far a greater problem for Fort Benning than drugs."[32] Low prices and availability of post liquor supplies added to the problem of alcohol abuse for many of their military customers. Kegs of beer offered by the Class VI store on post were easy to buy. This inspired eighteen-year-old military dependents living in Alabama, where the purchase of kegs was illegal, to smuggle their prized possessions over the state line.

Wanting to improve the fitness of volunteers, the army's chief of staff, General Bernard Rogers, ordered the Infantry School to develop three effective physical training programs for use army-wide—modified programs of Latham's regimen. Consequently, the baseline program was designed for soldiers whose jobs required little physical activity; the Military Occupational Specialty program for soldiers with special demands; and the unit program for those assigned to units requiring specific physical conditioning for the mission. For a brief time, Airborne students were allowed to run in sneakers, but protests from several members of the original test platoon, put the jump troops back into their boots.[33]

Though Latham was criticized for his physical training programs and for the number of suicides at the post during his watch, others rewarded his dedication. Columbus native Margaret Shirling, who worked at Fort Benning for nearly thirty-five years, admired his accomplishments—

---

[29] Marie Russo, "A drug problem at Benning," *Bayonet*, November 4 1977, 6.
[30] Ibid.
[31] Ibid.
[32] Ibid.
[33] Sgt. Maj. (Ret.) Bob Summers, interview by Peggy Stelpflug.

achievements made despite a cutback of nearly 300 officers and 600 civilian workers. "Before Latham came," according to Shirling, "the post had become a playground with litter all over the place. He really straightened up the place. Fort Benning looks like an Army post again."[34]

---

[34] Julie Casey, "Shirling watches Benning grow," *Bayonet*," October 27 1978, 16.

43.

OSUT vs. TST

Acronyms were an initial success; and in the latter states of the 1970s, they made their mark in the army and at Fort Benning. Consider this list of contemporary acronyms (in no particular order): OSUT, TST, POI, TRADOC, BT/AIT, IFV, OBC, LAW, NCOSI, PNCOC, NCOSI, RIF, ANCOC, OCS, AUSA, and VOLAR. But the one that dominated this period was OSUT.

OSUT stood for One Station Unit Training, a term often discussed by politicians and military leaders. OSUT was compared to TST or Two Station Training. The comparison put Fort Benning into the middle of the duel, just as it was in the planning stages of the all-volunteer army concept, more popularly known as VOLAR.

The evaluation of OSUT and TST was scheduled to occur between January 1978 and May 1979 to compare the effectiveness and efficiency of the two training plans. OSUT vs. TST began in the 1st Infantry Training Brigade, formerly known as the 1st Advanced Infantry Training Brigade. OSUT, proven successful in the training of armor, artillery, and engineer soldiers, trained soldiers to the entry skill level through an uninterrupted, integrated learning process with a single cadre—in one unit, at one station. With TST, training took place at two stations, using two cadres. Testing was ordered by Congress and was administered by the US Army Training and Doctrine Command (TRADOC).[1]

The army decided to adopt an integrated program of instruction (POI) for infantry trainees. It was designed to eliminate redundancies in training present under the Basic Training Advanced Individual Training (BT/AIT) system. Trainees under OSUT and TST followed the same POI for the

---

[1] "OSUT test begins here in August," *Bayonet*, June 16 1978, 2.

course of the test. The crucial difference between the groups was that one remained at Fort Benning for the entire training period.

Formal testing began at Benning and at Fort Knox, Kentucky, on January 5, and the secretary of the army sent the training and cost analysis to Congress in late August for members to decide which method was more effective.[2] Until the announcement was made by Congress, Benning and Knox continued with OSUT/TST mix.[3]

Under OSUT, soldiers were sent directly to Fort Benning from the Fort Jackson, South Carolina, Reception Station. At Benning they underwent an eleven-week program of instruction (POI) in fundamental and specialized infantry skills. Those selected for TST were sent from Jackson to Knox for the first training phase and then to Benning for the final phase. The curriculum was the same except that training was interrupted for the TST soldier while he changed stations. Under OSUT/TST, the soldier was introduced to the particular weapon system in which he would specialize five weeks after entering the army.

Soldiers in the test program for One Station Unit Training (OSUT) moved into new barracks at Sand Hill. Treadwell Barracks, named in honor of Medal of Honor recipient Colonel Jack Treadwell, housed the 7th Battalion of the 1st Infantry Training Brigade. The $7 million brick structure housed 1,200 people in 56-man bays, each with its own cadre room, study area, and bathing area. In addition, the building held administrative offices and the dining facility. If OSUT were selected, the cost of transferring soldiers from one duty station to another during training and duplication in cadre, equipment, and training facilities would be greatly reduced or eliminated.

Not everyone was involved with the OSUT vs. TST battle. In February 1978, OCS candidates Brenda Barton and Donna Shuffstall became the army's first women commissioned in a combat arms branch of service. Both were assigned to Air Defense Artillery units, deployed throughout the world in peacetime as a deterrent to enemy air attack.

With government money available for the volunteer army, construction continued on post. The dedication of the $1.5 million Salomon Dental Clinic in the Sand Hill area was held in February. Captain Ben Louis

[2] Pat Brown, "OSUT/TST testing analyzed," *Bayonet*, May 25 1979, 3.
[3] Ibid.

Salomon, Dental Corps, USA, was killed in action in Saipan during World War II. In June, Major General Orris E. Kelly, the chief of chaplains, dedicated the Sand Hill Chapel. The five-sided $900,000 brick structure sat 200 worshippers and featured a Roman garden, and a 60-foot tower with a computerized carillon that played songs every hour and chimes every half hour.[4]

In a change of command, Colonel John Estes Rogers, a Georgia native, was named assistant commandant of the Infantry School. A graduate of North Georgia College, Rogers received a bachelor of science degree in business administration and later a master's degree. He performed a variety of leadership roles at Benning from 1958 to 1960. In Vietnam he was a commander in the 101st Airborne Division (Airmobile). Before returning to Benning, he was deputy assistant chief of staff, 1 Corps, in Korea. Rogers replaced Brigadier General Fred K. Mahaffey, assigned in April as director of the Infantry Fighting Vehicle (IFV) Special Study Group, Fort Leavenworth.

In October 1978, Fort Benning celebrated its sixtieth birthday. One of the events was a presentation of a statue of Sergeant Alvin C. York, one of America's most famed infantrymen. Sculptor Felix de Weldon gave his creation to the US Army. Weldon was best known for the Iwo Jima Memorial, "the largest bronze statue in existence."[5] The York statue was placed on permanent display in the National Infantry Museum.[6]

In November 1978, Benning's 498th Medical Company provided medical and humanitarian assistance in Guyana when nearly 1,000 American followers of the Reverend Jim Jones drank poisoned Kool Aid in a mass suicide in Jonestown. Their deaths occurred after cult members murdered Congressman Leo Ryan of California. Major Clarence Cooper, commanding officer and head of the forty-four-man contingent, praised the performance of the 498th during the eerie operation. Cooper said, "although the operation involved gruesome experiences for all personnel who participated, there was overall satisfaction at having performed a

---

[4] "Sand Hill gets modern dental clinic," *Bayonet*, March 3 1978, 31.

[5] Pat Brown, "Alvin York statue is Benning's birthday gift," *Bayonet*, October 6 1978, 11.

[6] Ibid.

humanitarian mission such as this."[7]

Various Benning units were eliminated or altered their missions in 1978. Benning's Pathfinder School closed in October, and the 1st Battalion, 29th Infantry, transferred from the School Brigade to the 197th Infantry Brigade in November. The mission of the 1/29th was support of the US Army Infantry School in its field and hands-on training. However, the strength of the 1/29th was cut in half due to the reduction of forces following the end of the Vietnam conflict, so the unit merged with the 197th to have all school support under the same headquarters.[8]

Another change occurred in late November when the final 1st Advanced Individual Training (AIT) graduation was held on Dickman Field at Harmony Church, completing a phase-out of AIT training. More than 60,000 soldiers trained under the program prior to its name change to the 1st Infantry Training Brigade on July 1 under the OSUT/TST test program.

Three days before Christmas, President Jimmy Carter—the first Deep South president in 128 years and the first ever from Georgia—arrived at Lawson Field on Air Force One. He continued his trip home to Plains by helicopter. Fellow Georgians Livsey and Rogers officially greeted the commander-in-chief, who in turn greeted the public present at his first visit to Benning as president.[9]

Removed from conflict, the military experienced new popularity. Two year enlistments and assignments to Europe or overseas attracted young men and women to enter the army in 1979. With the offer of a $2,000 education fund "bonus," high school graduates who scored high on enlistment exams joined, agreeing to serve four years in the reserves after leaving service. The US Army proved satisfactory for Sergeant Gracie Howard and Private First Class Glenn Howard. They were the first brother and sister team to go through Benning's Airborne training together.[10]

---

[7] Larry Weese, "Benning soldiers assist in Guyana," *Bayonet*, December 1 1978, 23.

[8] Mike Daigle "1/29th attached to 197th at ceremony," *Bayonet*, November 23 1978, 8.

[9] "Carter to visit Benning," *Bayonet*, December 26 1978, 2.

[10] "1979," *Bayonet*, December 28 1979, 24.

As 1979 began, Brigadier General William B. Steele's military career ended. Although the commanding general of 5th Mechanized Infantry Division at Fort Polk, Louisiana, Steele chose to retire at Fort Benning, site of his military baptism in the early 1940s. At home in Columbus, Steele started a new career in the international division of AFLAC insurance Company, traveling overseas more than he did in the army.

In March 1979, a *Bayonet* reporter asked Livsey to name the most important course offered by the Infantry School. Without hesitating, he chose the advanced noncommissioned officers' course: "In that course we train NCOs to be platoon sergeants, and I can't see any Army effective in combat without good platoon sergeants."[11]

The first training level offered by the Noncommissioned Officer School of Infantry (NCOSI) was for corporal or specialist 4 under the heading of primary noncommissioned officers' course (PNCOC), a course designed to train skill level 1 personnel to become team or squad leaders. The second training level was the basic noncommissioned officers' course (BNCOC), a course designed to update E-5s and E-6s, already in a leadership position, on current army doctrine. The highest training level for the combat arms enlisted soldier at NCOSI was the advanced noncommissioned officers' course (ANCOC), exclusive to Benning. Here selected students improved leadership, management skills, and physical training.

In April, the 197th Infantry Brigade Replacement Detachment was reactivated at Kelley Hill after the first detachment was closed in September 1977. The 197th Replacement Detachment handled all arrival and departures for the brigade: "There is one thing that remains true for every soldier in the 197th Infantry Brigade; sooner or later every soldier will visit the replacement detachment in one capacity or another."[12]

In June, Livsey commended the selection of Major General David E. Grange, Jr., to follow him as Benning's commander. "Dave Grange is a veteran of three wars. He is a distinguished soldier, highly decorated

---

[11] Dale Wilson, "Livsey, Rogers speak," *Bayonet*, March 30 1979, 22.

[12] Robert C. Clouse, "197th re-activated at Kelley Hill," *Bayonet*, August 24 1979, 16.

infantryman and uniquely qualified to command the Infantry Center. Most of all, he is a soldier's soldier," Livsey said.[13]

This was Grange's fourth tour at Benning. In 1953, he was a Ranger instructor at the Infantry School and in 1955 attended the infantry officers' advanced course. From July 1971 until September 1973, he served as director of the Ranger Department. He entered the army in June 1943 and served as a paratrooper in World War II. He received his commission as a second lieutenant of infantry in May 1950. He fulfilled two combat tours during the Korean conflict and three during the Vietnam War. He served with a Special Forces Group in Germany, commanded US Army Readiness Region VIII, and led the 2nd Infantry Division in Korea before his assignment at Benning. Grange enjoyed fishing, hunting, and horseback riding—hobbies reminiscent of early post commandants. In fact, polo made a comeback at the post in 1979 with matches played on Blue Field. Commenting on her husband's assignment, Lois Grange said, "We've spent more time at Benning than any other post and it really was just like 'coming home!'"[14] She planned to open Riverside to the public as often as possible: "When we were here in 1950, I used to pass by and wonder what this house looked like inside. I really think the public deserves to see this beautiful place and I want to share it with them."[15]

It was a time of peace for the army and Fort Benning, but not everything was idyllic. A serviceman and his wife had reason to criticize the Main Post Theatre: "As we entered the theatre a stagnant, musty odor permeated the air, ruining even the stalest popcorn, making it impossible to relax and enjoy the movie."[16] The couple pointed out "howling soldiers from the School Brigade" also proved a distraction as well as two mice that were darting about.[17] Those discomforts were coupled with the discovery that "our shoes were welded to the floor by a sticky goo resulting from spilt drinks, candy, and other related items."[18] Post theatre authorities promptly

---

[13] "Livsey assigned to Germany," *Bayonet*, April 13 1979, 1.

[14] Pat Brown, "Lois Grange glad to be back," *Bayonet*, July 27 1979, 17.

[15] Ibid.

[16] J. Barham, "Fort Benning soldier slams Main Post Theater," *Bayonet*, November 9 1973, 4.

[17] Ibid.

[18] Ibid.

answered their letter, promising more help for crowd control, cleaner carpets, and the elimination of rodents and insects.[19]

In addition, an unusual article for the historically staid *Bayonet* appeared that November. This story announced that prostitution was alive and well on Victory Drive, just outside the gates of Fort Benning. "Two things that have been round Army posts for a long time are prostitutes and young soldiers who put themselves in a position to be ripped-off. Don't set yourself up for a 'bad scene,'" the writer implored.[20] The Armed Forces Disciplinary Control Boards investigated suspect shops and bars, placing them off limits if undesirable conditions were discovered.[21]

As the year ended, US Senator Sam Nunn addressed the local AUSA chapter at the new Columbus Iron Works Convention & Trade Center. He spoke about the Iranian militants who seized the US Embassy in Tehran, taking American hostages and casting a pall over Jimmy Carter's presidency. Nunn said the United States "must be prepared to take action and that action must be swift and certain" if American hostages were harmed or killed.[22]

In years to come, Nunn's remarks about Iran would hardly be the last words on that combative region of the world—a region that soon would become all too familiar to the American soldier and the American people.

---

[19] Ibid.

[20] Gary Jones, "Prostitution—Alive and well on Victory Drive," *Bayonet*, November 16 1979, 20.

[21] Ibid.

[22] Cliff Purcell, "Senator tours Benning," *Bayonet*, December 14 1979, 1.

44.

America Taken Hostage

Many Americans never knew the difference between Iran and Iraq, but Americans knew the difference in 1980, mainly because of Iran's leader—Ayatolla Ruholla Khomeini. The Ayatolla took hostage fifty-two Americans, holding them at their own embassy, while the world held its breath. The event changed the course of a presidency, put the United States on the brink of a Middle Eastern war, and caused Americans to study the culture and politics of a region whose volatility flows as freely as its oil and whose problems are as numerous as the grains of sand in its countryside.

Hostages were taken in November 1979 and by the next year President Jimmy Carter, concerned that the country might be going to war, reinstated a draft for the first time in five years, preparing for a potential Mid-East troop buildup. At first, men and women, ages nineteen and twenty-nine were to register. That created a stir. Women never had been issued a draft card. People were upset at the prospect of mothers and daughters going to war. The proposal to register women for the draft was defeated in the House Armed Services Military Personnel Subcommittee.[1]

In April 1980, an attempt was made to free the fifty-two Americans held hostage for nearly six months at the American Embassy in Teheran. However, secret operation Eagle's Claw, involving the army, navy, marines and air force, was called off after mechanical problems caused a shortage of helicopters required to transport the ninety-man team to Teheran. Fort Benning was on no special status after the aborted rescue.

During withdrawal of men involved in the mission, a helicopter collided with a C-130 cargo plane, resulting in the deaths of eight US servicemen in the Iranian desert. The ground commander of the rescue

---

[1] "President of the United States," *World Book Year Book* (Chicago: World Book-Childcraft International, Inc., 1981) 453.

party was Colonel Charles Beckwith, leader of the elite Blue Light antiterrorist unit at Fort Bragg. A volunteer for the Army Special Forces, Beckwith commanded the top-secret Delta Project in Vietnam, earning the nickname "Chargin' Charlie."[2] A former Ranger instructor at Fort Benning, Beckwith ran the third phase of the Ranger training course in 1966–1967 at Auxiliary Field 7 at Eglin Air Force Base, Florida. He "put the Florida phase of Ranger training into a Vietnam mode."[3]

With the hostage situation continuing in the Mid-East, an assault strip was built at Benning in September 1980. A 4,200-foot runway accommodating air force C-130s, the strip served the post in Emergency Readiness Exercises. In addition, the first nuclear, biological, and chemical (NBC) training building opened on post to accommodate the soldier, his vehicle, and all his gear in a chemical environment.[4]

In July 1980, Brigadier General Edward L. Trobaugh succeeded Brigadier General John E. Rogers as assistant commandant of the Infantry School. Rogers's new assignment was commander of the Berlin Brigade in Germany. Trobaugh, former assistant division commander for operations, 9th Infantry Division at Fort Lewis, attended the Infantry School basic and advanced courses as well as Airborne, Ranger, jumpmaster, and pathfinder courses. He served two tours of duty in Vietnam.[5]

For those in command positions, it was a busy time. When Secretary of the Army Clifford Alexander announced that One Station Unit Training (OSUT) would begin at Fort Benning in fiscal year 1981, nearly $6 million in appropriated funds was released for the building of a reception station to process OSUT recruits. Although another $3 million was "drastically needed" to complete the station, a $7.3 million savings in annual operating costs was expected to be gained by adopting the all-infantry OSUT over the Two Station Training (TST) formerly used at the post.[6]

---

[2] "Charlie Beckwith Was Not the Average Bear," *US News & World Report*, June 27 1994, 20.

[3] Col. Charlie A. Beckwith, USA (Ret.) and Donald Knox, *Delta Force* (New York: Harcourt Brace Jovanovich, 1983) 85.

[4] "*Bayonet*'s top stories of 1980 featured visits, training and competition," *Bayonet*, December 31 1980, 17.

[5] "New assistant commader installed," *Bayonet*, July 25 1980, 8.

[6] T. A. Sabel, "OSUT approved for Benning," *Bayonet*, August 22 1980, 1.

Since the recruiting command met its goal of 24,800 army recruits for the fiscal year 1980 by mid-July, General John Vessey, recruiting command vice-chief of staff, permitted an increase in recruits, allowing 4,500 to 5,000 extra soldiers. An economic downturn throughout the country contributed to the increase of new soldiers. A new battalion, the 8th Battalion, 1st Infantry Training Brigade, was activated at Benning for the influx of recruits, and a $15,523,690 contract was awarded for a trainee barracks facility. The following year the 9th battalion was formed with plans for the 10th battalion in 1982.[7]

To have personnel to train the additional troops, a School for Infantry Drill Sergeants originated on post. After finishing the eight-week course, selected soldiers were sent to the 1st Infantry Training Brigade. Another innovation was the recognition of the most outstanding noncommissioned officers. In 1980, Staff Sergeant James W. Wiehe was selected as the first post NCO of the quarter and Sergeant Phillip G. Johnston, Company D, 197th Infantry Brigade, was selected as Fort Benning's soldier of the year.[8]

After twenty-nine years of service, Norman F. Force, chief of Benning's forestry branch, retired. He arrived at the post in 1951, equipped with a bachelor of science degree in forestry and experience with the US Forest Service and Department of Defense. On post, he managed 129,000 acres of forestlands for the remainder of his career. "Fort Benning became one of the four biggest posts making money by selling timber.... From 1947 to 1965 we were filling orders for every military installation east of the Mississippi," Force said.[9] In addition to timber management, fire protection was a major part of Force's job. The use of simulators and flares during training exercises increased the risks of fire. Sometimes he had to deal with as many as 200 fires a year.[10]

On election day in 1980, Georgian Jimmy Carter was voted out of office. Because of his failure to free the hostages after nearly two years of captivity and because of the poor performance of the American economy, Carter lost his bid for re-election to Republican favorite Ronald Reagan,

---

[7] "New Brigade will be activated," *Bayonet*, May 21 1981, 1.

[8] "*Bayonet*'s top stories of 1980 featured visits, training and competition," *Bayonet*, December 31 1980, 15, 26.

[9] Becky Bulgrin, "1st post forester retires," *Bayonet*, August 29 1980, 10.

[10] Ibid.

actor and former California governor. On January 20, 1981, the same day Reagan took the oath as the fortieth president of the United States, Iran released the fifty-two hostages after 444 days in captivity. The immediate crisis in the Mid-East was over.

Although the United States was experiencing peace, the world was still a dangerous place. To prepare for this danger, Major Daniel D. Turner of the US Army Infantry Board, was the first American soldier to parachute wearing a protective mask, helping Airborne troops face threats of chemical warfare. Terrorism, another danger, was a way of life in many countries. Troops were often sent to these troubled lands in efforts to diffuse or end the conflicts.

In February, three soldiers from Company C, 1st Battalion, 58th Infantry (Mechanized), fired a new weapon system developed for the army. Private First Class Michael Miller, Private David Wright, and Private Wendall Perry were the first soldiers to test fire the Viper. The Viper was a shoulder-fired, short range, anti-tank weapon that promised improvement over the M72A2 light anti-tank weapon (LAW). Later in the year, Benning soldiers learned to use a new missile system called tubular-launched optically-tracked wire-guided anti-armor missile (TOW). In August, the multiple integrated laser system (MILES) arrived, and soldiers of the 197th Infantry Brigade were the first to operate the system. Soldiers wore the MILES equipment during exercises to simulate live-fire engagements by recording laser beam "hits."

Although electronic warfare was a major part of the army's future, traditional training concepts were not ignored. Bayonet training, dropped at Fort Benning in 1972 because of injuries to participating soldiers, was reinstated in 1981 "to foster aggressiveness, develop esprit-de-corps, and help build confidence."[11] A bayonet assault course, developed by engineers from the 2nd Platoon, Company C, 43rd Engineers, included a three-foot-wide ditch filled with concertina wire, a fifteen-foot-high dirt hill, a barbed wire tunnel crawl, and a log hurdle.

For soldiers of the 1st Infantry Training Brigade, the routine was filled with "military sounds of thudding boots, growling and grunting soldiers and cold steel and rifle butts hitting targets at the former Sand Hill golf

---

[11] Bill Walton, "Grunting soldiers replace groaning golfers," *Bayonet*, December 4 1981, 18.

course."[12] About a mile long, the course offered twenty-two obstacles; eight were bayonet targets. Each bayonet target was hit twice, with a long and short thrust. The average time for completing the assault course was five minutes. After finishing, a participant went through a second time.[13]

Fort Benning also continued its tradition of training troops from allied countries. In March 1981, the United States granted El Salvador $25 million in military aid and sent twenty additional military advisers to help combat left wing guerrillas. About 600 El Salvadoran officer candidates arrived at Fort Benning for four months of training in leadership, tactics, maintenance, and troop leading procedures. They trained under the Foreign Assistance Act of 1961 at a cost of $15 million.[14]

In May, Brigadier General Robert William RisCassi succeeded Major General Edward L. Trobaugh as commandant of the Infantry School. Trobaugh, named chief of the US Army Military Assistance Group in Madrid, Spain, received his second star during his farewell ceremony on York Field. RisCassi formerly served as assistant commander of the 8th Infantry Division (Mechanized), US Army, Europe. Earlier he commanded the 4th Battalion, 503rd Infantry, and 173rd Airborne Brigade in Vietnam. He also served in Washington, DC; attended Army War College; served as commander of the 4th Brigade, 4th Infantry Division, Europe; and was chief of staff, 8th Infantry Division.[15]

On June 16, the 2nd Infantry Training Brigade, formed by splitting the 1st Infantry Training Brigade, was activated with Colonel Howard Clark in command. Located in Harmony Church, Clark's headquarters was one of the World War II "temporary" buildings that served as headquarters of the 11th Air Assault Division in the 1960s. Also, the 1st Battalion, 29th Infantry, celebrated its eightieth birthday at Fort Benning. With its motto "We Lead the Way," it led training at the US Army Infantry School since arriving at Camp Benning in 1919. The 29th Infantry, attached to the 197th Brigade, supported school troops in 1981 with the infantry fighting vehicles, TOW, and Ranger platoons.

---

[12] Ibid.

[13] Ibid.

[14] "U.S. to train Salvadoran troops," *Bayonet*, December 30 1981, 3.

[15] "Gen. Riscass: here Monday," *Bayonet*, May 29 1981, 3.

In July, Secretary of the Army John O. Marsh, Jr., paid his first official visit to the post where he graduated from Infantry Officer Candidate School in 1945 and later completed Airborne training. "I give credit," Marsh said, "to what success I have had in life to the training received and the leadership abilities I learned while at Fort Benning."[16]

Another OCS graduate and important visitor to the post in 1981 was Secretary of Defense Caspar W. Weinberger, an inductee into the OCS Hall of Fame. He explained his reason for enlisting in the army in September 1941 after graduating from Harvard Law School: "I was simply struck with the belief that the way of the infantry was the only right and honorable way to serve."[17] Commissioned after graduating with class number fourteen from Fort Benning's OCS in 1942, Weinberger served in the Pacific, rising to the rank of captain. Praising the infantryman at Fort Benning, Weinberger said, "The combat infantryman in the United States knows better than anyone the carnage of the battlefield and the tragedy of war. It is the combat infantryman who carries the burden of war."[18]

Major General David E. Grange, Jr., commandant of Fort Benning, left the post in August to command the 6th Army at the Presidio in San Francisco. Grange, who received his third star, helped implement One Station Training at Fort Benning, consolidating all initial training of infantry soldiers at the post and fulfilling the post's logo, "Home of the Infantry." Grange parachuted over the post during a farewell leapfest held in his honor.

Major General Robert L. "Sam" Wetzel, previously assigned to the office of the army chief of staff in Washington, succeeded Grange. A commanding general of the 3rd Infantry Division (Mechanized) in Europe from July 1979 to March 1981, Wetzel also commanded the 4th Battalion, 31st Infantry; 196th Infantry Brigade; and 23rd Infantry Division (American) in Vietnam from June 1968 to January 1969.[19]

---

[16] "Army Secretary visits Benning," *Bayonet*, July 17, 1981, 4.

[17] Caspar Weinberger, *Fighting for Peace* (New York: Warner Books, Inc., 1990) 7.

[18] "Defense Secretary Conducted into OCS Hall of Fame," *Bayonet*, July 31, 1981, 1.

[19] Maj. Gen. (Ret.) Carmen Cavezza, interview by Peggy Stelpflug, June 17, 1998, Columbus Government Center.

In July 1981, Wetzel sent 2,500 soldiers from the 197th Infantry Brigade to the newly activated National Training Center (NTC) at Fort Irwin, California—the largest army post in the US. The unit engaged in live-fire maneuvers for forty-five days in the upper Mojave Desert. Colonel Carmen J. Cavezza, 197th commander since March, recalled, "We were the first brigade-sized unit to go to the National Training Center. They kind of used us as a test case. The weather and terrain were very stressful as well. It was a very hot summer out there in 1981. The training—it was like war—became an emotional thing for the soldiers…great combat training."[20]

On October 19, a nine-member squad from Fort Benning, attached to the Fighting Vehicles Systems Task Force, participated in a christening ceremony for the Bradley infantry fighting vehicle (IFV) at Fort Meyer, Virginia. Later that month, four Bradley IFVs were delivered to the army. The Bradley was not a tank but a fighting vehicle designed to operate with the Abrams tank. It excelled in firepower, mobility, and armored protection, surpassing the army's existing armored personnel carrier (M113). It was named for General of the Army Omar Bradley, a former Benning commandant and World War II leader. Bradley, the last of America's five-star generals, died April 8.

On December 4, 1981, a groundbreaking ceremony was held for the Fort Benning Reception Station, a multi-million dollar facility located behind Kimbro Gym at Sand Hill. It was another step toward OSUT. "For the day a young soldier puts on his first pair of combat boots until he stands proudly at graduation as a qualified infantryman, every hour of his in-processing and training will be conducted by Fort Benning's superb officers and NCOs," Wetzel said at the ceremony.[21]

The importance of the Bradleys continued to grow. On March 2, 1982, Company D, 1st Battalion, 29th Infantry Regiment, 197th Infantry Brigade—the army's first Bradley infantry fighting vehicle company—was activated at Benning on Presidential Field. On May 26, the first two production line models of the Bradley fighting vehicles arrived. "The Bradley, operating with the M-1 Abrams tank, artillery, and attack helicopters will significantly reduce the advantages of the enemy's numerical

---

[20] Ibid.

[21] Brian Adams, "Reception station groundbreaking," *Bayonet*, December 11, 1981, 4.

superiority," Wetzel said in remarks at the range.[22] The army expected to purchase 6,882 Bradleys with 40 available at Fort Benning by the fall of 1982.

The 5th Battalion, 1st Infantry Training Brigade moved into Albanese Barracks on Sand Hill in April. The barracks was named in honor of Private First Class Lewis Albanese, a member of Company B, 5th Battalion, 7th Cavalry, 1st Cavalry Division in Vietnam. Albanese, who saved his platoon from enemy fire, was posthumously awarded the Medal of Honor. Because it replaced the old World War II wooden barracks that housed thousands of soldiers during three wars, residents nicknamed the new building "the Starship" for its technology, including two large classrooms with TV monitors that provided training material on tape for the soldiers.

In addition to the new barracks, a new weapons storage area that provided security, maintenance, and storage facilities for more than 12,000 weapons was dedicated on Kelley Hills. It was named for Medal of Honor recipient Corporal Michael A. Crescenz. He served as rifleman in Company, 4th Battalion, 31st Infantry, 196th Infantry Brigade, Americal Division, in Vietnam. Crescenz was killed after assaulting three enemy bunkers, allowing his unit to complete its mission.[23]

Funds for these projects, including a multi-million dollar motor pool dedicated on Kelley Hill to house vehicles for the 1st Battalion, 29th Infantry, 197th Infantry Brigade, were part of a $200 billion military spending bill—the largest in US history. Although $15.5 million was provided for new Bradley infantry fighting vehicle ranges, funding for barracks, a clinic, and a post office intended for the Sand Hill area was delayed.

A change of command occurred at the post in April. Brigadier General Kenneth C. Leuer was welcomed as assistant commandant of the Infantry School, succeeding Major General Robert W. RisCassi as assistant commandant of the Infantry School. RisCassi left the post in February to take command of the US Army Readiness and Mobilization Region III, Fitzsimmons Army Medical Center, Aurora, Colorado. Previously, Leuer commanded the 193rd Infantry Brigade (Canal Zone) and the US Army Security Assistance Agency in Latin America. Other duties included the

---

[22] Tom Fuller, "First production line Bradleys arrive," *Bayonet*, May 28, 1982, 4.

[23] "1982: the year that was," *Bayonet*, December 29, 1982, 18.

82nd Airborne Division at Fort Bragg, the 8th Infantry Division in Germany, the 2nd Infantry Division in Korea, US Special Forces at Fort Bragg, the 173rd Airborne Brigade, and the 101st Airborne Division in Vietnam. After serving as chief of faculty development at the Infantry School, Leuer organized the first Ranger battalion since World War II.

Another change was the departure of the 121st Aviation Company for Germany. The mission of the unit remained that of resupplying and relocating troops with the Blackhawk helicopter—the most modern utility helicopter in the US Army. Shortly after fifteen Blackhawks were flown to Charleston, South Carolina, and loaded on a navy ship, thirty-six officers and eighty-nine enlisted soldiers departed Lawson Airfield for Germany. In November 1982, the post received seven Blackhawk helicopters in a trade-off for seven UH-Is to continue full time support of the Army Infantry School with "the most modern piece of aviation equipment available."[24] Fort Benning had fifteen pilots transitioned to fly the Blackhawks in addition to five crew chiefs and one maintenance sergeant.

For the second year in a row, Fort Benning's Lones W. Wigger, Jr., swept the rifle championships at the National Rifle Association's National Indoor Championships in July. Wigger held twenty-five world records, winning seventy-eight medals in international shooting as well as twice winning Olympic gold medals. In 1981, he became the first competitor to win all events in the rifle and pistol competitions at the National Indoor Championships.[25]

In another test of skill, Sergeants First Class Charles R. Light and Philip L. Sebay won the inaugural "Best Ranger" competition in May, receiving the Army Commendation Medal and a pair of engraved 9 mm pistols. The competition was named after former Fort Benning commander Lieutenant General David E. Grange—once an instructor and later director of the Ranger Department. A five-day endurance test held at Fort Benning and the Florida Ranger Camp proved the outstanding physical and mental condition of the competing soldiers. Colonel Eugene D. Hawkins, director

---

[24] Lt. Col. James H. Kenton, commander of Lawson Army Airfield, Rick Russell, "Blackhawks arrive at Benning," *Bayonet*, November 24 1982, 19.

[25] "Lones Wigger wins all NRA indoor titles," *Bayonet*, July 16 1982, 33.

of the Ranger Department, said "the Rangers course turns out the best combat leaders in the world."[26]

On July 20, the US Army Infantry Training Center (USAITC) was officially established and recognized as the sole proponent agency for infantry in the US Army. As a result, the title chief of infantry, first given to Camp Benning commandant Major General Charles Farnsworth in July 1920, returned to Fort Benning and its commandant, Major General Sam Wetzel.

The Law Enforcement Command, which trained the military police, underwent a major change early in 1983, becoming the Military Police Activity, part of the Department of the Army's plan to maximize mobilization capability to meet wartime requirements for deployable MP units. The Military Police Activity also trained a platoon of handpicked soldiers from several units in a concentrated two-week training course designed to improve the patrolling of restricted Fort Benning ranges. It patrolled nightly in two-man units using night surveillance techniques and devices to prevent thieves from taking "anything from training devices to bleachers."[27]

George Heberling, a twenty-eight-year civil service employee, was on the list of retirees in January 1983. The long-time post employee arrived at Fort Benning in 1944 as a lieutenant, attending the officers' basic course and later the Airborne School. Serving as a civilian procurement officer in Japan, Heberling was introduced to Kathryn, a native of Columbus. "When I met and married her," he said, "I married the South."[28] The first civilian appointed comptroller of an army post, Heberling accomplished much at Fort Benning. His best-known work, proving the cost effectiveness of One Station Unit Training (OSUT) saved the army $2.7 million yearly.[29]

In April 1983, Hollywood once again came to the post, this time to film the movie *Tank*. It starred well-known film and television stars James Garner and Shirley Jones. Fort Benning personnel played many of the extra

---

[26] Bill Reynolds, "Rangers compete for David E. Grange Award," *Bayonet*, May 7, 1982, 22.

[27] Col. Curtis Earp, post provost marshal, Robert McClain, "Security," *Bayonet*, March 4, 1983, 20.

[28] T. William Fuller, "Post money manager retiring after 27 years," *Bayonet*, January 21, 1983, 3.

[29] Ibid.

roles: three sergeants, a major, a barmaid, a food service specialist, a senior NCO in the medical field and two senior NCOs. Post locations used for filming included the Custer Terrace family housing area, the 2nd Battalion, 69th Armor Motor Pool, and post ranges.

On July 6, Johnston Hall, home of the Sand Hill Reception Station, was dedicated for Specialist 4th Class Donald R. Johnston, a Columbus native who was awarded the Medal of Honor posthumously for his heroic actions in Vietnam with the 1st Cavalry Division. When explosive charges were thrown at his company, he covered the detonations with his body, saving the lives of six comrades on March 21, 1969.[30]

In July, Major General James J. Lindsay, former commander of the 82nd Airborne Division at Fort Bragg, succeeded Wetzel, who became deputy commander of US Army Europe and 7th Army, Heidelberg, Germany. Lindsay enlisted in the army in 1952 and graduated from OCS at Fort Benning in 1953. He attended infantry officers' advanced course at the Infantry School, becoming Airborne, Ranger, and Pathfinder qualified. His other assignments included the office of the joint chiefs of staff, US Military Assistance Command in Thailand, and XVIII Airborne Corps. "I'm deeply moved by this assignment," Lindsay said, "I can't put into words how much it means to me. I'll do everything in my power to live up to the charge given me today."[31]

Leuer, the assistant school commander, was promoted to major general and a new assignment as assistant chief of staff, operations, 8th US Army/United Nations Command in Korea. His replacement was Brigadier General Edwin H. Burba, formerly the executive to the chief of staff, US Army. Burba, a 1959 US Military Academy graduate, received training at Benning in the Infantry Officers' School and Defense Language Institute at the Presidio in Monterey. He went to Vietnam in 1964 with the 1st Special Forces Group as chief of plans and operations and later was officer in charge of psychological warfare. In 1966, he was a company commander at the Infantry School and in 1967 was assigned to the 1st Brigade, 1st Cavalry Division in Vietnam.[32]

---

[30] "Johnston Hall dedicated at Benning," *Bayonet*, July 8, 1983, 1.

[31] Robert McClain, "Maj. Gen. Lindsay assumes command," *Bayonet*, July 15, 1983, 1.

[32] "Brig. Gen. Leuer welcomed," *Bayonet*, April 30, 1982, 1.

In November, Colonel Carmen J. Cavezza relinquished command of the 197th Infantry Brigade. While commanding the 5,000-member brigade, Cavezza supported the Infantry School and prepared the combat-ready brigade by maintenance programs and diverse training. Cavezza remained on post to serve as chief of staff, succeeding Colonel Bobby J. Harris. Retiring after thirty years of service, Harris said, "When I first came in the army we were a walking army. Now…the walking infantry is the minority. Everybody rides, and sophisticated equipment is assigned to each unit."[33]

New 197th commander, Colonel James A. Musselman, a ROTC graduate, attended Infantry Officer Basic and Airborne and Ranger Schools at Benning. He then served in Vietnam, taught at the Florida Ranger Camp, attended the infantry officers' advanced course, and served another combat tour in Vietnam. He was in the Pentagon's office of the deputy chief of staff for operations and plans prior to his new assignment.

On November 26, nearly 900 Columbus residents, Fort Benning soldiers, and US Marines gathered at Lakebottom Park in Columbus to honor 241 marines and fellow servicemen killed in Lebanon. They died in a terrorist truck bombing during a peacekeeping mission in Beirut on October 23. Eighteen servicemen who died in the US invasion of Grenada in October and November were also honored for rescuing Americans on the politically unstable island. Fourteen Georgia servicemen, including Beirut Marine Corporal Victor Mark Prevatt of Columbus, were among those honored. Remembering the fallen servicemen, who "died in the tradition of Valley Forge, Concord, and Iwo Jima, of Normandy and Vietnam," three soldiers placed a pair of empty boots in front of the speaker's platform with a combat helmet positioned on top of a rifle bayoneted into the ground.[34] The *Bayonet* said the death toll of the peacekeeping force in Beirut was the largest number of American casualties in a single day since January 13, 1968, when 246 servicemen were killed in Vietnam at the start of the Tet offensive.[35]

War no longer involved the world or massive forces, but war still produced casualties—as noted by author Daniel P. Bolger: "Men (and some women) killed in small wars are just as dead as those killed in big ones. It has

---

[33] Rick Russell, "Chief of staff bids post farewell," *Bayonet*, December 16 1983, 3.

[34] Maj. Gen. Roy E. Moss, fourth Marine division commander, Robert McClain, "Columbus honors fallen servicemen," *Bayonet*, December 2 1983, 1.

[35] Ibid.

always been a savage peace out there past the stockade gates. The work is
never clean or easy."[36]

---

[36] Daniel P. Bolger, *Savage Peace* (Novato CA: Presidio Press, 1995) 106.

45.

Protest at the Gate

Instead of a clerical collar, the Reverend Roy Bourgeois first arrived at Fort Benning in the uniform of a soldier—a choice of clothing that earned the outspoken Catholic priest an eighteen-month reservation in a federal prison.

That was 1983, the year before the School of Americas Bourgeois so fervently protested was relocated to Fort Benning from Panama. It was supposed to be a temporary home for the training center for Latin American soldiers and civilians. Temporary eventually became permanent and so did the civil disobedience of Bourgeois and his band of followers.[1]

The school originated at Fort Amador in Panama in 1946. Originally it was known as the Latin-American Training Center—Ground Division. Its principal mission then was to train US personnel stationed in the former Canal Zone. The first students from Latin America were trained in 1947. In 1949, the school moved to Fort Gulick. Instructors spoke in English until 1956 when Spanish became the official academic language. The US Army School of the Americas adopted its name in 1963. Between 1946 and 1984, it graduated 45,331 military personnel from twenty-two Latin American countries.[2]

On October 24, 1984, the Department of the Army announced that Fort Benning would be the transitional training site of the US Army School of the Americas. The training center was moving because the US gave up control of the Canal Zone. The center officially opened at the Georgia installation in December, and classes began in January 1985. Under

---

[1] Virginia Anderson, "Civil disobedience: Priest ready for prison," *Atlanta Constitution*, June 20 1996, B3.

[2] Marco Morales, "School of America's officially opens at Benning," *Bayonet*, December 21 1984, 4.

provisions of an agreement implementing the 1977 Panama Canal Treaty, the school closed its doors September 30, 1984, at Fort Gulick, Panama.[3]

Training foreign troops was nothing new at Fort Benning. The Infantry School had welcomed students from other countries for many years. The rainbow of uniforms and medals was a familiar sight on post and in the civilian community. A program that trained soldiers from El Salvador began in 1981—an obscure program that in 1983 made national newspaper headlines because of Bourgeois and three other protesters.[4]

Bourgeois was a Catholic priest in the Maryknoll Order. After joining the US Navy in 1964 and serving in Vietnam, the Louisiana native entered the seminary in 1966. In El Salvador in 1981, he saw atrocities committed by the armed forces and by extremists in the civil war—acts he attributed to training those soldiers received at the School of the Americas. Moved by what he had seen, Bourgeois began opposing the training of Salvadoran soldiers, who "keep the rich *rich* and the poor *poor*."[5] In the first act of civil disobedience at Fort Benning in 1983, Bourgeois protested the 1980 murder of Archbishop Oscar Romero in El Salvador. Bourgeois and three friends went to the barracks of Salvadoran soldiers on post and played a tape of Romero's last sermon in which he urged the military to lay down their guns. For trespassing and impersonating an officer, Bourgeois was arrested and sentenced to prison for eighteen months.[6]

The USARSA commandant was Colonel Michael J. Sierra, who assumed the duty in June 1984. A 1964 graduate of the Infantry Officer Candidate School, Sierra served two tours in Vietnam as an infantry platoon leader of the 101st Airborne Division and as a company commander of the 1st Cavalry Division. With his combat experience and his master's degree in international relations, Sierra was prepared to fulfill the school's purpose of conducting military training and of promoting cooperation among Latin American armed forces.[7]

---

[3] Ibid.

[4] Associated Press, "High court upholds convictions of Benning protesters," *Columbus Ledger-Enquirer*, March 8 1994, B2.

[5] Virginia Anderson, "Civil disobedience: Priest ready for prison," B3.

[6] Ibid.

[7] "School of Americas heading for Fort Benning," *Bayonet*, October 26 1984, 4.

Students from Latin America and the United States began training at the School of the Americas on January 24, 1985, with the command and general staff course—the equivalent of the course offered at Fort Leavenworth, Kansas. The primary difference was that it was taught in Spanish and was geared towards military application in Latin America. The thirty-three students enrolled represented ten countries: Peru, Colombia, Costa Rica, Paraguay, Dominican Republic, Panama, Guatemala, Honduras, Venezuela, and the US. Only four Latin American officers had been in the US before coming to Benning.

The forty-five-week command and general staff course prepared field grade officers for duty as commanders and general staff officers in their respective armed forces. General subjects included staff operations, management, tactics, logistics, strategic studies, joint and combined operations, security assistance, and internal defense. In addition, courses of study would include combat arms, military intelligence, resource management, NCO and cadet leadership, as well as patrolling and Ranger training. More than 1100 students from 15 Central and South American countries trained at USARSA in 1985.

Benning was among three contenders for the school's permanent location. Other posts desiring it were Fort Stewart, Georgia, and Fort Polk, Louisiana. Representative Richard Ray, who represented Muscogee County in Congress, worked with the Greater Columbus Chamber of Commerce to secure the school. Following the example of chamber members who "fought" for Camp Benning, local companies and businessmen wrote letters to Secretary of the Army John O. Marsh, Jr., "urging the Army to keep the school here."[8] Mayor Bill Feighner and others met with the under-secretary of the army and presented him 250 letters as well as a six-minute video stressing the city's support. Banks, car dealerships and other local companies hired Spanish-speaking executives to help students, teachers, and their families, who contributed nearly $2 million a month to the local economy.[9]

Colonel Miguel A. Garcia assumed command of the US Army School of the Americas on October 22, 1985, succeeding Michael J. Sierra, who was reassigned as commander of the 3rd Brigade, 25th Infantry Division in

---

[8] Pat Quinley, "School of the Americas gets warm welcome," *Columbus Ledger-Enquirer*, August 4 1985, D2.

[9] Ibid.

Hawaii. Sierra had been commandant of USARSA since June 1984. Garcia noted, "USARSA has gone through a very difficult period moving from Panama to Fort Benning...costly both in terms of money and some disruption in courses. It hasn't been perfect."[10] However, his immediate plans were "to continue, and improve if necessary, the fine record the School has had for thirty-nine years in the area of education and training officers, cadets, and non-commissioned officers from Latin America."[11]

A ROTC graduate of the University of Puerto Rico, Garcia graduated from the field artillery officers' advanced course, the US Army Command and General Staff College and the Defense Intelligence School's attaché course. He received a master's degree in Latin American studies from Georgetown University. Garcia also served in Panama; Washington, DC; and Europe.[12]

While city officials fought for the school, Bourgeois was fighting against it. This was the genesis for decades of protests. From that group of four in 1983, the movement grew into the School of Americas Watch. Every November thousands of eclectic protesters camp out at Benning's main gate and conduct a non-violent protest.[13] Demonstrations continued after the army shut the doors on the former School of the Americas. When the Department of the Defense reopened it as the Western Hemisphere Institute for Security and Cooperation under more stringent civilian controls, protesters coined the slogan, "New name, old shame."[14]

After the School of the Americas arrived, an old Fort Benning institution stabilized. Members of the Fort Benning Officers' Open Mess established a flat rate of $15 dues per month regardless of rank. The monthly fee included family golf, swimming, and tennis service. The drive for 2,700 members would insure financial stability and revitalize the club.

---

[10] "Newly-assigned USARSA commander shares views," *Bayonet*, November 15 1985, 7.

[11] Ibid.

[12] Ibid.

[13] Tony Adams, "School continues to draw fire," Benning Leader, November 24 1995, 11; Karen Jacobs, "Activists protest Army School in Georgia," CommonDreams.org Newscenter, November 17 2002, 1, google:http://www.commondreams.org/headlines02/1117-06.htm.

[14] "Congress closes US Army School of the Americas, gives ok to open new school," *Jesuits USA*, May 30 2000, google: Jesuit USA News: May 30 2000.

Major General Jim Lindsay noted, "Our goal is to provide a service to members and there is no reason why we cannot have the best club in the Army."[15]

Seeking to improve the post for all its residents, the Infantry Center staff reorganized to improve the quality of life for soldiers and their family members. On post the deputy post commander, assumed previously by the chief of staff, now was a separate duty appointed to oversee the Directorates of Personnel and Community Activities. The DPC, Colonel Neal Christensen, acted as the commanding general's representative for off-post community affairs.[16]

Chief of Staff Colonel Carmen Cavezza, responsible for mission, men, and resources, directly supervised the Directorates of Plans and Training as well as security and industrial operations. The Community Life Program (CLP) inspired the changes in the Infantry Center staff after Lieutenant Colonel John Pierce and Major John Ross gave new direction to the program. "Concern for the soldier and the military family is what the CLP is all about," Pierce stated.[17] Initially established at Fort Benning in 1973 and revitalized in 1983, the success of Benning's program resulted in the adoption of the Community Life Program army-wide.[18]

The announcement of Fort Benning's winning a $1 million first prize came in February. The Training Doctrine Command (TRADOC) installation that saved the most money during fiscal year 1983 won the prize. Project SPIRIT (Systematic Productivity and Improvement Review) competition on post produced a total savings of almost $25 million. The prize money added to Benning's budget funded many desired post projects.

In February 1984, a weapon exchange occurred when the post's 15th Cavalry and 2nd Battalion, 69th Armor turned in their M60A1s for the M60A3 tank. Able to fight in all conditions, the M60A3 used a laser ranging system so tank crews could determine exact ranges. "It's not an M-1

---

[15] "Officers' Club makes major changes," *Bayonet*, December 9 1983, 1.

[16] Roy Turgeon, "Fort Benning restaurants key positions," *Bayonet*, January 6 1984, 1.

[17] Bill Reynolds, "Benning program revitalized; local communities on upswing," *Bayonet*, September 9 1983, 17.

[18] Ibid.

Abrams, but I know if I can see a target, it hasn't got a chance," explained Master Gunner Clarence Woods of the 15th Cavalry.[19]

The 586th Engineer Company of the 36th Engineer Group, celebrating its forty-third year in 1984, spanned the Chattahoochee River one winter day, using twenty-two raft components to support a large bridge. Tanks of the 2nd Battalion, 69th Armor crossed successfully that afternoon. The 36th Engineer Group, reactivated in 1973, was one of the first army units to train in amphibious tactics.

Infantry School Commandant General James J. Lindsay, the second chief of infantry since the position was re-established at Benning, left in March for his assignment as commander of XVII Airborne Corps at Fort Bragg. On March 29, Major General John Foss succeeded Lindsay. Foss led the 7th Army Training Command in Germany prior to his assignment at Benning. His wife, Gloria, a native of Glasgow, Scotland, graduated from Columbus High School and Columbus Medical Center School of Nursing. The couple married at Fort Benning on April 6, 1957.[20]

Foss entered the army in 1951, enlisting as an infantryman. He received his commission from West Point in 1956. After attending the infantry officers' basic course and taking Airborne and Ranger training at Benning, he served with the Infantry School's Ranger Department. Following duty in Korea, he served as tactics instructor at West Point and taught at Sandhurst, England's Royal Military Academy. Foss was the first US exchange instructor at Sandhurst.

In June 1984, former commandant David E. Grange, Jr., returned for his retirement ceremony on Todd Field in Harmony Church. Called "the best Ranger," Grange was eighteen when he entered the army as an enlisted man in 1943.[21] He fought in World War II, Korea, and Vietnam. In 1971, he returned to Fort Benning as director of the Ranger Department, and again in 1979 to command the post until 1981. General Grange served his country forty-one years.

Bill Reynolds of Benning's Public Affairs Office described the respected general : "His uniform tells the story of his experience. He is a

---

[19] "15th Cavalry replaces aging tanks," *Bayonet*, February 17 1984, 11.

[20] "Gen. Foss eyes Fort Benning command," *Bayonet*, March 23 1984, 1.

[21] Billy Reynolds, "Army's 'Best Ranger' returns to Benning," *Bayonet*, June 29 1984, 1.

soldier who has earned the CIB with two stars, the black and gold Ranger tab, and the Master Parachutist Badge. His wings are covered with bronze stars signifying his jumps in combat."[22]

Also in June, a dedication ceremony was held for the multi-million dollar barracks for soldiers of 6th Battalion, 1st Infantry Training Brigade. The ultra-modern building in Sand Hill housed more than 1,150 soldiers. It was named for Medal of Honor recipient Sgt. John N. Holcomb, Company D, 2nd Battalion, 7th Cavalry, 1st Cavalry Division. He was killed in Vietnam after reporting the location of an enemy battalion his squad met after coming in on the "first bird."[23]

At York Field on October 3, Headquarters, 75th Infantry Regiment (Ranger) and 3rd Battalion, 75 Infantry (Ranger) were officially activated at Benning. Colonel Wayne A. Downing assumed command of the regiment and Lieutenant Colonel William C. Ohl II assumed command of the battalion. About 730 new personnel came to Benning because of the activation, 130 at regimental headquarters and 600 at 3rd Battalion. The well-attended ceremony included Secretary of the Army Marsh, who said, "The nature of conflict in the world today requires the expansion of United States special operations forces. The 75th Ranger Regiment is one of the cornerstones of that force."[24]

In December 1983, Lindsay sounded the final whistle on a Fort Benning tradition that dated back to its earliest years. After the team ended its season with a record of 9–2, the commanding general announced that Fort Benning would no longer support a post football team.[25] The $53,000 spent to support 70 or more Doughboys on the football squad did not benefit 24,000 soldiers who participated in the post athletic program. "We will, therefore, use our athletic program resources to build a better intramural program that involves all our soldiers playing on the teams (platoon or company) with which they will go to war if called upon," Lindsay said.[26]

---

[22] Ibid.

[23] "Post dedicates new ITB barracks," *Bayonet*, June 29 1984, 4.

[24] Robert Ashworth, "Ranger units activated at Benning," *Bayonet*, October 5 1984, 1.

[25] James J. Lindsay, "Post opts to cancel Doughboy football; decision aids post athletic programs," *Bayonet*, December 16 1983, 2.

[26] Ibid.

In the days before sports appeared on every television channel, Benning's football and baseball teams provided spectator sports for soldiers hungry for entertainment and diversion. The teams lived up to beliefs practiced at West Point where cadets were expected to participate in some kind of sports activity. Behind the scenes, post teams gave commanders bragging rights, sometimes to the point that particular bases wheeled and dealed to get outstanding players assigned to their particular units.

Doughboy Stadium, built in 1924 as a memorial to comrades who fell in World War I, was home to a team speckled with names familiar to football fans of their era. Dwight E. Eisenhower, a former West Point player, was an assistant coach for the Doughboys. Bill Meeks, a future head coach at Southern Methodist University and a Dallas Cowboy assistant, coached and played on the field. So did Bob Waterfield, a star quarterback of the Los Angeles Rams who perhaps is better remembered as the husband of Hollywood glamour star Jane Russell, who for a time was a Fort Benning spouse. Leeman Hall, a gun-slinging quarterback from West Point, filled its air with passes.

The 1946 Doughboys, made up of raw recruits just out of high school, won the service championship, outscoring opponents 353 to 45 in six games. Army captain Bill Meeks was coach, and his players included John Green, a member of the National Football League Hall of Fame, and Jack Stroud, who played eleven years with the New York Giants and appeared in three Pro Bowl games.

Perhaps the greatest era of Doughboy football came in the early 1960s. The 1962 team was Benning's first undefeated season, and 1963 looked even stronger. Pat Dye, an All-American guard at the University of Georgia in 1959 and 1960, was commissioned a second lieutenant upon graduating in 1962 and in January 1963 was assigned as a platoon leader to Fort Benning's 58th Infantry, 197th Infantry Brigade. Dye, along with guard Joe Wendryhoski, a University of Illinois football star, hoped to secure the Doughboy defense for the team's second consecutive undefeated season, but ended the season 5-2-1.[27] Dye—who went on to a successful coaching career at Auburn University—was selected to the *Army Times* All-Army football

---

[27] "Two Doughboys are All-Army; Wendryhoski on second team," *Bayonet*, December 20 1963, 31.

team along with Doughboy halfback Billy Williamson, a former Georgia Tech star. Wendryhoski was chosen for the All-Army second team.[28]

The 1964 Doughboy squad was invited to play in the Missile Bowl at Orlando, Florida, in the annual service football classic after defeating Fort Campbell's Screaming Eagles, 6-3. Benning's Mickey Carmack kicked two field goals, the last coming with forty-six seconds remaining in the game, leading the Big Blue squad to the victory. In the Missile Bowl, Benning defeated Fort Eustis with Dye winning the MVP award. Dye, Williamson, and tackle Greg Orth made the All-Army team. The Washington, DC, Touchdown Club selected Dye as the Armed Forces player of the year.[29]

The same month that Lindsay shut off the lights at Doughboy Stadium, Cavezza, chief of staff, left Benning to become Secretary of the Army March's executive officer. Colonel James R. Ellis, commander of the 29th Infantry Regiment replaced Cavezza.

To better utilize manpower and resources for training missions, the 29th Infantry Regiment was reorganized in December 1984. The regiment, composed of the 1st and 2nd Battalions, consolidated the Infantry Training Group, 1/29th Infantry, and weapons, gunnery and maintenance departments into an efficient, modern organization. Retired Sergeant Major Frank Plass bought what was once the 29th Infantry's mess hall where he ate while training in 1946, 1952, and 1956. Plass moved it to Ellerslie, Georgia, about sixteen miles north of Columbus, and made it into a barn. World War II buildings on post were sold for $50 apiece. Plass explained, "All you had to do was pay your $50 in Savannah and come out here and tear the building down and haul it off."[30]

On February 5, 1985, Carmouche Range, a computerized range for use by Bradley fighting vehicles, was officially opened. Foss, the commanding general, was the first to fire on the $5 million range that featured pop-up moving targets.[31]

---

[28] Dave Barun, "Dye Named Army's 1964 'Most Valuable Player'; Orth, Williamson Gain All-Army Football Berths," *Bayonet*, December 24 1964, 14.

[29] Dave Braun, "Dye selected by Touchdown Club for top grid honor, will receive Col. Joseph F. Escude Award at banquet," *Bayonet*, January 15 1965, 12.

[30] Norval Edwards, "In Harmony with the Past," *Columbus Ledger-Enquirer*, November 28 1994, A1.

[31] "CG officially opens new computerized Bradley range," *Bayonet*, February 8 1985, 7.

In April, Senator Barry Goldwater of Arizona a member of the Senate Armed Services Committee, viewed Ranger and Airborne demonstrations at Benning. He also attended a demonstration of the Bradley infantry fighting vehicle, which he came to assess. The former World War II pilot fired the Bradley's main gun and the M-60 and squad automatic weapon machine guns. After eating lunch with the 197th Infantry Brigade, Goldwater attended a COHORT (Cohesion, Operational Readiness and Training) unit's graduation. Although he saw the need to control the defense budget, he supported the Bradley, declaring, "It's a fabulous fighting weapon."[32]

In 1985, with the help of Senator Sam Nunn of Georgia and Representative William Nichols of Alabama, Goldwater worked on reorganization of the military: "Our reorganization sought to pin down a precise chain of command and the specific roles of officers in it. The chain itself was not to be altered, but it was to be much more accountable."[33] Goldwater soon found, "History and tradition were against us."[34] Eventually signed into law by President Reagan, the Goldwater-Nichols Department of Defense Reorganization Act of 1986 increased the powers of the Chairman of the Joint Chiefs and streamlined the military chain of command.[35]

Foss also addressed problems with his chain of command in an interview with a *Bayonet* reporter. He expressed a desire to overcome what he considered a detriment in the leadership of company commanders: "The weakness of many company commanders is the fact that they don't build a strong chain of command, a strong team. The company commander who runs a one-man show, who displays no faith or confidence in his subordinates will not succeed."[36]

Foss also supported the Bradley, urging men "to come forward and 'Make me Bradley Platoon leader.'"[37] Advising "a good mixture of light and mechanized infantry assignments" for a successful infantry career, he said,

---

[32] Mike Brazile, "Senator Goldwater visits Fort Benning," *Bayonet*, April 5 1985, 1.

[33] Barry M. Goldwater with Jack Casserly, *Goldwater* (New York: St. Martin's Press, 1988) 426.

[34] Ibid., 431.

[35] "Goldwater-Nichols Act," http://en.wikipedia.org/wiki/goldwater-nichols_act.

[36] Maj. Gen. John W. Foss, Fort Benning Commander, with Mike Brazile, "Post commander shares his views on leadership," *Bayonet*, October 4 1985, 2.

[37] Ibid.

"Our Army is now balancing out its light and mech forces, and officer and NCOs must be experienced enough in either light or mech if they want to be effective."[38]

In July, a Silver Wings Parachute Team member died in a tragic jump mishap before a large crowd during Fourth of July festivities.[39] Master Sergeant Clarence Faught died when his main and reserve parachutes failed to open. Soldiers from the 4th Airborne Training Battalion and Silver Wings were pallbearers at his funeral in a rural community near Birmingham. Faught, a Vietnam veteran, spent seven of his seventeen-year army career at Fort Benning as a Ranger, master parachutist, and expert infantryman. Over 200 people joined Faught's wife, Judith, and son David at a memorial service July 10 at the post's Airborne Chapel.[40]

Following the accident, the Silver Wings were grounded for three weeks. In future performances they were required to wear a new safety device that opened a reserve parachute at a certain altitude if a main parachute malfunctioned. The Silver Wings jumped from about 8,000 feet and opened main parachutes by 2,500 feet.[41] The automatic device was set to activate at 1,000 feet. Some team members expressed concern about the new device, which could malfunction, opening a reserve chute at the same time a main parachute opened. That could cause both parachutes to tangle so neither would work. Because of these concerns, Foss later ordered the use of the device stopped.[42]

The filming of *A Time for Triumph*, a made-for-television movie starring Patty Duke Austin, began on post on September 24. Actor Joe Bologna played Chuck Hasson and Austin played Concetta Hassan in the real-life story. Concetta joined the army in order to support her husband, Charles, a survivor of three heart attacks at the age of thirty-one. Concetta

---

[38] Ibid.

[39] "Independence Day activities marred by tragic death of army parachutist," *Bayonet*, July 12 1985, 1.

[40] "Fallen Silver Wing laid to rest," *Bayonet*, July 12 1985, 2.

[41] Bobbi Miller, "Silver Wings Soaring Again," *Columbus Ledger*, August 25 1985, B1.

[42] Bobbi Miller, "Silver Wings Skydivers Abandon Safety Device," *Columbus Ledger*, August 9 1985, 1.

Hassan, the oldest female warrant officer to hold a helicopter pilot's license, was on flight status during filming and acted as an adviser.[43]

In October, eighty-five soldiers of B Company, 1st Battalion, 58th Infantry, 197th Brigade began a two-week training exercise in Honduras. Cooks, medics, and an interpreter from the School of the Americas accompanied the unit, linking up with soldiers from the 16th Infantry Battalion of the Honduran army. Captain Carl Bailey, B Company commander, said the deployment was "an opportunity to prove that we are deployable worldwide."[44]

Engineers from the 43rd Engineer Battalion, 36th Engineer Group, returned from Honduras in September after building and upgrading gravel roads in support of Cabanas '85. "Rain, mud, and mosquitoes were a daily fact of life for the engineers, along with the 110 degree temperatures" at Camp Bulldog, ninety minutes by air from the nearest city.[45] The presence of American troops in Central America prompted Nicaragua, a country bordering Honduras, to charge the US with conducting a secret war by aiding rebel contra forces and mining Nicaraguan harbors. President Reagan withdrew the US from World Court proceedings in the case brought against it by Nicaragua.

In fall of 1985, the 197th Infantry Brigade received its first improved M-1 Abrams tanks. In addition, the Jeep was replaced by the high mobility multipurpose wheeled vehicle (HMMWV). Fort Benning's Infantry Board used HMMWV as a baseline for comparison with a light force vehicle, similar to a dune-buggy; and secondly, evaluated it as a "BMP [Soviet infantry fighting vehicle] Killer."[46]

In October, the 4th Airborne Training Battalion was redesignated as the 1st Battalion (Airborne), 507th Infantry, commanded by Lieutenant Colonel Leonard Scott. The 507th was activated on July 20, 1942, at Fort Benning as the Parachute Infantry Regiment. The unit saw combat in Normandy on D-Day and at the Battle of the Bulge. It later spearheaded

---

[43] Mike Brazile, "Filming of movie begins at Fort Benning Tuesday," *Bayonet*, September 20 1985, 16.

[44] Sally Toomey, "1–58th soldiers deploy for training exercise in Honduras," *Bayonet*, October 18 1985, 5.

[45] Becky Winters, "Welcome Home!" *Bayonet*, September 27 1985, 24.

[46] Mike Brazile, "Army begins replacing Jeeps with HMMWVS," *Bayonet*, October 18 1985, 10.

allied forces into Germany. At the ceremony, Secretary of the Army John Marsh said to the troops, "You are the future of the 507th. Our country needs you in a troubled world."[47]

A light infantry unit—the unit of choice in the 1980s—was created at Fort Benning when the 2nd Brigade/10th Mountain Division was activated in October. Expecting to remain on post three years, the 2nd Brigade made its temporary home at Sand Hill with the arrival of its first 100 men. More soldiers were to follow in 1986. After training together in One Station Unit Training, soldiers of the 2nd Brigade would stay together as a unit because of the COHORT concept. Fort Drum, New York, was the eventual home of the entire 10th Division.[48]

The stationing of the brigade at Fort Benning added about $30 million to the annual military payroll. The civilian payroll increased by about $4 million after Fort Benning employed 190 additional civilians. Colonel Michael Plummer, commander of the Benning brigade, spoke of the training of the light infantrymen when the unit was officially activated: "We will train leaders who will lead and fight from the front. We'll have the right soldiers who will be capable of leaving their boot prints wherever they are ordered to go."[49] Plummer, assisted in his mission by Sergeant Major Tom Cruise, proudly predicted, "We're gonna be the best damn soldiers in the Army."[50]

---

[47] Mike Brazile, "4th Airborne Training Battalion retires colors," *Bayonet*, November 1 1985, 1.

[48] Brazile, "10th Division brigade activates on post," *Bayonet*, October 11 1985, 1.

[49] Ibid.

[50] Brazile, "Commander wants only the best soldiers in new Fort Benning unit," September 27 1985, 9.

46.

Fighting for the Bradley

Though it carries one of infantry's most revered names, the Bradley infantry fighting vehicle has always carried more than its share of controversy. Defending the Bradley was one of Major General Edwin Burba's primary concerns as he rose to the position of Fort Benning's commander and chief of infantry in early 1986. Awaiting him were questions from Congress about the Bradley's future. Critics said it was "unsafe and unsuitable."[1] Senate and house members agreed to buy 720 new Bradleys in exchange for extra tests conducted by the US General Accounting Office. Elected officials wanted to confirm the vehicles' safety and capability. Burba was assistant commandant prior to becoming chief of infantry—a position he observed "is the quintessence of soldiering."[2]

Burba was an infantryman since 1959, following his graduation from West Point. Comparing infantry past and present, he said, "One is the impact of technology and how we fight.... The second big difference is the new doctrine of AirLand Battle, which is a doctrine of maneuver warfare, which we didn't have in 1959."[3] Defending Benning's new technology, especially the Infantry Center that helped design and maintain the Bradley as well as train Bradley crews, Burba argued, "You cannot have a doctrine of maneuver warfare based on mobility, agility, and firepower if you don't have the equipment to support it.... To succinctly put it, the Bradley is a winner in all field tests and computer war games. With the Bradley, our Army wins. Without the Bradley, we lose. It's as simple as that."[4]

---

[1] Mike Brazile, "Foss passes post command to Burba," *Bayonet*, January 10 1986, 1.

[2] Ibid.

[3] Maj. Gen. Edwin Burba and Mike Brazile, "New commander shares philosophy during interview," *Bayonet*, January 17 1986, 3.

[4] Ibid.

When Burba's predecessor, General John W. Foss, left to command the 82nd Airborne Division, he thanked "superiors, peers, subordinates, and friends...in helping me to make Fort Benning the good place it is."[5] Foss always praised the civilian community: "The relationship between the post and the civilian community is more open, honest, and supportive than you could find in many locations in the Army."[6] Foss explained, when the 75th Infantry (Rangers), the US Army School of Americas, and the 10th Mountain Division came to Fort Benning, "everybody had to give something up. Post support organizations were spread thinner and office and building spaces reassigned, but everybody on post responded in a favorable manner, including civilians, soldiers, and officers."[7]

With the nation in a recession, it was a period of belt-tightening. Because of the Gramm-Rudman bill passed by Congress in December 1985 calling on government to eliminate the federal deficit by 1991, sixty civilian temporary workers were laid off at Benning in March. Later in the year, eighty-seven cooks lost their jobs in reduction in force.

Brigadier General Barry McCaffrey succeeded Burba as Infantry School assistant commandant on January 14, 1986. A 1964 graduate of the US Military Academy, McCaffrey attended Ranger School at Fort Benning, receiving the Parachutist Badge and the Ranger Tab. He served with the 82nd Airborne Division, was an adviser to an Airborne battalion of the 2nd Vietnamese Airborne Division, and a company commander with B Troop, 2nd Battalion, 7th Infantry, 1st Cavalry Division in Vietnam. Burba praised McCaffrey, forty-three, as a soldier who "paid his dues."[8] Awarded the Distinguished Service Cross twice in Vietnam, McCaffrey also earned two Silver Stars and four Bronze Stars for valor as well as three Purple Hearts and the Combat Infantryman Badge. He returned to West Point in 1972 as executive of the Department of Social Sciences. Later he was with the 3rd Infantry Division (Mechanized) in Germany and served at Fort Lewis as

---

[5] Becky Winters, "Benning commander tapped to lead 82nd," *Bayonet*, January 3 1986, 3.

[6] Ibid.

[7] Ibid.

[8] "McCaffrey assumes new post duties," *Bayonet*, January 17 1986, 1.

assistant chief of staff, 9th Infantry Division and as commander, 3rd Brigade, 9th Infantry Division.[9]

In April, Secretary of the Army John O. Marsh spoke at the official dedication of the Airborne Memorial Walk at Eubanks Field. He said, "Paratroopers are just as important now as in World War II; they will be important in 1990 and in the future…. We need the airborne to support our national policy."[10] The Walk was built to honor soldiers in Airborne, glider, and troop carrier units. Bronze plaques on granite stands represented the insignias of the twenty-six paratrooper units. Red King, a member of Benning's Airborne Test Platoon and American's first enlisted paratrooper to drop over Fort Benning, attended the ceremony along with other Airborne soldiers from World War II, Korea, Vietnam, and Grenada.

When President Ronald Reagan arrived in Columbus on a thirteen-state campaign tour of the US in October, many people turned out to see him. The *Bayonet* reported, "Fort Benning played its part as host to the visit when the president's limo landed at Lawson Army Airfield complete with Secret Service crew."[11] Most thought it a privilege to see the president, but some viewed his political visit as somewhat extravagant: "When we figure the expense of the flying cars in, Air Force One, all the Secret Service people, installing special telephones and all—it was a waste of money."[12]

An audience of 5,300 was on hand at the Columbus Municipal Auditorium as Reagan campaigned for Georgia Senator Mack Mattingly's re-election. Nearly 500 people paid $100 for breakfast and a front seat at the auditorium. Prior to his speech, Reagan signed the Veterans' Benefits Improvement and Health-Care Authorization Act of 1986, a bill he planned to veto until pressure from veterans' groups changed his mind.[13] The bill provided a 1.5 percent cost-of-living increase for disabled veterans or their beneficiaries.

---

[9] Paul Timm, "New Inf. School assistant commandant comes to Benning from 9th ID," *Bayonet*, January 3 1986, 3.

[10] Mike Brazile, "Paratroopers' memorial dedicated," *Bayonet*, April 18 1986, 1.

[11] Mike Brazile, "'Out with old, in with new,'" *Bayonet*, December 31 1986, 19.

[12] H. Milton Landrum John Dagley, Rhonda Pines, and Harold Connett, "Some Couldn't Go, Some Didn't Want to," *Columbus Ledger*, October 29 1986, A-7.

[13] Russell Grantham, "Some in Reagan Camp Opposed Veterans Bill," *Columbus Ledger*, October 28 1986, B-1.

On November 25, 1986, the permanent stationing of the US Army School of the Americas at Fort Benning was recognized in a ceremony attended by Marsh and other dignitaries. Guests from Latin American countries represented at the school were in attendance as well as officials from the US government. Building 35, former site of the Infantry School, was to undergo a $12 million renovation. Major General Burba endorsed the school's permanent location, saying, "I think this is a great victory for Fort Benning. We have freedoms that they see and that they would like to aspire to obtain."[14]

A CBS *60 Minutes* crew arrived on post in January. Headed by commentator Morley Safer, the crew filmed a segment on the Bradley fighting vehicle. Soldiers from Company D, 1st Battalion, and 29th Infantry Regiment staged a live-fire exercise on Redcloud Range, pitting the BIFV against the M113 carmored personnel arrier. The Bradley "out-shot, out maneuvered and out-ran the M114 as the two tackled an obstacle course, of sorts, that was equipped with log walls, ditches, dirt berms and hay bales."[15] Safer interviewed Burba and members of the Bradley crew on camera, telling the crew, "Just try to pretend there are no officers here."[16] After filming at Redcloud, everyone went to Engineer Landing on the Chattahoochee River and watched four Bradleys enter the water, "dispelling a common misconception that the vehicle has a problem 'swimming.'"[17]

Burba, who served as assistant commander of the Infantry School from 1983 to 1986 and then became commanding general in 1986, left Fort Benning in June 1987 to command the 7th Infantry Division at Fort Ord, California. General Kenneth C. Leuer, a former Infantry School assistant commandant, succeeded Burba. Like General George C. Marshall, Leuer wanted to train soldiers to find solutions to problems that occurred in training or in battle. His expectations for his troops were high: "Every infantryman must be completely professional in his appearance and attitude, disciplined and physically fit. To be a good infantryman, he must have self-

---

[14] Mike Brazile and Laurie J. Hill, "School of the Americas on post permanently," *Bayonet*, August 8 1986, 1.

[15] Dawn Kilpatrick, "Fort Benning hosts '60 Minutes,'" *Bayonet*, January 16 1987, 1.

[16] Ibid.

[17] Ibid.

respect, pride in his uniform and country, a high sense of duty and obligation to his comrades and his superior, and a self-confidence born of demonstrated ability."[18] Leuer added, "All of us in positions of responsibility must help our soldiers and their families to grow. The health of our Army—its readiness—depends upon the health of its soldiers and their families."[19]

Sally Jean Leuer, the general's wife, described how she felt about returning: "It's very hard to be the new man on the block, no matter where you are, but I feel comfortable here because we have so many friends in the area."[20] She found more openness in young people in the 1980s, explaining, "When I was a young wife, I would never, ever, just walk up and say hello to the CG's wife. I find it exciting today because young people will walk up to you without being afraid.... Everybody loves it here. It's a youthful, beautiful post, with a history that adds to its charm."[21]

McCaffrey, Benning's assistant commander, left in December 1987 to become Deputy United States Representative to NATO in Brussels, Belgium. Colonel William W. Hartzog, nominated for his first star in July, succeeded him. Former commander of the 197th Infantry Brigade, Hartzog was at Benning since November 1985. A native of North Carolina, he was commissioned a second lieutenant upon his graduation from The Citadel in 1963, later earning a master's degree in psychology.

On September 1, 1988, Leuer reviewed Benning troops for the last time as commander after he announced his retirement August 19. At his farewell ceremony, he "urged the Army to continue the 'One Infantry Concept' he instituted."[22] He believed every infantry soldier should be trained in all aspects of infantry warfare rather than specializing in one type of duty: "We should really build the spirit of the infantry in its totality."[23]

---

[18] Becky Obert, "Leuer says hard work, dedication key to success," *Bayonet*, June 26 1987, A-3.

[19] Ibid.

[20] Becky Obert, "Benning's new 'first' lady brings grace, charm to Riverside," *Bayonet*, June 26 1987, A-3.

[21] Ibid.

[22] Kimball Perry, "'Soldier's soldier Leuer says goodbye," *Columbus Ledger-Enquirer*, September 2 1988, A-1.

[23] Ibid.

Major General Michael F. Spigelmire, fifty, succeeded Leuer, assuming the duties of commandant of the US Army Infantry School and commanding general of the US Army Infantry Center. Leuer described the post's fortieth commanding general as "a people person," adding, "He's one of our top infantry generals and this is the top infantry job."[24] Spigelmire, previously commander of the 24th Infantry Division at Fort Stewart, completed Airborne and Ranger School at Fort Benning and later served two tours in Vietnam—the first with the 1st Cavalry Division and the second as a district senior adviser. A former instructor at the Infantry School as well as deputy director for Combat Developments, he returned in the late 1970s to command the 197th Infantry Brigade.

When Spigelmire was ready to review his troops on September 21, there was a problem: his jeep didn't start. The same jeep had to be jump-started during Leuer's retirement ceremony three weeks earlier. Spigelmire remained undaunted. He "did what any good infantryman would do. He inspected his troops on foot."[25]

The pages of history continued to turn. In August, William "Red" King—the first enlisted man to officially jump as a US Army paratrooper—died at age seventy-one. King retired in 1960, lived in Columbus, and spoke at several Airborne graduations. He enjoyed telling how his "unscheduled" jump made Airborne history. William Ryder, the original test platoon leader, who had a distinguished career, joined other Airborne soldiers at King's funeral. Pallbearers were from 1st Battalion, 507th Parachute Infantry Regiment. King was buried at Fort Mitchell Cemetery—a site overlooking Lawson Airfield.

Some 2,400 soldiers from the 197th Infantry Brigade flew out of Lawson on September 5 to participate in exercises in Germany. The 197th, the largest infantry brigade in the US Army, was the only unit from Fort Benning to take part in the return of forces to Germany (REFORGER), "billed as a 'dress rehearsal' for war in Europe."[26] The unit sent over 3,000

---

[24] "Benning's ready to welcome its new commanding general," *Columbus Ledger-Enquirer*, September 21 1988, A-5.

[25] Kimball Perry, "General was ready, jeep wasn't," *Columbus Ledger-Enquirer*, September 22 1988, D-2.

[26] Kimball Perry, "Shipping out to Europe," *Columbus Ledger-Enquirer*, September 6 1988, A-3.

soldiers to Germany for a 6–8 week period. In addition, 1,000 brigade vehicles were sent to Europe, including 300 tracked vehicles. Nearly 17,000 American troops took part in REFORGER.[27]

That same year, J. D. Coleman, public affairs director for the Georgia Department of Public Safety and former information officer for the 1st Cavalry from 1963–1965, completed his book *Pleiku: the Dawn of Helicopter Warfare in Vietnam*.[28] Published twenty-five years after the air cavalry concept was put into practice at Fort Benning, his book gave a detailed account of the 1st Cav's first serious campaign. People from Columbus remembered much about the unit's organization and training at the post in the mid-1960s. Paul Stansel, one of the first area soldiers in Vietnam, said it was an exciting time: "There was a lot of money being spent on housing. There were contracts and experiments. We were forever doing things never done before or since."[29]

"There was whole new equipment," remembers Barry Henderson, who went over with a Chinook company. "We had our pick of folk, top people. There were four majors in our company. Never has any organization been better staffed. There were no maintenance or people problems."[30]

Larry Owen, a Chattahoochee Valley Community College instructor in 1988, said the city adopted them. "They sent us pizzas and sundry packs. They took care of our children and wives and this forged close family relationships. The way the wives were treated had a lot to do with why they came back here to retire. We had a lot of casualties as a result of Pleiku. It nearly wiped out Baker High School (fathers)."[31] In November 1965, there were eighty-eight "new" widows in Columbus whose husbands were members of the 1st Cav.

In his book, Coleman pointed out the "firsts" accomplished by the 1st Cav: the first time airmobility—transporting troops swiftly by helicopter—was put to the test, the first American engagement with a full-size regiment of enemy soldiers, and the first American victory of the

---

[27] Ibid.

[28] Priscilla Black Duncan, "'Pleiku': Special tale of a special unit," *Columbus Ledger-Enquirer*, October 2 1988, B7.

[29] Priscilla Black Duncan, "1st Cav changed the face of war," *Columbus Ledger-Enquirer*, October 2 1989, B-3.

[30] Ibid.

[31] Ibid.

Vietnam War.[32] The campaign also marked the takeover of the war by American soldiers, who previously were only advisers. In addition, the division was the first and only one in Vietnam to receive a Presidential Unit Citation and "was the only one to see action in all four military regions of Vietnam before it came home in March 1971."[33]

Columbus Ledger reporter Priscilla Black Duncan, whose late husband Charlie Black reported on the 1st Cav's activities, wrote: "There is little to note the once glorious 1st Cavalry Division at Fort Benning, although many of its men have retired nearby. The Harmony Church barracks are still in use, but the memorial fountain on Victory Drive is dry, rusting, and littered with trash."[34]

"Iron Mike" received better care. In November, the Follow Me statue (also called the Infantryman statue and "Iron Mike") was moved from Fort Benning to Jacksonville, Florida, for cleaning and restoration by the Atlantic Monument Company. Thoroughly "cured" of its extensive oxidation, the popular statue returned to its post in front of Building 4 where it stood guard for twenty-four years. Another famous post statue, the *Doughboy Statue*, was moved to the Noncommissioned Officers Academy, the former Faith Middle School, after standing watch for thirty years in front of Building 35. Two years older than "Iron Mike," it is a copy of the original *Doughboy Statue* in Berlin, dedicated on post in 1958.

In December, the US Army Infantry Board became part of TRADOC's new Test and Experimentation Command (TEXCOM), located at Fort Hood, Texas. With this unifying play, TEXCOM commanded nine test and experimentation boards, including the Infantry Board. Created in 1903, the Infantry Board's first home was Fort Leavenworth, Kansas, moving to Camp Benning in December 1919. Under the new organization, the Infantry Board remained at Benning until March 1991 when it left the post for Fort Hood. The mission of the Infantry Board remained the same, testing infantry organizations, analyzing training and doctrine, and perfecting the equipment used by individual soldiers.

---

[32] Priscilla Black Duncan, "'Pleiku': Special tale of a special unit," B-7.

[33] Priscilla Black Duncan, "Where are they now?" *Columbus Ledger-Enquirer*, October 2 1988, B-6.

[34] Ibid., B-3.

Wearing the star of a brigadier general, William M. Steele, a native of Atlanta, returned to Fort Benning in April as the new assistant commandant of the US Army Infantry School. He previously served as executive officer to the commanding general of the US Army Training and Doctrine Command (TRADOC). A graduate of The Citadel in 1967, Steele was at Fort Benning for many assignments. In 1989, Steele, forty-three, was ready to serve again at the familiar post.

"I'm an infantryman and I've been an infantryman for twenty-two years. My whole family is excited," Steele said. "My oldest was born in Atlanta and my youngest was born right there in Columbus. We're really excited about coming back. We consider it home."[35]

Steele succeeded Hartzog, who became director of operations for the US Southern Command at Quarry Heights, Panama, a country in turmoil under the leadership of General Manuel Noriega. Hartzog stayed on post for Spanish instructions. Because of Hartzog's support of TRADOC's SPIRIT competition, Sarah McLaney, a civilian employee, successfully guided Benning's wins in 1988 and in 1989, the only post to win the million-dollar award two years in a row. Carefully calculating and validating dollar savings at Fort Benning, she created a "can-do" atmosphere throughout the post.[36]

In October 1989, John Douglas Marshall, a former Infantry School student, returned, much more impressed than when he left there the first time. "This is no place I ever wanted to revisit," he said. "When I last left Fort Benning, it was with an immense sense of relief. I hated this place, this 'Home of the Infantry.' I counted the days until I could say farewell forever to Fort Benning."[37] When Marshall graduated from the Infantry School in 1969, his grandfather S. L. A. Marshall—famed for his military writings—gave the main speech. However, when young Marshall declared himself a conscientious objector and refused to serve in Vietnam, his grandfather renounced him. During his visit to Benning twenty years later,

---

[35] Kimball Perry, "Infantryman's return to Benning is star-studded," *Columbus Ledger-Enquirer*, April 19 1989, B1.

[36] Col. (Ret.) Burnet Quick, interview by Peggy Stelpflug, July 16 1998, Uptown Columbus GA.

[37] John Douglas Marshall, *Reconciliation Road* (Syracuse: Syracuse University Press, 1993) 106.

Marshall sat in a class in leadership taught in Infantry Hall. He wrote, "The lecture hall looks unchanged with broad risers stepping down to the stage, six lieutenants seated around each table covered with pale green linoleum, cinderblock walls painted the color of urine, faded blue drapes surrounding the stage and that perennial star of the Army educational system—the screen for the overhead projector."[38]

He was surprised at his reaction to the students: "I did not anticipate being so impressed with the lieutenants going through the Infantry School. After I became a conscientious objector, I viewed the military with suspicion and even derision for years, much as many people in the country did then.... I had been in the military. I knew the military traditions of buck-passing and ass-covering."[39] Marshall left with these thoughts: "I have felt respect for these lieutenants at Benning, their dedication, their reasoned approach to their work. If there are to be armies, then these are the kind of young leaders that armies should have."[40]

These young leaders were put to the test when more than 600 soldiers from Benning's 3rd Battalion, 75 Ranger Regiment and Headquarters, 75 Ranger Regiment, parachuted into Panama as part of "Operation Just Cause" on December 20, 1989. It was the largest combat operation since the Vietnam War.[41] In addition, the 988th Military Police Company, although not a part of "Just Cause," performed missions in support of combat operations. They arrived on December 13 as a part of a routine 128-day rotation.

Two Fort Benning Rangers, Staff Sergeant Larry R. Barnard 29, Company B, 3rd Battalion, 75 Ranger Regiment and Private First Class Roy D. Brown, 19, Company A, 3rd Battalion, 75 Ranger Regiment lost their lives. Sergeant Michael A. DeBlois, twenty-four, a soldier from Columbus, was also killed. A platoon sergeant with Company C of the 1st Airborne Battalion, 508th Infantry, Fort Bragg, DeBlois had been in Panama since June.

---

[38] Ibid., 107.

[39] Ibid., 114.

[40] Ibid., 115.

[41] Ann M. McDonald, "More than 600 Benning troops participate in 'Just Cause,'" *Bayonet*, December 29 1989, 1.

Though no longer an active soldier, a Columbus man with strong ties to Fort Benning died during this time. Maynard Ashworth, founder of the *Bayonet*, died at St. Francis Hospital in Columbus on the same day paratroopers and Rangers landed in Panama. He was ninety-five. Appropriately, he was buried with a copy of the *Bayonet*, which he helped start. Ashworth, a staunch supporter of the post since its earliest years, was publisher emeritus of the *Columbus Ledger-Enquirer*.

President George H. Bush ordered nearly 2,000 additional US troops to Panama to protect Americans from violence resulting from a disputed election. Following the successful invasion of Panama, Guillermo Endara was installed as president and ex-dictator Manuel Noriega was arrested January 3, 1990. Noriega's reputation as a drug dealer and ruthless dictator meant bad news for his alma mater—the US Army School of the Americas. The feisty ex-dictator of Panama graduated with the Class of '65 and '67 when the school was located in Panama. The school also drew criticism after the murders of a cook, her daughter, and six Jesuit priests who were critical of right-wing death squads during El Salvador's civil war.[42] They were killed at a Roman Catholic University in San Salvador in November 1989. Nineteen of the twenty-seven Salvadoran officers implicated in those killings were graduates of the US Army's School of the Americas.[43] Salvadoran officers trained at Benning were accused in other massacres during the war.[44]

In an effort to prevent such situations, the Department of Special Operations and Low Intensity Conflict was activated at the US Army School of Americas in March 1989. It emphasized the problems that terrorism, insurgency, and drug trafficking posed to Latin American allies. It was expanded to fit the needs of each Latin American country. Supporters of the school believed continued contact with Latin American armies was necessary

---

[42] Douglas Waller, "Running a 'School for Dictators,'" *Newsweek*, August 9 1993, 37.

[43] Ibid.

[44] Ibid.

to effect social and democratic values. Critics did not, and do not, agree. It is an argument debated by throngs of protesters every November on Benning Road.

47.

A Microcosm of the Army

Though it was a new year and a new decade, a soldier's life remained the same. As always, some were going and some were coming home. March 1991 was a microcosm of the decade ahead. Early that month, the first troops from Operation Desert Storm returned, greeted by post commander Major General Carmen Cavezza and General Edwin H. Burba, Jr., commander of the US Army Forces Command. Cavezza viewed Desert Storm as "a classic example of how to fight a war," believing it was fought properly with minimal casualties. Burba proclaimed, "It was a magnificent victory for our nation and the entire free world."[1]

Meanwhile, troops of the 70th Training Division were preparing to leave three months after their arrival. The 1,500-man unit made history as the first Army Reserve Training Division to mobilize at Fort Benning. Its Headquarters and Headquarters Detachment were recognized as the first reserve component headquarters to command and control six active-duty training battalions while supporting the Infantry Training Center during Operation Desert Storm.[2]

While army commanders were looking at the big picture, offering send-offs and welcomes, Roger Joyce of the 197th presented a more down-to-earth attitude when his unit came home: "The first thing I'm going to do is take a bath, get clean, and relax."[3]

During the 1990s, others shared Joyce's view. The decade began with Army Rangers returning from Panama and "Just Cause." Rangers conducted

---

[1] Jon R. Anderson, "Post welcomes returning soldiers—Desert Storm 'heroes' come home," *Bayonet*, March 15 1991, 1.

[2] Tom Hockaday, "70th Training Div. bids post farewell," *Bayonet*, March 22 1991, B1.

[3] Ibid.

two airborne assaults and captured 1,014 enemy prisoners and more than 16,000 weapons, all in a day's work for an Army Ranger. Wounded troops returned in early February, all the way from Panama to Martin Army Community Hospital. In early April, MPs from the 988th Military Police Company returned after a 120-day rotation in Panama, resuming duties on post after a 13-day leave. As other units were returning, soldiers from Company A, 43rd Engineer Battalion, 6th Engineer Group, departed for Honduras to participate in Joint Task Force Bravo in April, followed by Company C in August.

A change of command took place in June 1990 as Major General Michael F. Spigelmire, handed over his duties as commandant to Major General Carmen J. Cavezza. These two leaders previously exchanged salutes when Cavezza assumed command of the 197th Infantry Brigade from Spigelmire. Cavezza, who commanded the 7th Infantry Division in Panama during "Just Cause," also received the mantle of infantry chief. General John W. Foss, training and doctrine commander and a former CG at Benning, passed the colors of the US Army Infantry Center to Cavezza, his former chief of staff.[4]

Foss praised Spigelmire and described Spigelmire's wife, Diane, as the "epitome of an Army wife," awarding her a Department of the Army Outstanding Civilian Service Medal.[5] Ending the ceremony, Cavezza said, "There is a sign at the gate that says, 'Excellence Begins Here.' I submit the excellence is also sustained here and that Fort Benning and excellence are synonymous.... It's a great day to be in the Army at Fort Benning."[6]

Cavezza, a former commanding general of Fort Ord, California, was prepared to wear two hats at Benning, working with TRADOC and FORSCOM. While overseeing the deployment as well as the training of soldiers, Cavezza viewed Benning as a dual post, "a microcosm of what goes on in the Army every day. It all happens right here."[7]

---

[4] Ann M. McDonald, "Cavezza takes command," *Bayonet*, June 22 1990, 1.

[5] Ibid.

[6] Ibid.

[7] Maj. Gen. (Ret.) Carmen Cavezza, interview by Peggy Stelpflug, June 17 1998, Columbus Government Center, Columbus GA, handwritten transcript and audiocassette, Auburn AL.

The brief peace following the Panama conflict ended when Iraq's Saddam Hussein ordered his troops to invade Kuwait. The 197th Infantry Brigade, the largest mechanized infantry brigade in the army, received orders on August 13 to go to the Middle East as part of "Operation Desert Shield." The 197th Infantry Brigade, led by Colonel Ted Reid, deployed with the 24th Infantry Division as its round-out brigade. On August 21, 4,000 soldiers left Kelley Hill on 85 buses bound for Fort Stewart to undergo gunnery training with the 24th Infantry Division before the combined units deployed from Savannah, Fort Stewart's port of embarkation.

Consequently, soldiers from the 608th Ordnance Company, 36th Engineer Group were the first Benning troops to arrive overseas. They departed Lawson Field August 24 and arrived in the Middle East thirty-six hours later. In September, the 926th and 359th Medical Detachments, 34th Medical Battalion, left for Saudi Arabia. The 926th, the first element of Benning's 34th Medical Battalion to leave, specialized in preventative medicine. The 359th was a neurosurgical team.

Although they did not go overseas, soldiers from the 586th Engineer Battalion loaded ships bound for Saudi Arabia. They were located at the Port of Jacksonville, Florida. Personnel from Benning went temporary duty to Jacksonville where troops and civilians worked for 360 consecutive days. Later, Jacksonville civilians were hired to help load equipment and troops. Equipment included gear for chemical defense as well as camouflage suits for 6,000 soldiers, four sets each for a total of 24,000 suits.[8]

In early September, the army, unlike its policy during the Vietnam conflict, suspended separation from service, including those with critical skills or skills in short supply in the active army. Some civilians at the post left their positions, taking a cut in pay to serve in the Persian Gulf as reservists or members of the National Guard, returning to their jobs after the conflict. Benning's civilian employees contributed greatly to the Persian Gulf mission even though they faced limited promotions, reduced overtime, delayed training, and forced furloughs without pay due to the deficit reduction program.[9]

---

[8] Dale Ellis, telephone interview by Peggy Stelpflug, June 1998.

[9] Evelyn D. Harris, "Civilians brace for possible furlough," *Bayonet*, September 21 1990, 1.

On September 10, the 215th Finance Support Unit left for Saudi Arabia to provide services for commanders and soldiers, including individual pay concerns. Joining them were historians from the 44th Military History Detachment from Fort McPherson, Georgia, to ensure proper care of documents for army archives. On September 12, the Technical Supply Platoon of the 598th Maintenance Company left for Saudi Arabia. Fifty-one members of the 598th departed. Its mission was to supply class nine items, such as engines, tires, and other items necessary for large vehicle repair. On September 26, the 533rd Transportation Company and 361st Trailer Detachment, 36th Engineering Group, deployed with approximately 170 troops. The 533rd's mission was to transport ammunition, food, barriers, and sandbags. The 361st maintained trailers that loaded and unloaded equipment.

Female soldiers were deployed with the 533rd. After women did well in Panama—some were involved in fire-fights—their abilities were not questioned.[10] The only concern was how they would be perceived in Saudi Arabia, where the roles of females were dictated by a male-dominated culture. First Sergeant Bobbie J. Hollis of the 533rd said, "Our female soldiers are some of the best soldiers we have in this unit. Their morale has been at an all-time high and they are ready to move out."[11]

Women who stayed behind while their soldier husbands were deployed received advice from Trish Burba, wife of General Edwin H. Burba, Jr., former commander of the Infantry Center. She called her reminders the "Three G's" during a post visit in 1990: "Get a best friend—you have to have a friend; get out of the house—volunteering or whatever makes you happy; get in charge of the checkbook—men are always off and going somewhere, usually with short or no advance notice."[12]

On October 12, the Headquarters and Headquarters Company, 36th Engineering Group, as well as the 690th Medical Company, 498th Medical Company, 74th Medical Detachment, 5th Medical Detachment and Headquarters and Headquarters Company, all of the 34th Medical

---

[10] Alyanna B. Clay-Heard, "More Benning units deploy," *Bayonet*, September 28 1990, 1.

[11] Ibid.

[12] Paul Timm, "'3 G's advice for soldiers' wives," *Columbus Ledger-Enquirer*, March 31 1990, A-6.

Battalion, were deployed to Saudi Arabia. Shortly before Thanksgiving, the 675th Medical Dispensary Detachment, 34th Medical Battalion, left for the Mideast.

On Thanksgiving Day 1990, President George H. W. Bush and General Norman Schwarzkopf, commander of Operation Desert Shield, visited with troops of Fort Benning's 197th Infantry Brigade. Later in December, more Benning units were deployed to the Middle East. The 43rd Engineer Battalion (Combat) (Heavy) planned to build roads and airstrips. Also deploying with the 43rd were the 496th Chemical Detachment, Army Reserve, and the 317th Military History Detachment.

Reminiscent of Colonel George C. Marshall, who did not want the army to repeat the mistakes of World War I, Generals Schwarzkopf, Colin Powell, and Barry McCaffrey did not want to repeat mistakes made in Vietnam. Each had remained in the army in an effort to change things. During Desert Shield and Desert Storm, Schwarzkopf was the regional commander, Powell was chairman of the joint chiefs of staff, and McCaffrey commanded the 24th Infantry Division (Mechanized). Each had Benning connections. Powell was a student, Ranger graduate, instructor, and Infantry Board member. McCaffrey, a Ranger graduate, was assistant commandant of the Infantry School. While receiving advanced training in tactics at Benning, Schwarzkopf won the George C. Marshall Award for Excellence in Military Writing. His 1962 paper, "The Battered Helmet," was published in *Infantry*. It described Caesar's victory on the plains of Pharsalus in his battle with Pompey. In Desert Storm, Schwarzkopf used some of those same operations: "He [Caesar] had concentrated superior combat power at the decisive time and place. Above all, he had seized, retained, and exploited the initiative."[13]

In a televised address to the American people on January 16, 1991, President George H. W. Bush announced, "We have no choice but to force Saddam from Kuwait by force. We will not fail."[14] Thus began Operation Desert Storm, a massive attack on Iraq by allied military forces. By February 19, coalition forces had conducted an extensive air war against Iraqi targets.

---

[13] Capt. H. Norman Schwarzkopf, "The Battered Helmet," *Infantry* 52/4 (July/August 1962): 2.

[14] "American President: President George Herbert Walker Bush," http://www.millercenter.virginia.edu/academic/americanpresident/bush.

On February 24, the Gulf ground phase of Operation Desert Storm began. Benning troops, attached to the 24th Infantry Division (Mechanized), were in the largest US tank battle since World War II. The battle pitted "roughly 36,000 troops and 800 tanks" from the US 3rd Armored Division, the 101st Airborne Division (Air Assault) and the 24th Infantry Division (Mechanized) against the Republican Guard's Hammurabi Division, "composed of 800 tanks and about 10,000 troops."[15]

Fort Benning's 36th Combat Engineer Group and the 197th Infantry Brigade fought alongside the 24th Infantry Division (Mechanized), nicknamed the Victory Division. Writing to his troops, McCaffrey reviewed the mission to free Kuwait:

> On 24 February 1991, the 26,000 soldiers, 1,800 armored vehicles, and 6,800 wheeled vehicles of the 24th Infantry Division Combat Team and the attached 212th Field Artillery Brigade and 36th Engineer Group attacked into Iraq.... In just 100 hours of battle, you attacked 370 kilometers deep into the enemy's flank and rear...the 24th Infantry Division's attack spearheaded the ground offensive for the Allied coalition force. Our advance moved farther and faster than any other mechanized force in military history.... We must not forget our fallen comrades. Eight Victory Division soldiers were killed and thirty-six were wounded in this campaign. We will remember them with both dignity and honor.[16]

In mid-March, the 29th's Bradley crews returned, ready to drink beer and eat pork, items prohibited in Saudi Arabia.[17] The remainder of Benning's troops arrived as part of Operation Proud Return. By April, 14,065 Fort Benning soldiers had returned from Desert Storm, including the 535th Engineer Detachment that provided electrical power to patriot missile stations and to cease-fire talks in Iraq. Schwarzkopf, commander-in-chief of Operations Desert Shield and Desert Storm, described his feelings for troops who served him in Operation Desert Storm: "Through your courageous acts, your dedicated service, your determination, and love of

---

[15] Associated Press, "Saddam's best torn to tatters," *Columbus Ledger-Enquirer*, February 28 1991, 1.

[16] Paul Timm, "24th Infantry Division commander's letter describes U. S. success," *Columbus Ledger-Enquirer*, April 13 1991, A-6.

[17] Agatha Hudson James, "Heroes coming home," *Bayonet*, March 29 1991, 1.

country, you have written history in the desert sands that can never be blown away by the winds of time."[18]

Cavezza also expressed his feelings: "The Department of the Army takes great pride in honoring both military and civilians who served so effectively during Desert Storm. I take particular pride in honoring the military and civilians at Fort Benning who served and those who provided invaluable support here at home."[19] Among the hundreds of deserving civilians, Cavezza recalled Dale Ellis, the post's director of logistics: "Dale Ellis stands out in my mind as one of the truly outstanding civilian employees."[20] Considered a key player in the deployment of forces to Desert Shield and Desert Storm, Ellis arrived at Fort Benning in 1979. The Wyoming native began as chief of maintenance for the Directorate of Logistics but soon became its director. Responsible for transporting troops and equipment to the depot, Ellis helped deploy the 197th, the 36th, and the 34th Medical. Lawson Army Air Field, capable of flying C-5s and C-17s, was the principal aerial port of embarkation. "I'll never forget the feeling of pride when we put aircraft and soldiers on the ground during deployments," Ellis said.[21]

Lieutenant Colonel Russell Eno, who returned after a nine-month tour in Saudi Arabia, confirmed the job done by Ellis, his staff, and those similarly involved: "I was witness to the greatest logistical operation, in terms of moving personnel, material, weapons, in history."[22]

Once more, the army was changing, changing the way it deployed and the way it fought. At a Fort Benning conference in April 1991, army chief of staff General Carl E. Vuono said, "Gone are the times when all the infantry leader had to do was to stand at the head of a massed formation and point a

---

[18] Capt. H. Norman Schwarzkopf, "Schwarzkopf proud of Desert Storm troops," *Bayonet*, March 15 1991, A-2.

[19] Maj. Gen. (Ret.) Carmen Cavezza, "Benning salutes public service employees," *Bayonet*, May 3 1991, A-2.

[20] Cavezza interview.

[21] Dale Ellis, telephone interview by Peggy Stelpflug, June 1998.

[22] Alyanna B. Summers, "CATD officer returns from desert tour," *Bayonet*, November 22 1991, 1. Confirmed in Eno telephone interview with Peggy Stelpflug, June 1998.

sword, spear, or musket in the general direction of the enemy."[23] He urged troops to master all elements of combat power in order to win an air-land battle since they were part of "an Army that will be the smallest since the eve of World War II."[24]

At that same conference, Burba recalled the early years of the Bradley fighting vehicle as "a trail of tears...the great thing about the American system is that it works."[25] Foss agreed: "We were convinced that the Bradley was a good infantry fighting vehicle and it demonstrated that in Operation Desert Storm.... Concerns that the Bradley would not be able to withstand enemy fire or that the soldiers were not confident in its abilities proved to be unfounded through the test of combat."[26]

Cavezza also toiled for acceptance of the Bradley. After serving as Foss's chief of staff at Benning, he worked for the secretary of the army, seeing first hand the transformation of the Bradley from a personnel carrier to a fighting vehicle. He noted it was "a painful but logical progression" of a valued machine.[27]

For the third straight year, the post took top spot in the SPIRIT Award. More than 300 money-saving actions resulted in Benning saving $194.4 million. The post received the prize of $100,000. Sarah McLaney, a civilian employee, again skillfully guided the project.[28]

In May, Colonel Carl F. Ernst—on the promotion list for brigadier general—was selected as the post's next deputy commanding general, replacing Brigadier General William M. Steele, reassigned to the 8th Infantry Division in Europe. Ernst was former commander of the Battle Command Training Program at Fort Leavenworth and recently served as the deputy operations officer, Army Central Command. He served as chief of staff for the 3rd Army command post during Desert Storm and the restoration of Kuwait. The forty-seven-year-old Louisiana native was

---

[23] Gen. Carl E. Vuono, "The Army of the 1990s—Challenges of Change and Continuity," *Infantry* 81/3 (May/June 1991): 13.

[24] Ibid.

[25] Jon R. Anderson, "Major command leaders speak out," *Bayonet*, April 19 1991, A-4.

[26] Ibid.

[27] Cavezza interview.

[28] Alynna B. Clay-Heard, "Post takes top spot in SPIRIT," *Bayonet*, May 10 1991, 1.

commissioned into the army in 1966 after graduating from LSU. He later earned a master's degree at Shippensburg University in Pennsylvania. He attended Benning's officers' basic and advanced courses, as well as Airborne and Ranger schools. Ernst was chief of the Tactics Division and later, director of the Combined Arms and Tactics Department of the Infantry School.[29]

Bolstered by a decisive military victory, the post and the surrounding communities were ready to celebrate Armed Forces Day with one of the biggest parades in Columbus. Benning soldiers who had participated in Operations Desert Shield and Desert Storm proudly met cheering crowds. More than 2,000 soldiers from the 197th Infantry Brigade and 36th Engineer Group marched. *Bayonet* writer Clyde Snively voiced a concern of soldiers throughout the years: "If this parade is meant to honor soldiers, then the soldiers should sit in the bleachers and the civilians should march."[30] Snively described the parade as the "Mother of all parades," a take-off on Saddam Hussein's description of his proposed battle in the desert as the "Mother of all battles."[31]

Former secretary of the army John O. Marsh saw Desert Storm "as the first post-Cold War Conflict."[32] A guest of honor at the Officer Candidates School's fiftieth-anniversary ball held May 24 at the Columbus Ironworks Convention & Trade Center, Marsh enjoyed visiting with Cavezza, a friend who served as his executive officer in Washington. Cavezza, in turn, looked upon Marsh as a role model: "I really learned to respect the man because he loved the Army so much. He lived by example, inspiring and challenging others."[33]

In June 1991, the 197th Infantry Brigade was redesignated as the 3rd Brigade, 24th Infantry Division (Mechanized). Commanded by Colonel Ted Reid, it kept its nickname as the "Sledgehammer Brigade" and continued its mission of supporting the 11th Infantry Regiment. The change had little

---

[29] James C. Rupp, "Benning welcomes asst. commandant," *Bayonet*, May 17 1991, 1.

[30] Clyde Snively, "Mother of all Parades takes place Saturday," *Bayonet*, May 17 1991, A-2.

[31] Colin L. Powell with Joseph E. Persico, *My American Journey* (New York: Random House, 1995) 506.

[32] Brian Sutton, "500 attend OCS anniversary ball," *Bayonet*, May 31 1991, A3.

[33] Cavezza interview.

impact on Benning since less than 520 soldiers of the 5,000-troop brigade moved to Fort Stewart. During a June 14 ceremony on York Field, McCaffrey, commander of the 24th Division at Fort Stewart and former Infantry School assistant commander, declared, "I will tell you that the spirit of the 197th will live on in the 3rd Brigade."[34]

In the never-ending cycle of personnel moves, Betty Van Sickle, librarian at Donovan Technical Library for twenty-six years, retired in August, planning to read and to conduct independent research. Before coming to Benning, she was a librarian at the NCO Club Library at Fort Rucker which was near her family's Alabama farm where German prisoners worked during World War II. When Van Sickle came to Benning in 1964, she worked briefly at the main post library before moving to Donovan Library in Building 4 in December 1965. Along with John Cook, head librarian at Fort Benning's Sayres Library, she supplied books to troops during Desert Storm.

Another civilian, Willie Horace, a cook at Branch 2013 Infantry Hall Cafeteria in Building 4, retired after thirty-six years. He served as a utility man, porter, bus boy, snack bar attendant, food service worker, short-order cook, and main dinner cook.[35] Later in the year, contracting director Donald Goodroe retired after forty years of service, rising from a GS-2 clerk typist to GM-14. Raised on a farm near Columbus, he excelled in the Purchasing and Contracting Office, which increased from fifteen to seventy positions during his tenure.

On August 16, the 4th Battalion, 36th Infantry, became inactive after serving since August 1987 as one of the light infantry battalions of the Infantry Training Center. In four years the unit produced more than 12,000 qualified infantry soldiers.[36] Also during this time, the 675th Medical Detachment, 34th Medical Battalion returned after spending eight months in Saudi Arabia, replaced by its sister unit, the 676th Medical Detachment. The 10-person team treated approximately 15,000 soldiers on a sick-call

---

[34] Tom Wilkinson, "197th becomes 3rd Bde, 24th ID," *Bayonet*, June 21 1991, 1.

[35] Connie Bridges, "Cook lays down ladle after 36 years on job," *Bayonet*, September 13 1991, B1.

[36] Marilyn Balzarin, "4th Battalion, 36th Infantry becomes Inactive," *Bayonet*, August 16 1991, A1.

basis.[37] Though smaller detachments and individuals remained on the scene, the 598th of the 36th Engineer Group was the last Fort Benning unit to return from Saudi Arabia. Cavezza welcomed the unit that deployed in October 1990 and that varied from 190 men and women to 250 during its thirteen-month stay in the Gulf.[38]

Cavezza turned over command of Fort Benning to Major General Jerry A. White in a ceremony held October 4 in front of Infantry Hall. White, with thirty years of active service and two tours in Vietnam, previously served as commanding general of Fort Ord, California, and the 7th Infantry Division (Light). In his fifteen-month tour of duty, Cavezza saw Benning through Operation Desert Shield and Operation Desert Storm. He was scheduled for promotion and an assignment as commander of 1 Corps at Fort Lewis, Washington. Though the war was difficult, Cavezza said his most difficult task was the post-war reduction of the civilian work force, stating, "I hate to lose any of them."[39]

At the change of command ceremony, White said, "In the heart of each and every infantry man is the secret desire to come back to beautiful Fort Benning and to serve with the finest soldiers in the Army."[40]

Late in October, Reid handed over command of the 3rd Brigade, 24th Infantry Division to Colonel Robert J. S. Onge. Reid had commanded the Sledgehammer Brigade since October 1989. During his tenure, the 197th Infantry Brigade (Mechanized) (Separate) fought in the Persian Gulf War with the 24th Infantry Division, becoming its third brigade in June 1991.

Eloquent conservative spokesman William F. Buckley, Jr., visited the post in October. A former army officer, author, lecturer, host of TV's *Firing Line*, and editor of *National Review*, Buckley lectured students of the infantry officers' basic and advanced courses. Buckley, a graduate of Benning's Officer Candidate School, believed society needed to defend its freedoms and expressed concern about ending the war too early, a concern of many

[37] "34th med. Come home," *Bayonet*, April 19 1991, 1.

[38] "589th completes gulf tour," *Bayonet*, September 6 1991, 1.

[39] "Cavezza reflects on tour," *Bayonet*, October 4 1991, 3.

[40] Alyanna B. Summers, "Benning gets new commanding general," *Bayonet*, October 11 1991, 1.

Americans: "What we thought of as a conclusive victory appears to be less than that; Hussein is still in power."[41]

Illness became a controversial aftereffect of the Iraq conflict. Benning's health problems with troops returning from the Gulf first were noticed in November 1991. A rare disease caused by the parasite leishmania found in sand flies was discovered in twenty-two soldiers who served in the Gulf War.[42] Consequently, blood donations by Gulf veterans were halted. Martin Army Community Hospital reported no blood from soldiers who served in the Gulf since August 1, 1990, was present at its facility. Gulf War medical issues would be controversial for years to come, with some soldiers claiming they were exposed to deadly chemicals while serving in the Gulf.[43]

No one in 1991 could imagine that Fort Benning troops from another decade would put themselves in harm's way in that same desert, in search of that same elusive Saddam.

---

[41] Richard Brill, "Noted author visits post," *Bayonet*, November 8 1991, 1.

[42] J. Jan Hoffman, "Disease from Sandfly halts Gulf vets' blood donations," *Bayonet*, November 15 1991, 1.

[43] Mark S. Kalinoski, "Researchers wrestle with Gulf vets' syndrome," *Bayonet*, July 30 1993, A5; Ian Urbina, "Troops' exposure to nerve gas could have caused brain damage, scientists say," *New York Times*, May 17 2000, A18.

48.

Mother Goes to War

The uniform and the gear were that of a soldier. The eyes belonged to a mother. In combat gear, hat strapped on, Specialist 4th Class Hollie Vallance was ready for war. But in her arms was Cheyenne, her five-week-old daughter. In the Persian Gulf, the woman would be a soldier, a decorated medic. At Fort Benning that day in 1990, she was a mother tenderly saying goodbye to her baby.

Veteran *Columbus Ledger-Enquirer* photographer Allen Horne also was there, among the media marking the departure of Fort Benning's 197th Infantry Brigade to Kuwait. But first there were the clinging goodbyes. This was a scene played out in every war. Names of the battlefields change, but the faces of the young people who fight do not. Neither does the conflict on the faces of the ones left behind. Because that scene is the same, editors challenged Horne to bring back something different, something that captured that moment. Earlier that same week his colleague Lawrence Smith came away with a striking photo that made the front page in Columbus and around the country. August the 23rd was Horne's turn, and he sought something fresh and dramatic. Into the lens of his camera that day came mother and child. His photograph of Hollie and Cheyenne was only a single frame of hundreds snapped that day but that maternal moment became a lasting image that captured the difference between this war and wars of the past.[1] For this time, mother was going to war, leaving behind her baby and her husband, also a Fort Benning soldier.

Vallance signed up for the army as a high school junior in Galena, Michigan. She completed basic training then went on to college, continuing in the reserves. At the age of nineteen, she went from full-time college

---

[1] Richard Hyatt, "Allen Horne Photographs Memories," *Columbus Ledger-Enquirer*, May 31 1997, A4.

courses to active duty. Vallance married Anthony Kirk, also an army non-com, but she kept her maiden name. Cheyenne was born July 4, 1990, while her parents were stationed at Fort Benning. Less than a month later, Vallance received orders for Saudi Arabia for Operation Desert Shield.

Though Cheyenne was still a newborn, Vallance did not waver. "You chose the military. If they say you go, you go," Vallance said in an interview years after that deployment.[2] "When I found out I was going, I was prepared. I had gone in to the Army at seventeen, so my mindset was military all the way. The military came first. Besides, I had that twenty-year-old mentality that nothing was going to happen to me."[3] Those feelings of invincibility changed when on the grounds of Lawson Army Air Field she took her baby in her arms. At that moment, she was not only a soldier with duties to perform, she was a mother who loved her child. Nearby, Horne and camera were busy.

Horne learned the art of photography in the US Navy. He was assigned to an aircraft carrier where he took pictures of takeoffs and landings. If there was not a crash, he threw away the film. He rejoined the *Ledger-Enquirer* as a photographer in 1958. His assignments took him all over Georgia and Alabama, but his specialty was children. "Children show the good side of life and of the news," said Horne, who retired in 1997.[4]

"Pictures like that are just plain luck," a modest Horne said years later. "You just happen to be there. I saw it happening and I shot like crazy." His photograph of Vallance and her baby was on the front page of the *Ledger-Enquirer* the next morning and soon was transmitted around the world by the Associated Press.[5] For it, Horne won numerous awards, including the Green Eyeshade Award and the National Headliner Award. It became a two-page spread in *Life Magazine's* "Years in Pictures" and was reprinted in encyclopedias and a variety of books.[6] It even followed Vallance to war.

When Vallance and the 197th arrived at its camp near Rikyadh, the photograph was on the cover of an Arabic-language newspaper and

---

[2] Ibid.

[3] Holly Straley, telephone interview with Richard Hyatt, October 23 2002, *Columbus Ledger-Enquirer* Office, Columbus GA.

[4] Richard Hyatt, "Allen Horne Photographs & Memories," *Columbus Ledger-Enquirer*, May 31 1997, A4.

[5] Ibid.

[6] Ibid.

reproduced as a chalk drawing used as a poster for Women's History Month, a version she saw in a PX while she was still serving in the Gulf. Her mother, back home, told her the photograph was seen everywhere and soon Vallance was getting mail from schoolgirls and grandmothers alike. "My friends and I read every letter," she said; "They were touching."[7] While the photograph received worldwide distribution, Vallance's record as a soldier was not reported. She served in the desert until March 1991. As a medic with a field unit, she went forward and was part of an armored unit that took out an airport. For her service, she received the Combat Medics Badge, one of the first female soldiers to earn such an award.

Women in the Military

The man's world and the man's army began to change in 1943 with the establishment of the Women's Army Corps. President Franklin D. Roosevelt—with the support of army chief of staff George C. Marshall—signed that act into law in July 1943. With the president's signature, the Women's Army Auxiliary Corps (WAAC) was converted into the Women's Army Corps (WAC). Women, for the first time, had "pay, privileges, and protection" equal to what men received.[8] WACs, unlike WAACs were legally authorized to serve overseas with protection if captured or benefits if injured. In the coming years, female soldiers received high praise for their accomplishments in North Africa, Sicily, Italy, Great Britain, and the Pacific.[9]

Earlier, in March 1942, less than four months after Pearl Harbor, the army had 5 million troops on its rolls. Marshall knew they would need more. His goal was 8.2 million troops. With that increase in mind, the WAAC was authorized on May 14. Like the Army Nurse Corps, it was an adjunct to the army. Oveta Culp Hobby was sworn as the first WAAC on May 16, successfully organizing and directing the corps. After the war she was the

---

[7] Mick Walsh, "A Lifetime Ago," *Columbus Ledger-Enquirer*, October 24 2002, C3.

[8] "The Women's Army Corps," http://www.army.mil/cmh-pg/brochures/wac/wac.htm, 14

[9] Ibid., 16–17.

first woman to earn the Distinguished Service Medal for her work with the WAC having filled 239 types of noncombatant jobs.[10]

When World War II began, women had served at Fort Benning for more than twenty years. The first women assigned were nurses. Nearly all American women who served in the army during World War I were nurses, members of the Army Nurse Corps formed in 1901.[11] In 1921, twenty-three members of the Army Nurse Corps, all lieutenants, were part of the Camp Benning Medical Department. First Lieutenant Maude Bowman served as head nurse.

Nurses such as Major Ruth Anderson were committed to their army career. Anderson completed twenty-five years of service in the Army Nurse Corps while at Fort Benning Station Hospital in 1943. Colonel Edward A. Noyes, commanding officer of the Station Hospital, praised Anderson for her career and outstanding service.[12]

However, pin-up girls, not nurses, were regularly featured in the *Bayonet* during the early 1940s. At times, post civilian employees, selected as models, were headlined as "the Belles of Ft. Benning."[13] Sue Woodall, a cryptographer for the Signal Corps, was selected as "Chime One." She was a beauty whose vital statistics, listed in the newspaper, included a complexion "Fair as morning dew."[14] Mary Tedesco, who also worked for the Signal Corps was "Chime Two." A recent graduate of Columbus High School, Tedesco lived with her family at Fort Benning where her father served in the Infantry School. Barbara Posey was "Chime Three." A Columbus native, she was a civilian secretary in 3rd Battalion headquarters.[15]

But in March 1943, the newspaper featured women in an entirely different light. On March 5, the first WAAC unit arrived at Fort Benning. The 43rd Post Headquarters Company was composed of 135 members. First Lieutenant Evelyn A. Rothrock was the commanding officer. In June, 1st Lieutenant Gail A. Gaines succeeded Rothrock. Members of the unit worked with the 4th Service Command. An article in the *Bayonet* captured

---

[10] Ibid., 18.

[11] Tom Condon, "Corridor traces women's history in military," *Bayonet*, March 2 1984, 4.

[12] "Major Anderson completes 25 years service," *Bayonet*, May 20 1943, 9.

[13] "The Belles of Ft. Benning...Chime One," *Bayonet*, December 16 1943, 1.

[14] Ibid.

[15] Ibid.

the effect of the first women soldiers at the fort: "Main post personnel was getting back to normal again this week after having recovered from the initial shock of seeing women march around attired in GI khaki."[16] However, the WAACs were soon accepted "as just another part of the daily life at one of America's busiest posts."[17]

The 84th WAAC Post Headquarters Company commanded by Letitia Gentile followed on April 10. Three officers and 157 enlisted women were quartered in the Harmony Church area. The unit was composed of two clerical platoons and one headquarters platoon. The two clerical sections assumed duties with the Student Training Brigade. In June the 772nd WAAC Company was assigned to Lawson Field. Commanding officer of the unit was 1st Lieutenant Mary E. Herman. New barracks were built in the Lawson Field area for the company, which was attached to the Air Corps.

Many of the WAACs received their basic training at Daytona Beach, Florida, at the 2nd WAAC Training Center. They primarily trained in administration and other specialized duties. WAACs replaced soldiers in noncombatant assignments, holding clerical jobs, working at the post's theatres and service clubs, and serving as technicians in the hospital. WAACs also were on duty in the service club of the 10th Armored Division at Benning. They served as librarians, hostesses, receptionists, and clerks.[18] They also served behind the steam table in the cafeteria and at the soda fountain. Others acted as teletypers, printers, weather observers, photographers, and cooks.[19] During their free time, the women visited with friends or dated, but were back in the barracks for bed check at 10:45 P.M.

WAACs also rigged and maintained parachutes at the Benning's Parachute School. Nearly 100 women served as parachute riggers during World War II. However, unlike the men who were asked to jump with the chutes they packed, women were not allowed to jump. The WAACs did fly with paratrooper trainees, watching them jump with the chutes the women had packed. Female troops continued to arrive. Seven WAACs from Fort

---

[16] "Post Returns to Normal as WAAC Contingent Assumes Routine Duties," *Bayonet*, March 11 1943, 5.

[17] Ibid.

[18] "WAAC's on Duty in Service Club of Tenth Armoured," *Bayonet*, March 18 1943, 3.

[19] Ibid.

Des Moines, Iowa, the first to come to Benning for Officer Candidate School, came in April 1973.

When the WAC bill was signed into law in July 1943, all WAACs chose either to join the army as a member of the WAC or to return to civilian life. Lieutenant Gail A. Gaines, commanding officer of the detachment Station Complement was the first WAAC officer at Fort Benning to be sworn into the Women's Army Corps (WAC), receiving military benefits similar to enlisted men.[20]

The early WACs had varied backgrounds and education. Lucy M. Braga, a secretary at a Boston publishing company, worked on the Public Relations Staff of the Infantry School. Private Anna Jane Gray, a laboratory technician, graduated from Winthrop College. When Beatrice Strauss enlisted in 1942, she was a buyer of handmade hosiery for a New York company. In service she received training as a laboratory technician. She married Roy R. VanDusen, Jr., an instructor at the Infantry School.

Several WACs, like Strauss, married post soldiers. In August 1943, Private First Class Louise M. Martin of the 43rd WAC Detachment married Corporal Emery W. Lade in an early morning ceremony at the post Catholic Chapel. Friends of the bride and bridegroom were treated with two thirty-nine-pound wedding cakes—one at the Headquarters Company and one at the WAC Detachment.[21] After a wedding breakfast at the Ralston Hotel with their commanding officers, the newlyweds departed on their honeymoon, a five-day leave at Pine Mountain, Georgia. WACs married to soldiers were allowed to leave service when their husbands returned from their overseas assignments.

On September 9, the *Bayonet* announced the arrival of the first colored company of the WAC, three officers and twelve enlisted. These women replaced soldier personnel in the colored Reception Center at the post. By the following month, forty-four enlisted personnel, commanded by 2nd Lieutenant Lucille Mayo, joined them. Arriving from Fort Des Moines, Louisiana, the WACs became X-ray, lab, and surgical technicians at the Station Hospital, and clerks, drivers, mail clerks, and statisticians at the Reception Center.[22]

---

[20] "Lieut. Gaines 1st WAC officer sworn in here," *Bayonet*, September 2 1943, 1.
[21] "WAC-Soldier Wed at Post," *Bayonet*, August 26 1943, 2.
[22] "Colored WAC Adds Personnel," *Bayonet*, October 30 1943, 2.

By May 1944, six Women's Army Corps detachments were at Benning. At war's end, five detachments of the Women's Army Corps were on duty there. In 1945, at peak strength of about 100,000 WACs, several thousand WACs married to veterans were discharged. Women and men over thirty-eight years old could leave the army if they wished, and soon non-veteran husbands demanded the release of all married WACs. Less than 10,000 WACs remained in the army.[23] Jobs and responsibilities given women in the army changed little until the roles of women began to grow in society. As these roles for women emerged in the civilian world, they also emerged ever so slowly in the military.

In 1973, 1st Lieutenant Nancy Zizunas became one of the first female instructors ever assigned to the Infantry School. Zizunas taught race relations in the Leadership Department. In addition, Privates Diane Hinshaw and Nancy Abrams assumed duty with the 139th Military Police Company and Captain Jo Rusin became Fort Benning's first female protocol officer. The same year, Privates Joyce Kutch and Rita Johnson were the first women in the history of the US military to earn their Airborne Wings. Lemuel T. Pitts and George Ivy, pioneers in Fort Benning's original 1940 Airborne Test Platoon, pinned Airborne wings on the first two female graduates. Later Kutsch and Johnson received specialized training as parachute riggers, an option once reserved mainly for men.

By 1974, for the first time, army ROTC courses were opened to women in universities all over the country. In 1972, over 200 women were admitted to the program on a test basis conducted at 10 colleges. In 1973, enrollment was limited to 6,000. At Fort Benning, Corporals Patricia Hickerson and Theresa Netherton were the first women graduates of the infantry officers' advanced course. Netherton graduated with her husband, Corporal David Netherton, in 1973. After the WAC became a separate corps of the Regular Army in 1948, it remained part of the US Army organization until it was abolished in 1978. Women were then free to join the army and to participate in all branches except combat branches.

The roles for women in service continued to expand although the debate over a woman's role in combat continues today. That argument was raging when Hollie Vallance got her orders to the Gulf War. To her, such

---

[23] "The Women's Army Corp," http://www.army.mil/cmh-pg/brochures/wac/wac.htm, 19.

service should be a choice for women in the army. "If a woman wants that, hell yeah, but don't force them," she said. "Men make the choice of what kind of unit they join. So should women. If women choose a combat unit, that should be their choice."[24]

In the 1970s, the army adopted a policy that said married couples in service would be assigned, in the majority of cases, to locations where they could establish common households. In cases such as Kuwait, that certainly was not possible, so Vallance had to leave her husband and baby behind. That was not the only time she had to leave Cheyenne. After Kuwait, she was assigned to Korea and spent a year there without her daughter.[25] After Vallance and her first husband divorced, she married Shannon Straley, also a soldier. Their daughter, Cherokee, was three months old when Vallance got orders to Cuba. She told her superiors she would not go until Cherokee was six months old. That supposedly was the policy in 1990, but she was not aware of the regulation then: "I had friends in the Gulf who had babies younger than Cheyenne. I wasn't alone. I knew what it meant to me and to the others. But the policy was not out of sympathy. The six months was supposed to allow the new mother time to get back in shape."[26] So this time when the army gave her orders to leave, Vallance refused. That led her to leave the army in 1996 with a medical discharge.[27] Since then, she and her husband have moved to Colorado. He left the army two years after his wife and is a Colorado state trooper. Vallance completed her education at Colorado State University. She teaches agriculture at a high school near their home in Johnstown, Colorado.[28]

The *Ledger-Enquirer* gave Vallance an enlarged copy of Horne's photograph, and it still hangs in her dining room, a novelty to Cheyenne's friends. It is hard for the young people to believe that the soldier in the picture is Mrs. Straley. It's hard for her to believe, too. "That was a lifetime ago," she said.[29]

---

[24] Straley interview.

[25] Ibid.

[26] Ibid.

[27] Walsh, "A Lifetime Ago," C3.

[28] Ibid.

[29] Walsh, "A Lifetime Ago," C3.

When soldiers of another era were assigned to that same part of the world in 2002, a Columbus reporter called to get reaction to other women going to war. Hollie did not quibble, telling the newspaper reporter that she would probably go again if she were needed. Nor does she regret the years she spent in uniform. "The Army and the VA have been very good to me, all of my adult life," she said.[30] But what would she say if Cheyenne, now a teenager, came in and told her mother that she wanted to join the army as her mother did years ago? "Mom will say, 'Go to college. Go in as an officer.'"[31]

It's an answer that is no different than dads give their sons.

---

[30] Straley interview.
[31] Ibid.

49.

Proud to be a Soldier

His great-great grandfather first came to Fort Benning as an army general. John Joseph Pershing arrived a lowly private. But they shared more than a name.

John Joseph Pershing, a twenty-one-year-old private, was assigned to Company E, 1st Battalion, 38th Infantry Regiment, US Army Infantry Training Center in 1992. His family roots trace to General John Joseph "Blackjack" Pershing—a hero of World War I and of Fort Benning's early history. The younger Pershing said his National Guard drill sergeant helped him in his career choice. "I might not ever be as great of a soldier as my great-great grandfather," he admitted. "But I'm proud to be a soldier."[1]

On February 14, 1992, the $6 million renovation of the former Infantry School Headquarters, which housed the Infantry School from 1935 to 1964, was completed. In a ceremony hosted by Commandant Colonel Jose R. Feliciano, the School of the Americas (SOA) reopened its offices at Building 35 that had served as SOA headquarters since 1984. In another ceremony, the dedication of the SOA library honored the late John B. Amos, founder of American Family Life Assurance Corporation (AFLAC). Amos was one of the Columbus businessmen who supported relocation of the School of the Americas from Panama. Before his death in 1990, Amos received recognition for his business and civic accomplishments, including the Department of the Army Decoration for Distinguished Civilian Service. His wife, Elena, a native of Cuba, reminded the audience at the dedication that Amos would be pleased with this honor since his highest army rank was corporal. Senator Strom Thurmond of South Carolina, a close friend of the Amos family, was guest speaker.[2]

---

[1] Patrice Dawson, "A Pershing serves again," *Bayonet*, April 10 1992, C-1.
[2] "SOA to open new building," *Bayonet*, February 14 1992, 1.

Another attention-getting event was Major General Jerry White's acceptance of a bayonet from outer space. Lieutenant Colonel James S. Voss, an astronaut and infantry officer, carried the bayonet on his first space flight aboard the space shuttle *Atlantis* in 1991. A native of Opelika, Alabama, Voss graduated from Auburn University and attended infantry officers' basic course, the advanced infantry officers' course, and Ranger school at Benning. A veteran of 5 space flights, 201 days in space, and 4 spacewalks, Voss retired in 2003 to teach at Auburn and lecture around the United States.[3]

Fort Benning soldiers were called to all parts of the world. In spring, the 43rd Engineers went to Costa Rica as part of task force *Siempre Listo*, Always Ready, to help the country and to do jungle training in exercise *Caminos de la Paz*, Road of Peace. In addition, the 988th Military Police Company returned in May after four months in Panama. The unit of 155 soldiers maintained order in the troubled nation. Also in May, the 498th Medical Company, 34th Medical Battalion returned after a five-month deployment in Honduras and the 215th Finance Support Unit returned to the Middle East.[4]

In a downsizing following Desert Storm, the Infantry Training Center became the Infantry Training Brigade. The brigade consisted of six infantry-training battalions that trained more than 21,000 soldiers in basic military and infantry skills and administered to their health and welfare.

The US Rangers celebrated their 50th Anniversary in June with a three-day celebration that included a mass tactical parachute operation involving the entire 75th Ranger Regiment as well as dedication ceremonies for a Ranger Hall of Fame at its first induction ceremony held on Malvesti Field, located east of the ranger compound in Harmony Church. Normally used for PT and graduations, the field was dedicated the year before to the memory of Colonel Richard J. Malvesti who died in a parachuting accident at Fort Bragg. Inductees included individuals who made extraordinary contributions to the nation or to Ranger history:

---

[3] "Space traveler, army astronaut visits Fort Benning," *Bayonet*, February 21 1992, C1.

[4] Richard Brill, "498th returns," *Bayonet*, May 22 1992, 1.

PRE-WORLD WAR II
Captain Benjamin Church
Major Robert Rogers
Colonel John S. Mosby

WORLD WAR II EUROPE
Brigadier General William O. Darby
Major General James E. Rudder
Colonel Max Schneider

WORLD WAR II PACIFIC
Major General Frank D. Merrill
Colonel George A. McGee
Colonel Logan E. Weston

KOREA
Colonel Glenn M. Hall
Colonel Ralph Puckett
Sergeant Martin E. Watson

VIETNAM
Specialist 4th Class Robert D. Law
Staff Sergeant Robert J. Pruden
Staff Sergeant Laszlo Rabel

AT LARGE
Colonel Frances (Bull) Dawson
Major General Kenneth C. Leuer
Colonel Arthur D. Simons
General Richard E. Cavazos
Lieutenant General David E. Grange
Colonel Elliott P. Sydnor

In July, the US Army Physical Fitness School was relocated to Benning. Previously located at Fort Benjamin Harrison, Indiana, it offered a master fitness trainer course, a four-week class to train the trainers. With the downsizing of the army, existing personnel were required to stay in good condition and to pass the army physical fitness test administered by Louis Tomas, a research physiologist with a doctorate in sports medicine. In mid-July, the 34th Medical Battalion, at Benning since 1966, was inactivated after performing in Desert Shield and Desert Storm. Remaining units of the battalion were placed under the 36th Engineer Group. Also in July, the 63rd Engineer Company, 36th Engineer Group, was activated with 182 soldiers assigned to the unit.

Brigadier General Carl F. Ernst, deputy commanding general and assistant commandant of the US Army Infantry School, left in August for his new assignment as assistant division commander of the 82nd Airborne. Before Ernst's departure, White, the post's commanding general, offered a prediction: "This is the home of the infantry and one day, you will come home. When you do, your address will be Riverside."[5]

Former distinguished visiting professor at the School of the Americas Dr. Russell W. Ramsey, a 1957 graduate of the US Military Academy, became a permanent member of the faculty in August. Ramsey, who helped develop the counter-insurgency operations course in 1961 when the school was still in Panama, trained as a Ranger and senior parachutist and later was assigned to the 1st Air Cavalry at Fort Benning and in Vietnam.[6] Fluent in Spanish, Ramsey was developing a course in resource management to help Latin Americans adjust to a post-Cold War era. By instructing the military how to provide "equipment for development in rural areas," he said, "they can teach literacy and technical skills to youngsters, and only they can fight the drug lords."[7]

Busy in peacetime and war, the 498th Medical Company (Air Ambulance), under the command and control of the 13th Supply and Service Battalion—part of the 36th Engineer Group—deployed eighteen soldiers to Kuwait in mid-August. The 36th put out forest fires in Yellowstone National Park, dealt with Alaskan oil spills, supported Desert

---

[5] Alyanna B. Summers, "Deputy CG bids fond farewell," *Bayonet*, August 14 1992, A-3.

[6] Ibid.

[7] Daniel Maloney, "Visiting professor becomes permanent part of SOA staff," *Bayonet*, August 21 1992, B-6.

Shield and Desert Storm, and rotated to Joint Task Force, Bravo, in Honduras.[8]

The 43rd Engineer Battalion was deployed to Florida, August 31, to join reserve counterparts in cleaning up destruction left by Hurricane Andrew, a category 4 storm. The 63rd Combat Support Equipment Company accompanied the unit. The 988th Military Police also helped, staying in Goulds, Florida, north of Homestead, an area badly hit by Andrew.

In 1992, Fort Benning won first place in Training and Doctrine Command's Communities of Excellence Award for posts in the Extra Large Installation Category. Although the post won several million dollars in the TRADOC sponsored SPIRIT awards, winning as recently as 1991 (the final year of the SPIRIT program), this was Fort Benning's first time to win TRADOC's Communities of Excellence Award (ACOE). The belief in the past was that Benning was too big to win, that it was easier for smaller posts to pass inspections.[9] However, Chief of Staff Colonel Burnet (Burnie) Quick with the support of White and the expertise of Sarah McLaney, former director of the SPIRIT program, changed all that. Chosen by White to manage the post on a day-to- day basis, Quick arrived in January 1992. Quick believed the post could win in competition with other posts but when he called TRADOC to inquire about Benning's 1991 performance the observer said, "That's the worst installation in the Army." When Quick protested the harsh appraisal, the TRADOC spokesman insisted, "I'm telling you they're awful."[10]

Quick, determined to compete, asked Sarah McLaney to brief him on the SPIRIT program. Overcoming her anxiety of briefing a chief of staff or a general, McLaney was willing to explain a program she loved and to describe the people involved. After listening, Quick declared, "That's her. I want her to do my ACOE and I want her to do my quality program."[11] McLaney took on both projects in addition to her regular job. When Quick and McLaney went to see White, Quick blurted out a promise:

---

[8] "498th Medical Company deploys 18 to Kuwait," *Bayonet*, August 14 1992, 1.

[9] Col. (Ret.) Burnet Quick, interview by Peggy Stelpflug, July 16 1998, Uptown Columbus GA.

[10] Ibid.

[11] Ibid.

"General White we can win the award for the best installation in the Army," Quick said.

"You've got to be kidding," White said.

"Trust me. We can do this. All you have to do is get behind this. We could win $1.5 million, sir."

White turned to McLaney, "Can we do this, Sarah?"

"Absolutely," she said.[12]

McLaney lived in Phenix City since she was a child. A graduate of Central High School, she attended Perry Business School and worked for a Columbus insurance company before coming to Benning at age twenty-two as a GS-3 clerk-typist in the Finance and Accounting Office of the Directorate of Resource Management.[13]

"My friends said, 'You don't need to go out there and work with those soldiers. You're making a big mistake,'" recalled McLaney, "but I already had a friend who worked there and she encouraged me to come. Besides, the pay was much more than downtown."[14]

When Quick and McLaney went to work to win the ACOE. They drove all about the post, walked through every building and met with every organization. Preparing everybody on what to expect from investigating team members, they told them to say, "Welcome!" and encouraged them to believe in what they were doing and to think that they were the best. A woman at a post day care center announced to her team visitor, "I want you to come in and see our child care facility. We take care of America's greatest resources—our children."[15] Her words moved Quick. "If that doesn't put a tingle in your heart, nothing will."[16]

In June, Total Army Quality (TAQ) merged with the Army Communities of Excellence (ACOE) Program. Designed to streamline the army's quality effort, it met criticism. McLaney recalled having to brief General White for the first time about the ACOE:

---

[12] Sarah McLaney, interview by Peggy Stelpflug, December 11 1998, Building 66, Fort Benning GA.

[13] Ibid.

[14] Ibid.

[15] Ibid.

[16] Quick interview.

I was scared to death. I had been going all over the post trying to sell the program, but he had a room full of people who didn't want to do it. General White must have liked the talk because he banged his fist on the conference table and said, "You will support this lady and you will do this. Do you hear me?" The support was soon there. You cannot do the program without support, and we have had support at Fort Benning, beginning with Colonel Quick and General White. We became a winner with General White and Colonel Quick.[17]

Another one of Quick's duties as chief of staff was to supervise a contract to tear down World War II wooden buildings and get them off the books. Selling wood from them was not very successful because of the asbestos lining. Quick recalled,

We decided then we wanted to save some, but we didn't have the money to move them, so we asked the Department of Defense if we moved them to a new spot would that get them off the books. Otherwise, it was necessary to maintain them and that meant expensive paint and repair. They said yes. So we saved a World War II barracks, an orderly room, a supply room, a mess hall, and we had Patton's headquarters, including his small sleeping quarters behind it, all part of Patton's legacy from his days spent training the 2nd Armored Division at Fort Benning in World War II.[18]

Quick and White wanted to preserve at least a street of "old Fort Benning." They relocated the historic buildings to a spot near the National Infantry Museum. "Old folks, like me, who went to ROTC summer camp and helped keep fire watch on the buildings' coal-burning furnaces—and some even older—can go back out there and say, 'Oh, yeah, I slept in a barracks just like that,'" Quick said. "Those buildings took a lot of wear. There are a lot of soldiers who trained for war in those buildings during the years. But they're gone. History."[19]

As the year ended, Benning soldiers joined United Nations troops in Operation Restore Hope, an operation ordained by President George H. W. Bush in his last days in office. The UN force arrived in Somalia in early December to ensure the delivery of food to starving people caught in the

---

[17] McLaney interview.
[18] Quick interview.
[19] Ibid.

middle of warring Somali factions. At the end of 1992, troops from the 36th Engineer Group prepared to join this mission.

But peace soon turned to war.

50.

Death in Somalia

Six pairs of spit-shined combat boots and six black berets were on the stage atop M-16 rifles. It was a moment to remember six Fort Benning Rangers. Six were dead, killed in a conflict that began with efforts to feed a hungry people.

That peaceful effort to bring food to those who needed it brought Private Wilson Hoffer to Somalia. He was serving with the 36th Engineer Group, commanded by Colonel Phillip R. Anderson. They left Fort Benning in January 1993. That was what he described in a letter to his family back home. Hoffer's job was to sweep the roadways for mines. "Helping people is what it's all about," he wrote.[1]

Plans to help turned into a fight for survival, leading to that respectful ceremony in October. Hostile forces in Mogadishu, Somalia, killed six American soldiers. The deaths of the six Rangers marked the post's largest loss of life in combat since Vietnam.[2]

Though the year ended on a somber note, it began with a celebration. In April 1993, Fort Benning won the Chief of Staff of Army Award and Best Installation in the Continental United States, Large Category, with a prize of $1 million. Benning edged out Fort Sill, Oklahoma, and Fort Lewis, Washington. Organization and hard work by Jerry White, Burnie Quick, and Sarah McLaney created an all-post effort. It brought not only honor but also money for improvements, resulting in a better quality of life for post personnel. The win also fulfilled the ambition of Brigadier General Briant

---

[1] MSgt. Diana G. Willis, "36th soldiers send Valentine's greetings from Somalia," *Bayonet*, February 12 1993, A-2; Tom Wilkinson, "36th 'Sweeps' clean," *Bayonet*, February 12 1993, B-5.

[2] Clint Claybrook and Timothy Rogers, "Benning salutes fallen Rangers," *Columbus Ledger-Enquirer*, October 9 1993, A-1.

H. Wells, an early Infantry School commandant, who predicted Fort Benning would be known as "one of the finest posts in the Army."[3]

In May, Benning leaders attended the Army Chief of Staff Communities of Excellence Awards ceremony at the Pentagon, receiving a trophy, an ACOE flag, and $1 million. In addition, Fort Benning was recognized for winning Best Civilian Personnel Services and Best Military Personnel Services—an extra $50,000 for each. McLaney, Fort Benning's Communities of Excellence coordinator, said, "More important than the money that comes with winning the COE award is making our military community an excellent place to live, work, and play."[4]

Benning also took first place in the Training and Doctrine Command (TRADOC) extra-large installation category, repeating its 1992 accomplishment. In addition, eight Benning activities were first-place winners in the extra-large installation category, the best in TRADOC. After those victories, post leaders decided to compete for another Army Community of Excellence title, hoping to win the Commander-in-Chief (CINC) Award for the best army installation in the world and its $1.5 million cash award.

For Fort Benning Rangers, it was a time for a change of command when Colonel James T. Jackson, who served as commander of the 3rd Battalion, 75th Ranger Regiment in 1991, assumed the duties of Ranger commander. In the higher echelons, Brigadier General Jack P. Nix, Jr., former assistant division commander for operations of the 82nd Airborne Division, succeeded Brigadier General John Hendrix as deputy commanding general and assistant commandant of the Infantry School in July. Nix was a native of Gainesville, Georgia, and a graduate of Georgia Tech. Hendrix's new duty was as deputy chief of staff for operations, US Army Europe.

It was also time for an old friend to visit. Lieutenant General (Ret.) David E. Grange, Jr., former Benning commander and 1993 Doughboy Award Winner, was present when his son Colonel David L. Grange ended his tour as commander of the 75th Ranger Regiment on post in July 1993. At his farewell ceremony, Grange called his men a "tough and dependable band of brothers" and declared his tour, "the greatest years of soldering that

---

[3] LeRoy Yarborough in collaboration with Truman Smith, *A History of the Infantry School, Fort Benning, Georgia* (Ft. Benning: The Infantry School, 1931) 184.

[4] Ruth J. Spaller, "Post to try for World's Best," *Bayonet*, August 2 1993, A-1.

I have ever experienced."[5] He thanked his mother and his father for the standards they gave him. His wife, Holly, present with the couple's two sons, David and Matthew, was honored with a humanitarian service award for her work with soldiers and their families.[6]

Military Funds Cut

With the conclusion of Desert Storm, the demise of the Soviet Union, and the waning influence of Russia, the Clinton administration reduced military funding. To save money, post commander Jerry White made an agreement with Georgia Power Company to curtail energy use during hours when demand was the greatest. The post was the fourth-largest user of electricity in southwest Georgia and twelfth largest in the state. Although not without problems and complaints, the agreement produced saving of more than $1 million for the post. The post was able to save time and money when new arrivals were given a more efficient way to sign up with utility companies. The plan was to build a utility center on post hosted by utility companies at their own expense.[7]

As commanding general, White also made it a point to be active in civilian activities believing it a key to his success. White credited a little known group whose members met monthly in "a little hut in the woods to barbecue steaks, have a social hour, and sit there with their sleeves rolled up. You can't go unless you're a CEO. You can't send a representative." White, chief of the infantry and head of the Infantry School, also acted as post CEO and mayor of Fort Benning. "Of things that I was able to accomplish at Fort Benning," White said, "I credit to that group and that relationship I had."[8] Frank Lumpkin, Jr., a Columbus businessman and staunch Fort Benning supporter corroborated White's popularity. Asked if he thought there were other Benning commandants comparable to George Marshall or Omar

---

[5] Connie Bridges, "75th Regt: Rangers get new leader," *Bayonet*, July 30 1993, A-1.

[6] Ibid.

[7] William Riley Hall, "Post turns off air to save $$$," *Bayonet*, July 30 1993, 1; Maj. Gen. (Ret.) Jerry A. White, interview by Peggy Stelpflug, June 3 1998, United Way Office, Columbus GA.

[8] Ibid.

Bradley, he replied, "The one that's in there now [White] is doing a good job."[9]

As chief of infantry, White examined new technology for use in training or testing at the post such as the Javelin missile. Sergeant Anthony Morish, Company B, 1st Battalion, 29th Infantry Regiment, was chosen to shoulder-fire the Javelin missile at a moving T-72 tank.[10] Morish wanted "to be the first" to fire the Javelin. "I found out it works," he said. "I'll be on a high horse for awhile."[11] The Javelin, unlike the old anti-tank weapons that were wire-guided or short-range direct-fire systems, had a self-guiding imaging infrared (IIR) seeker.

"I can envision a soldier riding in a helicopter or in the back of a Bradley, plugged into the side of the vehicle with a video screen in front, providing him enemy information, friendly information, or tell exactly where he is and his orders," White mused. "As he dismounts the helicopter or Bradley, he will unplug and the information he saw before will light upon his visor. The soldier, able to transmit data, will be a complete system fully compatible with other systems on the battlefield."[12]

Preparing for the twenty-first century with new technology and doctrine, White also supported the Dismounted Warfighting Battle Lab that enabled the army in times of tight resources to get modern equipment to the soldiers at less cost and in less time. "Owning the Night" was the first battle lab project tasked by the Department of the Army and included testing combinations of various night vision devices and lasers.

By late summer 1993, the situation in Somalia grew more serious with the deaths of twenty-four Pakistani soldiers ambushed by Somali clan leader Mohamed Farah Aidid. Four Americans were killed by a land mine in August. Commander Lieutenant Colonel Murray J. Rupert wrote from Sword Base, Somalia: "We are hopeful that the United Nations will get Aidid under control in the near future so that life here can get back to

---

[9] Frank G. Lumpkin, Jr., interview by Peggy Stelpflug, spring 1994, Columbus GA.

[10] Sanford E. Parr, "Benning soldier first to shoulder-fire Javelin," *Bayonet*, August 13 1993 C-2.

[11] Ibid.

[12] Benning looks to quality future," *Bayonet*, October 8 1993, A-2.

normal."[13] Close to 460 members of the 13th Corps Support Battalion, 36th Engineer Group, deployed for a six-month rotation to Somalia to provide combat service support operations to the UN forces. By mid-August, 4,000 US troops were in Somalia with 24,000 peacekeepers, all involved in a mission now considered more dangerous.[14]

Elements of the 3rd Battalion, 75th Ranger Regiment were alerted for deployment to Somalia by President Clinton because of the escalating violence against UN forces in South Mogadishu, a decision recommended by Chairman of the Joint Chiefs of Staff General Colin Powell and Secretary of Defense Les Aspin.[15] A 400-soldier task force of Rangers and support personnel under Lieutenant Colonel Danny McKnight, 3rd Battalion, 75th Ranger Regiment commander, left Benning in late August to reinforce the Quick Reaction Force from the 10th Mountain Division. This was "the longest deployment for the Rangers since the Vietnam War."[16]

In late September, elements of 317th Engineer Battalion and other units of the 3rd Brigade, 24th Infantry Division (Mechanized), commanded by Lieutenant Colonel Kenneth S. Kasprisin, participated in a standard rotation deployment of troops to Somalia to provide combat and logistics support. The deployment included M-113 armored personnel carriers, utility trucks with trailers, earth-movers, and other engineer equipment.[17]

As the search for Aidid continued, Major General Tom Montgomery, US commander in Somalia, requested tanks and armored vehicles to protect supply convoys. Although Powell supported Montgomery's request, Aspin—believing former president Jimmy Carter was negotiating a US withdrawal from Somalia with Aidid—tabled the request, hoping to contain the problem rather than escalate it.[18]

---

[13] Lt. Col. Murray J. Rupert, "Somaliagram: 13th CSB settling in," *Bayonet*, August 27 1993, A-2.

[14] Associated Press, "Elite Army force heads to Somalia," *Montgomery Advertiser*, August 25 1993, 3A.

[15] Colin Powell with Joseph E. Persico, *My American Journey* (New York: Random House, 1995) 584.

[16] William Riley Hall, "Rangers to return," *Bayonet*, October 22 1993, A-1.

[17] Ruth J. Spaller, "Somalia Bound Engineers Deploy," *Bayonet*, October 1 1993, 1.

[18] Sidney Blumenthal, "Why Are We in Somalia?" *New Yorker*, October 25 1993, 48; "Aspin defends decision," *Montgomery Advertiser*, October 8 1999, A9.

A forty-man combat engineer platoon from 3rd Brigade, 24th Infantry Division, also departed for Somalia to provide combat and logistics support capabilities for the relief effort. Made up of elements of the 317th Engineer Battalion and other units of the 3rd Brigade, 24th Infantry Division (Mechanized), the unit left for Somalia at the end of September on a standard rotation deployment. On October 3, Rangers captured Aidid's top leaders, who were meeting near the Olympic Hotel in Mogadishu. Rangers dropped from four MH-60 Blackhawks and surrounded the hotel. McKnight and Delta Commander Major General William F. Garrison's task force, "led a twelve-vehicle convoy of three five-ton trucks and nine Humvees manned by over fifty Rangers, tasked to pick up and extract the raiders and detainees by ground."[19] After the Deltas secured their twenty-four prisoners, McKnight's ground convoy headed toward the secured target. During this time, the Somali National Alliance (SNA) began shooting, and a rocket-propelled grenade (RPG) hit a Blackhawk helicopter.

Staff Sergeant Edward Yurek, a squad leader in Company B of the 3rd Battalion, saw the chopper crash-land in an alley. As Somali crowds moved in, Yurek said, "We had to fight our way to it."[20] Yurek and Staff Sergeant Derrick W. Van Vugt, another squad leader in 2nd Platoon, Company B, and others, rescued the two chiefs and protected the bodies of the two pilots killed in the crash. Yurek, whose squad suffered no injuries, explained, "Tactically, by the numbers, maybe that doesn't make sense, but to us...he was our friend. He would have given his life for us, so we weren't going to leave him."[21]

McKnight, with the captives and wounded Rangers in his trucks, attempted to move his vehicles to the downed aircraft, but Garrison ordered McKnight to deliver the prisoners to the airfield. McKnight obeyed, fulfilling the mission but forcing him to leave his men fighting in the streets.[22]

---

[19] Daniel P. Bolger, *Savage Peace: Americans at War in the 1990s* (Novato CA: Presidio, 1995) 315.

[20] Ruth J. Spaller, "Combat," *Bayonet*, November 12 1993, A-1.

[21] Ibid.

[22] Daniel P. Bolger, *Savage Peace: Americans at War in the 1990s* (Novata CA: Presidio, 1995) 319.

An RPG hit another MH-60 helicopter about two miles from the Olympic Hotel. One of the men aboard, Chief Warrant Officer Michael Durant, later a captive, was kept alive by two Delta snipers, Master Sergeant Gary L. Gordon and Sergeant First Class Randall D. Shugart. Gordon and Shugart were awarded the Medal of Honor posthumously, "the first such honors accorded since the Vietnam War."[23]

Trying to organize a rescue team, Lieutenant Colonel William David, commander of 214th Infantry, 10th Mountain Division, called on UN allies, who were not informed earlier of the US plan to capture Aidid's leaders. Italy, Pakistan, and Malaysia offered tanks and armored cars. Members of the Delta unit—Major James Nixon, Jon Macejunas, Matt Rierson, and Chuck Esswein—led the columns of the rescue convoy.[24] During the sixteen-hour battle, six Benning Rangers gave their lives while forming a defensive perimeter around the injured helicopter crew. The Rangers who died were members of B Company: Sergeant James C. Joyce, Corporal James M. Cavaco, Sergeant Lorenzo M. Ruis, Corporal James E. Smith, Sergeant Dominick M. Pilla, and Specialist Richard W. Kowalewski Jr. Their deaths fell on the ninth anniversary of the 3rd Ranger Battalion, 75th Ranger Regiment, activated at Fort Benning on October 3, 1984.

US Senator Sam Nunn, D-Georgia, saw no US strategic interest in Somalia: "The Senate and the House ought to narrow that mission so that we have a definite ending point. I don't think capturing one person is going to end this."[25] On October 7, President Clinton announced that reinforcements, including several hundred fresh troops, heavy tanks, armed personnel carriers, helicopters, and gunships would be sent to ensure a safe withdrawal of US troops by March 31, 1994. Other UN contingents followed Clinton's policy. Aidid declared a cease-fire on October 9 and soon released Chief Warrant Officer Michael Durant.[26]

Eighteen servicemen died in battle, and eighty-four were wounded. There were hundreds of Somali casualties. As pictures of dead American

---

[23] Bolger, *Savage Peace: Americans at War in the 1990s*, 324.

[24] Mark Bowden, *Black Hawk Down* (New York: Atlantic Monthly Press, 1999) 272.

[25] Associated Press, "Nunn calls for definite end point of U.S. mission in Somalia," *Columbus Ledger-Enquirer*, September 27 1993, A-3.

[26] Bolger, *Savage Peace: Americans at War in the 1990s*, 327.

servicemen being dragged through the streets of Mogadishu were televised in the United States, the mission to help the people of Somalia paled, losing most of its supporters. On October 8, the wounded soldiers arrived at Martin Army Community Hospital. They were taken to a special ward on the fifth floor that was decorated for the occasion by wives from the 75th Ranger Regiment.[27] Many wives and family members of the wounded were already in the hospital, waiting for the soldiers before they arrived.[28] Nine wounded soldiers were released shortly after arrival at the hospital. Columbus businesses provided the wounded returning from Somalia with restaurant meals, games, magazines and other supplies.[29]

Eleven wounded Rangers from the 3rd Battalion received the Purple Heart. US Army chief of staff General Gordon R. Sullivan, presented the medals to the young soldiers. Larry Moores, a 1991 graduate of Benning's OCS and a member of the 3rd Battalion, received a Silver Star. He made two trips in a Humvee to help fallen soldiers, recalling, "It just seemed like it took forever to get the (rescue) mission going."[30]

Flights carrying more than 100 Rangers from Fort Benning's 3rd Battalion, 75th Ranger Regiment, landed at Lawson on October 22 from Mogadishu. Another 131 followed. Approximately 400 Rangers of the 600-member task force returned. While awaiting the arrival of her husband and his troops, Barbara McKnight declared, "They're our heroes...."[31] Deputy Secretary of Defense William J. Perry (who soon replaced Aspin) was at the airfield. Referring to their "difficult mission," Perry said, "All Americans are grateful for your courage and your service to our country."[32]

As contemporary history was being made, past history was being celebrated. Fort Benning's Diamond Jubilee anniversary began October 7 with a wreath-laying ceremony at the grave of General Henry Lewis Benning in Linwood Cemetery, near downtown Columbus. In addition, a

---

[27] Harry Franklin, "Wounded Rangers arrive at Benning hospital," *Columbus Ledger-Enquirer*, October 9 1993, A-1.

[28] Ibid.

[29] Ibid., A-1, A-5.

[30] Heidi Fedak, "Decorated Ranger recalls Somalia raid that went awry," *Benning Leader*, March 1 1996, 3.

[31] William Riley Hall, "Rangers to Return," *Bayonet*, October 22, 1994, 1.

[32] Ruth J. Spaller, "Benning welcomes Rangers," *Bayonet*, October 15 1993, 1.

historic marker was unveiled at a triangular part at the corner of Dixon and Macon Road in Columbus, marking the original site of Camp Benning.

Colonel Burnie Quick and Columbus mayor Frank Martin cut Fort Benning's seventy-fifth birthday cake on Broadway in Columbus during the city's Uptown Jam. Exhibits and demonstrations included the Silver Wings, Ranger hand-to-hand combat, K-9 demonstrations, the infantry band, and the infantry chorus.[33] Quick thought it appropriate to begin the celebration of Fort Benning's seventy-fifth birthday in Columbus (rather than on post) because it was the Columbus Chamber of Commerce that seventy-five years before asked the War Department to locate the School of Infantry in the area. Many graduates of the school and post now called Columbus "home." In 1993, approximately 9,900 former service members trained at the expense of the Department of Defense lived in the Columbus area.[34] Retirees were valued in the surrounding civilian work force and the economy.

For the seventy-fifth anniversary, Senator Nunn wrote,

> The secret of Fort Benning's success is that it has never stood still—it is dedicated to ensuring that American infantry soldiers will always be the best trained and equipped soldiers on any battlefield at any time.... Soldiers at Fort Benning are more than visitors in Georgia—they are friends and neighbors. Active duty and retired, they are the foundation of much of the life of our schools, our churches, our businesses and our civic affairs.... Make no mistake about it—for as long as there are those in the world who would challenge our freedom, there will be a US Army. And as long as there is an Army, there will be a Fort Benning.[35]

White agreed. He said, "Fort Benning will have bumps in the road and ups and downs, but Fort Benning will be here long after I'm gone." He also saw the continuing need of the soldier: "History has taught us that no one

---

[33] Ruth J. Spaller, "Diamond Jubilee: Celebration begins with wreath laying," *Bayonet*, October 15 1993, 1.

[34] Linda Bosley Dailey, "Retirees a valuable asset to community," *Benning Leader*, October 1 1993, 70.

[35] Sam Nunn, "Thanks, Home of the Infantry," Benning Leader, October 1 1993, 2.

ever really owns a piece of terrain until some infantry soldiers stood on it. This hasn't changed, and never will."[36]

Those who supported the soldiers' mission received recognition. At the quarterly Excellence Appreciation Day Breakfast at the Officers' Club in December, more than 100 Fort Benning employees and soldiers were honored, receiving paperweights engraved with "Quality Employee."[37] Dale Ellis, director of logistics, received a special commendation from General Wayne A. Downing, commander-in-chief, US Special Operations Command, and General Dennis J. E. Reimer, commander, Forces Command. Ellis and his staff were cited for "providing excellent support to soldiers."[38]

"That was the most successful thing we had done," Sarah McLaney recalled. "They [honored employees] would dress up in their best clothes and tell others. 'I'm getting my picture taken with the general.' The personal recognition helped sell the quality program. People like to be told they have done a good job. We didn't have a lot of money to give cash awards, so we had to recognize people to let them know."[39] No one thought McLaney could persuade an army general to participate in such a ceremony. McLaney explained, "When we started this, people said, 'Sarah, you'll never get a two-star general to stand up there. His time is too precious and his calendar is too crowded,' but General White said, 'Yeah, we'll do it.' At the first breakfast, I told him, 'We appreciate your time.' He replied, 'Sarah, it's worth every minute of it.'"[40]

With the holidays near, soldiers still in Somalia wanted to be home. Nearly 500 members of the 43rd Engineer Battalion and 13th Corps Support Battalion returned in mid-December.[41] Soldiers from the 36th Engineer Group made it three days before Christmas. Fifty members of the

---

[36] Connie Bridges, "Benning looks to quality future," *Bayonet*, 75th Anniversary Commemorative, October 8 1993, A-2.

[37] The practice of showing appreciation and recognition to post personnel began in 1992 when Quick awarded small paperweights with the letter Q for "quality employee."

[38] Cynthia Cheatham, "Post honors employees," *Bayonet*, December 17 1993, 1.

[39] Sarah McLaney, interview by Peggy Stelpflug, December 11 1998, Building 66, Fort Benning GA.

[40] Ibid.

[41] "Engineers to be home for the holidays," *Bayonet*, December 17 1993, 1.

608th Ordnance Company, 13th Corps Support Battalion, the last Fort Benning soldiers to leave Somalia, returned in March 1994. More than 1,500 Fort Benning soldiers served in Somalia during 1993–1994.[42] Over sixty served two tours of duty. Private First Class Michael Hogue of the 608th summed up the feeling of coming home from Somalia, "When I left (Fort Benning) I hated this place.... Now I'll never complain about it again."[43]

---

[42] Ibid.

[43] Ruth J. Spaller, "608th comes home," *Bayonet*, March 25 1994, A-3.

President Harry Truman laughs over an article in the *Columbus Ledger* during his 1950 visit to Columbus and Fort Benning.

Infantry Officer Candidate School students "enjoy" a square meal in the 1950s. OCS, reopened at Fort Benning in February 1951, was renamed First Officer Candidate Battalion, Second Student Regiment.

Eben Reid (left) Columbus Mayor Lawrence Shields, Major General Guy S. Meloy Jr., Dupont Kirven Sr. and Frank Kirven celebrate Fort Benning's 35th birthday, October 1953.

Friends gather at the Fifth Avenue YMCA-USO in November 1955: (L-R) Larry Horres, Eddie Bell Zonner, Louise Bynum and James E. Proctor.

Personnel at Out Post No.1 wave goodbye to Major General Joseph H. Harper, Infantry School commandant 1954-1956, as he leaves the post in May 1956.

Unveiled on April 1, 1958, on the 40th Anniversary of Fort Benning, the Doughboy Statue, a WWII soldier, stands at parade rest with his M-1 rifle in front of Building 35, the U.S. Army Infantry School. The German sculptor Ernst Kunst used Staff Sergeant Thomas E. Love as his model. The monument is a tribute to the American infantryman.

(L-R) I. Wallace, club host; Roena Blanton, volunteer service organization; Master Sergeant William Roberts, outstanding G.I for 1960; Mrs. Gordon H. Kitclong, Sr., hostess; and Ruby Washington, Miss USO 1960, meet at the 5th Avenue YMCA-USO.

Major General Harry W. O. Kinnard, commander of the 1st Cavalry Division Airmobile. talks with Mrs. Ben Dorcy, "mother of the 1st Cavalry," who designed its yellow and black patch in 1921. Her husband was a former 7th Cavalry commander.

On July 3, 1965, the colors of the 11th Air Assault Division were retired and its personnel along with members of the 2nd Infantry Division were transferred to the 1st Cavalry Division Airmobile. Over 10,000 civilian and military guests attended the ceremony. Later, on August 18, 1965, the unit held its farewell review before its deployment to the Republic of Vietnam.

Charlie Black, a Columbus reporter, gets his story. Adopted by troops of the Air Cav, Black spent time with the unit at Fort Benning and later in Viet Nam, keeping civilian and military families informed of their loved ones.

People gather in downtown Columbus to celebrate Fort Benning's 50th Anniversary in 1968. The float honors Columbus papers and Fort Benning's *Bayonet*.

Lieutenant William Calley (left), on trial for the My Lai incident, is assisted by military police when leaving the post stockade on March 30, 1971.

Major General Kenneth C. Leuer, Fort Benning commander from 1987–1988, speaks at a training exercise at Fort Benning, Georgia. In 1973-1974, Leuer organized the first Ranger Battalion since World War II.

Ina Balin (left) and Betty Tisdale comfort Vietnamese children brought to Fort Benning from Vietnam with the Tisdales' help in April 1975.

Vietnamese orphans (L-R) Vu-Tien Thong and Nguyen Mong Hoang stand at Wilbur School, April 13, 1975, the morning after their arrival on post.

Museum director Dick Grube (left) assists General of the Army Omar Bradley at the dedication of the National Infantry Museum, Building 396, on July 1, 1977. General Bradley gave his 5-star insignia to Grube to decorate Bradley's displayed uniform jacket.

Major General David E. Grange, Jr., commanding general, United States Army Infantry Center, Fort Benning, Georgia 1979-1981. poses for Army photographer Sergeant First Class Richard C. Maehr, Jr. on July 24, 1979.

Specialist 4 Hollie Vallance says goodbye to her 7-week old daughter Cheyenne and to her husband Anthony Kirk as she prepares to leave for Kuwait in August 1990 to support the U.S. role in the Persian Gulf crisis. The picture taken by Allen Horne, *Columbus Ledger-Enquirer* photographer, appeared in several publications throughout the country.

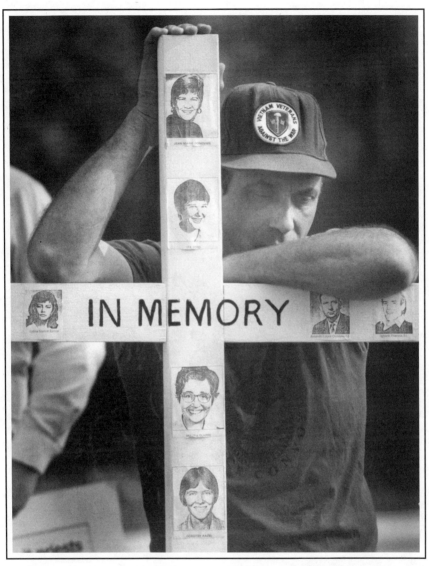

In November 1991, Louis DeBenedette, a member of Vietnam Veterans Against the War in El Salvador, joined protesters on the anniversary of the deaths of El Salvadoran priests and nuns. The group objected to the training of Salvadoran soldiers at the School of the Americas at Fort Benning.

General Colin Powell and his wife Alma revisit Fort Benning. An Infantry School graduate and instructor, Powell became Chief of Staff and later Secretary of State.

Fort Benning's main mission is to train soldiers. For proficiency, Private John Hudson practices stream crossings at Upatoi Creek in April 1993.

When the 498th Medical Company returned from Kuwait in May 1993, Warrant Officer Jeff DuPharme was reunited with baby Isaac, daughter Leah, and son Ethan.

Staff Sergeant Richard D. Merritt does the Commando Crawl on Darby Queen Obstacle Course in the 1993 Annual Best Ranger Competition.

The 317th Engineer Battalion loads its gear for its assignment in Somalia, departing from Lawson Field in late September 1993. The deployment included M-113 armored personnel carriers, engineer and utility trucks with trailers, and earthmovers.

Gunnery Sergeant Keith Oakes left. and Sergeant First Class William Patterson, 5th Ranger Training Battalion, take 1st place after crossing the finish line of the buddy run, the last event of Best Ranger 2001.

Reporter Joe Galloway (left) and Lieutenant General Harold "Hal" Moore center. authors of *We Were Soldiers Once...and Young*, reminisce with Colonel Ted Swett in October 2004, recalling their time in Vietnam with the 1st Cavalry Division.

People from the Columbus area express their support for Fort Benning units and other
U.S. troops fighting in Operation Iraqi Freedom in October 2004.

Following tradition of celebrating special events for Fort Benning units,
paratroopers fill the sky for a rendezvous in October 2004.

51.

Best in the World

Major General Jerry White was in command when the last UH-1 on post—No. 66-16854—flew its final mission March 4, 1994. The UH-1, known as the Huey, was a frequent sight around and above the post during the Vietnam War. Any vacant land was turned into a helicopter pad, so the ground was as crowded with Hueys as the Georgia sky. The Huey's final mission was to drop members of the Silver Wings onto Eubanks Field before joining other retired aircraft designated for donation to museums.[1]

Former National Infantry Museum Director Dick Grube, a member of the 1st Cavalry Division (Airmobile), found the UH-1 reliable and dependable in Vietnam: "It provided close-in technical support for the troops on ground...a very versatile little aircraft."[2] Grube said 434 Hueys were assigned to Benning during formation of the Air Assault Division. With the departure of the last Huey, six Blackhawk helicopters remained to support Infantry School training, fly visiting dignitaries around the post, and provide transportation for the Silver Wings.[3]

That spring, White welcomed the Army Community of Excellence evaluation team from Washington, DC, to Riverside. The military leaders ate barbecue at an outdoor reception while listening to music by the infantry band and the finance choir. The Whites made Riverside accessible to all. "I used to have people come knock on the door to come see Riverside," the commanding general explained. "I'd bring them in—soldiers and civilians

---

[1] Ruth J. Spaller, "Huey comes in for final landing," *Bayonet*, March 11 1994, A-3.

[2] Ibid.

[3] Ibid.

alike.... Riverside was especially nice. It was special for us. It was the most special time in our life."[4]

On April 8, Building 35, the Infantry School Building until 1964 and then home of the School of the Americas, was renamed Ridgway Hall in honor of General Matthew B. Ridgway, who died in his sleep in 1993 at age ninety-eight. A student during George C. Marshall's generation, Ridgway went on to lead the 82nd Airborne Division. As its first commander, he jumped with his troops on the eve of D-Day, June 6, 1944. Late in his career, Ridgway was appointed supreme commander of the Allied Powers of Europe by President Truman and later named US Army chief of staff in 1953 by President Eisenhower.[5] He retired in 1955.[6]

When Senator Sam Nunn visited the School of Americas in April, he commended its effort to train international leaders. Nunn directed his comments to SOA critics: "You don't close Cambridge because a dictator such as Oliver Cromwell went there. You don't close Princeton because of Aaron Burr. And you don't close the University of Heidelberg because of Joseph Goebbels. Therefore you don't close the School of Americas because a small minority of its students have been accused of wrong doing."[7]

When Fort Benning won the Commander-in-Chief's Award (CINC) as Best Army Installation in the World—an award predicted by Quick in 1992—mayors Frank Martin of Columbus and Sonny Coulter of Phenix City along with Colonel Burnie Quick announced the news at Infantry Hall.[8] White, Benning's first commanding general to win the CINC was at the National Training Center in Irwin, California. Along with $1.5 million, Benning activities awarded the Best in the Army (world titles) received $50,000 each for Best Military Personnel Services, Best Army Career and Alumni Program, Best Morale, Welfare and Recreation and Family Support Services.[9]

---

[4] Maj. Gen. (Ret.) Jerry A. White, interview by Peggy Stelpflug, June 3 1998, United Way Office, Columbus GA.

[5] Devon Kerbow, "Post names Bldg 35 Ridgway Hall," *Bayonet*, April 15 1994, A-3.

[6] Ibid.

[7] "Senator visits SOA," *Bayonet*, April 1 1994, 1.

[8] Karen S. Morarie, "Benning new world champ," *Bayonet*, April 15 1994, 1.

[9] Ibid.

For the second year in a row, the post won the Chief of Staff Army Award for Best Large Installation in the Continental United States. Inspired by these wins, Sarah McLaney, Communities of Excellence coordinator, looked to the future: "No other post has won the CINC [Commander-in-Chief] award twice, but that's our goal and we believe that if any installation can do it, it's Fort Benning. Fort Benning is the best. Hooah!"[10] In May, White accepted the Army Communities of Excellence Awards for the Commander-in-Chief's Award and Chief of Staff Army Award in Washington, DC. Award money was earmarked for the Audie Murphy Gym, Sand Hill Recreation Center, Soldiers' Plaza, Carey Pool at the Main NCO Club, playground equipment for family housing, and phase 1 of the Columbus Riverwalk and Recreation Trail Project.

Though not "real" money, White received a symbolic check for $4 million, representing money saved by 3,500 post volunteers at Fort Benning and Columbus. At a post Volunteer Recognition Ceremony, White noted, "What you [volunteers] do to take care of soldiers, to take care of soldiers' families, is absolutely critical to everything we stand for here, and that is to create a quality of life second to none."[11]

In June 1994, Brigadier General John J. Maher III, a former commander of the Ranger Training Brigade, succeeded Brigadier General Jack P. Nix, Jr., as deputy commanding general and assistant commandant of the United States Army Infantry Center and School. Nix reported to the United States Army Southern European Task Force and 5th Theatre Army Area Command as commanding general. A native of Atlanta, Maher was a 1970 distinguished military graduate of the University of Georgia. He later earned a master's degree in management and supervision from Central Michigan University. The Vietnam veteran previously served as assistant division commander, 24th Infantry Division (Mechanized), Fort Stewart, Georgia.

On June 30, the 36th Engineer Group gathered at York Field to witness the 43rd Combat Engineer Battalion as it "furls it [sic] colors" for

---

[10] Richard Brill, "Fort Benning wins best again," *Bayonet*, September 16 1994, A-1.

[11] Marc G. Turchin, "Fort Benning honors its volunteers," *Bayonet*, April 29 1994, C-6.

the last time."[12] The unit served twenty-eight years at Fort Benning, deploying to Somalia and to the Persian Gulf while commanded by Lieutenant Colonel Larry Davis. The post lost 635 soldiers when the 43rd was inactivated. Although spread out over the next five months, it was "the biggest one-time loss of soldiers from the post in recent years."[13]

In addition, the 2nd US Army Reserve Noncommissioned Officer Academy was inactivated in July due to downsizing of reserve forces. It trained more than 7,000 reserve and National Guard soldiers after relocating from Fort Bragg in 1989.[14] The Henry Caro Noncommissioned Officers Academy, unaffected by the change, saw Command Sergeant Major Allan R. Halstead, head of the NCOA since July 1992, pass command to Command Sergeant Major Willie G. Wells.[15]

A teary Burnet R. Quick retired July 8 in a ceremony at Infantry Hall's Marshall Auditorium. Quick recalled, "There are good feelings about Fort Benning," he said. "You can't go through that wonderful institution without feeling pride, without understanding the great men—whether it's Bradley or Eisenhower—whoever preceded you (not everyone is destined to be a general). But I can truly say the day I retired at Fort Benning, I couldn't get through my final speech. I cried and I wasn't embarrassed. I loved every day in the Army. I knew I'd miss the Army...but I don't look back."[16] As Quick began a new career as president of the Uptown Columbus Association, Colonel Gregory C. Camp, former deputy assistant commandant of the Infantry School, took Quick's place as chief of staff at Fort Benning.

During another ceremony, US Rangers dedicated the Ranger Memorial on August 25, following a twenty-two-month campaign to erect the memorial near Infantry Hall. The Ranger Memorial Walk featured a twenty-foot-tall bronze commando knife, designed and constructed by sculptor Steve Dickey, symbolizing Ranger strike operations. Along with granite monuments honoring various associations, cut and polished Georgia granite stones—etched with the names of fallen and living Rangers—made

---

[12] Clint Claybrook, "Fort Benning is losing 635-soldier battalion," *Columbus Ledger-Enquirer*, May 23 1994, B-1.

[13] Ibid.

[14] "1994 in review," *Bayonet*, January 6 1995, A-3.

[15] Ibid.

[16] Col. (Ret.) Burnet Quick, interview by Peggy Stelpflug, July 16 1998, Uptown Columbus GA.

up the Ranger Memorial Walk. The father of one of the six Fort Benning Rangers killed in Mogadishu, Somalia, in 1993, donated money so each of the six had his own stone in the walkway.[17]

Major General Kenneth Leuer, now a Columbus resident, headed the US Ranger Association and played a major role in raising the $550,000 for the memorial.[18] Young soldiers who wore the Ranger Tab met half the cost. Leuer noted, "There are plenty of people who want to ride the glory train; and there are those who want to be there on the winning day...but there are damn few who have the guts to give the sweat and blood that pave the road to victory!"[19]

The induction class of sixteen soldiers into Ranger Hall of Fame included Sergeant 1st Class Randall D. Shughart, a Ranger who died while guarding a wounded pilot after his helicopter crashed on the streets of Mogadishu in October 1993. Major James C. Queen made history by becoming the first African American inducted into the Ranger Hall of Fame. He served as an executive officer in an all-black company during the Korean War.[20]

Although the army had no female Rangers, it now had women drill sergeants. In 1968, the first woman earned the right to wear the drill sergeant hat, but it was not until 1994 that the first female drill sergeants were assigned to Benning. Sergeant 1st Class Angela M. Pitts and Staff Sergeant Regina Santiago were the first women to instruct drill sergeant candidates, teach classes, and make on-the-spot corrections. Another woman, Lieutenant Colonel Jeannie M. Picariello, former chief of health promotion, US Army Southern Command, Panama, headed the US Army Physical Fitness School. With a staff of twenty-one, the school offered inspections for units and conducted classes.

In 1994, Fort Benning was named the best extra-large installation in Training and Doctrine Command for the third consecutive year. In addition, several Fort Benning activities were named the best in TRADOC in the extra-large category. The money for Phase II of the Riverwalk

---

[17] Clint Claybrook, "Rangers dedicate their memorial," *Benning Leader*, September 2 1994, 11.

[18] Ibid.

[19] Ibid.

[20] Ibid.

construction was paid from ACOE prize money. With the Riverwalk, soldiers and family members could walk, jog, or bike from the post to the 14th Street Bridge in uptown Columbus, a distance of eight miles. Soldiers of the 36th Engineer Group helped complete the project for the 1996 Olympic Games.[21]

A full review and retirement ceremony was held on September 15 to mark White's thirty-five years of distinguished service. TRADOC Commander General Frederick M. Franks, Jr., described White as "a soldier of vision, a soldier of passion and a soldier of toughness" who "led his soldiers...with a 'Follow Me' spirit."[22] Although an avid supporter of new technologies, White believed soldiers, not technology, made a strong army. "When it's all said and done, regardless of the technology, there's going to be another dark night, and some soldier's going to have to walk through the mud and pull out his bayonet and take an objective."[23]

During White's command, Fort Benning won best extra-large installation in TRADOC three times, Best large army installation in the Continental United States twice and, for the first time, best army installation in the world. "There's no place better than Fort Benning," White said, adding, "Fort Benning has the best civilian work force...bar none. They are as dedicated as any soldier I have ever seen."[24] Praising his wife, White said, "She has suffered the highs and lows, enjoyed the good times and shared the bad times. Her concern for soldiers and families has been the same as mine. If I'm ever known for anything from my military experience, it will be my real love for soldiers. I tried to do everything I could to take care of soldiers."[25]

White admitted, "So many of the things that I took credit for, Linda did. If you came to visit Fort Benning, I expected your experience to be positive, wherever you stayed. My wife sort of took those things over. Her presence was felt at every facility of Fort Benning, from the commissary, to

---

[21] "Post helps with Riverwalk," *Columbus Ledger-Enquirer*, March 2 1994, A-3.

[22] Ruth J. Spaller, "USAIC gets new commander," *Bayonet*, September 16 1994, A-1.

[23] Karen S. Morarie, "CG nears retirement," *Bayonet*, August 19 1994, A-8.

[24] Ibid.

[25] White interview.

the PX, to the hospital, to all the quarters. She was there all the time, making sure they understood what the standards really were."[26]

White's successor as commanding general was Major General John W. Hendrix, a former deputy commandant. Hendrix returned to Benning after serving in Germany as deputy chief of staff for operations, US Army Europe and 7th Army. Born and raised in Georgia, he received a ROTC army commission at Georgia Tech. He and his wife, Cheri, also a native Georgian, looked forward to the assignment. He pledged that Benning would "continue to be the best post in the Army."[27] McLaney—with White and Quick retired—had another determined supporter for her ACOE program.

The Military Police Activity and Fort Benning Fire Department combined on October 1 to form the Directorate of Public Safety. The first class of the Fort Benning Law Enforcement Academy graduated in September. Approved by the Department of Veterans Affairs and sponsored by the Georgia Standards and Training Council, an academy program trained soldiers leaving the military for positions in law enforcement.

The 988th Military Police Company left Lawson Field for Haiti in September on Operation Uphold Democracy after the UN authorized force to rid Haiti of a military dictatorship and to return Jean-Bertrand Aristide to power. The 586th Engineer Company (Assault Float Bridge), 36th Engineer Group, soon followed. Its leader, Captain Carole L. Anderson, was the first female engineer bridge company commander ever deployed. The 535th Engineer Detachment—redesignated the 249th Engineer Battalion—also served in Haiti, producing electricity with portable generators.[28]

Soldiers from the 3rd Brigade, 24th Infantry Division left for Operation Vigilant Warrior, a major exercise held in the Middle East in 1994. This raised the number of 3rd Brigade soldiers who left for either Saudi Arabia or Kuwait to 2,060 in response to new threats by Iraqi president Saddam Hussein, who was defeated in Operation Desert Storm.[29]

---

[26] Ibid.

[27] Ruth J. Spaller, "USAIC gets new commander," 1.

[28] Jerry Macintire, "535th: Unit changes name not mission," *Bayonet*, December 9 1994, B-5.

[29] "Some Iraqui troops halt retreat," *Columbus Ledger-Enquirer*, October 14 1994, 1; "3rd Brigade troops headed to Mideast," *Columbus Ledger-Enquirer*, October 15 1994, A-6.

Saddam Hussein moved thousands of Iraqi troops close to his country's border with Kuwait in early October. After the 24th Infantry Division and other units sent troops to Kuwait and Saudi Arabia in mid-October and November, Hussein withdrew, and Operation Vigilant Warrior developed into a training exercise.[30] Showing his support for the troops, President Clinton visited with 1,571 soldiers of the 3rd Brigade, 24th Infantry Division in Kuwait in late October. Including the 1994 Kuwait deployment, Fort Benning deployed troops thirty-eight times since January 1992.[31]

Elements of the 3rd Brigade arrived at Benning before Thanksgiving for a holiday homecoming. These and other soldiers (about 17,000) enjoyed Thanksgiving dinner on post.[32] The menu called for 18,000 pounds of roasted turkey, 1,000 pounds of ham, 1,200 pounds of Cornish game hen, 1,082 pounds of peeled shrimp, 4 tons of fruit, 21 pounds of parsley, and 800 pounds of hard candy.[33] Ice carvings created from 300-pound blocks of ice were displayed.[34]

The largest contingent of Benning troops deployed to Kuwait following Desert Storm returned home December 7. In mid-December, the Infantry Training Brigade's 3rd Battalion, 32nd Infantry Regiment was inactivated. Companies C and D were the last two to graduate from the regiment that formerly trained more than 3,500 OSUT soldiers each year.[35] Unit colors went to the National Infantry Museum.

On January 31, 1995, Dick Grube put in his last day as director of the National Infantry Museum, a position he accepted in 1973 after retiring from the army as a lieutenant colonel. His successor was curator Z. Frank Hanner. Grube, Hanner said, taught him about history and the importance of preserving it "so soldiers can understand that the past plays an important part in shaping who they are today and so that civilians can appreciate the

---

[30] "US troops off alert for Mideast duty," *Columbus Ledger-Enquirer*, October 21 1994, A-1.

[31] "180 more troops off to duty in Mideast," *Columbus Ledger-Enquirer*, October 28 1994, A-5.

[32] Jerrie Macintire, "Thanksgiving Feast," November 23 1994 C-1.

[33] Ibid.

[34] Ibid.

[35] "ITB's 3rd Battalion Inactivated," *Bayonet*, December 16 1994, B-5.

suffering and heroism that helped make this nation great."[36] Hanner, who received a degree in history from Appalachian State University in Boone, North Carolina, came to the museum in 1981. He previously worked at the 24th Infantry Division (Mechanized) Museum at Fort Stewart and obtained a master's degree from Armstrong State College in Savannah.[37]

A Fort Benning institution older than the museum, but less venerable, closed its doors in February 1995. The Installation Detention Facility closed after operating fifty-five years as the post jail. Built in 1939 as a disciplinary barracks to handle 122 prisoners, the building is on the National Historic Register and cannot be destroyed. Only two cells, located inside the building now used as the Military Police Station, were kept for detention. In the facility's last four or five years, the average population was between ten and twenty inmates.[38] It also housed prisoners from three Georgia installations and two from Alabama.

Historically, two prisoners were sentenced to death by hanging. Private John J. O'Conner killed a guard while attempting to escape from a work detail, and Private Curn L. Jones killed an officer candidate outside a store in Columbus.[39] Old-timers said the hangings took place in the Engineering Warehouse where the gallows were erected. The executed prisoners were buried outside the cemetery walls but were included in the main cemetery when the wall by Terry Drive was extended in 1974.[40]

A tragic loss of life occurred in mid-February 1995. Four ranger students died during an exercise in the Florida swamps.[41] The students were in the final phase of Ranger School at Camp James E. Rudder, located at Eglin Air Force Base, Florida, operating in three thirty-four-man patrols. The Ranger School, headquartered at Benning, with camps in Dahlonega, Georgia; Fort Bliss, Texas; and Eglin, trained 2,600 soldiers in close combat skills each year. Killed were Ranger 2nd Lieutenant Spencer Dodge, twenty-

---

[36] Richard Brill, "Curator carries on Museum's history," *Bayonet*, February 17 1995, C-1.

[37] Ibid.

[38] Clint Claybrook, "Benning to close its detention facility," *Bayonet*, December 30 1994, 8.

[39] Lisa M. Hibbert, "Post cemetery mirrors military history," *Bayonet*, July 26 1995, A-7.

[40] Ibid.

[41] "Training became a nightmare," *Benning Leader*, April 7 1995, 12.

five, from Stanley, New York, and president of the class of 1994 at West Point; Captain Milton Palmer, twenty-seven, from Fishers, Indiana, a Citadel graduate; 2nd Lieutenant Curt Sansoucie, twenty-three, from Rochester, New Hampshire, a 1994 West Point graduate; and Sergeant Norman Tillman, twenty-eight, from Grenada, Mississippi, a mortar man with the 82nd Airborne Division, Fort Bragg, North Carolina.[42] Tillman was posthumously promoted to staff sergeant. All died of hypothermia after extended exposure of fifty- to fifty-nine-degree water during training in the Florida swamps.[43] All four deceased students received their Ranger tabs posthumously at the February 24 graduation ceremony with fellow Rangers accepting the tabs on their behalf.[44]

A six-week internal investigation, headed by Maher at the request of Hendrix, found "human judgment errors" and "a flawed decision making process" as the causes of the situation that led to the four training deaths.[45] Nine members of the Ranger Training Brigade's 6th Battalion, headquartered at Eglin were disciplined, including the battalion commander. In March, all nine were relieved of their duties with punishment ranging from counseling to letters of reprimand. The waterborne phase of Ranger training—with improvements—resumed in August, six months after it was halted.

Some good news for the post came when it won the Commander-in-Chief's Award for Best Army Installation in the World for a second year in a row—Sarah McLaney's goal. The Directorates of Military Personnel-Adjutant General, Community Activities' Morale, Welfare and Recreation, and Civilian Personnel also were named the best of their kind in the army.[46] Hendrix proudly accepted the installation of excellence flag and a wooden trophy at Commander-in-Chief's Annual Awards for Installation Excellence. "It doesn't get any better than this," Hendrix said.[47]

---

[42] "Ranger deaths: Five suspended," *Bayonet*, March 10 1995, A-3.

[43] Ibid.

[44] Mark G. Turchin, "Ranger class to graduate after training incident," *Bayonet*, February 24 1995, A-1.

[45] "Training became a nightmare," 12.

[46] Ruth J. Spaller and Lisa M. Hibbert, "Post collects more excellence awards," *Bayonet*, April 28 1995, 1.

[47] Agatha Hudson Debrow, "Fort Benning receives 'best' in world crown," *Bayonet*, May 19 1995, 1.

President Bill Clinton visited the post April 12, greeting soldiers and civilians at Lawson Army Airfield while on his way to Warm Springs, Georgia, to pay tribute to Franklin Delano Roosevelt on the fiftieth anniversary of his death. In a building where thousands of troops were deployed, Clinton thanked Fort Benning soldiers for their contributions in the Middle East, Somalia, and Haiti.[48] After brief remarks, the president saluted popular Command Sergeant Major William Acebes—Fort Benning's top enlisted man. The next day Acebes retired after a thirty-year career.

Spring was in full bloom when the city's annual Riverfest Weekend "went out with a bang" in April.[49] Members of the 4th Battalion, 41st Field Artillery, 24th Infantry Division set up four 105 mm howitzers on the Chattahoochee riverbank to accompany the Columbus Symphony Orchestra during its performance of Tchaikovsky's 1812 Overture. Retired Colonel Joe Bell, sitting in Phenix City's new amphitheatre that Saturday night, wondered what old soldiers would think about this setting and the classical music wafting over the river.[50] In days gone by, GIs believed a young man wasn't really a soldier until he had spent a rough and rowdy Saturday night in Phenix City. "Here I am, a Saturday night in Phenix City, listening to the symphony. What a change," Bell thought. "If those old soldiers—the brown shoe army—could see a symphony orchestra on the banks of the Chattahoochee on a Saturday night, I don't know what their reaction would be. I really don't know what they would think of today's Phenix City, Columbus, or Fort Benning."[51]

On May 23, a farewell ceremony was held for Assistant Commandant John Maher, named commanding general of the 25th Infantry Division (Light), Schofield Barracks, Hawaii. Brigadier General Robert T. Clark, assistant division commander of the same unit, replaced Maher. Clark, a graduate of Benning's infantry officers' basic and advanced courses, was a rifle platoon leader and company executive officer with the 1st Cavalry Division (Airmobile) in Vietnam. Later he commanded the 3rd Brigade,

[48] Clint Claybrook, "President compliments Benning soldiers," *Columbus Ledger-Enquirer*, April 13 1995, A6.

[49] "The Riverfest artillery," *Benning Leader*, May 5 1995, 11.

[50] Col. (Ret.) Joe Bell, interview by Peggy Stelpflug, November 6 1998, Donovan Library, Fort Benning GA.

[51] Ibid.

101st Airborne Division during Desert Shield and Desert Storm. Graduating with a degree in history from Texas Tech University, Clark was the distinguished military graduate.

Clark continued a family tradition. His father Retired Colonel H. A. Clark was commissioned in the horse cavalry in 1939 but transferred to the infantry after World War II. Clark's grandfathers served over thirty-five years each in the military. "I am very happy to be back," Clark said. "I grew up an Army brat. I lived at Fort Benning for ten years when my father was stationed here on two different occasions. I went to Don C. Faith Middle School. I learned how to play golf on the 'Follow Me' golf course. I played baseball on the fields here. I was born into the Army. I always wanted to be an Army officer like my father."[52]

Another familiar family also was represented on post. Lieutenant Paul B. Malone IV, an executive officer in the Ranger Brigade, was the great-grandson of General Paul Malone, a stalwart of early Benning history. Malone's sons Paul Jr. and A. J. fought in World War II and retired as colonels. Grandson Paul III, a West Point graduate, was wounded in Vietnam and became a college professor. Paul Malone IV served in Desert Storm prior to his assignment at Benning. He said the family's 100-year tradition of unbroken military service would be tested since his only child was a young daughter, Sandra. "She can join the Army and be the fifth generation to go to West Point if she wants, but that's going to be awhile."[53]

A new family tradition began when Lieutenant Colonel Robert Kissel and Lieutenant Colonel Deborah Kissel shared rank and a marriage license. Robert Kissel took command of 1st Battalion, 29th Infantry Regiment, and his wife, the post's only female battalion commander, took charge of the 30th Adjutant General Battalion, Infantry Training Brigade. In organizing recruits who come from all over the US, shipped to the army by 4,950 recruiters, she said, "We don't yell and scream at them, but we don't handle them with kid gloves, either. They're pretty well scared when they get here."[54]

---

[52] Lisa M. Hibbert, "Assistant commandant continues family tradition," *Bayonet*, October 6 1995, A-7.

[53] Shannon Day, "Family enjoys military tradition," *Bayonet*, July 28 1995, B-2.

[54] Claybrook, "Benning's new recruits break in new traditions," *Columbus Ledger-Enquirer*, October 30 1995, B-1.

While Kissel dealt with raw recruits, the 1995 Doughboy Award was presented to a dedicated veteran who took the infantry into the sky—eighty-year-old retired lieutenant general Harry W. O. Kinnard. Becoming a paratrooper for "the badge, the boots, and the buck," Kinnard went on to command the 1st Cavalry Division (Airmobile) formed at Fort Benning in the early 1960s.[55] "Like all my military awards, it really belongs to the wonderful men, living and dead, with whom I fought," he said.[56] He also was the first inductee into the Order of St. Maurice, the patron saint of the infantry. Established in 1994 by the National Infantry Association, it recognized individuals who made significant contributions to promote or enhance the infantry. Kinnard also explained his view of war: "Even though we have a tradition of fighting for just causes, I would never put a kind face on war; wars fought for whatever reasons are cruel and painful…. Men in close combat develop the feelings of deep mutual respect and brotherly love."[57]

In October, at the urging of local veterans, a thoroughfare through the heart of Columbus was renamed "Veterans Parkway." A dedication ceremony was held at the Eternal Flame Memorial at the Government Center. Columbus mayor Bobby Peters was "hoisted aloft" by a utility bucket at the intersection of Ninth Street and Fourth Avenue to unveil one of the new green and white street signs.[58] Wanda Funderburk, president of the Chattahoochee Valley Chapter of Gold Star Wives, helped her group of Vietnam widows place American flags along Veterans Parkway and Victory Drive. Members of the Chattahoochee Valley Retired Officer Association put up 126 flags, which were taken down after Veteran's Day. "We try to honor the American flag," explained Funderburk, "because our husbands paid the greatest sacrifice you can give, the ultimate sacrifice for your country."[59]

---

[55] Lisa M. Hibbert, "Retired general takes up infantry honor," *Bayonet*, June 23 1995, A-7.

[56] Ibid.

[57] Ibid.

[58] Tony Adams, "Parkway pays tribute to area veterans," *Benning Leader*, October 13 1995, 4.

[59] Jim Molis, "Flags again serve as tribute to veterans," *Columbus Ledger-Enquirer*, November 6 1995, B-1.

The army, through technology, was to transform itself into a smaller, rapidly deployable, yet lethal force. To perform this mission, the post was designated as an Individual Deployment Site (IDS) post by the US Army Training and Doctrine Command. The post was selected because of its power projection platform, airfield, central issue facility, and its experience as a replacement center.[60] Soldiers were prepared for movement in five days. If additional training was needed, the soldier remained longer. Active duty soldiers operated the IDS, coordinating every aspect of deploying an individual from housing, to training, to issuing theater specific equipment, and to certifying the soldiers' readiness. The 347th Personnel Replacement Battalion, an Illinois-based US Reserve Unit, later assumed this mission.

When twenty-seven Army Reserve and National Guard units were scheduled for processing, a mobilization group for units, rather than individuals, processed the troops. It was the only such unit in the army at that time. It ensured that a soldier's papers (such as wills, power of attorneys, and weapons qualifications) were all current before the soldier was shipped to Bosnia or Germany. In Bosnia, Fort Benning soldiers joined a 60,000-troop international peacekeeping effort to ease the conflict between Serbs, Muslims, and Croats caused by the breakup of Yugoslavia.[61]

Civilians and military members continued to come from all over the United States for processing before heading overseas to support Operation Joint Endeavor—the ongoing peace-keeping mission in Bosnia. Fort Benning's Soldier Readiness Processing Center, which began December 1995, processed 2,844 personnel by January 29, 1996, seeing to it that all individuals assigned to Germany or Bosnia met deployment criteria.

As a power projection base, the post sent combat troops to the world's trouble spots and readied troops from other services and other posts for major deployments. With Benning soldiers participating in Operation Joint Endeavor in 1995–1996 included several soldiers from the 988th Military Police Company went to Bosnia for a five-month deployment. President Clinton, who ordered the first Americans into Bosnia, explained the ongoing

---

[60] Lisa M. Hibbert, "Benning opens deployment centers," *Bayonet*, December 22 1995, 1.

[61] "Bosnian conflict: from beginning to present," *Bayonet*, December 15 1995, C-4; "As 586th heads to Bosnia, more units to follow," *Bayonet*, December 15 1995, C-4.

mission: "Our goals are to supervise the separation of the armies, maintain a cease fire, and provide a safe environment."[62] Troops that passed through Fort Benning were at the core of these goals.

---

[62] Lisa M. Hibbert, "586th joins Operation Joint Endeavor," *Bayonet*, December 15 1995, 1.

52.

Smaller But Lethal

With money in their pockets and time on their hands, contemporary soldiers spent those commodities in ways their ancestors would never have imagined.

Slowly vanishing from the south side of Columbus were the joints that featured cold beer and hot women and charged high prices for each. Lingerie shops with very few garments for sale were popular for a time, but they too went away. Gone were the days that a trainee, fortified with Saturday night drinks, would decorate his body with everything from "Mother" to "Airborne." It was getting to the point that even a self-respecting tattoo parlor had trouble making a living.

"Those days are gone," noted Bill Dubuc, owner of Columbus Superior Skin Art on Victory Drive. "Guys used to be lined up. We could have tattooed military day and night.... The people who are in the Army now are a lot different than they were then. It seems like now they're more preppy than they used to be. They don't even go to the go-go-bars like they used to. They go to the malls and play video games now. It's just a different type of people."[1]

The modern army was smaller but more lethal. From 1990 through 1998, the strength of the active-duty army declined by 37 percent, dropping from 781,000 in 1989 to 495,000 soldiers in 1996, according to the Center for Strategic and Budgetary Assessments.[2] The Army National Guard and Army Reserve declined by 22 percent, from 736,000 to 575,000, leaving a force larger than the active army.[3]

---

[1] Heidi Fedak, "Tattoos," *Benning Leader*, August 9 1996, 7.

[2] "Senate OKs boost for Guard, Reserves," *Montgomery Advertiser*, July 19 1996, 6A.

[3] Ibid.

Training of these forces became more regulated. TRADOC Regulation 350–6 and Fort Benning Regulation USAIC 600-3 permitted no degrading of soldiers by language, physical contact, or physical or verbal abuse.[4] Post regulations banned mass punishment and the use of excessive training as penalty. No more than twenty-five push-ups or fifty sit-ups were allowed in any five-minute period. Sexual harassment was taboo. Even with these improved conditions, potential recruits chose not to join the army because of its numerous and lengthy deployments, such as ones to the Persian Gulf War and missions to Somalia, Rwanda, Macedonia, Panama, and Haiti.[5] Former secretary of defense Caspar Weinberger wrote that Desert Storm's success caused a "Victory Disease," adding, "The US force that defeated Saddam Hussein no longer exists. What we have today is a military that is a shadow of its former self."[6] He also warned of Russia's 25,000 nuclear warheads that "could destroy the US in an afternoon."[7]

Benefits of servicewere an issue to the military's civilian workforce. Since 1989, Judy Pennington, chief of personnel management and head of the systems support division, had worked to secure the Southeast Civilian Personnel Operations Center (CPOC) for Fort Benning. It offered nearly 200 jobs to the area, but 44 of the 64 civilian personnel jobs on post faced extinction.The CPOC officially opened at Fort Benning in January 1996. The process of organizing a regional personnel office began—taking over the records, job applications, some hiring, and other operations involving about 40,000 army civilian employees in the Southeast by the end of September 1996.[8] The Fort Benning Directorate of Civilian Personnel continued to serve as adviser as well as a liaison with the CPOC. Theresa Gunter, head of the directorate until her retirement in Sepbember, received the 1995 Army Communities of Excellence Award for the Best Civilian Personnel Services and was also recognized in TRADOC's new award

---

[4] Heidi Fedak, "Abuse, profanity out of style," *Benning Ledger*, February 2 1996, 11.

[5] Ian Fisher, "For G.I.'s more time away from home fires," *New York Times*, December 24 1996, A1.

[6] Caspar Weinberger and Peter Schweizer, *The Next War* (Lanham MD: Regnery Publishers Incorporated, 1996) xv, xix.

[7] Ibid.

[8] Brian Voller, "Regional personnel office to cut ribbon," *Bayonet*, January 12 1996, 1.

category—the Sustained Leadership in Civilian Personnel Administration—because she kept winning the leadership award.[9] In 1974, Gunter was the second woman in the history of the Infantry Center promoted to the level of GS-13.[10]

In March 1996, the 3rd Brigade, 24th Infantry Division (Mechanized) was reflagged as the 3rd Brigade, 3rd Infantry Division (Mechanized). The 1st Infantry Division—"Big Red One"—replaced the 3rd Infantry Division, based in Germany since 1958. Called the "Rock of the Marne" or Marne Division for its several battles along the Marne River in World War I, the 3rd Infantry Division returned home to the US after thirty-eight years of foreign service. The division was stationed at Fort Stewart, Fort Benning, and Hunter Army Airfield. Created in 1917, the unit fought in six major battles in World War I and lost 16,450 men.[11] With the draw-down to ten divisions, the 3rd, with its proud history in World War I and World War II, found itself nearly eighty years later focusing on training soldiers to deploy anywhere in the world in twenty-four hours.

The 24th Infantry Division, the "Victory Division," helped liberate the Philippines in 1945, fought in South Korea, Grenada, and took part in Operation Desert Storm in 1991. As it ended its twenty-one-year relationship with Fort Stewart, 16,000 soldiers changed their insignia from 24th to 3rd Infantry Division.[12] The 3rd Brigade, 3rd Infantry Division was located at Kelley Hill.

In April, after competing with Forts Bragg and Sill, Fort Benning made news by winning the Chief of Staff of the Army Award as Best Large Army Installation in the United States for the fourth consecutive time. Sarah McLaney, directorate of Resource Management and Quality Improvement Office, received the Meritorious Civilian Service Award from Major General John W. Hendrix on York Field for spearheading the project.[13]

---

[9] Heidi Fedak, "Former civilian personnel chief to be honored," *Benning Leader*, September 27 1996, 16.

[10] "Fort Benning events of 1974," *Bayonet*, December 27 1974, 13.

[11] Robin A. Shawlinski, "3rd Bde remembers unit sacrifices," *Bayonet*, June 7 1996, 1.

[12] "3/24 now 3/3 ID," *Bayonet*, March 1 1996, 1.

[13] Lori Egan, "CG rewards excellence at monthly retreat," *Bayonet*, April 12 1996, A-6.

Colonel Richard L. Rutledge, garrison commander, accepted the Army Communities of Excellence bowl in May in Washington, DC, for the Chief of Staff Award. The 1996 ACOE award marked the first time that the post was judged on the Army Performance Improvement Criteria. APIC, an adaptation of the Malcolm Baldrige criteria, was implemented by the army in 1995. Baldrige, a proponent of quality management, was secretary of commerce from 1981–1987.

For the 1996 competition, Fort Benning had to submit a seventy-page application in which McLaney explained that the army embraced APIC out of necessity because "as resources diminish, the army has fewer dollars to spend and fewer people to get the job done. But we are also embracing APIC because it's a better way to do things."[14]

The Total Army Quality (TAQ), established in 1990 under Major General Carmen J. Cavezza's command, was key component of APIC evolution, providing quality products and services. "It took us from focusing solely on quality," McLaney explained, "to focusing on processes—how we do what we do."[15] The five key processes—infantry future, infantry doctrine, infantry training, force projection, and base operations—included all members of the post work force, "from the warehouse worker and rifleman up to the commanding general."[16] All shared, McLaney explained, "in the responsibility of providing the best possible service in our daily efforts and of looking for opportunities which lead to continuous improvement."[17]

The 1st Battalion, 29th Infantry Regiment won the army's Maintenance Excellence Award for the sixth time in eight years. The unit had nearly two battalion's worth of equipment (126 Bradley Fighting Vehicles and 78 wheeled vehicles). The motor pool averaged 150 vehicles a day for various missions. Although the unit constantly changed military personnel (a staff of 176 that repaired vehicles), it had a core of 22 civilians. Battalion maintenance officer, Chief Warrant Officer David Baker,

---

[14] "Army embraces APIC in quest for excellence," *Bayonet*, January 12 1996, A-3.

[15] Quality Performance Improvement Office, "Army embraces APIC in quest for excellence," *Bayonet*, January 12 1996, A-3.

[16] Ibid.

[17] Ibid.

explained, "We have a permanent staff of civilians that are the continuity of the unit. And they're the backbone of the maintenance."[18]

Two well-known soldiers were selected as recipients of the 1996 Doughboy Award on June 14. This marked the first time the award was presented to two infantrymen and the first time an enlisted soldier was a recipient. Retired General James J. Lindsay and Retired Command Sergeant Major Theodore L. Dobol received chrome-plated helmets for their outstanding contributions to the infantry. Lindsay, a former commanding general of Fort Benning who retired in 1990 with thirty-eight years of service, began his career at Fort Benning as a private in 1952 and graduated from OCS I 1953.

Dobol served in World War II, the Korean War, and the Vietnam War, earning four Silver Stars, five Purple Hearts, and eight Battle Stars. During his army career, he served twenty-six years, 1940–1966, with the 26th Infantry Regiment, the Blue Spaders. In 1959, Dobol was one of the first non-commissioned officer promoted to the pay grade E-9, serving as sergeant major.[19] While in Vietnam in April 1968, he was promoted from sergeant major to command sergeant major. He retired in 1969 after thirty-one years of service, largely spent with the 1st Infantry Division, the Big Red One.[20] On Veteran's Day, November 11, 1996, Camp LA Alicia in Bosnia-Herzegovina was renamed Camp Dobol in tribute to the honor command sergeant major-for-life of the 26th Infantry. On November 25, 1996, five months after receiving the Doughboy Award, Dobol died of a brain tumor.[21]

Carrying on a tradition of service set by Doughboys Lindsay and Dobol, soldiers from the 586th Engineer Company (Assault Float Bridge), 36th Engineer Group (Combat), returned in mid-June after six months in Bosnia building and maintaining pontoon float bridges. At Lawson Field,

---

[18] Heidi Fedak, "Call 'em super mechanics," *Benning Leader*, May 3 1996, 12.

[19] Dobol is sometimes listed as the first non-commissioned officer in the US Army to be appointed command sergeant major. However, the first CSM promotion list (8 January 1968) did include Sergeant Major William Woolridge, another of the esteemed NCOS produced by the 26th Infantry. Dobol, according to Woolridge, was not promoted to CSM until April 1968.

[20] Capt. Tawanna Brown, "Camp's new name honors Big Red One veteran," *The Talon*, November 22 1996, 4.

[21] Z. Frank Hanner, National Infantry Museum director, Fort Benning, GA, email to Peggy Stepflug, August 3 2004.

soldiers boarded buses to Audie Murphy Gymnasium where Hendrix welcomed them: "You all look a few pounds leaner than when you left here six months ago, but we are all damn proud of you, Hooah!"[22]

Soldiers who did not return safely from their missions were remembered at a new field of honor. Once home to a series of wooden, single-story hospital buildings, the 20-acre grassy field in front of the National Infantry Museum (former post hospital) was dedicated to soldiers who gave their lives in war and peace. At the June 14, 1996, ceremony, Brigadier General Robert Clark, Fort Benning's deputy commander, remembered the old hospital: "God only knows how many broken bones and broken bodies were mended in that hospital over the years. Thousands, literally thousands of men and women were treated here. That's the heritage of this field. This is a good field. This is a field of mercy, and it's now fittingly today, officially, Sacrifice Field."[23] Honored were Captain William R. Black, 1st Sergeant Glenn L. Harris, Captain M. McKenna, and Retired Major Wayne Wiley. Wiley, who had worked at Fort Benning's Directorate of Combat Development, was killed when a terrorist bomb blew up the US military training center of the Saudi Arabian National Guard in November 1995. Black, a company commander with the 2nd Battalion, 12th Cavalry, was killed in action in Vietnam, March 8, 1969. His wife, Anne, present at the ceremony, was a teacher at Loyd Elementary School. Harris died in an accident during a training exercise at Fort Benning in December 1994. The US Air Force mistakenly shot down McKenna, a graduate of Columbus High School, who was piloting a helicopter in a no-fly force zone over northern Iraq in April 1994.

Later in the year more than 250 veterans, Rangers and guests, dedicated the World War II Ranger memorial at Sacrifice Field. On it were the names of 580 Rangers who fell in World War II. Veteran Ranger Simon A. Loesh, one of the first to buy a memorial brick, said it was "the last word.... We laid down our lives for each other. This monument really means a lot to us."[24]

---

[22] "Welcome Home!" *Bayonet*, June 14 1996, A-1.

[23] Heidi Fedak, "Paying the 'ultimate sacrifice,'" Benning Leader, June 21 1996, 6.

[24] Lori Egan, "Veterans dedicate monument," *Bayonet*, November 22 1996, A-1.

Even soldiers who returned safely from their missions were at times subject to mission-related illnesses such as those who were exposed to Agent Orange in Vietnam. Some veterans of the Gulf War suffered illnesses that were yet unexplained.[25] In 1996, the Department of Defense released evidence that some chemical warfare agents may have been inadvertently released during the destruction of Iraqi weapons storage sites in 1991.[26] Martin Army Community Hospital remained one of nearly 160 military health facilities worldwide that evaluated and treated Gulf War veterans with problems related to Operation Desert Storm. Since the initiation of the program in June 1994, the hospital provided care to 466 patients through the Comprehensive Clinical Evaluation Program.[27]

Sacrifices made by soldiers were also on the mind of a former battalion commander led by General George S. Patton—retired Lieutenant Colonel Frank G. Lumpkin, Jr. The generous Columbus businessman promised $100,000 for reconstruction of a World War II village on the grounds of the National Infantry Museum. Patton's headquarters building, the dining facility, Patton's original sleeping quarters, a company office building, barracks used by Patton's troops when he commanded the 2nd Armored Division, and a guard post were to be part of a permanent addition to the museum.[28] Estimated cost of the project was $1 million for repair and authenticity.[29]

"I was fearful that the barracks were going to be destroyed because they couldn't get the money for the renovations," Lumpkin said. "Restoration of World War II barracks will become a showpiece for the Columbus and Fort Benning community…. The Infantry Museum is the best attraction Columbus has and the barracks will make it even better."[30]

The present post was a challenge of a different kind. For that, John L. Baggett, deputy director of the Directorate of Public Works (DPW), received the Georgia Society of Professional Engineers 1996 Engineer of

---

[25] Peter Cary and Mike Tharp, "The Gulf War's grave aura," *US News & World Report*, July 8 1996, 33; "Senators rip Pentagon over nerve gas exposure," *Benning Leader*, September 27 1996, 17.

[26] Ibid.

[27] "Hospital treats Gulf War vets," *Bayonet*, November 8 1996, 1.

[28] Brian R. Voller, "Post receives $100,000," *Bayonet*, July 4 1996, A-1.

[29] Ibid.

[30] Ibid.

the Year in government award. He managed an $80 million annual budget that provided all base operations support, including engineering services, master planning, utilities, and environmental services to a daily population of 100,000 soldiers and civilians.[31] Baggett, a member of DPW's work force since 1965, served as deputy director since 1985 with Colonel Dave Brown, director.

Carrying on a post tradition, Hendrix, attended by his friends and colleagues, took his final parachute jump as commander of Fort Benning. Hendrix left to lead the 3rd Infantry Division at Fort Stewart. "I've got the 75th Ranger Regiment on one side of me, the Airborne School on the other side and the 3rd ID in the east," Hendrix said.[32] "This is the home of the infantry and there is no other place where you get a better feeling of it than here," he said.[33] During his career, Hendrix followed the four C's: commitment, courage, competence, and candor.[34] As for his military training, Hendrix said Ralph Puckett, his combat commander in Vietnam, was a big influence on him.

Puckett, honorary colonel of the 75th Ranger Regiment in 1996, recalled Hendrix's transfer from a signal officer to the infantry in Vietnam. "He wanted a rifle company, so I told my brigade commander to give a rifle company to Captain Hendrix. I said 'He'll do all right. He'll be the best that you've seen.' After his first operation, my brigade commander was convinced Captain Hendrix really knew his stuff. Captain Hendrix—who's now Major General Jay Hendrix—was about as cool and calm under fire as anybody I'd ever seen."[35]

Hendrix's successor, Major General Carl F. Ernst previously served at Fort Monroe, Virginia, as deputy chief of staff at the Training and Doctrine Command. A former assistant commandant of the Infantry School, as well as the school's director of Combined Arms and Tactics, Ernst went on to command the Joint Task Forces in Somalia and serve as assistant

---

[31] Lori Egan, "DPW deputy director 1996 engineer of the year," *Bayonet*, June 7 1996, A-7.

[32] Lisa M. Hibbert, "CG reflects on home of the infantry," *Bayonet*, July 4 1996, A-1.

[33] Ibid.

[34] Ibid.

[35] Col. (Ret.) Ralph Puckett, interview by Peggy Stelpflug, May 28 1996, National Infantry Museum, Fort Benning GA.

commander of the 82nd Airborne Division. Former commandant General White was correct when he told Ernst in 1992, "one day, you will come home. When you do, your address will be Riverside."[36]

"I have a picture of my wife, Linda and I standing in front of Iron Mike when I was a second lieutenant in 1966 and at that time I had no idea I would become a general. I didn't even think I would make major!" Ernst said. "And here I am, back in front of this statue again. This is my fifth trip to Fort Benning and I'm going to keep doing it until I get it right. I'm glad to be back here. Fort Benning is place where you don't have to explain what *hooah* means—you live it."[37]

History was in the making when retired Lieutenant General Carmen Cavezza, executive director of Columbus '96, and Commandant Hendrix signed the contract for Fort Benning to host the Columbus Olympic Village for women's fast -pitch softball. Approximately 165 Olympians, athletes and officials lived on post from July 6 to August 3. They were housed in Henry Hall, Building 73. The village was six miles from Golden Park, the city's minor league baseball stadium that was converted into a softball venue. Sally Foley, a Columbus native, was Mayor of the Olympic Village, a diplomatic post set up to extend Southern hospitality to athletes and visiting dignitaries.

Of the twenty-nine local individuals who carried the Olympic flame for the 1996 Olympic torch relay on July 12, seven were affiliated with Fort Benning or the military: Sergeant First Class Joseph J. Wood, Company B, 2nd Battalion, 11th Infantry Regiment; Sergeant Willie Briskey, Headquarters and Headquarters Company, 3rd Battalion, 75 Ranger Regiment; Colonel Robert B. Nett (Ret.), World War II Medal of Honor Recipient for Company E, 305th Infantry, 77th Division; Owen T. Ditchfield, media specialist, Edward A. White Elementary School; Captain Glen Dubis, a 1984 Olympian from the Army Marksmanship Unit; Sergeant Major Laurence Mosley (Ret.), a 1960 Olympian from the Army Marksmanship Unit.; Master Sergeant Charles Davis (Ret.), a volunteer with the Atlanta Committee for the Olympic Games.

---

[36] Alyanna B. Summers, "Deputy CG bids fond farewell," *Bayonet*, August 14 1992, A-3.

[37] Lisa M. Hibbert, "Post gets new commander," *Bayonet*, July 12 1996, A-1.

Asked what carrying the Olympic flame meant to him, Nett replied, "It means continuing to serve with soldiers as I have done through three wars. It feel it's a tribute to them and I'd like to share it with them."[38]

Most of Fort Benning's troops performing Olympic duty came from 3rd Brigade, 3rd Infantry Division (Mechanized) with the majority of soldiers from 1st Battalion, 30th Infantry Regiment. The soldiers operated base camps, providing housing and all other facilities for 650 to 950 soldiers at each base camp. Later in August, soldiers of the 3rd Brigade operated a support unit to assist with the Paralympic Games.

Sacrifice of soldiers was brought home to troops, families, and friends when a monument was dedicated in August to honor twenty-two Rangers who died in combat or training since the 3rd Ranger Battalion was reactivated in 1984. The names of those who died in combat were sandblasted on one side of the black granite stone and those who lost their lives in training on the other side. Lieutenant Colonel Frank Kearney, battalion commander, noted the memorial stands in "the shadow of the barracks, under the shade of the oak trees, along the route to the mess hall" of the 75th Ranger Regiment. Remembering the fallen Rangers, Kearney said, "We, their brothers in arms who watched them bravely lead the way, humbly render this salute. May God watch over our fallen Rangers and bless their families."[39]

Family members at the dedication included Deanna Joyce-Beck whose twenty-four-year-old husband, Sergeant James Casey Joyce, lost his life while fighting in Mogadishu. For her, being there was difficult. "We lived here for three years and I used to drop my husband off every morning and it's hard to come back here and see all the soldiers.... You used to attend these things and your husband was right there beside you and that's very hard," she said.[40] "Time does heal.... it's hard in the beginning, but there's a

---

[38] Ann Oleska, "Local heroes to carry on Olympic tradition," *Bayonet*, March 1 1996, C-1.

[39] Marc G. Turchin, "Rangers remember fallen comrades with new memorial," *Bayonet*, June 14 1996, A-1.

[40] Marc G. Turchin, "Rangers remember fallen comrades with new memorial," *Bayonet*, June 14 1996, A-1.

point where you have to realize they're not coming back. But I'm thankful he was in the Army. I think he loved it here. I know he was proud."[41]

The memorial, in the works since 1993, largely was made possible by a $100,000 donation by Arthur W. "Bud" Brisciani, a member of the US Army Ranger Association. He made it after the battalion's return from Somalia, where six Rangers lost their lives attempting to recover fallen comrades. A Ranger carrying away the body of a fallen soldier was etched into the monument.

In late August, after the Olympics, the 29th Infantry Regiment moved from Kelley Hill and Harmony Church back to Main Post and the building it occupied between 1930 and 1943. "We moved into the cuartels as soon as construction finished in 1930," said Frank C. Plass, honorary command sergeant major for the 29th Infantry Regiment and president of the 29th Infantry Regimental Association.[42] "The regimental headquarters and the 1st Battalion occupied Olson Hall, and 2nd and 3rd Battalions lived in Henry Hall. We lived in those buildings until the regiment was moved to Iceland in 1943 during World War II."[43] With individual phone service in their rooms and private baths, the 29th had come a long way from the tents and muddy roads of early Camp Benning.

First Sergeant Leticia Westlake made history as the first female first sergeant in the annals of the 11th Infantry Regiment. Westlake, after serving eighteen years in the army, was proud to hold a leadership position and to inspire other women. "Being a female will not affect my role as first sergeant because I don't look at gender and I want to be treated the same way," Westlake said. "If she wants to be a soldier, she can be a soldier. If she wants to be a good soldier, she can be a good soldier."[44] As proof of this, Staff Sergeant Cynthia F. Jackson and Sergeant Denise A. Dillon, the first two women to attend drill sergeant school at Fort Benning, graduated in August 1995.[45]

---

[41] Heidi Fedak, "Saluting their fallen comrades," *Benning Leader*, June 14 1996, A-5.

[42] Lisa M. Hibbert, "29th Inf. Moves back to Main Post," *Bayonet*, August 30 1996, A-1.

[43] Ibid.

[44] Hibbert, "11th Inf Regt gets female 1st Sgt," *Bayonet*, July 4 1996, A-7.

[45] Shannon Day, "Benning graduates first two female Drill Sgts.," *Bayonet*, August 11 1995, C-4.

Two drill sergeants would continue to be good soldiers and to give orders long after their army careers had ended. The voices of Staff Sergeant John P. Lowthorpe and Sergeant First Class Christopher K. Greca, instructors at the drill sergeant school, became part of Fort Benning's permanent display at the Columbus Museum. "It is a good feeling that 100 years from now, as long as the exhibit still stands," Greca said, "my great-grand children will be able to enter that exhibit and hear my voice."[46]

Columbus and Fort Benning drew closer as Commanding General Carl Ernst, Columbus mayor Bobby Peters, and Phenix City mayor Sammy Howard took part in the grand opening of the Chattahoochee Riverwalk, extending from the National Infantry Museum to downtown Columbus. "The Riverwalk joins Fort Benning with Columbus and Phenix City.... They're one community now," Peters noted.[47] Unlike the dedication of the road joining Columbus to Fort Benning in 1925, no "marriage ceremony" ensued.

Soon celebrating the fiftieth anniversary of the Civilian Military Council (CMC), Peters, Phenix City's city manager Bobby Gaylor and Ernst signed a proclamation to continue the CMC, started by Louis Kunze and early supporters. Public affairs secretary Mary Joan Leighton, who died in 1991, helped arrange meetings of the CMC, calling key civilians and military leaders who met once a month to ensure good relations between town and post. Leighton also took calls from mothers asking about their sons' training in OSUT...and gave them answers.[48] Soldiers and their families appreciated Leighton's wholehearted involvement in the affairs of Fort Benning.[49]

For many, like Leighton, Fort Benning was more than just an employer. It was home of the infantry, an educational institution that trained soldiers, men and women, from basic training to noncommissioned officers to commissioned officers. Describing Fort Benning's updated

---

[46] Hibbert, "Soldiers bring exhibit to life," *Bayonet*, August 16 1996, A-3.

[47] Lori Egan, "Tricommunity members stroll, run Columbus Riverwalk," *Bayonet*, October 18 1996, B-1.

[48] Clyde Snively, "Snively fondly remembers a friend," *Bayonet*, April 5 1991, A-2.

[49] Ibid.

mission, Ernst said, "It is clear we must plan and train in order to project flexible, survivable combat power anywhere in the world on short notice."[50]

---

[50] Maj. Gen. Carl F. Ernst, chief of infantry, "Commandant's Note: Forced Entry and the Contingency Force," *Infantry* 87/3 (July/December 1997): 1.

53.

Putting Soldiers First

The road to Bosnia began at Benning. But the road did not end in Bosnia. This rocky road led to most of the world's hot spots. Rapid deployment was becoming a Fort Benning specialty. The CONUS Replacement Center's support of Operation Joint Endeavor—sending troops to Europe in support of Bosnia—was in place since December 1995.[1] As a power projection platform, the post deployed the 3rd Brigade, 3rd Infantry Division (Mechanized); the 75th Ranger Regiment; and the 36th Engineer Group (Combat) in every major deployment of US forces in the last decade.[2]

At the post, various services of the US Armed forces worked with the Joint Preparation for Onward Movement Center (JPOM), preparing individual members of their respective branches for duty in Bosnia or the European theater as part of Operation Joint Endeavor. The Infantry Center developed new doctrine and training innovations, testing new equipment and weapon systems for Force XXI. Defining the mission, General Ernst stated, "It is clear we must plan and train in order to project flexible survivable combat power anywhere in the world on short notice...and sustain and reinforce deployed forces as needed."[3] Deployments for wars, peacekeeping, and training were frequent and at times lengthy. As a result, Fort Benning's active-duty dependents, spouses, and children learned to adapt to those departures and homecomings.[4]

While troops were going and coming in 1997, so were the leaders, Brigadier General Robert Clark left his post as assistant commandant for an

---

[1] Donald Rothberg, "Troops for Bosnia," *Benning Leader*, September 27 1996, 17.

[2] Maj. Gen. Carl F. Ernst, Chief of Infantry, "Commandant's Note: Forced Entry and the Contingency Force," *Infantry* 87/3 (July–December 1997): 1.

[3] Ibid.

[4] Tony Adams, "498th 'ready for anything,'" *Benning Leader*, March 21 1997, 4.

assignment with TRADOC. During a January ceremony on York Field, Walter Wojdakowski celebrated his twenty-five-year career with a promotion to brigadier general and with his new job as deputy commanding general. His most recent assignments were in Germany where he served as the director of training, 7th Army Training Command and later commanded the Operations Group, Combat Maneuver Training Center.[5]

In addition to welcoming his new deputy commanding general, in February Major General Carl Ernst also welcomed Mack Vereen, the post's new command sergeant major. He served with Ernst in Somalia as command sergeant major of Joint Task Force, Somalia. Ernst said Vereen was one of the top soldiers in the army, serving as command sergeant major of US Army Alaska Command.[6] Earlier in his career, he graduated from Benning's Airborne and Ranger Schools, followed by tours that included Operation Just Cause in Panama and Operation Restore Hope in Somalia. Vereen, who held a bachelor of science degree and a masters of arts degree from a Baptist seminary, said, "This is a unique opportunity to serve as the chief enlisted infantryman in the US Army, and to fulfill the duties and responsibilities of a command sergeant major."[7] Hoping to keep Fort Benning "the best installation in the US Army," Vereen vowed, "Never will I allow my needs to take precedence over my soldiers, their family members, the civilian work force, or the community."[8]

As Wojdakowski and Vereen settled in, word was received that the All-Army wrestling team of eight soldier-wrestlers and a coach would leave the post in June 1997. It was relocated to Fort Carson, Colorado, which offered an army athlete training center and proximity to the US Olympic Training Center in Colorado Springs. Before its departure, the team finished first at the Armed Forces wrestling meet in March at the Pensacola Naval Air Station in Florida. The World Class Athlete Program was created in 1948 to give soldiers with exceptional athletic skills the opportunity to train full-time to reach their potential and to try out for the US Olympic team.[9]

---

[5] "Former 11th commander returns as deputy CG," *Bayonet*, January 17 1997, 1.

[6] Brian R. Voller, "Post CSM assumes duties," *Bayonet*, January 31 1997, A-2.

[7] Ibid.

[8] Ibid.

[9] Tony Adams, "All army wrestlers moving out," *Benning Leader*, January 17 1997, 5.

Though the wrestling team was no longer on post, the US Army Marksmanship Unit (USAMU) continued to add to Fort Benning's esprit de corps. The Chattahoochee Valley Sports Hall of Fame inducted retired Lieutenant Colonel Lones Wigger, Jr., a former US Army Marksmanship Unit shooter, into its ranks in February. A member of the US Army Marksmanship Unit's Hall of Fame, Wigger was considered the unit's greatest international rifleman.[10] In 1996 the US Olympic committee named him one of the top 100 Olympians of all time. Wigger won his first Olympic gold medal at Tokyo in 1964, setting a world record. In twenty years of international competition, he won sixty-five gold, thirty-eight silver, and eight bronze medals, including gold medals at the 1964 and 1972 Olympic games.[11] With fourteen world record-setting teams, he set thirteen individual world records and claimed eighty national championships, holding or co-holding thirty-two national records.[12]

Staff Sergeant James Todd Graves, a USAMU shotgun shooter, added to the unit's glory when he was named the 1997 Army Male Athlete of the Year. Graves was considered the best skeet shooter in the country and one of the top three in the world.[13] After enlisting in January 1984, Graves was assigned to the USAMU after basic and infantry training at Fort Benning. Graves, who competed in the 1992 and 1996 Olympics, hoped to fulfill his goal of Olympic gold. "If it wasn't for the Army, I couldn't have accomplished what I have," Graves said. "I'm proud to wear the green uniform. It would have been really hard to make it to the Olympics without the Army."[14]

More than 1,500 Rangers dropped onto Fryar Drop Zone for the annual three-day Ranger Rendezvous in June, bringing together all three Ranger battalions. Retired colonel Bob Nett was among fourteen former Rangers inducted into the Ranger Hall of Fame, then in its sixth year. During the rendezvous, a regimental change of command occurred when Colonel William J. Leszcznski, Jr., passed command of the 75th Ranger

---

[10] Anna O'Leska, "Former soldier inducted into Hall of Fame," *Bayonet*, February 28 1997, C-1.

[11] Ibid.

[12] Ibid.

[13] Paula J. Randall Pagan, "AMU Soldier wins Athlete of the Year title," *Bayonet*, October 31 1997, A-4.

[14] Ibid.

Regiment to Colonel Stanley A. McChrystal, its tenth commander. Leszczynski, assigned to Italy, said, "I wish I could turn back the clock and start over. I've been fortunate. Some people never meet a real hero in their whole life. I was surrounded by heroes, 2,364 of them."[15]

Some Benning leaders were ready to retire. Charlie O'Dell, one of the "fathers" of the Bradley fighting vehicle system, retired in July 1997 after more than forty years of service.[16] In 1968, he taught seven days a week in the Infantry Company Tactics Department at Fort Benning, training officers and NCOs for combat in Vietnam. In the late 70s, O'Dell took part as a Department of the Army civilian in General William DePuy's TRADOC (Training and Development Command) revolution that took the army from a post-Vietnam to the information-age army today. With its success in Desert Storm, the Bradley fighting vehicle system contributed greatly to that change. As former Fort Benning commander General Carmen Cavezza recalled, the development of the Bradley caused controversy because of time and money, but "it was definitely a machine that was needed."[17]

Command Sergeant Major Willie Wells relinquished his three-year command of the Henry Caro Noncommissioned Officer Academy to Command Sergeant Major George R. Monk. After his tour of twenty-seven years, Wells said young soldiers now were more intelligent compared to the draftees in the 1970s who "had no direction in their life."[18] Even with technology, Wells believed a soldier needed to "stand toe-to-toe and face-to-face with his enemy.... The 'spirit of the bayonet,' so to speak, will never go away."[19] The role of command sergeant major, according to Wells, was to set a good example for his men: "He's one who stands toe-to-toe with the colonel and says, 'Hey sir, we're not taking care of soldiers.'"[20]

---

[15] Elizabeth E. LaMonica, "75th Ranger Regt receives new boss," *Bayonet*, June 27 1997, A-3.

[16] Lt. Col. Tim Mishkofski, "Charter member of Bradley Fighting Vehicle System retires," *Bayonet*, July 18 1997, A-5.

[17] Maj. Gen. (Ret.) Carmen Cavezza, interview by Peggy Stelpflug, June 17 1998, Columbus Government Center, Columbus GA.

[18] Sgt. Marc G. Turchin, "NCOA Sergeant Major retires," *Bayonet*, November 21 1997, A-3.

[19] Ibid.

[20] Sgt. Marc G. Turchin, "NCOA Sergeant Major retires," A-3.

Command Sergeant Major Joe M. Heckard of the 11th Infantry Regiment echoed those observations, noting modern soldiers had to be smarter to keep pace with the use of computers and other new technology.[21] Heckard, who served with all three Ranger battalions was ready to retire. "It's been a long thirty years, a tough thirty years. I've never had an easy assignment, so now it's time for me to sit back and enjoy life for a while."[22]

After twenty-eight years of active service, Colonel John R. Reitzell, chief of staff of the US Army Infantry School, retired on March 13. Commissioned a second lieutenant in 1969, he attended the infantry officers' basic course, Ranger School, and Airborne School. In Vietnam, he was a rifle platoon commander—ten months out of college. From his experience, he reasoned, "Soldiers don't trust officers inherently and they damn sure don't trust lieutenants. That is, until a lieutenant does something to prove that A. they're capable; B. they care; and C. they're going to get 'em out of whatever predicament they get 'em into.... I made a couple of Fort Benning-educated decisions, some basic things they teach here, and it worked."[23] In Vietnam, he said, "Nobody wanted to be the last guy killed and nobody wanted to be the leader of the last guy killed."[24]

Responding on the army making do with less, Reitzell said, "It takes twenty-eight guys to run the drop zone out at Fryar for the basic Airborne course. Do we need all twenty-eight out there? I don't know, let's take two of them off and see if we kill somebody. So there are some tradeoffs there and you've got to apply common sense to it.... But by and large we are doing what we're supposed to do and we're doing it very damn well."[25] Reitzell believed the army would have to rely on more simulated training since it was less expensive than actual training. United States forces, he said, would be called on for more peacekeeping, humanitarian, and disaster relief missions, but added, "We simply can't lose the focus that we are in the business of winning the nation's shooting wars."[26]

---

[21] Brian R. Voller, "Retire," *Bayonet*, March 28 1997, A-5.

[22] Ibid.

[23] Tony Adams, "Reitzell hanging up his BDU's," *Benning Leader*, March 7 1997, 12.

[24] Ibid.

[25] Ibid.

[26] Ibid.

Units as well as individuals continued to come and go. One hundred soldiers with the 498th Medical Company (Air Ambulance), 36th Engineer Group (Combat) flew out of Lawson, March 18, headed for a peacekeeping mission in Bosnia.[27] In March 1997, an international force of about 31,000 troops, including about 8,500 Americans, replaced the troops that had prevented hostility in Bosnia since the Dayton Peace Accords of 1995.[28] The 832nd Medical Company, Air Ambulance, a National Guard unit from West Bend, Wisconsin, temporarily replaced the 498th on post.

As the 498th was returning, the 608th Ordnance Company, 36th Engineer Group (Combat) prepared to leave for Hungary. The company's mission was to support Operation Joint Guard Mission, supplying ammunition to units inside the Bosnian theatre. The seventy-five to eighty soldiers were prepared to stay six to twelve months or longer.[29]

In what was becoming a tradition, for the fifth year in a row, Fort Benning won the Army Chief of Staff Award. It recognized Benning as the best large installation in the army. And, after losing to New Jersey's Picatinny Arsenal in 1996, Fort Benning reclaimed its title as Best Large Army Installation in the World for the third time in four years by winning the Commander-in-Chief's Award. The cash award was $500,000 rather than the previous $1 million, a contribution for soldiers and their families and other improvements such as the night vision lab, land warrior and the digitized soldier.[30]

At a pep rally, the US Army Infantry band played the theme from *Rocky* as Ernst entered Marshall Auditorium, arms upraised in a victorious salute: "I can't tell you what an honor it is to be on this stage today for this purpose. You get to do a lot of things as the Commanding General of Fort Benning...but to be able to stand up in front of the folks who do the work to

---

[27] Brian R. Voller, "498th leaves post for Taszar, Hungary," *Bayonet*, March 21 1997, 1.

[28] Linda D. Kozaryn, Peace grows in Bosnia; Violence in Kosovo," *Bayonet*, May 29 1998, A-4.

[29] Tanya Holt-Wagner, "608 leaves Taszar, Hungary," *Bayonet*, October 17 1997, A-1.

[30] Heidi Fedak, "On top of the world again," *Benning Leader*, March 21 1997, 5.

make us the best Army installation in the whole world is real privilege and an honor."[31]

Added glory came in July when, on its first try, the post won the President's Quality Award (PQA), an award recognizing service to customers and commitment to excellence in the federal government. As the 1997 winner, the post was not allowed to resubmit a nomination packet for the award until the year 2001 since its mission as the winning base was to tell others how to succeed.

Sarah McLaney, who helped Benning win its first major award in 1992, summed up the significance of the PQA: "This is the top award in the federal government. It's the best of the best. We cannot do any better than this as far as awards...it shows that we do care and we do try to do the best that we can do."[32]

Recognizing leadership from its military neighbors, the Columbus Consolidated Government named former Fort Benning commandant Carmen Cavezza as its third city manager in three years. "I kind of stumbled into city manager," Cavezza explained. "When I came back from Fort Lewis, the Olympics were going on, and they asked me to run the Olympics softball venue which I did. After the Olympics were over we took the organization and converted it into the Greater Columbus Sports and Events Council, which still exists and continues to bring athletic events into Columbus."[33]

When Mayor Bobby Peters asked Cavezza if he was interested in the city manager's job, an appointed position, Cavezza said yes. "It seemed like the thing to do," he said. "I got caught up in it."[34] Hoping to build on the diversity of Columbus, Cavezza said, "I'm a persuasive leader. I feel if you have good people, let them be good. I want to give city employees their rein."[35]

---

[31] Elizabeth E. LaMonica, "Post commander praises community during rally," *Bayonet*, April 14 1997, 1.

[32] Marc G. Turchin, "Fort Benning wins quality award," *Bayonet*, July 18 1997, A-1.

[33] Cavezza interview.

[34] Wayne Partridge and Richard Hyatt, "Cavezza new city manager," *Columbus Ledger-Enquirer*, April 16 1997, A-8.

[35] Ibid.

Cavezza had commanded Fort Benning and the US Army Infantry School from June 1990 until October 1991. He held three advanced degrees, including a doctorate. His first visit to Columbus was in 1961 as a second lieutenant. He recalled,

> In 1961, Columbus was just a little town outside the gate.... That was my perspective. When I came back in 1965, it was getting better because there was a new mall—Columbus Square Mall. Now it started to get some personality, but it was still just a town outside the gate of Fort Benning. When I came back in the '80s, Interstate 85 helped it take on more personality, its own identity. Then again when I came back as CG, it really blossomed. So I saw this city transition over the years from something I really wouldn't want to be involved in to something I was excited about.[36]

Cavezza was not paid as much as his predecessor. His salary was $87,000 a year plus benefits for the responsibility of overseeing Columbus's daily operations and managing 2,200 employees.[37] That was Cavezza's decision. "I wanted to come in and see just what it was like, so I thought what they offered me was appropriate.... I got beat up a little bit in the community for that but my conscience was clean on it."[38]

Another civilian military link was made when Carl Patrick, Sr., chairman of Columbus-based Carmike Cinemas, was inducted into the Officer Candidate School's Hall of Fame. A graduate of OCS during World War II, Patrick did not obtain the rank of colonel or hold a Medal of Honor. But he helped start Columbus Tech, established a chair, funded the Patrick Theatre in the Columbus Museum, and donated a million dollars to St. Francis Hospital's cardiac unit. He also opened a ten-screen theatre on post, the first venture of its kind for the army. Patrick, who served more than four years in the army, donated the uniform he wore in Sicily to the National Infantry Museum.[39]

An expansion of a post unit was an additional special event in the summer of 1997. The Infantry Training Brigade (ITB) added another

---

[36] Cavezza interview.

[37] Ibid.

[38] Ibid.

[39] Heidi Fedak, "Theater mogul an OCS Hall of Famer," *Benning Leader*, September 19 1997, 10.

battalion: the 2nd Battalion, 19th Infantry Regiment with lineage and honors dating back to the Civil War. This expanded the ITB from five training battalions to six. From 1984 to 1987, ITB had ten battalions, fifty companies turning out recruits. In 1996, the five remaining training battalions had about 13,000 graduates.[40] With the new unit, ITB would process and train more than 21,000 One Station Unit Training soldiers for infantry units all over the world.[41]

Another outfit did not celebrate its eventful news. The 586th Engineer Company (Assault Float Bridge), a combat bridge-building unit with the 36th Engineer Group, had its last major operation—a two-week exercise to Camp Gruber, Oklahoma—before it was inactivated in September 1997. The 586th, constituted in 1945 in Mainland China, was inactivated at the end of World War II and reactivated in 1951. The unit, which moved to Fort Benning in 1972, deployed to Jacksonville, Florida, during Operations Desert Shield and Storm in 1990–1991 and received the Meritorious Unit Citation for its work supporting the post by helping deliver troops and equipment to the Mid-east.[42]

In 1992, the 586th's River Rats provided relief for victims of Hurricane Andrew in Florida and participated in Operation Uphold Democracy in Haiti in 1994. The unit made history when it built the longest ribbon bridge on record, spanning Croatia's Sava River during the movement of NATO peacekeeping troops into Bosnia in 1995–1996.[43]

A happier event, especially for children on post and in town, was the Easter egg hunt held at Riverside, home of Major General Carl F. Ernst and his wife, Linda. Post organizations provided entertainment and snacks for 2,500 people who gathered on Riverside's lawn to watch children find 7,000 eggs in less than ten minutes.[44]

Such occasions detracted from the post's problems. In 1997, downsizing of the army affected civilian and military employment. The Training and Doctrine Command, Fort Benning's higher headquarters, was directed

---

[40] Heidi Fedak, "Job Growth," *Benning Leader*, April 18 1997, 5.

[41] Ibid.

[42] Sgt. Marc G. Turchin, "36th bids farewell to bridge company," *Bayonet*, September 26 1997, A-1.

[43] Ibid.

[44] Lisa M. Hibbert, "Community searches for Easter eggs at Riverside," *Bayonet*, March 28 1997.

by the Department of the Army to make 1,841 reductions in the civilian work force over the next three fiscal years. As an incentive, Voluntary Separation Incentive pay and Voluntary Early Retirement Authority were approved for 1997. The army's total force of nearly 750,000 in 1989 was reduced by 36 percent in 1997. Medical and retirement benefits also were at risk. Government, that once promised to provide free lifetime medical care for soldiers, trimmed away benefits. Fewer soldiers performed more missions and worked longer hours. Many thought a return to the draft a solution to recruiting problems. Others like retired Colonel Ralph Puckett disagreed. "I have never met a commander at any level who wants to return to the draftee Army. Unanimously, they believe that the soldiers (and the Army) we now have are better than ever before. They give the all-volunteer force as a major reason."[45]

Puckett conceded, "the draft might diminish the lack of connection between civilians and the military since parents who have no children in the military have little or no interest in what is happening in the services."[46] But he disliked the fact that women would be subject to the draft in order to be politically correct. "What would be the effect on a rifle company with 50 percent women?" Puckett asked. "Returning to the draft may not have the commendable consequence promised. Instead the impact in a politically correct environment could be disastrous, a 'cure' worse than the 'disease.'"[47]

A persistent problem for the post since 1990 was the annual School of the Americas protest. In a prelude to its November 16 protest, seven activists vandalized the entrance to Fort Benning, using crowbars to pull letters from the post's entrance sign. Crosses and photos of the slain priest and two women co-workers were placed on the ground. The Reverend Roy Bourgeois, who spent six months in prison for a similar demonstration in 1995, stood by and watched the protesters, who were arrested for criminal trespassing and destruction of government property. Nearly 1,000 people

---

[45] Col. (Ret.) Ralph Puckett, "Hackworth only half right on recruiting dilemma," *Benning Leader*, September 5 1997, 2.

[46] Ibid.

[47] Ibid.

demonstrated outside the main gates, carrying empty black plywood coffins and white crosses in a mock funeral procession.[48]

Colonel Roy Trumble, the SOA commander, said, "The School of the Americas can't be held accountable for the conduct of a few graduates.... We believe SOA has had a positive effect on Latin America."[49] Since 1946, nearly 60,000 students graduated from the school with less than 300 linked to war crimes.[50] Congress passed the $4.2 million budget for the school by seven votes, providing an endorsement of the institution as a tool for the United States in advancing democracy and human rights in Latin America.

Still another problem, a "prickly" problem common to other posts and other services in various degrees, was of "blood pinning" or "blood wings" initiations. Though the practice was prohibited, some soldiers said the practice occurred at past Airborne School graduations and Expert Infantryman's Badge ceremonies. The procedure at Benning was relatively painless, compared usually to a bee sting.[51] The graduate who requested blood wings would have a friend "pin" the wings or the badge onto the graduate's chest by thumping it with the palm of the hand. Sweatshirts and t-shirts sold in local stores had pictures of blood dripping from the paratrooper's wings or expert infantryman's badge.[52]

In December, Phenix City and Russell County honored those who died in America's last five major conflicts—World Wars I and II, the Korean War, the Vietnam War, and the Persian Gulf War—with a memorial next to Garrett Stadium in Phenix City. Sam Nunn—a former US senator from Georgia and distinguished chairman of the Senate Armed Services Committee—was the primary speaker. Nunn believed a living monument was the appropriate way to remember those events. "It's because of them we are free each day to taste life," Nunn told the audience. "The best memorial

---

[48] Lori Egan, "SOA watch protesters demonstrate, trespass, leave Fort Benning," *Bayonet*, November 21 1997, A-1.

[49] Ibid.

[50] Ibid.

[51] Tony Adams, "Some Benning soldiers undergo 'blood pinning,'" *Benning Leader*, February 7 1997, 3.

[52] Ibid.

is to make this community a living monument of what they fought to preserve."[53]

[53] Mollie M. Herman, "Local area honors veterans with memorial," *Bayonet,* December 12 1997, A-3.

54.

Lines in the Sand

Good soldiers don't grow on trees. Boots are another matter. Fort Benning's trees were alive with orchards of combat boots. Old boots, army issue boots that had gone to war and back. It was a custom more than a crop, part of an interesting rite that became part of coming home from Bosnia, a way for returning troops to mark their farewell to the military and to Fort Benning. No one knew how it began, but once a returning soldier was cleared and processed, he would knot the laces on his old boots and sling them into the nearest tree. Soon boots were dangling like over-ripe fruit in trees around Harmony Church, near the processing facility that served troops coming from and going to Bosnia.

But Bosnia was not the only destination for troops passing through the processing center in 1998. In January, acting secretary of the army Robert M. Walker came to visit troops on their way to Kuwait. Walker, who took over after former army secretary Togo West moved to Veterans Affairs, returned to Fort Benning as the army's top civilian. "Never in my wildest imagination did I ever dream that Private Walker would some day become the acting secretary of the army. I wanted to come to Fort Benning as my first official trip as acting secretary because this is where it all began for me," Walker said.[1]

Walker, along with recently appointed sergeant major Robert M. Hall, visited 2,500 trainees at the Infantry Training Brigade and said goodbye to soldiers deploying to Kuwait.[2] More than 1,157 troops for the 3rd Brigade, 3rd Infantry Division (Mechanized) departed on chartered airplanes from

---

[1] Marc G. Turchin, "Army leaders visit post," *Bayonet*, January 9 1998, 1.

[2] Sgt. 1st Class Larry Lane, "Soldiers leave for Kuwait," *Bayonet*, January 9 1998, 1.

Lawson Army Airfield, January 11, on their way to Intrinsic Action, an annual four-month desert training exercise.[3]

Intrinsic Action, mainly a maneuvering exercise, included two Bradley companies, two tank companies, and a field artillery battery. An engineering company and combat support elements were also deployed to Kuwait. If problems with Iraq arose, troops could switch from a training mode to a wartime position. Exercises with the Kuwaiti military were planned for March. The 3rd Brigade was not alone. The 608th Ordnance, 36th Engineer Group (Combat) ran an ammunition supply depot for the Bosnia peacekeeping mission while the 75th Ranger Regiment's 3rd Battalion stood ready to launch anywhere in the world. In 1998, the Infantry School's 11th and 29th Regiments as well as Ranger training and infantry training brigades trained nearly 40,000 soldiers and prepared soldiers and civilians—reservists to civilian interpreters—for the mission.[4]

By January 1998, the NATO alliance in the Bosnian region numbered 34,000, including 8,000 Americans—far less than the 27,000 US troops initially deployed there.[5] Benning processed thousands of troops on their way in and out of the region. Processing included updating medical and personnel records, outfitting them with cold-weather gear, and briefing them on overseas customs and cultures. Fort Benning's Continental US Replacement Center (CRC) was the only active CRC in the states in 1998, preparing civilian reservists and active-duty troops of all military branches.[6]

A new director was in charge of deployments. The man so successful in moving personnel and equipment during Desert Shield and Desert Storm, Logistics Director Dale E. Ellis, said goodbye January 30, after holding the post's top logistics spot for thirteen years. Ellis recalled arriving at Benning in 1979: "I can still remember after all these years, stepping off the airplane,

---

[3] Staff Sgt. Clifton Kershaw, "Post unit to spend months in desert," *Bayonet*, January 16 1998, A-5; "Leavin' on a jet plane," *Bayonet*, January 16 1998, 1.

[4] Tony Adams, "I don't think it's time to leave," *Benning Leader*, January 9 1998, 5.

[5] Linda D. Kozaryn, "Peace grows in Bosnia; Violence in Kosovo," *Bayonet*, May 29 1998, A-4.

[6] Sgt. 1st Class Larry Lane, "CRC mission doesn't change in '98, continues deploying soldiers," *Bayonet*, January 9 1998, A-5.

feeling the hot air hit my face and thinking, 'What did I get myself into?'"[7] Explaining his reasons for retiring in Columbus, he said, "We have three daughters and all have married Georgia boys. They all have kids now, which kind of means I have a lot of roots in this part of the country. Whether I like it or not, Georgia is home now."[8] After almost thirty-seven years of civil service, Ellis ended his mission of sending troops off to training exercises, peacekeeping duty, and war with everything they needed for success. "You can't imagine the feeling of pride you get knowing that they're fully loaded and have all the proper gear and are ready to go," he said.[9] Ken Strumpler, chief of DOL's Maintenance Division, was Ellis's replacement.

Another post deployment occurred in February as 200 soldiers from the 3rd Brigade, 3rd Infantry Division (Mechanized) left for Kuwait and a possible confrontation with Iraq. Soldiers of the 2nd Battalion, 69th Armor Regiment, 3rd Brigade, 3rd Infantry Division (Mechanized) said their goodbyes at the Kelley Hill Recreation Center. "The waiting has been driving me nuts," said Christa Valencia whose husband, Private First Class Fernando Valencia, was with Company A, 2nd Battalion, 69th Armor Regiment. "We've been waiting for several days and finally you just want to say, 'Go already!'"[10]

Two Fort Benning companies of M1-A1 tank crews and support personnel joined 3,000 Fort Stewart soldiers on their way to Kuwait to deter potential aggression by Iraq in Operation Desert Thunder. It was the largest build-up of American troops since the Gulf War.[11] Colonel Jack Gardner, 3rd Brigade commander, said the "two great tank companies shoot as well as anybody in the Army."[12] Contracted civilian workers, deployed earlier, off-loaded equipment and prepared it before additional soldiers arrived in Kuwait. Commanding General Major General Carl F. Ernst said, "I pray for diplomacy to work but if diplomacy fails, the soldiers will be the line in the sand."[13]

---

[7] Michelle J. Davis, "Logistics director plans to retire," *Bayonet*, January 23 1998, A-4.

[8] Ibid.

[9] Ibid.

[10] Lori Egan, "Troops deploy to Kuwait," *Bayonet*, February 27 1998, 1.

[11] Ibid.

[12] Ibid.

[13] Ibid.

The US Forces command units at Benning were the first to get the anthrax vaccine ordered by Defense Secretary William Cohen for all 1.5 million men and women in uniform.[14] Members of the 3rd Brigade, 75th Ranger Regiment, and the 36th Engineer Group received a series of six shots administered over eighteen months with annual boosters to maintain immunity. Although troops were trained and equipped for chemical and biological war more than their counterparts in the 1991 conflict, they were still not fully prepared for the warfare of the twenty-first century.[15]

About 285 soldiers of the 3rd Brigade, 3rd Infantry Division, returned home in May. They were among the 1,000 3rd Brigade soldiers deployed to Kuwait in January. Other members of the unit returned in July, after five months in the desert, training in temperatures as high as 120 degrees.

The 608th Ordnance troops, 36th Engineer Group returned in August from Hungary after serving eleven months. Specialist Justin Devine, a native of Presque Isle, Maine, said of the 608th's Bosnia-related mission, "I think it's great they we're helping them out. But in my opinion, I think we should help out our own people first.... It makes sense to me that they want to believe in their own religion. It doesn't make sense why they would want to kill each other over it. You have to think about how lucky we are."[16]

Deployments, such as those to Kuwait, affected local businesses. When soldiers departed, dependents frequently left to visit "home," decreasing not only retail sales but also personal services. Before, Ranger Joe's barbershop did record business, but after deployment, things were quiet. Joe Kennedy, vice president of Budget Car Sales, saw business decline nearly 50 percent when troops were called to serve in Operation Desert Storm in 1991, observing, "The whole economy was affected."[17] Still one tradition thrived:

---

[14] "Gulf troops to receive anthrax vaccine," *Benning Leader*, March 6 1998, 7; Charles L. Cragin, "Anthrax vaccine proves to be save, effective tool," *Bayonet*, August 20 1999, A-3.

[15] Tony Adams, "Germ warfare team heads for Gulf," *Benning Leader*, February 20 1998, 5; David Hackworth, "Troops simply aren't ready for deadly gas," *Benning Leader*, December 5 1997, 2; Heidi Fedak, "Army grapples with NBC threat," *Benning Leader*, September 12 1997, 4–5; Spc. D. Stewart Howell, "Soldiers learn chemical protection, NBC training," *Bayonet*, May 22 1998, A-5.

[16] Meredith Hartley, "608th troops learn how lucky they have it," *Benning Leader*, August 21 1998, 5.

[17] Meredith Baker, Big Bucks," *Benning Leader*, March 20 1998, 10.

weddings at the Infantry Center Chapel. In 1997, eighty-eight Saturday weddings were performed, free of charge. Each wedding had two hours "to get in, set up, have the ceremony, clean up, and get out."[18] Prior to the wedding, couples attended premarital counseling offered by the Family Life Center.

Conventions in the area, many of them military reunions, counteracted post departures and brought people and money into the area. A significant portion of the 269 conventions and the 322,000 people who attended in 1997 were military-related. That meant $119 million to hotels, restaurants, and stores. Research revealed that with only half of the 16 million World War II veterans still alive, cities needed to promote gatherings for the Vietnam and Korean War generations.[19]

Competitive events also brought money into the community. Representative Mac Collins of Georgia initiated action in Congress to get $1.5 million added to the 1997 Defense Appropriations Act to buy equipment for the US Army Marksmanship Unit, including state-of-the-art computerized targeting equipment and the Suis Ascor targeting system used in the 1996 Olympics.[20] Because of the new equipment, the post presented major shooting events with an expected $1 million impact on the local economy. The first international event was the Columbus/Fort Benning 1998 Grand Prize in May, attracting 300 competitors and coaches from 60 nations.[21]

Approximately $81 million—in the form of salaries and operating expenses—went into the Columbus economy each month, adding up to about $972 million per year.[22] With 23,683 soldiers and 7,332 civilians working on post, nearly $1.4 billion was funneled into the local economy each year.[23] In addition, nearly 13,500 military retirees lived in the

---

[18] Meredith Hartley, "Benning chapel churns out newlyweds each Saturday," *Benning Leader*, May 8 1998, 15.

[19] Tony Adams, "Reunions bring back memories and money," *Benning Leader*, May 22, 1998, 3.

[20] Paula Randall Pagán, "Marksmanship unit gets new electronic target system," *Bayonet*, January 16 1998, A-3.

[21] Ibid.

[22] Baker, "Big Bucks," 10.

[23] Ibid.

Columbus-Phenix City area with an annual income of $210 million.[24] Georgia had the fastest growing population of military retirees in the nation. In 1998 around 165,000 military retirees lived in the state—29 percent of them over the age of sixty-five.[25]

In February 1998, Colonel Lawrence K. White, Jr., chief of staff, joined the list of retired military after nearly twenty-eight years of service. White, a troop commander in Vietnam with the 11th Armored Cavalry Regiment, was chief of staff at Fort Lewis before coming to Fort Benning in October 1996. Replacing White was Colonel John C. Latimer, chief of staff of the US Army Infantry School. Latimer, a 1972 graduate of The Citadel, served with the 82nd Airborne Division at Fort Bragg, US Forces Command at Fort McPherson, Georgia, and the US Central Command at MacDill Air Force Base. Ernst regarded White not only as an outstanding chief of staff but also as a friend. "Every once in a while you get lucky. You find someone you serve with that you really admire and respect. Not only a great soldier, but a friend," Ernst said.[26] Ernst, deputy commanding general when White was the 11th Infantry Regiment's commander, said, "Larry is the kind of soldier you'd want on your flank in a tough fight. Larry is the kind of soldier you'd give your children to as a combat leader, and know he'd lead them well. Larry is the type of soldier, you'd trust with your life."[27]

At his retirement ceremony, White jumped with the Silver Wings, Benning's Command Exhibition Parachute Team, landing in front of Infantry Hall. On his previous jump on York Field in 1993 he landed flat on his "derrière butt."[28] This time he did it right, but joked, "They're going to retire my jumpsuit. It's worn-out on the rear end."[29]

McKenna Village was the operations center for an important experiment in the summer of 1998. Soldiers of the 101st Airborne Division (Air Assault) from Fort Campbell, the 3rd Infantry Division (Mechanized) from Fort Stewart and the staff of the Dismounted Battle Space Battle Lab

---

[24] Meredith Hartley, "Do soldiers really feel they are appreciated?" *Benning Leader*, May 15 1998, 5.

[25] "Cleland includes healthcare plan in defense bill," *Benning Leader*, May 15 1998, 11.

[26] Marc G. Turchin, "Chief of staff retires," *Bayonet*, August 7 1998, 1.

[27] Ibid.

[28] Ibid.

[29] Ibid.

conducted the Rapid Force Projection Initiative (RFPI) field experiment, testing new light infantry technology. High-tech digitized sensors and shooters were connected by a light digital tactical operations center. RFPI ran three scenarios: Air Assault, Defense in Sector and Deliberate Defense.[30]

Troops simulated a traditional Soviet motorized rifle division attaching a brigade-size light force. Also involved were 250 civilian support personnel. Using simulation and reality, the two-week experiment looked at emerging technology and its use in Force XXI, the army program designed to field an infantryman equipped with high-tech optics, information systems and weapons for the battlefield of tomorrow.[31] A control center set up near the battle lab on Main Post helped gather information from the sensors to find the enemy earlier, using virtual reality.[32] "This [the RFPI field experiment] is the very first of its kind using virtual reality for the soldier and the Army," said Traci Jones, the project's lead engineer. "This is the logical place to do it because Fort Benning is the home of the soldier."[33]

The closest thing to a real battle was an assault at McKenna Village. Soldiers testing the equipment said the technology still had a long way to go to compete with reality.[34] Corporal Shawn Marsh, a participant, observed, "If you have a mission to clear a building, the Army could take aerial photos of it and they could print it out here so we could do a walk through. But as far as training, I believe reality is the best way to go."[35] Though pleased with results, Colonel Tim Bosse, deputy director of the Dismounted Battle Space Battle lab, said, "You can have all of the best sensors and the longest shooters in the world, but it's still going to come down to guys in foxholes shooting at targets to win the fight."[36]

Retired Colonel Al Garland, a critic close to home, criticized the army's use of advanced technology in the March issue of the *Benning Leader*,

---

[30] Sgt. 1st Class Larry Lane, "RFPI tests sensors, technology," *Bayonet*, August 7 1998, 1.

[31] Meredith Hartley, "Soldiers step onto the virtual battlefield," *Benning Leader*, July 31 1998, 6.

[32] Ibid.

[33] Ibid.

[34] Ibid.

[35] Ibid.

[36] Larry Lane, "RFPI lends hand to advance Technology," *Bayonet*, August 14 1998, 1.

which published its final edition in December 1998. "The only people getting warm and fuzzy...are the CEOs of the companies producing the gear.... I am probably too old and too far out of the loop to appreciate the Force XXI program. But I believe we are placing far too much faith in inanimate objects that have not proven successful under field operating conditions and will probably never do so."[37]

On October 1, army basic combat training expanded to nine weeks, providing more human relations and physical fitness training than in the past. In May, values-based training as well as thirty hours of human relations training was added to the instruction at army drill sergeant schools to help them instruct new soldiers in the seven army values: loyalty, duty, respect, selfless service, honor, integrity, and personal courage.[38]

Fort Benning's top drill sergeant in 1998, Staff Sergeant Clifford Drysdale, the son of a retired army first sergeant, learned army values at an early age. Drysdale, who grew up in Columbus, dropped out of Jordan High School in 1985 to join the army, serving in Germany, Somalia, and Haiti. Basic training at Sand Hill in 1985 had a profound effect on his life. Encouraged to take the job of drill sergeant, Drysdale worked seventeen hours a day, seven days a week in the thirteen-week Infantry Training Brigade program. He showed homesick teens how to make their bed properly or keep their rifles clean.[39] Drysdale explained the satisfaction of seeing changes in young recruits exposed to army values: "When they get here, they don't have a clue as to what's going on, they don't have the military discipline, but when you see them march across the graduation field and hear from their parents...you feel like you've accomplished a whole lot."[40]

When Rangers gathered earlier in the year for the sixteenth annual David E. Grange, Jr., Best Ranger competition, a pair of Fort Benning sergeants, part of the forty-team competition, came in first and won Colt .45 pistols. It was the fourth attempt for Sergeant 1st Class Eric Riley, a Ranger

---

[37] Al Garland, "Don't rely too much on high-tech combat," *Benning Leader*, March 6 1998, 15.

[38] Jim Caldwell, "Basic training extends to nine weeks," *Bayonet*, October 2 1998, 1.

[39] Tony Adams, "From dropout to top drill," *Benning Leader*, March 6 1998, 15.

[40] Ibid.

School instructor, and the first for Staff Sergeant Thomas Smith.[41] Smith, the "pack mule," gave the reason for their success: "He knew that I was physically strong enough to do it because he used to be my platoon sergeant. So I did all the physical stuff. But he's a very meticulous planner. He planned the whole competition, five different scenarios in his head before we even started."[42]

Riley, a native of Cincinnati, Ohio, and Smith from Dardanelle, Arkansas, excelled overall in jumping from a helicopter, marching twenty miles with sixty pounds of equipment on their backs, avoiding an enemy sniper, roping up and down a tower, tackling the Darby Queen obstacle course and land navigation.

In the first Jane Wayne day, fifty soldiers' wives from the 4th Ranger Training Battalion and other female participants tackled a 60-foot rappelling tower, a 40-foot log walk and rope drop, a 500-meter boat movement, a movement under direct fire, and a laser-tag type operation.[43] The final event was anti-armor ambush using M-60s and M-4s on a BTR-60 armored personnel carrier. Patty Smith gained an appreciation for her husband, Sergeant Scott Smith, and his job at the 4th Ranger Training Battalion. "I have never worn camouflage before," she said. "I hope I don't break out."

To add to the Ranger's list of things-to-do, since 1997, Ranger training required instruction in boxing. Each student went through three periods of hand-to-hand techniques. In the fourth, students fought a fifteen-round bout. Matches took place on a drop zone at Camp Darby. "We want to toughen our people up," said Lieutenant Colonel Eric Hutchings, 4th Ranger Training Battalion commander. "Our students need to be able to receive a blow and then return one."[44]

A new bayonet assault course for the 4th Ranger Training Battalion was named for retired Colonel Lewis L. Millet, recipient of the Medal of Honor for a successful bayonet charge in Korea. Accompanied by his son at the dedication, Millet said, "The bayonet is the ultimate last weapon…. To

---

[41] Adams, "Benning duo captures 'Best' title," *Benning Leader*, May 8 1998, 12.

[42] Ibid.

[43] Nicole Longstreath, "Women put in Ranger's boots during first Jane Wayne day," *Bayonet*, May 1 1998, A-4.

[44] Marc G. Turchin, "Boxing: Students 'put up their dukes' at Ranger School," *Bayonet*, March 6 1998, A-4.

be successful, you have to be strong and in good shape."[45] The Millett family first experienced its loss of a uniformed family member in 1675 during an Indian massacre in Massachusetts. The most recent was Millet's son Staff Sergeant John Millett, an army flight medic, killed in a 1985 airliner crash in at Gander, Newfoundland, returning from a successful peacekeeping mission in the Sinai Desert.[46]

On November 20, 1998, a tribute was held for all the men killed in combat and training maneuvers since the 75th Ranger Battalions were activated in the 1970s. Fifty-five Rangers were honored at the Fallen Comrade Memorial service. Five were killed in the restoration of democracy in Panama; eight died in Grenada, rescuing American students in the Caribbean; six were killed in a firefight in the streets of Mogadishu, Somalia; and thirty-six died in training accidents over the last two decades. Reflecting on those killed in training and those killed on the battlefield, Colonel Stanley McChrystal, 75th Ranger Regiment commander, said, "the sacrifice is the same."[47]

Work on the $33.7 million barracks for the 75th Ranger Regiment due for completion in May 2000, was delayed by the discovery of 1,057 hand grenades, 20 French rifle grenades, 3 US rifle grenades, 182 pounds of small arms ammunition, and 2 anti-tank rounds. The post's Explosive Ordnance Detachment blew up these occupational hazards. A munitions-removal contractor found and destroyed remaining buried ordnance with a magnitrometer, a device similar to a metal detector. During construction, most buried ordinance devices were found in former impact areas, designated places for artillery practice.

Such setbacks did not distract from the post's sixth straight win of the Chief of Staff of the Army, Army Communities of Excellence (ACOE) Award for "installation excellence." The post was designated the best large stateside army installation and awarded a $200,000 prize. In April, amidst cheers and applause from sixty post leaders and delegates from Columbus and Phenix City who traveled to Washington, Ernst and chief of the Quality Management Division, Sarah McLaney, received the winning trophy from

---

[45] Tony Adams, "Slashing and jabbing," *Benning Leader*, May 22 1998, 4.

[46] Ibid.

[47] Adams, "Rangers refuse to forget the fallen," *Benning Leader*, November 27 1998, 4.

army chief of staff General Dennis J. Reimer.[48] After Benning won the Commander-in-Chief Award—given for best large army installation in the world—in 1994, 1995, and 1997, a new rule prohibited repeat winners. The 1998 prize went to Fort Carson, Colorado.

Over a six-year period, Fort Benning won more than $5.2 million. The $500,000 won in 1997 went for the Better Opportunities for Single Soldiers (BOSS) program, playground equipment for housing areas, maintaining and enhancing post lake recreation sites, cleaning and painting Doughboy Stadium, restoring the Follow Me fitness trail, upgrading post chapels, general landscaping, supporting the post's continuance of the Army Community of Excellence program as well as the application fee for the Georgia Oglethorpe Award, a competition for the best industry in Georgia.[49]

Financial contributions to post medical facilities were made by members of the Officers' Wives Club who contributed to the post's improvement by raising $52,625 for various programs and agencies. With a membership of 308, the club established grants for $28,000 in scholarships.[50] Both enlisted and officers' family members were eligible. Additional contributions went to the army community for schools, American Red Cross, community services, Boy Scouts and Girl Scouts, AUSA, and other post projects.

Following the August 1998 bombings of US Embassies in Kenya and Tanzania, retaliatory strikes were made against targets in Afghanistan and Sudan. Fort Benning now exercised security measures with the Force Protection Plan. Martin Army Community Hospital was given added protection, and the 988th Military Police Company and the US Army Infantry Center (USAIC) Military Police Company manned post entrances twenty-four hours a day. The post usually operated at "Threat OM normal," the lowest level of security, but moved to Threat COM D, the highest level of security.[51]

---

[48] 1st Class Larry Lane, "Post picks up ACOE award," *Bayonet*, May 8 1998, 1.

[49] Ibid.

[50] Rashaan Dozier-Escalante, "OWC raises money for programs," *Bayonet*, June 5 1998, A-3.

[51] Tony Adams, "Frustration, goodwill at checkpoints," *Benning Leader*, September 4 1998, 4.

In addition to the hospital, Infantry Hall received protection along with Infantry Training Brigade barracks, the main exchange, and commissary. Entrances at Infantry Hall were reduced from fifteen to three to ensure that Benning, an open post, was safe for soldiers, families, civilian employees, retirees, and visitors.[52] The Directorate of Public Safety and the military police checked for valid registration decals, maintenance, driver's license, military IDs, and the destination of civilians entering the post. Contents of commercial and rental trucks were checked against the driver's shipping log.

About 100 officers staffed the 11 checkpoints while 2,000 vehicles passed through the I-85 site during rush hour, a problem since most posts do not have interstate highways running through them. Protecting an 183,000-acre installation with 60 access points was difficult, especially in intense summer heat. Individuals brought freshly baked cupcakes to the post protectors, and Royal Crown Cola donated 300 cases of soft drinks with Frito Lay and Tom's Food furnishing stock items.

Benning security would no longer be an issue for Brigadier General Walt Wojdakowski, deputy post commander since January 1997. He left for a new assignment as chief of the Office of Military Cooperation at the American Embassy in Kuwait City—a city he helped liberate as a battalion commander during the Gulf War. His replacement was Brigadier General Russel L. Honore, assistant commander of the 1st Cavalry Division, Fort Hood, Texas, who attended the infantry officers' basic and advanced courses at Fort Benning. A veteran of Desert Storm, Honore also served as senior mechanized infantry trainer at Fort Irwin's National Training Center and commanded the 1st Brigade of the 3rd Infantry Division at Fort Stewart. A graduate of Southern University Agriculture and Mechanical College in Baton Rouge, Louisiana, he earned a master's degree from Troy State University. On September 16, in front of Infantry Hall, Honore said, "Our role will be to continue to shape change for the Army…to adapt to new doctrine, write that doctrine and adapt the force structure to the Force XXI concept for the soldier of the future."[53]

---

[52] Ibid.

[53] Norval Edwards, "Benning gets new deputy commander," *Benning Leader*, September 18 1998, 3.

The soldier of the future certainly was on the mind of General Hugh Shelton, chairman of the joint chiefs of staff and President Clinton's top military adviser, when he placed a blue shoulder cord (the official designation of infantrymen since 1951) and army service ribbon on his son's uniform, signifying his son's transition from civilian to infantryman. Speaking at the graduation ceremony Shelton said, "Though many honors have come my way, I can tell you that no honor means more than being able to say I am an American infantryman. I am both proud and honored to be the first one to welcome each of you, including my son, Mark, to the infantry."[54]

Another 1998 visitor was General William W. Hartzog, commanding general of the US Army Training and Doctrine Command. Hartzog was stationed at Benning for nine of the thirty-five years he spent in service to his country. At his retreat ceremony he reflected, "When I first heard the poem, 'I am the Infantry,' I was standing where the Airborne School is now. It was then I began to understand what it was all about. We all are Iron Mikes. It is about the spirit, going forward, instead of backward."[55]

When Air Force Two carrying the vice president landed at Lawson Army Airfield in March, Vice President Al Gore shook hands and talked to the crowd before going to Columbus State University to discuss the school's Intellectual Capital Partnership Program to train workers for high-tech jobs. More than 200 third-, fourth-, and fifth-graders walked almost two miles from Wilson Elementary School to see the vice president, the highest-ranking government official to visit in 1998.[56]

Protesters, led by actor Martin Sheen, appeared again in November to remember those killed by former students of the School of Americas. No arrests were made for trespassing. Retired Major Ray Lopez, a former USARSA instructor and executive director of the School of the Americas Support Group, Inc., talked to protesters, telling them, "The School is

---

[54] Nicole M. Graham, "Chairman speaks at graduation," *Bayonet*, June 5 1998, A-3.

[55] Graham, "Post pays tribute to TRADOC commander during ceremony," *Bayonet*, August 28 1998, A-3.

[56] Meredith Baker, "Vice President stops at Benning," *Benning Leader*, March 6 1998, 12.

something our country can be proud of. I can't just stand by and let people stain its reputation."[57]

Colonel Roy Trumble, SOA commandant for over three years, defended the institution when he retired in July, saying, "I regret that there continues to be opposition of the most valuable foreign policy tool in the US government's arsenal to affect [sic] a positive change in Latin America. Knowledgeable people will realize that the attacks on the school are unwarranted."[58] Colonel Glenn R. Weidner, the school's new commander, previously served as the army's senior fellow at Harvard University's Weatherhead Center for International Affairs.

Many SOA graduates led the Honduran relief effort when Hurricane Mitch struck Nicaragua and Honduras in the fall of 1998. More than 9,000 people died from heavy winds, mudslides, and flooding caused by the storm, one of the deadliest hurricanes of the century.[59] Fort Benning's 498th Air Ambulance Company provided a twenty-four-hour MEDEVAC, and the 36th Engineer Group's Headquarters commanded US Army relief units in Nicaragua. The 63rd Combat Support Equipment Company, 36th Engineer Group, cleared and repaired road networks in Task Force Build Hope.

In December Colonel Abraham J. Turner relinquished command of the US Army Infantry Training Brigade (ITB) to Colonel John "Rusty" Schorsch. Schorsch's first command was to order drill sergeants to march their soldiers off the field so they could go to their barracks and pack for Christmas leave.[60] Nearly 3,000 ITB soldiers left for Operation Exodus, a two-week holiday break conducted for the past twenty-one years except during Operations Desert Storm and Desert Shield in the Gulf War.[61]

Peace was growing in Bosnia as the end of 1998 approached. Warring factions were separated at last and armies demobilized. The rule of law was taking hold. But problems were escalating in Kosovo: Serb president Slobodan Milosevic had installed a harsh police state and was determined to

---

[57] Michelle J. Davis, "Protest," *Bayonet*, November 25 1998, A-1.

[58] Meredith Hartley, "School gets new commander," *Benning Leader*, July 24 1998, 12.

[59] Pfc. Mitch Frazier, "Soldiers join relief efforts," *Bayonet*, December 4 1998, 1; "Servicemembers provide hurricane relief," *Bayonet*, November 13 1998, A-1.

[60] Pfc. Nicole M. Massie, "ITB receives new commander," *Bayonet*, December 18 1998, A-1.

[61] Ibid.

drive ethnic Albanians—representing 90 percent of the population—out of the country—dead or alive. His goal was ethnic cleansing, but in his way he would find Fort Benning troops.

55.

Civilians Have a Mission, Too

Civilian workers never wore ranks on their sleeves and never commanded a crisp salute. But since the days of leaky tents and muddy streets these people have been vital to Fort Benning's mission. Many of these workers never served a day in uniform while others joined the civil service workforce after retiring from active duty. In 1999, two men who contributed in both uniform and civvies were honored for their contributions. Later in the year, the woman who helped fill Fort Benning trophy cases with awards also would be honored.

Retired Lieutenant Colonel Charles McIntosh, with forty years of government service, was honored at Infantry Hall during an Honor Bayonet Ceremony in January. He was awarded the Order of St. Maurice and a Department of the Army Superior Service Award. During his twenty-four-year military career, including three years as a POW in Korea, he was decorated with the Distinguished Service Cross, two Silver Stars and three Bronze Stars for valor, four Purple Hearts, and two Vietnam Crosses of Gallantry.[1]

After retiring from the army in 1972, McIntosh served with the US Army Infantry Center's Directorate of Combat Development. As an employee with the Light Infantry Task Force team, he helped develop doctrine and core training strategies for light infantry battalions. As a combat development specialist with the Electronics and Special Developments Division, he led the development of a combat identification system to reduce fratricide and the shortstop electronic protection system to protect soldiers in foxholes from artillery threat.

---

[1] Pfc. Nicole M. Massie, "Post honors veteran for years of service," *Bayonet*, January 15 1999, A-1.

Honoring McIntosh, Deputy Commanding General Russel L. Honore said, "When we built the Follow Me statue, it was built with a soldier like this in mind. He is a true grunt. Mr. McIntosh is a living legacy to the infantry." McIntosh replied, "I have strived to do a service to the infantrymen and to make their job easier. I have received an education one cannot buy during my time of service."[2]

Charles Thornton, a division chief of Dismounted Battlespace Battle Lab, died that same month and was buried at Fort Mitchell National Cemetery in Seale, Alabama. He was posthumously awarded the Army Government Civilian Tester of the Year award for 1999 by the National Defense Industrial Association. Thornton was remembered in the *Bayonet*: "When Charlie said it would happen, it did.... We trusted in a man who did so much for soldiers throughout the years. He served, first, for twenty-two years on active duty, including three tours in Vietnam, and then, for the next eighteen years, in civil service, working to make visions reality. Many soldiers will never know our Charlie, but they have him to thank for making their training better, safer, and smarter. They'll never know of his many contributions to 'Owning the Night,' which gives us the edge on the battlefield at night."[3]

In January 1999, the Basic Combat Training Brigade (BCTB) was activated—the first time in more than thirty years that Sand Hill housed a brigade other than the Infantry Training Brigade (ITB). Commanded by Colonel Nolen Bivens, it contained three battalions and a headquarters service company. Two battalions consisted of five companies and one had four. Each had the capacity to train around 240 Basic Combat Training (BCT) soldiers per cycle. After the BCTB's activation, the 1st Battalion, 38th Infantry Regiment, Infantry Training Brigade transitioned to the new brigade. It became the BCTB's first operational battalion. In addition, three other companies from One Station Unit Training (OSUT) moved to BCT.

The Basic Combat Training Brigade (BCTB) welcomed another battalion to Sand Hill in April. The 3rd Battalion, 47th Infantry Regiment joined the 1st Battalion, 38th Infantry Regiment in training soldiers from more than 160 MOSs (Military Occupational Specialty). To train the 2,400 initial entry soldiers, more than fifty troops were assigned to serve as cadre

---

[2] Ibid.
[3] "In Memoriam," *Bayonet*, January 29 1999, A-2.

for the new battalion. At full capacity, the BCTB increased the number going through initial training by about 5,500. In early June, the 2nd Battalion, 47th Infantry Regiment joined the BCTB at Sand Hill, merging it with 1st Battalion, 38th Infantry Regiment and 3rd Battalion, 47th Infantry Regiment.

Away from home, the 63rd Engineer Company (Combat Support Equipment), 36th Engineer Group (Construction), attached to the 46th Engineer Battalion from Fort Polk, Louisiana, remained in Nicaragua repairing damage caused by Hurricane Mitch the preceding year. It reestablished secondary farm roads, erected temporary bridges, and built a replacement medical clinic as well as a building to house the doctors.

As a participant in Task Force Build Hope, Sergeant Michael Moore, described the emotions of being one of the first US troops in Nicaragua after twenty years. "Sometimes you may leave the base camp feeling down, but as soon as you pass through the gates heading out to the project site and see the smiling children shouting and waving, your spirits are lifted. You feel appreciated and you realize why we are really here."[4]

In March, a new army policy on fraternization took effect, giving officers and enlisted soldiers who were dating one year to marry or end their relationships. It revised Regulation 600-20. It also limited private business deals between officers and enlisted soldiers. A new post policy—US Army Infantry Center Regulation 210-5—defined rules for dependents under the age of eighteen. Youth were required to be in their quarters after 10 P.M. each night and remain there until 5 A.M. unless accompanied by their parent or guardian or en route to or from an organized function.[5] Families that did not comply were subject to losing on-post privileges and faced ejection from post housing.

Remodeling was a welcomed policy in 1999. The Officers' Wives Club Thrift Shop, located in Crain Hall, reopened after extensive renovation. The former NCO Club (and previous 1921 Biglerville Mess) was one of the first buildings on Camp Benning. Honorary Officers' Wives Club president Linda Ernst cut the ribbon of the shop, a shop awarded the Volunteer

---

[4] 1st Lt. Heather Andrews, "63 builds roads, friendships in Nicaragua," *Bayonet*, January 22 1999, A-6.

[5] Spc. Michelle J. Davis, "New Juvenile misconduct policy to take effect June 1," *Bayonet*, April 24 1998, 1.

Organization of Excellence Award in 1999. Profits from the store sponsored the club's scholarship program as well as other endeavors.

Doughboy Stadium, another post landmark, also had a facelift, requiring over 400 gallons of paint. Cost for repairing the 1925 structure came from $140,000 received from Army Communities of Excellence awards. The stadium, used primarily for physical training and intramural sports, was the site of Benning's 1999 Easter Sunrise Service.

More funds were available in March after the post won the 1999 Army Communities of Excellence Commandeer-in-Chief's (CINC) Award for the fourth time in five years. That secured $500,000 for improvements on post and to the quality of life for soldiers, family members and the civilian work force. Major General Carl Ernst also accepted the 1998 Oglethorpe Award from Georgia Governor Roy Barnes at the Second Georgia Oglethorpe Annual Conference and Awards Banquet in March, the post's first entry into a state contest. "We have a great work force, who every day does an awful lot with an awful little, in terms of resources," Ernst said.[6] He dedicated it to Sarah McLaney. Despite suffering a stroke in 1998, she worked hard for the Oglethorpe and CINC awards. "Sarah, this award is truly yours," Ernst said.[7]

In addition to the CINC award in 1999, Fort Benning was awarded the Chief of Staff of the Army (CSA) Award for the seventh consecutive year. Later that year, McLaney retired after thirty-three years of civilian service. She fulfilled her wish, with the help of others, "to win the Oglethorpe and the big CINC award."[8] Sarah Hodges succeeded her as chief of the Quality Management Division, Directorate of Resource Management.

McLaney was certain the team would succeed with Hodges. She said, "They will continue to be just as successful whether I'm here or not. I didn't do anything by myself. It takes a team working with you on all of this. Without a team, it falls apart. With the award program, the whole army will continue to improve. We shared information with the infantry, Department of Defense, the navy, the marines, and the Goddard Space Center. We sent them copies of everything we did. I couldn't tell you all the installations

---

[6] Pfc. Amy L. Nyland, "Benning accepts Oglethorpe Award," *Bayonet*, March 26 1999, A-1.

[7] Ibid.

[8] McLaney interview.

we've helped. The hope of this program is that the whole Army will improve."[9] In her retirement, she planned to spend time with her husband, Rex, her three children, and five granddaughters. She would continue playing piano and organ in the same church in Phenix City, a task she performed for forty years as of Easter Sunday 1999.

Charlotte Lovett worked thirty-nine years and seven months on post as a civilian employee. The Columbus native said, "I work eight to ten hours a day out here, and my co-workers are like a second family to me. That is what I am going to miss most." Passing the civil service exam during her senior year at Jordan High School, Lovett's first job in 1960 was as secretary for the School Brigade now known as the 11th Infantry Regiment.

She worked several jobs on post until Commanding Major General Robert Wetzel hired her as his secretary. She served sixteen years as secretary for Fort Benning commandants. Lovett found the volunteer army different from the "boot-strap Army" of the past. "We have career people who want to be here," she explained. "The post now offers soldiers and their families many community life programs unavailable in the boot-strap army." Spending time with her husband Gene and family of four children and seven grandchildren was her retirement goal. "I may find a part-time job," she said, "like being a greeter at Wal-Mart, so that I can see people."[10]

More than 1,200 soldiers left for Kuwait in April for a four-month deployment. Soldiers from 1st Battalion, 15th Infantry Regiment, 3rd Brigade, 3rd Infantry Division (Mechanized) operated one of the largest training forces in the Middle East as part of Operation Intrinsic Action. Lieutenant Colonel Bob Pricone, Task Force 1-15 commander, said, "We have some of the best troops in the Army going on this mission and some of the best leaders. Everyone can be confident that our soldiers will do their best and return safely."[11] Their primary mission was to maintain a presence to deter the Iraqi military from entering Kuwait. Occupying Dragon Base, a tent city thirty kilometers from the Iraqi border, the soldiers had outdoor

---

[9] Sarah McLaney, interview by Peggy Stelpflug, December 11 1998, Building 66, Fort Benning GA.

[10] Sally Shutt, "Secretary retires after 39 years on post," *Bayonet*, September 24 1999, A-8.

[11] Pfc. Mitch Frazier, "Brigade Soldiers leave for Kuwait," *Bayonet*, April 16 1999, A-1.

showers and latrines. Desert training, concerts, and trips kept soldiers occupied while 3,000 miles from home in record-setting high temperatures, averaging about 126 degrees and reaching a high of 143 degrees.

The Fort Benning Golf Counsel provided golf clubs, golf balls, and carpet squares to the "Can Do" International Golf Club opened at Camp Doha, Kuwait. The flagpoles were pickets, and the flags were sandbags. The 3,010-yard, nine-hole course featured narrow fairways, scenic views, variable winds, and multiple sand traps. First Lieutenant Mike Lindsey, Task Force battalion adjutant, 1st Battalion, 15th Infantry, and course creator, explained, "The hard-core golfers needed something to tide them over until they could return to the states."[12]

When soldiers from the 3rd Brigade, 3rd Infantry Division safely returned from Kuwait after four months as part of Operation Intrinsic Action and Operation Desert Spring, their homecoming was marred by the discovery of their damaged cars, vandalized in the deployment storage lot on post. Damages and loss of property were covered by prompt legal assistance. Private First Class Kevin Ruffin said, "It's devastating to return home from a real-world deployment and have to worry about our cars instead of spending time with friends and family. It's sad that people don't care and would do this type of thing for no reason."[13]

On a happier note, honors were extended to retired general William R. Richardson and retired command sergeant major Basil L. Plumley, two of the army's top infantrymen, during the 1999 Doughboy Award ceremony. In his thirty-five-year career, General Richardson led the development of the new AirLand Battle Doctrine, reorganizing the army's heavy divisions for the modern army. The former head of TRADOC said he learned about leadership, confidence, and warrior values at the Infantry School. Plumley, a Columbus resident, served for thirty-two years. During his career, Plumley made five combat jumps in Sicily, Normandy, and North Korea. He was sergeant major of the 1st Battalion, 7th Cavalry in Vietnam. After retirement in 1974, he worked as a civilian employee at Martin Army Community Hospital at Fort Benning for fifteen years.

---

[12] Spc. Brian Murphy, "Do whatever you 'Can Do,'" *Bayonet*, July 16 1999, C-1.

[13] Michele E. Hanson, "Vandals make Soldier's return less than joyous," *Bayonet*, August 20 1999, A-3.

Weather on post was hot in the summer of 1999, nearing 100 degrees with high humidity. Dealing with live-fire field exercises, forced marches, and outdoor classroom instruction, soldiers—especially those not acclimated—used the buddy system to monitor one another for dehydration or sunstroke.[14] One solution to the heat was the Close Combat Tactical Trainer (CCTT), located at Mabry hall. It offered more than thirty simulators for infantry weapons and vehicles while allowing units to practice inside before actual field training. In addition to no weather obstacles, the CCTT provided no fuel problems for its simulated vehicles, no maintenance problems, and an unlimited supply of bullets.

Brigadier General Paul Eaton, Fort Benning's new deputy commanding general, and his wife, P. J., arrived from Germany, where he served as assistant division commander for the 1st Armored Division. He succeeded Honore who left in August 1999 for duty on the support staff for the joint chiefs of staff in Washington, DC. The Eatons were in time for the honor bestowed on Columbus businessman and World War II veteran Frank G. Lumpkin in September 1999 for his support of Benning's historical World War II buildings. The National Infantry Association designated the courtyard surroundings the buildings as Frank G. Lumpkin Jr. Plaza. Infantry Museum director Z. Frank Hanner said, "Frank G. Lumpkin ensured that there would be a Fort Benning in 1918, and Frank G. Lumpkin, Jr., has ensured that Fort Benning history will be protected."[15] Ernst agreed. "No family has been more supportive of Fort Benning," he said. "There must be something in the DNA."[16]

On September 14, Major General John M. LeMoyne assumed command of Fort Benning from General Ernst, commandant since July 1996. Ernst, named special assistant to TRADOC's commanding general, would pursue strategies for light forces and military operations in urban terrain until his retirement in 2000. During Ernst's tenure, the post was presented two Commander-in-Chief's Awards, three Chief of Staff of the

---

[14] Meredith Hartley, "Soldiers trying to keep cool through broiling conditions," *Benning Leader*, July 10 1998, 6; "Post Outlines new heat policy," *Bayonet*, June 26 1998, 1.

[15] Sally Shutt, "Columbus family safeguards Fort Benning's history," *Bayonet*, September 17 1999, A-5.

[16] Ibid.

Army Awards, the Presidential Quality Award, and the Oglethorpe Award. Calling his tour "three years of magic," Ernst said he and his wife would truly miss the "soldiers, their families, volunteers, civilian employees, retirees, and those who support us in Columbus and Phenix City."[17]

Ernst confessed that he was a kid at heart. "I like shooting weapons; I like walking patrols with soldiers; and I like falling out of airplanes. There is just a lot of fun in this business of soldiering."[18] In his early years, his goal was "to survive a tour in Vietnam...to live to be twenty-five." Thinking of the present, he said, "I know I will never be back in uniform. I'll visit Fort Benning, but that's different because it's not like being a part of this marvelous institution. So that's going to be very difficult and very sad.... Keep doing what you're doing, because no one does it like Fort Benning."[19]

LeMoyne was at Benning in 1950 where he watched his father's tank battalion train before it deployed overseas. He enlisted, choosing to serve in Special Forces. He received his commission from the University of Florida in 1968. He was a Ranger instructor and operations officer for the 2nd Battalion, 75th Ranger Regiment at Fort Lewis. His Vietnam combat tours included commanding a company in the 25th Infantry Division and as adviser to a Vietnamese Airborne battalion. He participated in Operation Just Cause in Panama and later commanded the 1st Brigade, 24th Infantry Division during that unit's "end run" to the Euphrates River in Desert Storm. Prior to his Benning assignment, he was assistant deputy chief of staff for personnel for the US Army in Washington, DC. Le Moyne, who called his assignment a privilege, desired "to work with American soldiers and to work with those entrusted with our nation's sons and daughters."[20] He wanted Fort Benning "to continue to be the best place in the US Army to train, to work, to live, to raise a family."[21]

---

[17] Maj. Gen. Carl F. Ernst, commanding general, "CG says goodbye, thanks to community," *Bayonet*, September 10 1999, A-2.

[18] Pfc. Amy L. Nyland, "Former CG heads to TRADOC," *Bayonet*, September 17 1999, A-4.

[19] Ibid.

[20] Pfc. Mitch Frazier, "Ernst hands over reigns to Le Moyne," *Bayonet*, September 17 1999, A-1.

[21] Maj. Gen. John M. Le Moyne, commanding general, "New CG sets goals," *Bayonet*, September 17 1999, A-2.

Riverside, LeMoyne's new home, was renovated during the final ten months of Ernst's tenure. The Ernsts lived in the Marshall House, the post's quarters for distinguished visitors, while lead paint was removed and the exterior painted white, topped by an "infantry blue" tin roof. The house, with its surrounding twelve acres, had 6,000 square feet of living space, five bedrooms, three bathrooms, and five fireplaces. Major General John Hendrix, a previous commandant, wrote TRADOC that the house needed repairs more costly than the annual $25,000 operational expenses would allow. He urged TRADOC to fix the house or tear it down.[22]

Another historic post building, the National Infantry Museum, held an exhibition of war dogs in 1999. Retired Sergeant First Class Jesse Mendez, former chief instructor at Benning's 26th Scout Dog Platoon, urged museum director Z. Frank Hanner to tell the canine's story. Mendez, a three-tour Vietnam veteran, had conducted twelve-week courses for the dogs and their handlers. The dogs detected enemy movement, booby traps, land mines, and ambushes. "Had it not been for these dogs," Mendez said, "The Vietnam War Memorial in Washington would have a lot more names engraved on it."[23]

When Mendez retired to Columbus in 1969, his dog Pal was discharged with him, and lived with Mendez for ten more years. In 1975, only 200 dogs returned home from Vietnam out of 7,000 dogs belonging to the different services. "When they pulled out in 1975, everyone was in a hurry to save their butts," Mendez said. "They had to leave the dogs in their kennels or tied to a stake. You had a choice of euthanizing them or turning them over to the Vietnamese."[24]

As 1999 ended, Sergeant Nancy Sellers won Black Hat of the Year, an award for the best Airborne instructor at the US Army Airborne School. She was presented a special black hat with gold braid during the 1st Battalion (Airborne), 507th Infantry Regiment's holiday jump tower lighting ceremony. She was the first woman to serve as a master trainer with the 507th Infantry and first to win top honor. She kept alive a family tradition.

---

[22] Sally Shutt, "Historic Riverside receives facelift," *Bayonet*, October 22 1999, A-1, A-5.

[23] Sally Shutt, "Museum prepares exhibit for War Dogs," *Bayonet*, October 22 1999, A-3.

[24] Ibid.

Her grandfather was a World War II veteran and her father served three tours in Vietnam with the air force. "When I saw my first Black Hat, I wanted to be one of them," Sellers said. "I liked their professionalism, the way they carried themselves. They had that sense of knowing everything you could possibly know."[25]

Fort Benning, though classified an open post, needed to keep its training mission secure. Military Police operated checkpoints put into place eleven months before, ensuring the safety of soldiers, dependents, and civilians. Even then, years before terrorists struck on American soil, the post was seen as a potential target—as noted by Captain Jay Griffith, Directorate of Threat and Security: "We are a symbol of national power; a source of arms and ammunition; an open installation; host a variety of prominent national and international figures; and with our status as Best Installation in the World, can be considered a potential target that would add to a terrorist's reputation."[26]

---

[25] Shutt, "Female instructor earns top honors," *Bayonet*, December 17 1999, A-4.

[26] Capt. Jay Griffith, "Organizations use symbolic dates to carry out acts," *Bayonet*, June 25 1999, A-3.

56.

Just a Chaplain and a Bugle

With little fanfare and lots of history, Major General John Le Moyne sent out the invitations. Ceremony was involved, but as Fort Benning's commanding general, he also was looking for advice and counsel.

The army was making the transition to a new concept of Brigade Combat Team Initiative, and LeMoyne turned to leaders who had his job at other times and, in many ways, in other armies. The invitation went out to surviving commandants of the Infantry Center. Eleven accepted, bringing together at Fort Benning an unprecedented number of past post commanders.

Present were General John W. Hendrix, General James J. Lindsay, General John W. Foss, Lieutenant Orwin C. Talbott, Lieutenant General Michael F. Spigelmire, Lieutenant General Robert "Sam" Wetzel, Lieutenant General Carmen J. Cavezza, Major General Kenneth C. Leuer, Major General Jerry A. White, and Major General Carl F. Ernst. The exchange of ideas within this group aided Le Moyne in the upcoming Infantry Conference. For the retired generals, it was a chance to renew old ties. Hendrix had not seen Talbott since Hendrix was a captain in the advanced course years before. Of the "new" infantry, Hendrix said, "Our goal is to deploy a combat brigade in thirty hours, a division in ninety-six hours, and five divisions in thirty days."[1]

In 2000, Fort Benning continued to provide new tactical and technical ideas for the military. Its task, presented by Army Chief of Staff Eric Shinseki, was to redesign the infantry force. The Initial Brigade Combat Team (IBCT) would provide immediate deployment and the lethality of a heavy unit. It would meet a need for a unit between light and heavy forces.

---

[1] Karen Taylor, "General Speaks out on Army future," *Bayonet*, April 21 2000, 4.

Shinseki wanted to transform two brigades at Fort Lewis, Washington, into units capable of being on the ground anywhere in the world in ninety-six hours, using "off the shelf" vehicles to enhance the mobility and force protection of its infantry forces. At the Infantry Conference in June, Shinseki directed his speech to its theme: "Army Transformation and How It Affects the Infantry and Force Modernization."[2] Conveying ideas of a quicker, lighter army, he said previous heavy forces, designed for the plains of Europe during the Cold War, no longer met contemporary challenges.[3]

The year 2000 saw another Army Community of Excellence victory. The Chief of Staff Army Award brought $200,000 to the post. In April, civilian employees received time off for their help in winning the eighth ACOE Chief of Staff Army award.

Changes on post occurred when the Henry Caro Noncommissioned Officer Academy, commanded by Command Sergeant Major George R. Monk, moved to Infantry Hall, close to the Donovan Technical Library. Noncommissioned officer courses were now taught in one building. A bust of Henry Caro was put in the school's hallway, the lower west wing of Infantry Hall.

Colonel Rose Walker provided another change when she became the first woman inducted into the Officer Candidate School's Hall of Fame. She was one of the eighty-six members inducted in 2000. The first OCS class to include women graduates at Benning was OCS Class 1–77.

Controversy occurred when the US Army School of the Americas closed its doors at the end of 2000 and reopened under the auspices of the Department of Defense. It opened in early 2001 with a new name and a new commander, Colonel Richard Downie. Its new name was the Western Hemisphere Institute for Security Cooperation. The school's transition, allowing civilian and military police agencies in South and Central America to attend as well as military personnel, featured less military training, more education on the democratic process, and more oversight by members of Congress. In deference to protesters, the institute required at least eight hours of human rights education in each course.[4] Colonel Glenn Weidner, commandant of the former SOA, was prophetic concerning the changes and

---

[2] Lori Egan, "Post welcomes Army's top leaders," *Bayonet*, June 9 2000, 1.

[3] Mitch Frazier, "Top officer tackles Army's future," *Bayonet*, June 16 2000, A-9.

[4] Spc. Mitch Frazier, "Congress mandates changes," *Bayonet*, May 26 2000, 1.

their impact on future protests: "This will be a step forward for the school, but I don't think this will end the protest for the school. The problem is so loaded with emotion and misunderstanding. I don't think we will ever see it end."[5]

The Doughboy Award of 2000 went to Retired Lieutenant General Harold G. Moore and Command Sergeant Major William T. Mixon. Both were recognized for their years of military service and distinctive contributions to the infantry community. Moore retired in 1977 after more than thirty-two years. He served in Korea as a company commander and regimental S3 and in Vietnam as a battalion (1st Battalion, 7th Cavalry Regiment) and brigade commander. In Vietnam, Moore served with Sergeant Basil Plumley, a previous Doughboy Award winner.

Mixon, a native Georgian, recorded 1,500 jumps. He was a veteran of the Korean War and Vietnam and served at the Infantry Center, Ranger Department, and Airborne Department. His military career spanned thirty-five years and seventeen days, and he ended it as Command Sergeant Major of the XVIII Airborne Corps at Fort Bragg. During his career he spent seventeen years at Benning.

Reporter Joe Galloway, a former senior writer at *US News & World Report* was keynote speaker at the Infantry Conference along with Moore. They were together at Ia Drang in 1965, and Galloway received a Bronze Star Medal with "V" Device for rescuing a wounded soldier. On the ground during the four days of fighting, Galloway was the only civilian journalist to receive the medal. He and Moore co-authored *We Were Soldiers Once...and Young*, a 1992 book based on their Vietnam experience with the 1st Cavalry Division. Galloway said he learned from Moore "that you do your job right, love your troops, and let your career take care of itself."[6] Writer-director Randy Wallace adapted the book as a movie with Moore serving as technical adviser. To prepare to write the screenplay and to appreciate the training soldiers endure, the fifty-year-old Wallace spent two weeks with the Ranger Training Brigade. "I've got bruises all over my body," he said, "but it's the most thrilling experience I've ever lived through."[7] Moore believed

---

[5] Ibid.

[6] Sally Shutt, "Journalist praises veterans," *Bayonet*, June 23 2000, A-5.

[7] Mick Walsh, "Screenwriter learns role of Ranger," *Columbus Ledger-Enquirer*, May 25 2000, A3.

Wallace's experience at Fort Benning helped him "get it right" in the movie.[8]

Although the rhythm of the post continued in training, graduations and awards, its key players in Columbus were passing away. Frank Lumpkin, Jr., died in March 2000 at the age of ninety-two. With him died personal knowledge of the post's early history and the soldiers who served in those years. An enthusiastic and generous supporter of Columbus and Fort Benning, Elena Amos, the widow of AFLAC founder John B. Amos, died that May. A native of Cuba, she met Amos when they were students at the University of Miami. A torch-bearer in the 1996 Olympics, Elena Amos was a dedicated supporter of the School of Americas and a generous benefactor to many local and national projects. With Amos and Lumpkin died volumes of memories.

Robert Felton, a retired army lieutenant colonel, documented such memories by preserving thousands of photographs at the National Infantry Museum. He was the retiree Volunteer of Excellence winner in 1999. Spending three days a week in "the hole," he separated, identified, catalogued, and preserved the many unmarked photos. A 1958 graduate of OCS, he served in Korea and Vietnam.

Retired sergeant major James K. Hudson also stayed close to the post. Swimming daily in the indoor pool where he had been a lifeguard, he took advantage of many post facilities, including the Donovan Library. At the understaffed library, he assisted soldiers looking for books or material and aiding retirees in researching their former units. Hudson, who fought in Korea and Vietnam, received his master's degree in English after a twenty-six-year army career. Hudson summed up the post's significance to those who served there, writing, "Fort Benning's historic, eventful, and illustrious page of American history since World War I foretells the same kind of future performance. Those with strong emotional and personal memories of their military experience at Fort Benning can look forward to the coming years and decades of this new millennium Deep-South post."[9]

---

[8] Ibid.

[9] Sgt. Maj. (Ret.) James K. Hudson, personal papers, Columbus GA.

Over and over again, retired soldiers and their spouses say Benning was home, the place they were the happiest. John A. Sullivan, who presented his book *Toy Soldiers: Memoir of a Combat Platoon Leader in Korea* to the Donovan Library, wrote, "Trained for combat, was I? Ready to lead a platoon, was I? You bet your ass I was. Fort Benning, Georgia, housed the finest school I had ever attended: TIS, The Infantry School.... Those six months at Benning were probably the best six months of my life to date. The food was great, the living quarters clean and comfortable. And the army certainly put its best foot forward when it came to our training."[10]

Unfortunately, many retirees found it difficult to plan a burial at Fort Benning because of the limited grounds of the post cemetery. The need for more military cemeteries was addressed by Representative Terry Everett of Alabama, chairman of the House Veterans Affairs Investigations Subcommittee: "We're losing more than a thousand World War II veterans a day, more than 377,000 a year. Funding is millions of dollars short to meet their needs. We're going to run out of space early in the twenty-first century unless something is done."[11]

Matthew St. Clair, a soldier from the 1930s, was determined he would be buried in Fort Benning's cemetery where his German mother—formerly married to an American soldier—is buried. St. Clair, a former boxing champ, knew how he wanted to spend his eternity. He arrived at Fort Benning a frightened teen, scared at the prospect of being a horse soldier. With the help of his sergeant, he learned to love horses and this Georgia post. "I will be cremated and that urn will sit on top of my mother's coffin. I don't want to be anywhere except in that post cemetery. My wife knows this. I'll have a firing squad and a chaplain—he can be Jewish, Protestant or

---

[10] John A. Sullivan, *Toy Soldiers: Memoir of a Combat Platoon Leader in Korea* (Jefferson NC: McFarland Company, Inc., 1991) 5–6.
[11] Associated Press, "Veterans Groups warn of need for new cemeteries," *Birmingham News*, May 20 1999, 7A.

Catholic—I don't care. Just a chaplain and a bugle. That's all I want. After I'm dead and buried in the post cemetery, I plan to get up and ride my horse Dan around post grounds. That's where I want to be."[12]

---

[12] Matthew St. Clair, interview by Peggy Stelpflug, December 11 1998, Donovan Technical Library, Fort Benning GA.

57.

Stars over Columbus

They have in common the stars on their shoulders, the Green Suit, and the experiences. They have in common the battles they fought and the pride they share in an installation each commanded. They have in common a hometown they each adopted.

Sam Wetzel, Ken Leuer, Jerry White, and Carmen Cavezza earned the stars they wore as US Army generals. Those stars granted them lifetime membership in a fraternity of leaders that opens doors anywhere in the world. In retirement, each lives and works in saluting distance of Fort Benning—the post they commanded near the ends of their distinguished careers.

Of that quartet, three have held positions of leadership in the civilian community. Two directed non-profit agencies. One was the most powerful figure in city government. Only Wetzel chose a new career in business, though like the others he too was active in community service. Their backgrounds are similar. So are the lives they have led after storing their Green Suits in the closet.

SamWetzel retired in 1986 and returned to Columbus mainly because he asked his wife—a native of Idaho—where she wanted to live. Her answer was Columbus. That suited Wetzel and his new business, Wetzel International Corporation, Inc. Born from contacts he built after serving twelve years in Europe, his international consulting firm as well as a later venture, European Foods, both prospered. "An Army officer brings managerial experience, he brings personal experience, and he brings leadership," Wetzel said, attributing his success in business with his military background.[1]

---

[1] Jan Wesner Childs, "From Battlefield to Boardroom," *Columbus Ledger-Enquirer*, June 5 1995, D-8.

As a young person, Wetzel, was unable to complete the requirements of an Eagle Scout. It was during World War II and as he puts it, "Everyone left." Recognizing its values, he was active with the Boy Scouts of America throughout his army career, helping others attain that distinctive honor. In Columbus, he ultimately received one of the organization's highest honors, the Silver Beaver Award, awarded to an adult member of BSA for distinguished service to young people. Wetzel's involvement in Boy Scouts was indicative of the way Fort Benning retirees were involved in the local communities.

Wetzel viewed Columbus as home and Fort Benning as the best post in the United States. "Prizes attest to this honor," he said. "If military cutbacks prevail, Fort Benning will be the last to go."[2]

Ken Leuer, who served as assistant commandant under Wetzel, believed army retirees have "led to a normalization of the area." When interviewed in 1998, he saw problems that existed between the post and the community in World War II as irrelevant. "People no longer warn, 'Lock the daughters up, the soldiers are in town.' That's all gone," Leuer explained. "It's an open post. People come and go. The influence of the civilian work force going back and forth, living in the community and working on the post, also has contributed to the normalization of the area."[3]

"Benning is fortunate to have grown an experienced civilian labor force," Leuer stated. "When I say experienced, I mean second, third or fourth generations of families that have worked with the government. That's a real plus. By having that cultured work force available, it adds to the stability of the operations at Fort Benning. It adds to the overall community compatibility between Fort Benning and the community."[4]

Although Leuer believed local people feel positive about the post, he noted that each year the number of people who visit or have a true understanding of it decreases. Columbus citizens are invited to attend ceremonies, dedications, exhibits, and demonstrations. Yet, according to

---

[2] Lt. Gen. (Ret.) Robert L. "Sam" Wetzel, telephone interview by Peggy Stelpflug, August 20 1998.

[3] Maj. Gen. (Ret.) Kenneth Leuer, interview by Peggy Stelpflug, June 5 1998, Goodwill Industries, Columbus GA.

[4] Ibid.

Leuer, few actually visit. For that reason, many have no idea what goes on at the installation.

"When you could buy a drink at the Fort Benning Officers' Club and you could not buy one in downtown Columbus, we had an awful lot of members in the club as courtesy of the post," Leuer explained. "They congregated at Fort Benning, and kept that relationship. When Benning had two golf courses and Columbus had one, a lot of people played golf on post so the social memberships and the club memberships were conduits for a lot of the leadership of Columbus that no longer exists. Now Columbus has golf courses and clubs galore. The interface is not as great."[5]

For Leuer, the ties were still strong. He and his wife, Sally Jean, played golf there, and he remained active in the Ranger Memorial Foundation. Personal interests also kept him close. His son, Joseph, worked at the Western Hemisphere Institute for Security Cooperation—the renamed School of Americas. His daughter Linda Lee married an army officer. She also went through jump school at Fort Benning when Leuer was assistant commandant. Leuer commented,

> Everyone was worried to death. Linda was a teeny little thing, five-foot-one and 102 pounds, but she did the Iron Man and was a world-class tri-athlete. She passed the PT test handily and did the bonus point pushups. She ran the fastest mile any female had ever run at the time, so she did real well. She was joking about going to Ranger School. I would have had no problem with her going to Ranger School, but I would have a hell of a problem saying, "My daughter is jumping with the Rangers with the lead element and facing harm's way."[6]

Until retiring in 1999, Leuer was chief executive of Goodwill Industries in Columbus. Many of his key leaders were retired NCOs or retired officers.

The retired general supported the volunteer force at Fort Benning. It improved, he said, when pay improved, putting in place "the greatest Army we've ever had. That Army we put in Desert Storm was the best trained, ready to fight, highly led, highly motivated force we've ever put on a battlefield.... What we have to remember though is that Army was led by

---

[5] Ibid.
[6] Ibid.

people who gained experience in Vietnam. We don't have nearly that amount of experience remaining at this point in time. There are certain elements you can only learn having been there," he said, speaking before the war in Iraq.[7]

Some experiences harden the soldier.

"Many have not had the experience of having to touch someone who's dead, who you've known, and you've just talked to five minutes ago—the kind of experience that no one should have. But once you have it, it changes you. It changes your outlook on how you train. It changes your outlook on how you take care of people. How you take care of soldiers. For me that means that soldiers are well trained. Soldiers who complain never say 'You're not training me right,' but that's what they're signaling."[8]

At posts such as Benning, soldiers are trained before being put in harm's way. That was and is its role. Leuer continued to support that effort through the National Infantry Association. It was White who asked Leuer to serve as NIA's first president. Leuer believed Benning's role will not change. "It has everything that goes to make up an ideal campsite for military purposes," he said, listing attributes that were described in 1917. "Fort Benning is the best post in the world, the best of all US installations."[9]

Jerry White did not argue with that. He supported the post entering the competitions that led to its recognition in the contemporary army.[10] Much of that he attributed to the relationship between the army and the civilian community—something that impressed observers who came to judge the post. Acknowledging the installation's contribution to the area's economy, White said it goes beyond money, involving the strong dose of national pride found in the South.[11] "If we had Fort Benning in some other part of the country, it might not be the same," White said. "But here there's still that sort of pride. There's no outward animosity toward military people. They may be some but very little. It's not perfect by a long ways, but we're

---

[7] Ibid.

[8] Ibid.

[9] Ibid.

[10] Maj. Gen. (Ret.) Jerry White, interview by Peggy Stelpflug, June 3 1998, United Way Office, Columbus GA.

[11] Ibid.

sort of a model. Other posts ask, 'How did you get this relationship with your community?' It's different from any place I've ever been. It's closer."[12]

Like Benning, Columbus has grown, but as some people observe, it remains a large small town. White retired to Virginia in 1994, but returned to Columbus when he was asked to take the position of executive director of United Way. He directed local campaigns until 2002 when he was asked to lead the effort for a new National Infantry Museum to be built at a location off post, not far from Benning's main gate. He accepted to serve as president of the National Infantry Association and chairman of the National Infantry Foundation. His former chief of staff Gregory Camp and retired banker Ben Williams aided his efforts to bring the museum—and the Infantry—to Columbus.

At United Way, White cared for people, just as he did as commanding general, focusing on quality of life for people. "It's an extension of my military leadership. A lot of people build fine arts theaters, but I wanted to make sure people were being taken care of and provided for by the United Services. That was my purpose. After all, that's what the Army's all about and what war is all about: helping your troops."[13] Like Leuer, White believes in the volunteer army, an opinion he did not always share. "But I was proved wrong," he explained. "We have a much better army with the all-volunteer army. We made a lot of mistakes in the early 1970s. We tried to turn it into a fraternity. But once we got settled down and got the standards set where they out to be, it was all right."[14]

White believes a modern, interactive infantry museum will be "the hook for our community," describing a campus far beyond the traditional static museum.[15] In it, White hopes to capture the spirit of the infantry and to remove the mystery that accompanies a military installation. White said,

> There's something about a military post that's sort of scary to civilians downtown. When we lived in Riverside, I wanted it open to the public. Foreign generals, foreign troops, international visitors, everybody feels good about Fort Benning and about the United States Army. They love to come here. They love to come to

---

[12] Ibid.

[13] Ibid.

[14] Ibid.

[15] White interview.

Riverside. Being in command, you feel like you are making a significant contribution to your country, to the community, to your soldiers. We want to create a museum everyone would like to visit.[16]

Carmen Cavezza, another former Fort Benning Commandant who chose Columbus as his home, said commanding Fort Benning was the "toughest job I had in the Army."[17] As chief of infantry, he oversaw combat developments, training facilities, and the professional development of the officer corps. He was expected to remember volumes of information on a multitude of things. It was good training for his current position as city manager of Columbus, another job that required a multi-faceted person. After retiring from the military, Cavezza returned to Georgia as head of Columbus '96, the local organizing group for the Olympic women's fast pitch softball venue. He was chosen for his leadership and because of his connections to another retired Fort Benning commander, Michael Spigelmire.[18] Spigelmire was chief of venue operations for the Atlanta Committee for the Olympic Games. It was through Cavezza's relationship with the post that the local Olympic Village came together at Fort Benning.[19]

Cavezza's work drew praise from the international committees and from local officials.[20] He converted the Olympic group into the Greater Columbus Sports & Events Council and later was appointed city manager. Jerry White expressed what others thought: "You wouldn't see in most communities a retired commandant being made a city manager. It wouldn't happen."[21] By embracing Cavezza—a native of Elmira, New York—Columbus proved it had come a long way since the city's first city manager, a Yankee from Pennsylvania, was attacked and run out of town in 1922. Cavezza proved to be an outstanding public official. He worked

---

[16] Ibid.

[17] Lt. Gen. (Ret.) Carmen Cavezza, interview by Peggy Stelpflug, June 17 1998, Columbus Government Center.

[18] Jan Wesner Childs, "From Battlefield to Boardroom," *Columbus-Ledger Enquirer*, June 5 1995, D-8.

[19] Cavezza interview; Donna S. Budgenska, "Cavezza Olympics Leader," *Bayonet*, September 29 1995, A-5.

[20] Cavezza interview.

[21] White interview.

smoothly with citizens, the mayor, ten council members, and the city workforce. With his guidance, the city continued to make steady progress.

Wetzel, Leuer, White, and Cavezza were not alone. Many retired officers and enlisted personnel held positions in both the private and public sector—including Robert Poydasheff, a retired JAG colonel, who was elected mayor in 2002. Some applauded this use of talent. Some were resentful. "Take a senior NCO," Cavezza said. "They have a pretty good background. They may be a little older, but they bring a wealth of experience into the city. But to some people they're competing for jobs. They think retirees will accept a lower salary, making it more competitive and knocking other people out of the running. Some see the major role Fort Benning has played in the area and accept it. Others are critical."[22]

When Cavezza retired from the military, he put his stars in the dresser drawer. If anyone called him, "General Cavezza," he corrected the person. "Carmen," he said.[23] He has little to do with the post other than using the hospital and playing golf. "I don't go excessively because my philosophy is I commanded it once, and I don't want to try to do it again."[24]

With the federal government's Base Realignment and Closing (BRAC) at work in 2003, Cavezza along with other local and state leaders assembled data and information in support of keeping Georgia bases open—particularly Fort Benning, the brightest gem in a state dotted with military bases. Cavezza remained more than optimistic: "Fort Benning will be around. It's invaluable to the Army. The infantry is a basic element of the army. You can't do anything without it. I don't care how technical we get. I don't see anything happening to Fort Benning, except fiscal restraints. In my opinion, it is going to be around for a long, long time."[25]

---

[22] Cavezza interview.
[23] Ibid.
[24] Ibid.
[25] Ibid.

58.

September 11, 2001

There was no formal declaration from Congress, but the loss of thousands of American civilian lives and the crumbling demise of two symbolic skyscrapers on the island of Manhattan gave reason for war. Fort Benning—just as the rest of the world did—realized this on the morning of September 11, 2001, minutes after watching the twin towers of the World Trade Center go down and witnessing the damage and loss of life at the Pentagon building in Washington, DC.

As soon as leaders could sort out the events of September 11, Fort Benning began to assess its role. Major General John LeMoyne, the post commander, was in an airplane on his way from Fort Leavenworth that day when a pilot gave him the news. Believing the country would weather this attack and come out stronger, he said, "My personal estimate is it will take us about three weeks to work through the information that we have as a nation to begin to make some sense of what has happened and the impact on our American way of life because it will no longer be as it was before 8 o'clock this morning."[1]

Acting as Omar Bradley did after bombs fell on Pearl Harbor, LeMoyne informed every commander on post, as well as civilian department heads, to tell every person that day, before they left for home, that Fort Benning's priority was still the training of troops and the care of their families. It was that way in 1941 and it remained so in 2001. By 10:30 A.M., security on post was increased to "Force Protection Delta." Troops were on a heightened level of awareness. Check points were established. Cars were searched. Identification was required. Five Muscogee Country School buses bringing dependent children back home from school were searched that

---

[1] Dusty Nix, "Rules Have Changed," *Columbus Ledger-Enquirer*, September 12 2001, A11.

afternoon. Planes at Lawson were grounded. The last time Fort Benning had been on such high security was 1996, after terrorist bombings in Saudi Arabia killed nineteen US servicemen.

Plans to establish checkpoints on roads leading into the post by the following January were quickly moved up. Troops seemed to be hunkering down for the long haul. Military police Humvees were hauling trailers loaded with traffic signs and orange roadway cones. Soldiers hurriedly put up a tent next to portable toilets at a checkpoint on Benning Road. The sight of rifle-toting combat troops standing watch was chilling.

In 2001, there were 23,000 soldiers and family members at Fort Benning along with 7,000 civilian employees.[2] On September 12th, it seemed as if every one of them was in a vehicle on Interstate I-85, each of them trying to get on post. No one enjoyed it, but people were calm and orderly despite horrendous traffic that turned the commute to Benning into a tedious, all-day event.[3]

Fort Benning's school system was one of the hardest hit. Its children were on post waiting for the yellow school buses and waiting for school. Faculty and staff were somewhere outside the gates, lost in traffic. Superintendent Dell McMullen—who beat the traffic by leaving her Columbus home by 3:00 A.M. that day—was determined to keep life as normal as possible for the children of the soldiers who attended her school. For an alternative plan, she secured city buses from Columbus to pick up and return her teachers and staff to the parking lot of the Columbus Civic Center. The first bell rang later than usual, but by September 13 Fort Benning teachers and students were at school on time.[4]

Through it all, LeMoyne kept private the personal effect the plane hitting the Pentagon had on him and his family. Lieutenant General Timothy Maude, fifty-three, a close friend of LeMoyne's family, was the army's deputy chief of personnel, based in Washington. He was killed when American Airlines flight 77 hit the Pentagon. LeMoyne could not predict at

---

[2] S. Thorne Harper, "Fort Benning Tightens Security," *Columbus Ledger-Enquirer*, September 12 2001, A-11.

[3] Eddie Daniels, "Officials Discuss Post Security," *Columbus Ledger-Enquirer*, September 15 2001, B1.

[4] Ibid.

that moment that in a matter of weeks, in a peculiar twist of army fate, he would fill his buddy's job.

As LeMoyne forecasted, it did take weeks for the White House and the Pentagon to sort out the aftermath of the terrorism, giving time to reduce the rubble and bury the dead. It was also a time for American leaders to decide what type of action would be appropriate. At Fort Benning, training and preparation continued with a reinforced vigor. Soldiers and spouses alike were on edge, knowing deployment had to be near.

For four months, LeMoyne awaited Congressional approval of his promotion and his reassignment. Brigadier General Paul Eaton, a former deputy commanding officer at Benning was tabbed as LeMoyne's successor. Eaton, fifty-one, was deputy commander of the post in 1999–2000 before his assignment to Fort Lewis, Washington, where he was charged with assembling the army's first futuristic forces. He also served with distinction in Bosnia and Somalia. The army, he said, was the only career he had ever known.[5]

"I'm the son of a career fighter pilot. I'm the son of a career marine. I married a soldier. I have a son who's going to be an infantry lieutenant this coming summer. And I am a senior leader in a very large and well-organized outfit, and we're heavily armed.... Every night the citizens of America go to sleep comfortable with that fact...never fearing from their standing forces."[6]

After Eaton's father, the marine pilot, was killed in Vietnam, Eaton chose West Point, as had his father. He also married into a marine family. His father-in-law, a graduate of the US Naval Academy, was a marine colonel. "That made for Army-Navy fun," Eaton joked.[7]

Now it was his job to help Fort Benning and the infantry through a transition point. Eaton would command the training mission at the post, helping young soldiers prepare themselves for battle. He would be priming troops for the first battle of the next war, for on October 7, 2001, Operation Enduring Freedom began, an attack on the Taliban in Afghanistan for harboring and providing support for al Qaeda and its leader Osama bin Laden, who masterminded the bombing of US embassies in 1998 and the

---

[5] S. Thorne Harper, "It's All I've Ever Known," *Columbus Enquirer*, December 23 2001, A1.

[6] Ibid.

[7] Ibid.

2001 destruction of the twin towers and the Pentagon building. It was the first attack by the US in the "War on Terror" campaign.

The United States fought with the Afghan Northern Alliance (United Front), a multi-ethnic group opposed to the Taliban, and received additional support from the United Kingdom, Australia, and Canada. Though considerable numbers of Taliban surrendered, retreated, or escaped to tribal territory, some Taliban members continued to fight, and Osama bin Laden, organizer of the terrorist plane attacks, remained free. With the help of the coalition and US troops, thousands who were trained at Fort Benning, Afghanistan citizens held elections in December 2001, electing Hamid Karzai as chairman of Afghanistan's new transitional administration.

On a Tuesday, September 17, 2002, three young men came to a Columbus Council meeting to request a monument honoring Officer Candidate School alumni who made the supreme sacrifice in the war against terrorism. The young men, Chad Neibert, Paul Ramsay, and William Trevathan, leaders of the OCS Class 6-02, received a challenge from Lieutenant Colonel Daniel Kessler, their commander, to perform a worthwhile project on post or in the community before they graduated. They wanted the monument placed on a quarter-acre plot of city property on South Lumpkin Road. The centerpiece of the memorial would be a 5-foot by 3-foot chunk of black granite. On that rock would be an image of the World Trade Center with a double exposure of the rubble left in wake of the attack. City Manager Carmen Cavezza, called the cadets' approach "a classic ambush."[8] Cavezza approved of their project and called Eaton to commend the young men's spunk. Things then began to happen.

Biff Hadden of the Greater Columbus Chamber of Commerce, a former army officer, helped, and 135 members of the class 6-02 worked in shifts with supplies and equipment loaned, borrowed, or bought at cost.

On October 14, the War on Terrorism Memorial was dedicated—all put in place within twenty-four days. For the men and women in the graduating class, the names engraved on the slab were part of them, part of Benning's OCS heritage. At the ceremony, Kessler put faces to those names. Lieutenant General Timothy Maude, who died at the Pentagon, was the army's deputy chief of staff for personnel. He helped coin the recruiting

---

[8] Chuck Williams, "OCS Cadets Want to Build Memoria," *Columbus Ledger-Enquirer*, September 18 2002, C1.

slogan, "An Army of One."[9] Cyril Richard "Rick" Rescorla was a former member of the 7th Cav, the unit that fought so gallantly in the Ia Drang Valley of Vietnam. His picture was on the cover of *We Were Soldiers Once...and Young*, a book about that 1965 battle. Rescola died a hero, helping others escape from the towers in the World Trade Center.

Describing Hyland, Kessler got personal. They were pals, and just days before the plane crashed into the Pentagon, the two of them shared an unplanned visit in Washington. Hyland knew of Kessler's job at Fort Benning, and as they parted he offered his friend a challenge: "I'm an OCS grad and I expect the standards to remain high."[10] Kessler then added, "Six days later, he was dead."[11] The work done by Class 6-02 lived up to standards. The memorial, clearly visible from Lumpkin Road leading on to post is a tribute to those who died and to those who built it.

[9] Mick Walsh, "OCS Honors Fallen," *Columbus Ledger-Enquirer*, October 15 2002, C1.

[10] Ibid.

[11] Ibid.

59.

Past Meets Present

On a spiffy night in the nation's capital, men in black tie and dress blues escorted women in formal gowns, and the history of an army outpost that began in mud and clay and survived through peace and war converged at a single ceremonial dinner.

Being honored that night in November 2003 were two men forever linked by service to their country and tours of duty on the grounds of an army installation they equally loved. Formally presented that evening at the National Building Museum in Washington, DC, was the fourth George C. Marshall Foundation Award. Receiving it was Secretary of State Colin L. Powell.[1]

Each chose the United States Army as their career. Each moved through the ranks to become a general officer. Each was chairman of the joint chiefs of staff. Each led in time of war and conflict. Each continued his service as secretary of state. Each, of course, was a respected alumnus of Fort Benning.

The Marshall Award is presented every two years to an individual or organization that contributed to ameliorating "hunger, poverty, desperation, and chaos" around the world.[2] These things were foremost in Marshall's mind when he outlined his blueprint for postwar Europe in 1947. As Marshall spoke at Harvard, the world was recovering from war. As Powell accepted the award in 2003, the United States military was in Iraq after war was declared on March 19, 2003, because Iraq allegedly possessed weapons of mass destruction. The war—Operation Iraqi Freedom—began March 20

---

[1] Anne Applebaum, "Having It Both Ways," *Washington Post*, April 21 2004, A23.
[2] "The George C. Marshall Foundation Award," http://www.marshallfoundation.org/support/award.html.

when an air strike attempted to target Iraq's ruthless leader, Saddam Hussein, in Baghdad.

Powell, a respected soldier and statesman, played a big part, along with President George W. Bush, in a war beyond the boundaries of Afghanistan. In January 29, 2002, Bush identified Iraq, along with Iran and North Korea, as an "axis of evil."[3] On October 11, Congress authorized an attack on Iraq. In a speech at West Point in May, Bush introduced the new defense doctrine of preemption.

On February 5, 2003, Powell made the case to the United Nations for the war in Iraq.[4] When presenting US intelligence that was meant to prove that Saddam Hussein possessed weapons of mass destruction, Powell showed slides of what he was told were mobile bioweapons. To prepare for his presentation, he "went and lived at the CIA for about four days," meeting with then-CIA Director George Tenet and other top officials, trying to establish the accuracy of the accusations.[5] By March 2003 an estimated 200,000 troops were stationed in the Gulf with British and Australian troops. On March 19, 2003, the US declared war on Iraq. The war began 5:30 A.M. Baghdad time March 20, when the US launched Operation Iraqi Freedom. Baghdad fell April 9.

On May 1, the US declared an end to major combat operations, and on May 30, 2003, Secretary of State Colin Powell denied intelligence about Iraq's weapons of mass destruction was distorted or exaggerated to justify the attack since Iraq's WMD were an imminent threat to world security. But no weapons of mass destruction were found, and in the summer of 2003, Tenet called to tell Powell that intelligence sources also believed there were no mobile labs for making biological weapons.[6]

Throughout his life, Colin Powell was shaped by experiences—some positive, some not. The experience of enforced segregation is one neither he nor his generation can escape. It was there in 1967 when Powell returned to

---

[3] "President Delivers State of the Union Address," www.whitehouse.gove/news/releases/2002/01/20020129-11.html.

[4] "Secretary of State Addresses the U. N. Security Council," www.whitehouse.gove/news/releases/2003/20030205-1.html.

[5] Fred Kaplan, "The Tragedy of Colin Powell: How the Bush Presidency Destroyed Him," Slate.com, February 19 2004, http://www.slate.com/id/2095756/.

[6] "Former aide: Powell WMD speech 'lowest point in my life,'" CNN, August 23 2005, http://www.cnn.com/2005/WORLD/meast/08/19/powell.

Fort Benning as a member of the Infantry School faculty and it was certainly there eight years before when he was in the officers' basic course. These experiences he remembered much too well. As a soldier wearing army green, he was accepted. As a man of color, life was not so easy.

"I could go into Woolworth's in Columbus, Georgia, and buy anything I wanted, as long as I did not try to eat there. I could go into a department store and they would take my money, as long as I did not try to use the men's room. I could walk along the street, as long as I did not look at a white woman," he recalled later in his memoirs.[7] Segregation or not, Powell was determined to succeed. "I did not feel inferior, and I was not going to let anybody make me believe I was.... I occasionally felt hurt. I felt anger. But most of all I felt challenged. I'll show you!"[8] Show them he did; first with the stars on the shoulders of his army uniform. Then as chairman of the joint chiefs of staff during the Gulf War. Later as secretary of state under President George W. Bush during the attack on the World Trade Center and during the ensuing war in Iraq. Much of the foundation for these milestones was laid at Fort Benning.

Powell graduated from the basic course in the Top Ten of his class. He attended Ranger School where one of his instructors was 1st Lieutenant Vernon Coffee, an officer he still remembers. "Coffee was the first black officer I knew who was at the top of his game, the first so good that respect for him transcended race."[9]

Airborne training followed Ranger School. The young soldier made five jumps in two days. At graduation Powell wore "Corcoran commercial jump boots (paid for out of pocket, since no self-respecting paratrooper would be caught dead wearing Army-issue boots), and received paratrooper wings to complement our black-and-gold Ranger tabs."[10] He was now an Airborne Ranger, and, as he explains in his autobiography, "In all the American infantry, there is no cockier soldier."[11]

---

[7] Colin L. Powell with Joseph E. Persico, *My American Journal* (New York: Random House, 1995) 42.

[8] Ibid., 43.

[9] Ibid., 42.

[10] Ibid., 44.

[11] Ibid.

Powell joined the Infantry School faculty in 1966, making his return to Georgia. It was to be a pivotal experience in his development as an officer and a leader of men. Particularly important to him was the instructors' course: "For three intense weeks, we learned how to move before a class, use our hands, adopt an authoritative tone, hold center stage, project ourselves and transmit what was inside our heads into someone else's. We were peer-evaluated, merit-boarded, scored, graded, and critiqued to death. If I had to put my finger on the pivotal learning experience of my life, it could well be the instructors' course, where I graduated first in the class."[12] Powell also served as a test officer with the Infantry Board, testing new infantry weapons and equipment, judging them acceptable or not by using army RAM standards: Reliability, Availability, and Maintainability, criteria he used repeatedly.[13]

During their earlier tour at Benning, Colin and Alma Powell lived at 172-A Arrowhead Road, down the street from Jerry White, a future post commander. Linda, their second child, was born at Martin Army Hospital in 1964. On their final stint at Benning, the Powells lived in Phenix City, on a road that now bears his name.

Powell returned to Columbus and Phenix City to speak at the annual meeting of the Greater Columbus Chamber of Commerce on January 7, 1993.[14] He also attended the dedication of the Colin Powell Parkway, describing the house where he lived in the 1960s as "the first home that our family had."[15] At the ceremony, he gave this advice: "When you pass this sign, don't think of General Colin L. Powell, chairman of the joint chiefs of staff. Think of Captain Colin Powell and let that young captain remind you of today's captains, lieutenants, sergeants, and privates. Take care of them as you took care of me and keep them close to your heart always. They deserve it."[16]

Powell, former commander of the Armed Forces Command, was selected at age fifty-two to hold the highest US military post in 1989—chairman of the joint chiefs of staff. He succeeded Admiral William

---

[12] Ibid., 116–17.

[13] Ibid., 110.

[14] Karen S. Morarie, "Powell visits Fort Benning," *Bayonet*, January 15 1993, A-3.

[15] Ibid.

[16] Ibid.

J. Crowe, Jr., who was chairman when the US Congress passed the Goldwater-Nichols Military Reorganization Act in 1986. Powell, who served in that role until 1993, explained the significance: "I would be the first full-term chairman to possess Goldwater-Nichols powers. I was formally confirmed by the Senate on September 20 to become the youngest officer, the first African American, and the first ROTC graduate to fill this office."[17]

Reforms in the office were intended to resolve inter-service rivalry that impeded members of the joint chiefs during Vietnam and to foster clear and direct lines of command to avoid the tragedy that occurred in Beirut in 1983 and the military mishaps of Grenada. "Under Goldwater-Nichols," Powell said, "I was principal military adviser. I did not have to take a vote among the chiefs.... I did not even have to consult them."[18]

Powell returned to Benning as recipient of the 1994 Doughboy Award. In receiving infantry's highest honor, he said, "the most powerful memories that come to me late at night, when I reflect on all this, are of comrades that didn't make it—comrades who gave their lives. It is in their memory that I accept this award."[19]

In late June of that year, ABC-TV news correspondent Barbara Walters interviewed Powell at Benning for *20/20*. Three different post locations were used: The Airborne memorial at Eubanks Field, the Infantry Museum, and a short segment at the Follow Me statue in front of Infantry Hall. The program aired September 15, 1995.[20] His choice of Fort Benning said much for his feeling for the post. The American public was keenly interested in Powell, who wrote *My American Journey*, a book many believed laid the groundwork for a run for the presidency of the United States. It was a campaign that never took place.

Powell's experiences as a young soldier in segregated Columbus and Phenix City were little different from ones other African Americans experienced there. The race of a soldier had been a factor since the early days when black soldiers helped build a post on which they were relegated to

---

[17] Colin Powell with Joseph E. Perisco, *My American Journey*, 411–12.

[18] Ibid., 447.

[19] Marc G. Turchin, "Colin Powell accepts top infantry award in ceremony at York Field," *Bayonet*, August 12 1994, A-1.

[20] Lisa M. Hibbert, "Powell, Walters visit post," *Bayonet*, June 30 1995, 1.

shacks. Before interstate highways and before civil rights legislation, African-American officers assigned to Benning followed a prescribed route from Washington. They knew which restaurants would serve them, and they would plan to stay overnight in South Carolina at a hotel where they knew they were welcome.[21] Over the years, there were recurring racial problems at Fort Benning, just as there were in the world outside the gates. These incidents wore many faces. In 1931, the War Department ordered a temporary end of enlistments, reenlistments, and promotions for African-American soldiers—a situation that persisted until 1934.[22]

Tuskegee Institute president Robert R. Moton said reduction of black troops was unfair.[23] He also asked for the promotion of Colonel Benjamin O. Davis, a ROTC instructor at the historic black Alabama school located around sixty miles from Fort Benning. Moton explained Davis was "the highest ranking Negro officer in the United States Army...who, by reason of his color is denied service according to his rank and with his own regiment."[24] Moton mentioned the 24th Infantry when he wrote to President Herbert Hoover: "The original declaration was that these Negro troops from the 24th Infantry were transferred to Fort Benning as a special training unit. Whatever the original intention, this program has been entirely abandoned. Negro troops at Fort Benning are without arms or equipment of any sort that could be used in training for combat service. They are called out twice a week for what are virtually the rudiments of drill, the only elements of training which they get."[25]

Around this period, two black officers were flown to Fort Benning for a short refresher course. Some Benning officers circulated a petition demanding their withdrawal—which drew the ire of George C. Marshall. "Marshall denied it and the two officers remained," according to the general's biographer Forrest Pogue.[26] Later, one of the grateful visiting

---

[21] Ulysses Lee, *United States Army in World War II: The Employment of Negro Troops* (Washington DC: Office of the Chief of Military History United States Army, 1966) 25.

[22] Ibid.

[23] Ibid.

[24] Ibid., 27.

[25] Ibid., 26–27.

[26] Forrest C. Pogue, *George C. Marshall: Education of a General* (New York: Viking Press, 1963) 262.

officers wrote to Marshall: "Your quiet and courageous firmness, in this case has served to hold my belief in the eventual solution of problems which beset my people in their oftentimes pathetic attempts to be Americans."[27]

As Moton indicated, black soldiers were at Benning since its earliest years. White soldiers at Benning served as instructors, worked in the post exchange, at the range, and with the military police. Black soldiers worked as cooks, waiters, or janitors. In the 1940s, troops of the newly formed Infantry School Service Command were challenged by the needs of an expanding post. To meet this need, in January 1941, the "old" 3rd Battalion of the 24th Infantry Regiment was reactivated. The battalion was inactivated November 3, 1921, when the 24th—the Buffalo soldiers—left Camp Furlong, New Mexico. Because of the 1941 expansion, the regiment increased to 3,000 officers and men, most obtained under Selective Service.[28] The 24th continued its varied duties at the post. With war looming and the need for manpower acute, the government turned to a growing black population. On September 16, 1940—the same day the Selective Service Act was approved—a press release reported that 36,000 of the first 400,000 men called would be African American. Although black draftees would remain in separate units—a continuation of War Department policy—they would be represented in all arms and services.[29]

After the first influx of blacks began to enter the army as a result of the draft, "the first major example of racial violence occurred. In a wooded section of Fort Benning, Georgia, the body of a Negro soldier, Private Felix Hall, his hands tied behind him, was found hanging from a tree."[30] Two views followed this discovery in April 1941: the blacks believed he had been lynched, but post authorities thought it could have been suicide. An investigation revealed no clues: "speculation continued, but in the absence of foul play, no considerable agitation took place. A queasy uneasiness among Negro troops and the public lingered."[31]

---

[27] Ibid.

[28] L. Albert Scipio, *The 24th Infantry at Fort Benning* (Silver Springs MD: Roman Publications, 1986) 67.

[29] Lee, *United States Army in World War II: The Employment of Negro Troops*, 78.

[30] Ibid., 349.

[31] Ibid., 349.

At this same time, Secretary of War Henry Stimson appointed William Hastie, dean of the Howard University Law School, as his civilian aide on Negro affairs. Hastie would help the army "to expand its Negro strength with a minimum of difficulty."[32] With more black soldiers coming to the post, local black citizens wanted to help these soldiers improve their life outside of Fort Benning. As part of this effort, the Ninth Street USO was built, and the Army-Navy USO on Eleventh Street opened—the first all-black facilities in the country. Ninth Street was also the site of the nation's only Negro Army YMCA, financed by Lily Mae Lanceford, a prominent businesswoman. The Reverend W. A. Reid, pastor of Shady Grove Baptist Church in Columbus, offered the benediction at its dedication on July 27, 1941. The Ninth Street Branch YMCA, when built in 1907, was the second modern Negro YMCA building in the country and the first in the South.[33]

Less than a year later, after twenty years, Fort Benning said farewell to the men of the 24th Infantry Regiment, the first African-American unit assigned to the post. In April 1942, the 24th was the first black infantry regiment sent overseas. Historian L. Albert Scipio recalled the sad departure of the 24th:

> I returned from Tuskegee, where I was in school, for the occasion. Since I had come to Fort Benning with the regiment, I wanted to be there when it left. None of us knew at the time what a historic moment April 1, 1942, would be for the regiment. It was truly a sad occasion. I would venture to say that many were sad because they knew that the regiment was not ready for combat. A majority of the men were little more than raw recruits. What is more, immediately prior to departure, a number of hospital patients were prematurely returned to duty. Filler replacements were received but many of these were below regimental standards. Some of the replacements turned out to be disciplinary cases. At any rate, the 24th Infantry boarded the troop train and headed to San Francisco for departure to the South Pacific as part of Task Force 9156. Their assignment now was war.[34]

---

[32] Ibid., 78.

[33] "About the YMCAs of Columbus, GA," www.columbusymca.com/about.html. See "9th Street History."

[34] L. Albert Scipio, *The 24th Infantry at Ft. Benning* (Silver Spring MD: Roman Publications, 1986) 67.

An influx of young black men, recent high school graduates, came to Benning in 1943 to enroll in the Army Specialized Training Program (ASTP), Basic Training Center of the Infantry School. In June 1943, ASTP was ready to handle approximately 6,000 black troops for twelve- or thirteen-week training periods. Training was to provide advancement for those who neglected their education or were unable to receive an education. Sergeant William L. Graham, Headquarters, First Battalion, Special Training Regiment, was the unit's educational adviser. Holder of a master's degree from Northwestern University and a teacher's license from Georgia, Graham represented the "best educated men," black volunteer teachers, prepared to instruct these young men. By July, the training center, operating at full strength, had 12,000 troops.

In January 1944, the War Department announced plans to activate the first black parachute unit, the 555th Parachute Infantry Company at Fort Benning. Major James C. Queen, a former member of the battalion, said the War Department was reluctant to form the unit because "they didn't believe that black troops could become paratroopers, just like they didn't believe black soldiers could become airmen. They just didn't think we could do it."[35]

The first cadre of sixteen paratroopers graduated from their Airborne training on February 16, 1944.[36] Retired sergeant first class Carl Reeves, who made Columbus his home, said the original test platoon of twenty men, whittled down to "Sweet Sixteen," became his instructors "who dished out the same rough treatment" they received by their four white instructors "who tried to bust 'em."[37] Reeves rode in the train coach reserved for blacks on his way to Benning from New York. He sat "right behind the coal car, where soot blew in their faces."[38] In Columbus, Reeves explained, no hotels accepted blacks: "You had to find a boarding house or know someone who would take you in."[39] Since only black noncommissioned officers could get housing in barracks on post, a black soldier with a family had to find a place

---

[35] "Arlington home of memorial dedicated to black paratroopers," *Columbus Ledger-Enquirer*, August 17 1995, B-7.

[36] Connie Bridges, "'Triple Nickels' soldiers focus on black history," *Bayonet*, October 8 1993, D-1.

[37] Ibid.

[38] Ibid.

[39] Ibid.

off post. Also, Reeves recalled, "no blacks were allowed on Main Post without a pass."[40]

Retired Lieutenant Colonel Bradley Biggs, the first black officer accepted for Airborne duty, was a member of the "Triple Nickels"—the name given to the unit that grew into a 350-man battalion by late 1944 because of the large number of volunteers. Though not engaged in any battle of World War II, the 555th did see action in the Pacific Northwest "by dropping in to fight forest fires set by Japanese incendiary balloons."[41]

While the army was slowly changing for soldiers of color, Fort Benning was not. The army had put a stop to segregation in post exchanges, recreation facilities, troop trains, and troop ships. Benning, however, kept separate theatres and quarters. Near the end of the war, on the race across France, "artillery, armoured and tank destroyer units were intermingled without regard to race. Only the infantry had to catch up."[42] Integrated units were still in the future.

As war ended, efforts to improve conditions for black soldiers were made on and off post.–Moving faster than a society that still was separate, President Harry Truman moved to desegregate the military. On July 26, 1948, he signed Executive Order 9981, which created the committee on Equality of Treatment and Opportunity in the Armed Services. This policy clearly favored integration in America: "It is the declared policy of the President that there shall be equality of treatment and opportunity for all persons in the armed services without regard to race, color, religion, or national origin."[43] During a time of national segregation, noticeably in the South, the army promoted social mobility of minority groups.

Into the 1970s, Fort Benning enjoyed the support of congressional leaders such as Georgia Senator Richard B. Russell and Representative Carl Vinson. Russell first went to Washington in 1932. He was responsible for fifteen major military bases in Georgia that produced an annual civilian payroll of over $1 billion. Russell's strong influence also impeded integration on these posts since he was a leader of the Dixiecrats, a splinter

---

[40] Ibid.

[41] Ibid.

[42] Geoffrey Perret, *There's a War to Be Won* (New York: Random House, 1991) 454–55.

[43] "Truman Library—Executive Order 9981," www.trumanlibarry.org/9981.htm

political party that sprang up in 1948 with segregation as a major plank in its platform. Before the Korean conflict began, Russell attached an amendment to the draft extension bill that would allow soldiers to choose whether they would serve in integrated units.[44] The amendment was defeated. Even after Truman's edict of equality in the military, bases in the South lagged behind their counterparts throughout the country.

Military historian Clay Blair confirms, "the Army, which had strong emotional, economic and political ties to the Deep South, fought the order by every conceivable stratagem."[45] Although units in Korea were integrated by the end of 1951, it would be business as usual at army posts in the South, including Fort Benning.

At Benning, the "Triple Nickels" were deactivated after Truman's order. They became the 3rd Battalion, 505th Airborne Regiment. Then, as Ranger training was being reestablished at Fort Benning, the all-black 24th Infantry Regiment was inactivated in Chipori, Korea, on October 1, 1951—a month shy of its eighty-second birthday. L. Albert Scipio, who grew up at Fort Benning while his father was assigned to the 24th, points out that the unit "celebrated its eighty-first, and last anniversary on November 1, 1950, in the field in Korea."[46]

Scipio records the historical significance of the unit's final days in that faraway country: "So it was on October 1, 1951, the last of the six original Colored Regulars, created after the Civil War, was retired from army rolls. That was an historic day in Korea, one that would have saddened those men of the regiment who stormed up San Juan Hill.... With the elimination of separate black units in Korea, an era in American military history came to an end. While I welcome integration of the armed forces as an act decades overdue. I sorrow that the 24th Infantry Regiment is now extinct."[47]

In May 1954, a ruling of the United States Supreme Court that segregation of the races was unconstitutional supported Truman's earlier

---

[44] "Desegregation—4 Desegregation in the military," http://en.wikipedia.org/wiki/desegregation.

[45] Clay Blair, *The Forgotten War* (New York: Times Books, 1987) 150.

[46] L. Albert Scipio, *Last of the Black Regulars: a History of the 24th Infantry Regiment, 1869–1951* (Silver Spring MD: Roman Publications, 1983) 99.

[47] Ibid.

decision.[48] "Separate but equal" was no longer accepted. By June 1954, no separate Negro units existed at Benning, and the courses and training programs offered by the Infantry School were open without racial restrictions. Not that all problems were solved—there would be other incidents and in the 1970s, a special unit was created to deal with diversity, dealing with not only African Americans but also with the growing number of Hispanics in the military.[49]

Though the military strongly supported diversity of race, gender, and ethnicity, there were still obstacles, and minorities often felt compelled to prove their worth—an attitude expressed at the fortieth reunion of the black paratroopers of the 555th Parachute Infantry Battalion. Sergeant First Class Nathan Parks of Phenix City, a veteran of Korea and Vietnam, explained their success: "A lot of fellows had one thing in mind—to show the world we were just as good…a bullet doesn't know if you're purple or chartreuse."[50]

Colin Powell showed he was as good as many and better than most. While climbing the army ladder was not always easy, he reached pedestals few have achieved. He opposed the war in Iraq and expressed his thoughts to President Bush. He warned the president of acting unilaterally and to consider the economic and political consequences of war, particularly in the Mideast. However, the president, supported by others in his cabinet, pursued the war in Iraq. Powell stood by his president's decision.[51]

In November 2004, after President Bush's re-election, Colin Powell resigned as the sixty-fifth secretary of state and returned to private life.

Powell accepted the Marshall Foundation award November 12, 2003, eight months after the invasion of Iraq. Powell, who kept Marshall's picture in his office, said, "George C. Marshall is a personal hero of mine, and so this award will always mean a great deal to me.… When I sit in my office and I'm dealing with the most difficult problems, or I'm on the phone with somebody, I look straight at George.… Whether as a young cadet on the

---

[48] Gorton Carruth, "Racial segregation in public schools was declared unconstitutional by the U. S. Supreme Court," *What Happened When* (New York: Penguin Group, 1991) 850.

[49] Col. Gilberto Villahermosa, "America's Hispanics in America's Wars," *Army Magazine* 52/9 (September 2002): 63–66.

[50] Bobbi Miller, "Unique History Remembered at Black Paratroopers' Reunion," *Bayonet*, August 12 1984, B-1.

[51] Applebaum, "Having It Both Ways," A-23.

football team or as Secretary of State or as General Marshall, that same visage looks back at me, looking squarely back at me in a blue-gray business suit, ramrod straight, the very embodiment of dignity and steely resolve."[52]

---

[52] Colin L. Powell, "Remarks on Receiving the 2003 George C. Marshall Foundation Award," (speech, Washington DC, November 12 2003). Transcript available at http://www.state.gov/secretary/former/powell/remarks/2003/26126.htm.

60.

I Am the Infantry.

The death of Lieutenant Colonel Roy Lothner in January 2003 rekindled interest in the much-quoted poem *I Am the Infantry*. Lothner, a highly-decorated veteran of World War II and Korea, was director of Special Services at Fort Benning for nearly two decades. In 1956, still on active duty, he produced a stage show based on the poem that puts in chronological verse every war the US Infantry fought. His son Marc said, "Even to the end of his life, he was able to recite that poem verbatim."[1]

Lothner staged the poem, but he was not its author. According to Russ Eno, the editor of *Infantry Magazine*, authorship belonged to Lieutenant Colonel Stephen White, then-editor of the *Infantry School Quarterly*. Since appearing in White's magazine in July 1956, the poem was recited at graduations, special holidays, and special post events: "I am the Infantry—Queen of Battle! For two centuries I have kept our nation safe, purchasing freedom with my blood. To tyrants, I am the day of reckoning; to the oppressed, the hope of the future. Where the fighting is thick, there am I.... I am the Infantry! Follow Me."[2]

The infantry, in 2003, was in the thick of fighting in Iraq. US forces congregated in Kuwait in early March preparing for the inevitable. On March 20 the order came. Gathered near the border with Kuwait, 20,000 soldiers of Fort Benning's and Fort Stewart's 3rd Infantry Division, part of the largest US assault since the Persian Gulf War in 1991, began to move, signaling the start of the ground war in Iraq.[3] More than 600 combat

---

[1] Mick Walsh, "Original Poem Dates to 1956," *Columbus Ledger Enquirer*, January 22 2003, A1.

[2] "Queen of Battle," www.tomahawks.us/queen_of_battle.htm; Mick Walsh, "Original Poem Dates to 1956," A1.

[3] "2003 Iraq War Timeline," http://en.wikipedia/org/wiki/2003_Iraq_war_timeline.

vehicles, including M1A1 Abrams tanks and M2A2 Bradley fighting vehicles joined them. As the 3rd moved forward, there was resistance, but soon they were taking bridges and securing airports.[4] The division's three brigades leapfrogged one another in their race to Baghdad. In April the early stages of the battle for the ancient city began, blocked only by Saddam Hussein's Republican Guard. Movement was fast. "There's an eerie easiness to it," Specialist Timmy Melia told S. Thorne Harper, a *Columbus Ledger-Enquirer* reporter embedded with the Benning units.

"We're all at a certain place and a certain time," said Colonel Dan Allyn, commander of the unit's 3rd Brigade. "This is my calling. I hope to make the right decisions at the right time to protect my forces." Days later, his men entered the suburbs of Baghdad and the fighting grew, but on April 9, Baghdad fell and the statue of Saddam Hussein came down. Then came a change of direction. The mission was shifting towards a more humanitarian effort, and major operations were suspended. Most Iraqis looked on US troops as liberators and were thankful Saddam Hussein was removed from power and subject to a trial in a free Iraq.[5]

In June 2003, when Major General Paul Eaton left for Iraq, he passed the post colors to Brigadier General Stephen Layfield, interim post commander. The only face-to-face time he and his successor, Brigadier General Benjamin Freakley, had was in Mosul, a town on the Tigris River in northern Iraq. Freakley was ending his tour as assistant division commander of operations for the 101st Airborne Division in Iraq. General Eric Shinseki, army chief of staff, selected Eaton to train and rebuild the defeated Iraqi army. However, US Administrator Paul Bremer, with orders from the Bush administration, dissolved the Iraqi army as a de-Baathification effort.[6] This decision was contrary to Bremer's predecessor, retired general Jay Garner, who wanted to put the Iraqi army back together. Because of the disbandment, recruitment and training was painfully slow.

Freakley said he told Eaton "what to expect when trying to rebuild the army over there and he told me what to expect in my new job—a tremendous amount of leaders in the officer and non-commissioned officer

---

[4] Ibid.

[5] Bob Woodward, *State of Denial* (New York: Simon & Schuster, 2006) 202–203.

[6] Ibid., 193–94, 196, 197–98.

corps, a superb relationship with the communities around Fort Benning and quality living quarters."[7]

Freakley's quarters did improve. He went from a combat zone to Riverside, the stately plantation home reserved for post commanders. The new assignment also meant new responsibilities since his recent jobs were with combat units, the 24th Infantry Division in the first Gulf War and the 101st in Iraq. Not that Benning was new. Freakley, a native of Virginia and a 1975 West Point graduate, attended all the basic courses there, Airborne to Rangers. "I'm the new commander of the Infantry Center," he said as he took command. "This is the highlight of my career."[8]

The post in July 2003 was pulled in many directions for the many missions assigned to their soldiers.[9] Freakley was also torn. Men he served with in Iraq were dying, yet he was safe and secure. A month after he arrived, he spoke to the men and women of the 3rd Brigade, 3rd Infantry after their return from Iraq and the overthrow of Saddam. Feelings were raw that day: "We live in a country that sometimes misplaces loyalty and who it looks up to. Our heroes are rock stars, athletes, rich people, and professional wrestlers. But today's true heroes are the soldiers sitting right here."[10]

Sacrifices were made daily in the desert of Iraq as the postwar conflicts continued. Saddam's sons were dead, but the search for Saddam himself continued. As looting spread, questions were asked about troop strength, recalling army chief of staff Shinseki's advice for 400–500,000 troops in postwar Iraq rather than the 130–150,000 allowed by civilian leaders at the Department of Defense.[11] Shinseki, an advocate of the Initial Brigade Combat Team, supported a lighter army capable of immediate deployment in time of conflict, but he realized the need for "boots on the ground" to

---

[7] Mick Walsh, "Freakley Has His 'Highlight,'" *Columbus Ledger-Enquirer*, July 15 2003, A1.

[8] Ibid.

[9] S. Thorne Harper, "Faces of Freakley," *Columbus Ledger-Enquirer*, November 7 2003, A1.

[10] Ibid.

[11] Joseph L. Galloway, "Retired brass; Oust Rumsfeld," *Atlanta Journal Constitution*, April 14 2006, A-11.

keep the peace, especially in a divided country such as Iraq with Shiites, Sunnis, and Kurds all vying for power.[12]

In November, Ranger Joe himself showed up in Iraq. Paul Voorhees, owner of the legendary Ranger Joe's store on Victory Drive in Columbus, arrived on what he termed "a mission of love."[13] An ordained Baptist minister, he spent Thanksgiving in Baghdad, attending church services all over the ancient city. Two months before Voorhees made his trip, Benning troops honored him at his store for forty years of service to soldiers. Freakley proclaimed him "an exceptional friend of Fort Benning."[14]

Colonel William Kidd, commander of the Ranger Training Brigade, praised the merchant's generosity. "During this last big deployment, if people's boots didn't fit properly (when they were issued) he would exchange them free of charge at his store before they left," Kidd said. "He's really a kind of go-to guy for the combat soldier...."[15]

On December 14, news out of Iraq made the commanding general's annual Christmas celebration at Fort Benning more festive. American forces captured Saddam, flushing him out of a hole in the sand.[16] Freakley heard the news early that morning and immediately attached a computer-generated picture of Saddam to his Christmas tree. To Mick Walsh, a Columbus reporter who crashed the party at Riverside, Freakley was more reticent. He said he was not one to gloat but that having the Iraqi leader in custody was "strategically important to our mission."[17] Freakley said he had no strong personal feelings about Saddam but added "the last candle of resurgence has been extinguished."[18] As he finished his formal statement, the chest-pounding and fist-pumping erupted, putting the general in a holiday

---

[12] Paul D. Easton, "A Top-Down Review for the Pentagon," *New York Times*, March 19, 2006.

[13] Mick Walsh, "'Ranger Joe' Goes to Iraq," *Columbus Ledger-Enquirer*, November 21 2003, C3.

[14] Tony Adams, "GIs salute 'Joe,'" *Columbus Ledger-Enquirer*, September 19 2003, C8.

[15] Ibid.

[16] Mick Walsh, "Freakley: Intelligence Did It," *Columbus Ledger*-Enquirer, December 15 2003, A1.

[17] Ibid.

[18] Ibid.

mood. "I have to admit, this does make for a terrific Christmas present," Freakley said.[19]

In January 2004, David Kay, former head of the US weapons inspection teams in Iraq, informed a Senate committee that no weapons of mass destruction were found in Iraq and that prewar intelligence was "almost all wrong."[20] With no WMD to pursue, the rationale for war changed to regime change and the democratization of Iraq.

Speaking to the Rotary Club of Columbus on April 21, 2004, Ben Freakley spoke of the long struggle ahead to achieve this aim.[21] Rambling through a litany of subjects that noon—from terrorism to the press to Fort Benning's future, the general reserved his deepest emotions for his personal view on war and peace, warning the war being fought that day in Iraq—in an era of instant gratification—might last fifteen to twenty years. "There's a definite clash of ideas between those of us who love freedom and democracy and those who want to fight and destroy our way of life," Freakley said. "And time is of no concern to them. If we don't take the fight to our adversaries, they'll bring it to us, much like they did on 9/11."[22]

Though all Americans stood against terrorism, and most agreed on bringing the fight to Afghanistan where the Taliban supported al Qaeda, many questioned the need for troops staying in Iraq.[23] With the revelation of physical and sexual abuse of Iraqi prisoners at Abu Ghraib prison near Baghdad—the same prison Saddam used to torture anyone suspicious of undermining his regime—many in the States and around the world were outraged. Iraqis, many with family members held at the prison, distrusted America's intentions.[24] Though Iraqi enthusiasm lessened for Americans in their country, Eaton, continued to enlist young Iraqis. He told the *Bayonet* in a May 2004 interview that the Iraqi army was not yet where he wanted it

---

[19] Ibid.

[20] Julia Malone, "Prewar spying 'dead wrong,'" *Atlanta Journal Constitution*, April 1 2005, 1.

[21] Mick Walsh, "Benning mission to grow," *Columbus Ledger-Enquirer*, April 22 2004, C1.

[22] Ibid.

[23] John Kerry, "Two Deadlines and an Exit," *New York Times*, April 5 2006, http://www.nytimes.com/2006/04/05/opinion/05kerry.html.

[24] Woodward, *State of Denial*, 372–73.

to be, but "Eventually they will catch up." American soldiers kept busy staying alive and doing their jobs.

On Memorial Day, 2004, old soldiers were in good spirits at 0900 as they clustered together at Fort Benning's Main Post cemetery on the last day of May. Many of these former warriors were just off the bus from Washington, DC, where they went to offer tearful salutes at the opening of the long-anticipated World War II Memorial. Many of them helped bury old buddies on a week when the local obituary pages were filled with the names of men who in their youth fought in Europe or Japan. Now the old guys joined the men and women wearing today's uniforms. Such scenes regularly played around Fort Benning. Old men tell stories. Young men fight wars.

That same holiday weekend, at a shopping mall on the other side of Columbus, a ritual of another kind took place. Soldiers in uniform invaded Peachtree Mall, some with marksmanship medals on their shirts and pimples on their faces. Some walked the mall with proud mothers and fathers, in town for the holiday. Some held hands with girls from back home. On the fringe of the food court, at a bank of pay phones, soldiers armed with freshly bought phone cards waited their turn. When their turn came to use the telephone, they emptied the phone cards as fast as they did the cheap beers they guzzled the night before. Later in the day, folding into taxicabs, the soldiers were on their way to Benning, knowing they soon would be on their way to Baghdad.

Also on their way were 150 soldiers from 36th Engineer Group and the 598th Maintenance Company, going to Kuwait or Iraq. The 988th Military Police Company left for Afghanistan, and elements of the 13th Corps Support Battalion, including 223rd Heavy Equipment Transport Platoons and Detachment 31 of the 1207th US, Army Field hospital left for Southwest Asia. Later the 36th Engineer's Group Headquarters left for Iraq.

Many Americans and Iraqis friendly to Americans were killed daily, mainly in Baghdad. Postwar reconstruction, commandeered by contractors Halliburton and Bechel, was at a standstill because of "chaos, criminality, insurgency, and terrorism."[25] Clean water and electricity were often precious commodities. Insurgents killed contractors and soldiers almost daily. Road

---

[25] Larry Diamond, *Squandered Victory* (New York NY: Henry Holt & Company, 2005) 279.

bombs were all too common and all too deadly. Major General Paul Eaton, recalling his experience in Iraq, told an American journalist in October 2004, "This thing evolved in front of us. And each day it got incrementally worse until it exploded."[26]

After the assault on Falluja, a sacred place for many Iraqis, on October 25, 2004, by 10,000 American soldiers, many Iraqis felt Americans were trying to take over their country.[27] With the postwar conflict continuing, the 3rd Infantry Brigade returned to Iraq. As the Infantry Center band played, nearly 4,000 troops from Kelley Hill received a formal send off January 7, 2005, at Doughboy Stadium. A crowd of 8,000, composed of family, friends, dignitaries, and supporters from the surrounding communities, cheered the unit for their return to Iraq and their mission to help make Iraq free.

On January 30, 2005, Iraqis voted. The large turnout—58 percent of those eligible—indicated their desire to achieve a form of democracy for their country.[28] The United Iraq Alliance, a coalition of Shiites, received a majority. In April 2005, the Iraq Assembly named Shiite Ibrahim al-Jaafari as prime minister. Although General John Abizaid, commander of US forces in the Middle East, said the Iraq insurgency remained as strong as it had been six months earlier, Iraq had turned a corner.[29]

A general who served in Iraq, Major General Walter Wojdakowski, a former Fort Benning assistant commandant, assumed command of the post in August. One of his important missions at Benning was to continue to train and prepare national guard members and reservists for the war in Iraq. While in Iraq he served as deputy to Lieutenant General Ricardo Sanchez, top commander. In 1991, he took part in Operation Desert Storm, and later commanded Benning's 11th Infantry Regiment. A 1972 graduate of West Point, he married Candy Cooper, a Columbus girl, and his two children attended Columbus High School. His son Steven served in Iraq.

Iraq took a backseat to what many considered America's worst natural disaster in history. On August 29, Hurricane Katrina, category four, plowed into Mississippi, Louisiana, and Alabama, leveling buildings, homes, and

---

[26] Thomas E. Ricks, "General Reported Shortages in Iraq," *Washington Post*, October 18 2004, 1.

[27] Woodward, *State of Denial*, 206, 372–73.

[28] Ibid., 383.

[29] Ibid.

trees. Nearly 2,000 people died.[30] A levee breach in New Orleans caused downtown flooding and devastation. Soldiers serving in Iraq who lived in these states wondered if they would have a home to return to. A hero to many trying to find shelter and struggling to get their lives back together was a soldier well known at Fort Benning: Lieutenant General Russel Honore, former deputy commanding general and assistant commandant of Fort Benning. His recent assignment was commanding general of 1st United States Army at Fort Gillem, Forest Park, Georgia.

Dubbed "the Raging Cajun" by the media and as "one John Wayne dude" by New Orleans mayor Ray Nagin, Honore, a 1978 graduate of Tuskegee University, was commander of Joint Task Force Katrina. Providing the first real leadership victims experienced since their misery began, he told the survivors and his troops, "Let's get it on." Honore, a Louisiana native, headed military efforts to save and evacuate survivors from New Orleans. One of his first orders was for the military to point their weapons down, stressing their humanitarian mission to citizens of New Orleans. People applauded when they saw him on the street, valuing his efforts to provide comfort and security in an extreme situation that included looters and snipers.

Fort Benning's 14th Combat Support Hospital departed for New Orleans with more than 250 medical personnel. Their mission was to care for Department of Defense personnel, the several thousand troops from throughout the country supporting the effort. Earlier, the 489th Air Ambulance Company, a unit of the 14th, flew to New Orleans. The 14th, a field hospital when part of the 36 Engineer Group, now reported to the 44th Medical Command.

Post problems in 2005 were minimal compared to what was happening in Iraq and the southern Gulf states. The Base Realignment and Closure Process—BRAC—meant reduction and closure for many bases in the country, including some in Georgia, but Fort Benning—surviving the cut as so many predicted—faced the opposite problem: growth.[31] Post expansion

---

[30] "Hurricane Katrina," http://en.wikipedia.org/wiki/Hurricane_Katrina.

[31] "Columbus gears for growth surge," *Atlanta Journal-Constitution*, September 9 2005, D6; Tony Adams, "Shifting into high gear," *Columbus Ledger-Enquirer*, January 21 2006, 1.

could mean similar problems post personnel faced in early Fort Benning, finding quarters, homes, and schools for post personnel.

Many of the same players as years back, the Chamber of Commerce, post personnel, bankers, military leaders, real estate companies, contractors, etc., were preparing for new troops, civilian workers, and their families. A potential tent city was not out of question. Because of the thousands of reservists preparing for Iraq or Afghanistan, some trainees were living in modular housing or large air-conditioned tents.

Now not only Columbus and Phenix City were involved but counties such as Lee, Russell, Chattahoochee, and Barbour. People like Biff Hadden, vice president for economic development with the Greater Columbus Chamber of Commerce, presented facts to surrounding communities, accenting how their community will benefit: "Clearly every business in town benefits when your population grows," said Hadden.[32] Papers reported the probability of the largest troop expansion since the Vietnam War with thousands coming from closed European bases. Stores, such as barbershops and car dealers, welcomed the newcomers. Now they would have plenty of clients when major units, such as the 3rd Brigade, were away on missions. Over the next few years, the creation of 7,000 additional jobs seemed likely.[33]

In September 2005, the BRAC Commission recommended that the Army's Armor Center and School from Fort Knox, Kentucky, to Ft. Benning. The population was expected to grow to about 170,000 when the realignment was complete in 2011. With army and infantry combined—something former tankers General George Patton and Dwight D. Eisenhower would approve—their mission will prevail. The families would add spouses and children.[34]

As part of an eight-year, $1.7 billion project, plans were in place to tear down 4,000 housing units and built more modern units with most housing absorbed off base. Bob Poydasheff said, "All in all, it's a great time to be mayor of Columbus, Georgia." In anticipation of the influx of new troops, tracts of land were sold at inflated prices. The city, unlike early Columbus,

---

[32] "Columbus gears for growth surge," D6.

[33] Elliott Minor, "Getting Ready," *Opelika-Auburn*, November 28 2004, 1.

[34] Erica Walsh, "Chief of Infantry says combining arms is right move for Army," *Turret*, May 10 2007, 1.

no longer depended solely on "mills and military" but benefited also from universities and insurance technology.

Still another event promised to bring Columbus and Fort Benning closer. Plans for a spacious Infantry Museum, so sought after during the many years of the post, were finalized with one-third of its $70 million goal reached in 2004. Ground breaking was held September 21, 2004, with more than 1000 people attending the ceremony.[35] White said the idea for the museum started "only about eight years ago, when Frank Lumpkin offered us funds to restore seven historic buildings from the World War II era."[36] In addition to the Lumpkin family, Lieutenant General Manton S. Eddy's family made early donations. "My uncle made the Army his life, but he made Columbus his home," said nephew Ben Hardaway III, when he and Sarah Hughston and Mr. and Mrs. John Flournoy presented a million dollar gift.

The first corporate million dollar pledge was made by United Defense Industries, Inc., an Arlington, Virginia-based defense contracting company that supplies the army with the Bradley fighting vehicle as well as development of manned ground vehicles for the Future Combat Systems program. In May 2005, the foundation received a gift of $3.5 million from the Robert W. Woodruff Foundation.[37] Woodruff, born in Columbus, led the Coca-Cola Company from 1923 to his death in 1985. White said, "Their contribution provides a giant step in our quest to honor those great Americans who have fought for and defended the freedoms we all enjoy."

The National Infantry Museum and Heritage Park will be built on 200 acres donated by both Fort Benning and Columbus, connecting city and

---

[35] Three Medal of Honor recipients from World War II, Vietnam, and Korea participated as well as the youngest infantry soldier at Fort Benning, Private Richard S. Williams, 1st Battalion, 19th Infantry Regiment; Brigadier General Benjamin Freakley, post commander; Bill Turner, former chairman of W. C. Bradley Company; Medal of Honor recipient retired Colonel Bob Nett; Mike Gaymon, president of the Columbus Chamber of Commerce; Mayor Bob Poydasheff, and retired Major General Jerry White, chairman of the National Infantry Foundation.

[36] Spc. Eliamar Castanon, "Groundbreaking for National Infantry Museum," *Bayonet*, http://www.tradoc.army.mil/pao/TNSarchives/September04/093104.htm, September 27 2004.

[37] Miami based Knight Foundation donated 1 million to halp fund construction of NIM. Mick Walsh, "Knight Foundation donates $1 M," December 15 2006, http://www.ledger-enquirer.com/mld/ledgerenquirer/news/local/16243409.htm.

post. It will have a 150,000-square-foot museum, a memorial walk of honor, and a parade field where 30,000 soldiers (or more) will graduate from infantry training each year. Featuring a chapel for weddings and a hotel for those coming to reunions and graduations, the museum and park should attract 300,000 visitors from the Southeast, revitalizing the local communities.[38] Frank Hanner, Infantry Museum curator, who, more than anyone, realized the need for a new museum, believed the museum would be a "world-class attraction that will, in essence, help the American people and the world to know the epic story of the US infantryman and his sacrifice."[39]

In February 2005, seven World War II buildings, a barracks, a day room, a supply room, a mess hall, a chapel, and the headquarters and sleeping quarters used by General George Patton in 1941–42 were moved to the site of the new museum and park to create a World War II Company Street. The move took twelve hours over two days. The tightest spot was in front of Riverside.

Guided by Ben Williams, National Infantry Foundation executive director, Newton Aaron and Associates, Inc., signed on as project manager in 2004 to oversee the construction process, and E. Verner Johnson and Associates of Boston were chosen to design the new National Museum and Heritage Park. Columbus-based architects Hecht Burdeshaw Johnson Kidd and Clark signed up to assist. Midland Engineering of Columbus will help deal with all environmental and real estate issues. Larry French and Associates of Columbus, a landscape firm, will refine the master site plan. Chris Chadbourne and Associates have charge of the new National Infantry Museum's exhibits, featuring a day in the army, war settings, and the history of the infantry.[40] To capture the spirit of the infantry, Chadbourne went through boot camp in 2004 escorted by Staff Sergeant Arthur Fontenaux, Fort Benning's drill sergeant of the year. His fear of heights did not stop him from jumping from the thirty-four-foot Mock Door Tower.[41] After joining soldiers for the last mile of a long hike and observing them receiving

---

[38] Spc. Eliamar Castanon, "Groundbreaking for National Infantry Museum."

[39] Ibid.

[40] Cyndy Cerbin, "Museum Designers 'Enlist' in Infantry," National Infantry Foundation, http://www.nationalinfantryfoundation.org/nr_chadbourne.shtml, December 13 2004.

[41] Ibid.

Crossed Rifles, their first badge of honor, Chadbourne said, "I have a new appreciation for the role Fort Benning plays in our nation's security.... We're going to have to give the museum's Fort Benning gallery some extra special attention."[42] Perhaps an exhibit in the new museum built to honor the infantry may feature the popular poem Stephen White wrote and Roy Lothner staged: "Wherever brave men fight ...and die for freedom, you will find me. I am the bulwark of our nation's defense. I am always ready...now and forever. I am the Infantry—Queen of Battle!"

The new infantry museum, built to honor the infantry, will serve as another bond between post and town, partners for more than eighty-five years. Fort Benning has grown from 1918 Camp Benning to an immense army base. But whenever or wherever Fort Benning is mentioned, its dearest title is "Home of the Infantry," dearest in terms of endearment and of sacrifice.

---

[42] Ibid.

Acknowledgments

In 1993, Ed Williamson, a military historian and retired Auburn University history professor, asked if I wanted a writing project. He had been asked to write the history of Fort Benning, but because of other commitments, he declined. When Ed believed you could do something, you believed it too. So having taught high school and college English classes, I was eager to research, write, and edit this topic. As a wife of a retired military career officer, I was familiar with military life.

As the mother of US Marine, Lance Corporal Bill J. Stelpflug—one of the 241 marines and fellow servicemen who died in the 1983 marine barracks terrorist bombing in Beirut, Lebanon—I wanted to honor the men and women in military service.

Stalwarts Douglas Purcell, director of the Chattahoochee Historical Commission, the organization sponsoring the project, and board member Forrest Shivers approved Ed's recommendation. Director Dick Grube, museum director, and his assistant Z. Frank Hanner gave me a list of resources and after Dick's retirement, Frank, museum curator, continued his support, advising and editing. Becky Pennington, museum secretary, was also a mainstay during this period.

Fortified by the *Bayonet* and *Benning Leader*'s coverage of the seventy-fifth anniversary of the post and "An Outline History of Fort Benning, Georgia, and Infantry School Concept," a comprehensive chronology compiled by Robert Holcombe, I began my research. Fort Benning's Donovan Technical Library was a bonanza of post history and many outstanding Donovan librarians assisted me. The library held a treasure trove of old Infantry School newspapers, documents, and copies of the *Leader* and the *Bayonet*. I owe a great debt to the fine reporting of their staffs.

A History of the Infantry School by LeRoy W. Yarborough in collaboration with Truman Smith was an extremely helpful book for the post's early history to 1931. The discovery of Etta Blanchard Worsley's *Columbus on the Chattahoochee* proved an invaluable source of information of the early post and of its relationship to Columbus. Another fine source of

Home of the Infantry

post history was L. Albert Scipio's *The 24th Infantry at Fort Benning*. Auburn
University's library, the Bradley Library in Columbus, and the Columbus
State University Archives, then directed by Craig Lloyd, were fine
resources.

For a primary source, Grube and Hanner directed me to the late Frank
G. Lumpkin, Jr., a retired businessman who allowed me generous access to
his father's files. Frank G. Lumpkin, Sr., was influential in the creation of
Fort Benning and became good friends with its troops as well as its many
leaders. Frank G. Lumpkin, Jr., also relayed many memories of George
Patton, Omar Bradley, and others. His spirited observations of post and
town provided me personal access to the past. I deeply appreciate his
kindness.

I also wish to express my gratitude to all the interesting, caring, and
resourceful men and women I interviewed for this work. Their time,
patience, and desire to tell their stories continually renewed my appreciation
of the dedication of those directly involved with the post and of the need to
write its history.

Another person who influenced the project was Sergeant Major
(Retired) James E. Hudson, a veteran of Korea and Vietnam, who told me
about the "real" army. Having received his master's degree in English after
leaving the service, he enthusiastically corrected and inspired many topics in
the manuscript while we researched at Donovan Library, one of his favorite
places to spend the day on post.

In Auburn, I read much of my work to members of an informal weekly
writing club—Sheila Jones, Myra Provo, Margaret Cutchins, and our
fearless leader, Mary Belser. Their thoughtful recommendations and
corrections were always on mark. Fortunately they never complained about
listening to Fort Benning history.

I wish to thank Thomas and Shirley Curran, Sara Hudson, Ruth
Gynther, Peggy Walls, Lois Sampsel, Alice Pantarotto, and Elizabeth
Wetzel and other friends who expressed their interest and encouragement.

Family members also helped. Our daughters Laura, Kathy (who helped
edit the 1940s), and Christy, and their husbands, Al, Mike, and John were
highly supportive. My son Joe and his wife, Catherine, promised to read
every word. My sister Mary Lou and her husband, William Schmitzer, who
spent four years in the Pacific with the Coast Guard in World War II,

encouraged me; also my mother and step-dad, Riley and Abe Stone. Our nine grandchildren were careful not to disturb Grandma's papers.

My dad, Walter Blank—too young for World War I and too old for World War II—would have approved of my topic since he loved to tell tales of the time he spent at Camp McCoy, Wisconsin, as a member of the National Guard. My husband, Bill, a former aeronautical engineering professor at the Air Force Academy and an F-4 pilot in Vietnam, made all things possible for my research and writing of this manuscript.

While researching Fort Benning's history, I developed respect and affection for the "Home of the Infantry" and for the civilians and military who serve it. Thanks to Richard Hyatt, who revised the lengthy manuscript, the finished work has a voice. The history of Fort Benning goes on. Others writing from their own Fort Benning experience and collective memory will add to its heart and soul.

—Peggy Stelpflug
Auburn, Alabama

On my fifty-seventh birthday, I was a pallbearer. We met the first day of high school and were buddies from homeroom until graduation. Now I helped carry Fred Miller's body up a hillside in a majestic Atlantic cemetery. After the burial, talk turned to the past. I was there when Fred graduated OCS. I was there when he came home from Vietnam. I remembered him telling how he got off the ship in Saigon and the first person he met was Sergeant Willie Webb, our high school ROTC teacher. Webb saluted.

We first met Webb at Sylvan High School in Atlanta. Our first year of ROTC was also his. We tested him, and he said we were worse than the soldiers he trained at Fort Benning. I was a ringleader—such as the day we stood for the annual formal inspection. An army officer came down the line. In front of me, he stopped. I did a crisp inspection arms and he grabbed my weapon. It was clean.

"Name the branches of service," he said.

"Sir, the branches of service are the army, the navy, the marines, the air force...and the Salvation Army, Sir!"

Webb was at the officer's side. I glimpsed his face. It was ashen, then angry, then disappointed at this punk cadet who embarrassed him in front of a superior. I learned nothing. I thought I was cute. My epiphany came in a map reading class. We used maps that were Fort Benning hand-me-downs.

Webb called a pop quiz and said we needed our maps and tools. Mine were in my locker. If I was getting a zero, I was having fun. We had to find coordinates and benchmarks and identify what was located there. I made up places, including Dolly's, a house of ill repute I had heard of in Rome, Georgia.

Next day, with me in uniform, Sergeant Webb marched me to the principal's office. The principal, James C. Fain, asked me what Dolly's was.

"Eh, that's a restaurant in West End," I said.

"Well, good," he said. "I was afraid it was that whorehouse in Rome, Georgia."

Later I would wonder how straitlaced Mr. Fain knew about the whorehouse. Standing there I was too scared to think such things. I was going to be suspended. But Sarge interceded. I wasn't a bad boy, he said. He could salvage me if Mr. Fain said okay.

Reprieve granted, I shook Sergeant Webb's hand. No way was I going to let him down. And I didn't. A year later, we returned to the principal's office. This time, they announced I was being invited back to ROTC for my senior year—as an officer.

Decades later, I'm in Columbus, involved in writing a history of Fort Benning, the post whose maps I studied long ago. This time I need no map. Peggy Stelpflug has mapped out the research for me, and she did it well. The research and the facts are hers, the voice is mine. I believe our collaboration captures the post's history and spirit—spirit that is embodied in the men and women who pass through it. Some advance to greatness and rank. Some just move on. Each carries a piece of this place with them.

As a longtime newspaperman at the *Columbus Ledger-Enquirer*, I carry my own memories. I remember combat soldiers tenderly carrying babies off planes the night Betty Tisdale's orphans arrived from Vietnam. I remember a memorial at Main Post Chapel for Charlie Black and the war correspondents and generals who showed up. I remember a lonely funeral for Arthur Pue, an old sergeant who, when the vodka ran out on Sundays, would call and cry about all he had seen. I remember a receiving line near Air Force One, welcoming President Jimmy Carter to Lawson Field. I remember the saucy stories of my friend Frank Lumpkin, Jr., who knew Patton, Bradley, and Marshall as men—not heroes. I remember chanting protesters solemnly crossing on to post, met by stern soldiers who dutifully confronted them. I remember sitting in the commanding general's office two days after 9/11, as Major General John LeMoyne told me we were at war, never hinting that he had lost a friend at the Pentagon and that he would soon replace him. I remember the passion of Brigadier General Benjamin Freakley, recently returned from Iraq, unloading opinions about how the newspaper depicted his soldiers.

So the honor of recording Fort Benning's history is mine. Appreciation to Peggy Stelpflug for her years of work...to Carmen Cavezza for listening to endless tales...to Rich McDowell and his staff at Fort Benning's Public Affairs...to Doug Purcell for his tireless patience...to Jack Bassett for having an empty office...to Sam Harper, who went to war...and to John L. Davis who first introduced me to the post. Finally, there is William Webb, a sergeant who died a chief warrant officer, and Fred Miller, who in some ways never came home from war. They saluted in Vietnam. I salute them back.

—Richard Hyatt
Columbus, Georgia

Bibliography

Adams, Brian. "Reception station groundbreaking." *Bayonet*, December 11, 1981, 4.

Adams, Tony. "Benning's wooden barracks caught in a demolition war." *Benning Leader*, May 15, 1998, 3.

———. "GIs salute 'Joe.'" *Columbus Ledger-Enquirer*, September 19, 2003, C1.

———. "Rangers refuse to forget the fallen." *Benning Leader*, November 27, 1998, 4.

———. "Reitzell handing up his BDU's." *Benning Leader*, March 7, 1997, 12.

"Advanced Class, In Retrospection." *Infantry School News*, June 6, 1930, 6.

After Action Report, Exercise Air Assault II. Headquarters Exercise Director. Project TEAM. December 15, 1964. Documents, Donovan Technical Library, Fort Benning GA, X-1.

Aiken, Conrad. "IV: the Wars." *The Soldier*. Norfolk CT: New Directions, 1944.

"All-Army Awards Made by General Powell: Sergeant Set Five Records with Pistols." *Bayonet*, June 16, 1960, 1.

Ambrose, Stephen E. *Eisenhower.* New York: Simon & Schuster, 1983.

Anderson, Jon R. "Post welcomes returning soldiers–Desert Storm 'heroes' come home." *Bayonet*, March 15, 1999, 1.

Anderson, Sean, and Stephen Sloan. *Historical Dictionary of Terrorism.* Metuchen NJ: Scarecrow Press, 1995.

Anderson, Virginia. "Civil disobedience: Priest ready for prison." *Atlanta Journal*, June 20, 1996, B3.

Andrews, Heather, "63 builds roads, friendships in Nicaragua." *Bayonet*, January 22, 1999, A-6.

"Annual Class in Retrospection." *Infantry School News*, June 6, 1930, 1.

Annual Report of the Infantry School, June 30, 1930. Fort Benning folder titled "Office of the Commandant." Vault, Donovan Technical Library, Fort Benning GA, 28.

"Anthony Eden, General Marshall, Sir John Dill tour Fort Benning." *Bayonet*, March 25, 1943, 1.

Applebaum, Anne. "Having it Both Ways." *Washington Post*, April 21, 2004, A23.

"Appreciative Citizens Give Loving Cup and Check to Betjeman." *Columbus Enquirer-Sun*, December 7, 1918, 1.

"Arlington home of memorial dedicated to black paratroopers." *Columbus Ledger-Enquirer*, August 17, 1995, B-7.

"Army: Fort Suicide?" *Newsweek* (National Affairs), September 27, 1976, 36.

"Army, Infantry mark 185th Anniversary." *Bayonet*, June 9, 1960, 1.

"Army of 150,000 voted by Senate after Long Fight." *Columbus Enquirer-Sun*, January 15, 1921, 1.

"Army Sets New Hair Styles." *Bayonet*, June 5, 1970, 34.

"Army Swept Camp Perry Matches Taking Six Major Team Trophies." *Bayonet*, September 2, 1960, 1.

"Army to Retain 200,000 of the Drafted Men." *Columbus Enquirer-Sun*, March 9, 1919, 1.

Ashworth, Maynard R. "Why the Army plans 'OCS' Move." *Sunday Ledger-Enquirer*. December 15, 1946, 2–D.

Ashworth, Robert. "Ranger units activated at Benning." *Bayonet*, October 5, 1984, 1.

Associated Press. "Julia C. Moore, 75, outspoken Army wife." *Atlanta Journal Constitution*, April 21, 2004, B6.

———. "Nunn calls for definite end point of U.S. Mission in Somalia." *Columbus Ledger Enquirer*, September 27, 1993, A-3.

———. "Saddam's best torn to tatters." *Columbus Ledger-Enquirer*, February 28, 1991, 1.

———. "Veterans' Groups warn of need of new cemeteries." *Birmingham News*, May 20, 1999, 7A.

Aure, Kathy. "Death of General's Friend Marks End of Era." *Columbus-Enquirer*, December 9, 1971, 8.

Avery, Isaac Wheeler. *The History of the State of Georgia from 1850–1881*. New York: Brown and Derby, 1881.

Bailey, Virginia. "Columbus Lifts Lid in Big Celebration." *Columbus Enquirer*, August 15, 1945, 1.

Bank, Aaron. *From OSS to Green Berets*. Novato CA: Presidio Press, 1986.

Barham, J. "Fort Benning soldier slams Main Post Theatre." *Bayonet*, November 9, 1973, 4.

Barnes, Margaret Anne. *The Tragedy and the Triumph of Phenix City, Alabama*. Macon GA: Mercer University Press, 1998.

Bartley, Numan V. *The Creation of Modern Georgia*, second edition. Athens: University of Georgia Press, 1990.

Baumgartner, John W. "The Infantry and Its School." *Infantry School Quarterly* 39/1 (July 1951): 5.

"Bayonet Training makes comeback." *Bayonet*, September 11, 1981, 6.

Beckwith, Charlie A., and Donald Knox. *Delta Force*. New York: Harcourt Brace Jovanovich, 1983.

Bell, Joe. Interview by Peggy Stelpflug. November 6. Donovan Technical Library, Fort Benning GA. Handwritten transcript and audio cassette, Auburn AL, 1998.

Benning, Anna Caroline. "Henry Lewis Benning." *Men of Mark in Georgia*. Volume 3. Edited by William J. Northen. Atlanta: A. B. Caldwell, 1911. Reprint. Spartanburg SC: Reprint Co., 1974.

———"Seaborn Jones." *Men of Mark in Georgia*. Volume 2. Edited by William J. Northen. Atlanta: A.B. Caldwell, 1910. Reprint. Spartanburg SC: Reprint Co., 1974.

"Benning-Columbus Step to Wedding March." *Infantry School News*, June 5, 1925, 4.

Benning, Henry L. "Speech to the Virginia State Convention, February 13 1861," found in Fulton Anderson, *Addresses Delivered before the Virginia State Convention*. Richmond: Wyatt M. Elliott, Printer, 1861; microfilm: New Haven, Connecticut Research Publication in 1974, reel 62 no. 2257. Documentations: Ralph Brown Draughon Library, Auburn University, Auburn AL.

"Benning Makes Switch to Check Pay System." *Bayonet*, January 12, 1968, 1.

"Benning Paved Highway." *Fort Benning News*, February 2, 1923, 4.

"Benning Railroad, Combat Veteran, 8 Fogeys, Retires." *Bayonet*, November 28, 1946, 1.

"Benning to Reopen OCS." *Bayonet*, January 11, 1951, 1.

"Big Camp Site is Changed." *Columbus Ledger*, October 18, 1918, 1.

"Big Plantation Is Transformed within Six Years." *Infantry School News*, September 17, 1926, 13.

Biggs, Bradley. *Gavin*. Hamden CT: Archon Books, 1980.

Biographical Directory of the United States Congress 1774–1989. Bicentennial Edition. Washington: U. S. Government Printing Office, 1989.

Black, Charles L. "Truce Announcement Sometimes Is Slow." *Columbus Enquirer*, August 15, 1963, 1.

———. Introduction to unpublished manuscript. Personal papers. Columbus GA.

Black, Robert W. *Rangers in Korea*. New York: Ivy Books, 1989.

Blair, Clay. *Ridgway's Paratroopers: The American Airborne in World War II*. Garden City NY: The Dial Press, 1985.

———. *The Forgotten War*. New York: Times Books, 1987.

Blumenson, Martin. *Patton: The Man Behind the Legend 1885–1945*. New York: William Morrow & Company, Inc., 1985.

Bolger, Daniel P. *Savage Peace: Americans at War in the 1990s*. Novato CA: Presidio Press, 1995.

Booth, T. Michael, and Duncan Spencer. *Paratrooper*. New York: Simon & Schuster, 1994.

Bowden, Mark. *Black Hawk Down*. New York: Penguin Books, 1999.

Bradin, James W. *From Hot Air to Hellfire*. Novato CA: Presidio Press, 1994.

Bradley, Omar, with collaborator Clay Blair. *A General's Life*. New York: Simon & Schuster, 1983.

Brazile, Mike. "Paratroopers' memorial dedicated." *Bayonet*, April 18, 1986, 1.

———. "Ranger Association moves headquarters to Benning." *Bayonet*, April 12, 1985, 7.

———. "10th Division brigade activates on post." *Bayonet*, October 11, 1985, 1.

Brazile, Mike, and Laurie J. Hill. "School of the Americas on post permanently." *Bayonet*, August 8, 1986, 1.

Bridges, Connie. "Benning looks to quality future." *Bayonet*, October 8, 1993, 75th anniversary commemorative edition, A-2.

———. "Cook lays down ladle after 36 years on job." *Bayonet*, September 13, 1951, B-1.

Brill, Richard. "Calculator—'He made a better dog of us all.'" *Bayonet*, October 8, 1993, B-2.

———. "Fort Benning in the 1940s." *Bayonet*, October 8, 1993, B-5.

———. "Fort Benning wins best again." *Bayonet*, September 16, 1994, A-1.

Britts, Nicolas. "USARSA receives full funding." *Bayonet*, September 24, 1999, A-1.

Brown, Pat. "Alvin York statue is Benning's birthday gift." *Bayonet*, October 6, 1978, 11.

Bruk, Douglas O. "More Benning units deploy to Middle East." *Bayonet*, December 28, 1990, 1.

Bulgrin, Becky. "1st post forester retires." *Bayonet*, August 29, 1980, 10.

Bussey, Charles M. *Firefight at Yechon: Courage and Racism in the Korean War.* Washington: Brassey's Inc., 1991.

Butterworth, W. E. *Flying Army: The Modern Air Arm of the U. S. Army.* Garden City NY: Doubleday, 1971.

"Calculator—The School's 'Dog of All Dogs'—A Real Pal." *Bayonet*, September. 29, 1961, 34.

"Camp Benning Is Official Name of Camp." *Enquirer-Sun*, October 19, 1918, 2.

"Camp Perry Troops Here." *Columbus Ledger*, October 27, 1918, 1.

"Camp Site Is Changed to South of City." *Columbus Enquirer-Sun*, October 18, 1918, 1.

Campbell, Major Verne D. "Armor and Cavalry Music." Part 2. *Armor* 80/3 (May/June 1971): 37.

"Can VOLAR end the draft?" *Columbus Ledger*, March 28, 1971, 18.

"Capt. Brown Leaves Monday to Receive Medal of Honor." *Columbus Ledger*, August 16, 1945, 5.

Carr, Virginia Spencer. *The Lonely Hunter: A Biography of Carson McCullers.* Garden City NY: Doubleday & Company, Inc., 1975.

Carruth, Gorton. *What Happened When.* New York: Signet, 1991.

Castanon, Eliamar. "Groundbreaking for National Infantry Museum." *Bayonet*, http://www.tradoc.army.mil/pao/TNSarchives/September04/093104.htm. September 27, 2004.

Cavezza, Carmen. Interview by Peggy Stelpflug. Columbus Government Center. Handwritten transcript and audiocassette, Auburn AL, June 17, 1998.

Cerbin, Cyndy. "Museum Designers 'Enlist' in Infantry." *Bayonet*, http://www.nimfb.org/nr_chadbourne.shtml. September 27, 1994.

Chappell, Lucius Henry. "Brief Sketch of General Benning for Whom Camp at Columbus Has Been Named." *Columbus Ledger*, October 20, 1918, 5.

Chappell, Loretto Lamar. "Notes from Scrap-book Chamber of Commerce." Fort Benning Folders. Chappell File. Genealogy Department, Columbus Public Library, Columbus GA.

————. "The Establishment of the Infantry School at Columbus Georgia, June 1918–March 8, 1919." *Notes from Clippings, Telegrams, and Letters Preserved in Scrap-book Belonging to Mrs. John A. Betjeman.* Fort Benning Folders. Chappell File. Genealogy Department, Columbus Public Library, Columbus GA.

Cheatham, Cynthia. "Post honors employees." *Bayonet*, December 17, 1993, A-1.

Cherry, Rev. F. L. "The History of Opelika and her Agricultural Tributary Territory." *Alabama Historical Quarterly* 15/1 (Spring 1953): 183.

"Chief of Staff Taylor Gives the Word on the Future Challenges of Infantry." *Army Navy Air Force Journal* 96/14 (December 6, 1958): 11.

Claybrook, Clint. "Post has turned out its share of heroes." *Benning Leader*, October 1, 1993, 80

Claybrook, Clint, and Timothy Rogers. "Benning salutes fallen Rangers." *Columbus Ledger-Enquirer*, October 9, 1993, A-1.

"Client Kills Lawyer Who Charged $2,500." *New York Times*, June 5, 1928, 59:2.

Clodfelter, Micheal. *Vietnam in Military Statistics: A History of the Indochina Wars, 1772–1991.* Jefferson NC: McFarland & Co., 1995.

Clouse, Robert C. "197th re-activated at Kelley Hill." *Bayonet*, August 24, 1979, 16.

Clutterbuck, Richard L. *Guerrillas and Terrorists*. London: Faber & Faber Limited, 1977.

———. *Terrorism in an Unstable World*. New York: Routledge, 1994.

Cobb, James C. "The Making of a Secessionist; Henry L. Benning and the Coming of the Civil War." *Georgia History Quarterly* 60/4 (Winter 1976): 313–23.

Coleman, J. D. "Charlie Black–The Soldier's Friend in Vietnam." *The Journalist* 11/4, (November 1967): 6–7.

———. *Pleiku: The Dawn of Helicopter Warfare in Vietnam*. New York: St. Martin's Press, 1988.

"Colonel Marshall Goes to New Command." *Benning Herald*, June 17, 1932, 1.

"Columbus and General Benning." *Columbus Ledger*, October 20, 1918, 5.

"Columbus gears for growth surge." *Atlanta Journal-Constitution*, September 9, 2005, D1.

"Columbus Lands Georgia-Auburn Football Game." *Columbus Enquirer-Sun*, February 21, 1919, 1.

"Columbus on Verge Most Wonderful Era Prosperity in History." *Columbus Enquirer-Sun*, September 26, 1918, 1.

Connett, Skip. "America's sons and daughters and mothers head out." Includes photo of Hollie Vallance by Allen Horne. *Columbus Ledger*, August 24, 1990, 1.

Cray, Ed. *General of the Army*. New York: W.W. Norton & Company, 1990.

Cronenberg, Allen. *Forth to the Mighty Conflict*. Tuscaloosa: University of Alabama Press, 1995.

Cuneo, John R. *Robert Rogers of the Rangers*. New York: Oxford University Press, 1959.

"Curator Carries on Museum's History." *Bayonet*, February 17, 1995, C-1.

Daly, Mary. "Audie Murphy Arrives to Help Welcome Third." *Columbus-Ledger*, December 3, 1954, 26.

Dalfiume, Richard M. *Desegregation of the U. S. Armed Forces: Fighting in Two Fronts, 1939–1953*. Columbia: University of Missouri Press, 1969.

Daniels, Eddie. "Officials Discuss Post Security." *Columbus Ledger-Enquirer*, September 12, 2001, A11.

Darby, William O., and William H. Baumer. *We Led the Way*. San Rafael CA: Presidio Press, 1980.

Davis, Neil. Telephone interview by Peggy Stelpflug. Husband of Henrietta Worsley Davis and brother-in-law of Thomas Blanchard Worsley. Handwritten transcript, Auburn AL, November 29, 1995.

Debrow, Agatha Hudson. "Fort Benning receives 'best' in world crown." *Bayonet*, May 19, 1995, A-1.

De Camara, Bob. "Loss of President; A Terrible Blow." *Bayonet*, November 29, 1963, 15.

Decker, Bert. "Copter Cavalry." *Combat Forces Journal* 4/9 (April 1954): 36.

"Defense Secretary Conducted into OCS Hall of Fame." *Bayonet*, July 31, 1981, 1.

Derry, Joseph T. "Georgia." *Confederate Military History*. Volume 6. New York: Thomas Yoseloff, 1962.

D'Este, Carlo. *Patton—A Genius for War*. New York: HarperCollins, 1995.

Devlin, Gerard. *Paratrooper!* New York: St. Martin's Press, 1979.

Diamond, Larry. *Squandered Victory*. New York: Henry Holt & Company, 2005.

Diary. The Infantry School, Fort Benning GA, 1922–1934. 2 volumes. Unpublished. Bound Book: Typed entries about post activities. Vault, Donovan Library, Fort Benning GA.

Dictionary of American Military Biography. Edited by Roger J. Spiller. Westport CT: Greenwood Press, 1984.

Dix, Dusty. "Rules Have Changed." *Columbus Ledger-Enquirer*, September 12, 2001, A11.

"Doughboy Statue Unveiling Held; Stands as Infantry Memorial." *Bayonet*, April 3, 1958, 1.

Doughboy. Camp Benning GA: The Infantry School, 1921.

Doughboy. Fort Benning GA. The Infantry School Yearbook, 1922. Atlanta: Foote and Davies Co., 1922. National Infantry Museum, Fort Benning GA.

Duncan, Priscilla Black. "1st Cav changed the face of war." *Columbus Ledger-Enquirer*, October 2, 1989, B-3.

———. "Where are they now?" *Columbus Ledger-Enquirer*, October 2, 1988, B-6.

Dunkin, Tom. *The Trial of Lt. William Calley*. Columbus GA: R. W. Page Corporation, 1971.

Dupuy, R. Ernest. "Impact of George Marshall Remains on Army and World." *Army, Navy, Air Force Register* 80/4169 (October 31, 1959): 24.

"Early History of Fort Benning." *Army, Navy, Air Force Register* 76/3920 (January 22, 1955): 6.

Egan, Lori. "SOA watch protestors demonstrate, trespass, leave Fort Benning." *Bayonet*, November 21, 1997, A-1.

———. "Troops deploy to Kuwait." *Bayonet*, February 27, 1998, 1.

Einhorn, David. "Bradley Dedicates Museum." *Columbus Ledger*, July 1, 1977, l.

Eisenhower, Dwight D. *At Ease*. Garden City NY: Doubleday Company, Inc., 1967.

———. *The Historical Record of Eisenhower's Life*. New York: American Heritage Publishing Company, 1969.

"11th Air Assault Division Will Be Located on Post." *Bayonet*, February 8, 1963, 1

Elkins, John W. "War?" *Fort Benning News*, January 12, 1923, 4.

Ellis, Dale. Telephone interview by Peggy Stelpflug. Handwritten transcript, Auburn AL, June 1998.

Ellis, Rex. "Infantry Board to Observe 50th Anniversary." *Bayonet*, October 17, 1969, 21.

"Enlisted Men Are Top of Viet Casualty List." *Bayonet*, September 2, 1966, 11.

Ennis, Ned Baxter. "Charlie Black: The Ernie Pyle of the Vietnam War." Master's thesis, University of Georgia, 1987.

Everett, Arthur, Kathryn Johnson, and Harry F. Rosenthal. *Calley*. New York: Dell Publishing Company, Inc., 1971.

"Faculty Doffs Its Dignity at Picnic Besides the Upatoi." *Infantry School News*, May 23, 1930, 1, 3.

Fall, Bernard B. *Street Without Joy*. Harrisburg PA: Stackpole, 1964.

———. *Hell in a Very Small Place*. New York: Vintage Books, 1966.

"Family of 'Atomic Pilot' Thrilled by Jap Offer." *Columbus Ledger*, August 10, 1945, 9.

"Fifty Years Ago." *Bayonet*, February 4, 1972, 18.

"1st Cavalry's 'Mother' Hopes to Restyle Patch." *Bayonet*, July 9, 1965, 24.

"First Death at Temporary Camp." *Columbus Enquirer-Sun*, October 25, 1918, 2.

Floyd, Cyril. *Dr. Floyd's Journal: Memoirs of Dr. Cyril Floyd, 1925–1941*. Copy of unpublished, handwritten manuscript. Accession No. 93-31, Auburn University Library Archives, Auburn AL.

"'Fly-by' of 50 Called Largest Ever in Army." *Bayonet*, July 28, 1961, 1.

"Fort Benning." *Army–Navy Register*, October 28, 1944, 2.

"Fort Benning, Georgia, 'America's most Colorful post.'" *Pictorial Revue*, Columbus GA: Columbus Office Supply Company, 1942. Booklet. Located in Special Collections (UA 26.B48P52 1942), Auburn University Library, Auburn AL.

"Franklin Delano Roosevelt." *The American Experience*. TV-PBS. October 11, 1994.

Franklin, Harry. "Waverly Hall: A Heap of History." *Columbus Ledger-Enquirer*, March 7, 1993, A-5.

Frazier, Mitch, PFC. "Brigade Soldiers Leave for Kuwait." *Bayonet*, April 16, 1999, A1.

———. "Military police working dogs train for success." *Bayonet*, October 29, 1999, A-8.

Fulbright, James William. *Arrogance of Power*. New York: Random House, 1966.

Fuller, Tom. "15th Cavalry replaces aging tanks." *Bayonet*, February 17, 1984, 11.

———. "First production line Bradleys arrive." *Bayonet*, May 28, 1982, 4.

Fussell, Paul. *Doing Battle: the Making of a Skeptic*. Boston: Little Brown & Company, 1996.

———. "My War." *The Norton Reader*, 7th ed. New York: W.W. Norton & Company, 1988.

Galloway, Joseph L. "Rest in peace, Julie Moore." *Columbus Ledger-Enquirer*, April 25, 2004, F4.

Garland, Albert N. "Don't rely too much on high-tech combat." *Benning Leader*, March 6, 1998, 15.

———. Interview by Peggy Stelpflug at National Infantry Museum. Handwritten transcript, Auburn AL, 1994.

———. Telephone interview by Peggy Stelpflug. Handwritten notes, Auburn AL, March 28, 1997.

Gavin, James. *On to Berlin*. New York: Bantam Books, 1978.

"Gen. Kinnard Gets Official Farewell." *Bayonet*, August 20, 1965, 1.

"General Marshall Opposes Large Standing Army." *Army and Navy Journal* 82/2 (September 9, 1944): 31.

Georgia Department of Agriculture. *Georgia: Historical and Industrial*. Atlanta: Geo. W. Harrison State Printer, The Franklin Printing and Publishing Co., 1901.

Georgia, The WPA Guide to Its Towns and Countryside. Compiled by workers of the Work Program Administration in the State of Georgia. Athens: University of Georgia Press, 1940. Reprint. Columbia: University of South Carolina Press, 1990.

Gersh, Don. "197th bids goodbye to Col. Cavezza." *Bayonet*, November 18, 1983, 1.

Gibbons, William Conrad. *The U.S. Government and the Vietnam War, Part IV (1965–1968)*. Princeton: Princeton University Press, 1995.

"Git or Git Got." *Newsweek*, December 6, 1965, 88.

"Gowdy Field to Be Dedicated in Game with Georgia Today." *Infantry School News*, March 27, 1925, 1.

Greene, Bob. *Duty: a father, his son, and the man who won the war.* New York: HarperCollins Publishers, 2000.

Griminger, Charles O. "The Armed Helicopter Story," *Army Aviation Digest* 17/11 (November 1971): 17.

Grimes, Millard. "Charlie Black Knew a Secret." *Columbus Ledger*, November 28, 1982, B11.

Grube, Dick. Interview by Peggy Stelpflug. National Infantry Museum, Fort Benning GA. Typed transcript and audio cassette, Auburn AL, January 17, 1996.

Hackworth, David. *About Face.* New York: Simon & Schuster, 1989.

———. *Hazardous Duty:* New York: William Morrow, 1996.

"Hair Trigger Action at Camp Says Major Jones." *Enquirer-Sun*, September 26, 1918, 1.

Halberstadt, Hans. *Green Berets: Unconventional Warriors.* Novato CA: Presidio Press, 1988.

Halberstram, David. *The Best and the Brightest.* New York: Random House, 1972.

———. *The Making of a Quagmire.* New York: Random House, 1965.

Hanner, Z. Frank. National Infantry Museum Curator. Interviews by Peggy Stelpflug 1993–2000. Reader and contributor to *Home of the Infantry* manuscript. Typed transcripts, Auburn AL.

Harding, Forrest. "The Flair." *Benning Herald*, June 2, 1933, 4.

"Harding would make Benning Permanent." *Columbus Enquirer-Sun*, January 6, 1921, 1.

Harper Encyclopedia of Military Biography. Edited by Trevor N. Dupuy, Curt Johnson, and David L. Bongard. New York: HarperCollins, 1993.

Harper Encyclopedia of Military History. Edited by Trevor N. Dupuy and Ernest Dupuy. New York: Harper Collins, 1993.

Harper, S. Thorne. "Faces of Freakley." *Columbus Ledger-Enquirer*, November 7, 2003, A1.

———. "It's All I've Ever Known." *Columbus Enquirer*, December 23, 2001, A1.

Harris, Julian. "Lynchings in 1920." Editorial. *Columbus Enquirer-Sun*, January 4, 1921, 4.

Hartley, Meredith. "Soldiers step on to the virtual battlefield." *Benning Leader*, July 31, 1998, 6.

Heaton, Dean R. *Four Stars: The Super Stars of United States Military History.* Baltimore MD: Gateway Press, Inc., 1995.

Helms, Jesse. "Columbus Woman's Husband Flies First Plane to Drop Atomic Bomb." *Columbus Enquirer*, August 8, 1945, 1.

Hepburn, Lawrence R., principal contributor. *Contemporary Georgia*, 2nd edition. Carl Vinson Institute of Government. Athens: University of Georgia, 1992.

Hibbert, Lisa M. "586th Joins Operation Joint Endeavor." *Bayonet*, December 15, 1995, 1.

——— "29th Inf. Moves back to main post." *Bayonet*, August 30, 1996, A-1.

——— "11th Inf. Regt. gets female 1st Sgt." *Bayonet*, July 4, 1996, A-7.

Hillman, Major R. L. "A Haphazard Review of Some Tribulations Which Beset The Infantry School in the Early Years and Have Been, In Part, Retained." Correspondents: Maj. Gen. Charles S. Farnsworth, Brig. Gen. Walter H.

Gordon, and Col. Paul B. Malone 1920–1921. Donovan Library, Fort Benning GA.

Hillman, Rolfe, "Dinky Line." *Sunday Ledger-Enquirer Magazine*, December 18, 1960, 12.

"Hiroshima/Nagasaki." *Dothan Eagle*, August 6, 1995, 8–A.

History of the Infantry School (1927–1932) Folder. WPA Historical Record Survey Relating to Fort Benning. Located in Donovan Technical Library, Fort Benning GA.

History of Georgia, 2nd edition. Edited by Kenneth Coleman. Athens: University of Georgia Press, 1991.

"Hobson Praises Naming Highway 'Victory Drive.'" *Columbus Ledger*, August 20, 1945, 2

Hogan, David W. Jr. *Raiders or Elite Infantry?* Westport CT: Greenwood Press, 1992.

Holcombe, Robert, Jr. *An Outline History of Fort Benning, Georgia, and the Infantry School Concept.* Unpublished manuscript. Compiled for the National Infantry Museum, Fort Benning GA, 1990.

Holland, John. "Infantry School Building Finally Becomes a Reality After Spending 13 Years in Planning and Construction." *Bayonet*, June 5, 1964, 8.

Holmes, William F. *A History of Georgia.* 2nd edition. Edited by Kenneth Coleman. Athens: University of Georgia Press, 1991.

Holmes, Richard. *The World Atlas of Warfare.* New York: Viking Studio Books, 1988.

Houston, Donald E. *Hell on Wheels.* San Rafael CA: Presidio Press, 1977.

"Howell Cobb Papers." Edited by R. P. Brooks. *Georgia Historical Quarterly* 5/3 (September 1921): 37–40.

Howze, Gen. Hamilton. "Tactical Employment of the Air Assault Division." *Army* 14/2 (September 1963): 53.

Hudson, James K. Sgt. Maj. (Ret.) USA. Interview by Peggy Stelpflug. Donovan Technical Library, Fort Benning GA. Handwritten transcript and audio cassette, Auburn AL, April 13, 1997.

———— Private Papers. Columbus GA.

Hume, Edgar Erskine. "The History of Fort Benning." *Infantry School News*, May 25, 1928, 1, 13.

Hyatt, Richard. "Allen Horne Photographs & Memories." *Columbus Ledger-Enquirer*, May 31, 1997, A4.

————. "Life Will Never Be the Way It Was." *Columbus Ledger-Enquirer*, September 13, 2001, A1.

"Infantry School Chief Names 'Copter Board.'" *Army, Navy, Air Force Journal* 92/6 (October 1954): 152.

"Infantry School Will be Small Next Year." *Fort Benning News*, April 7, 1923, 1.

"Infantryman's Aerial Friend–the Caribou." *Bayonet*, September 22, 1961, 5.

"Influenza Epidemic of 1918." Collection of undated clippings and typed reports related to findings of influenza study made at the Post Hospital at Auburn Polytechnic Institute. File #119. Department of Archives, Auburn University, Auburn AL.

"Instruction at the Infantry School." *Army and Navy Register* 90/2675 (October 31, 1931): 409.

International Military and Defense Encyclopedia. 6 volumes. Edited by Trevor N. Dupuy. Washington: Brassey's, Inc., 1993.

Jameson, Charles. "Initial Mass Jump Made by Division Paratroopers." *Bayonet,* August 6, 1965, 1.

Jessup, John E., and Louise B. Ketz. *Encyclopedia of the American Military.* Volume 3. New York: Charles Scribner's Sons, 1994.

"Jim Woodruff—citizen, patriot, friend." *Bayonet,* October 22, 1976, 1.

Jones, Gary. "Prostitution—Alive and Well on Victory Drive." *Bayonet,* November 16, 1979, 20.

Jones, John Paul. "Final Report of Major J. Paul Jones of the Construction of Camp Benning, GA." December 8, 1919. Microfilm Udgg FU (Item 4). Donovan Technical Library, Fort Benning GA.

Jowers, Vic. "We Beheld Atom Blast in Nevada." *Bayonet,* June 4, 1953, 1.

"Jump School Is 20; Celebration Planned." *Bayonet,* May 18, 1962, 1.

Kane, Sharyn, and Richard Keeton. *Fort Benning: The Land and the People.* Tallahassee FL: Southeast Archeological Center, 2003.

Kay, W. K. "Army Aviation Story." *Army Aviation Digest* 7/6 (June 1961): 1.

Keegan, John. *A History of Warfare.* New York: Alfred A. Knopf, 1993.

———. *Book Notes.* Television interview by Brian Lamb, May 8, 1994. C-Span. http://www.booknotes.org/Transcript/?ProgramID=1198.

———. *The Face of Battle.* New York: Viking Penquin Inc., 1976.

Kerrison, Marie W. *Henry Lewis Benning: States Rights Advocate and Soldier.* Master's thesis, Emory University, 1937.

King, Campbell. "The Progress of Infantry Development." *Infantry Journal* 38/3 (March/April 1931): 165.

King, Edward L. *Death of the Army.* New York: Saturday Review Press, 1972.

Kocian, Gene. *Memories of Jazz: The History of Swing & Jazz in the Columbus, Georgia, Area.* New York: Sewell Printers, 1989.

Krepinevich, Andrew F. Jr., *The Army and Vietnam.* Baltimore: John Hopkins University Press, 1986.

Kyle, Clason F. *Images, A Pictorial History of Columbus, Georgia.* Norfolk VA: Donning Company, 1986.

Lane, Deputy Sgt. 1st Class Larry. "Post picks up ACOE award." *Bayonet,* May 8, 1998, 1.

Lang, Thomas M. "Army Aviation Story: Rotary Wing Aircraft." *Army Aviation Digest* 8/9 (September 1962): 28.

Laurence, Janice H., and Peter F. Ramsberger. *Low-Aptitude Men in the Military.* New York: Praeger, 1991.

Lavendar, Paul W. "Airborne test platoon fades into history." *Bayonet,* March 15, 1991, A-5.

Lee, R. Alton. *Dwight D. Eisenhower, Soldier and Statesman.* Chicago: Nelson-Hall, 1981.

Lee, Ulysses. *United States Army in World War II: The Employment of Negro Troops.* Washington DC: Office of the Chief of Military History United States Army, 1966.

Lee, William C. "Introduction." In *Airborne Warfare,* by Maj. Gen. James M. Gavin, ix. Washington: Infantry Journal Press, 1947.

Leuer, Kenneth. Interview by Peggy Stelpflug. Goodwill Industries, Columbus GA. Handwritten transcript and audio cassette, Auburn AL, June 5, 1998.

Lewy, Guenter. *America in Vietnam*. New York: Oxford University Press, 1978.

Levy, David W. *The Debate over Vietnam*. 2nd edition. Baltimore: John Hopkins University Press, 1995.

Lovett, Ralph B. "Up from the Primitive." *Infantry Journal* 42/3 (May/June 1935): 217–21.

Lowenhagen, Chuck. "Local Paper's Modern 'War' Correspondent Follows Sky Soldier Division Field Exercise." *Bayonet*, October 16, 1964, 29.

Lumpkin, Frank G., Sr. Collected personal papers, 1918–1958, Columbus GA.

———. 1994. Interview by Peggy Stelpflug in Lumpkin's Columbus GA office. Handwritten transcript and audio cassette, Auburn AL.

———. Interviews and private conversations with Richard Hyatt 1980s–1990s. Typed transcript, Columbus GA.

Lupold, John S. *Chattahoochee Valley Sources and Resources. An Annotated Bibliography*. Volume 1. Dexter MI: Thomson-Shore, Inc., 1988.

"Mac Patch Buried Near Dad's Army." *Columbus Ledger*, October 24, 1944, 1.

MacLean, Nancy. *Behind the Mask of Chivalry: The Making of the Second Ku Klux Klan*. New York: Oxford University Press, 1994.

Mahan, Joseph B. *Columbus: Georgia's Fall Line "Trading Town."* Northridge CA: Windsor Publications, Inc., 1986.

Mahoney, Larry. "Marshall: His years at the School of Infantry led to leadership in war and peace." *Bayonet*, January 19, 1968, 18.

Mailing List 1921. Edited by Major R. H. Kelley. Camp Benning GA: The Infantry School, 1921.

Malone, Paul. "What Camp Benning Means to the Infantry." *Infantry Journal* 16/6 (December 1919): 440.

Mannock, Robin. "'Charlie Black Club' in VN Is Least Exclusive in Highlands; Generals, Privates Are Members." *Columbus Enquirer*, October 9, 1965, 1.

"Marines Realize Their Five Year Dream and Defeat the Doughboys." *Infantry School News*, November 19, 1926, 12.

Marshall, George C. *The Papers of George Catlett Marshall*. Edited by Larry I. Bland. Baltimore: John Hopkins University Press, 1981.

———. *Interviews and Reminiscences for Forrest C. Pogue*. Edited by Larry I. Bland. Lexington VA: George C. Marshall Research Foundation, 1991.

———. "Profiting by War Experiences." *Infantry Journal* 18/1 (January 1921): 36.

———. "Report on the Army," July 1, 1939 to June 30, 1943. Biennial Report of General George C. Marshall, chief of staff of the United States Army to the secretary of war. Washington: Infantry Journal Press, 1943.

———. *Selected Speeches and Statements of General of the Army George C. Marshall*. Washington: Infantry Journal Press, 1945.

Marshall, John Douglas. *Reconciliation Road*. Syracuse: Syracuse University Press, 1993.

Marshall, Katherine Tupper. *Together: Annals of An Army Wife*. New York: Tupper and Love, Inc., 1946.

Martin, John H. *Columbus, Georgia: From its selection as a "Trading Town" in 1827 to its Partial Destruction by Wilson's Raid in 1865. Part I : 1846–1865*. Vidalia GA:

Georgia Genealogical Reprints, 1972. First published 1875 by Thos. Gilbert, Printer, Columbus GA.

Mast, Gerald. *A Short History of the Movies*. 3rd edition. Indianapolis: Bobbs-Merrill Educational Publishing, 1981.

McCullers, Carson. *Reflections in a Golden Eye*. Cambridge: Houghton Mifflin Company, 1941.

McDonald, Ann M. "Cavezza takes command." *Bayonet*, June 22, 1990, 1.

———. "First Airborne test platoon paratrooper dies." *Bayonet*, September 2, 1988, 1.

McDowell, Margaret B. *Carson McCullers*. Boston: Twayne Publishers, 1980.

McFarlane, Robert C. with Zofia Smardz. *Special Trust*. New York: Cadell & Davies, 1994.

McKenney, Alfred E. "The New Benning." *Infantry Journal* 48/3 (January 1941): 6–13.

McLaney, Sara. Interview by Peggy Stelpflug. Building 66, Fort Benning GA. Typed transcript and audio cassette, Auburn AL, December 11, 1998.

McMaster, H. R. *Dereliction of Duty*. New York: HarperCollins Publishers, Inc., 1997.

McNamara, Robert Sr. with Brian Van DeMark. *In Retrospect*. New York: Times Books, 1995.

"Memorial Addresses on William J. Harris," H. doc 370 (72-1) 9545. Tribute to Senator Harris from members of the Senate. Washington: United States Government Printing Office, 1932.

"Memorial Tablets To Be Established at Cross Roads." *Infantry School News*, February 26, 1926, 1.

Mertel, Kenneth D. *Year of the Horse: Vietnam—1st Air Cavalry in the Highlands*. New York: Exposition Press, 1968.

Miller, Merle. *Ike the Soldier*. New York: G. P. Putnam's Sons, 1987.

"Moore, Buried among those she honored." *Columbus Ledger-Enquirer*, April 23, 2004, A3.

Moore, Lt. Gen. Harold G., and Joseph L. Galloway. *We Were Soldiers Once...and Young*. New York: Harper Perennial, 1993.

———. Telephone Interview by Peggy Stelpflug. Handwritten Notes, Auburn AL, 1996.

Morarie, Karen S. "Benning now world champ." *Bayonet*, April 15, 1994, 1.

———. "Powell visits Fort Benning." *Bayonet*, January 15, 1993, A-3.

———. "Post detention facility to close by February 28." *Bayonet*, January 20, 1995, A-1.

Morgan, Elizabeth Shelfer. *Uncertain Seasons*. Tuscaloosa: University of Alabama Press, 1994.

Morris, Willie. "From James Jones: A Friendship." *Modern War*. Edited by Paul Fussell. New York: W.W. Norton Company, 1991.

Moseley, Clemont Charlton. "The Political Influence of the Ku Klux Klan in Georgia 1915–1925." *Georgia Historical Quarterly* 57/2 (Summer 1973): 237.

Moskos, Charles C., and John Sibley Butler. *All That We Can Be: Black Leadership and Racial Integration the Army Way*. New York: Basic Books, 1996.

Mowat, Farley. *My Father's Son*. Toronto: Seal Books, 1992.

"Mrs. Kinnard Plans to Remain as Division's 'Mama.'" *Bayonet*, August 6, 1965, 24.

National Infantry Museum Official Tour Guide. Fort Benning GA.

Nichols, Ben. "Marching Units, Helicopters, Equipment Pass in Review on 11th's Organization Day." *Bayonet*, May 10, 1963, 1.

Northen, William J., ed. *Men of Mark in Georgia*. 7 vols. Atlanta GA: A. B. Caldwell, 1906–12. Reprint. Spartanburg SC: Reprint Co., 1974.

Notes from Clipping, Telegrams, and Letters Preserved in a Scrapbook Belonging to Mrs. John A. Betjeman. Fort Benning Folder. Chappell File. Geneaology Department, Columbus Public Library, Columbus GA.

Norwood, Leonard L. "Why Fort Benning Built a Monument to a Dog." *Atlanta Constitution*, November 2, 1958, 50

Nunn, Sam. "Thanks, Home of the Infantry." *Benning Leader* 3/5. Special Edition. October 1, 1993, 2.

Nye, Roger H. *The Patton Mind*. Garden City Parks NY: Avery Publishing Group Inc., 1993.

Nye, Joseph S. Jr., and Roger K. Smith. *After the Storm*. Lanham MD: Madison Books, 1992.

Nyland, Amy L. "Benning accepts Oglethorpe Award." *Bayonet*, March 26, 1999, A-1.

"OCS Is Resumed." *Benning Herald*, March 1951, 19.

Palmer, Bruce Jr. *The 25-Year War*. Lexington: University Press of Kentucky, 1984.

Partridge, Wayne, and Richard Hyatt. "Cavezza new city manager." *Columbus Ledger-Enquirer*, April 16, 1997, A-8.

Patton, George S. *War As I Knew It*. Boston: Houghton Mifflin Company, 1947.

Payne, Robert. *The Marshall Story*. New York: Prentice-Hall, 1951.

Pearson, F. J. "Intimate Glimpses of Garrison Life." *Infantry Journal* 27/4 (October 1925): 409–13.

———. *George C. Marshall: Statesman*. New York: Viking, 1987.

Peers, William. *The My Lai Inquiry*. New York: W. W. Norton & Company, 1979.

"Pentomic Army Changes Ahead." *Army Navy Air Force Journal* 98/28 (March 11, 1961): 1, 9.

Perret, Geoffrey. *There's a War to Be Won*. New York: Random House, 1991.

Perry, Kimball. "Soldier's soldier Leuer says goodbye." *Columbus Ledger-Enquirer*, September 2, 1988, A-1.

"Post evolves from plantation to modern facility." *Bayonet*, October 8, 1993, A-7.

"Post Returns to Normal as WAAC Contingent Assumes Routine Duties." *Bayonet*, March 11, 1943, 5.

"Post Straightens Up Following LBJ Visit." *Bayonet*, November 17, 1967, 1.

"Post to try for World's Best." *Bayonet*, August 27, 1993, A-1.

Powell, Colin L. with Joseph E. Persico. *My American Journal*. New York: Random House, 1995.

———. "Remarks on Receiving the 2003 George C. Marshall Foundation Award." National Building Museum, Washington DC, November 12, 2003. Transcript available at http://www.state.gov/secretary/former/powell/remarks/2003/26126.htm.

Powell, Herbert B. "The Army's Infantry Center Takes an Atomic Age Look Ahead." *Army Navy Air Force Journal* 94/26 (February 23, 1957): 27.

Powers, P. W. "Pentomic Army's Missile Power." *Army* 7/9 (April 1957): 15.

Puckett, Ralph. Interview by Peggy Stelpflug. National Infantry Museum, Fort Benning GA. Handwritten transcript and audio cassette, Auburn AL, May 28, 1996.

"Purchase of Bussey Plantation." *Columbus-Enquirer-Sun*, October 20, 1918, 6.

Quarterman, Joseph "J. Q." Interview by Peggy Stelpflug. Donovan Technical Library, Fort Benning GA. Handwritten transcript and audio cassette, Auburn AL, February 3, 1997.

Quick, Burnet R. Interview by Peggy Stelpflug. Uptown Columbus, Columbus GA. Handwritten transcript and audio cassette, Auburn AL, July 16, 1998.

Ramsey, Russell W. *Some Keys to the Vietnam Puzzle*. Gainesville: University of Florida Libraries, 1968.

———. Interview by Peggy Stelpflug. School of the Americas, Fort Benning GA. Handwritten transcript and audio cassette, Auburn AL, March 4, 1997.

"Ranger Gets Perfect Score." *Bayonet*, June 4, 1953, 7.

Ranger Manual, US Army Infantry School. Documents, Donovan Technical Library, Fort Benning GA.

"Rangers Lead the Way: 75th Ranger Regiment Information Booklet," Documents, Donovan Technical Library, Fort Benning GA.

Regan, Geoffrey. *A History of Friendly Fire*. New York: Avon Books, 1995.

Register of Graduates and Former Cadets of the United States Military Academy, 1802–1971. State of Maryland: West Point Alumni Foundation,1972.

"Report of Board of Officers: Ranger Training, the Infantry School." August 31, 1951. Infantry School, Fort Benning GA.

"Reservation." *Infantry School News*, March 13, 1925, 4.

Ricks, Thomas E. "General Reported Shortages in Iraq. *Washington Post*, October 18, 2004, 1, 14.

Rishell, Lyle. *With a Black Platoon in Combat, Korean War, 1950–1953*. College Station: Texas A&M University Press, 1993.

Rogers, Robert. *Journals of Major Robert Rogers*. New York: Corinth Books, 1961.

Russell, Rick. "Blackhawks arrive at Benning." *Bayonet*, November 24, 1982, 19.

Russo, Marie. "A drug problem at Benning." *Bayonet*, November 4, 1977, 6.

Rutledge, Jerry. "1918—Camp Benning is born." *Benning Leader*, October 1, 1993, 6.

———. "Poydasheff building bridges to Benning." *Columbus Ledger-Enquirer*, September 20, 1993, D-3.

Ryan, Pat Abbott. "Top Lady Soldier." *Sunday Columbus Ledger-Enquirer Magazine*, June 18, 1961,10.

Ryan, Paul B. *The Iranian Rescue Mission: Why It Failed*. Annapolis: Naval Institution Press, 1985.

Sack, John. *Lieutenant Calley*. New York: Viking Press, 1971.

St. Clair, Matthew. Interview with Peggy Stelpflug. Donovan Technical Library, Fort Benning GA. Typed transcript and audio cassette, Auburn AL, December 11, 1998.

Schmitzer, William P. Conversation with Peggy Stelpflug. Handwritten notes, Auburn AL, Summer 1993.

Schwarzkopf, H. Norman. *It Doesn't Take a Hero*. New York: Bantom Books, 1992.

———. "The Battered Helmet." *Infantry* 52/4 (July/August 1962): 2.

———. "Schwarzkopf Proud of Desert Storm troops." *Bayonet*, March 15, 1991, A-2.
Scipio, L. Albert. *Last of the Black Regulars: A History of the 24th Infantry Regiment
     (1869–1951)*. Silver Spring MD: Roman Publication, 1983.
———. *The 24th Infantry at Ft. Benning*. Silver Spring MD: Roman Publications,
     1986.
"School Came to Benning." *Benning Herald* 20/30 (October 1949): 14.
*Selected Speeches and Statements of General of the Army George C. Marshall, Chief Of
     Staff United States Army*. Edited by Major H. A. DeWeerd. Washington: The
     Infantry Journal Press, 1945.
"Segregation Outlawed," *Columbus Enquirer*, May 18, 1954, 1.
75th Ranger Regiment: Rangers Lead the Way. Information Booklet, Vertical File.
     Donovan Library, Fort Benning GA.
"Sgt. Major Ferguson First E-9 to Re-Up." *Bayonet*, April 30, 1959, 1.
Sheehan, Neil. *A Bright Shining Lie*. New York: Random House, 1988.
Shutt, Sally. "Columbus Family Safeguards Fort Benning's History." *Bayonet*,
     September 17, 1999, A-5.
———. "Female instructor earns top honors." *Bayonet*, December 17, 1999, A-4.
———. "Museum prepares exhibit for War Dogs." *Bayonet*, October 22, 1999, A-3.
———. "Secretary retires after 39 years on post." *Bayonet*, September 24, 1999, A-8.
Siddons, Anne Rivers. *Heartbreak Hotel*. New York: Simon & Schuster, 1976.
Simple, Madonna. "Woman named year's top soldier." *Bayonet*, August 5, 1977, 6.
Simpson, Charles M. III. *Inside the Green Berets*. New York: Berkley Books, 1988.
Simpson, Harold B. *Audie Murphy, American Soldier*. Hillsboro TX: Hill Jr. College
     Press, 1975.
Singleton, Asa L. "The Future of Fort Benning." *Infantry Journal* 27/4 (October
     1925): 414–19.
"Site for Fort Benning was Suggested to Col. Eames by B .S. Miller." *Industrial
     Index*, July 28, 1954, 59.
Siter, Bridgett. "Secretary inducted into Ranger Hall of fame." *Bayonet*, May 28,
     2004, 1.
Smyser, William. "Student Brigade Marks 20th Year." *Bayonet*, October 26, 1962, 9.
Snively, Clyde. "Infantry Test Board Bids Farewell." *Bayonet*, March 22, 1991, A-2.
"Soldier Dead, Seven Poisoned by Bad Alcohol. *Columbus Enquirer-Sun*, December
     20, 1920, 1.
"Soldier Out-Races His Own Engine to Save a Baby's Life." *Infantry School News*,
     March 5, 1926, 1.
"Soldiers Help in Preserving Girard's Order." *Columbus Enquirer-Sun*, March 4,
     1919, 1.
Spaller, Ruth J. "Huey comes in for final landing." *Bayonet*, March 11, 1994, A-3.
Spano, Sara. *I Could've Written Gone with the Wind, But Cousin Margaret Beat Me To
     It*. Ann Arbor: McNaughton & Gunn, Inc., 1990.
———. Telephone interview by Peggy Stelpflug. Handwritten notes, Auburn AL,
     1994.
"Status of Air Assault Unit Clarified." *Bayonet*, April 3, 1964, 2.
Steele, William B. Interview by Peggy Stelpflug. Donovan Technical Library, Fort
     Benning GA. Handwritten transcript and audio cassette, Auburn AL, October 5,
     1998.

Stevens, O. B., R. F. Wright, and Georgia Department of Agriculture. *Georgia: Historical and Industrial.* Atlanta: George W. Harrison, State Printer, 1901.

"Stevens Sees OK of New Draft Plan." *Columbus Ledger-Enquirer*, December 4, 1954, 3.

"Story of Fort Benning, Home of the Infantry School of the U. S. Army." *Industrial Index* 34/24 (November 29, 1939): 50.

Straley, Hollie. Telephone interview by Richard Hyatt. Typed transcript, Columbus GA, October 23, 2002.

Strickland, Edwin, and Gene Wortsman. *Phenix City, the Wickedest City in America.* Birmingham: Vulcan Press, 1955.

Sullivan, John A. *Toy Soldiers: Memoir of a Combat Platoon Leader in Korea.* Jefferson NC: McFarland Company, Inc., 1991.

Summers, Bob. Interview by Peggy Stelpflug. Donovan Technical Library, Infantry Hall, Fort Benning GA. Handwritten transcript and audio cassette, Auburn AL, February 24, 2000.

Sutherland, Henry DeLeon , Jr., and Jerry Elijah Brown. *The Federal Road through Georgia, the Creek Nation and Alabama 1806–1836.* Tuscaloosa: University of Alabama Press, 1989.

Sutton, Brian C. "Infantry Board Goes." *Bayonet*, April 5, 1991, A-4.

Symes, Joseph. Conversation with Peggy Stelpflug. Auburn AL, 1994.

"Tank School at Fort Benning." *Army & Navy Register*, December 19, 1931, 584.

Taylor, Maxwell D. *The Uncertain Trumpet.* New York: Harper & Brothers, 1960.

Telfair, Nancy (Louise Gunby Jones DuBose). *A History of Columbus, Georgia 1828–1928.* Columbus: Historical Publishing Company, 1929.

———. "Women in Columbus 1828–1928." Manuscript in Columbus State University College Archives, MCI, Folder 1.

"Tests of Semi-Automatic Rifles." *History of the Infantry School*. Donovan Technical Library, Fort Benning GA, 16.

"30th Becomes 29th, 47th Due to Become 3rd." *Columbus Ledger*, December 2, 1954, 6.

Tierney, Richard. *Army Aviation Study.* Northport AL: Colonial Press, 1963.

Tilden, Richard, and Rosalind Roulston. *A History of the Infantry School.* Unpublished. Written for Fort Benning, 1945. Microfilm. Udgg fu U423 T.45 PU. Donovan Technical Library, Fort Benning GA.

Tolson, Lt. Gen. John J. *Vietnam Studies: Airmobility, 1961–1971.* Washington DC: Department of the Army, 1973.

Toombs, Robert, Alexander H. Stephens, and Howell Cobb. *Correspondence of Robert Toombs, Alexander H. Stephens and Howell Cobb.* New York: Da Capo Press, 1970.

Toomey, Sally. "1–58th soldiers deploy for training exercise in Honduras," *Bayonet*, October 18, 1985, 5.

"Troops Reach Columbus." *Columbus Ledger*, October 6, 1918, 1.

"Truman Concludes Benning Visit." *Bayonet*, April 27, 1950, 1.

Truscott, L. K., Jr. *Command Missions.* New York: E.P. Dutton & Company, Inc., 1954.

Turchin, Marc G. "Boxing: Students 'put up their dukes' at Ranger School." *Bayonet*, March 6, 1998, A-4.

———. "Fort Benning honors its volunteers." *Bayonet*, April 29, 1994, C-6.

———. "Rangers remember fallen comrades with new Memorial." *Bayonet*, June 14, 1996, A-1.

Turow, Scott. "Where Have All the Radicals Gone?" *Newsweek*, September 2, 1996, 1.

U. S. Congress. Senate. Committee on Military Affairs. "Land for Artillery Training Fields: Hearings before the Committee on Military Affairs on Acquiring Land for Establishment Of Mobilization and Training Fields for Artillery and Small Arms." 65th Cong., 3rd sess., January 7, 10, 14, 16, 1919.

"U. S. Files Petition in Federal Court to Condemn Camp Lands." *Enquirer-Sun*, November 17, 1918, 4.

Van Sickle, Betty. Interview by Peggy Stelpflug. Donovan Technical Library, Fort Benning GA. Handwritten transcript and audio cassette, Auburn AL, 1994.

Van Slyke, Jerry. "AIT Brigade received first trainees." *Bayonet*, March 19, 1976, 1.

Vanderpool, Jay D. "We Armed the Helicopter." *Army Aviation Digest* 17/6 (June 1971): 2.

Vaughn, Glenn. "Amazing Legend of Charlie Remembered." *Columbus Ledger-Enquirer*, August 30, 1987, B10.

Voller, Brian R. "Post receives $100,000." *Bayonet*, July 4, 1996, A-1.

Vuono, Carl E. "The Army of the 1990s—Challenges of Change and Continuity." *Infantry* 81/3 (May/June 1991): 13.

Wade, Wyn Craig. *The Fiery Cross: The Ku Klux Klan in America*. New York: Simon & Schuster, 1987.

Waller, Douglas. "Running a 'School for Dictators.'" *Newsweek*, August 9, 1993, 37.

Walsh, Mick. "Benning mission to grow." *Columbus Ledger-Enquirer*, April 22, 2004, C1.

———. "A Lifetime Ago." *Columbus Ledger-Enquirer*, October 24, 2002, C3.

———. "Freakley Has His 'Highlight.'" *Columbus Ledger-Enquirer*, July 15, 2003, A1.

———. "OCS Honors Fallen." *Columbus Ledger-Enquirer*, October 15, 2002, C1.

———. "Original Poem Dates to 1956." *Columbus Ledger Enquirer*, January 22, 2003, A1.

Walston, Kathleen Anne. "A Case for Revival of the Civilian Conservation Corps in Florida." Master's thesis, University of Florida, 1986.

Webster's American Military Biographies. Springfield MA: G. C. Merriam Company, 1978.

Weese, Larry. "Benning soldiers assist in Guyana." *Bayonet*, December 1, 1978, 23.

Weigley, Russell F. *History of the United States Army*. Bloomington: Indiana University Press, 1984.

Weinberger, Caspar. *Fighting for Peace*. New York: Warner Books, Inc., 1990.

Weinberger, Caspar, and Peter Schweizer. *The Next War*. Lanham MD: Regnery Publishers, 1996.

Westmoreland, William. "Gen. Westmoreland Lauds Troops for Tet Victory." *Bayonet*, March 6, 1968, 12.

———. *A Soldier Reports*. New York: Da Capo, 1989.

Wetzel, Robert L. "Sam." Telephone interview by Peggy Stelpflug. Handwritten transcript and audio cassette, Auburn AL, August 20, 1998.

White, Charles E. "The Origins of Fort Benning." Speech and panel discussion with Dick Grube and Dr. John Lupold. Columbus College (Columbus State

University), Columbus GA, March 1988. Typed transcript at National Infantry Museum, Fort Benning GA.

———. Interview by Peggy Stelpflug. US Army Infantry Center, Fort Benning GA. Handwritten transcript and audio cassette, Auburn AL, June 22, 1994.

White, Jerry A. Interview by Peggy Stelpflug. United Way Office, Columbus GA. Handwritten transcript and audio cassette, Auburn AL, June 3, 1998.

White, Terry. *The Making of the World's Elite Forces*. London: Sidgwick & Jackson, 1992.

Whitehead, Margaret Laney, and Barbara Bogart. *City of Progress, a History of Columbus, Georgia, 1828–1978*. Columbus GA: Columbus Office Supply Company, 1979.

"Who's Who." *Infantry School News*, October 15, 1926, 7.

Wilcox, Dennis L., Phillip H. Ault, Warren K. Agee. *Public Relations Strategies and Tactics*. New York: Harper Collins Publishers, Inc., 1992.

"Wiley Carrier 'Belly Flopper,'" *National Infantry Museum Official Tour Guide*, Fort Benning GA, 1–12.

Wilkinson, Tom. "197th becomes 3rd Bde, 24th I D." *Bayonet*, June 21, 1991, 1.

Williamson, Ed. Interview by Peggy Stelpflug. Typed transcript and audio cassette, Auburn University Library Archives, Spring 1995.

Winn, Billy. "Rambling Through Old Times." *Columbus Ledger-Enquirer*, April 15, 1994, A-10.

"With Impressive Ceremony Flag Formally Presented to Fort Benning Thursday." *Columbus Enquirer-Sun*, December 13, 1918, 1.

Wolf, Marv. "A Man Called Charlie Black." *Military Media Review* 10/4 (October 1983): 22.

Woodall, William C. *Home Town*. Columbus GA: Columbus Office Supply Company, 1935.

Worsley, Etta Blanchard. *Columbus on the Chattahoochee*. Columbus GA: Columbus Office Supply Company, 1951.

Yarborough, LeRoy, in collaboration with Truman Smith. *A History of the Infantry School, Fort Benning, Georgia*. Ft. Benning: The Infantry School, 1931.

"Year in Retrospect, 1934." *Benning Herald*, December 28, 1934, 1.

"Yes!!! The drill sergeant is back." *Bayonet*, June 11, 1976, 15.

Zadak, S. "Lynching for 1918." Letter to the Editor. *Montgomery Advertiser*, January 10, 1919, 4.

Zedric, Lance Q., and Michael F. Dilley. *Elite Warriors*. Ventura CA: Pathfinder Publishing, 1996.

———. "Military Metropolis." *Infantry School News*, February 14, 1930, 6.

Index